Operating System Concepts THIRD EDITION

Abraham Silberschatz University of Texas at Austin

James L. Peterson IBM Corporation

Peter B. Galvin Brown University

Addison-Wesley Publishing Company

Reading, Massachusetts   ■   Menlo Park, California   ■   New York
Don Mills, Ontario   ■   Wokingham, England   ■   Amsterdam   ■   Bonn
Sydney   ■   Singapore   ■   Tokyo   ■   Madrid   ■   San Juan   ■   Milan   ■   Paris

WORLD STUDENT SERIES EDITION

This book is in the Addison-Wesley Series in Computer Science.
Consulting Editor: Michael Harrison

VMS is a trademark of Digital Equipment Corporation. UNIX is a registered trademark of AT&T Bell Laboratories. OS/2 is a registered trademark of International Business Machines Corporation. MS/DOS is a registered trademark of Microsoft Corporation. NFS is a registered trademark of Sun Microsystems, Inc. Macintosh is a registered trademark licensed to Apple Computer, Inc.

Many of the designations used by manufacturers and sellers to distinguish their products are claimed as trademarks. Where those designations appear in this book, and Addison-Wesley was aware of a trademark claim, the designations have been printed in initial caps or all caps.

The programs and applications presented in this book have been included for their instructional value. They have been tested with care, but are not guaranteed for any particular purpose. The publisher does not offer any warranties or representations, nor does it accept any liabilities with respect to the programs or applications.

Fig. 3.8 from Iaccobucci, *OS/2 Programmer's Guide*, © 1988, McGraw-Hill, Inc., New York, New York. Fig. 1.7, p. 20. Reprinted with permission of the publisher.

Fig. 8.15 reprinted with permission from *IBM Systems Journal*, Vol. 10, No. 3, © 1971 International Business Machines Corporation.

Fig. 15.1 from Leffler/McKusick/Karels/Quarterman, *The Design and Implementation of the 4.3BSD UNIX Operating System*, © 1989, Addison-Wesley Publishing Co., Inc., Reading, Massachusetts. Fig. 1.1. Reprinted with permission of the publisher.

Figs. 16.1, 16.5, and 16.6 reproduced with permission from Open Software Foundation, Inc. Excerpted from Mach Lecture Series, OSF, October 1989, Cambridge, Massachusetts. Figs. 16.1 and 16.6 presented by R. Rashid of Carnegie-Mellon University and Fig. 16.5 presented by D. Julin of Carnegie-Mellon University.

Fig. 16.4 from Accetta/Baron/Bolosky/Golub/Rashid/Tevanian/Young, "Mach: a new kernal foundation for UNIX development," *Proceedings of Summer USENIX*, June 1986, Atlanta, Georgia. Reprinted with permission of the authors.

ISBN 0-201-54873-9
2 3 4 5 6 7 8 9 10 DO 9594939291

To my parents, Wira and Mietek,
  my wife, Haya,
  and my children, Lemor, Sivan and Aaron.

Avi Silberschatz

To my wife, Jeanne,
  and my children, Jennifer and Kathryn.

Jim Peterson

To Carla.

Peter Galvin

P R E F A C E

Operating systems are an essential part of a computer system. Similarly, a course on operating systems is an essential part of a computer-science education. This book is intended as a text for an introductory course in operating systems at the junior or senior undergraduate level, or first-year-graduate level. It provides a clear description of the *concepts* that underlie operating systems.

This book does not concentrate on any particular operating system or hardware. Instead, it discusses fundamental concepts that are applicable to a variety of systems.

Content of this Book

As prerequisites, we assume the reader is familiar with general assembly-language programming and computer organization. The text is organized in six major parts:

- **Overview** (Chapters 1 to 3). These chapters explain what operating systems *are*, what they *do*, and how they are *designed* and *constructed*. These chapters explain how the concept of an operating system has developed, what the common features of an operating system are, what an operating system does for the user, and what it does for the computer-system operator. The presentation is motivational, historical, and explanatory in nature. We have avoided a discussion of how things are done internally in these chapters. Therefore, they are suitable for individuals or lower-level classes who want to learn what an operating system is, without getting into the details of the internal algorithms.

- **Process management** (Chapters 4 to 6). The process concept and concurrency are at the very heart of modern operating systems. A *process* is the unit of work in a system. Such a system consists of a collection of *concurrently* executing processes, some of which are operating-system processes (those that execute system code), and the rest of which are user processes (those that execute user code). These chapters cover various methods for process management, CPU scheduling, process synchronization and communication, and deadlock handling.

- **Storage management** (Chapters 7 to 9). These chapters deal with the classic internal algorithms and structures of storage management. They provide a firm practical understanding of the algorithms used — the properties, advantages, and disadvantages. The algorithms are presented in a natural order, so that new, more complicated systems can be built on the understanding of simpler systems.

- **Files and protection** (Chapters 10 and 11). A *file* is a collection of related information defined by its creator. Files are mapped, by the operating system, onto physical devices. Protection mechanisms provide controlled access by limiting the types of file access that can be made by the various users. Protection must also be available to ensure that the besides files, memory segments, CPU, and other resources can be operated on by only those processes that have gained proper authorization from the operating system.

- **Distributed systems** (Chapters 12 to 14). A *distributed system* is a collection of processors that do not share memory or a clock. Such a system provides the user with access to the various resources the system maintains. Access to a shared resource allows computation speedup and improved data availability and reliability. A distributed system must provide various mechanisms for process synchronization and communication, for dealing with the deadlock problem and variety of failures that are not encountered in a centralized system.

- **Case studies** (Chapters 15 to 17). These chapters illustrate how the many concepts described can be put together in a real system. Two UNIX-based operating systems are covered in detail — Berkeley's 4.3BSD and Mach. These operating systems were chosen in part because UNIX at one time was almost small enough to understand and yet is not a toy operating system. Most of its internal algorithms were selected for *simplicity*, not for speed or sophistication. UNIX is readily available to computer-science departments, so many students have access to it. Mach provides an opportunity for us to study a modern operating system that provides compatibility with 4.3BSD but has a drastically different design and implementation. Chapter 17 briefly describes some of the most influential operating systems.

Organization

Operating systems first began to appear in the late 1950s, and for 20 years underwent major changes in concepts and technology. As a result, the first-generation operating-system textbooks that appeared during this period (such as Brinch Hansen [1973a], Madnick and Donovan [1974], Shaw [1974], Tsichritzis and Bernstein [1974], and Habermann [1976]) tried to explain a subject that was changing even as the books were being written.

Over time, however, operating-system theory and practice appeared to mature and stabilize. The fundamental operating-system concepts seemed well defined and well understood. The basic approaches to process management, CPU scheduling, process coordination, memory management, file systems, and so on, appeared unlikely to change. At this point, a second generation of operating-systems texts appeared (such as Deitel [1983] and the first edition of this book, Peterson and Silberschatz [1983]).

For the first edition, our primary goal was to present well-understood, agreed-on, classic operating-system material. The basic concepts were organized and presented carefully; the material flowed naturally from basic principles to more sophisticated ones. The bibliographic notes contained pointers to the research papers in which results were first presented.

The fundamental concepts and algorithms covered in the first edition were often based on those used in existing commercial or experimental operating systems. Our aim was to present these concepts and algorithms in a general setting that was not tied to one particular operating system. While the general presentation in the first edition was well-received, there was a strong demand for a more complete practical example, and so in the second edition, Peterson and Silberschatz [1985] we added a chapter on the UNIX operating system.

The first and second editions were organized to stress the basic practical aspects of operating systems (CPU scheduling and memory management) before presenting the unifying theoretical concept of the process model for operating systems. An alternate edition, Silberschatz and Peterson [1988], which reordered the presentation to discuss the process concept very early, was well-received, and eventually replaced the second edition.

The Third Edition

Many comments and suggestions were forwarded to us concerning our previous editions. These, together with our own observations while teaching at the University of Texas and IBM, have prodded us to produce this third edition, which is based on the alternate edition. Our basic procedure was to reorganize and rewrite the material in each chapter, to bring some of the older material up-to-date, to improve the exercises, to add new references, and to add two new chapters — one on distributed file system and the other on the Mach operating system.

Substantive revisions were made in the following chapters

- **Chapter 2**. This is a new chapter that discusses basic computer organization. Some of the material in this chapter was previously scattered in a number of different chapters, which resulted in some confusion. New material also has been added.

- **Chapter 4**. This chapter introduces the process concept and CPU scheduling. The material in this chapter appeared in parts of old Chapters 3 and 4. We thought that the material on scheduling should precede the material on process coordination.

- **Chapter 5**. This is a new organization of the old Chapter 3. The Accent IPC example was replaced with the IPC scheme of Mach.

- **Chapter 12**. We created a separate chapter on the basic structure of distributed systems. The bulk of the material came from the old Chapter 11.

- **Chapter 13**. We created a separate chapter on distributed communication and synchronization. The bulk of the material came from the old Chapter 11.

- **Chapter 14**. This is a new chapter on distributed file system. We discuss the various ways a distributed file system can be designed and implemented. First, we discuss common concepts on which distributed file systems are based. Then, we illustrate our concepts by examining the UNIX United, NSF, Andrew, Sprite, and Locus distributed file systems.

- **Chapter 15**. This chapter discusses UNIX 4.3BSD. The material is a revision of the material on UNIX 4.2BSD previously covered in the old Chapter 12.

- **Chapter 16**. This is a new chapter on the Mach operating system. This system is designed to incorporate the many recent innovations in operating-system research to produce a fully functional, technically advanced operating system. Unlike UNIX, which was developed without regard for multiprocessing, Mach incorporates multiprocessing support throughout. Its multiprocessing support is also very flexible, ranging from shared memory systems to systems with no memory shared between processors. Mach is designed to run on computer systems ranging from one to thousands of processors. In addition, Mach is easily ported to many varied computer architectures. A key goal of Mach is to be a distributed operating system capable of functioning on heterogeneous hardware. Although there are many experimental operating systems being designed, built, and used, Mach is able to satisfy the needs of the masses better than they are because it is fully compatible with UNIX 4.3BSD. As such, it provides a unique opportunity for us to compare two functionally similar, but internally dissimilar, operating systems.

Errata

This book has benefited from the careful reading and thoughtful comments of many people in the previous editions. We have attempted to clean up every error in this new edition, but — as happens with operating systems — there will undoubtedly still be some obscure bugs. We would appreciate it if you, the reader, would notify us of any errors or omissions in the book. If you would like to suggest improvements or to contribute exercises, we would be glad to hear from you. Any correspondence should be sent to A. Silberschatz, Department of Computer Sciences, The University of Texas at Austin, Austin, TX 78712 (e-mail — avi@cs.utexas.edu).

Acknowledgments

This book is derived from the previous editions, and so has been helped by many people, including Jeff Brumfield, Gael Buckley, Ajoy Kumar Datta, Rebecca Hartman, Richard Kieburtz, Carol Kroll, John Leggett, Michael Molloy, John Quarterman, Sara Strandtman, Charles Oualline, John Stankovic, and John Werth.

Lyn Dupré copyedited the book; Karen Shaffer edited our text into troff format. Karen Myer was very helpful with the book production.

Chapter 14 is derived from a paper by Levy and Silberschatz [1990]. John Quarterman helped us to convert the material on UNIX 4.2BSD to UNIX 4.3BSD.

We thank the following people, all of whom reviewed this edition of the book, David Black, Randy Bentson, Joseph Boykin, Wayne Hathaway, Christopher Haynes, Steven Stepanek, Louis Stevens, G. Scott Graham, Thomas LeBlanc, Robert Fowler, and Thomas Casavant.

A.S.
J.P.
P.G.

CONTENTS

PART 1 ■ Overview

CHAPTER 1 ▭ Introduction

1.1 What Is an Operating System? 3

1.2 Early Systems 6

1.3 Simple Monitor 8

1.4 Off-Line Operation 11

1.5 Buffering and Spooling 14

1.6 Multiprogramming 17

1.7 Time Sharing 18

1.8 Distributed Systems 21

1.9 Real-Time Systems 23

1.10 Single-User Systems 24

1.11 Summary 24

Exercises 25

Bibliographic Notes 26

CHAPTER 2 ▭ Computer System Structures

2.1 Interrupt-Based Systems 29

2.2 I/O Structure 34

2.3   Dual-Mode Operation   36

2.4   Hardware Protection   38

2.5   General System Architecture   42

2.6   Different Classes of Computers   43

2.7   Summary   48

Exercises   49

Bibliographic Notes   50

CHAPTER ☐ **Operating System Structures**

3

3.1   System Components   51

3.2   Operating-System Services   57

3.3   System Calls   59

3.4   System Programs   67

3.5   System Structure   70

3.6   Virtual Machines   75

3.7   System Design and Implementation   79

3.8   System Generation   81

3.9   Summary   83

Exercises   84

Bibliographic Notes   84

PART 2 ■ Process Management

CHAPTER ☐ **Processes**

4

4.1   Process Concept   89

4.2   Concurrent Processes   93

4.3   Scheduling Concepts   97

4.4   CPU Scheduling   103

4.5   Scheduling Algorithms   106

4.6   Multiple Processor Scheduling   121

4.7   Algorithm Evaluation   122

4.8   Summary   128

Exercises   **129**

Bibliographic Notes   **132**

CHAPTER ▢ **Process Coordination**

5

5.1   Background   **135**

5.2   The Critical-Section Problem   **139**

5.3   Synchronization Hardware   **147**

5.4   Semaphores   **149**

5.5   Classical Problems of Synchronization   **155**

5.6   Language Constructs   **160**

5.7   Interprocess Communication   **175**

5.8   Summary   **186**

Exercises   **186**

Bibliographic Notes   **192**

CHAPTER ▢ **Deadlocks**

6

6.1   System Model   **195**

6.2   Deadlock Characterization   **197**

6.3   Deadlock Prevention   **201**

6.4   Deadlock Avoidance   **204**

6.5   Deadlock Detection   **211**

6.6   Recovery from Deadlock   **216**

6.7   Combined Approach to Deadlock Handling   **218**

6.8   Summary   **219**

Exercises   **220**

Bibliographic Notes   **224**

PART 3 ■ Storage Management

CHAPTER ▢ **Memory Management**

7

7.1   Background   **229**

7.2   Swapping   **235**

7.3   Single-Partition Allocation **238**

7.4   Multiple-Partition Allocation **242**

7.5   Multiple Base Registers **249**

7.6   Paging **250**

7.7   Segmentation **260**

7.8   Paged Segmentation **267**

7.9   Summary **269**

Exercises **270**

Bibliographic Notes **274**

CHAPTER □ **Virtual Memory**

8

8.1   Motivation **275**

8.2   Demand Paging **277**

8.3   Performance of Demand Paging **284**

8.4   Page Replacement **286**

8.5   Page-Replacement Algorithms **290**

8.6   Allocation of Frames **301**

8.7   Thrashing **304**

8.8   Other Considerations **310**

8.9   Demand Segmentation **318**

8.10   Summary **319**

Exercises **320**

Bibliographic Notes **327**

CHAPTER □ **Secondary Storage Management**

9

9.1   Background **329**

9.2   Disk Structure **330**

9.3   Free-Space Management **334**

9.4   Allocation Methods **336**

9.5   Disk Scheduling **345**

9.6   Selecting a Disk-Scheduling Algorithm **350**

9.7   Sector Queueing **352**

9.8   Performance and Reliability Improvements **353**

9.9   Storage Hierarchy   **354**

9.10   Summary   **356**

Exercises   **357**

Bibliographic Notes   **360**

PART 4 ■■ Files and Protection

CHAPTER ▢ **File Systems**

10

10.1   File-System Organization   **365**

10.2   File Operations   **370**

10.3   Access Methods   **372**

10.4   Consistency Semantics   **375**

10.5   Directory-Structure Organization   **376**

10.6   File Protection   **386**

10.7   Implementation Issues   **390**

10.8   Summary   **392**

Exercises   **393**

Bibliographic Notes   **394**

CHAPTER ▢ **Protection**

11

11.1   Goals of Protection   **397**

11.2   Access Matrix   **400**

11.3   Dynamic Protection Structures   **405**

11.4   Revocation   **410**

11.5   Existing Systems   **411**

11.6   Language-Based Protection   **417**

11.7   Protection Problems   **422**

11.8   Security   **425**

11.9   Encryption   **427**

11.10 Summary   **430**

Exercises   **430**

Bibliographic Notes   **432**

PART 5 ▪ Distributed Systems

CHAPTER □ **Distributed System Structures**

12

12.1   Motivation   **437**

12.2   Topology   **439**

12.3   Communication   **444**

12.4   Network Types   **449**

12.5   Types of Operating Systems   **452**

12.6   Design Issues   **456**

12.7   Summary   **458**

    Exercises   **459**

    Bibliographic Notes   **460**

CHAPTER □ **Distributed Coordination**

13

13.1   Event Ordering   **463**

13.2   Mutual Exclusion   **466**

13.3   Deadlock Prevention   **470**

13.4   Deadlock Detection   **471**

13.5   Robustness   **480**

13.6   Reaching Agreement   **482**

13.7   Election Algorithms   **485**

13.8   Summary   **488**

    Exercises   **488**

    Bibliographic Notes   **489**

CHAPTER □ **Distributed File Systems**

14

14.1   Background   **491**

14.2   Naming and Transparency   **493**

14.3   Remote Services   **497**

14.4   Caching   **499**

14.5   Stateful versus Stateless Service   **505**

14.6   File Replication   **507**

14.7   Example Systems   **508**

14.8   Summary **539**

Exercises **540**

Bibliographic Notes **540**

PART 6 ■ Case Studies

CHAPTER ☐ **The UNIX Operating System**
15

15.1   History **545**

15.2   Design Principles **551**

15.3   Programmer Interface **553**

15.4   User Interface **562**

15.5   Process Management **566**

15.6   Memory Management **571**

15.7   File System **574**

15.8   I/O System **583**

15.9   Interprocess Communication **587**

15.10   Summary **594**

Exercises **594**

Bibliographic Notes **595**

CHAPTER ☐ **The Mach Operating System**
16

16.1   History **597**

16.2   Design Principles **599**

16.3   System Components **601**

16.4   Process Management **604**

16.5   Interprocess Communication **611**

16.6   Memory Management **617**

16.7   Programmer Interface **623**

16.8   Implementation Details **624**

16.9   Summary **627**

Exercises **628**

Bibliographic Notes **628**

CHAPTER 17   **Historical Perspective**

17.1   Atlas   **631**

17.2   XDS-940   **633**

17.3   THE   **633**

17.4   RC 4000   **634**

17.5   CTSS   **636**

17.6   MULTICS   **636**

17.7   OS/360   **637**

17.8   Other Systems   **639**

Bibliography   641

Index   679

PART 1

Overview

An *operating system* is a program that acts as an intermediary between a user of a computer and the computer hardware. The purpose of an operating system is to provide an environment in which a user can execute programs in a *convenient* and *efficient* manner.

We trace the development of operating systems from the first hands-on systems to current multiprogrammed and time-shared systems. Understanding the reasons behind the development of operating systems gives us an appreciation for what an operating system does and how it does it.

The operating system must ensure the correct operation of the computer system. To prevent user programs from interfering with the proper operation of the system, the hardware must provide appropriate mechanisms to ensure such proper behavior. We describe the basic computer architecture that makes it possible to write a correct operating system.

The operating system provides certain services to programs and to the users of those programs in order to make the programming task easier. The specific services provided will, of course, differ from one operating system to another, but there are some common classes of services that we identify and explore.

Introduction

An *operating system* is a program that acts as an intermediary between a user of a computer and the computer hardware. The purpose of an operating system is to provide an environment in which a user can execute programs. The primary goal of an operating system is thus to make the computer system *convenient* to use. A secondary goal is to use the computer hardware in an *efficient* manner.

To understand what operating systems are, we must first understand how they have developed. In this chapter, we trace the development of operating systems from the first hands-on systems to current multiprogrammed and time-shared systems. As we move through the various stages, we see how the components of operating systems evolved as natural solutions to problems in early computer systems. Understanding the reasons behind the development of operating systems gives an appreciation for what tasks an operating system does and how it does them.

1.1 What Is an Operating System?

An operating system is an important part of almost every computer system. A computer system can be roughly divided into four components: the *hardware*, the *operating system*, the *applications programs*, and the *users* (Figure 1.1).

The hardware (the central processing unit (CPU), memory, and input/output (I/O) devices) provides the basic computing resources. The

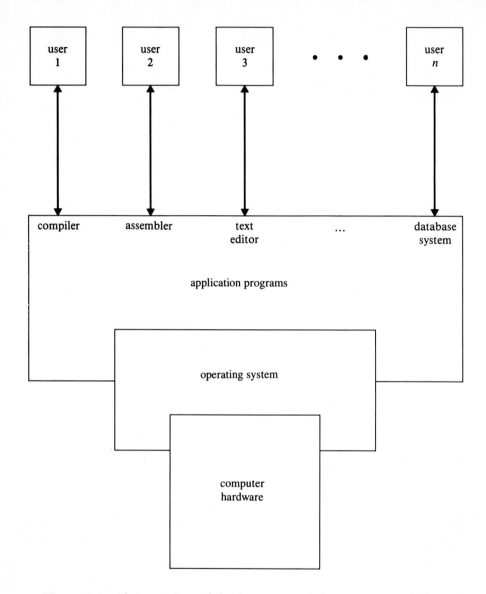

Figure 1.1   Abstract view of the components of a computer system.

applications programs (compilers, database systems, video games, and business programs) define the ways in which these resources are used to solve the computing problems of the users. There may be many different users (people, machines, other computers) trying to solve different problems. Accordingly, there may be many different applications programs. The operating system controls and coordinates the use of the hardware among the various application programs for the various users.

An operating system is similar to a *government*. The components of a computer system are its hardware, software, and data. The operating system provides the means for the proper use of these resources in the operation of the computer system. Like a government, the operating system performs no useful function by itself. It simply provides an *environment* within which other programs can do useful work.

We can view an operating system as a *resource allocator*. A computer system has many resources (hardware and software) that may be required to solve a problem: CPU time, memory space, file storage space, I/O devices, and so on. The operating system acts as the manager of these resources and allocates them to specific programs and users as necessary for the latter's tasks. Since there may be many, possibly conflicting, requests for resources, the operating system must decide which requests are allocated resources to operate the computer system efficiently and fairly.

A slightly different view of an operating system focuses on the need to control the various I/O devices and user programs. An operating system is a *control program*. A control program controls the execution of user programs to prevent errors and improper use of the computer. It is especially concerned with the operation and control of I/O devices.

In general, however, there is no completely adequate definition of an operating system. Operating systems exist because they are a reasonable way to solve the problem of creating a usable computing system. The fundamental goal of computer systems is to execute user programs and to make solving user problems easier. Toward this goal, computer hardware is constructed. Since bare hardware alone is not very easy to use, applications programs are developed. These various programs require certain common operations, such as controlling the I/O devices. The common functions of controlling and allocating resources are then brought together into one piece of software: the operating system.

There is also no universally accepted definition of what is part of the operating system and what is not. A simple viewpoint is that everything a vendor ships when you order "the operating system" should be considered. The memory requirements and features included, however, vary greatly between systems. Some take up less than 1 megabyte of space and lack even a full-screen editor, whereas others require hundreds of megabytes of space and include spelling checkers and entire window systems. A more common definition is that the operating system is the one program running at all times on the computer (usually called the *kernel*), with all else being application programs. The latter is more common and is the one we generally follow.

It is perhaps easier to define operating systems by what they *do*, rather than what they *are*. The primary goal of an operating system is *convenience for the user*. Operating systems exist because they are supposed to make it easier to compute with one than without one. This is particularly clear when you look at operating systems for small personal computers.

A secondary goal is *efficient* operation of the computer system. This goal is particularly important for large, shared multiuser systems. These systems are typically very expensive, and so it is desirable to make them as efficient as possible. These two goals, convenience and efficiency, are sometimes contradictory. In the past, efficiency considerations were often more important than convenience. Thus, much of operating-system theory concentrates on optimal use of computing resources.

To see what operating systems are and what operating systems do, let us consider how they have developed over the last 30 years. By tracing that evolution, we can identify the common elements of operating systems and see how and why these systems have developed as they have.

Operating systems and computer architecture have had a great deal of influence on each other. To facilitate the use of the hardware, operating systems were developed. As operating systems were designed and used, it became obvious that changes in the design of the hardware could simplify them. In this short historical review, notice how the introduction of new hardware features is the natural solution to many operating-system problems.

1.2 Early Systems

Initially, there was only computer hardware. Early computers were (physically) very large machines run from a console. The programmer would write a program and then operate the program directly from the operator's console. First, the program would be manually loaded into memory, from the front panel switches (one instruction at a time), from paper tape, or from punched cards. Then the appropriate buttons would be pushed to set the starting address and to start the execution of the program. As the program ran, the programmer/operator could monitor its execution by the display lights on the console. If errors were discovered, the programmer could halt the program, examine the contents of memory and registers, and debug the program directly from the console. Output was printed, or was punched onto paper tape or cards for later printing.

An important aspect of this environment was its *hands-on* interactive nature. The programmer was also the operator of the computer system. Most systems used a sign-up or *reservation scheme* for allocating machine time. If you wanted to use the computer, you went to the sign-up sheet, looked for the next convenient free time on the machine, and signed up for it.

There were, however, certain problems with this approach. Suppose you had signed up for 1 hour of computer time to run a program that you were developing. You might run into a particularly nasty bug and be unable to finish in 1 hour. If someone had reserved the following block of time, you would have to stop, collect what you could, and return at a later time to continue. On the other hand, if your program ran smoothly, you might finish in 35 minutes. Since you had thought you might need the machine longer, you had signed up for 1 hour, and so the machine would now sit idle for 25 minutes.

As time went on, additional software and hardware were developed. Card readers, line printers, and magnetic tape became commonplace. Assemblers, loaders, and linkers were designed to ease the programming task. Libraries of common functions were created. Common functions could then be copied into a new program without having to be written again.

The routines that performed I/O were especially important. Each new I/O device had its own characteristics, requiring careful programming. A special subroutine was written for each I/O device. Such a subroutine is called a *device driver*. A device driver knows how the buffers, flags, registers, control bits, and status bits for a particular device should be used. Each different type of device has its own driver. A simple task, such as reading a character from a paper-tape reader, might involve complex sequences of device-specific operations. Rather than the necessary code being written every time, the device driver was simply used from the library.

Later, compilers for FORTRAN, COBOL, and other languages appeared, making the programming task much easier, but the operation of the computer more complex. To prepare a FORTRAN program for execution, for example, the programmer would first need to load the FORTRAN compiler into the computer. The compiler was normally kept on magnetic tape, so the proper tape would need to be mounted on a tape drive. The program would be read through the card reader and written onto another tape. The FORTRAN compiler produced assembly-language output, which then needed to be assembled. This required mounting another tape with the assembler. The output of the assembler would need to be linked to supporting library routines. Finally, the binary object form of the program would be ready to execute. It could be loaded into memory and debugged from the console, as before.

Notice that there could be a significant amount of *set-up time* involved in the running of a job. Each job consisted of many separate steps: loading the FORTRAN compiler tape, running the compiler, unloading the compiler tape, loading the assembler tape, running the assembler, unloading the assembler tape, loading the object program, and running the object program. If an error occurred during any step, you might have to start over at the beginning. Each job step might involve the loading and unloading of magnetic tapes, paper tapes, and/or punch cards.

1.3 Simple Monitor

The job set-up time was a real problem. During the time that tapes were being mounted or the programmer was operating the console, the CPU sat idle. Remember that, in the early days, very few computers were available, and they were very expensive (they cost millions of dollars). In addition, there were the operational costs of power, cooling, programmers, and so on. Thus, computer time was very valuable, and owners wanted their computers to be used as much as possible. They needed high *utilization* to get as much as they could from their investments.

The solution was two-fold. First, a professional computer operator was hired. The programmer no longer operated the machine. As soon as one job was finished, the operator could start the next; there was no idle time due to reserving of computer time that turned out not to be needed. Since the operator had more experience with mounting tapes than a programmer, set-up time was reduced. The user provided whatever cards or tapes were needed, as well as a short description of how the job was to be run. Of course, the operator could not debug an incorrect program at the console, since the operator would not understand the program. Therefore, in the case of program error, a dump of memory and registers was taken, and the programmer had to debug from the dump. This allowed the operator to continue immediately with the next job, but left the programmer with a much more difficult debugging problem.

The second major time savings involved reducing set-up time. Jobs with similar needs were *batched* together and run through the computer as a group. For instance, suppose the operator received one FORTRAN job, one COBOL job, and another FORTRAN job. If he ran them in that order, he would have to set up for FORTRAN (load the compiler tapes, and so on), then set up for COBOL, and then set up for FORTRAN again. If he ran the two FORTRAN programs as a batch, however, he could set up only once for FORTRAN, saving operator time.

These changes, making the operator distinct from the user and batching similar jobs, improved utilization quite a bit. Programmers would leave their programs with the operator. The operator would sort them into batches with similar requirements and, as the computer became available, would run each batch. The output from each job would be sent back to the appropriate programmer.

But there were still problems. For example, when a job stopped, the operator would have to notice that fact by observing the console, determine why the program stopped (normal or abnormal termination), take a dump if necessary, and then load the card reader or paper-tape reader with the next job and restart the computer.   During this transition from one job to the next, the CPU sat idle.

To overcome this idle time, people developed *automatic job sequencing*; with this technique, the first rudimentary operating systems were created. What was desired was a procedure for automatically transferring control from one job to the next. A small program, called a *resident monitor*, was created for this purpose (Figure 1.2). The resident monitor is always (resident) in memory.

Initially (when the computer was turned on), the resident monitor was invoked, and it would transfer control to a program. When the program terminated, it would return control to the resident monitor,

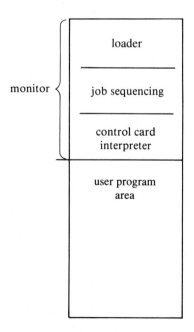

Figure 1.2   Memory layout for a resident monitor.

which would then go on to the next program. Thus, the resident monitor would automatically sequence from one program to another and from one job to another.

But how would the resident monitor know which program to execute? Previously, the operator had been given a short description of what programs were to be run on what data. So that this information could be provided directly to the monitor, *control cards* were introduced. The idea is quite simple. In addition to the program or data for a job, we include special cards (control cards), which are directives to the resident monitor indicating what program is to be run. For example, a normal user program might require one of three programs to run: the FORTRAN compiler (FTN), the assembler (ASM), or the user's program (RUN). We could use a separate control card for each of these:

> $FTN — Execute the FORTRAN compiler.
> $ASM — Execute the assembler.
> $RUN — Execute the user program.

These cards tell the resident monitor which programs to run.

We can use two additional control cards to define the boundaries of each job:

> $JOB — First card of a job.
> $END — Last card of a job.

These two cards might be useful for accounting for the machine resources used by the programmer. Parameters can be used to define the job name, account number to be charged, and so on. Other control cards can be defined for other functions, such as asking the operator to load or unload a tape.

One problem with control cards is how to distinguish them from data or program cards. The usual solution is to identify them by a special character or pattern on the card. Several systems used the dollar-sign character ($) in the first column to identify a control card. Others used a different code. IBM's Job Control Language (JCL) used slash marks (//) in the first two columns. Figure 1.3 shows a sample card-deck setup for a simple batch system.

A resident monitor thus has several identifiable parts. One major part is the *control-card interpreter* that is responsible for reading and carrying out the instructions on the cards at the point of execution. The control-card interpreter at intervals invokes a loader to load systems programs and applications programs into memory. Thus, a loader is a part of the resident monitor. Both the control-card interpreter and the loader need to perform I/O, so the resident monitor has a set of device drivers for the system's I/O devices. Often, the system and application

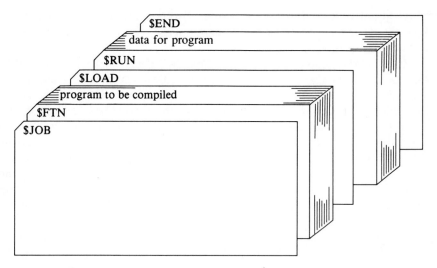

Figure 1.3   Card deck for a simple batch system.

programs are linked to these same device drivers, providing continuity in their operation, as well as saving memory space and programming time.

These batch systems work fairly well. The resident monitor provides automatic job sequencing as indicated by the control cards. When a control card indicates that a program is to be run, the monitor loads the program into memory and transfers control to it. When the program completes, it transfers control back to the monitor, which reads the next control card, loads the appropriate program, and so on. This cycle is repeated until all control cards are interpreted for the job. Then the monitor automatically continues with the next job.

1.4 Off-Line Operation

Computers, especially large mainframes, have traditionally been very expensive machines. Accordingly, the owners of these machines have wanted to get as much computation done as possible. The same is true even for today's cheaper microcomputers. Although microcomputers may not be very expensive, it is still desirable to get as much computing done as possible.

The switch to batch systems with automatic job sequencing was made to improve performance. The problem, quite simply, is that humans are extremely slow (relative to the computer, of course).

Consequently, it is desirable to replace human operation by operating-system software. Automatic job sequencing eliminates the need for human set-up time and job sequencing.

Even with automatic job sequencing, however, the CPU is often idle. The problem is the speed of the mechanical I/O devices, which are intrinsically slower than electronic devices. Even a slow CPU works in the microsecond range, with millions of instructions executed per second. A fast card reader, on the other hand, might read 1000 cards per minute (17 cards per second). Thus, the difference in speed between the CPU and its I/O devices may be three orders of magnitude or more.

The slowness of the I/O devices can mean that the CPU is often waiting for I/O. As an example, an assembler or compiler may be able to process 300 or more cards per second. A fast card reader, on the other hand, may be able to read only 1200 cards per minute (or 20 cards per second). This means that assembling a 1200 card program would require only 4 seconds of CPU time, but 60 seconds to read. Thus, the CPU is idle for 56 out of 60 seconds, or 93.3 percent of the time. The resulting CPU utilization is only 6.7 percent. The process is similar for output operations. The problem is that, while an I/O operation is occurring, the CPU is idle, waiting for the I/O to complete; while the CPU is executing, the I/O devices are idle.

Over time, of course, improvements in technology resulted in faster I/O devices. But CPU speeds increased even faster, so that the problem was not only unresolved, but also exacerbated.

One common solution was to replace the very slow card readers (input devices) and line printers (output devices) with magnetic-tape units. The majority of computer systems in the late 1950s and early 1960s were batch systems reading from card readers and writing to line printers or card punches. Rather than have the CPU read directly from cards, however, the cards were first copied onto a magnetic tape. When the tape was sufficiently full, it was taken down and carried over to the computer. When a card was needed for input to a program, the equivalent record was read from the tape. Similarly, output was written to the tape and the contents of the tape would be printed later. The card readers and line printers were operated *off-line*, not by the main computer (Figure 1.4).

Two approaches to off-line processing were used. Special-purpose devices (card readers, line printers) were developed that output directly to or input directly from magnetic tape. These devices had additional hardware designed specifically for this task. The other approach was to dedicate a small computer (such as the IBM 1401) to the task of copying to and from tape. The small computer was a satellite of the main computer. *Satellite processing* was one of the first cases of multiple computer systems working together to improve performance.

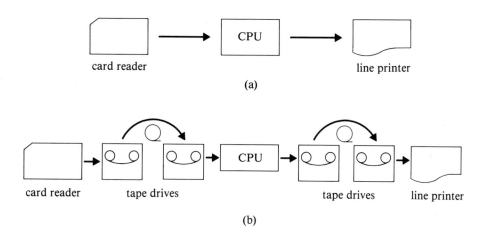

Figure 1.4 (a) On-line and (b) off-line operation of I/O devices.

The main advantage of off-line operation was that the main computer was no longer constrained by the speed of the card readers and line printers, but was limited by only the speed of the much faster magnetic tape units. This technique of using magnetic tape for all I/O could be applied with any unit record equipment (card readers, card punches, plotters, paper tape, printers).

In addition, no changes need be made to the application programs to change from direct to off-line I/O operation. Consider a program that runs on a system with an attached card reader. When it wants a card, it calls the card-reader device driver in the resident monitor. If we change to off-line operation of the card reader, only the device driver must be changed. When the program needs an input card, it calls the same system routine as before. However, now the code for that routine is not the card-reader driver, but rather is a call to the magnetic tape driver. The application program receives the same card image in either case.

This ability to run a program with different I/O devices is called *device independence*. Device independence is made possible by having the operating system determine which device a program actually uses when it requests I/O. Programs are written to use *logical* I/O devices. Control cards (or other commands) indicate how the logical devices should be mapped onto physical devices.

The real gain in off-line operation comes from the possibility of using multiple reader-to-tape and tape-to-printer systems for one CPU. If the CPU can process input twice as fast as the reader can read cards, then two readers working simultaneously can produce enough tape to keep the CPU busy. On the other hand, there is now a longer delay in getting a particular job run. It must first be read onto tape. Then there is a delay until enough other jobs are read onto the tape to "fill" it. The tape must then be rewound, unloaded, hand-carried to the CPU, and mounted on a free tape drive. This is not unreasonable for batch systems, of course. Many similar jobs can be batched onto a tape before it is taken to the computer.

1.5 Buffering and Spooling

Off-line processing allows overlap of CPU and I/O operations by executing those two actions on two independent machines. If we desire to achieve such an overlap in one single machine, constructs must be placed between the devices and the CPU to allow a similar separation of execution. Also, a suitable architecture must be developed to allow for this buffering. This architecture is discussed in Chapter 2.

1.5.1 Buffering

Buffering is a method of overlapping the I/O of a job with its own computation. The idea is quite simple. After data have been read and the CPU is about to start operating on them, the input device is instructed to begin the next input immediately. The CPU and input device are then both busy. With luck, by the time that the CPU is ready for the next data item (record), the input device will have finished reading it. The CPU can then begin processing the newly read data, while the input device starts to read the following data. Similarly this can be done for output. In this case, the CPU creates data that are put into a buffer until an output device can accept them.

In practice, buffering seldom keeps both the CPU and its I/O devices busy all the time, since either the CPU or the input device will finish first. If the CPU finishes first, it must wait; it cannot proceed until the next record is read and is in memory ready to be processed. Notice, however, that the CPU may not have to sit idle for long; in the worst case, it is idle no longer than it would be without buffering. If the input device finishes first, then either it must wait or it may proceed with reading the next record. The buffers that hold records that have been read but not yet processed (or processed but not yet output) are often made large enough to hold several records (for example a 255-character buffer, or a 10-card buffer). Thus, an input device can read several records ahead of the CPU. If the input device is consistently faster than the CPU, however, the buffer will eventually become full and the input device will have to wait.

Buffering is generally an operating-system function. The resident monitor or the device drivers include system I/O buffers for each I/O device. Subroutine calls to the device driver by applications programs (I/O requests) normally cause only a transfer to or from a system buffer. The actual I/O operation either has already been done, or will be done later, as soon as the device is available.

How does buffering affect performance? Buffering mainly helps to smooth over variations in the time it takes to process a record. If the average speeds (in records per second) of the CPU and the I/O devices are the same, then buffering allows the CPU to get slightly ahead of or behind the I/O devices, with both still processing everything at full speed.

However, if the CPU is, on the average, much faster than an input device, buffering is of little use. If the CPU is always faster, then it will always find an empty buffer and have to wait for the input device. For output, the CPU can proceed at full speed until, eventually, all system buffers are full. Then the CPU must wait for the output device. This situation occurs with *I/O-bound* jobs, where the amount of I/O, relative to computation, is very great. Since the CPU is faster than the I/O device, the speed of execution is bounded by the speed of the I/O device, not by the speed of the CPU.

On the other hand, the amount of computation is so high for a *CPU-bound* job that the input buffers are always full and the output buffers always empty; the CPU cannot keep up with the I/O devices.

Consequently, buffering can be of some help, but it is seldom sufficient. Most jobs were I/O bound in early computer systems. Buffering helped somewhat, but the I/O devices (such as card readers, line printers, and paper-tape readers and punches) were simply too slow to keep up with the CPU.

1.5.2 Spooling

Although off-line preparation of jobs continued for some time, it was quickly replaced in most systems. Disk systems became widely available and greatly improved on off-line operation. The problem with tape systems was that the card reader could not write onto one end of the tape while the CPU read from the other. The entire tape had to be written before it was rewound and read. Disk systems eliminated this problem. Because the head is moved from one area of the disk to another, a disk can rapidly switch from the area on the disk being used by the card reader to store new cards to the position needed by the CPU to read the "next" card.

In a disk system, cards are read directly from the card reader onto the disk. The location of card images is recorded in a table kept by the operating system. When a job is executed, the operating system satisfies its requests for card reader input by reading from the disk. Similarly, when the job requests the printer to output a line, that line is copied into a system buffer and is written to the disk. When the job is completed, the output is actually printed.

This form of processing is called *spooling* (Figure 1.5). The name is an acronym for **s**imultaneous **p**eripheral **o**peration **on-l**ine. Spooling essentially uses the disk as a very large buffer, for reading as far ahead as possible on input devices and for storing output files until the output devices are able to accept them. Spooling is also used for processing data at remote sites. The CPU sends the data via communications paths to a remote printer (or accepts an entire input job from a remote card reader). The remote processing is done at its own speed with no CPU intervention. The CPU just needs to be notified when the processing is completed so that it can spool the next batch of data.

Unlike spooling, buffering overlaps the I/O of a job with its own computation. The advantage of spooling over buffering is that spooling overlaps the I/O of one job with the computation of other jobs. Even in a simple system, the spooler may be reading the input of one job while printing the output of a different job. During this time, still another job (or jobs) may be executed, reading their "cards" from disk and "printing" their output lines onto the disk. Buffering can overlap the I/O of a job with only its *own* computation and I/O; spooling can overlap the I/O and computation of many jobs.

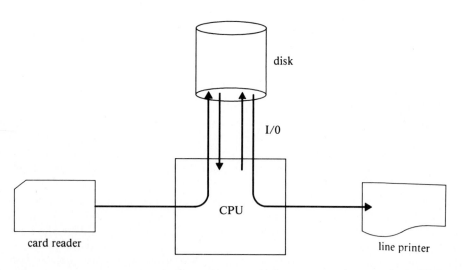

Figure 1.5 Spooling.

An extreme form of spooling can be done with magnetic tape. It is possible to read the entire contents of a magnetic tape onto disk before using it. All operations then occur on the disk copy, at higher speeds, and with no wear to the tape. This scheme is known as *staging* a tape.

Spooling has a direct beneficial effect on the performance of the system. For the cost of some disk space and a few tables, the CPU can overlap the computation of one job with the I/O of other jobs. Thus, spooling can keep both the CPU and the I/O devices working at much higher rates, particularly if there is a mix of CPU-bound and I/O-bound jobs to be run.

In addition, spooling provides a very important data structure: a *job pool*. Spooling will generally result in several jobs that have already been read waiting on disk, ready to run. A pool of jobs on disk allows the operating system to select which job to run next, in order to increase CPU utilization. When jobs come in directly on cards or even on magnetic tape, it is not possible to skip around and to run jobs in a different order. Jobs must be run sequentially, on a first-come, first-served basis. However, when several jobs are on a direct-access device, such as a disk, *job scheduling* becomes possible. We discuss job and CPU scheduling in greater detail in Chapter 4; a few important aspects are covered here.

1.6 Multiprogramming

The most important aspect of job scheduling is the ability to *multiprogram*. Off-line operation, buffering, and spooling for overlapped I/O have their limitations. A single user cannot, in general, keep either the CPU or the I/O devices busy at all times. Multiprogramming increases CPU utilization by organizing jobs so that the CPU always has something to execute.

The idea is as follows. The operating system picks and begins to execute one of the jobs in the job pool. Eventually, the job may have to wait for some task, such as a tape to be mounted, a command to be typed on a keyboard, or an I/O operation to complete. In a non-multiprogrammed system (uniprogramming), the CPU would sit idle. In a multiprogramming system, the operating system simply switches to and executes another job. When *that* job needs to wait, the CPU is switched to another job, and so on. Eventually, the first job finishes waiting and gets the CPU back. As long as there is always some job to execute, the CPU will never be idle.

This idea is quite common in other life situations. A lawyer does not have only one client at a time. Rather, several clients may be in the process of being served at the same time. While one case is waiting to go to trial or to have papers typed, the lawyer can work on another case. With enough clients, a lawyer need never be idle. (Idle lawyers tend to become politicians, so there is a certain social value in keeping lawyers busy.)

Multiprogrammed operating systems are fairly sophisticated. To have several jobs ready to run, the system must keep all of them in memory simultaneously (Figure 1.6). Having several programs in memory at the same time requires some form of memory management, which is covered in Chapters 7 and 8. In addition, if several jobs are ready to run at the same time, the system must choose among them. This decision is *CPU scheduling*, which is discussed in Chapter 4. Finally, multiple jobs running concurrently require that their ability to affect one another be limited in all phases of the operating system, including process scheduling, disk storage, and memory management.

1.7 Time Sharing

Time sharing (or *multitasking*) is a logical extension of multiprogramming. Multiple jobs are executed by the CPU switching between them, but the switches occur so frequently that the users may interact with

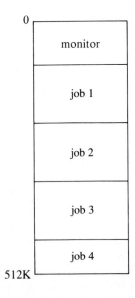

Figure 1.6   Memory layout for a multiprogramming system.

each program while it is running. To understand the difference, we will first review the batch method.

When batch systems were first developed, they were defined by the "batching" together of similar jobs. Card- and tape-based systems allowed only sequential access to programs and data, so only one application package (the FORTRAN compiler, linker, and loader, or the COBOL equivalents, for instance) could be used at a time. As on-line disk storage became feasible, it was possible to provide immediate access to all of the application package. Modern batch systems are no longer defined by the batching together of similar jobs; other characteristics are used instead.

A batch operating system normally reads a stream of separate jobs (from a card reader, for example), each with its own control cards that predefine what the job does. When the job is complete, its output is usually printed (on a line printer, for example). The definitive feature of a batch system is the *lack* of interaction between the user and the job while that job is executing. The job is prepared and submitted. At some later time (perhaps minutes, hours, or days), the output appears. The delay between job submission and job completion (called *turnaround* time) may result from the amount of computing needed, or from delays before the operating system starts processing the job.

There are some difficulties with a batch system from the point of view of the programmer or user, however. Since the user cannot interact with the job when it is executing, the user must set up the control cards to handle all possible outcomes. In a multistep job, subsequent steps may depend on the result of earlier ones. The running of a program, for example, may depend on its successful compilation. It can be difficult to define completely what to do in all cases.

Another difficulty in a batch system is that programs must be debugged statically, from snapshot dumps. A programmer cannot modify a program as it executes to study its behavior. A long turnaround time inhibits experimentation with a program. (Conversely, this situation may instill a certain amount of discipline into the writing and testing of programs.)

An *interactive*, or *hands-on*, computer system provides on-line communication between the user and the system. The user gives instructions to the operating system or to a program directly, and receives an immediate response. Usually, a keyboard is used to provide input, and a printer or display screen (such as a cathode-ray tube (CRT)) is used to provide output. When the operating system finishes the execution of one command, it seeks the next "control statement" not from a card reader, but rather from the user's keyboard. The user gives a command, waits for the response, and decides on the next command, based on the result of the previous one. The user can easily experiment, and can see results immediately. Most systems have an interactive text editor for entering programs and an interactive debugger for assisting in debugging programs.

If users are to be able to access both data and code conveniently, an *on-line file system* must be available. A *file* is a collection of related information defined by its creator. Commonly, files represent programs (both source and object forms) and data. Data files may be numeric, alphabetic, or alphanumeric. Files may be free-form, such as text files, or may be rigidly formatted. In general, a file is a sequence of bits, bytes, lines, or records whose meaning is defined by its creator and user. The operating system implements the abstract concept of a file by managing mass storage devices, such as tapes and disks. Files are normally organized into logical clusters, or *directories*, which makes them easier to use. Since multiple users have access to files, it is desirable to control by whom and in what ways files may be accessed.

Batch systems are quite appropriate for executing large jobs that need little interaction. The user can submit jobs and return later for the results; it is not necessary to wait while the job is processed. Interactive jobs tend to be composed of many short actions, where the results of the next command may be unpredictable. The user submits the command and then waits for the results. Accordingly, the *response* time should be quite short — on the order of seconds at most. An interactive system is used when a short response time is required.

Early computers were interactive systems. That is, the entire system was at the immediate disposal of the programmer/operator. This allowed the programmer great flexibility and freedom in program testing and development. But, as we saw, this arrangement resulted in substantial idle time while the CPU waited for some action to be taken by the programmer/operator. Because of the high cost of these early computers, idle CPU time was undesirable. Batch operating systems were developed to avoid this problem. Batch systems improved system utilization for the owners of the computer systems.

Time-sharing systems were developed to provide interactive use of a computer system at a reasonable cost. A time-shared operating system uses CPU scheduling and multiprogramming to provide each user with a small portion of a time-shared computer. Each user has a separate program in memory. When a program executes, it typically executes for only a short time before it either finishes or needs to perform I/O. I/O may be interactive; that is, output is to a display for the user and input is from a user keyboard. Since interactive I/O typically runs at people speeds, it may take a long time to complete. Input, for example, may be bounded by the user's typing speed; five characters per second is fairly fast for people, but is very slow for computers. Rather than let the CPU sit idle when this happens, the operating system will rapidly switch the CPU to the program of some other user.

A time-shared operating system allows the many users to *share* the computer simultaneously. Since each action or command in a time-shared system tends to be short, only a little CPU time is needed for each user. As the system switches rapidly from one user to the next, each user is given the impression that he has his own computer, whereas actually one computer is being shared among many users.

The idea of time sharing was demonstrated as early as 1960, but since time-shared systems are more difficult and expensive to build (due to the numerous I/O devices needed), they did not become common until the early 1970s. As the popularity of time sharing has grown, researchers have attempted to merge batch and time-shared systems into one system. Many computer systems that were designed as primarily batch systems have been modified to create a time-sharing subsystem. For example, IBM's OS/360, a batch system, was modified to support the Time-Sharing Option (TSO). At the same time, time-sharing systems have often added a batch subsystem. Today, most systems provide both batch processing and time sharing, although their basic design and use tends to be one or the other type.

Time-sharing operating systems are sophisticated. They provide a mechanism for concurrent execution (Chapters 4 and 5). Also, as in multiprogramming, several jobs must be kept simultaneously in memory, which requires some form of memory management, protection, and CPU scheduling. So that a reasonable response time can be obtained, jobs may have to be swapped in and out of main memory to the disk that now serves as a backing store for main memory. Hence, disk management must also be provided (Chapter 9). Time-sharing systems must also provide an on-line file system (Chapter 10) and protection (Chapter 11). Multiprogramming and time sharing are the central themes of modern operating systems, and the central themes of this book.

1.8 Distributed Systems

A recent trend in computer systems is to distribute computation among several physical processors. There are basically two schemes for building such systems. In a *tightly coupled* system, the processors share memory and a clock. In these multiprocessor systems, communication usually takes place through the shared memory.

In a *loosely coupled* system, the processors do not share memory or a clock. Instead, each processor has its own local memory. The processors communicate with one another through various communication lines, such as high-speed buses or telephone lines. These systems are usually referred to as *distributed* systems.

The processors in a distributed system may vary in size and function. They may include small microprocessors, work stations, minicomputers, and large general-purpose computer systems. These processors are referred to by a number of different names, such as *sites*, *nodes*, *computers*, and so on, depending on the context in which they are mentioned.

There are a variety of reasons for building distributed systems, the major ones being these:

- **Resource sharing**. If a number of different sites (with different capabilities) are connected to one another, then a user at one site may be able to use the resources available at another. For example, a user at site A may be using a laser printer available only at site B. Meanwhile, a user at B may access a file that resides at A. In general, resource sharing in a distributed system provides mechanisms for sharing files at remote sites, processing information in a distributed database, printing files at remote sites, using remote specialized hardware devices (such as a high-speed array processor), and performing other operations.

- **Computation speed up**. If a particular computation can be partitioned into a number of subcomputations that can run concurrently, then a distributed system may allow us to distribute the computation among the various sites, to run it concurrently. In addition, if a particular site is currently overloaded with jobs, some of them may be moved to other, lightly loaded, sites. This movement of jobs is called *load sharing*.

- **Reliability**. If one site fails in a distributed system, the remaining sites can potentially continue operating. If the system is composed of a number of large autonomous installations (that is, general-purpose computers), the failure of one of them should not affect the rest. If, on the other hand, the system is composed of a number of small machines, each of which is responsible for some crucial system function (such as terminal character I/O or the file system), then a single failure may effectively halt the operation of the whole system. In general, if enough redundancy exists in the system (in both hardware and data), the system can continue with its operation, even if some of its sites have failed.

- **Communication**. There are many instances in which programs need to exchange data with one another on one system. Window systems are one example, since they frequently share data or transfer data between windows. When a number of sites are connected to one another by a communication network, the processes at different sites have the opportunity to exchange information. Users may initiate file transfers or communicate with one another via *electronic mail*. A user can send mail to another user at the same site or at a different site. *Mail* is text that is not interpreted by the operating system.

Distributed systems are discussed in great detail in Chapter 12 through Chapter 14.

1.9 Real-Time Systems

Still another form of an operating system is the *real-time* system. A real-time system is often used as a control device in a dedicated application. Sensors bring data to the computer. The computer must analyze the data and possibly adjust controls to modify the sensor inputs. Systems that control scientific experiments, medical imaging systems, industrial control systems, and some display systems are real-time systems. Also included are some automobile-engine fuel-injection systems, home appliances controllers, and weapon systems. A real-time operating system has well-defined fixed-time constraints. Processing *must* be done within the defined constraints or the system will fail. For instance, it would not do for a robot arm to be instructed to halt *after* it had smashed into the car it was building. Contrast this requirement to a time-sharing system, where it is desirable (but not mandatory) to respond quickly, or to a batch system, where there may be no time constraints at all.

Such time constraints dictate the facilities that are usually available in real-time systems. Secondary storage of any sort is usually limited or missing, with data instead being stored in short-term memory, or read-only memory (ROM). ROM is a nonvolatile storage device that retains its content even in the case of electric outage; most other types of memory are volatile. Most advanced operating-system features are absent too, since they tend to separate the user further from the hardware and that separation results in uncertainty as to the amount of time an operation will take. For instance, virtual memory (discussed in Chapter 8) is almost never found on real-time systems.

Although people have attempted to mix time-sharing and real-time functionality in one operating system, the results have been compromises in features and utility because of the obvious conflicts in the requirements of the two types.

1.10 Single-User Systems

As hardware costs have decreased, it has once again become feasible to have a computer system dedicated to a single user. These types of computer systems are usually referred to as *personal computers*. The I/O devices have certainly changed, with panels of switches and card readers replaced with typewriter-like keyboards and mice. Line printers and card punches have succumbed to display screens and small, fast printers.

Until recently, the CPUs of these types of computer systems have been lacking the features needed to protect an operating system, including dual-mode instructions. Their operating systems have therefore been neither multiuser nor multitasking. However, the goals of these operating systems have changed with time; instead of trying to maximize CPU and peripheral utilization, the systems opt for user convenience and responsiveness. These systems include both the IBM PC family of computers running the MS-DOS operating system, and the Apple Macintosh and its software. The circle is now being completed again, with MS-DOS being succeeded by the OS/2 multitasking system and similar features being added to the new Macintoshes.

1.11 Summary

Operating systems have developed over the past 40 years for two main purposes. First, operating systems attempt to schedule computational activities to ensure good performance of the computing system. Second, they provide a convenient environment for the development and execution of programs.

Initially, computers were used from the front console. Software such as assemblers, loaders, and compilers improved the convenience of programming the system, but also required substantial set-up time. To reduce the set-up time, facilities hired operators and batched similar jobs.

Batch systems allowed automatic job sequencing by a resident monitor and improved the overall utilization of the computer greatly. The computer no longer had to wait for human operation. CPU utilization was still low, however, because of the slow speed of the I/O devices relative to that of the CPU. Off-line operation of slow devices was tried. Buffering was another approach to improving system performance by overlapping the input, output, and computation of a single job. Finally, spooling allowed the CPU to overlap the input of one job with the computation and output of other jobs.

To improve the overall performance of the system, developers introduced the concept of multiprogramming. With multiprogramming, several jobs are kept in memory at one time; the CPU is switched back and forth between them to increase CPU utilization and to decrease the total time needed to execute the jobs.

Multiprogramming, which was developed to improve performance, also allows time sharing. Time-shared operating systems allow many users (from one to several hundred) to use a computer system interactively at the same time. Other operating-system types include distributed systems and real-time systems.

We have shown logical progression of operating-system development, driven by inclusion of features in the CPU hardware that are needed for advanced operating-system functionality. This trend can be seen today in the evolution of personal computers, with inexpensive hardware being improved enough to allow, in turn, improved characteristics.

Exercises

1.1 What are the three main purposes of an operating system?

1.2 List the four steps that are necessary to run a program on a completely dedicated machine.

1.3 In a multiprogramming and time-sharing environment, several users share the system simultaneously. This situation can result in various security problems.

   a. What are two such problems?

   b. Can we ensure the same degree of security in a time-shared machine as we have in a dedicated machine? Explain your answer.

1.4 What is the main advantage of multiprogramming?

1.5 Why is spooling necessary for batch multiprogramming? Is it needed for a time-shared system? Explain your answer.

1.6 One of the drawbacks of early operating systems (for example, batch systems) was that the users lost the ability to directly interact with their jobs. In what ways do modern operating systems overcome this problem?

1.7 Define the essential properties of the following types of operating systems:

a. Batch

b. Interactive

c. Time-sharing

d. Real-time

e. Distributed

1.8 What is the main difficulty a person must overcome in writing an operating system for a real-time environment?

Bibliographic Notes

A general overview of operating-system functions and concepts is presented by Hoare [1972a]. Discussions concerning the historical evolution of computer hardware and software systems are presented by Rosen [1969], Rosin [1969], Denning [1971], and Weizer [1981].

An early batch-processing system is described by Bratman and Boldt [1959]. Off-line systems (satellite processing) were used by the IBM FORTRAN Monitor system from the late 1950s to the middle of 1960. Job-control languages are discussed by Brown [1970] and Barron [1974].

Spooling was pioneered on the Atlas computer system at Manchester University [Kilburn et al. 1961]. Spooling was also used on the Univac EXEC II system [1972a]. Spooling is now a standard feature of most systems, but it was not an integral part of IBM's OS/360 operating system for the 360 family of computers when OS/360 was introduced in the early sixties. Instead, spooling was a special feature added by the Houston computation center of the National Aeronautics and Space Administration (NASA). Hence, it is known as the Houston Automatic Spooling Priority (HASP) system.

Time-sharing systems were first proposed by Strachey [1959]. The earliest time-sharing systems were the Compatible Time-sharing System (CTSS) system developed at the Massachusetts Institute of Technology (MIT) [Corbato et al. 1962] and the SDC Q-32 system built by the System Development Corporation [Schwartz et al. 1964, Schwartz and Weissman 1967]. Other early, but more sophisticated, systems include the MULTIplexed Information and Computing Services (MULTICS) system developed at MIT [Corbato and Vyssotsky 1965], the XDS-940 system developed at the University of California at Berkeley [Lichtenberger and

Pirtle 1965], and the IBM TSS/360 system [Lett and Konigsford 1968]. General discussions concerning time-sharing systems are offered by Watson [1970].

Stone [1980] argued that the development of inexpensive microprocessors and of inexpensive memory eventually would make operating systems, and courses that teach them, obsolete. Denning [1980b, 1982a] replied that the basic old concepts of operating systems are simply being refined, and are being put to good use on contemporary hardware.

There are numerous up-to-date general textbooks on operating systems. These include Comer [1984], Tanenbaum [1987], Maekawa et al. [1987], Bic and Shaw [1988], Finkel [1988], Krakowiak [1988], and Deitel [1990].

Useful bibliographies on various operating-system topics are presented by Smith [1978, 1981], Newton [1979], Metzner [1982], Zobel [1983], and Brumfield [1986].

2

Computer System Structures

We need to have a general knowledge of the structure of a computer system before we can explore the details of system operation. In this chapter, several disparate parts of this structure are presented to round out our background knowledge. Since multiprogramming and time-sharing systems benefit from the overlap of CPU and I/O operations, the two standard machine architectures used to accomplish this overlap are outlined first.

The operating system must also ensure the correct operation of the computer system. So that user programs will not interfere with the proper operation of the system, the hardware must provide appropriate mechanisms to ensure correct behavior. Later in this chapter, we describe the basic computer architecture that makes it is possible to write a functional operating system. We also discuss different classes of computers and their respective operating systems.

2.1 Interrupt-Based Systems

For CPU and I/O operations to overlap, they must have a mechanism to allow a desynchronization and resynchronization of operation. Either of the following methods can be used; some systems use both:

- Interrupt-driven data transfer
- Direct-memory-access (DMA) data transfer

In contrast, in older systems, such data transfer was under the CPU control. The CPU had to execute, or at least to monitor, the data transfer, disallowing the overlapping of CPU and I/O operations. As an example, consider the steps needed to print data from memory:

1. Check whether the printer is ready for the next character.

2. If the printer is not ready, go to step 1.

3. If printer is ready, check whether there is another character to print.

4. If there is another character, go to step 1.

5. If there are no further characters, we are done with the printing.

This overlap method is known as *busy waiting*, since the CPU must keep checking the status of the I/O, and is therefore busy while it waits for each I/O to complete. Although it is true that in theory the CPU could do other processing and come back to print the next character later, this is not always possible in practice. Consider a fast input device that is being used. The CPU must still be faster, and thus will need to wait between inputs. If, however, the CPU switches to some other task to avoid this waste of time, it might risk missing some input, since two inputs may arrive during that time. Interrupt-based I/O is the perfect solution to this scenario.

The general structure of an interrupt-based system is depicted in Figure 2.1. Each device controller is in charge of a specific type of device (for example, disk drives, tape drives, line printers). A device controller maintains some local buffer storage and a set of special-purpose registers. The device controller is responsible for moving data between the peripheral device it controls and its local buffer storage.

To start an I/O, the CPU loads the appropriate registers within the device controller and then resumes its normal operation. The device controller, in turn, examines the contents of these registers to determine what action to take. For example, if it finds a read request, the controller will start the transfer of data from the device to its local buffer. Once the transfer of data is complete, the device controller informs the CPU that its has finished its operation. It accomplishes this communication by causing an *interrupt*.

When the CPU is interrupted, it stops what it is doing and immediately transfers execution to a fixed location. The fixed location usually contains the starting address where the service routine for the interrupt is located. The interrupt service routine transfers data from the local buffer of the device controller to main memory. Once this transfer is accomplished, the CPU can then resume the interrupted

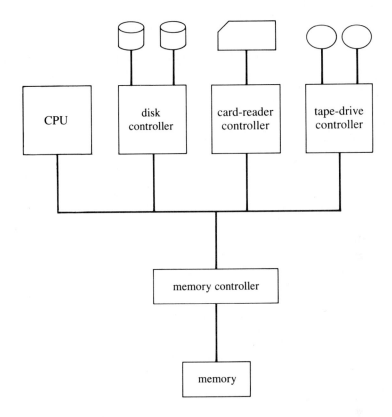

Figure 2.1 Interrupt-based computer system.

computation. In this way, I/O devices and the CPU can be operated concurrently. A time line of this operation is shown in Figure 2.2.

Interrupts are an important part of a computer architecture. Each computer design has its own interrupt mechanism, but several functions are common. The interrupt must transfer control to the interrupt service routine. Generally, this is done through reservation of a set of locations in low memory (the first 100 or so locations) to hold the addresses of the interrupt service routines for the various devices. This array, or *vector* of addresses is then indexed by a unique device number given with the interrupt request to provide the address of the interrupt service routine for the interrupting device.

The interrupt architecture must also save the address of the interrupted instruction. Many old designs simply stored the interrupt address in a fixed location or in a location indexed by the device

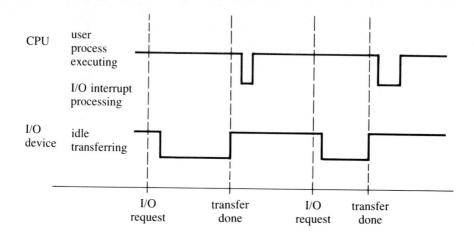

Figure 2.2   Interrupt time line.

number. More recent architectures store the return address on the system stack. Other registers, such as accumulators or index registers, may need to be explicitly saved and restored by the interrupt service routine. After the interrupt is serviced, a jump back to the saved return address will resume the interrupted computation as though the interrupt had not occurred. Usually, interrupts are *disabled* while an interrupt is being processed, delaying the incoming interrupt until the operating system is done with the current one and interrupts are *enabled*. If they were not thus disabled, the processing of the second interrupt while the first was being serviced would overwrite the first's data, and the first would be a *lost interrupt*. Sophisticated interrupt architectures allow for one interrupt to be processed during another, often by a priority scheme in which request types are assigned priorities according to their relative importance, and interrupt processing information is stored separately for each priority. A higher-priority interrupt will be taken even if a lower-priority interrupt is active, but interrupts at the same or lower levels are *masked*, or selectively disabled, to prevent lost interrupts or unnecessary ones.

For example, consider a simple terminal input driver. When a line is to be read from the terminal, the first character typed is sent to the computer. When that character is received, the asynchronous communication (or serial port) device to which the terminal line is connected will interrupt the CPU. When the interrupt request from the terminal arrives, the CPU will be about to execute some instruction. (If the CPU is in the middle of executing an instruction, the interrupt is normally held pending until the instruction execution is complete.) The address of this interrupted instruction is saved, and control is transferred to the interrupt service routine for the device.

The interrupt service routine saves the contents of any registers it will need to use. It checks for any error conditions that might have resulted from the last input operation. It then takes the character from the device and stores it in a buffer. The interrupt routine must also adjust pointer and counter variables, to be sure the next input character will be stored at the next location in the buffer. The interrupt routine next sets a flag in memory indicating to the other parts of the operating system that new input has been received. The other parts are responsible for processing the data in the buffer and transferring the characters to the program requesting input (see Section 2.5). Then, the interrupt service routine restores the contents of any saved registers and transfers control back to the interrupted instruction.

If characters are being typed to a 1200-baud terminal, the terminal can accept and transfer one character approximately every 8 milliseconds, or 8000 microseconds. A well-written interrupt service routine to input characters into a buffer may require 20 microseconds per character, leaving 7980 microseconds out of every 8000 for CPU computation (and servicing of other interrupts). Given this disparity, asynchronous I/O is usually assigned a low interrupt priority, allowing other, more important interrupts to be processed first, or even to preempt the current interrupt for another. A high-speed device, however, such as a tape, disk, or communications network, may be able to transmit information at close to memory speeds; the CPU would need 20 microseconds to respond to each interrupt, with interrupts arriving every 4 microseconds (for example).

To solve this problem, direct-memory access (DMA) is used for high-speed I/O devices. After setting up buffers, pointers, and counters for the I/O device, the device controller transfers an entire block of data to or from its own buffer storage to memory directly, with no intervention by the CPU. Only one interrupt is generated per block, rather than the one interrupt per byte (or word) generated for low-speed devices.

The basic operation of the CPU is the same. A user program, or the operating system itself, may request data transfer. The operating system finds a buffer (an empty buffer for input or a full buffer for output) from a queue of buffers for the transfer. (A buffer is typically 128 to 4096 bytes, depending on the device type.) The DMA controller then has its registers set to the appropriate source and destination addresses, and transfer length. This is usually done by a device driver, which knows exactly how this information is to be provided to the controller. The DMA controller is then instructed (via control bits in a control register) to start the I/O operation. The DMA controller interrupts the CPU when the transfer has been completed.

2.2 I/O Structure

If there are no jobs to execute, no I/O devices to service, and no users to whom to respond, an operating system will sit quietly, waiting for something to happen. Events are almost always signaled by the occurrence of an interrupt, or a trap. A *trap* (or an exception) is a software-generated interrupt caused either by an error (for example, division by zero or invalid memory access), or by a specific request from a user program that an operating-system service be performed.

Thus, an operating system is *interrupt driven*. The interrupt-driven nature of an operating system defines that system's general structure. When an interrupt (or trap) occurs, the hardware transfers control to the operating system. First, the operating system preserves the state of the CPU by storing registers and the program counter. Then, it determines which type of interrupt has occurred. This determination may require *polling*, the querying of all I/O devices to detect which requested service, or it may be a natural result of a vectored interrupt system. For each type of interrupt, separate segments of code in the operating system determine what action should be taken.

A major class of events that an operating system must handle is that of I/O interrupts. An I/O device will interrupt when it has finished an I/O request. This situation will occur, in general, as the result of a user program requesting I/O. Once the I/O is started, two courses of action are possible. In the simplest case, the I/O is started; then, at I/O completion, control is returned to the user program. The other possibility is to return control to the user program without waiting for the I/O to complete.

Waiting for I/O completion may be accomplished in one of two ways. Some computers have a special **wait** instruction that idles the CPU until the next interrupt. Machines that do not have such an instruction may have a wait loop:

Loop: **jmp** *Loop*

This very tight loop simply continues until an interrupt occurs, transferring control to another part of the operating system. The **wait** instruction is probably better, since a wait loop generates a series of instruction fetches, which may cause significant contention for memory access. The contention is caused by the I/O device transferring information and the CPU transferring instructions.

One major advantage of always waiting for I/O completion is that at most one I/O request is outstanding at a time. Thus, whenever an I/O interrupt occurs, the operating system knows exactly which device is interrupting. On the other hand, this approach excludes simultaneous I/O processing.

An alternative is to start the I/O and immediately to return control to the user program. A *system call* (a request to the operating system) is then needed to allow the user to wait for I/O completion. Hence, we still require the wait code that we needed before. We also need to be able to keep track of many I/O requests at the same time. For this purpose, the operating system uses a table containing an entry for each I/O device: the *device-status table* (Figure 2.3). Each table entry indicates the device's type, its address, and state (not functioning, idle, or busy). If the device is busy with a request, the type of request and other parameters will be stored in the table entry for that device. Since it is possible for a program to issue several requests to the same device, we may have a list or chain of waiting requests. Thus, in addition to the I/O device table, an operating system may have a request list for each device.

An I/O device interrupts when it needs service. When an interrupt occurs, the operating system first determines which I/O device caused the interrupt. It then indexes into the I/O device table to determine the status of that device, and modifies the table entry to reflect the occurrence of the interrupt. For most devices, an interrupt signals

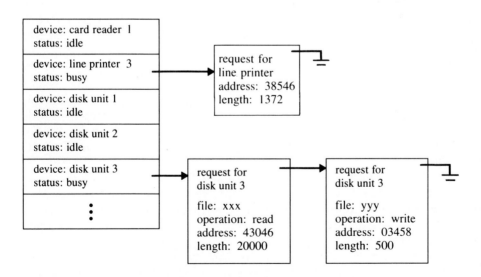

Figure 2.3   Device-status table.

completion of an I/O request. If there is an additional request waiting for this device, the operating system starts processing that request.

Finally, control is returned from the I/O interrupt. If a program was waiting for this request to complete (as recorded in the device-status table), we may now return control to it. Otherwise, we return to whatever we were doing before the I/O interrupt: to the execution of the user program (the program started an I/O operation and that operation has now finished, but the program has not yet waited for the operation to complete) or to the wait loop (the program started two or more I/O operations and is waiting for a particular one to finish, but this interrupt was from one of the others).

The schemes used by some input devices may vary from this one. Many interactive systems allow users to type ahead, or to enter data before they are requested, on their terminal. In this case, interrupts may occur, signaling the arrival of characters from the terminal, while the device-status block indicates that no program has requested input from this device. If type ahead is to be allowed, then a buffer must be provided to store the type-ahead characters until some program wants them. In general, we may need a buffer for each input terminal.

2.3 Dual-Mode Operation

Early computer systems were single-user programmer-operated systems. When the programmers operated the computer from the console, they had complete control over the system. As operating systems developed, however, this control was given to the operating system. Starting with the resident monitor, the operating system began performing many of the functions, especially I/O, for which the programmer had been responsible previously.

In addition, to improve system utilization, the operating system began to *share* system resources among several programs simultaneously. With spooling, one program might have been executing while I/O occurred for other jobs; the disk simultaneously held data for many jobs. Multiprogramming put several programs in memory at the same time.

This sharing created both improved utilization and increased problems. When the system was run without sharing, an error in a program could cause problems for only the one program that was running. With sharing, many jobs could be (adversely) affected by a bug in one program.

For example, consider the earliest resident monitor, providing nothing more than automatic job sequencing (Section 1.3). Suppose a program gets stuck in a loop reading input cards. The program will read through all of its data and, unless something stops it, will continue reading the cards of the next job, and the next, and so on. This could prevent the correct operation of many jobs.

Even more subtle errors could occur in a multiprogramming system, where one erroneous program might modify the program or data of another program, or even the resident monitor itself.

Without protection against these sorts of errors, either the computer must execute only one job at a time, or all output must be suspect. A properly designed operating system must ensure that an incorrect (or malicious) program cannot cause other programs to execute incorrectly.

Many programming errors are detected by the hardware. These errors are normally handled by the operating system. If a user program fails in some ways — such as an attempt either to execute an illegal instruction, or to access memory that is not in the user's address space — then the hardware will trap to the operating system. The trap transfers control through the interrupt vector to the operating system just like an interrupt. Whenever a program error occurs, the operating system must abnormally terminate the program. This situation is handled by the same code as is a user-requested abnormal termination. An appropriate error message is given, and the memory of the program is dumped. In a batch system, the memory dump may be printed, allowing the user to try to find the cause of the error by examining the printed dump. In an interactive system, the memory dump may be written to a file. The user may then print it or examine it on-line, and perhaps correct and restart the program.

This approach works fine as long as the error is detected by the hardware. We must be sure, however, that *all* errors are detected. We must protect the operating system and all other programs and their data from any malfunctioning program. Protection is needed for any shared resource. The approach taken is to provide hardware support to allow one to differentiate between various modes of executions. At the very least, we need two separate *modes* of operation: *user mode* and *monitor mode* (also called *supervisor mode* or *system mode*). A bit, called *mode-bit*, is added to the hardware of the computer to indicate the current mode: monitor (0) or user (1). With the mode-bit, we are able to distinguish between an execution that is done on behalf of the operating system, and one that is done on behalf of the user. As will be shown in Section 2.4, this ability is useful for many other aspects of system operation.

Whenever a trap or interrupt occurs, the hardware switches from user mode to monitor mode (that is, changes the state of the mode-bit to be 0). Thus, whenever the operating system gains control of the computer, it is in monitor mode. The system always switches to user mode (by setting the mode bit to 1) before passing control to a user program.

The dual mode of operation provides us with the means for protecting the operating system from errant users, and errant users from one another. We accomplish this protection by designating some of the machine instructions that may cause harm as *privileged instructions*. The hardware allows privileged instructions to be executed only in monitor mode. If an attempt is made to execute a privileged instruction in user mode, the hardware does not execute the instruction, but rather treats it as an illegal instruction and traps to the operating system.

The lack of a hardware-supported dual mode can cause serious shortcomings in an operating system. For instance, MS-DOS was written for the Intel 8088 architecture, which has no mode bit, and therefore no dual mode. A user program running awry can wipe out the operating system by writing over it with data, and multiple programs are able to write to a device at the same time, with possibly disastrous results.

2.4 Hardware Protection

A user program may disrupt the normal operation of the system by issuing illegal I/O instructions, by accessing memory locations within the operating system itself, or by refusing to relinquish the CPU. In the following paragraphs, we describe various mechanisms to ensure that such disruptions cannot take place in the system.

To prevent a user from performing illegal I/O, we define all I/O instructions to be privileged instructions. Thus, users cannot issue I/O instructions directly; they must do it through the operating system. For I/O protection to be complete, we must be sure that a user program can never gain control of the computer in monitor mode. If the computer is executing in user mode, it will switch to monitor mode whenever an interrupt or trap occurs, jumping to the address determined from the interrupt vector. Suppose a user program, as part of its execution, stores a new address in the interrupt vector. This new address could overwrite the previous address with an address in the user program. Then, when a corresponding trap or interrupt occurred, the hardware would switch to monitor mode, and would transfer control through the (modified) interrupt vector to the user program! The user program could gain control of the computer in monitor mode.

We must protect the interrupt vector from modification by a user program. In addition, we must also protect the interrupt service routines in the operating system from modification. Otherwise, a user program might overwrite instructions in the interrupt service routine with jumps to the user program, thus gaining control from the interrupt service routine that was executing in monitor mode. Even if the user did not gain unauthorized control of the computer, modifying the interrupt service routines would probably disrupt the proper operation of the computer system and of its spooling and buffering.

We see then that we must provide memory protection at least for the interrupt vector and the interrupt service routines of the operating system. In general, however, we want to protect the operating system from access by user programs, and, in addition, to protect user programs from one another. This protection must be provided by the hardware. It can be implemented in several ways, as we will see in Chapter 7. Here, we outline one such possible implementation.

What is needed to separate each program's memory space is an ability to determine the range of legal addresses the program may access, and to protect the memory outside that space. This protection can be provided by using two registers, usually a *base* and a *limit*, as illustrated in Figure 2.4. The base register holds the smallest legal physical memory address, and the limit register contains the size of the

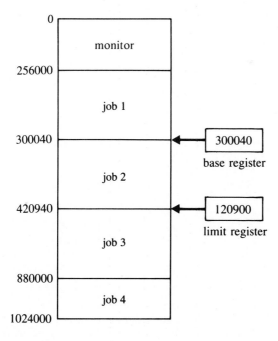

Figure 2.4   A base and a limit register define a logical address space.

range. For example, if the base registers holds 300040 and limit register is 120900, then the program can legally access all addresses from 300040 through 420940 inclusive.

This protection is accomplished by the CPU hardware comparing *every* address generated in user mode with the registers. Any attempt by a program executing in user mode to access monitor memory or other users' memory results in a trap to the monitor, which treats the attempt as a fatal error (Figure 2.5). This prevents the user program from (accidentally or deliberately) modifying the code or data structures of either the operating system or other users.

The base and limit registers can be loaded by the operating system, which uses a special privileged instruction. Since privileged instructions can be executed only in monitor mode, and since only the operating system executes in monitor mode, only the operating system can load the base and limit registers. This scheme allows the monitor to change the value of the registers, but prevents user programs from changing the registers' contents.

The operating system, executing in monitor mode, is given unrestricted access to both monitor and users' memory. This provision allows the operating system to load users' programs into users' memory,

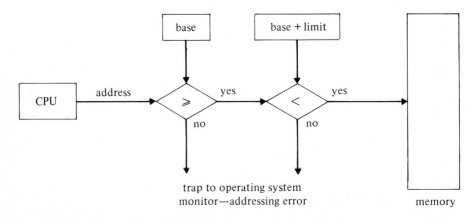

Figure 2.5   Hardware address protection with base and limit registers.

to dump them out in case of errors, to access and modify parameters of system calls, and so on.

To ensure that the operating system maintains control, we must prevent a user program from getting stuck in an infinite loop, and never returning control to the operating system. To accomplish this, we can use a *timer*. A timer can be set to interrupt the computer after a specified period. The period may be fixed (for example, 1/60 second) or variable (for example, from 1 millisecond to 1 second, in increments of 1 millisecond). A variable timer is generally implemented by a fixed-rate clock and a counter. The operating system sets the counter. Every time the clock ticks, the counter is decremented. When the counter reaches zero, an interrupt occurs. A 10-bit counter with a 1-millisecond clock would allow interrupts at intervals from 1 millisecond to 1024 milliseconds, in steps of 1 millisecond.

Before turning over control to the user, the operating system ensures that the timer is set to interrupt. If the timer interrupts, control transfers automatically to the operating system, which may treat the interrupt as a fatal error or decide to give the program more time. Instructions that modify the operation of the timer are clearly privileged.

Thus, the timer can be used to prevent a user program from running too long. A simple technique is to initialize a counter with the amount of time that a program is allowed to run. A program with a 7-minute time limit, for example, would have its counter initialized to 420. Every second, the timer interrupts and the counter is decremented by one. As long as the counter is positive, control is returned to the user program. When the counter becomes negative, we terminate the program for exceeding its time limit.

A more common use of a timer is to implement time sharing. In the most straightforward case, the timer could be set to interrupt every N milliseconds where N is the *time-slice* each user is allowed to execute before the next user gets control of the CPU. The operating system is invoked at the end of each time-slice to perform various housekeeping tasks, such as adding the value N to the record that specifies (for accounting purposes) the amount of time the user program has executed thus far. The operating system also resets registers, internal variables, and buffers, and changes several other parameters to prepare for the next program to run. Following this, the next program continues with its execution from the point at which it left off (when its previous time-slice ran out).

Another use of the timer is to compute the current time. A timer interrupt signals the passage of some period, allowing the operating system to compute the current time in reference to some initial time. If we have interrupts every 1 second, and we have had 1427 interrupts since we were told it was 1:00 P.M., then we can compute that the current time is 1:23:47 P.M. Some computers determine the current time in this manner, but the calculations must be done carefully for the time to be kept accurately, since the interrupt-processing time (and other times when interrupts are disabled) tends to cause the clock to slow down. Most computers have a separate hardware time-of-day clock that is independent of the operating system.

2.5 General System Architecture

The desire to reduce set-up time and to improve utilization of the computer system led to batching of jobs, to buffering and spooling, and eventually to multiprogramming and time sharing. These approaches share the resources of the computer system among many different programs and jobs. Sharing led directly to modifications of the basic computer architecture, to allow the operating system to maintain control over the computer system and especially over I/O. Control must be maintained if we are to provide continuous, consistent, and correct operation.

To maintain control, developers introduced a dual mode of execution (user mode and monitor mode). This scheme supports the concept of privileged instructions, which can be executed in only monitor mode. I/O instructions and instructions to modify the memory-management registers or the timer are privileged instructions.

As you can imagine, several other instructions are also classified as privileged. For instance, the **halt** instruction is privileged; a user program should never be able to halt the computer. The instructions to turn the interrupt system on and off are also privileged, since proper operation of the timer and I/O depends on the ability to respond to interrupts correctly. The instruction to change from user mode to monitor mode is privileged, and on many machines any change to the mode-bit is privileged.

Since I/O instructions are privileged, they can be executed by only the operating system. Then how does the user program perform I/O? By making I/O instructions privileged, we have prevented user programs from doing any I/O, either valid or invalid. The solution to this problem is that, since only the monitor can do I/O, the user must *ask* the monitor to do I/O on the user's behalf.

Most modern computers have a special instruction called a *system call* (also called a *monitor call*). Prior to having these special instructions, system calls were sometimes triggered by the user program executing an undefined instruction code — a code with no hardware operation defined for it. This generated an "illegal instruction" trap, resulting in transfer of control to the monitor. The TOPS-10 operating system depended exclusively on this technique.

When a system call is executed, it is treated by the hardware as a software interrupt. Control passes through the interrupt vector to a service routine in the operating system, and the mode-bit is set to monitor mode. The system-call service routine is a part of the operating system. The monitor examines the interrupting instruction to determine that system call has occurred. A parameter indicates what type of service the user program is requesting. Additional information needed for the request may be passed in registers or in memory (with pointers to the memory locations passed in registers). The monitor executes the request and returns control to the instruction following the system call.

Thus, to do I/O, a user program executes a system call to request that the operating system perform I/O on its behalf (Figure 2.6). The operating system, executing in monitor mode, checks that the request is valid, and (if it is valid) does the I/O requested. The operating system then returns to the user.

2.6 Different Classes of Computers

Until now, our discussions have concerned general-purpose computer systems. In this section, we discuss different classes of computers and their respective operating systems.

2.6.1 Multiprocessor Systems

Most systems to date are single-processor systems; that is, they have only one main CPU. However, there is an increasing trend toward multiprocessor systems. Such systems have more than one CPU in close communication, sharing the computer bus, and sometimes memory and peripheral devices.

There are several reasons for building such systems. One advantage is increased *throughput*. By increasing the number of processors, we would hope to get more work done in a shorter period of time. The speed-up ratio with n processors is not n, however, but rather less than n. When multiple processors cooperate on a task, a certain amount of overhead is incurred in keeping everything working correctly. This overhead, plus contention for shared resources, lowers the expected gain from additional processors. Similarly, a group of n programmers working closely together does not result in n times the amount of work being accomplished.

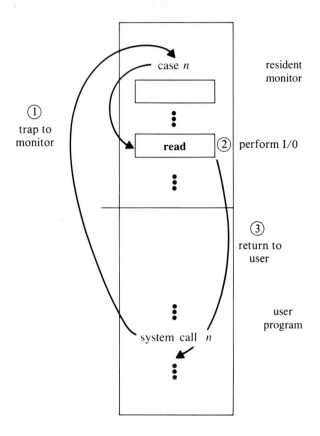

Figure 2.6   Use of a system call to perform I/O.

Another reason for multiprocessor systems is reliability. If functions can be distributed properly among several processors, then the failure of one processor will not halt the system, but will only slow it down. If we have 10 processors and one fails, then each of the remaining nine processors must pick up a share of the work of the failed processor. Thus, the entire system runs only 10 percent slower, rather than failing altogether. This ability to continue providing service proportional to the level of nonfailed hardware is called *graceful degradation*. Systems that are designed for graceful degradation are also called *fail-soft*.

Continued operation in the presence of failures requires a mechanism to allow the failure to be detected, diagnosed, and corrected (if possible). The Tandem system uses both hardware and software duplication to ensure continued operation despite faults. The system consists of two identical processors, each with its own local memory. The processors are connected by a bus. One processor is the primary and the other is the backup. Two copies are kept of each process; one on the primary machine and the other on the backup. At fixed checkpoints in the execution of the system, the state information of each job (including a copy of the memory image) is copied from the primary machine to the backup. If a failure is detected, the backup copy is activated and restarted from the most recent checkpoint. This is obviously an expensive solution, since there is considerable hardware duplication.

The most common multiple processor systems now use the *symmetric multiprocessing* model, in which each processor runs an identical copy of the operating system, and these copies communicate with one another as needed. Some systems use *asymmetric multiprocessing*, in which each processor is assigned a specific task. A master processor controls the system; the other processors either look to the master for instruction or have predefined tasks. This scheme defines a master-slave relationship. The master processor schedules and allocates work to the slave processors.

An example of the symmetric multiprocessing system is Encore's version of UNIX for the Multimax computer. This computer can be configured to employ dozens of processors, all running a copy of UNIX. The benefit of this model is that many processes can run at once (N processes if there are N CPUs) without causing a deterioration of performance. However, we must carefully control I/O to ensure that data reaches the appropriate processor. Also, since the CPUs are separate, one may be sitting idle while another is overloaded, resulting in inefficiencies. To avoid these inefficiencies, the processors can share certain data structures. A multiprocessor system of this form will allow jobs and resources to be shared dynamically among the various processors, and can lower the variance among the systems. However, such a system must be written carefully, as we shall see in Chapter 5.

Asymmetric multiprocessing is more common in very large systems, where one of the most time-consuming activities is simply processing I/O. In older batch systems, small processors, located at some distance from the main CPU, were used to run card readers and line printers and to transfer these jobs to and from the main computer. These locations are called remote job entry (RJE) sites. In a time-sharing system, a main I/O activity is processing the I/O of characters between the terminals and the computer. If the main CPU must be interrupted for every character for every terminal, it may spend all its time simply processing characters. So that this situation is avoided, most systems have a separate front-end processor that handles all the terminal I/O. For example, a large IBM system might use an IBM Series/1 minicomputer as a front-end. The front-end acts as a buffer between the terminals and the main CPU, allowing the main CPU to handle lines and blocks of characters, instead of individual characters. Such systems suffer from decreased reliability through increased specialization.

As microprocessors become less expensive and more powerful, additional operating-system functions are off-loaded to slave processors (or "back ends"). For example, it is fairly easy to add a microprocessor with its own memory to manage a disk system. The microprocessor could receive a sequence of requests from the main CPU and implement its own disk queue and scheduling algorithm. This arrangement relieves the main CPU of the overhead of disk scheduling. The IBM PC contains a microprocessor in its keyboard to convert the key strokes into codes to be sent to the CPU. In fact, this use of microprocessors has become so common that it is no longer considered multiprocessing.

2.6.2 Personal Computers

Personal computers appeared in the 1970s. Personal computers are microcomputers that are considerably smaller and less expensive than mainframe systems. Operating systems for these computers have benefited from the development of operating systems for mainframes in several ways. Microcomputers were immediately able to adopt the technology developed for larger operating systems. Buffering and spooling are present in many microcomputer systems; some personal computers even include multitasking.

On the other hand, the hardware costs for microcomputers are sufficiently low that individuals have sole use of the computer, and CPU utilization is no longer a prime concern. Thus, some of the design decisions that are made in operating systems for mainframes may not be appropriate for smaller systems. For example, file protection may not seem necessary on a personal machine. MS-DOS, the world's most common operating system, provides no such protection. It also lacks memory protection, multitasking, and dual-mode operation.

The Apple Macintosh operating system also does not provide these forms of protection. This is no coincidence, since the CPUs for which these operating systems were originally written do not provide the hardware support necessary for most forms of protection. As shown previously, without appropriate aid from the hardware, an operating system cannot provide this functionality. In recent years, the Apple Macintosh operating system has been ported to more advanced hardware, and now includes new features. Microsoft, the vendor of MS-DOS, has produced OS/2 as a follow-on system, rather than trying to retrofit MS-DOS.

memory and peripheral devices. The main reasons for building such systems are increased throughput and enhanced reliability. The most common multiprocessor systems now use the *symmetric multiprocessing* model, in which each processor runs an identical copy of the operating system, and these copies communicate with one another as needed. Some systems use *asymmetric multiprocessing*, in which each processor is assigned a specific task.

Personal computers are microcomputers that are considerably smaller and less expensive than mainframe systems. Operating systems for these computers have benefited from the development of operating systems for mainframes in several ways. However, since the hardware costs for microcomputers are sufficiently low, individuals can have sole use of the computer, and CPU utilization is no longer a prime concern. Hence, some of the design decisions that are made in operating systems for mainframes may not be appropriate for smaller systems.

Exercises

2.1 The concept of multiprogramming was not useful (that is, could not be used to gain more performance from a computing system) until the DMA channel was developed. Explain why this is true.

2.2 Show how a desire for control cards leads naturally to the creation of separate user and monitor modes of operation.

2.3 How does the distinction between monitor mode and user mode function as a rudimentary form of protection (security) system?

2.4 Which of the following instructions are privileged?

    a. Set value of timer.

    b. Read the clock.

    c. Clear memory.

    d. Turn off interrupts.

    e. Switch from user to monitor mode.

2.5 Some early computers protected the operating system by placing it in a memory partition that could not be modified by either the user job or the operating system itself. Describe two difficulties that you think could arise with such a scheme.

2.6 Many computer systems do not provide dual-mode operation in hardware. Consider whether it is possible to construct a secure operating system for these computers. Give arguments both that it is and that it is not possible.

2.7 Protecting the operating system is crucial to ensuring that the computer system operates correctly. Provision of this protection is the reason behind dual-mode operation, memory protection, and the timer. To allow maximum flexibility, however, we would also like to place minimal constraints on the user. The following is a list of operations that are normally protected. What is the *minimal* set of instructions that must be protected?

a. Change to user mode.

b. Change to monitor mode.

c. Read from monitor memory.

d. Write into monitor memory.

e. Fetch an instruction from monitor memory.

f. Turn on timer interrupt.

g. Turn off timer interrupt.

2.8 Writing an operating system that can operate without interference from malicious or undebugged user programs requires some hardware assistance. Name three hardware aids for writing an operating system, and describe how they may be used together to protect the operating system.

Bibliographic Notes

A detailed description of I/O devices such as channels and DMA appears in [Baer 1980]. A good discussion concerning I/O control interfaces can be found in [Stone 1982].

General discussions concerning multiprocessing are given by Nutt [1977], Enslow [1977], Gula [1978], and Jones and Schwarz [1980]. Multiprocessor hardware is discussed by Satyanarayanan [1980a, 1980b]. Performance of multiprocessor systems is presented by Maples [1985], Sanguinetti [1986], Agrawal et al. [1986], and Bhuyan et al. [1989].

The MS-DOS and the IBM-PC family are described by Norton [1986], and [Norton and Wilton 1988]. 1988]. An overview of the Apple Macintosh hardware and software is found in [Apple 1987]. The OS/2 operating system is covered in [Microsoft 1989].

3

Operating System Structures

An operating system provides the environment within which programs are executed. To construct such an environment, we partition the operating system logically into small modules and create a well-defined interface for these programs. Internally, operating systems vary greatly in their makeup, being organized along many different lines. The design of a new operating system is a major task. It is important that the goals of the system be well defined before the design begins. The type of system desired is the foundation for choices among various algorithms and strategies that will be necessary. In this chapter, we consider what services an operating system provides and how they are provided. We also describe various methodologies for designing such systems.

3.1 System Components

We can create a system as large and complex as an operating system only by partitioning it into smaller pieces. Each of these pieces should be a well-defined portion of the system, with carefully defined inputs, outputs, and function. Obviously, not all systems have the same structure. However, many modern operating systems share the goal of supporting the types of system components outlined in Sections 3.1.1 through 3.1.8.

3.1.1 Process Management

The CPU executes a large number of programs. Although its main concern is the execution of user programs, the CPU is also needed for other system activities. These activities are called *processes*. A process is a program in execution. Typically, a batch job is a process. A time-shared user program is a process. A system task, such as spooling, also is a process. For now, a process may be considered as a job or a time-shared program, but the concept is actually more general. As we shall see in Chapter 4, it is possible to provide system calls that allow processes to create subprocesses to execute concurrently.

In general, a process needs certain resources, including CPU time, memory, files, and I/O devices, to accomplish its task. These resources are either given to the process when it is created, or allocated to it while it is running. In addition to the various physical and logical resources that a process obtains when it is created, some initialization data (input) may be passed along. For example, a process whose function is to display on the screen of a terminal the status of a file, say F1, will get as an input the name of the file F1, and will execute the appropriate program to obtain the desired information.

We emphasize that a program by itself is not a process; a program is a *passive* entity, such as the contents of a file stored on disk, whereas a process is an *active* entity, with a *program counter* specifying the next instruction to execute. The execution of a process must progress in a sequential fashion. That is, at any point in time, at most one instruction is executed on behalf of the process. Thus, although two processes may be associated with the same program, they are nevertheless considered two separate execution sequences. It is common to have a program that spawns many processes as it runs.

A process is the unit of work in a system. Such a system consists of a collection of processes, some of which are operating-system processes (those that execute system code) and the rest of which are user processes (those that execute user code). All these processes can potentially execute concurrently, by multiplexing the CPU among them.

The operating system is responsible for the following activities in connection with process management:

- The creation and deletion of both user and system processes

- The suspension and resumption of processes

- The provision of mechanisms for process synchronization

- The provision of mechanisms for process communication

- The provision of mechanisms for deadlock handling

Process-management techniques will be discussed in great detail in Chapters 4 to 6.

3.1.2 Main-Memory Management

As discussed in Chapter 1, memory is central to the operation of a modern computer system. Memory is a large array of words or bytes, each with its own address. It is a repository of quickly accessible data shared by the CPU and I/O devices. The central processor reads instructions from main memory during the instruction-fetch cycle, and both reads and writes data from main memory during the data-fetch cycle. I/O implemented via DMA also reads and writes data in main memory. Main memory is generally the only storage device that the CPU is able to address directly. For example, for the CPU to process data from disk, those data must first be transferred to main memory by CPU-generated I/O calls. Equivalently, instructions must be in memory for the CPU to execute them.

For a program to be executed, it must be mapped to absolute addresses and loaded into memory. As the program executes, it accesses program instructions and data from memory by generating these absolute addresses. Eventually, the program terminates, its memory space is declared available, and the next program can be loaded and executed.

To improve both the utilization of CPU and the speed of the computer's response to its users, we must keep several programs in memory. There are many different memory-management schemes. These schemes reflect various approaches to memory management, and the effectiveness of the different algorithms depends on the particular situation. Selection of a memory-management scheme for a specific system depends on many factors, but especially on the *hardware* design of the system. Each algorithm requires its own hardware support.

The operating system is responsible for the following activities in connection with memory management:

- Keep track of which parts of memory are currently being used and by whom
- Decide which processes are to be loaded into memory when memory space becomes available
- Allocate and deallocate memory space as needed

Memory-management techniques will be discussed in great detail in Chapters 7 and 8.

3.1.3 Secondary-Storage Management

The main purpose of a computer system is to execute programs. These programs, with the data they access, must be in main memory during execution. Since main memory is too small to accommodate all data and programs permanently, the computer system must provide secondary storage to back up main memory. Most modern computer systems use disks as the primary on-line storage medium, for both programs and data. Most programs — including compilers, assemblers, sort routines, editors, and formatters — are stored on a disk until loaded into memory, and then use the disk as both the source and destination of their processing. Hence, the proper management of disk storage is of central importance to a computer system.

The operating system is responsible for the following activities in connection with disk management:

- Free-space management
- Storage allocation
- Disk scheduling

Techniques for secondary-storage management will be discussed in great detail in Chapter 9.

3.1.4 I/O System Management

One of the purposes of an operating system is to hide the peculiarities of specific hardware devices from the user. For example, in UNIX, the peculiarities of I/O devices are hidden from the bulk of the operating system itself by the *I/O system*. The I/O system consists of

- A buffer-caching system
- A general device-driver interface
- Drivers for specific hardware devices

Only the device driver knows the peculiarities of the specific device to which it is assigned.

We have already discussed in Chapter 2 how interrupt handlers and device drivers are used in the construction of efficient I/O systems. In Chapter 9, we shall discuss in great length how a particular device (the disk) is managed effectively.

3.1.5 File Management

File management is one of the most visible components of an operating system. Computers can store information in several different physical forms; magnetic tape, magnetic disk, and optical disk are the most common forms. Each of these devices has its own characteristics and physical organization.

For convenient use of the computer system, the operating system provides a uniform logical view of information storage. The operating system abstracts from the physical properties of its storage devices to define a logical storage unit, the *file*. Files are mapped, by the operating system, onto physical devices.

A file is a collection of related information defined by its creator. Commonly, files represent programs (both source and object forms) and data. Data files may be numeric, alphabetic, or alphanumeric. Files may be free-form, such as text files, or may be formatted rigidly. They consist of a sequence of bits, bytes, lines, or records whose meanings are defined by their creators. The concept of a file is a very general one.

The operating system implements the abstract concept of a file by managing mass storage devices, such as tapes and disks. Also files are normally organized into directories to ease their use. Finally, when multiple users have access to files, it may be desirable to control by whom and in what ways files may be accessed.

The operating system is responsible for the following activities in connection with file management:

- The creation and deletion of files
- The creation and deletion of directories
- The support of primitives for manipulating files and directories
- The mapping of files onto secondary storage
- The backup of files on stable (nonvolatile) storage media

File-management techniques will be discussed in Chapter 10.

3.1.6 Protection System

The various processes in an operating system must be protected from one another's activities. For that purpose, mechanisms are provided to ensure that the files, memory segments, CPU, and other resources can be operated on by only those processes that have gained proper authorization from the operating system.

For example, memory-addressing hardware ensures that a process can execute only within its own address space. The timer ensures that no process can gain control of the CPU without eventually relinquishing control. Finally, users are not allowed to do their own I/O, so that the integrity of the various peripheral devices is protected.

Protection refers to a mechanism for controlling the access of programs, processes, or users to the resources defined by a computer system. This mechanism must provide a means for specification of the controls to be imposed, together with a means of enforcement.

Protection can improve reliability by detecting latent errors at the interfaces between component subsystems. Early detection of interface errors can often prevent contamination of a healthy subsystem by a subsystem that is malfunctioning. An unprotected resource cannot defend against use (or misuse) by an unauthorized or incompetent user. A protection-oriented system provides a means to distinguish between authorized and unauthorized usage, as will be discussed in Chapter 11.

3.1.7 Networking

A *distributed* system is a collection of processors that do not share memory or a clock. Instead, each processor has its own local memory, and the processors communicate with one another through various communication lines, such as high-speed buses or telephone lines. The processors in a distributed system vary in size and function. They may include small microprocessors, work stations, minicomputers, and large general-purpose computer systems.

The processors in the system are connected through a *communication network*, which can be configured in a number of different ways. The network may be fully or partially connected. The communication-network design must consider routing and connection strategies, and the problems of contention and security.

A distributed system provides the user with access to the various resources that the system maintains. Access to a shared resource allows computation speedup, increased data availability, and enhanced reliability. Operating systems usually generalize network access as a form of file access, with the details of networking being contained in the network interface's device driver.

Discussions concerning network and distributed systems are presented in Chapters 12 to 14.

3.1.8 Command-Interpreter System

One of the most important system programs for an operating system is the *command interpreter*. Some operating systems, especially those on microcomputers such as MS-DOS and Apple's Macintosh system, include the command interpreter in the kernel. Other operating systems, usually those on larger computers, treat the command interpreter as a special program that is running when a job is initiated, or when a user first logs on (on time-sharing systems).

Many commands are given to the operating system by *control statements*. When a new job is started in a batch system, or when a user logs on to a time-shared system, a program that reads and interprets control statements is executed automatically. This program is variously called the control-card interpreter, the command-line interpreter, the shell (in UNIX), and so on. Its function is quite simple: Get the next command statement and execute it.

Operating systems are frequently differentiated in the area of command interpretation, with a user-friendly interpreter making the system more agreeable to some users. An example of this is the Macintosh interpreter, a window and menu system that is almost exclusively mouse-based. The user uses the mouse to point with the cursor to images (or *icons*) on the screen that represent programs, files, and system functions. Depending on the cursor location, clicking the mouse's button can invoke a program, select a file or directory (known as a *folder*), or pull down a menu containing commands. More powerful, complex, and difficult-to-learn interpreters endear themselves to other, more sophisticated users. On these, commands are typed on a keyboard and displayed on a screen or printing terminal, with the enter (or return) key signaling that a command is complete and is ready to be executed. The UNIX shells run in this mode.

The command statements themselves deal with process management, I/O handling, secondary-storage management, main memory management, file-system access, protection, and networking.

3.2 Operating-System Services

An operating system provides an environment for the execution of programs. The operating system provides certain services to programs and to the users of those programs. The specific services provided will, of course, differ from one operating system to another, but there are some common classes that we can identify. These operating-system services are provided for the convenience of the programmer, to make the programming task easier.

- **Program execution**. The system must be able to load a program into memory and to run it. The program must be able to end its execution, either normally or abnormally.

- **I/O operations**. A running program may require I/O. This I/O may involve a file or an I/O device. For specific devices, special functions may be desired (such as rewind a tape drive, or blank the screen on a CRT). Since a user program cannot execute I/O operations directly, the operating system must provide some means to do I/O.

- **File-system manipulation**. The file system is of particular interest. It should be obvious that programs need to read and write files. They also need to create and delete files by name. The file system is discussed fully in Chapter 10.

- **Communications**. There are many circumstances in which one process needs to exchange information with another process. There are two major ways in which such communication can occur. The first takes place between processes executing on the same computer; the second takes place between processes executing on different computer systems that are tied together by a computer network. Communications may be implemented via *shared memory*, or by the less general technique of *message passing*, in which packets of information are moved between processes by the operating system.

- **Error detection**. The operating system constantly needs to be aware of possible errors. Errors may occur in the CPU and memory hardware (such as a memory error or a power failure), in I/O devices (such as a parity error on tape, a card jam in the card reader, or lack of paper in the printer), or in the user program (such as an arithmetic overflow, an attempt to access an illegal memory location, or a too great use of CPU time). For each type of error, the operating system should take the appropriate action to ensure correct and consistent computing.

In addition, another set of operating-system functions exist not for helping the user, but rather for ensuring the efficient operation of the system itself. Systems with multiple users can gain efficiency by sharing the computer resources among the users.

- **Resource allocation**. When there are multiple users or multiple jobs running at the same time, resources must be allocated to each of them. Many different types of resources are managed by the operating system. Some (such as CPU cycles, main memory, and file storage) may have special allocation code, whereas others (such as I/O devices) may have much more general request and release code. For instance, in determining how to best utilize the CPU, operating systems have CPU-scheduling routines that take into account the speed of the CPU, the jobs that must be executed, the number of registers available, and other factors. There might also be routines to allocate a tape drive for use by a job. One such routine locates an unused tape drive and marks an internal table to record the drive's new user. Another routine is used to clear that table. These routines may also be used to allocate plotters, modems, and other peripheral devices.

- **Accounting**. We want to keep track of which users use how much and what kinds of computer resources. This record keeping may be for accounting (so that users can be billed) or simply for accumulating usage statistics. Usage statistics may be a valuable tool for researchers who wish to reconfigure the system to improve computing services.

- **Protection**. The owners of information stored in a multiuser computer system may want to control its use. When several disjoint jobs are being executed simultaneously, it should not be possible for one job to interfere with the others, or with the operating system itself. Protection involves checking all parameters passed in system calls for validity, and ensuring that all access to system resources is controlled. Security of the system from outsiders is also important. Such security starts with users having to specify passwords to be allowed access to the resources. It extends to defending external I/O devices, including modems and network adapters, from invalid access attempts, and to recording all such connections for detection of breakins. If a system is to be protected and secure, precautions must be instituted throughout it. A chain is only as strong as its weakest link.

3.3 System Calls

System calls provide the interface between a running program and the operating system. These calls are generally available as assembly-language instructions, and are usually listed in the manuals used by assembly-language programmers.

Some systems may allow system calls to be made directly from a higher-level language program, in which case the calls normally resemble predefined function or subroutine calls. They may generate a call to a special run-time routine that makes the system call, or the system call may be generated directly in-line.

Several languages, such as C, Bliss, and PL/360, have been defined to replace assembly language for systems programming. These languages allow system calls to be made directly. Some Pascal systems also provide an ability to make system calls directly from a Pascal program to the operating system. Most FORTRAN systems provide similar capabilities, often by a set of library routines.

As an example of how system calls are used, consider writing a simple program to read data from one file and to copy them to another file. The first thing the program will need is the names of the two files: the input file and the output file. These can be specified in many ways, depending on the operating-system design. One approach is for the program to ask the user for the names of the two files. In an interactive system, this will require a sequence of system calls, first to write a prompting message on the screen, and then to read from the keyboard the characters that define the two files. Another approach, frequently used for batch systems, is to specify the names of the files with control cards. In this case, there must be a mechanism for passing these parameters from the control cards to the executing program. On mouse-based and icon-based systems, a menu of file names is usually displayed in a window. The user can then use the mouse to select the source name, and a window could be opened for the destination name to be specified.

Once the two file names are obtained, the program must open the input file and create the output file. Each of these operations requires another system call. There are also possible error conditions for each operation. When the program tries to open the input file, it may find that there is no file of that name or that the file is protected against access. In these cases, the program should print a message on the console (another sequence of system calls) and then terminate abnormally (another system call). If the input file exists, then we must create a new output file. We may find that there is already an output file with the same name. This situation may cause the program to abort (a system call), or we may delete the existing file (another system call) and create a new one (another system call). Another option, in an interactive system, is to ask the user (a sequence of system calls to output the prompting message and read the response from the terminal) whether to replace the existing file or to abort.

Now that both files are set up, we enter a loop that reads from the input file (a system call) and writes to the output file (another system call). Each read and write must return status information regarding various possible error conditions. On input, the program may find that the end of the file has been reached, or that there was a hardware failure in the read (such as a parity error). The write operation may encounter various errors, depending on the output device (no more disk space, physical end of tape, printer out of paper, and so on).

Finally, after the entire file is copied, the program may close both files (another system call), write a message to the console (more system calls), and finally terminate normally (the last system call). As we can see, programs may make heavy use of the operating system. All interactions between the program and its environment must occur as the result of requests from the program to the operating system.

Most users never see this level of detail, however. The run-time support system for most programming languages provides a much simpler interface. For example, a *write* statement in Pascal or FORTRAN most likely is compiled into a call to a run-time support routine that issues the necessary system calls, checks for errors, and finally returns to the user program. Thus, most of the details of the operating system interface are hidden from the user programmer by the compiler and its run-time support package.

System calls occur in different ways, depending on the computer in use. Often, more information is required than simply the identity of the desired system call. The exact type and amount of information vary according to the particular operating system and call. For example, to get input, we may need to specify the file or device to use as the source, and the address and length of the memory buffer into which it should be read. Of course, the device or file and length may be implicit in the call.

Three general methods are used to pass parameters to the operating system. The simplest approach is to pass the parameters in *registers*. In some cases, however, there may be more parameters than registers. In these cases, the parameters are generally stored in a *block* or table in memory, and the address of the block is passed as a parameter in a register (Figure 3.1). Parameters also may be placed, or *pushed*, onto the *stack* by the program, and *popped* off the stack by the operating system. Some operating systems prefer the block or stack methods, since they do not limit the number or length of parameters being passed.

System calls can be roughly grouped into five major categories: *process control*, *file manipulation*, *device manipulation*, *information maintenance*, and *communications*. In Sections 3.3.1 to 3.3.5, we briefly discuss the types of system calls that may be provided by an operating system. Unfortunately, our description may seem somewhat shallow, since at this point most of these system calls support, or are supported by, concepts and functions that are discussed in later chapters. Figure 3.2 summarizes the types of system calls normally provided by an operating system.

3.3.1 Process and Job Control

A running program needs to be able to halt its execution either normally (**end**) or abnormally (**abort**). If a system call is made to terminate the currently running program abnormally, or if the program runs into a

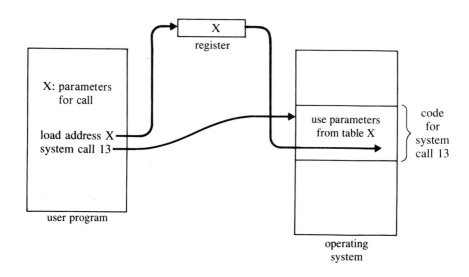

Figure 3.1   Passing of parameters as a table.

problem and causes an error trap, a dump of memory is sometimes taken and an error message generated. Under either normal or abnormal circumstances, the operating system must transfer control to the command interpreter. The command interpreter then reads the next command. In an interactive system, the command interpreter simply continues with the next command; it is assumed that the user will issue an appropriate command to respond to any error. In a batch system, the command interpreter usually terminates the entire job and continues with the next job. Some systems allow control cards to indicate special recovery actions in case an error occurs. If the program discovers an error in its input and wants to terminate abnormally, it may also want to define an error level. More severe errors can be indicated by a higher-level error parameter. It is then possible to combine normal and abnormal termination by defining a normal termination as error at level 0. The command interpreter or a following program can use this error level to determine the next action automatically.

A process or job executing one program may want to **load** and **execute** another program. This allows the command interpreter to execute a program as directed by, for example, a user command, the click of a mouse, or a batch command. An interesting question is where to return control when the loaded program terminates. This question is related to the problem of whether the existing program is lost, saved, or allowed to continue execution concurrently with the new program.

- Process Control
  - End, Abort
  - Load, Execute
  - Create Process, Terminate Process
  - Get Process Attributes, Set Process Attributes
  - Wait for Time
  - Wait Event, Signal Event
  - Allocate and Free Memory

- File Manipulation
  - Create File, Delete File
  - Open, Close
  - Read, Write, Reposition
  - Get File Attributes, Set File Attributes

- Device Manipulation
  - Request Device, Release Device
  - Read, Write, Reposition
  - Get Device Attributes, Set Device Attributes
  - Logically Attach or Detach Devices

- Information Maintenance
  - Get Time or Date, Set Time or Date
  - Get System Data, Set System Data
  - Get Process, File, or Device Attributes, Set Process, File, or Device Attributes

- Communications
  - Create, Delete Communication Connection
  - Send, Receive Messages
  - Transfer Status Information
  - Attach or Detach Remove Devices

Figure 3.2 Types of system calls.

If control returns to the existing program when the new program terminates, we must save the memory image of the existing program and thus have effectively created a mechanism for one program to call another program. If both programs continue concurrently, we have created a new job or process to be multiprogrammed. Often, there is a system call specifically for this purpose (**create process** or **submit job**).

If we create a new job or process, or perhaps even a set of jobs or processes, we should be able to control its execution. This control requires the ability to determine and reset the attributes of a job or process, including the job's priority, its maximum allowable execution time, and so on (**get process attributes** and **set process attributes**). We may also want to terminate a job or process that we created (**terminate process**) if we find that it is incorrect or is no longer needed.

Having created new jobs or processes, we may need to wait for them to finish execution. We may want to wait for a certain amount of time (**wait time**), but more likely we want to wait for a specific event (**wait event**). The jobs or processes should then signal when that event has occurred (**signal event**). System calls of this type, dealing with the coordination of concurrent processes, are discussed in more detail in Chapter 5.

Another set of system calls is helpful in debugging a program. Many systems provide system calls to **dump** memory. This provision is useful for assembly-language or machine-language debugging, particularly in a batch system. A program **trace** lists each instruction as it is executed; it is provided by fewer systems. Even microprocessors provide a CPU mode known as *single step*, in which a trap is executed by the CPU after every instruction. The trap is usually caught by a debugger, which is a system program designed to aid the programmer in finding and correcting bugs.

A time profile of a program is provided by many systems. It indicates the amount of time that the program executes at a particular location or set of locations. A time profile requires either a tracing facility or regular timer interrupts. At every occurrence of the timer interrupt, the value of the program counter is recorded. With frequent enough timer interrupts, a statistical picture of the time spent on various parts of the program can be obtained.

There are so many facets of and variations in process and job control that we shall use examples to clarify these concepts. The MS-DOS operating system is an example of a single-tasking system, which has a command interpreter that is invoked when the computer is started. Since MS-DOS is single-tasking, it uses a simple method to run a program, and does not create a new process. It loads the program into memory, writing over most of itself to give the program as much memory as possible. It then sets the instruction pointer to the first instruction of the program. The program then runs and either an error causes a trap, or the program executes a system call to terminate. In either case, the error code is saved in the system memory for later use. Following this, the small portion of the command interpreter that was not overwritten resumes execution. Its first task is to reload the rest of the command interpreter from disk. Once this is accomplished, the command interpreter makes the previous error code available to the user or to the next program.

Berkeley UNIX, on the other hand, is an example of a multitasking system. When a user logs on to the system, a command interpreter (called a *shell*) of the user's choice is run. This shell is similar to the MS-DOS command interpreter (in fact, MS-DOS is modeled after UNIX) in that it accepts commands and executes programs that the user requests. However, since UNIX is a multitasking system, the command interpreter may continue running while another program is executed. To start a new process, the shell executes a system call. Then, the selected program is loaded into memory via another system call, and the program is then executed. Depending on the way the command was issued, the shell then either waits for the process to finish, or runs the process "in the background." In the latter case, the shell immediately requests another command. When a process is running in the background, it cannot receive input directly from the user, since the shell is expecting input also. I/O is therefore done through files. Meanwhile, the user is free to ask the shell to run other programs, to monitor the progress of the running process, to change that program's priority, and so on. When the process is done, it executes a system call to terminate, returning to the invoking process a status code of 0, or a nonzero error code. This status or error code is then available to the shell or other programs.

3.3.2 File Manipulation

The file system will be discussed in more detail in Chapter 10. We can identify several common system calls dealing with files, however. Their exact meaning will become more clear when you read Chapter 10.

We first need to be able to **create** and **delete** files. Either system call requires the name of the file and perhaps some of the file's attributes. Once the file is created, we need to **open** it and to use it. We may also **read**, **write**, or **reposition** (rewinding or skipping to the end of the file, for example). Finally, we need to **close** the file, indicating that we are no longer using it.

We may need these same sets of operations for directories if we have a directory structure in the file system. In addition, for either files or directories, we need to be able to determine the values of various attributes, and perhaps to reset them if necessary. File attributes include the file name, a file type, protection codes, accounting information, and so on. Two system calls, **get file attribute** and **set file attribute**, are required for this function.

3.3.3 Device Management

A program, as it is running, may need additional resources in order to proceed. Additional resources may be more memory, tape drives, access to files, and so on. If the resources are available, they can be granted, and control can be returned to the user program; otherwise the program will have to wait until sufficient resources are available.

Files can be thought of as abstract or virtual devices. Thus, many of the system calls for files are also needed for devices. If there are multiple users of the system, however, we must first **request** the device, to ensure that we have exclusive use of it. After we are finished with the device, we must **release** it. These functions are similar to the **open/close** system calls for files.

Once the device has been requested (and allocated to us), we can **read**, **write**, and (possibly) **reposition** the device, just as we can with files. In fact, the similarity between I/O devices and files is so great that many operating systems merge the two into a combined file/device structure. In this case, I/O devices are identified by special file names.

3.3.4 Information Maintenance

Many system calls exist simply for the purpose of transferring information between the user program and the operating system. For example, most systems have a system call to return the current **time** and **date**. Other system calls may return information about the system, such as the number of current users, the version number of the operating system, the amount of free memory or disk space, and so on.

In addition, the operating system keeps information about all its jobs and processes, and there are system calls to access this information. Generally, there are also calls to reset it (**get process attributes** and **set process attributes**). In Section 4.1.3, we discuss what information is normally kept.

3.3.5 Communication

There are two common models of communication. In the *message-passing* model, information is exchanged through an interprocess communication facility provided by the operating system. Before communication can take place, a connection must be opened. The name of the other communicator must be known, be it another process on the same CPU, or a process on another computer. Each computer in a network has a *host name* by which it is commonly known. Similarly, each process has a *process name*, which is translated into an equivalent identifier by which the operating system can refer to it. The **get hostid**, and **get processid** system calls do this translation. These identifiers are then passed to the general-purpose **open** and **close** calls provided by the file system, or to specific **open connection** and **close connection** system calls. The recipient process usually must give its permission for communication to take place with an **accept connection** call. Most processes that will be receiving connections are special purpose *daemons*, which are system programs provided for that purpose. They execute a **wait for connection** call and are awakened when a connection is made. The source of the communication, known as the *client*, and the receiving daemon, known as a *server*, then exchange messages by **read message** and **write message** system calls. The **close connection** call terminates the communication.

In the *shared-memory* model, processes use *map-memory* system calls to gain access to regions of memory owned by other processes. Recall that, normally, the operating system tries to prevent one process from accessing another process's memory. Shared memory requires that two or more processes agree to remove this restriction. They may then exchange information by reading and writing data in these shared areas. The form of the data and the location are determined by these processes and are not under the operating system's control. The processes are also responsible for ensuring that they are not writing to the same location simultaneously. Such mechanisms are discussed in Chapter 5.

Both of these methods are common in operating systems, and some systems even implement both. Message passing is useful when smaller numbers of data need to be exchanged, since no conflicts need to be avoided. It is also easier to implement than is shared memory for intercomputer communication. Shared memory allows maximum speed and convenience of communication, since it can be done at memory speeds. Problems exist, however, in the areas of protection and synchronization.

3.4 System Programs

Another aspect of a modern system is its collection of system programs. Recall Figure 1.1, which depicted the logical computer hierarchy. At the lowest level is hardware, of course. Next is the operating system, then the systems programs, and finally the application programs. System programs provide a more convenient environment for program development and execution. They can be divided into several categories:

- **File manipulation**. These programs create, delete, copy, rename, print, dump, list, and generally manipulate files and directories.

- **Status information**. Some programs simply ask the system for the date, time, amount of available memory or disk space, number of users, or similar status information. That information is then formatted and printed to the terminal or other output device or file.

- **File modification**. Several text editors may be available to create and modify the content of files stored on disk or tape.

- **Programming-language support**. Compilers, assemblers, and interpreters for common programming languages (such as FORTRAN, COBOL, Pascal, BASIC, C, LISP, and so on) are often provided with the operating system. Recently, many of these programs have been priced and provided separately.

- **Program loading and execution**. Once a program is assembled or compiled, it must be loaded into memory to be executed. The system may provide absolute loaders, relocatable loaders, linkage editors, and overlay loaders. Debugging systems for either higher-level languages or machine language are needed also.

- **Communications**. These programs provide the mechanism for creating virtual connections among processes, users, and different computer systems. They allow users to send messages to each other's screens, to send larger messages as electronic mail, or to transfer files from one machine to another, and even to log on remotely to other computers.

- **Application programs**. Most operating systems are supplied with programs that are useful to solve common problems, or to perform common operations. Such programs include compiler compilers, text formatters, plotting packages, database systems, spreadsheets, statistical-analysis packages, games, and so on.

Perhaps the most important system program for an operating system is the *command interpreter*, the main function of which is to get the next user-specified command and to execute it.

Many of the commands given at this level manipulate files: create, delete, list, print, copy, execute, and so on. There are two general ways in which these commands can be implemented. In one approach, the command interpreter itself contains the code to execute the command. For example, a command to delete a file may cause the command interpreter to jump to a section of its code that sets up the parameters and makes the appropriate system call. In this case, the number of commands that can be given determines the size of the command interpreter, since each command requires its own implementing code.

An alternative approach used by UNIX, among other operating systems, implements all commands by special systems programs. In this case, the command interpreter does not "understand" the command in any way; it merely uses the command to identify a file to be loaded into memory and executed. Thus, a command

delete G

would search for a file called *delete*, load the file into memory, and execute it with the parameter G. The function associated with the **delete** command would be completely defined by the code in the file *delete*. In this way, programmers can add new commands to the system easily by creating new files of the proper name. The command-interpreter program, which can now be quite small, need not be changed for new commands to be added.

There are problems with this approach to the design of a command interpreter. Notice first that, since the code to execute a command is a separate system program, the operating system must provide a mechanism for passing parameters from the command interpreter to the system program. This task can often be quite clumsy, since the command interpreter and the system program may not both be in memory at the same time. Also, it is slower to load a program and execute it than simply jump to another section of code within the current program.

Another problem is that the interpretation of the parameters is left up to the programmer of the system program. This may mean that parameters are inconsistently provided across programs that appear similar to the user, but that were written at different times by different programmers.

The view of the operating system seen by most users is thus defined by the systems programs, not by the actual system calls. Consequently, this view may be quite removed from the actual system. Designing a useful and friendly user interface is therefore not a direct function of the operating system. In this book, we shall concentrate on the fundamental problems of providing adequate service to user programs. From the point of view of the operating system, we do not distinguish between user programs and systems programs.

3.5 System Structure

A system as large and complex as a modern operating system must be engineered carefully if it is to function properly and to be modified easily. A common approach is to partition the task into small pieces. Each of these pieces should be a well-defined portion of the system, with carefully defined inputs, outputs, and function. We have already briefly discussed the common components of operating systems (Section 3.1). In this section, we discuss the way that these components are interconnected and melded into a kernel.

3.5.1 Simple Structure

There are numerous commercial systems that do not have a well-defined structure. Frequently, such operating systems started as small, simple, and limited systems that grew beyond their original scope. An example of such a system is MS-DOS, the best-selling microcomputer operating system. MS-DOS was originally designed and implemented by a few people who had no idea that it would become so popular. It was written to provide the most functionality in the least space, so it was not divided into modules carefully. Figure 3.3 shows its current structure.

Although MS-DOS does have some structure, its interfaces and levels of functionality are not well separated. For instance, applications

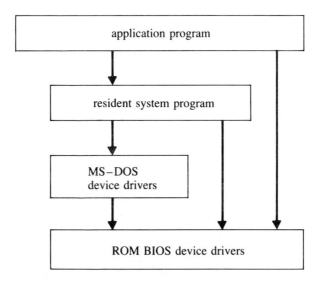

Figure 3.3 MS-DOS layer structure.

programs are able to access the basic I/O routines to write directly to the display and disk drives. Such freedom leaves MS-DOS vulnerable to errant programs, causing entire system crashes or disk erasures when user programs fail. Of course, MS-DOS is also limited by the hardware on which it runs. Since the Intel 8088 for which it was written provides no dual mode and no hardware protection, the designers of MS-DOS had no choice but to leave the base hardware accessible.

Another example of limited structuring is the original UNIX operating system. UNIX is another system that initially was limited by hardware functionality. It consists of two separable parts: the kernel and the systems programs. The kernel is further separated into a series of interfaces and device drivers, which have been added and expanded over the years as UNIX has evolved. We can view the UNIX operating system as being layered as shown in Figure 3.4. Everything below the system-call interface and above the physical hardware is the kernel. The kernel provides the file system, CPU scheduling, memory management, and other operating-system functions through system calls. Taken in sum, that is a very large amount of functionality to be combined into one level. Systems programs use the kernel-supported system calls to provide useful functions, such as compilation and file manipulation.

System calls define the *programmer interface* to UNIX; the set of systems programs commonly available defines the *user interface*. The programmer and user interfaces define the context that the kernel must support. Several versions of UNIX have been developed in which the

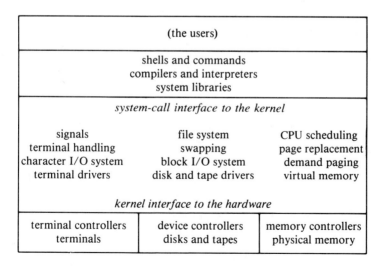

Figure 3.4 UNIX system structure.

kernel is partitioned further along functional boundaries. The AIX operating system, IBM's version of UNIX, separates the kernel into two parts. Mach, from Carnegie-Mellon University, reduces the kernel to a small set of core functions by moving all nonessentials into systems and even into user-level programs.

3.5.2 Layered Approach

These new UNIX versions are designed to use more advanced hardware. Given proper hardware support, operating systems may be broken into smaller, more appropriate pieces than those allowed by the original MS-DOS or UNIX. This allows the operating system to retain much greater control over the computer and the applications that make use of it. It also gives implementors more freedom to make changes to the inner workings of the system. Familiar techniques are used to aid in the creation of modular operating systems. Using the top-down approach, the overall functionality and features may be determined and separated into components. Information hiding is also important, leaving programmers free to implement the low-level routines as they see fit, provided the external interface of the routine stays unchanged and the routine itself performs the advertised task.

The modularization of a system can be done in many ways, but the most appealing is the layered approach, which consists of breaking the operating system into a number of layers (levels), each built on top of lower layers. The bottom layer (layer 0) is the hardware; the highest (layer N) is the user interface.

An operating-system layer is an implementation of an abstract object that is the encapsulation of data and operations that can manipulate those data. A typical operating-system layer — say layer M — is depicted in Figure 3.5. It consists of some data structures and a set of routines that can be invoked by higher-level layers. Layer M, in return, can invoke operations on lower-level layers.

The main advantage of the layered approach is *modularity*. The layers are selected such that each uses functions (operations) and services of only lower-level layers. This approach can make the debugging and verification of the system much easier. The first level can be debugged without any concern for the rest of the system, since, by definition, it uses only the basic hardware (which is assumed correct) to implement its functions. Once the first level is debugged, its correct functioning can be assumed while the second level is worked on, and so on. If an error is found during the debugging of a particular level, we know that the error must be on that level, since the levels below it are already debugged. Thus, the design and implementation of the system is simplified when the system is broken down into layers.

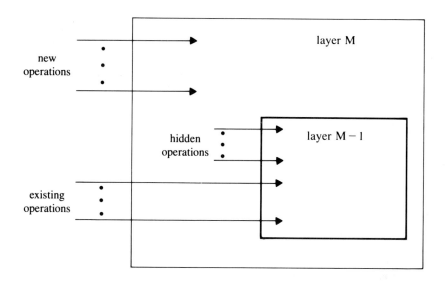

Figure 3.5 An operating-system layer.

Each layer is implemented using only those operations provided by lower-level layers. A layer does not need to know how these operations are implemented; it needs to know only what these operations do. Hence, each layer hides the existence of certain data structures, operations, and hardware from higher-level layers.

The layer approach to design was first used in the THE operating system at the Technische Hogeschool Eindhoven. The THE system was defined in six layers, as shown in Figure 3.6. The bottom layer was the hardware. The next layer implemented CPU scheduling. The next layer implemented memory management. The memory-management scheme was virtual memory (Chapter 8). Level 3 contained the device driver for the operator's console. Because it, as well as the I/O buffering, was placed at level 4, above memory management, the device buffers could be placed in virtual memory. The I/O buffering was also above the operator's console, so that I/O error conditions could be output to the operator's console.

This approach can be used in many ways. For example, the Venus system was also designed using a layered approach. The lower levels (0 to 4), dealing with CPU scheduling and memory management, were then put into microcode. This decision provided the advantages of additional speed of execution and a clearly defined interface between the microcoded levels and the higher levels (Figure 3.7).

Level 5:	user programs
Level 4:	buffering for input and output devices
Level 3:	operator-console device driver
Level 2:	memory management
Level 1:	CPU scheduling
Level 0:	hardware

Figure 3.6   THE layer structure.

The major difficulty with the layered approach involves defining the levels. Since a layer can only use layers at a lower level, careful planning is necessary. For example, the device driver for the backing store (disk space used by virtual-memory algorithms) must be at a level lower than that of the memory-management routines, since memory management requires the ability to use the backing store.

Other requirements may not be so obvious. The backing-store driver would normally be above the CPU scheduler, since the driver may need to wait for I/O and the CPU can be rescheduled during this time. However, on a large system, the CPU scheduler may have more information about all the active processes than can fit in memory. Therefore, this information may need to be swapped in and out of memory, requiring the backing-store driver routine to be below the CPU scheduler.

Level 6:	user programs
Level 5:	device drivers and schedulers
Level 4:	virtual memory
Level 3:	I/O channel
Level 2:	CPU scheduling
Level 1:	instruction interpreter
Level 0:	hardware

Figure 3.7   Venus layer structure.

These limitations have caused a small backlash against layering in recent years. Fewer layers with more functionality are being designed, providing most of the advantages of modularized code while avoiding the difficult problems of layer definition and interaction. OS/2, a direct descendant of MS-DOS, was created to overcome the limitations of MS-DOS. OS/2 adds multitasking and dual-mode operation, as well as other new features. Because of this added complexity and the more powerful hardware for which OS/2 was designed, the system was implemented in a more layered fashion. Contrast the MS-DOS structure to that shown in Figure 3.8. It should be clear that, from both the system-design and implementation standpoints, OS/2 has the advantage. For instance, direct user access to low-level facilities is not allowed, providing the operating system with more control over the hardware and more knowledge of which resources each user program is utilizing.

3.6 Virtual Machines

Conceptually, a computer system is made up of layers. The hardware is the lowest level in all such systems. The kernel running at the next level uses the hardware instructions to create a set of system calls for use by outer layers. The systems programs above the kernel are therefore able to use either system calls or hardware instructions, and in some ways these programs do not differentiate between these two. Thus, although they are accessed differently they both provide functionality that the program may use to create even more advanced functions. System programs, in turn, treat the hardware and the systems calls as though they were at the same level.

Some systems carry this scheme even a step further by allowing the system programs to be called easily by the application programs. As before, although the system programs are at a level higher than that of the other routines, the application programs may view everything under them in the hierarchy as though the latter were part of the machine itself. This layered approach is taken to its logical conclusion in the concept of a *virtual machine*. The VM operating system for IBM systems is the best example of the virtual-machine concept, since IBM pioneered the work in this area.

By using CPU scheduling (Chapter 4) and virtual-memory techniques (Chapter 8), an operating system can create the illusion of multiple processes, each executing on its own processor with its own (virtual) memory. Of course, normally, the process has additional features, such as system calls and a file system, which are not provided by the bare hardware. The virtual-machine approach, on the other hand, does not provide any additional function, but rather provides an interface that is

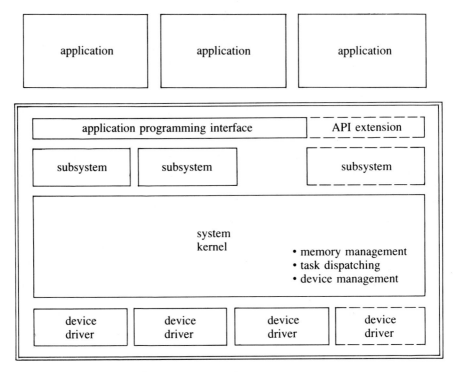

Figure 3.8   OS/2 layer structure.

identical to the underlying bare hardware. Each process is provided with a (virtual) copy of the underlying computer.

The resources of the physical computer are shared to create the virtual machines. CPU scheduling can be used to share the CPU and to create the appearance that users have their own processor. Spooling and a file system can provide virtual card readers and virtual line printers. A normal user time-sharing terminal provides the function of the virtual machine operator's console.

A major difficulty involves disk systems. Suppose the physical machine has three disk drivers but wants to support seven virtual machines. Clearly, it cannot allocate a disk drive to each virtual machine. Remember that the virtual-machine software itself will need substantial disk space to provide virtual memory and spooling. The solution is to provide virtual disks, which are identical in all respects except size. These are termed *minidisks* in IBM's VM operating system. The system implements each minidisk by allocating as many tracks as the minidisk needs on the physical disks. Obviously, the sum of the sizes of all minidisks must be less than the actual amount of physical disk space available.

Users thus are given their own virtual machine. They can then run any of the software packages that are available on the underlying machine. For the IBM VM system, a user normally runs CMS, a single-user interactive operating system. The virtual-machine software is concerned with multiprogramming multiple virtual machines onto a physical machine, but does not need to consider any user-support software. This arrangement may provide a useful partitioning of the problem of designing a multiuser interactive system into two smaller pieces.

Although the virtual machine concept is useful, it is difficult to implement. Much effort is required to provide an *exact* duplicate of the underlying machine. Remember, for example, that the underlying machine has two modes: user mode and monitor mode. The virtual-machine software can run in monitor mode, since it is the operating system. The virtual machine itself can execute in only user mode. Just as the physical machine has two modes, however, so must the virtual machine. Consequently, we must have a virtual user mode and a virtual monitor mode, both of which run in a physical user mode. Those actions that cause a transfer from user mode to monitor mode on a real machine (such as a system call or an attempt to execute a privileged instruction) must also cause a transfer from virtual user mode to virtual monitor mode on a virtual machine.

This transfer can generally be done fairly easily. When a system call, for example, is made by a program running on a virtual machine in virtual user mode, it will cause a transfer to the virtual-machine monitor in the real machine. The virtual user mode is also a physical user mode. When the virtual-machine monitor gains control, it can change the register contents and program counter for the virtual machine to simulate the effect of the system call. It can then restart the virtual machine, noting that it is now in virtual monitor mode. If the virtual machine then tries, for example, to read from its virtual card reader, it will execute a privileged I/O instruction. Since the virtual machine is running in physical user mode, this instruction will trap to the virtual-machine monitor. The virtual-machine monitor must then simulate the effect of the I/O instruction. First, it finds the spooled file that implements the virtual card reader. Then, it translates the read of the virtual card reader into a read on the spooled disk file, and transfers the next virtual "card image" into the virtual memory of the virtual machine. Finally, it can restart the virtual machine. The state of the virtual machine has been modified exactly as though the I/O instruction had been executed with a real card reader for a real machine executing in a real monitor mode.

The major difference is, of course, time. Whereas the real I/O might have taken 100 milliseconds, the virtual I/O might take less time (since it is spooled) or more (since it is interpreted). In addition, the CPU is being multiprogrammed among many virtual machines, further slowing down the virtual machines in unpredictable ways. In the extreme case, it may be necessary to simulate all instructions to provide a true virtual machine. VM works for IBM machines because normal instructions for the virtual machines can execute directly on the hardware. Only the privileged instructions (needed mainly for I/O) must be simulated and hence execute more slowly.

The virtual-machine concept has several advantages. Notice that in this environment there is complete protection of the various system resources. Each virtual machine is completely isolated from all other virtual machines, so there are no security problems. On the other hand, there is no direct sharing of resources. To provide sharing, two approaches have been implemented. First, it is possible to share a minidisk. This scheme is modeled after a physical shared disk, but is implemented by software. With this technique, files can be shared. Second, it is possible to define a network of virtual machines, each of which can send information over the virtual communications network. Again, the network is modeled after physical communication networks, but is implemented in software.

Such a virtual-machine system is a perfect vehicle for operating-systems research and development. Normally, changing an operating system is a difficult task. Since operating systems are large and complex programs, it is difficult to be sure that a change in one point will not cause obscure bugs in some other part. This situation can be particularly dangerous because of the power of the operating system. Since the operating system executes in monitor mode, a wrong change in a pointer could cause an error that would destroy the entire file system. Thus, it is necessary to test all changes to the operating system carefully.

But the operating system runs on and controls the entire machine. Therefore, the current system must be stopped and taken out of use while changes are made and tested. This period is commonly called *system-development time*. Since it makes the system unavailable to users, system-development time is often scheduled late at night or on weekends.

A virtual-machine system can eliminate much of this problem. System programmers are given their own virtual machine, and system development is done on the virtual machine, instead of on a physical machine. Normal system operation seldom needs to be disrupted for system development.

3.7 System Design and Implementation

In this section, we discuss the problems of designing and implementing a system. There are, of course, no complete solutions to the design problems, but there are approaches that have been successful.

3.7.1 Design Goals

The first problem in designing a system is to define the goals and specifications of the system. At the highest level, the design of the system will be significantly affected by the choice of hardware and type of system: batch, time-shared, single-user, multiuser, distributed, real-time, or general purpose.

Beyond this highest design level, on the other hand, the requirements may be much harder to specify. The requirements can basically be divided into two groups: *user* goals and *system* goals.

Users desire certain obvious properties in a system: The system should be convenient to use, easy to learn, easy to use, reliable, safe, and fast. Of course, these specifications are not very useful in the system design, since there is no general agreement on how to achieve these goals.

A similar set of requirements can be defined by those people who must design, create, maintain, and operate the system: The operating system should be easy to design, implement, and maintain; it should be flexible, reliable, error-free, and efficient. Again, these requirements are vague and have no general solution.

There is no unique solution to the problem of defining the requirements for an operating system. The wide range of systems shows that different requirements can result in a large variety of solutions for different environments. For example, the requirements for MS-DOS, a single-user system for microcomputers, must have been quite different from those for MVS, the large multiuser, multiaccess operating system for IBM mainframes.

The specification and design of an operating system is a highly creative task. No mere textbook can solve that problem. There are, however, some general principles that have been suggested. *Software engineering* is the general field for these principles; certain ideas from this field are especially applicable to operating systems.

3.7.2 Mechanisms and Policies

One very important principle is the separation of *policy* from *mechanism*. Mechanisms determine *how* to do something. In contrast, policies decide *what* will be done.

For example, a mechanism for ensuring CPU protection is the timer construct (see Section 2.3). The decision of for how long the timer is set for a particular user, on the other hand, is a policy decision.

The separation of policy and mechanism is very important for flexibility. Policies are likely to change from place to place or time to time. In the worst case, each change in policy would require a change in the underlying mechanism. A general mechanism would be more desirable. A change in policy would then require redefining only certain parameters of the system. For instance, if, in one computer system, a policy decision is made that I/O-intensive programs should have priority over CPU-intensive ones, then the opposite policy could easily be instituted at some other computer system if the mechanism were properly separated and were policy independent.

Policy decisions are important for all resource allocation and scheduling problems. Whenever it is necessary to decide whether or not to allocate a resource, a policy decision must be made. Whenever the question is "how" rather than "what," it is a mechanism that must be determined.

3.7.3 Implementation

Once an operating system is designed, it must be implemented. Traditionally, operating systems have been written in assembly language. However, that is generally no longer true. Operating systems can now be written in higher-level languages.

The first system that was not written in assembly language was probably the Master Control Program (MCP) for Burroughs computers. MCP was written in a variant of ALGOL. MULTICS, developed at MIT, was written mainly in PL/1. The UNIX operating system and OS/2 are mainly written in C. Only some 900 lines of code of the original UNIX were in assembly language, most of which constituted the dispatcher and device drivers. The Primos operating system for Prime computers is written in a dialect of FORTRAN. The Solo operating system is written in Concurrent Pascal.

The advantages of using a higher-level language, or at least a systems-implementation language, for implementing operating systems are the same as those accrued when the language is used for application programs: The code can be written faster, is more compact, and is easier to understand and debug. The major claimed disadvantages are reduced speed and increased storage requirements. Although no compiler can produce consistently better code than can an expert assembly-language programmer, a compiler often can produce code at least as good as that written by the average assembly-language programmer. In addition, replacing the compiler with a better compiler will uniformly improve the generated code for the entire operating system by simple recompilation. Finally, an operating system is far easier to *port* — to move to some other hardware — if it is written in a high-level language. For example, MS-DOS was written in Intel 8088 assembly language. Consequently, it is available on only the Intel family of CPUs. The UNIX operating system, which is written mostly in C, on the other hand, is available on a number of different CPUs, including Intel, Motorola, SPARC, and Mips.

As with other systems, major performance improvements are more likely to be the result of better data structures and algorithms than of cleaner coding. In addition, although operating systems are very large systems, only a small amount of the code is critical to high performance; the memory manager and the CPU scheduler are probably the most critical routines. After the system is written and is working correctly, bottleneck routines can be identified, and can be replaced with assembly-language equivalents.

To identify bottlenecks, we must be able to monitor the system performance. Code must be added to compute and display measures of system behavior. In a number of systems, the operating system does this task by producing trace listings of system behavior. All interesting events are logged with their time and important parameters, and are written to a file. Later, an analysis program can process the log file to determine system performance and to identify bottlenecks and inefficiencies. These same traces could also be run as input for a simulation of a suggested improved system. Traces also can be useful in finding errors in operating-system behavior.

An alternative possibility is to compute and display performance measures in real time. This approach may allow the system operators to become more familiar with system behavior and to modify system operation in real time.

3.8 System Generation

It is possible to design, code, and implement an operating system specifically for one machine at one site. More commonly, however, operating systems are designed to run on any of a class of machines at a variety of sites with a variety of peripheral configurations. The system must then be configured or generated for each specific computer site. This process is known as *system generation* (SYSGEN).

The operating system is normally distributed on tape or disk. To generate a system, we use a special program. The system-generation program reads from a file or asks the operator for information concerning the specific configuration of the hardware system:

- What CPU is to be used? What options (extended instruction sets, floating-point arithmetic, and so on) are installed? For multiple CPU systems, each CPU must be described.

- How much memory is available? Some systems will determine this value themselves by referencing memory location after memory location until an "illegal address" fault is generated. This procedure defines the final legal address and hence the amount of available memory.

- What devices are available? The system will need to know how to address each device (the device number), the device interrupt number, the device's type and model, and any special device characteristics.

- What operating system options are desired or what parameter values are to be used? These might include how many buffers of which sizes should be used, what CPU-scheduling algorithm is desired, what the maximum number of processes to be supported is, and so on.

Once this information is defined, it can be used in several ways. At one extreme, it may be used to modify a copy of the source code of the operating system. The operating system would then be completely compiled. Data declarations, initializations, and constants, along with conditional compilation, would produce an output object version of the operating system that is tailored to the system described.

At a slightly less tailored level, the system description could cause the creation of tables and the selection of modules from a precompiled library. These modules would be linked together to form the generated operating system. Selection would allow the library to contain the device drivers for all supported I/O devices, but only those actually needed would be linked into the operating system. Since the system would not be recompiled, system generation would be faster, but might result in a system with more generality than was actually needed.

At the other extreme, it would be possible to construct a system that was completely table driven. All the code would always be a part of the system, and selection would occur at execution time, not at compile or link time. System generation involves simply creating the appropriate tables to describe the system.

The major differences among these approaches are the size and generality of the generated system and the ease of modification as the hardware configuration changes. Consider the cost of modifying the system to support a newly acquired graphics terminal or another disk drive. Balanced against that cost, of course, is the frequency (or infrequency) of such changes.

3.9 Summary

Operating systems provide a number of services. At the lowest level, system calls allow a running program to make requests from the operating system directly. At a higher level, the command interpreter provides a mechanism for a user to issue a request without writing a program. Commands may come from cards (in a batch system) or directly from a terminal (in an interactive or time-shared system). Systems programs provide another mechanism for satisfying user requests.

The types of requests vary according to the level of the request. The system-call level must provide the basic functions, such as process control and file and device manipulation. Higher-level requests, satisfied by the command interpreter or systems programs, are translated into a sequence of system calls. System services can be classified into several categories: program control, status requests, and I/O requests. Program errors can be considered implicit requests for service.

Once the system services are defined, the structure of the operating system can be developed. Various tables are needed to record the information that defines the state of the computer system and the status of the system's jobs.

The design of a new operating system is a major task. It is important that the goals of the system be well defined before the design begins. The type of system desired is the foundation for choices among various algorithms and strategies that will be necessary.

Since an operating system is large, modularity is important. The design of a system as a sequence of layers is considered an important design technique. The virtual-machine concept takes the layered approach to heart and treats the kernel of the operating system and the hardware as though they were all hardware. Even other operating systems may be loaded on top of this virtual machine.

Throughout the entire operating-system design cycle, we must be careful to separate policy decisions from implementation details. This allows maximum flexibility if policy decisions are to be changed later.

Operating systems are now almost always written in a systems implementation language or a higher-level language. This feature improves their implementation, maintenance, and portability. To create an operating system for a particular machine configuration, we must perform system generation.

Exercises

3.1 What are the five major activities of an operating system in regard to process management?

3.2 What are the three major activities of an operating system in regard to memory management?

3.3 What are the three major activities of an operating system in regard to secondary-storage management?

3.4 What are the five major activities of an operating system in regard to file management?

3.5 What is the purpose of the command interpreter?

3.6 List five services provided by an operating system. Explain how each provides convenience to the users. In each case, explain where it would be impossible for user-level programs to provide these services.

3.7 What is the purpose of system calls?

3.8 What is the purpose of system programs?

3.9 What is the main advantage of the layered approach to system design?

3.10 What is the main advantage for an operating-system designer of using a virtual-machine architecture? What is the main advantage for a user?

3.11 Why is the separation of mechanism and policy a desirable property?

Bibliographic Notes

To see actual operating-system code, you might look at Madnick and Donovan [1974, Chapter 7] (a sample multiprogramming system for an IBM/360), Brinch Hansen [1977] (the Solo operating system for the PDP-11 written in Concurrent Pascal), or Brinch Hansen [1983] (the Edison system for the IBM PC). Comer [1984] and Tanenbaum [1987] also include the source code of sample operating systems.

Unger [1975] is concerned with various aspects of command languages. Particularly interesting is the survey of Gram and Hertweck [1975]. Brown [1978] provides a somewhat more recent summary of developments with command languages. A general discussion of command interpretation is presented by Finkel [1988, Chapter 7].

Command languages can be seen as special-purpose programming languages. Brunt and Tuffs [1976] argue that a command language should provide a rich set of functions; Frank [1976] argues for a more limited, simpler command language. An excellent case study is the UNIX shell, as described by Bourne [1978].

The layered approach to operating-system design has been advocated by Dijkstra [1968]. A good general discussion of the overall philosophy has been presented by Saxena and Bredt [1975], Habermann et al. [1976], and Denning [1976]. The THE system is described in [Dijkstra 1968b]; the Venus system is described in [Liskov 1972].

Brinch Hansen [1970] was an early proponent of the construction of an operating system as a kernel (or nucleus) on which can be built more complete systems. A computer architecture for supporting level-structured operating systems was described by Bernstein and Siegel [1975].

The first operating system to provide a virtual machine was the CP/67 on an IBM 360/67 and is described by Meyer and Seawright [1970]. CP/67 provided each user with a virtual 360 Model 65, including I/O devices. The commercially available IBM VM/370 operating system is derived from CP/67 and is described by Seawright and MacKinnon [1979], Holley et al. [1979] and Creasy [1981]. Hall et al. [1980] promoted the use of virtual machines for increasing operating-system portability. Jones [1978] suggested the use of virtual machines to enforce the isolation of processes for protection purposes. General discussions concerning virtual machines are presented by Hendricks and Hartmann [1979], MacKinnon [1979], Schultz [1988], and Goldberg [1974].

MS-DOS, Version 3.1, is described in [Microsoft 1986]. The Apple Macintosh operating system is described in [Apple 1987]. Berkeley UNIX is described in [CSRG 1986]. The standard AT&T UNIX system V is described in [AT&T 1986]. A good description of OS/2 is given in [Iacobucci 1988]. Mach is introduced in [Accetta 1986], and AIX is presented in [Loucks and Sauer 1987].

The issue of operating-system portability has been discussed by Cox [1975] and Cheriton et al. [1979] (the Thoth portable operating system).

Wulf et al. [1971], and Sammet [1971] have discussed higher-level system-implementation languages. A variant of ALGOL was used in writing the Burroughs MCP operating system. PL/1 was used in writing the MULTICS system. A variant of FORTRAN was used in writing the Primos operating system. The TI 990 operating system was written in a Pascal-like language with features for controlling concurrency. Numerous higher-level languages have been designed specifically for system implementation. These languages include PL/360 [Wirth 1968] for the IBM system/360 family of computers, SAL [Lang 1969] for the Atlas II computer, BCPL [Richards 1969] for the KDF9 computer, Bliss [Wulf et al. 1971] for the PDP-10 computer, and C [Kernighan and Ritchie 1978] for the UNIX operating system.

PART 2

Process Management

A *process* is a program in execution. In general, a process will need certain resources — such as CPU time, memory, files, and I/O devices — to accomplish its task. These resources are allocated to the process either when it is created, or while it is executing.

A process is the unit of work in most systems. Such a system consists of a collection of processes: Operating-system processes execute system code, and user processes execute user code. All these processes can potentially execute concurrently.

The operating system is responsible for the following activities in connection with process management: the creation and deletion of both user and system processes; the scheduling of processes; and the provision of mechanisms for synchronization, communication, and deadlock handling for processes.

4

Processes

The CPU executes a large number of programs. Although its main concern is the execution of user programs, the CPU is also needed for other system activities. These activities are called *processes*. A process is the unit of work in a system. Such a system consists of a collection of processes: Operating-system processes execute system code, and user processes execute user code. All these processes can potentially execute concurrently, the CPU (or CPUs) is multiplexed among them. By switching the CPU between processes, the operating system can make the computer more productive.

4.1 Process Concept

One hindrance to the discussion of operating systems is the question of what to call all the CPU activities. A batch system executes *jobs*, whereas a time-shared system has *user programs*, or *tasks*. Even on a single-user system, such as MS-DOS and Macintosh OS, a user may be able to run several programs at one time: one interactive and several batch programs. Even if the user can execute only one program at a time, the operating system may need to support its own internal programmed activities, such as spooling. In many respects, all of these activities are similar, so we call all of them *processes*.

The terms *job* and *process* are used almost interchangeably in this text. Although we personally prefer the term *process*, much of the operating system theory and terminology was developed during a time when the major activity of operating systems was job processing. It would be misleading to avoid the use of commonly accepted terms that include the word *job* (such as job scheduling) simply because the term *process* has superseded it.

4.1.1 Sequential Process

Informally, a *sequential process* is a program in execution. The execution of a process must progress in a sequential fashion. That is, at any point in time, at most one instruction is executed on behalf of the process.

A process is more than the program code plus the current activity. A process generally also includes the process *stack* containing temporary data (such as subroutine parameters, return addresses, and temporary variables), and a *data section* containing global variables.

We emphasize that a program by itself is not a process; a program is a *passive* entity, such as the contents of a file stored on disk, whereas a process is an *active* entity, with a *program counter* specifying the next instruction to execute.

Although two processes may be associated with the same program, they are nevertheless considered two separate execution sequences. It is common to have a process that spawns many processes as it runs. This issue will be further discussed in Section 4.2

4.1.2 Process State

As a process executes, it changes *state*. The state of a process is defined in part by that proccess's current activity. Each sequential process may be in one of the following three states:

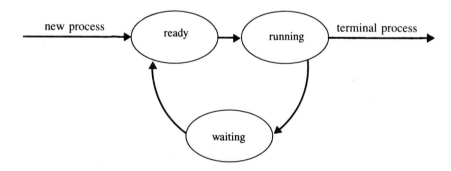

Figure 4.1   Process state diagram.

- **Running**. Instructions are being executed.

- **Waiting**. The process is waiting for some event to occur (such as an I/O completion).

- **Ready**. The process is waiting to be assigned to a processor.

These names are rather arbitrary, and vary between operating systems. The states they represent are found on all systems, however. It is important to realize that only one process can be *running* at any instant. Many processes may be *ready* and *waiting*, however. The state diagram corresponding to these three states is presented in Figure 4.1.

4.1.3 Process Control Block

Each process is represented in the operating system by its own *process control block* (PCB; also called a task control block; Figure 4.2). A PCB is a data block or record containing many pieces of the information associated with a specific process, including

- **Process state**. The state may be new, ready, running, waiting, or halted.

- **Program counter**. The counter indicates the address of the next instruction to be executed for this process.

- CPU **registers**. The registers vary in number and type, depending on the computer architecture. They include accumulators, index registers, stack pointers, and general-purpose registers, plus any condition-code information. Along with the program counter, this

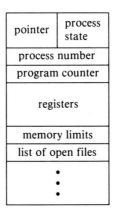

Figure 4.2 Process control block.

state information must be saved when an interrupt occurs, to allow the process to be continued correctly afterward (Figure 4.3).

- **CPU scheduling information**. This information includes a process priority, pointers to scheduling queues, and any other scheduling parameters.

- **Memory-management information**. This information includes limit registers or page tables (Chapter 7).

- **Accounting information**. This information includes the amount of CPU and real time used, time limits, account numbers, job or process numbers, and so on.

- **I/O status information**. The information includes outstanding I/O requests, I/O devices (such as tape drives) allocated to this process, a list of open files, and so on.

The PCB simply serves as the repository for any information that may vary from process to process.

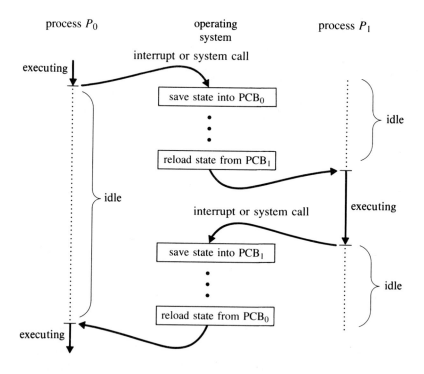

Figure 4.3   The CPU can be switched from process to process.

4.2 Concurrent Processes

The processes in the system can execute concurrently; that is, many processes may be multitasked on a CPU. There are several reasons for allowing concurrent execution:

- **Physical resource sharing**. Since the computer hardware resources are limited, we may be forced to share them in a multiuser environment.

- **Logical resource sharing**. Since several users may be interested in the same piece of information (for instance, a shared file), we must provide an environment to allow concurrent access to these types of resources.

- **Computation speedup**. If we want a particular task to run faster, we must break it into subtasks, each of which will be executing in parallel with the others. Notice that such a speedup can be achieved only if the computer has multiple processing elements (such as CPUs or channels).

- **Modularity**. We may want to construct the system in a modular fashion, dividing the system functions into separate processes, as was discussed in Chapter 3.

- **Convenience**. Even an individual user may have many tasks to work on at one time. For instance, a user may be editing, printing, and compiling in parallel.

Concurrent execution that requires cooperation among the processes requires a mechanism for process synchronization and communication. This mechanism is discussed in Chapter 5.

4.2.1 Process Creation and Termination

To obtain concurrent execution, we must have a mechanism for process creation and termination.

Process Creation

A process may create several new processes, via a create-process system call, during the course of execution. The creating process is called a *parent* process, whereas the new processes are called the *children* of that process. Each of these new processes may in turn create other processes.

In general, a process will need certain resources (CPU time, memory, files, I/O devices) to accomplish its task. When a process creates a subprocess, the subprocess may be able to obtain its resources directly from the operating system, or it may be constrained to a subset of the resources of the parent process. The parent may have to partition its resources among its children, or it may be able to share some resources (such as memory or files) among several of its children. Restricting a child process to a subset of the parent's resources prevents any process from overloading the system by creating too many subprocesses.

In addition to the various physical and logical resources that a process obtains when it is created, initialization data (input) may be passed along by the parent process to the child process. For example, a process whose function is to display on the screen of a terminal the status of a file, say *F1*, will get (when it is created) as an input from its parent process the name of the file *F1*, and will execute using that datum to obtain the desired information.

When a process creates a new process, two common implementations exist in terms of execution:

- The parent continues to execute concurrently with its children.
- The parent waits until all its children have terminated.

To illustrate these different implementations, let us consider the UNIX operating system. In UNIX, each process is identified by its *process identifier*, which is a unique integer. A new process is created by the **fork** system call. The new process consists of a copy of the address space of the original process. This mechanism allows the parent process to communicate easily with its child process. Both processes (the parent and the child) continue execution at the instruction after the **fork** with one difference: the return code for the **fork** is zero for the new (child) process, whereas the (nonzero) process identifier of the child is returned to the parent.

Typically, the **execve** system call is used after a **fork** by one of the two processes to replace the process's memory space with a new program. The **execve** system call loads a binary file into memory (destroying the memory image of the program containing the **execve** system call) and starts its execution.

Process Termination

A process terminates when it finishes executing its last statement and asks the operating system to delete the process. At that point, the process may return data (output) to its parent process (via the aforementioned system call).   There are additional circumstances when termination occurs.   A process can cause the termination of another process via an appropriate system call (for example, **abort**).   Usually, such a system call can be invoked by only the parent of the process that is to be terminated. Note that a parent needs to know the identities of its children. Thus, when one process creates a new process, the identity of the newly created process is passed to the parent.

A parent may terminate the execution of one of its children for a variety of reasons, such as

- The child has exceeded its usage of some of the resources it has been allocated.

- The task assigned to the child is no longer required.

To determine the first case, the parent must have a mechanism to inspect the state of its children.

Many systems do not allow a child to exist if its parent has terminated. In such systems, if a process terminates (either normally or abnormally), then all its children must also be terminated. This phenomenon is referred to as *cascading termination* and is normally initiated by the operating system.

To illustrate cascading termination, let us consider again the UNIX system. In UNIX, a process may terminate by using the *exit* system call, and its parent process may wait for that event by using the *wait* system call. The wait system call returns the process identifier of a terminated child, so that the parent can tell which of the possibly many children has terminated. A parent does not need to partition its resources among its children: Each child is scheduled separately by UNIX, and competes with the other processes equally for limited resources (memory, disk access).

4.2.2 Relation Between Processes

The processes executing in the operating system may be either independent processes or cooperating processes.

A process is *independent* if it cannot affect or be affected by the other processes executing in the system. Such a process has the following characteristics:

- Its state is not shared in any way by any other process.

- Its execution is deterministic; that is, the result of the execution depends solely on the input state.

- Its execution is reproducible; that is, the result of the execution will always be the same for the same input.

- Its execution can be stopped and restarted without causing ill effects.

Clearly, any process that does not share any data (temporary or persistent) with any other process is independent.

A process is *cooperating* if it can affect or be affected by the other processes executing in the system. Such a process has the following characteristics:

- Its state is shared among other processes.

- The result of its execution cannot be predicted in advance, since it depends on relative execution sequence.

- The result of its execution is nondeterministic since it will not always be the same for the same input.

Clearly, any process that shares data with other processes is a cooperating process.

Cooperating processes may either directly share a logical address space (that is, both code and data), or be allowed to share data only through files. The former case is achieved through the use of *lightweight* processes or *threads*, described in Section 4.2.3.

4.2.3 Threads

Recall that a process is defined by the resources it uses and by the location at which it is executing. There are many instances, however, in which it would be useful for resources to be shared and accessed concurrently. This situation is similar to the case where a **fork** system call is invoked with a new thread of control executing within the same virtual address space. This concept is so useful that several new operating systems are providing a mechanism to support it through the *thread* facility. A *thread* is a basic unit of CPU utilization. It has little nonshared state. A group of peer threads share code, address space, and operating-system resources. The environment in which a thread executes is called a *task*. A traditional (*heavyweight*) process is equal to a task with one thread. A task does nothing if no threads are in it, and a thread must be in exactly one task. An individual thread has at least its own register state, and usually its own stack. The extensive sharing makes CPU switching among peer threads and threads' creations inexpensive, compared with context switches among heavyweight processes. Thus, blocking a thread and switching to another thread is a reasonable solution to the problem of how a server can efficiently handle many requests.

The abstraction presented by a group of lightweight processes is that of multiple threads of control associated with several shared resources. There are many alternatives regarding threads; we mention a few of them briefly. Threads can be supported by the kernel (as in the Mach and OS/2 operating systems). In this case, a set of system calls similar to those for processes is provided. Alternatively, they can be supported above the kernel, via a set of library calls at the user level (as is done in Andrew).

Threads are gaining in popularity because they have some of the characteristics of heavyweight processes but can execute more efficiently. There are many applications where this combination is useful. For instance, the UNIX kernel is single-tasking: Only one task can be executing code in the kernel at a time. Many problems, such as synchronization of data access (locking of data structures while they are being modified) are avoided because only one process is allowed to be doing the modification (more on this in Chapter 5). Mach, on the other hand, is multithreaded, allowing the kernel to service many requests simultaneously. In this case, the threads themselves are synchronous: another thread in the same group may run only if the currently executing thread relinquishes control. Of course, the current thread would relinquish control only when it was not modifying shared data. On systems on which threads are asynchronous, some explicit locking mechanism must be used, just as in systems where multiple processes share data.

4.3 Scheduling Concepts

The objective of multiprogramming is to have some process running at all times, to maximize CPU utilization. For a uniprocessor system, there will never be more than one running process. If there are more processes, the rest will have to wait until the CPU is free and can be rescheduled.

The idea of multiprogramming is relatively simple. A process is executed until it must wait, typically for the completion of some I/O request. In a simple computer system, the CPU would then just sit idle. All this waiting time is wasted; no useful work is accomplished. With multiprogramming, we try to use this time productively. Several processes are kept in memory at one time. When one process has to wait, the operating system takes the CPU away from that process and gives it to another process. This pattern continues. Every time one process has to wait, another process may take over the use of the CPU.

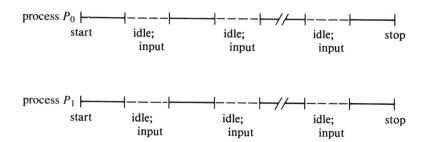

Figure 4.4   Two processes, P_0 and P_1, ready for execution.

The benefits of multiprogramming are increased CPU utilization and higher *throughput*. Throughput is the amount of work accomplished in a given time interval (for example, 17 processes per hour). As an extreme example, assume we have two processes, P_0 and P_1, to be executed (Figure 4.4). Each process executes for 1 second, then waits for 1 second. This pattern is repeated 60 times. If we run first process P_0 and then process P_1, one after the other, it will take 4 minutes to run the two processes (Figure 4.5); process P_0 takes 2 minutes to run, then process P_1 takes 2 minutes to run. We actually compute for only 2 minutes of this time, however; the other 2 minutes are idle time. Our CPU utilization is thus only 50 percent.

If we multiprogram process P_0 and process P_1, we can greatly improve the system performance (Figure 4.6). We start with process P_0, which executes for 1 second. Then, while process P_0 waits for 1 second, we execute process P_1. When process P_1 waits, process P_0 is ready to run. Now the elapsed time to execute both processes is only 2 minutes,

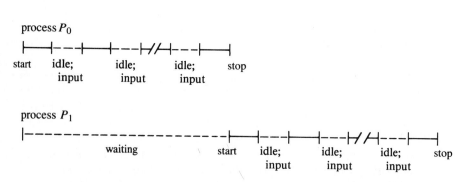

Figure 4.5   Process execution without multiprogramming.

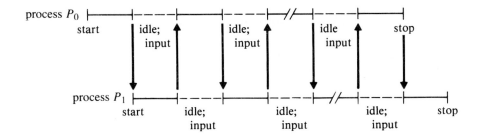

Figure 4.6 Process execution with multiprogramming.

and there is no idle CPU time. Thus, we have improved CPU utilization from 50 percent to 100 percent, increasing throughput at the same time. Notice that process P_0 finishes no earlier, but process P_1 is now finished in 2 minutes.

This example is an extreme case, and is highly unlikely to occur in practice. It does, however, illustrate the concept of multiprogramming. In Section 4.4, we examine CPU scheduling in much greater detail.

4.3.1 Scheduling Queues

As processes enter the system, they are put into a *job queue*. This queue consists of all processes residing on mass storage awaiting allocation of main memory. The processes that are residing in main memory and are ready and waiting to execute are kept on a list called the *ready queue*. This list is generally a linked list. A ready-queue header will contain pointers to the first and last PCBs in the list. Each PCB has a pointer field that points to the next process in the ready queue.

There are also other queues in the system. When a process is allocated the CPU, it executes for awhile and eventually either quits or waits for the occurrence of a particular event, such as the completion of an I/O request. In the case of an I/O request, such a request may be to a dedicated tape drive, or to a shared device, such as a disk. Since there are many processes in the system, the disk may be busy with the I/O request of some other process. Thus, the process may have to wait for the disk. The list of processes waiting for a particular I/O device is called a *device queue*. Each device has its own device queue (Figure 4.7). If the device is a dedicated device, as is a tape drive, the device queue will never have more than one process in it. If the device is sharable, as is a disk, several processes may be in the device queue.

A common representation for a discussion of process scheduling is a *queueing diagram*, such as that in Figure 4.8. Each rectangular box

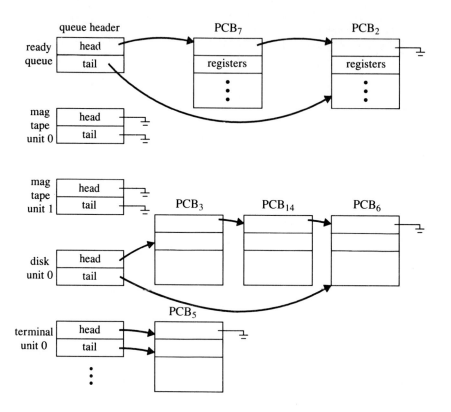

Figure 4.7   The ready queue and various I/O device queues.

represents a queue. Two types of queues are present: the ready queue and a set of device queues. The circles represent the resources that serve the queues, and the arrows indicate the flow of processes in the system.

A new process is initially put in the ready queue. It waits in the ready queue until it is selected for execution and is given the CPU. Once the process is allocated the CPU and is executing, one of several events could occur:

- The process could issue an I/O request, and then be placed in an I/O queue.

- The process could fork a new process and wait for the latter's termination.

- The process could be forcibly removed from the CPU, as a result of an interrupt, and be put back in the ready queue.

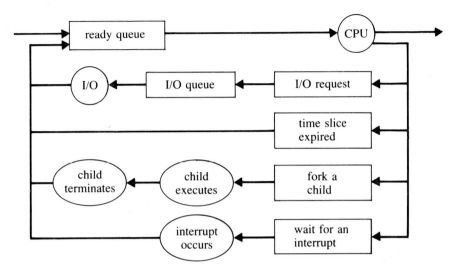

Figure 4.8   Queueing-diagram representation of process scheduling.

In the first two cases, the process eventually switches from the waiting state to the ready state and is then put back in the ready queue. A process continues this cycle until it terminates, at which time it exits from the system.

4.3.2 Schedulers

A process migrates between the various scheduling queues throughout its lifetime. The operating system must select processes from these queues in some fashion. The selection processes is carried out by the appropriate *scheduler*.

In a batch system, there are often more processes submitted than can be executed immediately. These processes are spooled to a mass storage device (typically a disk), where they are kept for later execution. The *long-term scheduler* (or *job scheduler*) selects processes from this pool and loads them into memory for execution. The *short-term scheduler* (or CPU *scheduler*) selects from among the processes that are ready to execute, and allocates the CPU to one of them.

The primary distinction between these two schedulers is the frequency of their execution. The short-term scheduler must select a new process for the CPU quite often. A process may execute for only a few milliseconds before waiting for an I/O request. Often, the short-term scheduler executes at least once every 10 milliseconds. Because of the short duration of time between executions, the short-term scheduler must be very fast. If it takes 1 millisecond to decide to execute a process for 10 milliseconds, then $1/(10 + 1) = 9$ percent of the CPU is being used (wasted) simply for scheduling the work.

The long-term scheduler, on the other hand, executes much less frequently. There may be minutes between the creation of new processes in the system. The long-term scheduler controls the *degree of multiprogramming* (the number of processes in memory). If the degree of multiprogramming is stable, then the average rate of process creation must be equal to the average departure rate of processes leaving the system. Thus, the long-term scheduler may need to be invoked only when a process leaves the system. Because of the longer interval between executions, the long-term scheduler can afford to take more time to decide which process should be selected for execution.

It may also be more important that the long-term scheduler make a careful selection. In general, most processes can be described as either I/O bound or CPU bound. An I/O-bound process is one that spends more of its time doing I/O than it spends doing computations. A CPU-bound process, on the other hand, is one that generates I/O requests infrequently, using more of its time doing computation than an I/O-bound process uses. It is important that the long-term scheduler select a good *process mix* of I/O-bound and CPU-bound processes. If all processes are I/O bound, the ready queue will almost always be empty, and the short-term scheduler will have little to do. If all processes are CPU bound, the I/O waiting queue will almost always be empty, and again the system will be unbalanced. The system with the best performance will have a combination of CPU-bound and I/O-bound processes.

On some systems, the long-term scheduler may be absent or minimal. For example, time-sharing systems often have no long-term scheduler, but simply put every new process in memory for the short-term scheduler. The stability of these systems depends either on a physical limitation (such as a limited number of available terminals) or on the self-adjusting nature of human users. If the performance declines to unacceptable levels, some users will simply quit, and will do something else.

Some operating systems, such as time-sharing systems, may introduce an additional, intermediate level of scheduling. This *medium-term scheduler* is diagrammed in Figure 4.9. The key idea behind a medium-term scheduler is that sometimes it can be advantageous to remove processes from memory (and from active contention for the CPU) and thus to reduce the degree of multiprogramming. At some later time, the process can be reintroduced into memory and its execution can be continued where it left off. This scheme is often called *swapping*. The process is swapped out and swapped in later by the medium-term scheduler. Swapping may be necessary to improve the process mix, or

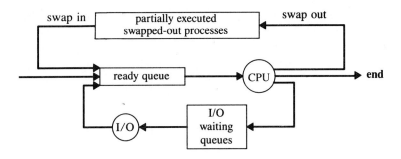

Figure 4.9 Addition of medium-term scheduling to the queueing diagram.

because a change in memory requirements has overcommitted available memory, requiring memory to be freed up. Swapping is discussed in more detail in Chapter 7.

4.4 CPU Scheduling

Scheduling is a fundamental operating-system function. Almost all computer resources are scheduled before use. The CPU is, of course, one of the primary computer resources. Thus, its scheduling is central to operating-system design.

4.4.1 CPU-I/O Burst Cycle

The success of CPU scheduling depends on the following observed property of processes: Process execution consists of a *cycle* of CPU execution and I/O wait. Processes alternate back and forth between these two states. Process execution begins with a *CPU burst*. That is followed by an *I/O burst*, which is followed by another CPU burst, then another I/O burst, and so on. Eventually, the last CPU burst will end with a system request to terminate execution, rather than with another I/O burst (Figure 4.10).

The durations of these CPU bursts have been measured. Although they vary greatly from process to process and computer to computer, they tend to have a frequency curve similar to that shown in Figure 4.11. The curve is generally characterized as exponential or hyperexponential. There is a very large number of very short CPU bursts, and there is a small number of very long CPU bursts. An I/O-bound program would typically have many very short CPU bursts. A CPU-bound

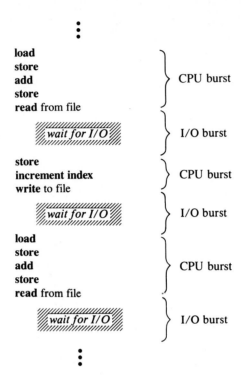

Figure 4.10   Alternating sequence of CPU and I/O bursts.

program might have a few very long CPU bursts. This distribution can be quite important in selecting an appropriate CPU-scheduling algorithm.

4.4.2 CPU Scheduler

Whenever the CPU becomes idle, the operating system must select one of the processes in the ready queue to be executed. The selection processes is carried out by the *short-term scheduler* (or CPU scheduler). The scheduler selects from among the processes in memory that are ready to execute, and allocates the CPU to one of them.

Note that the ready queue is not necessarily a first-in-first-out (FIFO) queue. As we shall see when we consider the various scheduling algorithms, a ready queue may be implemented as a FIFO queue, a priority queue, a tree, or simply an unordered linked list. Conceptually, however, all the processes in the ready queue are lined up waiting for a chance to run on the CPU. The records in the queues are generally PCBs of the processes.

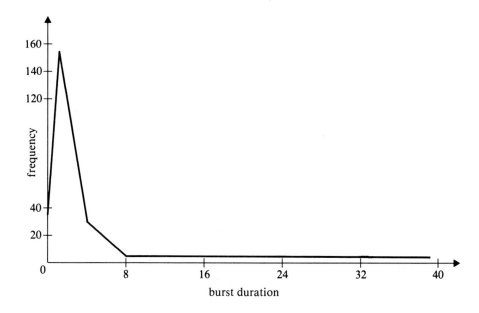

Figure 4.11 Histogram of CPU-burst times.

4.4.3 Scheduling Structure

CPU scheduling decisions may take place under the following four circumstances:

1. When a process switches from the running state to the waiting state (for example, I/O request, invocation of wait for the termination of one of the child processes)

2. When a process switches from the running state to the ready state (for example, when an interrupt occurs)

3. When a process switches from the waiting state to the ready state (for example, completion of I/O)

4. When a process terminates

For circumstances 1 and 4, there is no choice in terms of scheduling. A new process (if one exists in the ready queue) must be selected for execution. This, however, is not the case for circumstances 2 and 3.

When scheduling takes place only under circumstances 1 and 4, we say the scheduling scheme is *nonpreemptive;* otherwise, the scheduling scheme is *preemptive.* Under nonpreemptive scheduling, once the CPU has been allocated to a process, the process keeps the CPU until it releases the CPU either by terminating or by switching to the waiting state.

4.4.4 Context Switch

Switching the CPU to another process requires saving the state of the old process and loading the saved state for the new process. This task is known as a *context switch*. Context-switch time is pure overhead. It varies from machine to machine, depending on the memory speed, the number of registers, and the existence of special instructions (such as a single instruction to load or store all registers). Typically, it ranges from 1 to 100 microseconds.

Context-switch times are very dependent on hardware support. For instance, some processors provide multiple sets of registers. A context switch simply involves changing the pointer to the current register set. Of course, if there are more active processes than there are register sets, the system resorts to copying register data to and from memory, as before. Also, the more complex the operating system, the more work must be done during a context switch. As we shall see in later chapters, advanced memory-management techniques may require extra data to be switched with each context.

4.4.5 Dispatcher

Another component involved in the CPU-scheduling function is the *dispatcher*. The dispatcher is the module that actually gives control of the CPU to the process selected by the short-term scheduler. This function involves

- Switching context
- Switching to user mode
- Jumping to the proper location in the user program to restart that program

Obviously, the dispatcher should be as fast as possible.

4.5 Scheduling Algorithms

CPU scheduling deals with the problem of deciding which of the processes in the ready queue is to be allocated the CPU. There are many different CPU-scheduling algorithms. In this section, we describe several of these algorithms.

Different scheduling algorithms have different properties and may favor one class of processes over another. In choosing which algorithm to use in a particular situation, we must consider the properties of the various algorithms.

Many criteria have been suggested for comparing CPU-scheduling algorithms. Which characteristics are used for comparison can make a substantial difference in the determination of the best algorithm. Criteria that are used include the following:

- **CPU utilization**. We want to keep the CPU as busy as possible. CPU utilization may range from 0 to 100 percent. In a real system, it should range from 40 percent (for a lightly loaded system) to 90 percent (for a heavily used system).

- **Throughput**. If the CPU is busy, then work is being done. One measure of work is the number of processes that are completed per time unit, called throughput. For long processes, this rate may be one process per hour; for short transactions, throughput might be 10 processes per second.

- **Turnaround time**. From the point of view of a particular process, the important criterion is how long it takes to execute that process. The interval from the time of submission to the time of completion is the *turnaround time*. Turnaround time is the sum of the periods spent waiting to get into memory, waiting in the ready queue, executing on the CPU, and doing I/O.

- **Waiting time**. The CPU-scheduling algorithm does not really affect the amount of time during which a process executes or does I/O. The algorithm affects only the amount of time that a process spends waiting in the ready queue. Thus, rather than looking at turnaround time, we might simply consider the waiting time for each process.

- **Response time**. In an interactive system, turnaround time may not be the best criterion. Often, a process can produce some output fairly early and can continue computing new results while previous results are being output to the user. Thus, another measure is the time from the submission of a request until the first response is produced. This measure, called *response time*, is the amount of time it takes to start responding, but not the time that it takes to output that response. The turnaround time is generally limited by the speed of the output device.

It is desirable to maximize CPU utilization and throughput, and to minimize turnaround time, waiting time, and response time. In most cases, we optimize the average measure. However, it may sometimes be desirable to optimize the minimum or maximum values, rather than the average. For example, to guarantee that all users get good service, we may want to minimize the maximum response time.

It has also been suggested that, for interactive systems (such as time-sharing systems), it is more important to minimize the *variance* in the response time than it is to minimize the average response time. A system with reasonable and *predictable* response time may be considered more desirable than a system that is faster on the average, but is highly variable. However, there has been little work done on CPU-scheduling algorithms to minimize variance.

As we discuss various CPU-scheduling algorithms, we want to illustrate their operation. An accurate illustration should involve many processes, each being a sequence of several hundred CPU bursts and I/O bursts. For simplicity of illustration, we consider only one CPU burst (in milliseconds) per process in our examples. Our measure of comparison is the average waiting time. More elaborate evaluation mechanisms are discussed in Section 4.7.

4.5.1 First-Come, First-Served Scheduling

By far the simplest CPU-scheduling algorithm is the *first-come, first-served scheduling* (FCFS) algorithm. With this scheme, the process that requests the CPU first is allocated the CPU first. The implementation of the FCFS policy is easily managed with a FIFO queue. When a process enters the ready queue, its PCB is linked onto the tail of the queue. When the CPU is free, it is allocated to the process at the head of the ready queue. The running process is then removed from the ready queue. The code for FCFS scheduling is simple to write and understand.

The average waiting time under the FCFS policy, however, is often quite long. Consider the following set of processes that arrive at time 0, with the length of the CPU burst time given in milliseconds:

Process	Burst Time
P_1	24
P_2	3
P_3	3

If the processes arrive in the order P_1, P_2, P_3, and are served in FCFS order, we get the result shown in the following *Gantt chart*:

P_1	P_2	P_3

0   24   27   30

The waiting time is 0 milliseconds for process P_1, 24 milliseconds for process P_2, and 27 milliseconds for process P_3. Thus, the average waiting time is $(0 + 24 + 27)/3 = 17$ milliseconds. If the processes arrive in the order P_2, P_3, P_1, however, the results will be as shown in the following Gantt chart:

The average waiting time is now $(6 + 0 + 3)/3 = 3$ milliseconds. This reduction is substantial. Thus, the average waiting time under a FCFS policy is generally not minimal, and may vary substantially if the process CPU-burst times vary greatly.

In addition, consider the performance of FCFS scheduling in a dynamic situation. Assume we have one CPU-bound process and many I/O-bound processes. As the processes flow around the system, the following scenario may result. The CPU-bound process will get the CPU and hold it. During this time, all the other processes will finish their I/O and move into the ready queue, waiting for the CPU. While they wait in the ready queue, the I/O devices are idle. Eventually, the CPU-bound process finishes its CPU burst and moves to an I/O device. All the I/O-bound processes, which have very short CPU bursts, execute quickly and move back to the I/O queues. At this point the CPU sits idle. The CPU-bound process will then move back to the ready queue and be allocated the CPU. Again, all the I/O processes end up waiting in the ready queue until the CPU-bound process is done. There is a *convoy effect*, as all the other processes wait for the one big process to get off the CPU. This effect results in lower CPU and device utilization than might be possible if the shorter processes were allowed to go first.

The FCFS scheduling algorithm is nonpreemptive. Once the CPU has been allocated to a process, that process keeps the CPU until it wants to release the CPU, either by terminating or by requesting I/O. The FCFS algorithm is particularly troublesome for time-sharing systems, where it is important that each user get a share of the CPU at regular intervals. It would be disastrous to allow one process to keep the CPU for an extended period.

4.5.2 Shortest-Job-First Scheduling

A different approach to CPU scheduling is the *shortest-job-first* (SJF) algorithm. (We do not use the term *shortest process first* because most people and textbooks refer to this type of scheduling discipline as *shortest job first*.) This algorithm associates with each process the length of the latter's next CPU burst. When the CPU is available, it is assigned to the process that has the smallest next CPU burst. If two processes have the same length next CPU burst, FCFS scheduling is used to break the tie.

As an example, consider the following set of processes, with the length of the CPU burst time given in milliseconds:

Process	Burst Time
P_1	6
P_2	8
P_3	7
P_4	3

Using SJF scheduling, we would schedule these processes according to the following Gantt chart:

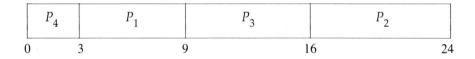

P_4	P_1	P_3	P_2

0   3   9   16   24

The waiting time is 3 milliseconds for process P_1, 16 milliseconds for process P_2, 9 milliseconds for process P_3, and 0 milliseconds for process P_4. Thus, the average waiting time is $(3 + 16 + 9 + 0)/4 = 7$ milliseconds. If we were using the FCFS scheduling, then the average waiting time would be 10.25 milliseconds.

The SJF scheduling algorithm is provably *optimal*, in that it gives the minimum average waiting time for a given set of processes. The proof shows that moving a short process before a long one decreases the waiting time of the short process more than it increases the waiting time of the long process (Figure 4.12). Consequently, the *average* waiting time decreases.

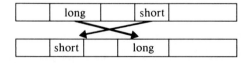

Figure 4.12   Proof that the SJF scheduling algorithm is optimal.

The real difficulty with the SJF algorithm is knowing the length of the next CPU request. For long-term (job) scheduling in a batch system, we can use the process time limit. Thus, users are motivated to estimate the process time limit accurately, since a lower value may mean faster response. (Too low a value will cause a "time-limit-exceeded" error and require resubmission.) SJF scheduling is used frequently in process scheduling.

Although the SJF algorithm is optimal, it cannot be implemented at the level of short-term CPU scheduling. There is no way to know the length of the next CPU burst. One approach is to try to approximate SJF scheduling. We may not *know* the length of the next CPU burst, but we may be able to *predict* its value. We expect that the next CPU burst will be similar in length to the previous ones. Thus, by computing an approximation of the length of the next CPU burst, we can pick the process with the shortest predicted CPU burst.

The next CPU burst is generally predicted as an exponential average of the measured lengths of previous CPU bursts. Let t_n be the length of the nth CPU burst, and let τ_{n+1} be our predicted value for the next CPU burst. Then, for α, $0 \leq \alpha \leq 1$, define

$$\tau_{n+1} = \alpha t_n + (1 - \alpha)\tau_n.$$

This formula defines an *exponential average*. The value of t_n contains our most recent information; τ_n stores the past history. The parameter α controls the relative weight of recent and past history in our prediction. If $\alpha = 0$, then $\tau_{n+1} = \tau_n$, and recent history has no effect (current conditions are assumed to be transient); if $\alpha = 1$, then $\tau_{n+1} = t_n$, and only the most recent CPU burst matters (history is assumed to be old and irrelevant). More commonly, $\alpha = 1/2$, so recent history and past history are equally weighted. Figure 4.13 shows an exponential average with $\alpha = 1/2$. The initial τ_0 can be defined as a constant or as an overall system average.

To understand the behavior of the exponential average, we can expand the formula for τ_{n+1} by substituting for τ_n, to find

$$\tau_{n+1} = \alpha t_n + (1-\alpha)\alpha t_{n-1} + \ldots + (1-\alpha)^j \alpha t_{n-j} + \ldots + (1-\alpha)^{n+1}\tau_0.$$

Since both α and $(1 - \alpha)$ are less than or equal to 1, each successive term has less weight than its predecessor.

The SJF algorithm may be either *preemptive* or *nonpreemptive*. The choice arises when a new process arrives at the ready queue while a previous process is executing. The new process may have a shorter next CPU burst than what is left of the currently executing process. A preemptive SJF algorithm will preempt the currently executing process,

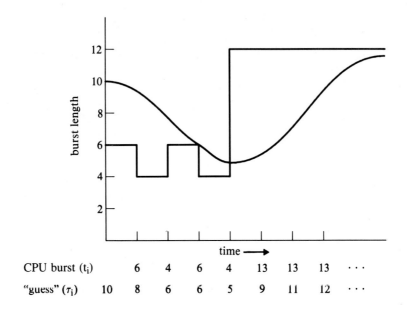

CPU burst (t_i)		6	4	6	4	13	13	13	$\cdots$
"guess" (τ_i)	10	8	6	6	5	9	11	12	$\cdots$

Figure 4.13   Predicting the next CPU burst using an exponential average.

whereas a nonpreemptive SJF algorithm will allow the currently running process to finish its CPU burst. Preemptive SJF scheduling is sometimes called *shortest-remaining-time-first* scheduling.

As an example, consider the following four processes, with the length of the CPU burst time given in milliseconds:

Process	Arrival Time	Burst Time
P_1	0	8
P_2	1	4
P_3	2	9
P_4	3	5

If the processes arrive at the ready queue at the times shown and need the indicated burst times, then the resulting preemptive SJF schedule is as depicted in the following Gantt chart:

P_1	P_2	P_4	P_1	P_3

0   1   5   10   17   26

Process P_1 is started at time 0, since it is the only process in the queue. Process P_2 arrives at time 1. The remaining time for process P_1 (7 milliseconds) is larger than the time required by process P_2 (4 milliseconds), so process P_1 is preempted, and process P_2 is scheduled. The average waiting time for this example is $((10 - 1) + (1 - 1) + (17 - 2) + (5 - 3))/4 = 26/4 = 6.5$ milliseconds. A nonpreemptive SJF scheduling would result in an average waiting time of 7.75 milliseconds.

4.5.3 Priority Scheduling

The SJF algorithm is a special case of the general *priority* scheduling algorithm. A priority is associated with each process, and the CPU is allocated to the process with the highest priority. Equal-priority processes are scheduled in FCFS order.

An SJF algorithm is simply a priority algorithm where the priority (p) is the inverse of the (predicted) next CPU burst (τ): $p = 1/\tau$. The larger the CPU burst, the lower the priority, and vice versa.

Note that we discuss scheduling in terms of *high* priority and *low* priority. Priorities are generally some fixed range of numbers, such as 0 to 7, or 0 to 4095. However, there is no general agreement on whether 0 is the highest or lowest priority. Some systems use low numbers to represent low priority; others use low numbers for high priority. This difference can lead to confusion. In this text, we assume that low numbers represent high priority.

As an example, consider the following set of processes, assumed to have arrived at time 0, in the order P_1, P_2, ..., P_5, with the length of the CPU burst time given in milliseconds:

Process	Burst Time	Priority
P_1	10	3
P_2	1	1
P_3	2	3
P_4	1	4
P_5	5	2

Using priority scheduling, we would schedule these processes according to the following Gantt chart:

P_2	P_5	P_1	P_3	P_4

0   1   6   16   18   19

The average waiting time is 8.2 milliseconds.

Priorities can be defined either internally or externally. Internally defined priorities use some measurable quantity or quantities to compute the priority of a process. For example, time limits, memory requirements, the number of open files, and the ratio of average I/O burst to average CPU burst have been used in computing priorities. External priorities are set by criteria that are external to the operating system, such as the importance of the process, the type and amount of funds being paid for computer use, the department sponsoring the work, and other, often political, factors.

Priority scheduling can be either preemptive or nonpreemptive. When a process arrives at the ready queue, its priority is compared with the priority of the currently running process. A preemptive priority scheduling algorithm will preempt the CPU if the priority of the newly arrived process is higher than the priority of the currently running process. A nonpreemptive priority scheduling algorithm will simply put the new process at the head of the ready queue.

A major problem with priority scheduling algorithms is *indefinite blocking* or *starvation*. A process that is ready to run but lacking the CPU can be considered blocked, waiting for the CPU. A priority scheduling algorithm can leave some low-priority processes waiting indefinitely for the CPU. In a heavily loaded computer system, a steady stream of higher-priority processes can prevent a low-priority process from ever getting the CPU. Generally, one of two things will happen. Either the process will eventually be run (at 2 A.M. Sunday, when the system is finally lightly loaded) or the computer system will eventually crash and lose all unfinished low-priority processes. (Rumor has it that, when they closed down the IBM 7094 at MIT in 1973, they found a low-priority process that had been submitted in 1967 and had not yet been run.)

A solution to the problem of indefinite blockage of low-priority processes is *aging*. Aging is a technique of gradually increasing the priority of processes that wait in the system for a long time. For example, if priorities range from 0 (low) to 127 (high), we could increment a waiting process's priority by 1 every 15 minutes. Eventually, even a process with an initial priority of 0 would have the highest priority in the system and would be executed. In fact, it would take no more than 32 hours for a priority 0 process to age to a priority 127 process.

4.5.4 Round-Robin Scheduling

The *round-robin* (RR) scheduling algorithm is designed especially for time-sharing systems. A small unit of time, called a *time quantum* or time slice, is defined. A time quantum is generally from 10 to 100 milliseconds. The ready queue is treated as a circular queue. The CPU scheduler goes around the ready queue, allocating the CPU to each process for a time interval of up to 1 time quantum.

To implement RR scheduling, we keep the ready queue as first-in, first-out (FIFO) queue of processes. New processes are added to the tail of the ready queue. The CPU scheduler picks the first process from the ready queue, sets a timer to interrupt after 1 time quantum, and dispatches the process.

One of two things will then happen. The process may have a CPU burst of less than 1 time quantum. In this case, the process itself will release the CPU voluntarily. The scheduler will then proceed to the next process in the ready queue. Otherwise, if the CPU burst of the currently running process is longer than 1 time quantum, the timer will go off and will cause an interrupt to the operating system. A context switch will be executed, and the process will be put at the *tail* of the ready queue. The CPU scheduler will then select the next process in the ready queue.

The average waiting time under the RR policy, however, is often quite long. Consider the following set of processes that arrive at time 0, with the length of the CPU burst time given in milliseconds:

Process	Burst Time
P_1	24
P_2	3
P_3	3

If we use a time quantum of 4 milliseconds, then process P_1 gets the first 4 milliseconds. Since it requires another 20 milliseconds, it is preempted after the first time quantum, and the CPU is given to the next process in the queue, process P_2. Since process P_2 does not need 4 milliseconds, it quits before its time quantum expires. The CPU is then given to the next process, process P_3. Once each process has received 1 time quantum, the CPU is returned to process P_1 for an additional time quantum. The resulting RR schedule is

P_1	P_2	P_3	P_1	P_1	P_1	P_1	P_1

0   4   7   10   14   18   22   26   30

The average waiting time is $17/3 = 5.66$ milliseconds.

In the RR scheduling algorithm, no process is allocated the CPU for more than 1 time quantum in a row. If a process's CPU burst exceeds 1 time quantum, that process is *preempted* and is put back in the ready queue. The RR scheduling algorithm is preemptive.

If there are *n* processes in the ready queue and the time quantum is *q*, then each process gets $1/n$ of the CPU time in chunks of at most *q* time units. Each process must wait no longer than $(n - 1) \times q$ time units until its next time quantum. For example, if there are five processes, with a time quantum of 20 milliseconds, then each process will get up to 20 milliseconds every 100 milliseconds.

The performance of the RR algorithm depends heavily on the size of the time quantum. At one extreme, if the time quantum is very large (infinite), the RR policy is the same as the FCFS policy. If the time quantum is very small (say 1 microsecond), the RR approach is called *processor sharing*, and appears (in theory) to the users as though each of *n* processes has its own processor running at $1/n$ the speed of the real processor. This approach was used in Control Data Corporation (CDC) hardware to implement 10 peripheral processors with only one set of hardware and 10 sets of registers. The hardware executes one instruction for one set of registers, then goes on to the next. This cycle continues, resulting in 10 slow processors rather than one fast one. (Actually, since the processor was much faster than memory and each instruction referenced memory, the processors were not much slower than a single processor would have been.)

In software, however, we need also to consider the effect of context switching on the performance of RR scheduling. Let us assume that we have only one process of 10 time units. If the quantum is 12 time units, the process finishes in less than 1 time quantum, with no overhead. If the quantum is 6 time units, however, the process requires 2 quanta, resulting in a context switch. If the time quantum is 1 time unit, then

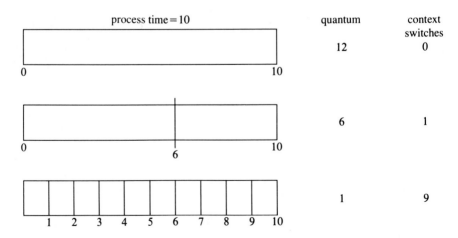

Figure 4.14   A smaller time quantum increases context switches.

nine context switches will occur, slowing the execution of the process accordingly (Figure 4.14).

Thus, we want the time quantum to be large with respect to the context-switch time. If the context-switch time is approximately 10 percent of the time quantum, then about 10 percent of the CPU time will be spent in context switch.

Turnaround time also depends on the size of the time quantum. As we can see from Figure 4.15, the average turnaround time of a set of processes does not necessarily improve as the time-quantum size increases. In general, the average turnaround time can be improved if most processes finish their next CPU burst in a single time quantum. For example, given three processes of 10 time units each and a quantum of 1 time unit, the average turnaround time is 29. If the time quantum is 10, however, the average turnaround time drops to 20. If context-switch

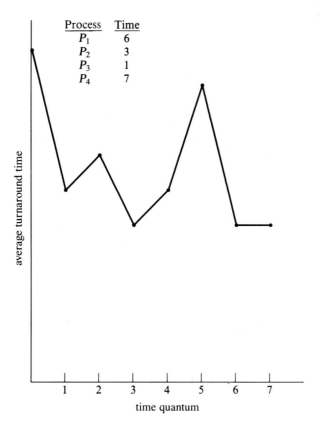

Figure 4.15   The average turnaround time varies with the time quantum.

time is added in, the average turnaround time increases for a smaller time quantum, since more context switches will be required.

On the other hand, if the time quantum is too large, RR scheduling degenerates to FCFS policy. A rule of thumb is that 80 percent of the CPU bursts should be shorter than the time quantum.

4.5.5 Multilevel Queue Scheduling

Another class of scheduling algorithms has been created for situations in which processes are easily classified into different groups. For example, a common division is made between *foreground* (interactive) processes and *background* (batch) processes. These two types of processes have quite different response-time requirements, and so might have different scheduling needs. In addition, foreground processes may have priority (externally defined) over background processes.

A *multilevel queue scheduling algorithm* partitions the ready queue into separate queues (Figure 4.16). Processes are permanently assigned to one queue, generally based on some property of the process, such as memory size or process type. Each queue has its own scheduling

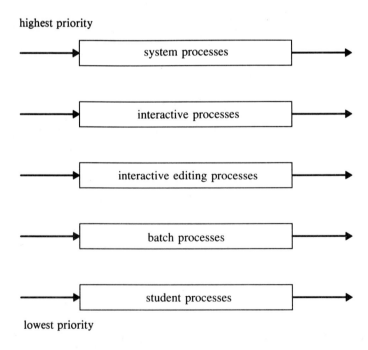

Figure 4.16   Multilevel queue scheduling.

algorithm. For example, separate queues might be used for foreground and background processes. The foreground queue might be scheduled by a RR algorithm, while the background queue is scheduled by an FCFS algorithm.

In addition, there must be scheduling between the queues. This is commonly a fixed-priority preemptive scheduling. For example, the foreground queue may have absolute priority over the background queue.

Let us look at an example of a multilevel queue scheduling algorithm with five queues:

- System processes

- Interactive processes

- Interactive editing processes

- Batch processes

- Student processes

Each queue had absolute priority over lower-priority queues. No process in the batch queue, for example, could run unless the queues for system processes, interactive processes, and interactive editing processes were all empty. If an interactive editing process entered the ready queue while a batch process was running, the batch process would be preempted.

Another possibility is to time slice between the queues. Each queue gets a certain portion of the CPU time, which it can then schedule among the various processes in its queue. For instance, in the foreground-background queue example, the foreground queue can be given 80 percent of the CPU time for RR scheduling among its processes, while the background queue receives 20 percent of the CPU to give to its processes in a FCFS manner.

4.5.6 Multilevel Feedback Queue Scheduling

Normally, in a multilevel queue scheduling algorithm, processes are permanently assigned to a queue on entry to the system. Processes do not move between queues. If there are separate queues for foreground and background processes, for example, processes do not move from one queue to the other, since processes do not change their foreground or background nature. This setup has the advantage of low scheduling overhead, but is inflexible.

Multilevel feedback queue scheduling, however, allow a process to move between queues. The idea is to separate processes with different CPU-burst characteristics. If a process uses too much CPU time, it will be moved to a lower-priority queue. This scheme leaves I/O-bound and interactive processes in the higher-priority queues. Similarly, a process that waits too long in a lower-priority queue may be moved to a higher-priority queue. This is a form of aging that would prevent starvation.

For example, consider a multilevel feedback queue scheduler with three queues, numbered from 0 to 2 (Figure 4.17). The scheduler first executes all processes in queue 0. Only when queue 0 is empty will it execute processes in queue 1. Similarly, processes in queue 2 will only be executed if queues 0 and 1 are empty. A process that arrives for queue 1 will preempt a process in queue 2. A process in queue 1 will in turn be preempted by a process arriving for queue 0.

A process entering the ready queue is put in queue 0. A process in queue 0 is given a time quantum of 8 milliseconds. If it does not finish within this time, it is moved to the tail of queue 1. If queue 0 is empty, the process at the head of queue 1 is given a quantum of 16 milliseconds. If it does not complete, it is preempted and is put into queue 2. Processes in queue 2 are run on an FCFS basis, only when queues 0 and 1 are empty.

This scheduling algorithm gives highest priority to any process with a CPU burst of 8 milliseconds or less. Such a process will quickly get the CPU, finish its CPU burst, and go off to its next I/O burst. Processes that need more than 8, but less than 24, milliseconds are also served quickly, although with lower priority than shorter processes. Long processes

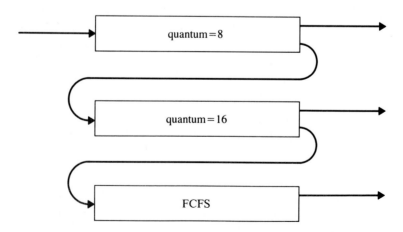

Figure 4.17 Multilevel feedback queues.

automatically sink to queue 2 and are served in FCFS order with any CPU cycles left over from queues 0 and 1.

In general, a multilevel feedback queue scheduler is defined by the following parameters:

- The number of queues

- The scheduling algorithm for each queue

- The method used to determine when to upgrade a process to a higher-priority queue

- The method used to determine when to demote a process to a lower-priority queue

- The method used to determine which queue a process will enter when that process needs service

The definition of a multilevel feedback queue scheduler makes it the most general CPU-scheduling algorithm. It can be configured to match a specific system under design. Unfortunately, it also requires some means of selecting values for all the parameters to define the best scheduler. Although a multilevel feedback queue is the most general scheme, it is also the most complex.

4.6   Multiple Processor Scheduling

Our discussion thus far has focused on the problems of scheduling the CPU in a system with a single processor. If multiple CPUs are available, the scheduling problem is correspondingly more complex. Many possibilities have been tried, and, as we saw with single-processor CPU scheduling, there is no one best solution. In the following, we briefly discuss some of the issues concerning multiprocessor scheduling. A complete coverage is beyond the scope of this text.

One major factor is the types of processors involved. The processors may be identical (a *homogeneous* system) or different (a *heterogeneous* system). If the processors are different, the options are relatively limited. Each processor has its own queue and its own scheduling algorithm. Processes are intrinsically typed by their structure; they must be run on a particular processor. A program written in VAX assembly language cannot be run on an IBM Series/1; it must be run on a VAX. Hence, the processes are self-segregating, and each processor can schedule itself.

If several identical processors are available, then *load sharing* can occur. It would be possible to provide a separate queue for each processor. In this case, however, one processor could be idle, with an empty queue, while another processor was very busy. To prevent this situation, we use a common ready queue. All processes go into one queue and are scheduled onto any available processor.

In such a scheme, one of two scheduling approaches may be used. In one approach, each processor is self-scheduling. Each processor examines the common ready queue and selects a process to execute. As we shall see in Chapter 5, if we have multiple processors trying to access and update a common data structure, each processor must be programmed very carefully. We must ensure that two processors do not choose the same process, and that processes are not lost from the queue. The other approach avoids this problem by appointing one processor as scheduler for the other processors, thus creating a master-slave structure. This is *asymmetric multiprocessing*.

4.7 Algorithm Evaluation

How do we select a CPU-scheduling algorithm for a particular system? As we saw in Section 4.5, there are many scheduling algorithms, each with its own parameters. As a result, selecting an algorithm can be quite difficult.

The first problem is defining the criteria to be used in selecting an algorithm. As we saw in Section 4.5, criteria are often defined in terms of CPU utilization, response time, or throughput. To select an algorithm, we must first define the relative importance of these measures. Our criteria may include several measures, such as

- Maximize CPU utilization under the constraint that the maximum response time is 1 second

- Maximize throughput such that turnaround time is (on average) linearly proportional to total execution time

Once the selection criteria have been defined, we want to evaluate the various algorithms under consideration. There are a number of different evaluation methods, which we describe in Sections 4.7.1 through 4.7.3.

4.7.1 Analytic Evaluation

One major class of evaluation methods is called *analytic evaluation*. Analytic evaluation uses the algorithm and the system workload to produce a formula or number that evaluates the performance of the algorithm for that workload.

Deterministic Modeling

One type of analytic evaluation is *deterministic modeling*. This method takes a particular predetermined workload and defines the performance of each algorithm for that workload.

For example, assume we have the workload shown. All five processes arrive at time 0, in the order given, with the length of the CPU burst time given in milliseconds:

Process	Burst Time
P_1	10
P_2	29
P_3	3
P_4	7
P_5	12

Consider the FCFS, SJF, and RR (quantum = 10 milliseconds) scheduling algorithms for this set of processes. Which algorithm would give the minimum average waiting time?

For the FCFS algorithm, we would execute the processes as

P_1	P_2	P_3	P_4	P_5

0   10   39   42   49   61

The waiting time is 0 milliseconds for process P_1, 10 milliseconds for process P_2, 39 milliseconds for process P_3, 42 milliseconds for process P_4, and 49 milliseconds for process P_5. Thus, the average waiting time is $(0 + 10 + 39 + 42 + 49)/5 = 28$ milliseconds.

With nonpreemptive SJF scheduling, we execute the processes as

P_3	P_4	P_1	P_5	P_2

0   3   10   20   32   61

The waiting time is 10 milliseconds for process P_1, 32 milliseconds for process P_2, 0 milliseconds for process P_3, 3 milliseconds for process P_4, and 20 milliseconds for process P_5. Thus, the average waiting time is $(10 + 32 + 0 + 3 + 20)/5 = 13$ milliseconds.

With the RR algorithm, we start process P_2, but preempt it after 10 milliseconds, putting it in the back of the queue:

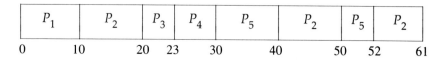

The waiting time is 0 milliseconds for process P_1, 32 milliseconds for process P_2, 20 milliseconds for process P_3, 23 milliseconds for process P_4, and 40 milliseconds for process P_5. Thus, the average waiting time is $(0 + 32 + 20 + 23 + 40)/5 = 23$ milliseconds.

We see that, *in this case*, the SJF policy results in less than one-half the average waiting time obtained with FCFS scheduling; the RR algorithm gives us an intermediate value.

Deterministic modeling is simple and fast. It gives exact numbers, allowing the algorithms to be compared. However, it requires exact numbers for input, and its answers apply to only those cases. The main use of deterministic modeling is in describing scheduling algorithms and providing examples. In cases where we may be running the same programs over and over again and can measure the program's processing requirements exactly, we may be able to use deterministic modeling to select a scheduling algorithm. Over a set of examples, deterministic modeling may indicate trends that can then be analyzed and proved separately. For example, it can be shown that, for the environment described (all processes and their times available at time 0), the SJF policy will always result in the minimum waiting time.

In general, however, deterministic modeling is too specific, and requires too much exact knowledge, to be useful.

Queueing Models

The processes that are run on many systems vary from day to day, so there is no static set of processes (and times) to use for deterministic modeling. What can be determined, however, is the distribution of CPU and I/O bursts. These distributions may be measured and then approximated or simply estimated. The result is a mathematical formula describing the probability of a particular CPU burst. Commonly, this distribution is exponential and is described by its mean. Similarly, the distribution of times when processes arrive in the system (the arrival-time distribution) must be given. From these two distributions, it is possible to compute the average throughput, utilization, waiting time, and so on for most algorithms.

The computer system is described as a network of servers. Each server has a queue of waiting processes. The CPU is a server with its ready queue, as is the I/O system with its device queues. Knowing arrival rates and service rates, we can compute utilization, average queue length, average wait time, and so on. This area of study is called *queueing-network analysis*.

As an example, let n be the average queue length (excluding the process being serviced), let W be the average waiting time in the queue, and let λ be the average arrival rate for new processes in the queue (such as three processes per second). Then, we expect that, during the time, W, that a process waits, $\lambda \times W$ new processes will arrive in the queue. If the system is in a steady state, then the number of processes leaving the queue must be equal to the number of processes that arrive. Thus,

$$n = \lambda \times W.$$

This equation is known as *Little's formula*. Little's formula is particularly useful because it is true for any scheduling algorithm and arrival distribution.

We can use Little's formula to compute one of the three variables, if we know the other two. For example, if we know that seven processes arrive every second (on average), and that there are normally 14 processes in the queue, then we can compute the average waiting time per process as 2 seconds.

Queueing analysis can be quite useful in comparing scheduling algorithms, but it also has its limitations. At the moment, the classes of algorithms and distributions that can be handled are fairly limited. The mathematics of complicated algorithms or distributions can be difficult to work with. Thus, arrival and service distributions are often defined in unrealistic, but mathematically tractable, ways. It is also generally necessary to make a number of independent assumptions, which may not be accurate. Thus, so that they will be able to compute an answer, queueing models are often only an approximation of a real system. As a result, the accuracy of the computed results may be questionable.

4.7.2 Simulations

To get a more accurate evaluation of scheduling algorithms, we can use *simulations*. Simulations involve programming a model of the computer system. Software data structures represent the major components of the system. The simulator has a variable representing a clock, and as this variable's value is increased, the simulator modifies the system state to reflect the activities of the devices, the processes, and the scheduler. As the simulation executes, statistics that indicate algorithm performance are gathered and printed.

The data to drive the simulation can be generated in several ways. The most common method uses a random number generator, which is programmed to generate processes, CPU-burst times, arrivals, departures, and so on, according to probability distributions. The distributions may be defined mathematically (uniform, exponential, Poisson) or empirically. If the distribution is to be defined empirically, measurements of the actual system under study are taken. The results are used to define the actual distribution of events in the real system, and this distribution can then be used to drive the simulation.

However, a distribution-driven simulation may be inaccurate, due to relationships between successive events in the real system. The frequency distribution indicates only how many of each event occur; it does not indicate anything about the order of their occurrence. To correct this problem, we can use *trace tapes*. We create a trace tape by monitoring the real system, recording the sequence of actual events (Figure 4.18). This sequence is then used to drive the simulation. Trace tapes are an excellent way to compare two algorithms on exactly the same set of real inputs. This method can produce very accurate results for its inputs.

Simulations can be very expensive, however, often requiring hours of computer time. A more detailed simulation provides more accurate results, but also requires more computer time. In addition, trace tapes

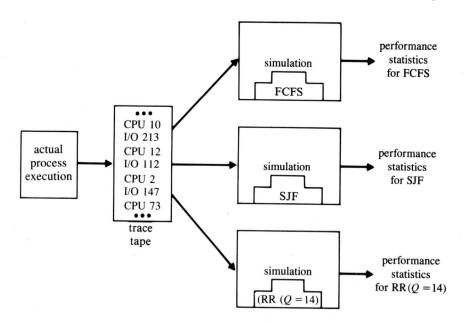

Figure 4.18   Evaluation of CPU schedulers by simulation.

can require large amounts of storage space. Finally, the design, coding, and debugging of the simulator can be a major task.

4.7.3 Implementation

Even a simulation is of limited accuracy. The only completely accurate way of evaluating a scheduling algorithm is to code it up and to put it in the operating system to see how it works. This approach puts the actual algorithm in the real system for evaluation under real operating conditions.

The major difficulty is the cost of this approach. The expense is incurred not only in coding the algorithm and modifying the operating system to support it as well as its required data structures, but also in the reaction of the users to a constantly changing operating system. Most users are not interested in building a better operating system; they merely want to get their processes executed and to use their results. A constantly changing operating system does not help the users get their work done.

The other difficulty with any algorithm evaluation is that the environment in which the algorithm is used will change. The environment will change not only in the usual way, as new programs are written and the types of problems change, but also as a result of the performance of the scheduler. If short processes are given priority, then users may break larger processes, into sets of smaller processes. If interactive processes are given priority over noninteractive processes, then users may switch to interactive use.

For example, researchers tried designing one system to classify interactive and noninteractive processes automatically by looking at the amount of terminal I/O. If a process did not input or output to the terminal in a 1-second interval, it was classified as noninteractive and was moved to a lower-priority queue. As a result, one programmer modified his programs to write an arbitrary character to the terminal at regular intervals of less than 1 second. The system gave his programs a high priority, even though the terminal output was completely meaningless.

The most flexible scheduling algorithms can be altered by the system managers. During operating-system build time, boot time, or run time, the variables used by the schedulers can be changed to reflect the expected future use of the system. For instance, if paychecks need to be processed and printed immediately, but are normally done as a low priority batch job, the batch queue could be given a higher priority temporarily. Unfortunately, few operating systems allow this type of tunable scheduling.

4.8 Summary

A *sequential process* is a program in execution. As a process executes, it changes *state*. The state of a process is defined by that process's current activity. Each process may be in one of the following states: *new, ready, running, waiting,* or *halted*. Each process is represented in the operating system by its own *process control block* (PCB).

The processes in the system can execute in parallel. There are several reasons for allowing concurrent execution: physical resource sharing, logical resource sharing, computation speedup, and modularity. Concurrent execution requires a mechanism for process creation and deletion.

The processes executing in the operating system may be either independent processes or cooperating processes. Cooperating processes may either directly share a logical address space or be allowed to share data only through files. The former setup is achieved through the use of light-weight processes or threads.

CPU scheduling is the task of selecting a waiting process and allocating the CPU to it. Each process is represented by a PCB. The PCBs can be linked together to form queues of processes. There are two major classes of queues in an operating system: I/O request queues and the ready queue. The ready queue contains all the processes that are ready to execute and are waiting for the CPU.

Long-term (job) scheduling is the selection of processes to be allowed to contend for the CPU. Normally, long-term scheduling is heavily influenced by resource-allocation considerations, especially memory management. Short-term (CPU) scheduling is the selection of one process from the ready queue. The CPU is allocated to the selected process by the dispatcher.

First-come, first-served (FCFS) scheduling is the simplest scheduling algorithm, but it can cause short processes to wait for very long processes. Shortest-job-first (SJF) scheduling is provably optimal, providing the shortest average waiting time. Implementing SJF scheduling is difficult because predicting the length of the next CPU burst is difficult. The SJF algorithm is a special case of the general priority scheduling algorithm, which simply allocates the CPU to the highest-priority process. Both priority and SJF scheduling may suffer from starvation. Aging is a technique to prevent starvation.

Round-robin (RR) scheduling is more appropriate for a time-shared system. RR scheduling allocates the CPU to the first process in the ready queue for q time units, where q is the time quantum. After q time units, the CPU is preempted and the process is put at the tail of the ready queue. The major problem is the selection of the time quantum. If the quantum is too large, RR scheduling degenerates to FCFS scheduling; if the quantum is too small, scheduling overhead in the form of context-switch time becomes excessive.

The FCFS algorithm is nonpreemptive; the RR algorithm is preemptive. The SJF and priority algorithms may be either preemptive or nonpreemptive.

Multilevel queue algorithms allow different algorithms to be used for various classes of processes. The most common is a foreground interactive queue, which uses RR scheduling, and a background batch queue, which uses FCFS scheduling. Multilevel feedback queues allow processes to move from one queue to another.

The wide variety of scheduling algorithms demands that we have methods to select among algorithms. Analytic methods use mathematical analysis to determine the performance of an algorithm. Simulation methods determine performance by imitating the scheduling algorithm on a "representative" sample of processes, and computing the resulting performance.

Exercises

4.1 Several popular microcomputer operating systems provide little or no means of concurrent processing. Discuss the major complications that concurrent processing adds to an operating system.

4.2 What two advantages do threads have over multiple processes? What major disadvantage do they have? Suggest one application that would benefit from the use of threads, and one that would not.

4.3 Describe the differences among short-term, medium-term, and long-term scheduling.

4.4 A CPU-scheduling algorithm determines an order for the execution of its scheduled processes. Given n processes to be scheduled on one processor, how many possible different schedules are there? Give a formula in terms of n.

4.5 What advantage is there in having different time quantum sizes on different levels of a multilevel queueing system?

4.6 Define the difference between preemptive and nonpreemptive scheduling. State why strict nonpreemptive scheduling is unlikely to be used in a computer center.

4.7 Explain the operation of multilevel scheduling.

4.8 Consider the following set of processes, with the length of the CPU-burst time given in milliseconds:

Process	Burst Time	Priority
P_1	10	3
P_2	1	1
P_3	2	3
P_4	1	4
P_5	5	2

The processes are assumed to have arrived in the order P_1, P_2, P_3, P_4, P_5, all at time 0.

a. Draw four Gantt charts illustrating the execution of these processes using FCFS, SJF, a nonpreemptive priority (a smaller priority number implies a higher priority), and RR (quantum = 1) scheduling.

b. What is the turnaround time of each process for each of the scheduling algorithms in part a?

c. What is the waiting time of each process for each of the scheduling algorithms in part a?

d. Which of the schedules in part a results in the minimal average waiting time (over all processes)?

4.9 Suppose the following processes arrive for execution at the times indicated. Each process will run the listed amount of time. In answering the questions, use nonpreemptive scheduling and base all decisions on the information you have at the time the decision must be made.

Process	Arrival Time	Burst Time
P_1	0.0	8
P_2	0.4	4
P_3	1.0	1

a. What is the average turnaround time for these processes with the FCFS scheduling algorithm?

b. What is the average turnaround time for these processes with the SJF scheduling algorithm?

c. The SJF algorithm is supposed to improve performance, but notice that we chose to run process P_1 at time 0 because we did not know that two shorter processes would arrive soon. Compute what the average turnaround time will be if the CPU is left idle for the first 1 unit and then SJF scheduling is used. Remember that processes P_1 and P_2 are waiting during this idle time, so their waiting time may increase. This algorithm could be known as future-knowledge-scheduling.

4.10 Consider a variant of the RR scheduling algorithm where the entries in the ready queue are pointers to the PCBs.

a. What would be the effect of putting two pointers to the same process in the ready queue?

b. What would be the major advantages and disadvantages of this scheme?

c. How would you modify the basic RR algorithm to achieve the same effect without the duplicate pointers?

4.11 Many CPU-scheduling algorithms are parameterized. For example, the RR algorithm requires a parameter to indicate the time slice. Multilevel feedback queues require parameters to define the number of queues, the scheduling algorithms for each queue, the criteria used to move processes between queues, and so on.

These algorithms are thus really sets of algorithms (for example, the set of RR algorithms for all time slices, and so on). One set of algorithms may include another (for example, the FCFS algorithm is the RR algorithm with an infinite time quantum). What (if any) relation holds between the following pairs of sets of algorithms?

a. Priority and SJF

b. Multilevel feedback queues and FCFS

c. Priority and FCFS

d. RR and SJF

4.12 Consider the following preemptive priority scheduling algorithm based on dynamically changing priorities. Larger priority numbers imply higher priority. When a process is waiting for the CPU (in the ready queue, but not running), its priority changes at a rate α; when it is running, its priority changes at a rate β. All processes are given a priority of 0 when they enter the ready queue. The parameters α and β can be set to give many different scheduling algorithms.

a. What is the algorithm that results from β > α > 0?

b. What is the algorithm that results from α < β < 0?

4.13 Suppose a scheduling algorithm (at the level of short-term CPU scheduling) favors those processes that have used little processor time in the recent past. Why will this algorithm favor I/O-bound programs and yet not permanently starve CPU-bound programs?

4.14 Differentiate between a multilevel feedback scheduling algorithm and a multilevel queue (foreground-background) CPU-scheduling algorithm that uses RR scheduling for the foreground and a preemptive priority algorithm for the background.

4.15 Explain the differences in the degree to which the following scheduling algorithms discriminate in favor of short processes:

a. FCFS

b. RR

c. Multilevel feedback queues

Bibliographic Notes

General discussions concerning the process concept and its implementation are given by Horning and Randell [1973], Brinch Hansen [1970] (the RC 4000 system), Dijkstra [1968] (the THE system), and Liskov [1972] (the Venus system). Tutorial and survey articles include those by Presser [1975] and Atwood [1976].

General discussions concerning scheduling have been written by Lampson [1968], Coffman and Kleinrock [1968a], Bunt [1976], and Shneiderman [1984]. More formal treatments of scheduling theory are contained in Conway et al. [1967], Coffman and Denning [1973], Kleinrock [1975], Sauer and Chandy [1981], and Lazowska et al. [1984]. A unifying approach to scheduling is presented by Ruschitzka and Fabry [1977].

Process scheduling has been discussed by Lampson [1968], Coffman and Kleinrock [1968a], Kleinrock [1970], Baskett [1971], Buzen [1973], and Lauesen [1973].

The preemptive priority-scheduling algorithm of Exercise 4.12 was suggested by Kleinrock [1975].

Discussions concerning scheduling in real-time systems are offered by Liu and Layland [1973], Abbot [1984], and Jensen et al. [1985]. Fair share schedulers are covered by Kay and Lauder [1988]. Little's formula is due to Little [1961].

Priority CPU scheduling has been discussed by Lampson [1968], Coffman and Kleinrock [1968a], and Kleinrock [1970]. Multilevel feedback queues were originally implemented on the CTSS system described in [Corbato et al. 1962]. This queueing system was analyzed by Schrage [1967]; variations on multilevel feedback queues were studied by Coffman and Kleinrock [1968b]. Additional studies were presented by Coffman and Denning [1973] and Svobodova [1976]. A data structure for manipulating priority queues was presented by Vuillemin [1978].

Lynch [1972c] provided a discussion of the practical aspects and goals of performance evaluation. A survey on performance evaluation was written by Lucas [1971]. Discussions concerning queueing system models have been given by McKinney [1969] and Coffman and Denning [1973].

5

Process Coordination

Concurrent processing is the basis of multiprogrammed operating systems. In this chapter, we discuss the issues of concurrency in great detail. Concurrent systems consist of a collection of processes: Operating-system processes execute system code, and user processes execute user code. All these processes can potentially execute concurrently.

To ensure orderly execution, the system must provide mechanisms for process synchronization and communication. In this chapter we discuss a number of different schemes for achieving this.

5.1 Background

In Chapter 4, we developed a model of a system consisting of a number of cooperating sequential processes, all running asynchronously and possibly sharing data. Let us illustrate this model with a simple example that is representative of operating systems.

Producer-consumer processes are common in operating systems. A *producer* process produces information that is consumed by a *consumer* process. For example, a print program produces characters that are consumed by the printer driver. A compiler may produce assembly code, which is consumed by an assembler. The assembler, in turn, may produce object modules, which are consumed by the loader.

To allow producer and consumer processes to run concurrently, we must create a pool of buffers that can be filled by the producer and emptied by the consumer. A producer can produce into one buffer while the consumer is consuming from another buffer. The producer and consumer must be synchronized, so that the consumer does not try to consume items that have not yet been produced. In this situation, the consumer must wait until an item is produced.

The *unbounded-buffer* producer-consumer problem places no practical limit on the number of buffers. The consumer may have to wait for new items, but the producer can always produce new items; there are always empty buffers. The *bounded-buffer* producer-consumer problem assumes that there is a fixed number of buffers. In this case, the consumer must wait if all the buffers are empty and the producer must wait if all the buffers are full.

In the following solution to the bounded-buffer problem, the shared variables are

```
var n;
type item = ... ;
var  buffer: array [0..n−1] of item;
in, out: 0..n−1;
```

with *in*, *out* initialized to the value 0. The shared pool of buffers is implemented as a circular array with two logical pointers: *in* and *out*. The variable *in* points to the next free buffer; *out* points to the first full buffer. The pool is empty when *in* = *out*; the pool is full when *in* + 1 **mod** *n* = *out*.

The code for the producer and consumer processes follows. The *no-op* is a do-nothing instruction. Thus, **while** *condition* **do** *no-op* simply tests the condition repetitively until it becomes false.

The producer process has a local variable *nextp* in which the new item to be produced is stored:

```
repeat
      ...
    produce an item in nextp
      ...
    while in+1 mod n = out do no-op;
    buffer[in] := nextp;
    in := in+1 mod n;
until false;
```

The consumer process has a local variable *nextc* in which the item to be consumed is stored.

```
repeat
    while in = out do no-op;
    nextc := buffer[out];
    out := out+1 mod n;
        ...
    consume the item in nextc
        ...
until false;
```

This scheme allows at most $n - 1$ buffers to be full at the same time. Suppose that we wanted to modify the algorithm to remedy this deficiency. One possibility is to add an integer variable *counter*, initialized to 0. *Counter* is incremented every time we add a new full buffer to the pool, and is decremented every time we remove one of the full buffers from the pool. The code for the producer process can be modified as follows:

```
repeat
        ...
    produce an item in nextp
        ...
    while counter = n do no-op;
    buffer[in] := nextp;
    in := in+1 mod n;
    counter := counter + 1;
until false;
```

The code for the consumer process can be modified as follows:

```
repeat
    while counter = 0 do no-op;
    nextc := buffer[out];
    out := out+1 mod n;
    counter := counter - 1;
        ...
    consume the item in nextc
        ...
until false;
```

Although both the producer and consumer routines are correct separately, they may not function correctly when executed concurrently. As an illustration, suppose that the value of variable *counter* is currently 5 and that the producer and consumer processes execute the statements "*counter := counter + 1*" and "*counter := counter − 1*" concurrently.

Following the execution of these two statements, the value of the variable *counter* may be 4, 5, or 6! The only correct result is *counter* = 5, which is generated correctly if the producer and consumer execute separately.

We can show that *counter* may be incorrect, as follows. Note that the statement "*counter* := *counter*+1" may be implemented in machine language (on a typical machine) as

$$register_1 := counter;$$
$$register_1 := register_1 + 1;$$
$$counter := register_1$$

where $register_1$ is a local CPU register. Similarly, the statement "*counter* := *counter* − 1" is implemented as follows:

$$register_2 := counter$$
$$register_2 := register_2 - 1;$$
$$counter := register_2$$

where again $register_2$ is a local CPU register. Even though $register_1$ and $register_2$ may be the same physical registers (an accumulator, say), remember that the contents of this register will be saved and restored by the interrupt handler (Section 2.1).

The concurrent execution of the statements "*counter* := *counter* + 1" and "*counter* := *counter* − 1" is equivalent to a sequential execution where the lower-level statements presented previously are interleaved in some arbitrary order (but the order within each high-level statement is preserved). One such interleaving is

T_0:	producer	**execute**	$register_1 := counter$	$\{register_1 = 5\}$
T_1:	producer	**execute**	$register_1 := register_1 + 1$	$\{register_1 = 6\}$
T_2:	consumer	**execute**	$register_2 := counter$	$\{register_2 = 5\}$
T_3:	consumer	**execute**	$register_2 := register_2 - 1$	$\{register_2 = 4\}$
T_4:	producer	**execute**	$counter := register_1$	$\{counter = 6\}$
T_5:	consumer	**execute**	$counter := register_2$	$\{counter = 4\}$

Notice that we have arrived at the incorrect state "*counter* = 4," recording that there are four full buffers when in fact there are five full buffers. If we reversed the order of the statements at T_4 and T_5, we would arrive at the incorrect state "*counter* = 6."

We would arrive at this incorrect state because we allowed both processes to manipulate the variable *counter* concurrently. To remedy this difficulty, we need to ensure that only one process at a time can be manipulating the variable *counter*. This requires some form of synchronization of the processes. A major portion of this chapter is concerned with the issue of process synchronization and coordination.

5.2 The Critical-Section Problem

Consider a system consisting of n processes $\{P_0, P_1, ..., P_{n-1}\}$. Each process has a segment of code, called a *critical section*, in which the process may be changing common variables, updating a table, writing a file, and so on. The important feature of the system is that, when one process is executing in its critical section, no other process is to be allowed to execute in its critical section. Thus, the execution of critical sections by the processes is *mutually exclusive* in time. The critical-section problem is to design a protocol that the processes can use to cooperate. Each process must request permission to enter its critical section. The section of code implementing this request is the *entry* section. The critical section may be followed by an *exit* section. The remaining code is the *remainder* section.

A solution to the critical-section problem must satisfy the following three requirements:

1. **Mutual Exclusion**. If process P_i is executing in its critical section, then no other processes can be executing in their critical sections.

2. **Progress**. If no process is executing in its critical section and there exist some processes that wish to enter their critical sections, then only those processes that are not executing in their remainder section can participate in the decision as to which will enter its critical section next, and this selection cannot be postponed indefinitely.

3. **Bounded Waiting**. There must exist a bound on the number of times that other processes are allowed to enter their critical sections after a process has made a request to enter its critical section and before that request is granted.

It is assumed that each process is executing at a nonzero speed. However, no assumption can be made concerning the *relative* speed of the n processes.

In Sections 5.2.1 and 5.2.2, we work up to solutions to the critical-section problem that satisfy these three requirements. The solutions do not rely on any assumptions concerning the hardware instructions or the number of processors the hardware supports. We do, however, assume that the basic machine-language instructions (the primitive instructions such as load, store, and test) are executed atomically. That is, if two such instructions are executed concurrently, the result is equivalent to their sequential execution in some unknown order. Thus, if a load and a store are executed concurrently, the load will get either the old value or the new value, but not some combination of the two.

When presenting an algorithm, we define only the variables used for synchronization purposes, and describe only a typical process P_i whose general structure is

repeat

| entry section |

critical section

| exit section |

remainder section

until *false*;

The *entry section* and *exit section* are enclosed in boxes to highlight the important segments of code.

5.2.1 Two-Process Solutions

In this section, we restrict our attention to algorithms that are applicable to only two processes at a time. The processes are numbered P_0 and P_1. For convenience, when presenting P_i, we use P_j to denote the other process; that is, $j = 1 - i$.

Algorithm 1

Our first approach is to let the processes share a common integer variable *turn* initialized to 0 (or 1). If *turn* = i, then process P_i is allowed to execute in its critical section. The structure of process P_i is shown in Figure 5.1.

This solution ensures that only one process at a time can be in its critical section. However, it does not satisfy the progress requirement, since it requires strict alternation of processes in the execution of the critical section. For example, if *turn* = 0 and P_1 is ready to enter its critical section, it cannot do so, even though P_0 may be in its remainder section.

repeat

$$\boxed{\textbf{while } \mathit{turn} \neq i \textbf{ do } \mathit{no\text{-}op};}$$

critical section

$$\boxed{\mathit{turn} := j;}$$

remainder section

until *false*;

Figure 5.1   The structure of process P_i in algorithm 1.

Algorithm 2

The problem with algorithm 1 is that it does not keep sufficient information about the state of each process; it remembers only which process is allowed to enter its critical section. To remedy this problem, we can replace the variable *turn* with the following array:

var *flag*: **array** [0..1] **of** *boolean*;

The elements of the array are initialized to *false*. If *flag[i]* is *true,* .this indicates that P_i is *ready* to enter the critical section. The structure of process P_i is shown in Figure 5.2.

In this algorithm, process P_i first sets *flag[i]* to be *true*, signaling that it is ready to enter its critical section. Following this, P_i checks to verify that process P_i is not also ready to enter its critical section. If P_i were ready, then P_i would wait until P_i had indicated that it no longer needed to be in the critical section (that is, *flag[j]* is *false*). At this point, P_i would enter the critical section. On exiting the critical section, P_i would set its *flag* to be *false*, allowing the other process (if it is waiting) to enter its critical section.

In this solution, the mutual-exclusion requirement is satisfied. Unfortunately, the progress requirement is not met. To illustrate this problem, we consider the following execution sequence.

$$
\begin{aligned}
T_0: & \quad P_0 \text{ sets } \mathit{flag}[0] = \mathit{true} \\
T_1: & \quad P_1 \text{ sets } \mathit{flag}[1] = \mathit{true}
\end{aligned}
$$

Now P_0 and P_1 are looping forever in their respective **while** statements.

repeat

> $flag[i] := true;$
> **while** $flag[j]$ **do** *no-op;*

critical section

> $flag[i] := false;$

remainder section

until *false;*

Figure 5.2   The structure of process P_i in algorithm 2.

This algorithm is crucially dependent on the exact timing of the two processes. The sequence could have been derived in an environment where there are several processors executing concurrently, or where an interrupt (such as a timer interrupt) has occurred immediately after step T_0 was executed, and the CPU is switched from one process to another.

Note that switching the order of the instructions for setting $flag[i]$, and testing the value of a $flag[j]$, will not solve our problem. It will result in a situation where it is possible for both processes to be in the critical section at the same time, violating the mutual-exclusion requirement.

Algorithm 3

By combining the key ideas of algorithm 1 and algorithm 2 we obtain a correct solution to the critical-section problem where all three requirement are met. The processes share two variables:

var *flag*: **array** [0..1] **of** *boolean;*
turn: 0..1;

Initially $flag[0] = flag[1] = false$, and the value of *turn* is immaterial (but is either 0 or 1). The structure of process P_i is shown in Figure 5.3.

To enter the critical section, process P_i first sets $flag[i]$ to be *true*, and then asserts that it is the other process's turn to enter if appropriate (*turn* = *j*). If both processes try to enter at the same time, *turn* will be set to both *i* and *j* at roughly the same time. Only one of these assignments will last; the other will occur, but be immediately

repeat

> $flag[i] := true;$
> $turn := j;$
> **while** ($flag[j]$ **and** $turn=j$) **do** *no-op*;

critical section

> $flag[i] := false;$

remainder section

until *false*;

Figure 5.3   The structure of process P_i in algorithm 3.

overwritten. The eventual value of *turn* decides which of the two processes is allowed to enter its critical section first.

We now prove that this solution is correct. We need to show that (1) mutual exclusion is preserved, (2) the progress requirement is satisfied, and (3) the bounded-waiting requirement is met.

To prove property (1), we note that each P_i enters its critical section only if either $flag[j]$ = *false* or *turn* = i. Also note that, if both processes can be executing in their critical sections at the same time, then $flag[0]$ = $flag[1]$ = *true*. These two observations imply that P_0 and P_1 could not have successfully executed their while statement at about the same time, since the value of *turn* can be either 0 or 1, but not both. Hence, one of the processes, say P_j, must have successfully executed the while statement, whereas P_i had to execute at least one additional statement ("*turn* = j"). However, since at that time $flag[j]$ = *true*, and *turn* = i, and this condition will persist as long as P_j is in its critical section, the result follows: Mutual exclusion is preserved.

To prove properties (2) and (3), we note that a process P_i can be prevented from entering the critical section only if it is stuck in the while loop with the condition $flag[j]$ = *true* and *turn* = j; this is the only loop. If P_j is not ready to enter the critical section, then $flag[j]$ = *false*, and P_i can enter its critical section. If P_j has set $flag[j]$ = *true* and is also executing in its while statement, then either *turn* = i or *turn* = j. If *turn* = i, then P_i will enter the critical section. If *turn* = j, then P_j will enter the critical section. However, once P_j exits its critical section, it will reset $flag[j]$ to *false*, allowing P_i to enter its critical section. If P_j resets $flag[j]$ to *true*, it must also set *turn* = *i*. Thus, since P_i does not change the value of the variable *turn* while executing the while statement, P_i will enter the critical section (progress) after at most one entry by P_j (bounded waiting).

5.2.2 Multiple-Process Solutions

We have seen that algorithm 3 solves the critical-section problem for two processes. Now let us develop two different algorithms for solving the critical-section problem for *n* processes.

Algorithm 4

The common data structures are

$$\text{var } flag: \textbf{array } [0..n-1] \textbf{ of } (idle, want\text{-}in, in\text{-}cs);$$
$$turn: 0..n-1;$$

All the elements of *flag* are initially *idle*; the initial value of *turn* is immaterial (between 0 and $n-1$). The structure of process P_i is shown in Figure 5.4.

To prove that this algorithm is correct, we need to show that (1) mutual exclusion is preserved, (2) the progress requirement is satisfied, and (3) the bounded-waiting requirement is met.

To prove property (1), we note that each P_i enters its critical section only if $flag[j] \neq in\text{-}cs$ for all $j \neq i$. Since only P_i can set $flag[i] = in\text{-}cs$, and since P_i inspects $flag[j]$ only while $flag[i] = in\text{-}cs$, the result follows.

To prove property (2), we observe that the value of *turn* can be modified only when a process enters its critical section and when it leaves its critical section. Thus, if no process is executing or leaving its critical section, the value of *turn* remains constant. The first contending process in the cyclic ordering (*turn*, *turn*+1, ..., $n-1$, 0, ..., *turn*-1) will enter the critical section.

To prove property (3) we observe that, when a process leaves the critical section, it must designate as its unique successor the first contending process in the cyclic ordering *turn* + 1, ..., $n - 1$, 0, ..., *turn* - 1, *turn*, ensuring that any process wanting to enter its critical section will do so within $n - 1$ turns.

Algorithm 5

A different approach to the critical-section problem is the *bakery algorithm*, which is based on a scheduling algorithm commonly used in bakeries, ice-cream stores, meat markets, and similar domains. This

var *j*: 0..*n*;
repeat

```
repeat
    flag[i] := want-in;
    j := turn;
    while j ≠ i
        do if flag[j] ≠ idle
                then j := turn
                else j := j+1 mod n;
    flag[i] := in-cs;
    j := 0;
    while (j < n) and (j = i or flag[j] ≠ in-cs) do j := j+1;
until (j ≥ n) and (turn = i or flag[turn] = idle);
turn := i;
```

critical section

```
j := turn+1 mod n;
while (flag[j] = idle) do j := j+1 mod n;
turn := j;
flag[i] := idle;
```

remainder section

until *false*;

Figure 5.4   The structure of process P_i in algorithm 4.

algorithm was developed for a distributed environment. We are concerned with only those aspects of the algorithm that pertain to a centralized environment.

On entering the store, each customer receives a number. The customer with the lowest number is served next. Unfortunately, the bakery algorithm cannot guarantee that two processes (customers) do not receive the same number. In the case of a tie, the process with the lowest name is served first. That is, if P_i and P_j receive the same number and if $i < j$, then P_i is served first. Since process names are unique and totally ordered, our algorithm is completely deterministic.

The common data structures are

$$\text{var } choosing: \textbf{array } [0..n-1] \textbf{ of } boolean;$$
$$number: \textbf{array } [0..n-1] \textbf{ of } integer;$$

Initially, these data structures are initialized to *false* and 0, respectively. For convenience, we define the following notation:

- $(a,b) < (c,d)$ if $a < c$ or if $a = c$ and $b < d$.

- $max(a_0, ..., a_{n-1})$ is a number, k, such that $k \geq a_i$ for $i = 0, ..., n-1$.

The structure of process P_i is shown in Figure 5.5.

To prove that the bakery algorithm is correct, we need first to show that, if P_i is in its critical section and P_k ($k \neq i$) has already chosen its $number[k] \neq 0$, then $(number[i],i) < (number[k],k)$. The proof of this is left to you in Exercise 5.4.

Given this result, it is now simple to show that mutual exclusion is observed. Indeed, consider P_i in its critical section and P_k trying to enter

repeat

```
choosing[i] := true;
number[i] := max(number[0], number[1], ..., number[n−1]) + 1;
choosing[i] := false;
for j := 0 to n−1
    do begin
            while choosing[j] do no-op;
            while number[j] ≠ 0
                and (number[j],j) < (number[i],i) do no-op;
    end;
```

critical section

```
number[i] := 0;
```

remainder section

until *false*;

Figure 5.5   The structure of process P_i in algorithm 5.

the critical section. When process P_k executes the second while statement for $j = i$, it finds that

- *number*[*i*] $\neq$ 0 and

- (*number*[*i*],*i*) < (*number*[*k*],*k*).

Thus, it continues looping in the while statement until P_i leaves its critical section.

If we wish to show that the progress and bounded-waiting requirements are preserved, and that the algorithm ensures fairness, it is sufficient to observe that the processes enter their critical section on a first-come, first-served basis.

5.3 Synchronization Hardware

In this section, we present some simple hardware instructions that are available on many systems, and show how they can be used effectively in solving the critical-section problem.

The critical-section problem could be solved simply if we could disallow interrupts to occur while a shared variable is being modified. Unfortunately, this solution is not always feasible. Many machines therefore provide special hardware instructions that allow us either to test and modify the content of a word, or to swap the contents of two words, atomically. These special instructions can be used to solve the critical-section problem in a relatively simple manner. Rather than discussing one specific instruction for one specific machine, let us abstract the main concepts behind these types of instructions. The *Test-and-Set* instruction can be defined as follows:

```
function Test-and-Set (var target: boolean): boolean;
    begin
        Test-and-Set := target;
        target := true;
    end;
```

The important characteristic is that this instruction is executed atomically; that is, as one uninterruptable unit. Thus, if two *Test-and-Set* instructions are executed simultaneously (each on a different CPU), they will be executed sequentially in some arbitrary order.

If the machine supports the *Test-and-Set* instruction, then we can implement mutual exclusion by declaring a Boolean variable *lock*, initialized to *false*. The structure of process P_i is shown in Figure 5.6.

repeat

> **while** *Test-and-Set(lock)* **do** *no-op;*

critical section

> *lock := false;*

remainder section

until *false;*

Figure 5.6   Mutual exclusion implementation with *Test-and-Set.*

The *Swap* instruction swaps the contents of two words, atomically, and is defined as follows:

> **procedure** *Swap* (**var** *a, b: boolean*);
>   **var** *temp: boolean;*
>   **begin**
>   *temp := a;*
>   *a := b;*
>   *b := temp;*
>   **end;**

As in the case of the *Test-and-Set* instruction, the *Swap* instruction is also executed atomically.

If the machine supports the *Swap* instruction, then mutual exclusion can be provided as follows. A global Boolean variable *lock* is declared and is initialized to *false*. In addition, each process also has a local Boolean variable *key*. The structure of process P_i is shown in Figure 5.7.

These algorithms do not satisfy the bounded-waiting requirement. We present an algorithm that uses the *Test-and-Set* instruction in Figure 5.8. This algorithm satisfies all the critical-section requirements. The common data structures are

> **var** *waiting:* **array** $[0..n-1]$ **of** *boolean*
>   *lock:* **boolean**

These data structures are initialized to *false*.

repeat

```
key := true;
repeat
     Swap(lock,key);
until key = false;
```

critical section

```
lock := false;
```

remainder section

until *false*;

Figure 5.7 Mutual exclusion implementation with the *Swap* instruction.

To prove that the mutual-exclusion requirement is met, we note that process P_i can enter its critical section only if either *waiting*[i] = *false* or *key* = *false*. *Key* can become *false* only if the *Test-and-Set* is executed. The first process to execute the *Test-and-Set* will find *key* = *false*; all others must wait. The variable *waiting*[i] can become false only if another process leaves its critical section; only one *waiting*[i] is set to *false*, maintaining the mutual-exclusion requirement.

To prove the progress requirement, we note that the arguments presented for mutual exclusion also apply here, since a process exiting the critical section either sets *lock* to *false*, or sets *waiting*[j] to *false*. Both allow a process that is waiting to enter its critical section to proceed.

To prove bounded waiting, we note that, when a process leaves its critical section, it scans the array *waiting* in the cyclic ordering ($i + 1$, $i + 2$, ..., $n - 1$, 0, ..., $i - 1$). It designates the first process in this ordering that is in the entry section (*waiting*[j] = *true*) as the next one to enter the critical section. Any process waiting to enter its critical section will thus do so within $n - 1$ turns.

5.4 Semaphores

The solutions to the critical-section problem presented in the previous section are not easy to generalize to more complex problems. To overcome this difficulty, we can use a synchronization tool, called a

var j: $0..n-1$;
   key: *boolean*;
repeat

> *waiting*[i] := *true*;
> *key* := *true*;
> **while** *waiting*[i] **and** *key* **do** *key* := *Test-and-Set*(*lock*);
> *waiting*[i] := *false*;

    critical section

> j := i+1 **mod** n;
> **while** ($j \neq i$) **and** (**not** *waiting*[j]) **do** j := j+1 **mod** n;
> **if** $j = i$ **then** *lock* := *false*
>   **else** *waiting*[j] := *false*;

    remainder section

until *false*;

Figure 5.8   Bounded-waiting mutual exclusion with *Test-and-Set*.

semaphore. A semaphore S is an integer variable that, apart from initialization, is accessed only through two standard *atomic* operations: *wait* and *signal*. (These operations were originally termed *P* (for *wait*) and *V* (for *signal*). These names come from the Dutch *proberen* (to test) and *verhogen* (to increment).) The classical definitions of *wait* and *signal* are

$$wait(S): \textbf{ while } S \leq 0 \textbf{ do } no\text{-}op;$$
$$S := S - 1;$$

$$signal(S): S := S + 1;$$

Modifications to the integer value of the semaphore in the *wait* and *signal* operations are executed indivisibly. That is, when one process modifies the semaphore value, no other process can simultaneously modify that same semaphore value. In addition, in the case of the *wait*(S), the testing of the integer value of S ($S \leq 0$), and its possible modification ($S := S - 1$), must also be executed without interruption.

repeat

> $wait(mutex);$

critical section

> $signal(mutex);$

remainder section

until *false;*

Figure 5.9   Mutual exclusion implementation with semaphores.

We shall see how these operations can be implemented in Section 5.4.2; first, let us see how semaphores can be used.

5.4.1 Usage

Semaphores can be used in dealing with the n-process critical-section problem. The n processes share a common semaphore, *mutex* (standing for *mut*ual *ex*clusion), initialized to 1. Each process P_i is organized as shown in Figure 5.9.

Semaphores can also be used in solving various synchronization problems. For example, consider two concurrently running processes: P_1 with a statement S_1, and P_2 with a statement S_2. Suppose that we require that S_2 be executed only after S_1 has completed. We can implement this scheme readily by letting P_1 and P_2 share a common semaphore *synch*, initialized to 0, and by inserting the statements

$$S_1;$$
$$signal(synch);$$

in process P_1, and the statements

$$wait(synch);$$
$$S_2;$$

in process P_2. Since *synch* is initialized to 0, P_2 will execute S_2 only after P_1 has invoked *signal(synch)*, which is after S_1.

5.4.2 Implementation

The main disadvantage of the mutual-exclusion solutions of Section 5.2, and of the semaphore definition given here, is that they all require *busy waiting*. While a process is in its critical section, any other process that tries to enter its critical section must continuously loop in the entry code. This is clearly a problem in a real multiprogramming system, where a single CPU is shared among many processes. Busy waiting wastes CPU cycles that some other process might be able to use productively. This type of semaphore is also called a *spinlock* (since the process "spins" while waiting for the lock). Spinlocks are useful in multiprocessor systems, as shown in Chapter 16. The advantage of a spinlock is that no context switch is required when a process must wait on a lock (a context switch may take considerable time). Thus, when locks are expected to be held for very short times, spinlocks are quite useful.

To overcome the need for busy waiting, we can modify the definition of the *wait* and *signal* semaphore operations. When a process executes the *wait* operation and finds that the semaphore value is not positive, it must wait. However, rather than busy waiting, the process can *block* itself. The block operation places a process into a waiting queue associated with the semaphore, and the state of the process is switched to the waiting state. Following this, control is transferred to the CPU scheduler, which selects another process to execute.

A process that is blocked, waiting on a semaphore *S*, should be restarted by the execution of a *signal* operation by some other process. The process is restarted by a *wakeup* operation, which changes the state of the process from the waiting state to the ready state. The process is then placed in the ready queue. (The CPU may or may not be switched from the running process to the newly ready process, depending on the CPU-scheduling algorithm.)

To implement semaphores under this definition, we define a semaphore as a record:

> **type** *semaphore* = **record**
> > *value*: *integer*;
> > *L*: **list of** *process*;
> **end**;

Each semaphore has an integer value and a list of processes. When a process must wait on a semaphore, it is added to the list of processes. A *signal* operation removes one process from the list of waiting processes and awakens it.

The semaphore operations can now be defined as

$wait(S)$: $S.value := S.value - 1$;
      if $S.value < 0$
        then begin
            add this process to $S.L$;
            $block$;
        end;

$signal(S)$: $S.value := S.value + 1$;
        if $S.value \leq 0$
         then begin
             remove a process P from $S.L$;
             $wakeup(P)$;
         end;

The *block* operation suspends the process that invokes it. The *wakeup(P)* operation resumes the execution of a blocked process *P*. These two operations are provided by the operating system as basic system calls.

Note that, while the classical definition of semaphores with busy waiting is such that the semaphore value is never negative, this implementation may have negative semaphore values. If the semaphore value is negative, its magnitude is the number of processes waiting on that semaphore. This fact is a result of the switching of the order of the decrement and the test in the implementation of the *wait* operation.

The list of processes can be easily implemented by a link field in each process control block (PCB). Each semaphore contains an integer value and a pointer to a list of PCBs. One way to add and remove processes from the list, which ensures bounded waiting, would be first-in, first-out (FIFO; a queue), where the semaphore contains both head and tail pointers to the queue. In general, however, the list may use *any* queueing strategy (FIFO, last-in, first-out (LIFO), priority, and so on). Correct usage of semaphores does not depend on a particular queueing strategy for the semaphore lists.

The critical aspect of semaphores is that they are executed atomically. We must guarantee that no two processes can execute *wait* and *signal* operations on the same semaphore at the same time. This situation is a critical-section problem, and can be solved in either of two ways.

In a uniprocessor environment (that is, where only one CPU exists), we can simply inhibit interrupts during the time the *wait* and *signal* operations are executing. This scheme works in a uniprocessor environment because, once interrupts are inhibited, instructions from different processes cannot be interleaved.

In a multiprocessor environment, inhibiting interrupts does not work. Instructions from different processes (running on different processors) may be interleaved in some arbitrary way. If the hardware does not provide any special instructions, we can employ any of the correct software solutions for the critical-section problem (Section 5.2), where the critical sections consist of the *wait* and *signal* procedures.

It is important to admit that we have not completely eliminated busy waiting with this definition of the *wait* and *signal* operations. Rather, we have removed busy waiting from the entry to the critical sections of application programs. Furthermore, we have limited it to only the critical sections of the *wait* and *signal* operations, which are quite short. (If properly coded, they should be no more than about 10 instructions.) Thus, the critical section is almost always empty, and virtually no busy waiting ever occurs. When busy waiting does occur, it does so for only a short time. An entirely different situation exists with application programs whose critical sections may be quite long (hours) or may be almost always occupied. In this case, busy waiting is extremely inefficient.

5.4.3 Deadlocks and Starvation

The implementation of a semaphore with a waiting queue may result in a situation where two or more processes are waiting indefinitely for an event that can be caused by only one of the waiting processes. The event in question is the execution of a *signal* operation. When such a state is reached, these processes are said to be *deadlocked*.

To illustrate this, we consider a system consisting of two processes, P_0 and P_1, each accessing two semaphores, S and Q, set to the value 1:

P_0	P_1
wait(S);	*wait(Q)*;
wait(Q);	*wait(S)*;
.	.
.	.
.	.
signal(S);	*signal(Q)*;
signal(Q);	*signal(S)*;

Suppose that P_0 executes *wait(S)* and then P_1 executes *wait(Q)*. When P_0 executes *wait(Q)*, it must wait until P_1 executes *signal(Q)*. Similarly, when P_1 executes *wait(S)*, it must wait until P_0 executes *signal(S)*. Since these signal operations cannot be executed, P_0 and P_1 are deadlocked.

We say that a set of processes is in a deadlock state when every process in the set is waiting for an event that can be caused only by another process in the set. The events with which we are mainly concerned here are resource acquisition and release. However, other types of events may result in deadlocks, as will be shown in Chapter 6. In that chapter, we shall describe various mechanisms for dealing with the deadlock problem.

Another problem related to deadlocks is *indefinite blocking* or *starvation*, a situation where processes wait indefinitely within the semaphore. Indefinite blocking may occur if we add and remove processes from the list associated with a semaphore in LIFO order.

5.5 Classical Problems of Synchronization

In this section, we present a number of different synchronization problems that are important mainly because they are examples for a large class of concurrency-control problems. These problems are used for testing nearly every newly proposed synchronization scheme. Semaphores are used for synchronization in our solutions.

5.5.1 The Bounded-Buffer Problem

The bounded-buffer problem was introduced in Section 5.1; it is commonly used to illustrate the power of synchronization primitives. We present here a general structure of this scheme, without committing ourselves to any particular implementation. We assume that the pool consists of n buffers, each capable of holding one item. The *mutex* semaphore provides mutual exclusion for accesses to the buffer pool and is initialized to the value 1. The *empty* and *full* semaphores count the number of empty and full buffers, respectively. The semaphore *empty* is initialized to the value n; the semaphore *full* is initialized to the value 0.

The code for the producer process is shown in Figure 5.10, while the code for the consumer process is shown in Figure 5.11. Note the symmetry between the producer and the consumer. We can interpret this code as the producer producing full buffers for the consumer, or as the consumer producing empty buffers for the producer.

5.5.2 The Readers and Writers Problem

A data object (such as a file or record) is to be shared among several concurrent processes. Some of these processes may want only to read the content of the shared object, whereas others may want to update (that is, to read and write) the shared object. We distinguish between

repeat
...
    produce an item in *nextp*
...
wait(empty);
wait(mutex);
...
add *nextp* to *buffer*
...
signal(mutex);
signal(full);
until *false;*

Figure 5.10   The structure of the producer process.

these two types of processes by referring to those processes that are interested in only reading as *readers* and to the rest as *writers*. Obviously, if two readers access the shared data object simultaneously, no adverse effects will result. However, if a writer and some other process (either a reader or a writer) access the shared object simultaneously, chaos may ensue.

To ensure that these difficulties do not arise, we require that the writers have exclusive access to the shared object. This synchronization problem is referred to as the *readers-writers* problem. Since it was originally stated, it has been used to test nearly every new synchronization primitive. The readers-writers problem has several

repeat
wait(full);
wait(mutex);
...
remove an item from *buffer* to *nextc*
...
signal(mutex);
signal(empty);
...
consume the item in *nextc*
...
until *false;*

Figure 5.11   The structure of the consumer process.

wait(wrt);

...

writing is performed

...

signal(wrt);

Figure 5.12 The structure of a writer process.

variations, all involving priorities. The simplest one, referred to as the *first* readers-writers problem, requires that no reader will be kept waiting unless a writer has already obtained permission to use the shared object. In other words, no reader should wait for other readers to finish simply because a writer is waiting. The *second* readers-writers problem requires that, once a writer is ready, that writer performs its write as soon as possible. In other words, if a writer is waiting to access the object, no new readers may start reading.

We note that a solution to either problem may result in *starvation*. In the first case, writers may starve; in the second case, readers may starve. For this reason other variants of the problem have been proposed. In this section, we present a solution to the first readers-writers problem. In Section 5.6.1, we present a solution that avoids starvation to a variant of the second readers-writers problem.

In this solution to the first readers-writers problem, the reader processes share the following data structures:

var *mutex, wrt: semaphore;*
readcount : integer;

The semaphores *mutex* and *wrt* are initialized to 1; *readcount* is initialized to 0. The semaphore *wrt* is common to both the reader and writer processes. The *mutex* semaphore is used to ensure mutual exclusion when the variable *readcount* is updated. *Readcount* keeps track of how many processes are currently reading the object. The semaphore *wrt* functions as a mutual exclusion semaphore for the writers. It also is used by the first or last reader that enters or exits the critical section. It is not used by readers who enter or exit while other readers are in their critical sections.

The general structure of a writer process is shown in Figure 5.12; the general structure of a reader process is shown in Figure 5.13. Note that, if a writer is in the critical section and n readers are waiting, then one reader is queued on *wrt*, and $n - 1$ readers are queued on *mutex*. Also

```
wait(mutex);
    readcount := readcount + 1;
    if readcount = 1 then wait(wrt);
signal(mutex);

        ...

    reading is performed

        ...
wait(mutex);
    readcount := readcount − 1;
    if readcount = 0 then signal(wrt);
signal(mutex);
```

Figure 5.13   The structure of a reader process.

observe that, when a writer executes *signal(wrt)*, we may resume the execution of either the waiting readers or a single waiting writer. The selection is made by to the scheduler.

5.5.3 The Dining-Philosophers Problem

Five philosophers spend their lives thinking and eating. The philosophers share a common circular table surrounded by five chairs, each belonging to one philosopher. In the center of the table there is a bowl of rice, and the table is laid with five single chopsticks (Figure 5.14). When a philosopher thinks, he does not interact with his

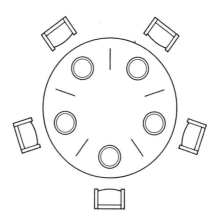

Figure 5.14   The situation of the dining philosophers.

colleagues. From time to time, a philosopher gets hungry and tries to pick up the two chopsticks that are closest to him (the chopsticks that are between him and his left and right neighbors). A philosopher may only pick up one chopstick at a time. Obviously, he cannot pick up a chopstick that is already in the hand of a neighbor. When a hungry philosopher has both his chopsticks at the same time, he eats without releasing his chopsticks. When he is finished eating, he puts down both of his chopsticks and starts thinking again.

The dining-philosophers problem is considered a classic synchronization problem, not because of its practical importance, but because it is an example for a large class of concurrency-control problems.

One simple solution is to represent each chopstick by a semaphore. A philosopher tries to grab the chopstick by executing a *wait* operation on that semaphore; he releases his chopsticks by executing *signals* on the appropriate semaphores. Thus, the shared data are

var *chopstick*: **array** [0..4] **of** *semaphore*;

where all the elements of *chopstick* are initialized to 1. The structure of philosopher i is shown in Figure 5.15.

Although this solution guarantees that no two neighbors are eating simultaneously, it nevertheless must be rejected because of the possibility of creating a deadlock. Suppose that all five philosophers become hungry simultaneously, and each grabs his left chopstick. All the elements of *chopstick* will now be equal to zero. When each philosopher tries to grab his right chopstick, he will be delayed forever.

```
repeat
    wait(chopstick[i]);
    wait(chopstick[i+1 mod 5]);
        ...
    eat
        ...
    signal(chopstick[i]);
    signal(chopstick[i+1 mod 5]);
        ...
    think
        ...
until false;
```

Figure 5.15   The structure of philosopher i.

Several possible remedies to the deadlock problem are listed next. In Section 5.6.2 we present an algorithm that ensures freedom from deadlocks.

- Allow at most four philosophers to be sitting simultaneously at the table

- Allow a philosopher to pick up his chopsticks only if both of them are available (note that this must be done in a critical section)

- Use an asymmetric solution; that is, an odd philosopher picks up first his left chopstick and then his right chopstick, while an even philosopher picks up his right chopstick and then his left chopstick

Finally, any satisfactory solution to the dining-philosophers problem must guard against the possibility that one of the philosophers will starve to death. A deadlock-free solution does not necessarily eliminate the possibility of starvation.

5.6 Language Constructs

Although semaphores provide a convenient and effective mechanism for process synchronization, their incorrect use can still result in timing errors that are difficult to detect, since these errors happen only if some particular execution sequences take place, and these sequences do not always occur.

We have seen an example of such types of errors in the use of counters in our solution to the producer-consumer problem. In that example, the timing problem happened only rarely, and even then the counter value appeared to be a reasonable value, just off by 1. Nevertheless, this is obviously not an acceptable solution. It is for this reason that semaphores were introduced in the first place.

Unfortunately, such timing errors can still occur with the use of semaphores. To illustrate how, let us review the solution to the critical-section problem using semaphores. All processes share a semaphore variable *mutex*, which is initialized to 1. Each process must execute *wait(mutex)* before entering the critical section, and *signal(mutex)* afterward. If this sequence is not observed, two processes may be in their critical sections simultaneously.

Let us examine the various difficulties that may result. Note that these difficulties will arise even if a *single* process is not well behaved. This situation may be the result of an honest programming error or an uncooperative programmer.

- Suppose that a process interchanges the order in which the *wait* and *signal* operations on the semaphore *mutex* are executed, resulting in the execution:

$$signal(mutex);$$

$$\cdots$$

critical section

$$\cdots$$

$$wait(mutex);$$

In this situation, several processes may be executing in their critical section simultaneously, violating the mutual-exclusion requirement. This error may be discovered only if several processes are simultaneously active in their critical sections. Note that this situation may not always be reproducible.

- Suppose that a process replaces *signal(mutex)* with *wait(mutex)*. That is, it executes

$$wait(mutex);$$

$$\cdots$$

critical section

$$\cdots$$

$$wait(mutex);$$

In this case, a deadlock will occur.

- Suppose that a process omits the *wait(mutex)*, or the *signal(mutex)*, or both. In this case, either mutual exclusion is violated or a deadlock will occur.

These examples illustrate that various types of errors can be generated easily when semaphores are used incorrectly to solve the critical-section problem. Similar problems may arise in the other synchronization schemes we discussed in Section 5.5.

To deal with the type of errors we have outlined, researchers have introduced many language constructs. In the following, we describe several such constructs. In our presentation, we shall assume that a process consists of some local data, and a sequential program that can operate on the data. The local data can be accessed by only the sequential program that is encapsulated within the same process. That is, one process cannot directly access the local data of another process. Processes can, however, share global data.

5.6.1 Critical Regions

The first high-level synchronization construct is the *critical region*. A variable v of type T, which is to be shared among many processes, can be declared:

var v: **shared** T;

The variable v can be accessed only inside a *region* statement of the following form:

region v **do** S;

This construct means that, while statement S is being executed, no other process can access the variable v. Thus, if the two statements,

region v **do** $S1$;
region v **do** $S2$;

are executed concurrently in distinct sequential processes, the result will be equivalent to the sequential execution "$S1$ followed by $S2$," or "$S2$ followed by $S1$."

The critical-region construct guards against some simple errors associated with the semaphore solution to the critical-section problem that may be made by a programmer. Note that it does not necessarily eliminate all synchronization errors; rather, it reduces their number. If errors occur in the logic of the program, reproducing a particular sequence of events may not be simple.

Let us illustrate now how a compiler could implement the critical-region construct. For each declaration

var v: **shared** T;

the compiler generates a semaphore $v\text{-}mutex$ initialized to 1. For each statement

region v **do** S;

the compiler generates the following code:

```
wait(v-mutex);
S;
signal(v-mutex);
```

Clearly, mutual exclusion is preserved as required by the semantics of the critical-region statement.

Critical regions may also be nested. In this case, however, deadlocks may result. To illustrate this problem, we let x and y be two shared variables accessed through the following two concurrent processes:

$$Q: \textbf{region } x \textbf{ do region } y \textbf{ do } S1;$$

$$R: \textbf{region } y \textbf{ do region } x \textbf{ do } S2;$$

If Q and R enter the regions x and y, respectively, at about the same time, a deadlock will occur. Consider the following execution sequence, using semaphores to implement the critical region construct:

T_0: Q executes $wait(x\text{-}mutex)$.
T_1: R executes $wait(y\text{-}mutex)$.
T_2: R executes $wait(x\text{-}mutex)$, R waits since $x\text{-}mutex = 0$.
T_3: Q executes $wait(y\text{-}mutex)$, Q waits since $y\text{-}mutex = 0$.

We now have a deadlock situation involving Q and R. The deadlock occurs because region x is nested in region y, and vice versa. To prevent such a situation, we can impose a resource ordering scheme (Section 7.3.4). If no such ordering can be constructed, deadlocks may occur. The compiler can detect the possibility of such deadlocks and issue error messages notifying the programmer of the situation. The compiler would use the nesting of two regions to define a binary relation as follows. If we have two regions x and y such that **region** y is nested in **region** x, then we define $y < x$. If this binary relation is a partial ordering, then no deadlock can occur.

The critical-region construct can be used effectively to solve the critical-section problem. It cannot, however, be used to solve some general synchronization problems. For this purpose, the *conditional critical region* must be used. The major difference between the critical-region and the conditional critical-region constructs is in the region statement, which now has the form

$$\textbf{region } v \textbf{ when } B \textbf{ do } S;$$

where B is a Boolean expression. As before, regions referring to the same shared variable exclude each other in time. Now, however, when a process enters the critical-section region, the Boolean expression B is evaluated. If the expression is true, statement S is executed. If it is false, the process relinquishes the mutual exclusion and is delayed until B becomes true and no other process is in the region associated with v.

Let us illustrate these concepts by coding the bounded-buffer problem. The buffer space and its pointers are encapsulated in

```
var buffer: shared record
                  pool: array [0..n−1] of item;
                  count,in,out: integer;
            end;
```

The producer process inserts a new item *nextp* into the shared buffer by executing

```
region buffer when count < n
    do begin
            pool[in] := nextp;
            in := in+1 mod n;
            count := count + 1;
        end;
```

The consumer process removes an item from the shared buffer and puts it in *nextc* by executing

```
region buffer when count > 0
    do begin
            nextc := pool[out];
            out := out+1 mod n;
            count := count − 1;
        end;
```

Let us illustrate how the conditional critical region could be implemented by a compiler. With each shared variable x, the following variables are associated:

```
var x-mutex, x-delay: semaphore;
    x-count, x-temp: integer;
```

Mutually exclusive access to the critical section is provided by *x-mutex*. If a process cannot enter the critical section because the Boolean condition B is false, it waits on the *x-delay* semaphore. We keep track of the number of processes waiting on *x-delay*, with *x-count*.

When a process leaves the critical section, it may have changed the value of some Boolean condition B that prevented another process from entering the critical section. Accordingly, we must trace through the queue of processes waiting on *x-delay*, allowing each process to test its

Boolean condition. When a process tests its Boolean condition (during this trace), it may discover that the latter now evaluates to the value *true*. In this case, the process enters its critical section. Otherwise, it must wait again on the *x-delay* semaphore. The variable *x-temp* is used to count the number of processes that have been allowed to test their Boolean condition during one trace. Accordingly, *x-mutex* is initialized to 1, and *x-delay*, *x-count*, and *x-temp* are initialized to 0. The statement

region *x* **when** *B* **do** *S*;

can be implemented as shown in Figure 5.16 This implementation assumes a FIFO ordering in the queueing of processes for a semaphore. For an arbitrary queueing discipline, a more complicated implementation is required.

Note that this implementation requires the reevaluation of the expression *B* for any waiting processes every time a process leaves the critical region. If several processes are delayed, waiting for their

```
wait(x-mutex);
if not B
   then begin
              x-count := x-count + 1;
              signal(x-mutex);
              wait(x-delay);
              while not B
                 do begin
                           x-temp := x-temp + 1;
                           if x-temp < x-count
                              then signal(x-delay)
                              else signal(x-mutex);
                           wait(x-delay);
                    end;
              x-count := x-count - 1;
        end;
S;
if x-count > 0
   then begin
              x-temp := 0;
              signal(x-delay);
        end;
   else signal(x-mutex);
```

Figure 5.16 Implementation of the conditional region construct.

respective Boolean expressions to become true, this reevaluation overhead may result in inefficient code. There are various optimization methods that can be used to reduce this overhead. Refer to the Bibliographic Notes for relevant references.

The conditional critical-region construct just described allows processes to be delayed only at the beginning of a critical region. There are, however, circumstances where synchronization conditions must be placed somewhere within the critical region. This observation led to the following new region construct:

region *v*
　　do begin
　　　　S1;
　　　　await(*B*);
　　　　S2;
　　end;

When a process enters the region, it executes statement *S1* (*S1* may be null). It then evaluates *B*. If *B* is true, *S2* is executed. If *B* is false, the process relinquishes mutual exclusion and is delayed until *B* becomes true and no other process is in the region associated with *v*.

We illustrate this new construct by coding a variant of the second readers-writers problem for accessing a shared file. The second readers-writers problem requires that, once a writer is ready, that writer writes as soon as possible. Thus, a reader can enter its critical section only if there is no writer in the critical section and there are no writers waiting to enter the critical section. The shared synchronization variables are

region *v*
　　do begin
　　　　await(*nwriters* = 0);
　　　　nreaders := *nreaders* + 1;
　　end;
　　　...
　　read file
　　　...
region *v*
　　do begin
　　　　nreaders := *nreaders* − 1;
　　end;

Figure 5.17   Reader process.

> **var** *v*: **shared record**
> > *nreaders, nwriters: integer;*
> > *busy: boolean;*
>
> **end**;

The variable *busy* is initialized to *false;* the variables *nreaders* and *nwriters* are initialized to 0.

A reader process waiting to access the shared file must execute as shown in Figure 5.17. Similarly, a writer process wishing to access the shared file must execute as shown in Figure 5.18.

Unfortunately, the critical-region scheme cannot guarantee that the preceding access sequences will be observed. In particular,

- A process might operate on the file without first gaining access permission to that file (by a direct call to read or to write the file).

- A process might never release the file once it has been granted access to that file.

- A process might attempt to release a file that it never requested.

- A process might request the same file twice (without first releasing that file).

Note that we have now encountered difficulties that are similar in nature to those that encouraged us to develop the critical-region construct in the first place. Previously, we had to worry about the

```
region v
   do begin
         nwriters := nwriters + 1;
         await((not busy) and (nreaders = 0));
         busy := true;
   end;
      ...
   write file
      ...
region v
   do begin
         nwriters := nwriters - 1;
         busy := false;
   end;
```

Figure 5.18   Writer process.

correct use of semaphores. Now, we have to worry about the correct use of higher-level programmer-defined operations, with which the compiler can no longer assist us.

5.6.2 Monitors

Another high-level synchronization construct is the *monitor* type. A monitor is characterized by a set of programmer-defined operators. The representation of a monitor type consists of declarations of variables whose values define the state of an instance of the type, as well as the bodies of procedures or functions that implement operations on the type. The syntax of a monitor is

> **type** *monitor-name* = **monitor**
>   variable declarations
>
>   **procedure entry** *P1* (...);
>   **begin** ... **end**;
>
>   **procedure entry** *P2* (...);
>   **begin** ... **end**;
>
>   ·
>
>   ·
>
>   ·
>
>   **procedure entry** *Pn* (...);
>   **begin** ... **end**;
>
>   **begin**
>   initialization code
>   **end**.

The representation of a monitor type cannot be used directly by the various processes. Thus, a procedure defined within a monitor can access only those variables declared locally within the monitor and the formal parameters. Similarly, the local variables of a monitor can be accessed by only the local procedures.

The monitor construct ensures that only one process at a time can be active within the monitor. Consequently, the programmer does not need to code this synchronization constraint explicitly (Figure 5.19). Thus, the monitor, as defined so far, is similar in many respects to the critical region. As we have seen, the critical region is not sufficiently powerful for modeling some synchronization schemes, and has thus been extended to the conditional critical region. Similarly, we need additional mechanisms with monitors for synchronization. These mechanisms are

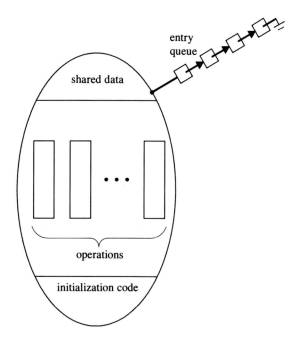

Figure 5.19   Schematic view of a monitor.

provided by the *condition* construct. A programmer who needs to write her own tailor-made synchronization scheme can define one or more variables of type *condition*:

$$\textbf{var } x,y: condition;$$

The only operations that can be invoked on a condition variable are *wait* and *signal*. The operation

$$x.wait;$$

means that the process invoking this operation is suspended until another process invokes

$$x.signal;$$

The *x.signal* operation resumes exactly one suspended process. If no process is suspended, then the *signal* operation has no effect; that is, the state of *x* is as though the operation was never executed (Figure 5.20).

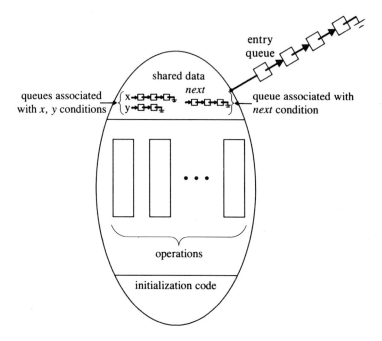

Figure 5.20   Monitor with condition variables.

Contrast this with the *wait* operation associated with semaphores, which always affects the state of the semaphore.

Now suppose that, when the *x.signal* operation is invoked by a process P, there is a suspended process Q associated with condition x. Clearly, if the suspended process Q is allowed to resume its execution, the signaling process P must wait. Otherwise, both P and Q will be active simultaneously within the monitor. Note, however, that both processes can conceptually continue with their execution. Two possibilities exist:

1. P waits until Q either leaves the monitor, or waits for another condition.

2. Q waits until P either leaves the monitor, or waits for another condition.

There are reasonable arguments in favor of adopting either (1) or (2). Since P was already executing in the monitor, choice (2) seems more reasonable. However, if we allow process P to continue, the "logical" condition for which Q was waiting may no longer hold by the time Q is resumed.

Choice (1) was advocated by Hoare, mainly because the preceding argument in favor of it translates directly to simpler and more elegant proof rules. A compromise between these two choices was adopted in the language Concurrent Pascal. When process P executes the *signal* operation, it immediately leaves the monitor. Hence, Q is immediately resumed. This scheme is less powerful than Hoare's, since a process cannot signal more than once during a single procedure call.

Let us illustrate these concepts by presenting a deadlock-free solution to the dining-philosophers problem. Recall that a philosopher is allowed to pick up his chopsticks only if both of them are available. To code this solution, we need to distinguish between three states that a philosopher may be in. For this purpose, we introduce the following data structure:

> **var** *state*: **array** [0..4] **of** (*thinking, hungry, eating*);

Philosopher i can set the variable *state*[i] $=$ *eating* only if his two neighbors are not eating (that is, *state*[i+4 **mod** 5] $\neq$ *eating* **and** *state*[i+1 **mod** 5] $\neq$ *eating*).

We also need to declare

> **var** *self*: **array** [0..4] **of** *condition*;

where philosopher i can delay himself when he is hungry, but is unable to obtain the chopsticks he needs.

We are now in a position to describe our solution. The distribution of the chopsticks is controlled by the monitor shown in Figure 5.21. Philosopher i must invoke the operations *pickup* and *putdown* on an instance *dp* of the *dining-philosophers* monitor in the following sequence:

> *dp.pickup(i);*
> ...
> eat
> ...
> *dp.putdown(i);*

It is easy to show that this solution ensures that no two neighbors are eating simultaneously, and that no deadlocks will occur. We note, however, that

- It is possible for a philosopher to starve to death. We shall not present a solution to this problem, but rather leave it as an exercise for you.

● If the philosophers fail to observe the sequence shown, this may result in timing errors. We shall say more on this subject when we discuss language-based protection in Chapter 11.

We shall now consider a possible implementation of the monitor mechanism using semaphores. For each monitor, a semaphore *mutex* (initialized to 1) is provided. A process must execute *wait(mutex)* before

```
type dining-philosophers = monitor
    var state : array [0..4] of (thinking, hungry, eating);
    var self : array [0..4] of condition;

    procedure entry pickup (i: 0..4);
        begin
            state[i] := hungry;
            test (i);
            if state[i] ≠ eating then self[i].wait;
        end;

    procedure entry putdown (i: 0..4);
        begin
            state[i] := thinking;
            test (i+4 mod 5);
            test (i+1 mod 5);
        end;

    procedure test (k: 0..4);
        begin
            if state[k+4 mod 5] ≠ eating
            and state[k] = hungry
            and state[k+1 mod 5] ≠ eating
            then begin
                    state[k] := eating;
                    self[k].signal;
                end;
        end;

    begin
        for i := 0 to 4
            do state[i] := thinking;
    end.
```

Figure 5.21   A monitor solution to the dining-philosopher problem.

entering the monitor, and must execute *signal(mutex)* after leaving the monitor.

Since a signaling process must wait until the resumed process either leaves or waits, an additional semaphore, *next*, is introduced, initialized to 0, on which the signaling processes may suspend themselves. An integer variable *next-count* will also be provided to count the number of processes suspended on *next*. Thus, each external procedure *F* will be replaced by

$$wait(mutex);$$
$$...$$
$$\text{body of } F;$$
$$...$$
$$\textbf{if } next\text{-}count > 0$$
$$\quad \textbf{then } signal(next)$$
$$\quad \textbf{else } signal(mutex);$$

Mutual exclusion within a monitor is ensured.

We can now describe how condition variables are implemented. For each condition *x*, we introduce a semaphore *x-sem* and an integer variable *x-count*, both initialized to 0. The operation *x.wait* can now be implemented as

$$x\text{-}count := x\text{-}count + 1;$$
$$\textbf{if } next\text{-}count > 0$$
$$\quad \textbf{then } signal(next)$$
$$\quad \textbf{else } signal(mutex);$$
$$wait(x\text{-}sem);$$
$$x\text{-}count := x\text{-}count - 1;$$

The operation *x.signal* can be implemented as

$$\textbf{if } x\text{-}count > 0$$
$$\quad \textbf{then begin}$$
$$\qquad next\text{-}count := next\text{-}count + 1;$$
$$\qquad signal(x\text{-}sem);$$
$$\qquad wait(next);$$
$$\qquad next\text{-}count := next\text{-}count - 1;$$
$$\quad \textbf{end};$$

This implementation is applicable to the definitions of monitors given by both Hoare and Brinch Hansen. In some cases, however, the generality of the implementation is unnecessary, and a significant improvement in efficiency is possible. We leave this problem to you in Exercise 5.22.

We turn now to the subject of process-resumption order within a monitor. If several processes are suspended on condition x, and an *x.signal* operation is executed by some process, then how do we determine which of the suspended processes should be resumed next? One simple solution is to use an FCFS scheme, so that the process waiting the longest is resumed first. There are, however, many circumstances in which such a simple scheduling scheme is not adequate. For this purpose, the *conditional-wait* construct can be used; it has the form

$$x.wait(c);$$

where c is an integer expression that is evaluated when the wait operation is executed. The value of c, which is called a *priority number*, is then stored with the name of the process that is suspended. When *x.signal* is executed, the process with the smallest associated priority number is resumed next.

To illustrate this new mechanism, consider the monitor shown in Figure 5.22 that controls the allocation of a single resource among competing processes. Each process, when requesting an allocation of its resources, specifies the maximum time it plans to use the resource. The

```
type resource-allocation = monitor
    var busy: boolean;
        x: condition;

    procedure entry acquire (time: integer);
        begin
            if busy then x.wait(time);
            busy := true;
        end;

    procedure entry release;
        begin
            busy := false;
            x.signal;
        end;

    begin
        busy := false;
    end.
```

Figure 5.22   A monitor to allocate a single resource.

monitor allocates the resource to that process that has the shortest time-allocation request.

A process that needs to access the resource in question must observe the following sequence:

$$R.acquire;$$

$$...$$

access the resource;

$$...$$

$$R.release;$$

where R is an instance of type *resource-allocation*.

As in the readers-writers solution with critical regions presented in Section 5.6.1, failure to observe this sequence may result in timing errors. One possible solution is to include the resource-access operations within *resource-allocation* monitor. However, this solution will result in scheduling being done according to the built-in monitor-scheduling algorithm, rather than the one we have coded.

To ensure that the processes observe the appropriate sequences, we must inspect all the programs that make use of the *resource-allocation* monitor and its managed resource. There are two conditions that must be checked to establish the correctness of this system. First, user processes must always make their calls on the monitor in a correct sequence. Second, we must be sure that an uncooperative process does not simply ignore the mutual-exclusion gateway provided by the monitor, and try to access the shared resource directly, without using the access protocols. Only if these two conditions can be ensured can we guarantee that no time-dependent errors will occur, and that the scheduling algorithm will not be defeated.

Although this inspection may be possible for a small, static system, it is not reasonable for a large system or for a dynamic system. This *access-control problem* can be solved only by additional mechanisms that will be elaborated in Chapter 11.

5.7 Interprocess Communication

Many of the problems that we have described, and more, are presented as synchronization problems. In a larger sense, however, they are simple examples of the larger problem of allowing *communication* between processes that wish to cooperate. In this section, we are concerned with the general problem of interprocess communication. Principally, there exist two complementary communication schemes: shared memory and message systems.

Shared-memory systems require communicating processes to share some variables. The processes are expected to exchange information through the use of these shared variables. For example, the bounded-buffer scheme discussed in Section 5.1 could be used for this purpose. In a shared-memory system, the responsibility for providing communication rests with the application programmers; the operating system needs to provide only the shared memory. The *message-system* method allows the processes to exchange messages. The responsibility for providing communication then rests with the operating system itself.

Obviously, these two schemes are not mutually exclusive, and could be used simultaneously within a single operating system. In this section, we focus primarily on message systems, since shared memory is basically application oriented. Also, we consider only systems with processes whose logical address spaces are disjoint.

The function of a message system is to allow processes to communicate with each other without the need to resort to shared variables. An interprocess communication facility basically provides two operations: **send**(*message*) and **receive**(*message*).

Messages sent by a process can be either fixed sized or variable sized. If only fixed-sized messages can be sent, the physical implementation is straightforward. This restriction, however, makes the task of programming more difficult. On the other hand, variable-sized messages require a more complex physical implementation, but the programming task becomes simpler.

If processes P and Q want to communicate, they must send messages to and receive messages from each other; a *communication link* must exist between them. This link can be implemented in a variety of ways. We are concerned here not with the link's physical implementation (such as shared memory, hardware bus, or network, which are covered in Chapter 12), but rather with the issues of its logical implementation, such as its logical properties. Some basic implementation questions are these:

- How are links established?

- Can a link be associated with more than two processes?

- How many links can there be between every pair of processes?

- What is the capacity of a link? That is, does the link have some buffer space? If it does, how much?

- What is the size of messages? Can the link accommodate variable-sized or fixed-sized messages?

- Is a link unidirectional or bidirectional? That is, if a link exists between P and Q, can messages flow in only one direction (such as only from P to Q) or in both directions?

The definition of *unidirectional* must be stated more carefully, since a link may be associated with more than two processes. Thus, we say that a link is unidirectional only if each process connected to the link can either send or receive, but not both, and each link has at least one receiver process connected to it.

In addition, there are several methods for logically implementing a link and the **send/receive** operations:

- Direct or indirect communication

- Symmetric or asymmetric communication

- Automatic or explicit buffering

- Send by copy or send by reference

- Fixed-sized or variable-sized messages

In the following discussion, we elaborate on these types of message systems.

5.7.1 Naming

Processes that want to communicate must have a way to refer to each other. They can use either *direct communication* or *indirect communication*, as we shall discuss in the next two subsections.

Direct Communication

In the direct communication discipline, each process that wants to send or receive a message must explicitly name the recipient or sender of the communication. In this scheme, the **send** and **receive** primitives are defined as follows:

> **send**(P, *message*). Send a *message* to process P.
> **receive**(Q, *message*). Receive a *message* from process Q.

A communication link in this scheme has the following properties:

- A link is established automatically between every pair of processes that want to communicate. The processes need know only each other's identity to communicate.

- A link is associated with exactly two processes.

- Between each pair of communicating processes, there exists exactly one link.

- The link is bidirectional.

For example, the producer-consumer problem can be coded in this scheme in the following way. The producer process is defined as

> **repeat**
> ...
> produce an item in *nextp*
> ...
> **send**(*consumer,nextp*);
> **until** *false*;

The consumer process is defined as

> **repeat**
> **receive**(*producer,nextc*);
> ...
> consume the item in *nextc*
> ...
> **until** *false*;

If this example is considered as a bounded-buffer scheme, then the size of the buffer is equal to the capacity of the communication link.

This scheme exhibits a symmetry in addressing; that is, both the sender and the receiver have to name each other in order to communicate. A variant of this scheme employs asymmetry in addressing. Only the sender names the recipient; the recipient is not required to name the sender. In this scheme, the **send** and **receive** primitives are defined as follows:

- **send**(*P, message*). Send a *message* to process *P*.

- **receive**(*id, message*). Receive a *message* from any process; *id* is set to the name of the process with whom communication has taken place.

The disadvantage in both of these schemes (symmetric and asymmetric) is the limited modularity of the resulting process definitions. Changing the name of a process may necessitate examining all other process definitions. All references to the old name must be found, so that they can be modified to the new name. This situation is not desirable from the viewpoint of separate compilation.

Indirect Communication

With indirect communication, the messages are sent to and received from mailboxes (also referred to as *ports*). A mailbox can be abstractly viewed as an object into which messages may be placed by processes and from which messages may be removed. Each mailbox has a unique identification. In this scheme, a process may communicate with some other process by a number of different mailboxes. Two processes may communicate only if they have a shared mailbox. The **send** and **receive** primitives are defined as follows:

> **send**(A, *message*). Send a *message* to mailbox A.
> **receive**(A, *message*). Receive a *message* from mailbox A.

In this scheme, a communication link has the following properties:

- A link is established between a pair of processes only if they have a shared mailbox.
- A link may be associated with more than two processes.
- Between each pair of communicating processes, there may be a number of different links, each corresponding to one mailbox.
- A link may be either unidirectional or bidirectional.

Now suppose that processes P_1, P_2, and P_3 all share mailbox A. Process P_1 sends a message to A, while P_2 and P_3 each execute a **receive** from A. Which process will receive the message sent by P_1? This question can be resolved in a variety of ways:

- Allow a link to be associated with at most two processes.
- Allow at most one process at a time to execute a **receive** operation.
- Allow the system to select arbitrarily which process will receive the message (that is, either P_2 or P_3, but not both, will receive the message). The system may identify the receiver to the sender.

A mailbox may be owned either by a process or by the system. If the mailbox is owned by a process (that is, the mailbox is attached to or defined as part of the process), then we distinguish between the owner (who can only receive messages through this mailbox) and the user of the mailbox (who can only send messages to the mailbox). Since each mailbox has a unique owner, there can be no confusion about who should receive a message sent to this mailbox. When a process that owns a mailbox terminates, the mailbox disappears. Any process that subsequently sends a message to this mailbox must be notified that the mailbox no longer exists (via exception handling).

There are a number of ways to designate the owner and users of a particular mailbox. One possibility is to allow a process to declare variables of type *mailbox*. The process that declares a mailbox is that mailbox's owner. Any other process that knows the name of this mailbox can use this mailbox.

On the other hand, a mailbox that is owned by the operating system has an existence of its own. It is independent, and is not "attached" to any particular process. The operating system provides a mechanism that allows a process

- To create a new mailbox

- To send and receive messages through the mailbox

- To destroy a mailbox

The process that creates a new mailbox is that mailbox's owner by default. Initially, the owner is the only process that can receive messages through this mailbox. However, the ownership and receive privilege may be passed to other processes through appropriate system calls. Of course, this provision could result in multiple receivers for each mailbox. Processes may also share a mailbox through the process-creation facility. For example, if process P created mailbox A, and then created a new process Q, P and Q may share mailbox A. Since all processes with access rights to a mailbox may ultimately terminate, after some time a mailbox may no longer be accessible by any process. In this case, the operating system should reclaim whatever space was used for the mailbox. This task may require some form of garbage collection.

5.7.2 Buffering

A link has some capacity that determines the number of messages that can temporarily reside in it. This property can be viewed as a queue of messages attached to the link. Basically, there are three ways such a queue can be implemented:

- **Zero capacity**. The queue has maximum length 0; thus, the link cannot have any messages waiting in it. In this case, the sender must wait until the recipient receives the message. The two processes must be synchronized for a message transfer to take place. This synchronization is called a *rendezvous*.

- **Bounded capacity**. The queue has finite length n; thus, at most n messages can reside in it. If the queue is not full when a new message is sent, the latter is placed in the queue (either the message is copied or a pointer to the message is kept), and the sender can continue execution without waiting. The link has a finite capacity, however. If the link is full, the sender must be delayed until space is available in the queue.

- **Unbounded capacity**. The queue has potentially infinite length; thus, any number of messages can wait in it. The sender is never delayed.

The zero-capacity case is sometimes referred to as a message system with no buffering; the other cases provide automatic buffering.

We note that, in the nonzero capacity cases, a process does not know whether a message has arrived at its destination after the **send** operation is completed. If this information is crucial for the computation, the sender must communicate explicitly with the receiver to find out whether the latter received the message. For example, suppose process P sends a message to process Q and can continue its execution only after the message is received. Process P executes the sequence

> **send**(Q ,*message*);
> **receive**(Q, *message*);

Process Q executes

> **receive**(P, *message*);
> **send**(P, "acknowledgment");

Such processes are said to communicate *asynchronously*.

There are special cases that do not directly fit into any of the categories we have discussed.

- The process sending a message is never delayed. However, if the receiver has not received the message before the sending process sends another message, the first message is lost. The advantage of this scheme is that large messages do not need to be copied more than once. The main disadvantage is that the programming task becomes more difficult. Processes need to synchronize explicitly, to ensure both that messages are not lost and that the sender and receiver do not manipulate the message buffer simultaneously.

- The process sending a message is delayed until it receives a reply. This scheme was adopted in the Thoth operating system. In this system, messages are of fixed size (eight words). A process *P* that sends a message is blocked until the receiving process has received the message and sent back an eight-word reply by the **reply**(*P*, *message*) primitive. The reply message overwrites the original message buffer. The only difference between the **send** and **reply** primitives is that a **send** causes the sending process to be blocked, whereas the **reply** allows both the sending process and the receiving process to continue with their executions immediately.

This synchronous communication method is easily expanded into a full-featured *remote procedure call*, or RPC, system. RPC is based on the realization that a subroutine or procedure call in a single-processor system acts exactly like a message system in which the sender blocks until it receives a reply. The message is then like a subroutine call, and the return message contains the value of the subroutine computed. The next logical step, therefore, is for concurrent processes to be able to call each other as subroutines using RPC. In fact, we will see in Chapter 14 that RPC can be used between processes running on separate computers to allow multiple computers to work together in a mutually beneficial way.

5.7.3 Exception Conditions

A message system is particularly useful in a distributed environment, where processes may reside at different sites (machines). In such an environment, the probability that an error will occur during communication (and processing) is much larger than in a single-machine environment. In a single-machine environment, messages are usually implemented in shared memory. If a failure occurs, the entire system fails. In a distributed environment, however, messages are usually handled by communication lines, and the failure of one site (or link) does not necessarily result in the failure of the entire system.

When a failure occurs in either a centralized or distributed system, some error recovery (exception-condition handling) must take place. Let us briefly discuss some of the exception conditions that a system must handle in the context of a message scheme.

Process Terminates

Either a sender or receiver may terminate before a message is processed. This situation will leave messages that will never be received or processes waiting for messages that will never be sent. We consider two cases here:

1. A receiver process P may wait for a message from a process Q that has terminated. If no action is taken, P will be blocked forever. (Notice that this condition is not a deadlock in the classical definition, since there is no circular wait.) In this case, the system may either terminate P or notify P that Q has terminated.

2. Process P may send a message to a process Q that has terminated. In the automatic-buffering scheme, no harm is done; P simply continues with its execution. If P needs to know that its message has been processed by Q, it must explicitly program for an acknowledgment. In the no-buffering case, P will be blocked forever. As in case 1, the system may either terminate P or notify P that Q has terminated.

Lost messages

A message from process P to process Q may become lost somewhere in the communications network, due to a hardware or communication-line failure. There are three basic methods for dealing with this event:

1. The operating system is responsible for detecting this event and for resending the message.

2. The sending process is responsible for detecting this event and for retransmitting the message, if it so wants.

3. The operating system is responsible for detecting this event; it then notifies the sending process that the message has been lost. The sending process can proceed as it wants.

It is not always necessary to detect lost messages. In fact, some network protocols specify that messages are unreliable, whereas some guarantee reliability (see Chapter 12). The user must specify (that is, either notify the system, or program this requirement itself) that such a detection should take place.

How do we detect that a message is lost? The most common detection method is to use *timeouts*. When a message is sent out, a reply message, acknowledging reception of the message, is always sent back. The operating system or a process may then specify a time interval during which it expects the acknowledgment message to arrive. If this time period elapses before the acknowledgment arrives, the operating system (or process) may assume that the message is lost, and the message is resent. It is possible, however, that a message did not get lost, but simply took a little longer than expected to travel through the network. In this case, we may have multiple copies of the same message flowing through the network. A mechanism must exist to distinguish between these various types of messages. This problem is discussed in more detail in Chapter 12.

Scrambled messages

The message may be delivered to its destination, but be scrambled on the way (for example, because of noise in the communications channel). This case is similar to the case of a lost message. Either the operating system will retransmit the original message, or it will notify the process of this event. Checksums (such as parity or CRC) are commonly used to detect this type of error.

5.7.4 An Example: Mach

As an example of a message-based operating system, consider the Mach operating system, developed at Carnegie Mellon University. The Mach kernel supports the creation and destruction of multiple tasks, which are similar to processes but have multiple threads of control. Most communication in Mach, including most of the system calls and all inter-task information, is done by *messages*. Messages are sent to and received from *mailboxes* (called ports in Mach).

Even system calls are made by messages. When each task is created, two special mailboxes, the Kernel mailbox and the Notify mailbox, are also created. The Kernel mailbox is used by the kernel to communicate with the task. The kernel sends notification of event occurrences to the Notify port. Only three system calls are needed for message transfer. The *msg_send* call sends a message to a mailbox. A message is received via *msg_receive*. Remote procedure calls are executed via *msg_rpc*, which sends a message and waits for exactly one return message from the sender.

The *port_allocate* system call creates a new mailbox and allocates space for its queue of messages. The maximum size of the message queue defaults to eight messages. The task that creates the mailbox is that mailbox's owner. The owner also is given receive access to the mailbox. Only one task at a time can either own or receive from a mailbox, but these rights can be sent to other tasks if desired.

The mailbox has an initially empty queue of messages. As messages are sent to the mailbox, the messages are copied into the mailbox. Messages are queued by priority. All messages have the same priority. Mach guarantees that multiple messages from the same sender are queued in FIFO order, but guarantees no absolute ordering. For instance, a message sent from each of two senders may be queued in any order.

The messages themselves consist of a fixed-length header, followed by a variable-length data portion. The header includes the length of the message and two mailbox names. When a message is sent, one mailbox name is the mailbox to which the message is being sent. Commonly, the sending thread expects a reply; the mailbox name of the sender is passed on to the receiving task, which may use it as a "return address" to send messages back.

The variable part of a message is a list of typed data items. Each entry in the list has a type, size, and value. The type of the objects specified in the message is important, since operating-system defined objects — such as the ownership or receive access rights, task states, and memory segments — may be sent in messages.

The send and receive operations themselves are quite flexible. When a message is sent to a mailbox, the mailbox may be full. If the mailbox is not full, the message is copied to the mailbox and the sending thread continues. If the mailbox is full, the sending thread has four options:

1. Wait indefinitely until there is room in the mailbox.

2. Wait at most n milliseconds.

3. Do not wait at all, but return immediately.

4. Temporarily cache a message. One message can be given to the operating system to keep even though the mailbox to which it is being sent is full. When the operating system can actually put the message in the mailbox, a message is sent back to the sender; only one such message to a full mailbox can be pending at any time for a given sending thread.

The last option is meant for server tasks, such as a line-printer driver. After finishing a request, these tasks may need to send a one-time reply to the task that had requested service, but must also continue with other service requests, even if the reply mailbox for a client is full.

The receive operation must specify from which mailbox or mailbox set to receive a message. A mailbox set is a collection of mailboxes, as declared by the task, which can be grouped together and treated as one mailbox for the purposes of the task. Threads in a task can receive only from a mailbox or mailbox set for which it has receive access. A *port_status* system call returns the number of messages in a given mailbox. The receive operation attempts to receive from (1) any mailbox in a mailbox set or (2) a specific (named) mailbox. If no message is waiting to be received, the receiving thread may wait, wait at most n milliseconds, or not wait.

The Mach system was especially designed for distributed systems, which we discuss in Chapters 12 through 14, but Mach is also suitable for single processor systems. The major problem with message systems has generally been poor performance caused by copying the message first from the sender to the mailbox, and then from the mailer to the receiver. The Mach message system attempts to avoid double copy operations by using virtual-memory management techniques (Chapter 8). Essentially, Mach points the message receiver to the message in the sender's address space. The message itself is never actually copied. This provides a large performance boost. The Mach operating system is discussed in detail in Chapter 16.

5.8 Summary

Given a collection of cooperating sequential processes that share some data, mutual exclusion must be provided. Different algorithms exist for solving the critical-section problem, with the assumption that only storage interlock is available.

The main disadvantage of these solutions is that they all require *busy waiting*. Semaphores overcome this difficulty. Semaphores can be used to solve various synchronization problems, and can be implemented efficiently.

A number of different synchronization problems (such as the bounded-buffer problem, the readers-writers problem, and the dining-philosophers problem) are important mainly because they are examples for a large class of concurrency-control problems. These problems are used to test nearly every newly proposed synchronization scheme.

The operating system must provide the means to guard against timing errors. Several language constructs have been proposed to deal with these problems. Critical regions can be used to implement mutual exclusion and arbitrary synchronization problems safely and efficiently. Monitors provide the synchronization mechanism for sharing abstract data types.

Interprocess communication provides a mechanism to allow processes to communicate and synchronize their actions. Interprocess communication is best provided by a message system. Message systems can be defined in many different ways. Message-passing systems also have other advantages, as will be shown in Chapter 12.

Exercises

5.1 What is the meaning of the term *busy waiting*? What other kinds of waiting are there? Can busy waiting be avoided altogether?

5.2 The correct producer-consumer algorithm presented in Section 5.1 allows only $n - 1$ buffers to be full at any point in time. Modify the algorithm to allow all the buffers to be fully utilized. Do not use semaphores in your solution.

5.3 The following algorithm, developed by Dekker, is the first known correct software solution to the critical-section problem for two processes. The two processes, P_0 and P_1, share the following variables:

> **var** *flag*: **array** [0..1] **of** *boolean*; (* initially false *)
>   *turn*: 0..1;

The following program is for process P_i ($i = 0$ or 1), with P_j ($j = 1$ or 0) being the other process:

```
repeat
    flag[i] := true;
    while flag[j]
        do if turn = j
            then begin
                    flag[i] := false;
                    while turn = j do no-op;
                    flag[i] := true;
                end;
        ...
    critical section
        ...
    turn := j;
    flag[i] := false;
        ...
    remainder section
        ...
until false;
```

Prove that the algorithm satisfies all three requirements for the critical-section problem.

5.4 Prove that, in the bakery algorithm (Section 5.2.2), the following property holds: If P_i is in its critical section and P_k ($k \neq i$) has already chosen its *number*[k] $\neq$ 0, then (*number*[i],i) < (*number*[k],k).

5.5 The following "solution" to the critical-section problem was presented by Hyman [1966]. Determine its correctness. If it is incorrect, show an example that violates one of the three requirements for the critical-section problem.

The two processes P_0 and P_1 share the following variables:

> **var** *flag*: **array** [0..1] **of** *boolean*; (* initially false *)
> *turn*: 0..1;

The following program is for process P_i (i = 0 or 1), with P_j (j = 1 or 0) being the other process.

```
repeat
    flag[i]:= true;
    while turn ≠ i
        do begin
                while flag[j] do no-op
                turn:= i;
            end
        …
        critical section
        …
    flag[i]:= false
        …
    remainder section
        …
until false;
```

5.6 Show that, if the *wait* and *signal* operations are not executed atomically, then mutual exclusion may be violated.

5.7 A *binary* semaphore is a semaphore whose integer value can range only between 0 and 1. Show how a general semaphore can be implemented using binary semaphores.

5.8 Semaphore waiting lists are often implemented as queues served in FIFO order. Could they be implemented as stacks? What problems might this implementation cause?

5.9 Consider a set of sequential processes that cannot share any variables except semaphores. Can these processes communicate with one another? (Hint: It will suffice to consider the transmission of a single bit.)

5.10 Is busy waiting a property of the *wait-signal* solution to process synchronization and mutual exclusion?

5.11 Two synchronization primitives, ENQ and DEQ, are defined as follows: *r* is a resource object, *P* is a process, *queue*(*r*) is a FIFO queue of processes waiting to acquire resource r, and $inuse(r)$ is a Boolean variable.

$ENQ(r)$: **if** $inuse(r)$
  then begin
    insert P in $queue(r)$;
    block P;
  end
  else $inuse(r):=$ $true$;

$DEQ(r)$: $P:=$ head of $queue(r)$;
  if $P \neq nil$
    then activate P;
    else $inuse(r):=$ $false$;

Construct an implementation of ENQ/DEQ using semaphores. Be sure that the ordering implicit in the reactivation of the process is implemented properly. Use any additional data structures and variables you need.

5.12 Write an algorithm for implementing semaphores using

  a. The Swap instruction

  b. The Test-and-Set instruction

5.13 A multiple semaphore allows the *wait* and *signal* primitives to operate on several semaphores simultaneously. It is useful for acquiring and releasing several resources in one atomic operation. Thus, the *wait* primitive (for two semaphores) can be defined as follows:

$wait(S,R)$: **while** $(S \leq 0$ **or** $R \leq 0)$ **do** *no-op*;
  $S:= S - 1$;
  $R:= R - 1$;

Show how a multiple semaphore can be implemented using regular semaphores.

5.14 *The Sleeping-Barber Problem.* A barbershop consists of a waiting room with n chairs, and the barber room containing the barber chair. If there are no customers to be served, the barber goes to sleep. If a customer enters the barbershop and all chairs are occupied, then the customer leaves the shop. If the barber is busy, but chairs are available, then the customer sits in one of the free chairs. If the barber is asleep, the customer wakes up the barber. Write a program to coordinate the barber and the customers.

5.15 *The Cigarette-Smokers Problem.* Consider a system with three *smoker* processes and one *agent* process. Each smoker continuously makes a cigarette and smokes it. But to make a cigarette, the smoker needs three ingredients: tobacco, paper, and matches. One of the smoker processes has paper, another has tobacco, and the third has matches. The agent has an infinite supply of all three materials. The agent places two of the ingredients on the table. The smoker who has the remaining ingredient then makes and smokes a cigarette, signaling the agent on completion. The agent then puts out another two of the three ingredients, and the cycle repeats. Write a program to synchronize the agent and the smokers.

5.16 Demonstrate that monitors, conditional critical regions, and semaphores are all equivalent, insofar as the same types of synchronization problems can be implemented with them.

5.17 Transform the *wait* and *signal* operations on a semaphore S into equivalent critical regions without busy waiting.

5.18 Write a bounded-buffer monitor in which the buffers (portions) are embedded within the monitor itself.

5.19 The strict mutual exclusion within a monitor makes the bounded-buffer monitor of Exercise 5.18 mainly suitable for small portions.

   a. Explain why this assertion is true.

   b. Design a new scheme that is suitable for larger portions.

5.20 Suppose that the *signal* statement can appear as only the last statement in a monitor procedure. How can the implementation suggested in Section 5.6.2 be simplified?

5.21 Consider a system consisting of processes P_1, P_2, ..., P_n, each of which has a unique priority number. Write a monitor that allocates three identical line printers to these processes, using the priority numbers for deciding the order of allocation.

5.22 A spooling system consists of an input process I, a user process U, and an output process O, which exchanges data through two bounded-buffer monitors *in* and *out* (Figure 5.23). Write a program to implement such a scheme, assuming that the *read* and *write* operations allow you to read from the card reader and to write to the printer.

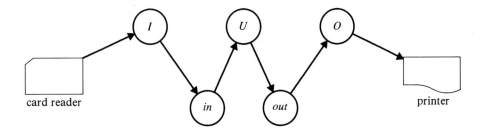

Figure 5.23   Spooling system for Exercise 5.21.

5.23 A file is to be shared among different processes, each of which has a unique number. The file can be accessed simultaneously by several processes, subject to the following constraint: The sum of all unique numbers associated with all the processes currently accessing the file must be less than n. Write a monitor to coordinate the access to the file.

5.24 Suppose that we replace the *wait* and *signal* operations of monitors with a single construct **await**(B), where B is a general Boolean expression that causes the process executing it to wait until B becomes true.

   a. Write a monitor using this scheme to implement the readers-writers problem.

   b. Explain why, in general, this construct cannot be implemented efficiently.

   c. What restrictions need to be put on the await statement so that it can be implemented efficiently? (Hint: Restrict the generality of B; see Kessels [1977].)

5.25 Write a monitor that implements an *alarm clock* that enables a calling program to delay itself for a specified number of time units (*ticks*). You may assume the existence of a real hardware clock, which invokes a procedure *tick* in your monitor at regular intervals.

5.26 Explain why, although a monitor ensures mutual exclusion, the procedures must be reentrant.

5.27 Consider a system that supports an interprocess-communication scheme but does not provide semaphores. Indicate what declarations and code would be needed to program an interaction that wants to use *wait* and *signal* operations on semaphores, rather than **send** and **receive**. You must show how to represent the *wait* and *signal* operations and semaphores using the **send** and **receive** operations and messages.

5.28 Consider the interprocess-communication scheme using mailboxes.

  a. Suppose a process P wants to wait for a message from mailbox A and from mailbox B (one from each). What sequence of **send** and **receives** should it do?

  b. What sequence of **send** and **receive** should be done if P wants to wait for a message either from mailbox A or from mailbox B (or from both).

  c. A **receive** operation makes a process wait until the mailbox is nonempty. Devise a scheme (if possible) that allows a process to wait until a mailbox is empty.

Bibliographic Notes

The mutual-exclusion algorithms 1 to 2 for two processes were first discussed in the classical paper by Dijkstra [1965a]. Dekker's algorithm (Exercise 5.3) — the first correct software solution to the two-process mutual-exclusion problem — was developed by the Dutch mathematician T. Dekker. This algorithm was also discussed by Dijkstra [1965a]. Simpler solutions to the two-process mutual-exclusion problem have since been presented by Doran and Thomas [1980], and Peterson [1981] (algorithm 3).

The first solution to the mutual-exclusion problem for n processes was presented by Dijkstra [1965b]. A simpler solution has been given by Peterson [1981]. Neither of these solutions, however, has an upper bound on the amount of time a process must wait before that process is allowed to enter the critical section. Knuth [1966] presented the first algorithm with a bound; his bound was 2^n turns. A refinement of Knuth's algorithm by deBruijn [1967] reduced the waiting time to n^2 turns, after which Eisenberg and McGuire [1972] (algorithm 4) succeeded in reducing the time to the lower bound of $n - 1$ turns. The bakery algorithm (algorithm 5) was developed by Lamport [1974]; it also requires $n - 1$ turns, but it is easier to program and understand. The hardware-solution algorithm that satisfies the bounded waiting requirement was developed by Burns [1978].

General discussions concerning the mutual exclusion problem are offered by Lamport [1986a, 1986b]. A collection of algorithms for mutual exclusion are given by Raynal [1986]. Complexity results concerning the number of shared variables needed to implement the various n-process mutual-exclusion algorithms are presented by Burns [1978], Burns and Lynch [1980], and Burns et al. [1982].

Discussions concerning the various aspects of semaphores are offered by Dijkstra [1965a, 1968, 1971] and Habermann [1972]. Patil [1971] examined the question of whether semaphores can solve all possible synchronization problems. Parnas [1975] discussed some of the flaws in Patil's arguments. Kosaraju [1973] followed up on Patil's work to produce a problem that cannot be solved by *wait* and *signal* operations. Lipton [1974] has discussed the limitation of various synchronization primitives, such as PV multiple [Patil 1971], PV general [Cerf 1972] and PV chunk [Vantilborgh and Van Lamsweerde 1972]. Additional results concerning these issues are described by Henderson and Zalcstein [1980].

The classic process-coordination problems we have described are paradigms for a large class of concurrency-control problems. The bounded-buffer problem, the dining-philosophers problem, and the sleeping-barber problem (Exercise 5.14) were suggested by Dijkstra [1965a, 1971]. The cigarette-smokers problem (Exercise 5.15) was developed by Patil [1971]. The readers-writers problem was suggested by Courtois et al. [1971]. The issue of concurrent reading and writing is discussed by Lamport [1977]. The problem of synchronization of independent processes is discussed by Lamport [1976].

The critical-region concept was suggested by Hoare [1972b] and Brinch Hansen [1972b]. The conditional critical region was proposed by Hoare [1972b] and was generalized by Brinch Hansen [1972b]. A comparison of the semaphore, critical-region, and conditional critical-region concepts is given by Brinch Hansen [1972a]. General discussions have been written by Brinch Hansen [1973a, 1973b]. The issue of efficient implementation of conditional critical region has been considered by Brinch Hansen [1972b] and Schmid [1976].

The monitor concept was developed by Brinch Hansen [1973a]. A complete description of the monitor was given by Hoare [1974]. A discussion concerning the various ways that signals can be implemented was offered by Howard [1976]. An extension to the monitor to allow automatic signaling was proposed by Kessels [1977]. Implementation issues were discussed by Lister and Maynard [1976] and Schmid [1976]. Monitors are used in the Concurrent Pascal language, which was developed by Brinch Hansen [1975] as an extension to Pascal. The language was used successfully in the writing of three different types of operating systems [Brinch Hansen 1977].

Another synchronization concept, the *coroutine*, was invented by Conway [1963] and illustrated by Knuth [1973]. This construct is mainly suited to a strictly interleaved execution of processes on a single processor and is the basic concept of pipes in the UNIX operating system.

The subject of interprocess communication is discussed by Brinch Hansen [1970] (the RC 4000 system), Cheriton et al. [1979] (the Thoth real-time operating system), Rashid and Robertson [1981] (the Accent operating system), and Accetta et al [1986] (the Mach operating system). Schlichting and Schneider [1982] discussed asynchronous message passing primitives. Brinch Hansen [1970] was the first person to suggest the use of messages for synchronization. Discussions concerning the implementation of remote procedure calls are presented by Birrell and Nelson [1984]. Stankovic [1982] and Staustrup [1982] discussed the issues of procedure calls versus message passing communication.

Deadlocks

In a multiprogramming environment, several processes may compete for a finite number of resources. A process requests resources, and if the resources are not available at that time, the process enters a wait state. It may happen that waiting processes will never again change state, because the resources they have requested are held by other waiting processes. This situation is called a *deadlock*. We have already briefly discussed this issue in Chapter 5 in connection with semaphores.

Perhaps the best illustration of a deadlock can be drawn from a law passed by the Kansas legislature early this century. It said in part: "When two trains approach each other at a crossing, both shall come to a full stop and neither shall start up again until the other has gone."

In this chapter, we describe methods that an operating system may use to deal with the deadlock problem. Note, however, that most current operating systems do not provide deadlock-prevention facilities. Such features probably will be added over time, as deadlock problems become more common. Several trends will cause this to happen, including larger numbers of processes, many more resources (including CPUs) within a system, and the emphasis on timesharing rather than batch systems.

6.1 System Model

A system consists of a finite number of resources to be distributed among a number of competing processes. The resources are partitioned into several types, each of which consists of some number of identical instances. CPU cycles, memory space, files, and I/O devices (such as printers and tape drives) are examples of resource types. If a system has two CPUs, then the resource type *CPU* has two instances. Similarly, the resource type *printer* may have five instances.

If a process requests an instance of a resource type, the allocation of *any* instance of the type will satisfy the request. If this is not the case, then the instances are not identical, and the resource type classes have not been properly defined. For example, a system may have two printers. These two printers may be defined to be in the same resource class if no one cares which printer prints which output. However, if one printer is on the ninth floor and the other is in the basement, then people on the ninth floor may not see both printers as equivalent, and separate resource classes may need to be defined for each printer.

A process must request a resource before using it and release the resource after using it. A process may request as many resources as it requires to carry out its designated task. Obviously, the number of resources requested may not exceed the total number of resources available in the system. In other words, a process cannot request three printers if the system only has two.

Under the normal mode of operation, a process may utilize a resource in only the following sequence:

1. **Request**. If the request cannot be immediately granted (for example, the resource is being used by another process), then the requesting process must wait until it can acquire the resource.

2. **Use**. The process can operate on the resource (for example, if the resource is a printer, the process can print on the printer).

3. **Release**. The process releases the resource.

The request and release of resources are system calls, as explained in Chapter 3. Examples are the Request and Release Device, Open and Close File, and Allocate and Free Memory system calls. Request and release of other resources may be accomplished through the *wait* and *signal* operations on semaphores. The use of resources also can be done only through system calls (for example, to read or write a file or I/O device). Therefore, for each use, the operating system checks to make sure that the using process has requested and been allocated the resource. A system table records whether each resource is free or allocated, and, if it is allocated, to which process. If a process requests a resource that is currently allocated to another process, it can be added to a queue of processes waiting for this resource.

A set of processes is in a deadlock state when every process in the set is waiting for an event that can be caused only by another process in the set. The events with which we are mainly concerned here are resource acquisition and release. The resources may be either physical resources (for example, printers, tape drives, memory space, and CPU cycles) or logical resources (for example, files, semaphores, and monitors). However, other types of events may result in deadlocks (for example, the IPC facility discussed in Chapter 5).

To illustrate a deadlock state, we consider a system with three tape drives. Suppose that there are three processes, each holding one of these tape drives. If each process now requests another tape drive, the three processes will be in a deadlock state. Each is waiting for the event "tape drive is released," which can be caused by only one of the other waiting processes. This example illustrates a deadlock involving processes competing for the same resource type.

Deadlocks may also involve different resource types. For example, consider a system with one printer and one tape drive. Suppose that process P_i is holding the tape drive and process P_j is holding the printer. If P_i now requests the printer and P_j requests the tape drive, a deadlock occurs.

6.2 Deadlock Characterization

It should be obvious that deadlocks are undesirable. In a deadlock, processes never finish executing and system resources are tied up, preventing other jobs from ever starting. Before we discuss the various methods for dealing with the deadlock problem, we shall describe features that characterize deadlocks.

6.2.1 Necessary Conditions

A deadlock situation can arise if and only if the following four conditions hold simultaneously in a system:

1. **Mutual exclusion**. At least one resource must be held in a nonsharable mode; that is, only one process at a time can use the resource. If another process requests that resource, the requesting process must be delayed until the resource has been released.

2. **Hold and wait**. There must exist a process that is holding at least one resource and is waiting to acquire additional resources that are currently being held by other processes.

3. **No preemption**. Resources cannot be preempted; that is, a resource can be released only voluntarily by the process holding it, after the process has completed its task.

4. **Circular wait**. There must exist a set $\{P_0, P_1, ..., P_n\}$ of waiting processes such that P_0 is waiting for a resource that is held by P_1, P_1 is waiting for a resource that is held by P_2, ..., P_{n-1} is waiting for a resource that is held by P_n, and P_n is waiting for a resource that is held by P_0.

We emphasize that all four conditions must hold for a deadlock to occur. The circular-wait condition implies the hold-and-wait condition, so the four conditions are not completely independent. We shall see in Section 6.3, however, that it is quite useful to consider each condition separately.

6.2.2 Resource-Allocation Graph

Deadlocks can be described more precisely in terms of a directed graph called a *system resource-allocation graph*. This graph consists of a set of vertices V and a set of edges E. The set of vertices V is partitioned into two types $P = \{P_1, P_2, ..., P_n\}$, the set consisting of all the processes in the system, and $R = \{R_1, R_2, ..., R_m\}$, the set consisting of all resource types in the system.

A directed edge from process P_i to resource type R_j is denoted by $P_i \rightarrow R_j$ it signifies that process P_i requested an instance of resource type

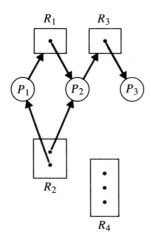

Figure 6.1   Resource-allocation graph.

R_j and is currently waiting for that resource. A directed edge from resource type R_j to process P_i is denoted by $R_j \rightarrow P_i$, signifying that an instance of resource type R_j has been allocated to process P_i. A directed edge $P_i \rightarrow R_j$ is called a *request edge*; a directed edge $R_j \rightarrow P_i$ is called an *assignment edge*.

Pictorially, we represent each process P_i as a circle and each resource type R_j as a square. Since resource type R_j may have more than one instance, we represent each such instance as a dot within the square. Note that a request edge points to only the square R_j, whereas an assignment edge must also designate one of the dots in the square.

When process P_i requests an instance of resource type R_j, a request edge is inserted in the resource-allocation graph. When this request can be fulfilled, the request edge is *instantaneously* transformed to an assignment edge. When the process later releases the resource, the assignment edge is deleted.

The resource-allocation graph in Figure 6.1 depicts the following situation.

- The sets P, R, and E:
  - $P = \{P_1, P_2, P_3\}$.
  - $R = \{R_1, R_2, R_3, R_4\}$.
  - $E = \{P_1 \rightarrow R_1, P_2 \rightarrow R_3, R_1 \rightarrow P_2, R_2 \rightarrow P_2, R_2 \rightarrow P_1, R_3 \rightarrow P_3\}$.

- Resource instances:
  - One instance of resource type R_1
  - Two instances of resource type R_2
  - One instance of resource type R_3
  - Three instances of resource type R_4

- Process states:
  - Process P_1 is holding an instance of resource type R_2, and is waiting for an instance of resource type R_1.
  - Process P_2 is holding an instance of R_1 and R_2, and is waiting for an instance of resource type R_3.
  - Process P_3 is holding an instance of R_3.

Given the definition of a resource-allocation graph, it can be easily shown that, if the graph contains no cycles, then no process in the system is deadlocked. If, on the other hand, the graph contains a cycle, then a deadlock may exist.

If each resource type has exactly one instance, then a cycle implies that a deadlock has occurred. If the cycle involves only a set of resource types, each of which have only a single instance, then a deadlock has occurred. Each process involved in the cycle is deadlocked. In this case, a cycle in the graph is both a necessary and a sufficient condition for the existence of deadlock.

If each resource type has several instances, then a cycle does not necessarily imply that a deadlock occurred. In this case, a cycle in the graph is a necessary but not a sufficient condition for the existence of deadlock.

To illustrate this concept, let us return to the resource-allocation graph depicted in Figure 6.1. Suppose that process P_3 requests an instance of resource type R_2. Since no resource instance is available, a request edge $P_3 \rightarrow R_2$ is added to the graph (Figure 6.2). At this point, two minimal cycles exist in the system:

$$P_1 \rightarrow R_1 \rightarrow P_2 \rightarrow R_3 \rightarrow P_3 \rightarrow R_2 \rightarrow P_1$$
$$P_2 \rightarrow R_3 \rightarrow P_3 \rightarrow R_2 \rightarrow P_2$$

Processes P_1, P_2, and P_3 are deadlocked. Process P_2 is waiting for the resource R_3, which is held by process P_3. Process P_3, on the other hand, is waiting for either process P_1 or process P_2 to release resource R_2. In addition, process P_1 is waiting for process P_2 to release resource R_1.

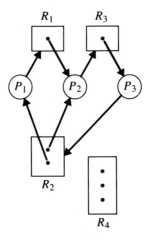

Figure 6.2   Resource-allocation graph with a deadlock.

Now consider Figure 6.3. In this example, we also have a cycle

$$P_1 \rightarrow R_1 \rightarrow P_3 \rightarrow R_2 \rightarrow P_1$$

However, there is no deadlock. Observe that process P_4 may release its instance of resource type R_2. That resource can then be allocated to P_3, breaking the cycle.

In summary, if a resource-allocation graph does not have a cycle, then the system is *not* in a deadlock state. On the other hand, if there is a cycle, then the system may or may not be in a deadlock state. This observation is important in dealing with the deadlock problem.

6.2.3 Methods for Handling Deadlocks

Principally, there are two methods for dealing with the deadlock problem. We can use some protocol to ensure that the system will *never* enter a deadlock state. Alternatively, we can allow the system to enter a deadlock state and then recover. As we show in Section 6.6, recovery from a deadlock may be difficult and expensive. Therefore, we first consider methods of ensuring that deadlocks never occur. There are two common methods: deadlock prevention and deadlock avoidance.

6.3 Deadlock Prevention

As we noted in Section 6.2.1, for a deadlock to occur, each of the four necessary conditions must hold. By ensuring that at least one of these

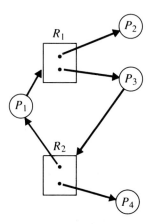

Figure 6.3   Resource-allocation graph with a cycle but no deadlock.

conditions cannot hold, we can *prevent* the occurrence of a deadlock. Let us elaborate on this approach by examining each of the four necessary conditions separately.

6.3.1 Mutual Exclusion

The mutual-exclusion condition must hold for nonsharable resources. For example, a printer cannot be simultaneously shared by several processes. Sharable resources, on the other hand, do not require mutually exclusive access, and thus cannot be involved in a deadlock. Read-only files are a good example of a sharable resource. If several processes attempt to open a read-only file at the same time, they can be granted simultaneous access to the file. A process never needs to wait for a sharable resource. In general, however, it is not possible to prevent deadlocks by denying the mutual-exclusion condition. Some resources are intrinsically nonsharable.

6.3.2 Hold and Wait

To ensure that the hold-and-wait condition never holds in the system, we must guarantee that, whenever a process requests a resource, it does not hold any other resources. One protocol that can be used requires each process to request and be allocated all of its resources before it begins execution. We can implement this provision by requiring that system calls requesting resources for a process precede all other system calls.

An alternative protocol allows a process to request resources only when the process has none. A process may request some resources and use them. Before it can request any additional resources, however, it must release all the resources that it is currently allocated.

To illustrate the difference between these two protocols, we consider a process that copies data from a tape drive to a disk file, sorts the disk file, and then prints the results to a printer. If all resources must be requested at the beginning of the process, then the process must initially request the tape drive, disk file, and the printer. It will hold the printer for its entire execution, even though it needs the printer only at the end.

The second method allows the process to request initially only the tape drive and disk file. It copies from the tape drive to the disk, then releases both the tape drive and the disk file. The process must then again request the disk file and the printer. After copying the disk file to the printer, it releases these two resources and terminates.

There are two main disadvantages to these protocols. First, *resource utilization* may be very low, since many of the resources may be allocated but unused for a long period. In the example given, for instance, we can release the tape drive and disk file, and then again request the disk file and printer, only if we can be sure that our data will remain on the disk file. If we cannot be assured that they will, then we must request all resources at the beginning for both protocols.

Second, *starvation* is possible. A process that needs several popular resources may have to wait indefinitely because at least one of the resources that it needs is always allocated to some other process.

6.3.3 No Preemption

The third necessary condition is that there be no preemption of resources that have already been allocated. To ensure that this condition does not hold, we can use the following protocol. If a process that is holding some resources requests another resource that cannot be immediately allocated to it (that is, the process must wait), then all resources currently being held are preempted. That is, these resources are implicitly released. The preempted resources are added to the list of resources for which the process is waiting. The process will be restarted only when it can regain its old resources, as well as the new ones that it is requesting.

Alternatively, if a process requests some resources, we first check whether they are available. If they are, we allocate them. If they are not available, we check whether they are allocated to some other process that is waiting for additional resources. If so, we preempt the desired resources from the waiting process and allocate them to the requesting process. If the resources are not either available or held by a waiting process, the requesting process must wait. While it is waiting, some of its resources may be preempted, but only if another process requests them. A process can be restarted only when it is allocated the new resources it is requesting and recovers any resources that were preempted while it was waiting.

This protocol is often applied to resources whose state can be easily saved and restored later, such as CPU registers and memory space. It cannot generally be applied to such resources as printers and tape drives.

6.3.4 Circular Wait

One way to ensure that the circular-wait condition never holds is to impose a total ordering of all resource types, and to require that each process requests resources in an increasing order of enumeration.

Let $R = \{R_1, R_2, ..., R_m\}$ be the set of resource types. We assign to each resource type a unique integer number, which allows us to compare two resources and to determine whether one precedes another in our ordering. Formally, we define a one-to-one function $F: R \rightarrow N$, where N is the set of natural numbers. For example, if the set of resource types R includes tape drives, disk drives, and printers, then the function F might be defined as follows:

$$F(\text{tape drive}) = 1,$$
$$F(\text{disk drive}) = 5,$$
$$F(\text{printer}) = 12.$$

We can now consider the following protocol to prevent deadlocks: Each process can request resources only in an increasing order of enumeration. That is, a process can initially request any number of instances of a resource type, say R_i. After that, the process can request instances of resource type R_j if and only if $F(R_j) > F(R_i)$. If several instances of the same resource type are needed, a *single* request for all of them must be issued. For example, using the function defined previously, a process that wants to use the tape drive and printer at the same time must first request the tape drive and then request the printer.

Alternatively, we can simply require that, whenever a process requests an instance of resource type R_j, it has released any resources R_i such that $F(R_i) \geq F(R_j)$.

If these protocols are used, the circular-wait condition cannot hold. We can demonstrate this fact by assuming that a circular wait exists (proof by contradiction). Let the set of processes in the circular wait be $\{P_0, P_1, ..., P_n\}$, where P_i is waiting for a resource R_i, which is held by process P_{i+1}. (Modulo arithmetic is used on the indexes, so that P_n is waiting for a resource R_n held by P_0.) Then, since process P_{i+1} is holding resource R_i while requesting resource R_{i+1}, we must have $F(R_i) < F(R_{i+1})$, for all i. But this means that $F(R_0) < F(R_1) < ... < F(R_n) < F(R_0)$. By transitivity, $F(R_0) < F(R_0)$, which is impossible. Therefore, there can be no circular wait.

Note that, the function F should be defined according to the normal order of usage of the resources in a system. For example, since the tape drive is usually needed before the printer, it would be reasonable to define $F(\text{tape drive}) < F(\text{printer})$.

6.4 Deadlock Avoidance

Deadlock-prevention algorithms, as discussed in Section 6.3, prevent deadlocks by restraining how requests can be made. The restraints ensure that at least one of the necessary conditions for deadlock cannot occur, and, hence, that deadlocks cannot hold. Possible side effects of preventing deadlocks by this method, however, are low device utilization and reduced system throughput.

An alternative method for avoiding deadlocks is to require additional information about how resources are to be requested. For example, in a system with one tape drive and one printer, we might be told that process P will request first the tape drive, and later the printer, before releasing both resources. Process Q, on the other hand, will request first the printer, and then the tape drive. With this knowledge of the complete sequence of requests and releases for each process, we can decide for each request whether or not the process should wait. Each request requires that the system consider the resources currently available, the resources currently allocated to each process, and the future requests and releases of each process, to decide whether the current request can be satisfied or must wait to avoid a possible future deadlock.

The various algorithms differ in the amount and type of information required. The simplest and most useful model requires that each process declare the *maximum number* of resources of each type that it may need. Given a priori information, for each process, about the maximum number of resources of each type that may be requested, it is possible to construct an algorithm that ensures that the system will never enter a deadlock state. This algorithm defines the *deadlock-avoidance* approach. A deadlock-avoidance algorithm dynamically examines the resource-allocation state to ensure that there can never be a circular-wait condition. The resource-allocation *state* is defined by the number of available and allocated resources, and the maximum demands of the processes. A state is *safe* if the system can allocate resources to each process (up to its maximum) in some order and still avoid a deadlock.

More formally, a system is in a safe state only if there exists a *safe sequence*. A sequence of processes $<P_1, P_2, ..., P_n>$ is a safe sequence for the current allocation state if, for each P_i, the resources that P_i can still request can be satisfied by the currently available resources plus the resources held by all the P_j, with $j < i$. In this situation, if the resources that process P_i needs are not immediately available, then P_i can wait until all P_j have finished. When they have finished, P_i can obtain all of its needed resources, complete its designated task, return its allocated resources, and terminate. When P_i terminates, P_{i+1} can obtain its needed resources, and so on. If no such sequence exists, then the system state is said to be *unsafe*.

A safe state is not a deadlock state. Conversely, a deadlock state is an unsafe state. Not all unsafe states are deadlocks, however (Figure 6.4). An unsafe state *may* lead to a deadlock. As long as the state is safe, the operating system can avoid unsafe (and deadlock) states. In an unsafe state, the operating system cannot prevent processes from requesting resources such that a deadlock occurs: The behavior of the processes controls unsafe states.

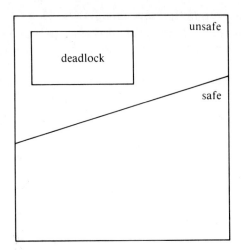

Figure 6.4   Safe, unsafe, and deadlock state spaces.

To illustrate, we consider a system with 12 magnetic tape drives and three processes: P_0, P_1, and P_2. Process P_0 requires 10 tape drives, process P_1 may need as many as four, and process P_2 may need up to nine tape drives. Suppose that, at time t_0, process P_0 is holding five tape drives, process P_1 is holding two, and process P_2 is holding two. (Thus, there are three free tape drives.)

	Maximum Needs	Current Needs
P_0	10	5
P_1	4	2
P_2	9	2

At time t_0, the system is in a safe state. The sequence $<P_1, P_0, P_2>$ satisfies the safety condition, since process P_1 can immediately be allocated all its tape drives and then return them (the system will then have five available tape drives), process P_0 can get all its tape drives and return them (the system will then have 10 available tape drives), and finally process P_2 could get all its tape drives and return them (the system will then have all 12 tape drives available).

Note that it is possible to go from a safe state to an unsafe state. Suppose that, at time t_1, process P_2 requests and is allocated one more tape drive. The system is no longer in a safe state. At this point, only process P_1 can be allocated all its tape drives. When it returns them, the system will have only four available tape drives. Since process P_0 is allocated five tape drives, but has a maximum of 10, it may then request five more. Since they are unavailable, process P_0 must wait. Similarly, process P_2 may request an additional six tape drives and have to wait, resulting in a deadlock.

Our mistake is in granting the request from process P_2 for one more tape drive. If we had made P_2 wait until either of the other processes had finished and released its resources, then we could have avoided the deadlock situation.

Given the concept of a safe state, we can define avoidance algorithms that ensure that the system will never deadlock. The idea is simply to ensure that the system will always remain in a safe state. Initially, the system is in a safe state. Whenever a process requests a resource that is currently available, the system must decide whether the resource can be allocated immediately or whether the process must wait. The request is granted only if the allocation leaves the system in a safe state.

Note that, in this scheme, if a process requests a resource that is currently available, it may still have to wait. Thus, resource utilization may be lower than it would be without a deadlock-avoidance algorithm.

6.4.1 Several Instances of a Resource Type

The deadlock-avoidance algorithm we describe next is commonly known as the *banker's algorithm*. The name was chosen because this algorithm could be used in a banking system to ensure that the bank never allocates its available cash such that it can no longer satisfy the needs of all its customers.

When a new process enters the system, it must declare the maximum number of instances of each resource type that it may need. This number may not exceed the total number of resources in the system. When a user requests a set of resources, the system must determine whether the allocation of these resources will leave the system in a safe state. If it will, the resources are allocated; otherwise, the process must wait until some other process releases enough resources.

Several data structures must be maintained to implement the banker's algorithm. These data structures encode the state of the resource allocation system. Let n be the number of processes in the system and m be the number of resource types. We need the following data structures:

- *Available*. A vector of length m indicating the number of available resources of each type. If *Available*$[j] = k$, there are k instances of resource type R_j available.

- *Max*. An $n \times m$ matrix defining the maximum demand of each process. If $Max[i,j] = k$, then process P_i may request at most k instances of resource type R_j.

- *Allocation*. An $n \times m$ matrix defining the number of resources of each type currently allocated to each process. If $Allocation[i,j] = k$, then process P_i is currently allocated k instances of resource type R_j.

- *Need*. An $n \times m$ matrix indicating the remaining resource need of each process. If $Need[i,j] = k$, then process P_i may need k more instances of resource type R_i in order to complete its task. Note that $Need[i,j] = Max[i,j] - Allocation[i,j]$.

These data structures vary in both size and value as time progresses.

To simplify the presentation of the algorithm, let us establish some notation. Let X and Y be vectors of length n. We say that $X \leq Y$ if and only if $X[i] \leq Y[i]$ for all $i = 1, 2, ..., n$. For example, if $X = (1,7,3,2)$ and $Y = (0,3,2,1)$, then $Y \leq X$. $Y < X$ if $Y \leq X$ and $Y \neq X$.

We can treat each row in the matrices *Allocation* and *Need* as vectors and refer to them as *Allocation*$_i$ and *Need*$_i$, respectively. *Allocation*$_i$ specifies the resources currently allocated to process P_i; *Need*$_i$ specifies the additional resources that process P_i may still request in order to complete its task.

Banker's algorithm

Let *Request*$_i$ be the request vector for process P_i. If *Request*$_i[j] = k$, then process P_i wants k instances of resource type R_j. When a request for resources is made by process P_i, the following actions are taken:

1. If *Request*$_i \leq$ *Need*$_i$, go to step 2. Otherwise, raise an error condition, since the process has exceeded its maximum claim.

2. If *Request*$_i \leq$ *Available*, go to step 3. Otherwise, P_i must wait, since the resources are not available.

3. The system pretends to have allocated the requested resources to process P_i by modifying the state as follows:

$$Available := Available - Request_i;$$
$$Allocation_i := Allocation_i + Request_i;$$
$$Need_i := Need_i - Request_i;$$

If the resulting resource-allocation state is safe, the transaction is completed and process P_i is allocated its resources. However, if the new state is unsafe, then P_i must wait for *Request*$_i$ and the old resource-allocation state is restored.

Safety algorithm

The algorithm for finding out whether or not a system is in a safe state can be described as follows:

1. Let *Work* and *Finish* be vectors of length m and n, respectively. Initialize *Work* := *Available* and *Finish*[i] := *false* for i = 1, 2, ..., n.

2. Find an i such that both

   a. *Finish*[i] = *false*

   b. *Need$_i$* $\leq$ *Work*.

   If no such i exists, go to step 4.

3. *Work* := *Work* + *Allocation$_i$*
   Finish[i] := *true*
   go to step 2.

4. If *Finish*[i] = *true* for all i, then the system is in a safe state.

An illustrative example

Consider a system with five processes P_0 through P_4 and three resource types A, B, C. Resource type A has 10 instances, resource type B has five instances, and resource type C has seven instances. Suppose that, at time T_0, the following snapshot of the system has been taken:

	Allocation	Max	Available
	A B C	A B C	A B C
P_0	0 1 0	7 5 3	3 3 2
P_1	2 0 0	3 2 2	
P_2	3 0 2	9 0 2	
P_3	2 1 1	2 2 2	
P_4	0 0 2	4 3 3	

The content of the matrix *Need* is defined to be *Max* − *Allocation* and is

	Need
	A B C
P_0	7 4 3
P_1	1 2 2
P_2	6 0 0
P_3	0 1 1
P_4	4 3 1

We claim that the system is currently in a safe state. Indeed, the sequence $<P_1, P_3, P_4, P_2, P_0>$ satisfies the safety criteria.

Suppose now that process P_1 requests one additional instance of resource type A and two instances of resource type C, so $Request_1$ = (1,0,2). To decide whether this request can be immediately granted, we first check that $Request_1 \leq Available$ (that is, (1,0,2) $\leq$ (3,3,2)), which is true. We then pretend that this request has been fulfilled and arrive at the following new state:

	Allocation	Need	Available
	A B C	A B C	A B C
P_0	0 1 0	7 4 3	2 3 0
P_1	3 0 2	0 2 0	
P_2	3 0 2	6 0 0	
P_3	2 1 1	0 1 1	
P_4	0 0 2	4 3 1	

We must determine whether this new system state is safe. To do so, we execute our safety algorithm and find that the sequence $<P_1, P_3, P_4, P_0, P_2>$ satisfies our safety requirement. Hence, we can immediately grant the request of process P_1.

You should be able to see, however, that when the system is in this state, a request for (3,3,0) by P_4 cannot be granted since the resources are not available. A request for (0,2,0) by P_0 cannot be granted, even though the resources are available, since the resulting state is unsafe.

6.4.2 Single Instance of Each Resource Type

Although the banker's algorithm is quite general and will work for any resource-allocation system, it may require $m \times n^2$ operations to decide whether a state is safe. If we have a resource-allocation system with only one instance of each resource type, a more efficient algorithm can be defined.

This algorithm uses a variant of the resource-allocation graph defined in Section 6.2.2. In addition to the request and assignment edges, we introduce a new type of edge, called a *claim edge*. A claim edge $P_i \rightarrow R_j$ indicates that process P_i may request resource R_j at sometime in the future. This edge resembles a request edge in direction, but is represented by a dashed line. When process P_i requests resource R_j, the claim edge $P_i \rightarrow R_j$ is converted to a request edge. Similarly, when a resource R_j is released by P_i, the assignment edge $R_j \rightarrow P_i$ is reconverted to a claim edge $P_i \rightarrow R_j$. We note that the resources must be claimed a priori in the system. That is, before process P_i starts executing, all its claim edges must already appear in the resource-allocation graph. We can relax this condition by allowing a claim edge $P_i \rightarrow R_j$ to be added to the graph only if all the edges associated with process P_i are claim edges.

Suppose that process P_i requests resource R_j. The request can be granted only if converting the request edge $P_i \xrightarrow{j} R_j$ to an assignment edge $R_j \rightarrow P_i$ does not result in the formation of a cycle in the resource-allocation graph. Note that we check for safety by using a cycle-detection algorithm. An algorithm for detecting a cycle in this graph requires an order of n^2 operation, where n is the number of processes in the system.

If no cycle exists, then the allocation of the resource will leave the system in a safe state. If a cycle is found, then the allocation will put the system in an unsafe state. Therefore, process P_i will have to wait for its requests to be satisfied.

To illustrate this algorithm, we consider the resource-allocation graph of Figure 6.5. Suppose that P_2 requests R_2. Although R_2 is currently free, we cannot allocate it to P_2, since this action will create a cycle in the graph (Figure 6.6). A cycle indicates that the system is in an unsafe state. If P_1 then requests R_2, a deadlock will occur.

6.5 Deadlock Detection

If a system does not employ either a deadlock-prevention or a deadlock-avoidance algorithm, then a deadlock situation may occur. In this environment, the system must provide

- An algorithm that examines the state of the system to determine whether a deadlock has occurred

- An algorithm to recover from the deadlock

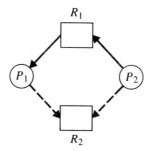

Figure 6.5   Resource-allocation graph for deadlock avoidance.

In the following discussion, we elaborate on these two issues as they pertain to systems with several instances of each resource type, as well as to systems with only a single instance of each resource type. At this point, however, let us note that a detection and recovery scheme requires overhead that includes not only the run-time costs of maintaining the necessary information and executing the detection algorithm, but also the potential losses inherent in recovering from a deadlock.

6.5.1 Several Instances of a Resource Type

The detection algorithm employs several time-varying data structures that are similar to those used in the banker's algorithm (Section 6.4.1):

- *Available*. A vector of length m indicating the number of available resources of each type.

- *Allocation*. An $n \times m$ matrix defining the number of resources of each type currently allocated to each process.

- *Request*. An $n \times m$ matrix indicating the current request of each process. If $Request[i,j] = k$, then process P_i is requesting k more instances of resource type R_j.

The less-than relation ($<$) between two vectors is defined as in Section 6.4.1. To simplify notation, we shall again treat the rows in the matrices *Allocation* and *Request* as vectors, and shall refer to them as *Allocation*$_i$ and *Request*$_i$, respectively. The detection algorithm described here simply investigates every possible allocation sequence for the processes that remain to be completed. Compare this algorithm with the banker's algorithm of Section 6.4.1.

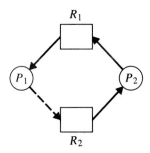

Figure 6.6   An unsafe state in a resource-allocation graph.

1. Let *Work* and *Finish* be vectors of length m and n, respectively. Initialize *Work* := *Available*. For $i = 1, 2, ..., n$, if $Allocation_i \neq 0$, then *Finish*[i] := *false*; otherwise, *Finish*[i] := *true*.

2. Find an index i such that both

   a. *Finish*[i] = *false*

   b. $Request_i \leq Work$.

   If no such i exists, go to step 4.

3. *Work* := *Work* + $Allocation_i$
   Finish[i] := *true*
   go to step 2.

4. If *Finish*[i] = false, for some i, $1 \leq i \leq n$, then the system is in a deadlock state. Moreover, if *Finish*[i] = *false*, then process P_i is deadlocked.

You may wonder why we reclaim the resources of process P_i (in step 3) as soon as we determine that $Request_i \leq Work$ (in step 2b). We know that P_i is currently *not* involved in a deadlock (since $Request_i \leq Work$). Thus, we take an optimistic attitude, and assume that P_i will require no more resources to complete its task; it will thus soon return all currently allocated resources to the system. If this is not the case, a deadlock may occur later. That deadlock will be detected the next time the deadlock-detection algorithm is invoked.

To illustrate this algorithm, we consider a system with five processes P_0 through P_4 and three resource types A, B, C. Resource type A has seven instances, resource type B has two instances, and resource type C has six instances. Suppose that, at time T_0, we have the following resource-allocation state:

	Allocation	Request	Available
	A B C	A B C	A B C
P_0	0 1 0	0 0 0	0 0 0
P_1	2 0 0	2 0 2	
P_2	3 0 3	0 0 0	
P_3	2 1 1	1 0 0	
P_4	0 0 2	0 0 2	

We claim that the system is not in a deadlocked state. Indeed, if we execute our algorithm, we will find that the sequence $<P_0, P_2, P_3, P_1, P_4>$ will result in *Finish*[i] = true for all i.

Suppose now that process P_2 makes one additional request for an instance of type C. The *Request* matrix is modified as follows:

	Request		
	A	B	C
P_0	0	0	0
P_1	2	0	2
P_2	0	0	1
P_3	1	0	0
P_4	0	0	2

We claim that the system is now deadlocked. Although we can reclaim the resources held by process P_0, the number of available resources is not sufficient to fulfill the requests of the other processes. Thus, a deadlock exists, consisting of processes P_1, P_2, P_3, and P_4.

6.5.2 Single Instance of Each Resource Type

The deadlock-detection algorithm of Section 6.5.1 is of order $m \times n^2$. If all resources have only a single instance, however, we can define a faster algorithm. Again, we will use a variant of the resource-allocation graph, called a *wait-for* graph. We obtain this graph from the resource-allocation graph by removing the nodes of type resource and collapsing the appropriate edges.

More precisely, an edge from P_i to P_j in a wait-for graph implies that process P_i is waiting for process P_j to release a resource that it needs. An edge $P_i \rightarrow P_j$ exists in a wait-for graph if and only if the corresponding resource-allocation graph contains two edges $P_i \rightarrow R_q$ and $R_q \rightarrow P_j$ for some resource R_q. For example, in Figure 6.7, we present a resource-allocation graph and its corresponding wait-for graph.

As before, a deadlock exists in the system if and only if the wait-for graph contains a cycle. To detect deadlocks, the system needs to *maintain* the wait-for graph and periodically to *invoke an algorithm* that searches for a cycle in the graph.

An algorithm to detect a cycle in a graph requires an order of n^2 operations, where n is the number of vertices in the graph. Although this cost is less than that of the general deadlock algorithm of Section 6.5.1, there is still considerable overhead in detecting such cycles.

6.5.3 Detection-Algorithm Usage

When should we invoke the detection algorithm? The answer depends on two factors:

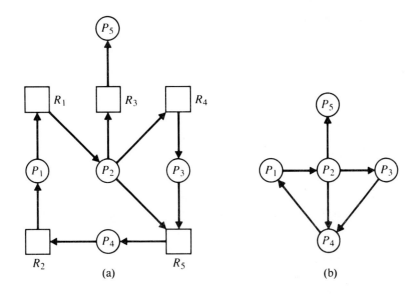

Figure 6.7   Resource-allocation graph (a) and its wait-for graph (b).

1. How *often* is a deadlock likely to occur?

2. How *many* processes will be affected by deadlock when it happens?

If deadlocks occur frequently, then the detection algorithm should be invoked more frequently. Resources allocated to deadlocked processes will be idle until the deadlock can be broken. In addition, the number of processes involved in the deadlock cycle may grow.

Deadlocks can come into being only when some process makes a request that cannot be granted immediately. It is possible that this request is the final request that completes a chain of waiting processes. In the extreme, we could invoke the deadlock-detection algorithm every time a request for allocation cannot be granted immediately. In this case, we can identify not only the set of processes that is deadlocked, but also the specific process that "caused" the deadlock. (In reality, each of the deadlocked processes is a link in the cycle in the resource graph, so all of them, jointly, caused the deadlock.) If there are many different resource types, one request may cause many cycles in the resource graph, each cycle completed by the most recent request, and "caused" by the one identifiable process.

Of course, invoking the deadlock-detection algorithm for every request may incur a considerable overhead in computation time. A less expensive alternative is simply to invoke it at less frequent intervals —

for example, once per hour, or whenever CPU utilization drops below 40 percent. (A deadlock eventually cripples system throughput and will cause CPU utilization to drop.) If the detection algorithm is invoked at arbitrary points in time, there may be many cycles in the resource graph. We would generally not be able to tell which of the many deadlocked processes "caused" the deadlock.

6.6 Recovery from Deadlock

When a detection algorithm determines that a deadlock exists, several alternatives exist. One possibility is to inform the operator that a deadlock has occurred, and to let the operator deal with it manually. The other possibility is to let the system *recover* from the deadlock automatically. There are two options for breaking a deadlock. One solution is simply to abort one or more processes in order to break the circular wait. The second option is to preempt some resources from one or more of the deadlocked processes.

6.6.1 Process Termination

To eliminate deadlocks by aborting a process, we use one of two methods. In both methods, the system reclaims all resources allocated to the terminated processes.

- **Abort all deadlocked processes.** This method clearly will break the deadlock cycle, but at a great expense, since these processes may have computed for a long time, and the results of these partial computations must be discarded, and probably must be recomputed later.

- **Abort one process at a time until the deadlock cycle is eliminated.** This method incurs considerable overhead, since, after each process is aborted, a deadlock-detection algorithm must be invoked to determine whether any processes are still deadlocked.

Notice that aborting a process may not be easy. If the process was in the midst of updating a file, terminating it in the middle will leave that file in an incorrect state. Similarly, if the process was in the midst of printing data on the printer, the system must reset the state of the printer to a correct state before proceeding with the printing of the next job.

If the partial termination method is used, then, given a set of deadlocked processes, we must determine which process (or processes) should be terminated in an attempt to break the deadlock. This is a policy decision, similar to CPU-scheduling problems. The question is basically an economical one; we should abort those processes, the termination of which will incur the minimum cost. Unfortunately, the term *minimum cost* is not a precise one. Many factors may determine which process is chosen, including

1. The priority of the process

2. How long the process has computed, and how much longer the process will compute before completing its designated task

3. How many and what type of resources the process has used (for example, whether the resources are simple to preempt)

4. How many more resources the process needs in order to complete

5. How many processes will need to be terminated

6. Whether the process is interactive or batch

6.6.2 Resource Preemption

To eliminate deadlocks using resource preemption, we successively preempt some resources from processes and give these resources to other processes until the deadlock cycle is broken.

If preemption is required to deal with deadlocks, then three issues need to be addressed:

1. **Selecting a victim**. Which resources and which processes are to be preempted? As in process termination, we must determine the order of preemption to minimize cost. Cost factors may include such parameters as the number of resources a deadlock process is holding, and the amount of time a deadlocked process has thus far consumed during its execution.

2. **Rollback**. If we preempt a resource from a process, what should be done with that process? Clearly, it cannot continue with its normal execution; it is missing some needed resource. We must roll back the process to some safe state, and restart it from that state.

   Since in general it is difficult to determine what a safe state is, the simplest solution is a total rollback: Abort the process and then restart it. However, it is more effective to roll back the process only as far as necessary to break the deadlock. On the other hand, this method requires the system to keep more information about the state of all the running processes.

3. **Starvation**. How do we ensure that starvation will not occur? That is, how can we guarantee that resources will not always be preempted from the same process?

   In a system where victim selection is based primarily on cost factors, it may happen that the same process is always picked as a victim. As a result, this process never completes its designated task, a *starvation* situation that needs to be dealt with in any practical system. Clearly, we must ensure that a process can be picked as a victim only a (small) finite number of times. The most common solution is to include the number of rollbacks in the cost factor.

6.7 Combined Approach to Deadlock Handling

It has been argued that none of the basic approaches for handling deadlocks (prevention, avoidance, and detection) alone is appropriate for the entire spectrum of resource-allocation problems encountered in operating systems. One possibility is to combine the three basic approaches, allowing the use of the optimal approach for each class of resources in the system. The proposed method is based on the notion that resources can be partitioned into classes that are hierarchically ordered. A resource-ordering technique (Section 6.3.4) is applied to the classes. Within each class, the most appropriate technique for handling deadlocks can be used.

It is easy to show that a system that employs this strategy will not be subjected to deadlocks. Indeed, a deadlock cannot involve more than one class, since the resource-ordering technique is used. Within each class, one of the basic approaches is used. Consequently, the system is not subject to deadlocks.

To illustrate this technique, we consider a system that consists of the following four classes of resources:

- **Internal resources**. Resources used by the system, such as a process control block

- **Central memory**. Memory used by a user job

- **Job resources**. Assignable devices (such as a tape drive) and files

- **Swappable space**. Space for each user job on the backing store

One mixed deadlock solution for this system orders the classes as shown, and uses the following approaches to each class:

- **Internal resources**. Prevention through resource ordering can be used, since run-time choices between pending requests are unnecessary.

- **Central memory**. Prevention through preemption can be used, since a job can always be swapped out, and the central memory can be preempted.

- **Job resources**. Avoidance can be used, since the information needed about resource requirements can be obtained from the job-control cards.

- **Swappable space**. Preallocation can be used, since the maximum storage requirements are usually known.

This example shows how various basic approaches can be mixed within the framework of resource ordering, to obtain an effective solution to the deadlock problem.

6.8 Summary

A deadlock state occurs when two or more processes are waiting indefinitely for an event that can be caused only by one of the waiting processes. Principally, there are two methods for dealing with deadlocks:

- Use some protocol to ensure that the system will never enter a deadlock state

- Allow the system to enter deadlock state and then recover

A deadlock situation may occur if and only if four necessary conditions hold simultaneously in the system: mutual exclusion, hold and wait, no preemption, and circular wait. To prevent deadlocks, we ensure that at least one of the necessary conditions never holds. There are three basic methods for deadlock prevention.

- **Hold and wait**. Before proceeding with its execution, each process must acquire all the resources it needs.

- **No preemption**. If a process is holding some resources and requests another resource, and this resource cannot be immediately allocated to that process (that is, the process must wait), then the process must release all the resources it is currently holding.

- **Circular wait**. Impose a linear ordering on all resource types. Each process can request resources only in an increasing order.

Another method for avoiding deadlocks that is less stringent than the preceding prevention algorithm is to have a priori information on how each process will be utilizing the resources. The banker's algorithm needs to know the maximum number of each resource class that may be requested by each process. Using this information, we can define a deadlock-avoidance algorithm.

If a system does not employ some protocol to ensure that deadlocks will never occur, then a detection and recovery scheme must be employed. A deadlock-detection algorithm must be invoked to determine whether a deadlock has occurred. If a deadlock is detected, the system must recover either by terminating some of the deadlocked processes or by preempting resources from some of the deadlocked processes.

In a system that selects victims for rollback primarily on the basis of cost factors, starvation may occur. As a result, the selected process never completes its designated task.

Finally, it has been argued that none of these basic approaches alone is appropriate for the entire spectrum of resource-allocation problems in operating systems. The basic approaches can be combined, allowing the separate selection of an optimal one for each class of resources in a system.

Exercises

6.1 List 3 examples of deadlocks that are not related to a computer-system environment.

6.2 Are all of the necessary conditions introduced in Section 6.2.1 independent, or does one or more of them have to hold for another to hold? Explain your answer.

6.3 Is it possible to have a deadlock involving only one single process? Explain your answer.

6.4 Hardware is not unbreakable. How does the failure of a device affect each of the three methods for handling deadlocks (prevention, avoidance, and detection)? What steps can be taken (if any are necessary) to improve the situation after a device goes down?

6.5 Prove that the safety algorithm of Section 6.4.1 requires an order of $m \times n^2$ operations.

6.6 People have said that proper spooling would eliminate deadlocks. Certainly, it eliminates card readers, plotters, printers, and so on from contention. It is even possible to spool tapes (called *staging* them), which would leave the resources of CPU time, memory, and disk space. Is it possible to have a deadlock involving these resources? If so, how could such a deadlock occur? What deadlock scheme would seem best to eliminate these deadlocks (if any are possible), or what condition is violated (if they are not possible)?

6.7 Consider the traffic deadlock depicted in Figure 6.8.

a. Show that the four necessary conditions for deadlock indeed hold in this example.

b. State a simple rule that will avoid deadlocks in this system.

6.8 Consider a system consisting of four resources of the same type that are shared by three processes, each of which needs at most two resources. Show that the system is deadlock-free.

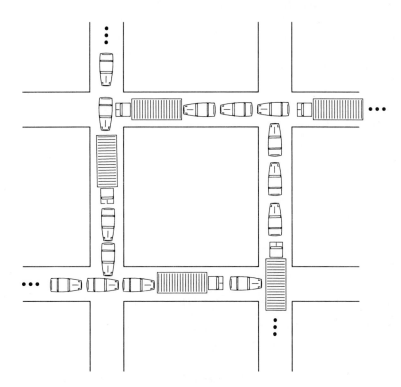

Figure 6.8 Traffic deadlock for Exercise 6.7.

6.9 Consider a system consisting of m resources of the same type, being shared by n processes. Resources can be requested and released by processes only one at a time. Show that the system is deadlock free if the following two conditions hold:

a. The maximum need of each process is between 1 and m resources.

b. The sum of all maximum needs is less than $m + n$.

6.10 What is the main difference between deadlock and starvation?

6.11 What difficulties may arise when a process is rolled back as the result of a deadlock?

6.12 Suppose that a system is in an unsafe state. Show that it is possible for the processes to complete their execution without entering a deadlock state.

6.13 In a real computer system, neither the resources available nor the demands of processes for resources are consistent over long periods (months). Resources break or are replaced, new processes come and go, new resources are bought and added to the system. If deadlock is controlled by the banker's algorithm, which of the following changes can be made safely (without introducing the possibility of deadlock), and under what circumstances?

a. Increase *Available* (new resources added).

b. Decrease *Available* (resource permanently removed from system).

c. Increase *Max* for one process (the process needs more resources than allowed, it may want more).

d. Decrease *Max* for one process (the process decides it does not need that many resources).

e. Increase the number of processes.

f. Decrease the number of processes.

6.14 Consider a system that runs 5000 jobs per month with no deadlock-prevention or deadlock-avoidance scheme. Deadlocks occur about twice per month, and the operator must terminate and rerun about 10 jobs per deadlock. Each job is worth about $2 (in CPU time), and the jobs terminated tend to be about half-done when they are aborted.

A systems programmer has estimated that a deadlock-avoidance algorithm (like the banker's algorithm) would be installed in the system with an increase in the average execution time per job of about 10 percent. Since the machine currently has 30-percent idle time, all 5000 jobs per month could still be run, although turnaround time would increase by about 20 percent on average.

a. What are the arguments for installing the deadlock-avoidance algorithm?

b. What are the arguments against installing the deadlock avoidance algorithm?

6.15 Consider the following snapshot of a system:

	Allocation	Max	Available
	A B C D	A B C D	A B C D
P_0	0 0 1 2	0 0 1 2	1 5 2 0
P_1	1 0 0 0	1 7 5 0	
P_2	1 3 5 4	2 3 5 6	
P_3	0 6 3 2	0 6 5 2	
P_4	0 0 1 4	0 6 5 6	

Answer the following questions using the banker's algorithm:

a. What is the content of the matrix *Need*?

b. Is the system in a safe state?

c. If a request from process P_1 arrives for (0,4,2,0), can the request be granted immediately?

6.16 Consider the following resource-allocation policy. Requests and releases for resources are allowed at any time. If a request for resources cannot be satisfied because the resources are not available, then we check any processes that are blocked, waiting for resources. If they have the desired resources, then these resources are taken away from them and are given to the requesting process. The vector of resources for which the waiting process is waiting is increased to include the resources that were taken away.

For example, consider a system with three resource types and the vector *Available* initialized to (4,2,2). If process P_0 asks for (2,2,1), it gets them. If P_1 asks for (1,0,1), it gets them. Then, if P_0 asks for $(0,0,1)$, it is blocked (resource not available). If P_2 now asks for $(2,0,0)$, it gets the available one $(1,0,0)$ and one that was allocated to P_0 (since P_0 is blocked). P_0's *Allocation* vector goes down to $(1,2,1)$, and its *Need* vector goes up to $(1,0,1)$.

    a. Can deadlock occur? If so, give an example. If not, which necessary condition cannot occur?

    b. Can indefinite blocking occur?

6.17 Can a system detect that some of its processes are starving? If you answer "yes," explain how it can. If you answer "no," explain how the system can deal with the starvation problem.

6.18 We can obtain the banker's algorithm for a single resource type from the general banker's algorithm simply by reducing the dimensionality of the various arrays by 1. Show through an example that the multiple-resource-type banker's scheme cannot be implemented by individual application of the single-resource-type scheme to each resource type.

6.19 Suppose that you have coded the deadlock-avoidance safety algorithm and now wish to implement the deadlock-detection algorithm. Can you do so by simply using the safety algorithm code and redefining $Max_i = Waiting_i + Allocation_i$, where $Waiting_i$ is a vector specifying the resources process i is waiting for, and $Allocation_i$ is as defined in Section 6.4? Explain your answer.

Bibliographic Notes

Dijkstra [1965a] was one of the first and most influential contributors in the deadlock area. Holt [1971b, 1972] was the first person to formalize the notion of deadlocks in terms of a graph-theoretical model similar to the one presented in this chapter. The issue of starvation is covered by Holt [1972] and Lauesen [1973].

The various prevention algorithms were suggested by Havender [1968], who has devised the resource-ordering scheme for the IBM OS/360 system.

The banker's algorithm for avoiding deadlocks was developed for a single resource type by Dijkstra [1965a], and was extended to multiple resource types by Habermann [1969]. General discussions concerning avoiding deadlocks by stating claims have been written by Habermann [1969], Holt [1971a, 1972], and Parnas and Habermann [1972]. Exercises 6.8 and 6.9 are from Holt [1971a].

A parallel deadlock-avoidance scheme was presented by Fontao [1971]. A practical approach to managing resources and avoiding deadlocks was discussed by Frailey [1973]. A deadlock-avoidance scheme in which the system resources are partitioned into subsystems, each of which can be scheduled independently, was presented by Lomet [1980].

The deadlock-detection algorithm for multiple instances of a resource type, which was described in Section 6.5.1, was written by Shoshani and Coffman [1970].

The issue of computational intractability of some deadlock-avoidance algorithms has been studied by Devillers [1977], Gold [1978], and Minoura [1982]. The issue of testing for freedom from deadlocks in a computer system was discussed by Kameda [1980]. The combined approach to deadlocks described in Section 6.7 was originally suggested by Howard [1973].

Survey papers have been written by Coffman, et al. [1971] and Isloor, et al. [1980]. A classifying bibliography of the deadlock problem is presented by Zoble [1983].

PART 3

Storage Management

The main purpose of a computer system is to execute programs. These programs, together with the data they access, must be in main memory (at least partially) during execution.

To improve both the utilization of CPU and the speed of its response to its users, the computer must keep several processes in memory. There are many different memory-management schemes. These schemes reflect various approaches to memory management, and the effectiveness of the different algorithms depends on the particular situation. Selection of a memory-management scheme for a specific system depends on many factors, especially on the *hardware* design of the system. Each algorithm requires its own hardware support.

Since main memory is usually too small to accommodate all data and programs permanently, the computer system must provide secondary storage to back up main memory. Most modern computer systems use disks as the primary on-line storage medium for information (both programs and data). Hence, the proper management of disk storage is of central importance to a computer system.

7

Memory Management

In Chapter 4, we showed how the CPU can be shared by a set of processes. As a result of CPU scheduling, we can improve both the utilization of the CPU and the speed of the computer's response to its users. To realize this increase in performance, however, we must keep several processes in memory; we must *share* memory.

In this chapter, we discuss various ways to manage memory. The memory-management algorithms vary from a primitive bare-machine approach to paging and segmentation strategies. Each approach has its own advantages and disadvantages. Selection of a memory-management scheme for a specific system depends on many factors, especially on the *hardware* design of the system. As we shall see, each algorithm requires its own hardware support.

The memory-management algorithms described in this chapter have one basic requirement: The entire program of a process must be in physical memory before the process can execute. This restriction limits the size of a process to the size of physical memory.

7.1 Background

As was shown in Chapter 1, memory is central to the operation of a modern computer system. Memory is a large array of words or bytes, each with its own address. Interaction is achieved through a sequence of reads or writes to specific memory addresses. The CPU fetches from and stores in memory.

229

A typical instruction execution cycle, for example, will first fetch an instruction from memory. The instruction is then decoded and may cause operands to be fetched from memory. After the instruction on the operands has been executed, results may be stored back in memory. Notice that the memory unit sees only a stream of memory addresses; it does not know how they are generated (the instruction counter, indexing, indirection, literal addresses, and so on) or what they are for (instructions or data). Accordingly, we can ignore *how* a memory address is generated by a program. We are interested in only the sequence of memory addresses generated by the running program.

7.1.1 Address Binding

A process must be loaded into memory to be executed. Usually, the process resides on a disk as a binary executable file. The collection of processes on the disk that are waiting to be brought into memory for execution form the *input queue.*

The normal procedure is to select one of the processes in the input queue and to load it into memory. This technique sometimes may result in relocating addresses, or linking external references to entry points as needed. As the process is executed, it accesses instructions and data from memory. Eventually, the process terminates and its memory space is declared available.

A user process may reside in any part of the physical memory. Thus, although the address space of the computer starts at 00000, the first address of the user process does not need to be 00000. This arrangement affects the addresses that the user program can use. In most cases, a user program will go through several steps (some of which may be optional) before being executed (Figure 7.1). Addresses may be represented in different ways during these steps. Addresses in the source program are generally symbolic (such as *I*). A compiler will typically *bind* these symbolic addresses to relocatable addresses (such as 14 bytes from the beginning of this module). The linkage editor or loader will in turn bind these relocatable addresses to absolute addresses (such as 74014). Each binding is a mapping from one address space to another.

Classically, the *binding* of instructions and data to memory addresses can be done at any step along the way:

- **Compile time**. If it is known at compile time where the process will reside in memory, then *absolute* code can be generated. For example, if it is known a priori that a user process resides starting at location *R*, then the generated compiler code will start at that location and extend up from there. If, at some later time, the starting location

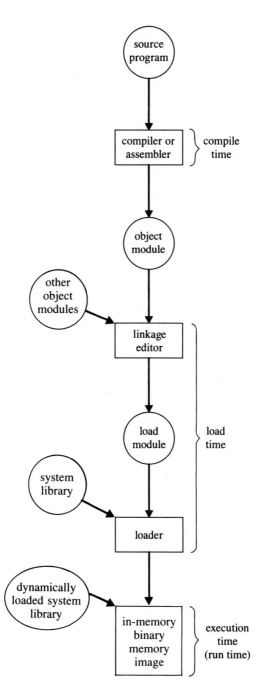

Figure 7.1 Multistep processing of a user program.

changes, then it will be necessary to recompile this code. The MS-DOS .COM-format programs are absolute code bound at compile time.

- **Load time**. If it is not known at compile time where the process will reside in memory, then the compiler must generate *relocatable* code. In this case, final binding is delayed until load time. If the starting address changes, we need only to reload the user code to incorporate this changed value.

- **Execution time**. If the process can be moved during its execution from one memory segment to another, then binding must be delayed until run time. Special hardware must be available for this scheme to work, as will be discussed later.

A major portion of this chapter is devoted to showing how these various bindings can be implemented effectively in a computer system.

7.1.2 Dynamic Loading

To obtain better memory space utilization, we can use *dynamic loading*. With dynamic loading, a routine is not loaded until it is called. All routines are kept on disk in a relocatable load format. The main program is loaded into memory and is executed. When a routine needs to call another routine, the calling routine first checks to see whether the other routine has been loaded. If it has not been, the relocatable linking loader is called to load the desired routine into memory and update the tables to reflect this change. Then control is passed to the newly loaded routine.

The advantage of dynamic loading is that an unused routine is never loaded. This scheme is particularly useful when large amounts of code are needed to handle infrequently occurring cases, such as various error routines. In this case, although the total program size may be large, the portion that is actually used (and hence actually loaded) may be much smaller.

Dynamic loading does not require special support from the operating system. It is the responsibility of the users to design their programs to take advantage of such a scheme.

7.1.3 Dynamic Linking

Notice that Figure 7.1 also shows *dynamically linked* libraries. Most operating systems support only static linking, in which system language libraries are treated like any other object module and are combined by the loader into the binary program image. The concept of dynamic linking is similar to that of dynamic loading. Rather than loading being postponed until execution time, linking is postponed. This feature is usually used with system libraries, such as language subroutine libraries. Without this facility, all programs on a system need to have a copy of their language library (or at least the routines referenced) included in the executable image. This requirement wastes both disk space and main memory. With dynamic linking, a *stub* is included in the image for each library-routine reference. This stub is a small piece of code that indicates how to locate the appropriate memory-resident library routine. When this stub is executed, it replaces itself with the address of the routine and executes the routine. Thus, the next time that that code segment is reached, the library routine is executed directly, with no cost being incurred by dynamic linking. Under this scheme, all processes that use a language library execute only one copy of the library code.

This feature can be extended to library updates (such as bug fixes). A library may be replaced by a new version, and all programs that reference the library will automatically use the new version. Without dynamic linking, all such programs would need to be relinked to gain access to the new library. So that programs will not accidentally execute new, incompatible versions of libraries, version information is included in both the program and the library. More than one version of a library may be loaded into memory, and each program uses this version information to decide which copy of the library to use. Minor changes retain the same version number, whereas major changes increment the version number. Thus, only programs that are compiled with the new library version are affected by the incompatible changes incorporated in it. Other programs linked before the new library was installed will continue using the older library. This system is also known as *shared libraries*.

7.1.4 Overlays

Since the entire logical address space of a process must be in physical memory before the process can execute, the size of a process is limited to the size of physical memory. So that a process can be larger than the amount of memory allocated to it, a technique called *overlays* is sometimes used. The idea of overlays is to keep in memory only those instructions and data that are needed at any given time. When other instructions are needed, they are loaded into space that was previously occupied by instructions that are no longer needed.

As an example, consider a two-pass assembler. During pass 1, it constructs a symbol table; then, during pass 2, it generates machine-language code. We may be able to partition such an assembler into pass 1 code, pass 2 code, the symbol table, and common support routines used by both pass 1 and pass 2. Assume the sizes of these components are as follows (K stands for "kilobyte," which is 1024 bytes):

Pass 1	70K
Pass 2	80K
Symbol table	20K
Common routines	30K

To load everything at once, we would require 200K of memory. If only 150K is available, we cannot run our process. However, notice that pass 1 and pass 2 do not need to be in memory at the same time. We thus define two overlays: (A) the symbol table, common routines, and pass 1, and (B) the symbol table, common routines, and pass 2.

We add an overlay driver (10K) and start with overlay A in memory. When we finish pass 1, we jump to the overlay driver, which reads overlay B into memory, overwriting overlay A, and then transfers control to pass 2. Overlay A needs only 120K, whereas overlay B needs 130K (Figure 7.2). We can now run our assembler in the 150K of memory available. However, it will run somewhat more slowly, due to the extra I/O to read the code for overlay B over the code for overlay A.

The code for overlay A and the code for overlay B are kept on disk as absolute memory images, and are read by the overlay driver as needed. Special relocation and linking algorithms are needed to construct the overlays.

As in dynamic loading, overlays do not require any special support from the operating system. They can be implemented completely by the user with simple file structures, reading from the files into memory and then jumping to that memory and executing the newly read instructions. The operating system notices only that there is more I/O than usual.

The programmer, on the other hand, must design and program the overlay structure properly. This task can be a major undertaking, requiring complete knowledge of the structure of the program, its code, and its data structures. Since the program is, by definition, large (small programs do not need to be overlayed), obtaining a sufficient understanding of the program may be very difficult. For these reasons, the use of overlays is currently limited to microcomputer and other systems that have limited amounts of physical memory and that lack hardware support for more advanced techniques. Automatic techniques to run large programs in limited amounts of physical memory are certainly preferable.

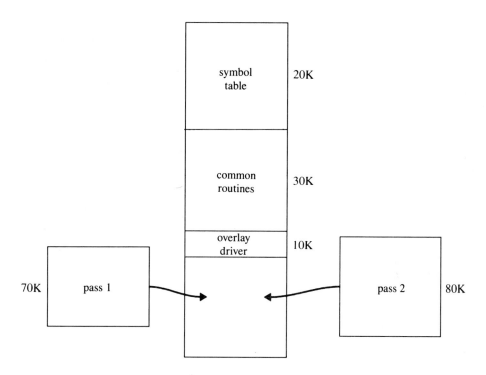

Figure 7.2 Overlays for a two-pass assembler.

7.2 Swapping

A process needs to be in memory to be executed. A process, however, can be *swapped* temporarily out of memory to a *backing store*, and then brought back into memory for continued execution. For example, assume a multiprogramming environment with a round-robin CPU-scheduling algorithm. When a quantum expires, the memory manager will start to swap out the process that just finished, and to swap in another process to the memory space that has been freed (Figure 7.3). In the meantime, the CPU scheduler will allocate a time slice to some other process in memory. When each process finishes its quantum, it will be swapped with another process. Ideally, the memory manager can swap processes fast enough that there are always processes in memory, ready to execute, when the CPU scheduler wants to reschedule the CPU. The quantum must also be sufficiently large that reasonable amounts of computing are done between swaps.

A variant of this swapping policy is used for priority-based scheduling algorithms. If a higher-priority process arrives and wants

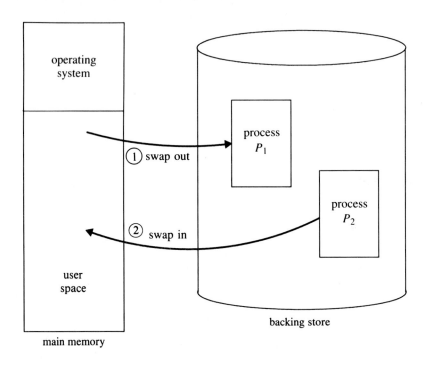

Figure 7.3   Swapping of two processes using a disk as a backing store.

service, the memory manager can swap out the lower-priority process in order to load and execute the higher-priority process. When the higher-priority process finishes, the lower-priority process can be swapped back in and continued. This variant of swapping is sometimes called *roll-out, roll-in*.

Normally a process that is swapped out will be swapped back into the same memory space that it occupied previously This restriction is dictated by the method of address binding. If binding is done at assembly or load time, then the process cannot be moved to different locations. If execution-time binding is being used, then it is possible to swap a process into a different memory space.

Swapping requires a *backing store*. The backing store is commonly a fast disk. It must be large enough to accommodate copies of all memory images for all users, and must provide direct access to these memory images. The system maintains a *ready queue* consisting of all processes whose memory images are on the backing store or in memory and are ready to run. Whenever the CPU scheduler decides to execute a process, it calls the dispatcher. The dispatcher checks to see whether the next process in the queue is in memory. If the process is not, and there is no free memory region, the dispatcher swaps out a process currently in memory and swaps in the desired process. It then reloads registers as normal and transfers control to the selected process.

It should be clear that the context-switch time in such a swapping system is fairly high. To get an idea of the context-switch time, assume that the user process is of size 100K and the backing store is a standard head disk with a transfer rate of 1 megabyte per second. The actual transfer of the 100K process to or from memory takes

$$100K \ / \ 1,000K \text{ per second } = \ 1/10 \text{ second}$$
$$= \ 100 \text{ milliseconds}$$

Assuming an average latency of 8 milliseconds, the swap time takes 108 milliseconds. Since we must both swap out and swap in, the total swap time is then about 216 milliseconds.

For efficient CPU utilization, we want our execution time for each process to be long relative to the swap time. Thus, in a round-robin CPU-scheduling algorithm, for example, the time quantum should be substantially larger than 0.216 seconds.

Notice that the major part of the swap time is transfer time. The total transfer time is directly proportional to the *amount* of memory swapped. If we have a computer system with 1 megabyte of main memory and a resident operating system taking 100K, the maximum size of the user process is 900K. However, many user processes may be much smaller than this size — say, 100K. A 100K process could be swapped out in 108 milliseconds, compared to the 908 milliseconds for swapping 900K. Therefore, it would be useful to know exactly how much memory a user process *is* using, not simply how much it *might be* using. Then, we would need to swap only what is actually used, reducing swap time. For this scheme to be effective, the user must keep the operating system informed of any changes in memory requirements. Thus, a process with dynamic memory requirements will need to issue system calls (**request memory** and **release memory**) to inform the operating system of its changing memory needs.

There are other constraints on swapping. If we want to swap a process, we must be sure that it is completely idle. Of particular concern is any pending I/O. If a process is waiting for an I/O operation, we may want to swap that process to free up its memory. However, if the I/O is asynchronously accessing the user memory for I/O buffers, then the process cannot be swapped. Assume that the I/O operation was queued, because the device was busy. Then, if we were to swap out process P_1 and swap in process P_2, the I/O operation might then attempt to use memory that now belongs to process P_2. The two main solutions to this problem are (1) never to swap a process with pending I/O, or (2) to execute I/O operations only into operating-system buffers. Transfers between operating-system and process memory then occurs only when the process is swapped in.

A modification of swapping was made in an early version of UNIX. Swapping was normally disabled, but would start if many processes were running and were using a threshold amount of memory. Swapping would again be halted if the load on the system was reduced. Currently, standard swapping is used in very few systems.

7.3 Single-Partition Allocation

By far the simplest memory-management scheme is *none*. The user is provided with the bare machine and has complete control over the entire memory space.

This approach has some definite advantages. It provides maximum flexibility to the user: The user can control the use of memory in whatever manner desired. It has maximum simplicity and minimum cost. There is no need for special hardware for this approach to memory management. Nor is there a need for operating-system software.

This system has its limitations, also: It provides no services. The user has complete control over the computer, but the operating system has no control over interrupts, no mechanism to process system calls or errors, and no space to provide multiprogramming. This approach is generally used only on dedicated systems where the users require flexibility and simplicity and are willing to program their own support routines.

The next simplest scheme is to divide memory into two partitions, one for the user and one for the resident operating system. It is possible to place the operating system in either low memory or high memory. The major factor affecting this decision is generally the location of the interrupt vector. Since the interrupt vector is often in low memory, it is more common to place the operating system in low memory. Thus, we shall discuss only the situation where the operating system resides in low memory (Figure 7.4). The development of the other situation is similar.

If the operating system is residing in low memory and a user process is executing in high memory, we need to protect the operating-system code and data from changes (accidental or malicious) by the user process. This protection must be provided by the hardware and can be implemented using a base- and limit-register scheme, as described in Section 2.4. Note that, since we have only one user in memory, the limit register is not necessarily needed here.

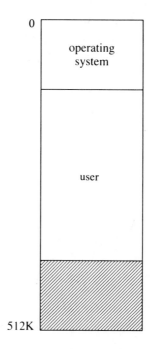

Figure 7.4 Single-user system.

Another problem to consider is the loading of user processes. Although the address space of the computer starts at 00000, the first address of the user program is not 00000, but rather is the first address beyond the base-register value. If the base address is known at compile time, absolute code can be generated. This code will start at the base address and extend up from there. If the base address subsequently changes, however, it will be necessary to recompile this code. As an alternative, the compiler may generate relocatable code. In this case, binding is delayed until load time. If the base address changes, the user code needs only to be reloaded for this changed value to be incorporated.

One difficulty with this scheme is that the base value must be *static* during the execution of the program. Clearly, if the user addresses are bound to physical addresses by use of the base, then these addresses will be invalid if the base changes. Thus, the base address can be changed only when no user program is executing. There are cases, however, when it is desirable to change the size of the operating system (and hence the base location) during program execution. For example, the operating system contains code and buffer space for device drivers. If a device driver (or other operating-system service) is not commonly used, it is undesirable to keep that code and data in memory, since we might be able to use that space for other purposes. Such code is sometimes called *transient* operating-system code; it comes and goes as needed. Thus, using this code changes the size of the operating system during program execution.

There are two ways to modify the basic scheme that we have presented to allow the operating system size to change dynamically. One method is to load the user process into high memory down toward the base-register value, rather than from the base toward high memory (Figure 7.5). The advantage here is that all unused space is in the middle and either the user or the operating system can expand into this unused memory, as necessary.

A more general approach is to delay address binding until *execution* time. This scheme requires slightly different hardware support, as illustrated in Figure 7.6. The base register is now called a *relocation* register. The value in the base register is *added* to every address generated by a user process at the time it is sent to memory. For example, if the base is at 14,000, then an attempt by the user to address location 0 is dynamically relocated to location 14,000; an access to location 346 is relocated to location 14346.

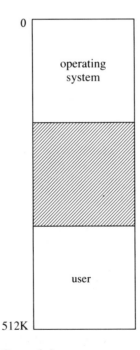

Figure 7.5 Loading of the user process into high memory.

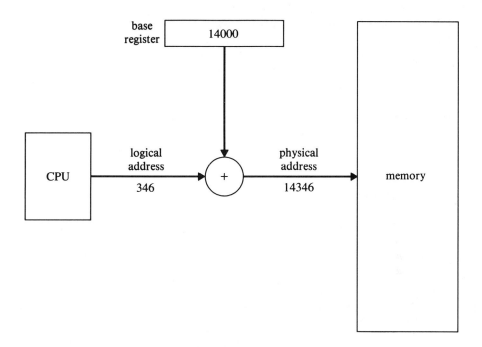

Figure 7.6 Dynamic relocation using a relocation register.

Notice that the user program never sees the *real* physical addresses. The program can create a pointer to location 346, store it in memory, manipulate it, compare it to other addresses — all as the number 346. Only when it is used as a memory address (in an indirect load or store perhaps) is it relocated relative to the base register. The user program deals with *logical* addresses. The memory-mapping hardware converts logical addresses into physical addresses. This form of execution-time binding was discussed in Section 7.1.1. The final location of a referenced memory address is not determined until the reference is made.

For this hardware, a change in the starting location requires only a change in the base register and a move of all user memory to the correct locations relative to the new base value. This scheme may require a significant amount of memory to be copied, but it allows the base to be changed at any time.

Notice also that we now have two different types of addresses: logical addresses (in the range 0 to *max*) and physical addresses (in the range $R + 0$ to $R + max$ for a base value R). The user generates only logical addresses and thinks that the process runs in locations 0 to *max*.

The operating system knows better, and can access physical memory directly in monitor mode. All information passed from the user process to the operating system (such as buffer addresses in system calls) must be relocated explicitly by operating system software before it is used. This requirement is especially important for addresses given to the I/O devices. The user program supplies logical addresses; these logical addresses must be mapped to physical addresses before they are used.

The concept of a *logical address space* that is bound to a separate *physical address space* is central to proper memory management.

7.4 Multiple-Partition Allocation

In a multiprogramming system, many different processes reside in memory, and the CPU is switched rapidly back and forth among these processes. The memory-management problem is to allocate memory to the various processes that are in the input queue waiting to be brought into memory.

One of the simplest schemes for memory allocation is to divide memory into a number of fixed-sized *partitions*. Each partition may contain exactly one process. Thus, the degree of multiprogramming is bounded by the number of partitions. When a partition is free, a process is selected from the input queue and is loaded into the free partition. When the process terminates, the partition becomes available for another process. This scheme was originally used by the IBM OS/360 operating system (called MFT); it is no longer in use. The scheme described in this section is a generalization of the fixed-partition scheme and is used primarily in a batch environment.

7.4.1 Basic Scheme

The operating system keeps a table indicating which parts of memory are available and which are occupied. Initially, all memory is available for user processes, and is considered as one large block of available memory, a *hole*. When a process arrives and needs memory, we search for a hole large enough for this process. If we find one, we allocate only as much memory as is needed, keeping the rest available to satisfy future requests.

For example, assume that we have 2560K of memory available and a resident operating system of 400K. This situation leaves 2160K for user processes, as shown in Figure 7.7. Given the input queue in the figure, and FCFS job scheduling, we can immediately allocate memory to processes P_1, P_2, and P_3, creating the memory map of Figure 7.8(a). We have a hole of size 260K that cannot be used by any of the remaining

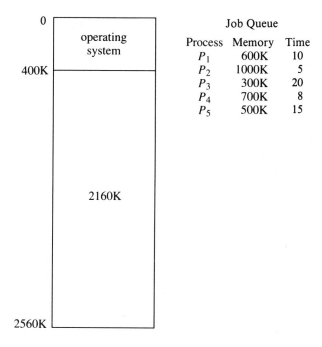

Figure 7.7   Scheduling example.

processes in the input queue. Using a round-robin CPU-scheduling algorithm with a quantum of 1 time unit, process P_2 will terminate at time 14, releasing its memory allocation. This situation is illustrated in Figure 7.8(b). We then return to our job queue and schedule the next process, process P_4, to produce the memory map of Figure 7.8(c). Process P_1 will terminate at time 28 to produce Figure 7.8(d); process P_5 is then scheduled, producing Figure 7.8(e).

This example illustrates several points. In general, there is at any time a *set* of holes, of various sizes, scattered throughout memory. When a process arrives and needs memory, we search this set for a hole that is large enough for this process. If the hole is too large, it is split into two: One part is allocated to the arriving process; the other is returned to the set of holes. When a process terminates, it releases its block of memory, which is then placed back in the set of holes. If the new hole is adjacent to other holes, we merge these adjacent holes to form one larger hole. At this point, we may need to check whether there are processes waiting for memory and whether this newly freed and recombined memory could satisfy the demands of any of these waiting processes.

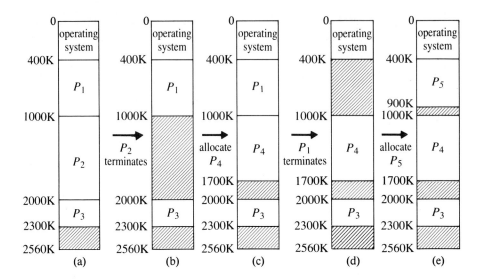

Figure 7.8   Memory allocation and long-term scheduling.

This is a particular application of the general *dynamic storage-allocation* problem, which is how to satisfy a request of size n from a list of free holes. There are many solutions to this problem. The set of holes is searched to determine which hole is best to allocate. *First-fit*, *best-fit*, and *worst-fit* are the most common strategies used to select a free hole from the set of available holes.

- **First-fit**. Allocate the *first* hole that is big enough. Searching can start either at the beginning of the set of holes or where the previous first-fit search ended. We can stop searching as soon as we find a free hole that is large enough.

- **Best-fit**. Allocate the *smallest* hole that is big enough. We must search the entire list, unless the list is kept ordered by size. This strategy produces the smallest leftover hole.

- **Worst-fit**. Allocate the *largest* hole. Again, we must search the entire list, unless it is sorted by size. This strategy produces the largest leftover hole, which may be more useful than the smaller leftover hole from a best-fit approach.

Simulations have shown that both first-fit and best-fit are better than worst-fit in terms of decreasing both time and storage utilization. Neither first-fit nor best-fit is clearly best in terms of storage utilization, but first-fit is generally faster.

These algorithms suffer from *external fragmentation*. As processes are loaded and removed from memory, the free memory space is broken into little pieces. External fragmentation exists when enough total memory space exists to satisfy a request, but it is not contiguous; storage is fragmented into a large number of small holes. Depending on the total amount of memory storage and the average process size, external fragmentation may be either a minor or a major problem. Statistical analysis of first-fit, for instance, reveals that, even with some optimization, given N allocated blocks, another $0.5N$ blocks will be lost due to fragmentation. That is, one-third of memory may be unusable! This is known as the *50-percent rule*.

Once a block of memory has been allocated to a process, the process can be loaded into that space and executed.

Since several processes reside in memory at the same time, memory protection must be available. We can provide this protection by using base and limit registers, similar to those discussed in Section 2.4. The base and limit registers allow dynamic relocation at run time. The base register contains the value of the smallest physical address; the limit register contains the range of logical addresses (for example, base = 100,040 and limit = 74,600). With base and limit registers, each logical address must be less than the limit register; we *dynamically* relocate the logical address by adding the value in the base register. This relocated address is sent to memory (Figure 7.9).

When the CPU scheduler selects this process, the dispatcher loads the base and limit registers with the correct values. Since every address generated by the CPU is checked against these registers, we can protect other users' programs and data from being modified by this running process.

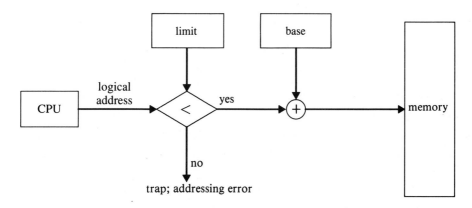

Figure 7.9   Hardware support for base and limit registers.

Another problem that arises with this scheme is illustrated by Figure 7.10. Consider the hole of 18,464 bytes. Suppose that the next process requests 18,462 bytes. If we allocate exactly the requested block, we are left with a hole of 2 bytes. The overhead to keep track of this hole will be substantially larger than the hole itself. The general approach is to allocate very small holes as part of the larger request. Thus, the allocated memory may be slightly larger than the requested memory. The difference between these two numbers is *internal fragmentation* — memory that is internal to a partition, but is not being used.

7.4.2 Long-Term Scheduling

As processes enter the system, they are put into an input queue. The long-term scheduler takes into account the memory requirements of each process and the amount of available memory space in determining which processes are allocated memory. When a process is allocated space, it is loaded into memory (and is relocated if necessary). It can then compete for the CPU. When a process terminates, it releases its memory, which the job scheduler may then fill with another process from the input queue.

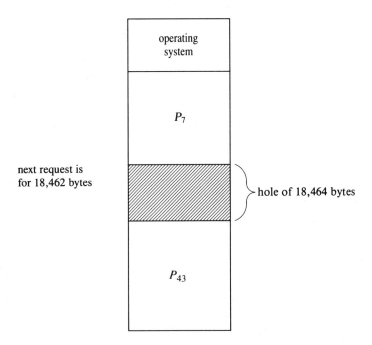

Figure 7.10   Memory allocation made in some multiple of bytes.

At any given time, we have a list of available block sizes and the input queue. The long-term scheduler can order the input queue according to a scheduling algorithm. Memory is allocated to processes until, finally, the memory requirements of the next process cannot be satisfied; no available block of memory (hole) is large enough to hold that process. The long-term scheduler can then wait until a large enough block is available, or it can skip down the input queue to see whether the smaller memory requirements of some lower-priority process can be met. This decision produces a choice between CPU scheduling with and without skip.

With this scheme, there is little or no internal fragmentation, since the partitions are created to be the size requested by the process. However, we can have external fragmentation. Looking back at Figure 7.8, we can see two such situations. In Figure 7.8(a), there is a total external fragmentation of 260K, a space that is too small to satisfy the requests of either of the two remaining processes, P_4 and P_5. In Figure 7.8(c), however, we have a total external fragmentation of 560K (= 300K + 260K). This space would be large enough to run process P_5 (which needs 500K), *except* that this free memory is not contiguous. The free memory space is fragmented into two pieces, neither one of which is large enough, by itself, to satisfy the memory request of process P_5.

This fragmentation problem can be severe. In the worst case, we could have a block of free (wasted) memory between every two processes. If all this memory were in one big free block, we might be able to run several more processes. The selection of first-fit versus best-fit can affect the amount of fragmentation. (First-fit is better for some systems, and best-fit is better for others.) Another factor is which end of a free block is allocated (which is the leftover piece — the one on the top, or the one on the bottom?). No matter which algorithms are used, however, external fragmentation will be a problem.

7.4.3 Compaction

One solution to the problem of external fragmentation is *compaction*. The goal is to shuffle the memory contents to place all free memory together in one large block. For example, the memory map of Figure 7.8(e) can be compacted, as shown in Figure 7.11. The three holes of sizes 100K, 300K, and 260K can be compacted into one hole of size 660K.

Compaction is not always possible. Notice that, in Figure 7.11, we moved processes P_4 and P_3. For these processes to be able to execute in their new locations, all internal addresses must be relocated. If relocation is static and is done at assembly or load time, compaction cannot be done; compaction is possible *only* if relocation is dynamic, and is done at execution time.

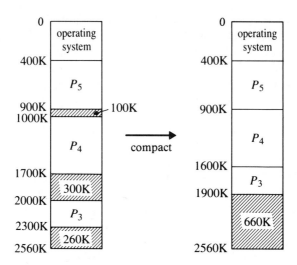

Figure 7.11   Compaction.

If addresses are relocated dynamically, relocation requires only moving the program and data, and then changing the base register to reflect the new base address.

When compaction is possible, we must determine its cost. The simplest compaction algorithm is simply to move all processes toward one end of memory; all holes move in the other direction, producing one large hole of available memory. This scheme can be quite expensive.

Consider the memory allocation shown in Figure 7.12. If we use this simple algorithm, we must move processes P_3 and P_4, for a total of 600K moved. In this situation, we could simply move process P_4 above process P_3, moving only 400K, or move process P_3 below process P_4, moving only 200K. Note that, in this last instance, our one large hole of available memory is not at the end of memory, but rather is in the middle. Also notice that, if the queue contained only one process that wanted 450K, we could satisfy that *particular* request by moving process P_2 somewhere else (such as below process P_4). Although this solution does not create a single large hole, it does create a hole big enough to satisfy the immediate request. Selecting an optimal compaction strategy is quite difficult.

Swapping can also be combined with compaction. A process can be rolled out of main memory to a backing store and rolled in again later. When the process is rolled out, its memory is released, and perhaps is reused for another process. When the process is to be rolled back in, several problems may arise. If static relocation is used, the process must

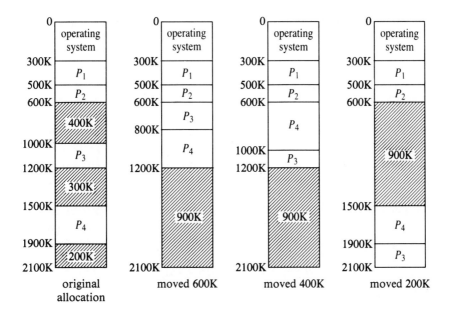

Figure 7.12 Comparison of some different ways to compact memory.

be rolled into the exact same memory locations that it occupied previously. This restriction may require that other processes be rolled out to free that memory.

If dynamic relocation (such as with base and limit registers) is used, then a process can be rolled into a different location. In this case, we find a free block, compacting if necessary, and roll in the process.

One approach to compaction is to roll out those processes to be moved, and to roll them into different memory locations. If swapping or roll-in, roll-out is already a part of the system, the additional code for compaction may be minimal.

7.5 Multiple Base Registers

The main problem with the variable-sized partition scheme is external fragmentation. One way to reduce the average amount of external fragmentation is to break the memory that a process needs into several parts. Each part is smaller than the whole, and thus is easier to pack in memory. For this approach, multiple base registers must be provided with a mechanism for address translation from logical to physical addresses.

One way to accomplish this, is to divide the memory into two disjoint parts. The system has two pairs of base and limit registers. Memory is split in half by use of the high-order address bit. Low memory is relocated and limited by base-limit register pair 0; high memory is relocated and limited by base-limit register pair 1. By convention, compilers and assemblers put read-only values (such as constants and instructions) in high memory and variables in low memory. Protection bits are associated with each register pair and can enforce the read-only nature of high memory. This arrangement allows programs (stored in high memory as read-only) to be shared among many user processes, each with its own separate low-memory segment.

Another way to accomplish this is to separate a program into two parts: code and data. The CPU knows whether it wants an instruction (instruction fetch) or data (data fetch or store). Therefore, two base-limit register pairs are provided: one for instructions and one for data. The instruction base-limit register pair is automatically read-only, so programs can be shared among different users.

In these schemes, by separating the instructions and data, and relocating each separately, we can share programs among different users. Thus, we make better use of memory, by reducing both fragmentation and multiple copies of the same code — particularly commonly used code such as compilers, editors, and so on.

7.6 Paging

The variable-sized partition scheme suffers from external fragmentation. Generally, this situation occurs when available memory is not contiguous, but rather is fragmented into many scattered blocks. Since the memory allocated to a particular process must be contiguous, this scattered, noncontiguous memory cannot be used. This problem has two general solutions. *Compaction* changes the allocation of memory to make free space contiguous, and hence useful. *Paging* permits a process's memory to be noncontiguous, thus allowing a process to be allocated physical memory wherever the latter is available. Paging avoids the considerable problem of fitting the varying-sized memory chunks onto the backing store, from which most of the previous memory-management schemes suffered. When some code fragments or data residing in main memory need to be swapped out, space must be found on the backing store. The fragmentation problems discussed in connection with main memory are also prevalent with backing store, except that access is much slower, so compaction is impossible. Because of its advantages over the previous methods, paging in its various forms is commonly used in many operating systems.

7.6.1 Hardware

Physical memory is broken into fixed-sized blocks called *frames*. Logical memory is also broken into blocks of the same size called *pages*. When a process is to be executed, its pages are loaded into any available frames from the backing store. The backing store is divided into fixed-sized blocks that are of the same size as the memory frames.

The hardware support for paging is illustrated in Figure 7.13. Every address generated by the CPU is divided into two parts: a *page number* (*p*) and a *page offset* (*d*). The page number is used as an index into a *page table*. The page table contains the base address of each page in physical memory. This base address is combined with the page offset to define the physical memory address that is sent to the memory unit. The paging model of memory is shown in Figure 7.14.

The page size (like the frame size) is defined by the hardware. The size of a page is typically a power of 2 varying between 512 words to

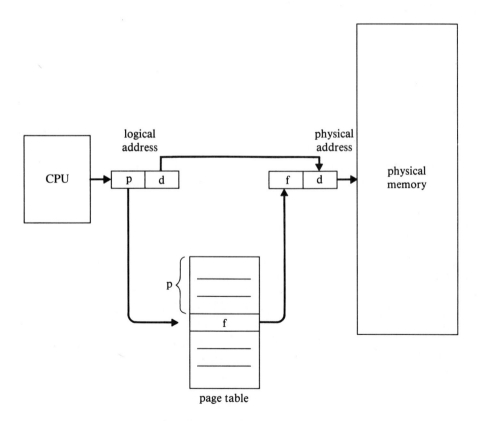

Figure 7.13 Paging hardware.

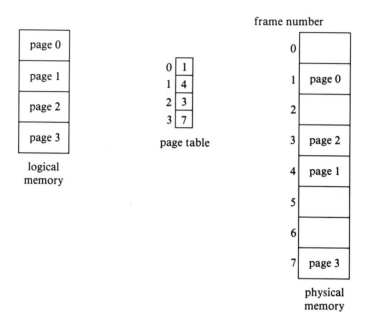

Figure 7.14   Paging model of logical and physical memory.

2048 words per page, depending on the computer architecture. The selection of a power of 2 as a page size makes the translation of a logical address into a page number and page offset particularly easy. If a page size is 2^n addressing units (bytes or words), then the low-order n bits of a logical address designate the page offset, and the remaining, high-order, bits designate the page number.

For a concrete, although minuscule, example, consider the memory of Figure 7.15. Using a page size of four words and a physical memory of 32 words (eight pages), we show an example of how the user's view of memory can be mapped into physical memory. Logical address 0 is page 0, offset 0. Indexing into the page table, we find that page 0 is in frame 5. Thus, logical address 0 maps to physical address 20 (= (5 × 4) + 0). Logical address 3 (page 0, offset 3) maps to physical address 23 (= (5 × 4) + 3). Logical address 4 is page 1, offset 0; according to the page table, page 1 is mapped to frame 6. Thus, logical address 4 maps to physical address 24 (= (6 × 4) + 0). Logical address 13 maps to physical address 9.

Notice that paging itself is a form of dynamic relocation. Every logical address is bound by the paging hardware to some physical address. The observant reader will have realized that paging is similar to using a table of base registers, one for each frame of memory.

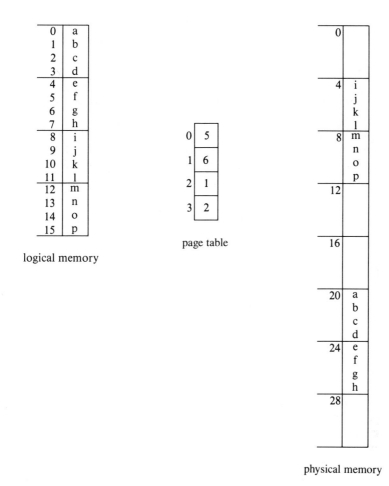

logical memory

page table

physical memory

Figure 7.15 Paging example for a 32-word memory with 4-word pages.

7.6.2 Long-Term Scheduling

The memory-management scheme influences the long-term scheduler. When a process arrives to be executed, the long-term scheduler examines its size. The size of the process is expressed in pages. The long-term scheduler then looks at available memory, which is kept as a list of unallocated frames. Each user page needs one frame. Thus, if the process requires n pages, there must be n frames available in memory. If there are n frames available, the long-term scheduler allocates them to this process. The first page of the process is loaded into one of the allocated frames, and the frame number is put in the page table for this process. The next page is loaded into another frame, and its frame number is put into the page table, and so on (Figure 7.16).

When we use a paging scheme, we have no external fragmentation: *Any* free frame can be allocated to a process that needs it. However, we may have some internal fragmentation. Notice that frames are allocated as units. If the memory requirements of a process do not happen to fall on page boundaries, the *last* frame allocated may not be completely full. For example, if pages are 2048 bytes, a process of 72,766 bytes would need 35 pages plus 1086 bytes. It would be allocated 36 frames, resulting in an internal fragmentation of 2048 − 1086 = 962 bytes. In the worst case, a process would need n pages plus one word. It would be allocated $n + 1$ frames, resulting in an internal fragmentation of almost an entire frame. If process size is independent of page size, we expect internal fragmentation of one-half page per process. This consideration suggests that small page sizes are desirable. However, there is quite a bit of overhead involved in each page-table entry, and this overhead is reduced as the size of the pages increases.

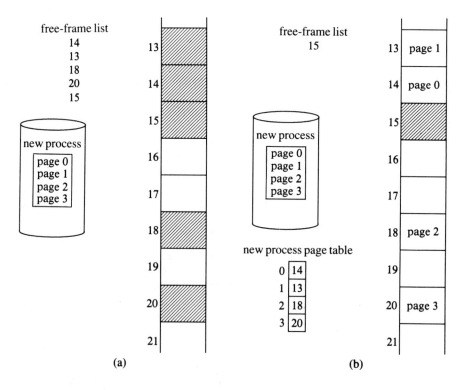

Figure 7.16   Free frames (a) before and (b) after allocation.

Each operating system has its own methods for storing page tables. Most allocate a page table for each process. A pointer to the page table is stored with the other register values (like the instruction counter) in the process control block. When the dispatcher is told to start a process, it must reload the user registers and define the correct hardware page-table values from the stored user page table.

7.6.3 Implementation of the Page Table

The hardware implementation of the page table can be done in a number of different ways. In the simplest case, the page table is implemented as a set of dedicated *registers*. These registers should be built from very high-speed logic to allow the paging address translation to be very efficient. Since every access to memory must go through the paging map, efficiency is a major consideration. The CPU dispatcher reloads these registers just as it reloads the other registers. Instructions to load or modify the page-table registers are, of course, privileged, so that only the operating system can change the memory map.

The use of registers for the page table is satisfactory if the page table is reasonably small (for example, 256 entries). Most contemporary computers, however, allow the page table to be very large (for example, 1 million entries). For these machines, the use of fast registers to implement the page table is not feasible. Rather, the page table is kept in main memory, and a *page-table base register* (PTBR) points to the page table. Changing page tables requires changing only this one register, substantially reducing context-switch time.

The problem with this approach is the time required to access a user memory location. If we want to access location *i*, we must first index into the page table, using the value in the PTBR offset by the page number for *i*. This task requires a memory access. It provides us with the frame number, which is combined with the page offset to produce the actual address. We can then access the desired place in memory. With this scheme, *two* memory accesses are needed to access a word (one for the page-table entry, one for the word). Thus, memory access is slowed by a factor of 2. This delay would be intolerable under most circumstances.

The standard solution to this problem is to use a special, small, hardware memory, variously called *associative registers* or *translation look-aside buffers* (TLBs). A set of associative registers is built of especially high-speed memory. Each register consists of two parts: a key and a value. When the associative registers are presented with an item, it is compared with all keys simultaneously. If the item is found, the corresponding value field is output. The search is very fast; the hardware, however, is quite expensive.

Associative registers are used with page tables in the following way. The associative registers contain only a few of the page table entries. When a logical address is generated by the CPU, its page number is presented to a set of associative registers that contain page numbers and their corresponding frame numbers. If the page number is found in the associative registers, its frame number is immediately available and is used to access memory. The whole task may take less than 10 percent longer than an unmapped memory reference.

If the page number is not in the associative registers, a memory reference to the page table must be made. When the frame number is obtained, we can use it to access memory (as desired). In addition, we add the page number and frame number to the associative registers, so that they will be found very quickly on the next reference.

The percentage of times that a page number is found in the associative registers is called the *hit ratio*. An 80 percent hit ratio means that we find the desired page number in the associative registers 80 percent of the time. If it takes 20 nanoseconds to search the associative registers, and 100 nanoseconds to access memory, then a mapped memory access takes 120 nanoseconds when the page number is in the associative registers. If we fail to find the page number in the associative registers (20 nanoseconds), then we must first access memory for the page table and frame number (100 nanoseconds), and then access the desired word in memory (100 nanoseconds), for a total of 220 nanoseconds. To find the *effective memory access time*, we must weigh each case by its probability:

$$\text{effective access time} = 0.80 \times 120 + 0.20 \times 220$$
$$= 140 \text{ nanoseconds.}$$

In this example, we suffer a 29-percent slowdown in memory access time (from 100 to 140 nanoseconds).

For a 90-percent hit ratio, we have

$$\text{effective access time} = 0.90 \times 120 + 0.10 \times 220$$
$$= 130 \text{ nanoseconds.}$$

This increased hit rate produces only a 23-percent slowdown in memory access time.

The hit ratio is clearly related to the number of associative registers. With between 16 and 512 associative registers, a hit ratio of 80 to 98 percent can be obtained. The Motorola 68030 processor has a 22-entry TLB. The Intel 80486 CPU has 32 registers and claims a 98-percent hit ratio.

7.6.4 Shared Pages

Another advantage of paging is the possibility of *sharing* common code. This consideration is particularly important in a time-sharing environment. Consider a system that supports 40 users, each of whom executes a text editor. If the text editor consists of 150K of code and 50K of data space, we would need 8000K to support the 40 users. If the code is *reentrant*, however, it can be shared, as shown in Figure 7.17. Here we see a three-page editor (each page of size 50K; the large page size is used to simplify the figure) being shared among three processes. Each process has its own data page.

Reentrant code (also called pure code) is non-self-modifying code. If the code is reentrant, then it never changes during execution. Thus, two or more processes can execute the same code at the same time. Each process has its own copy of registers and data storage to hold the data for its execution. The data for two different processes will of course vary for each process.

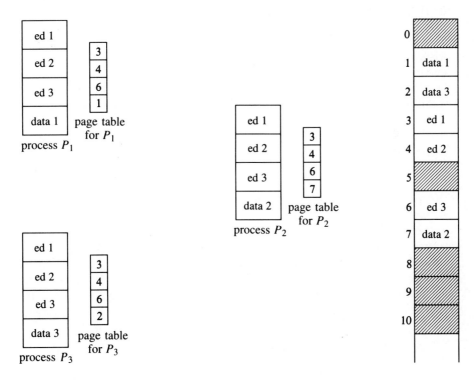

Figure 7.17 Sharing of code in a paging environment.

Only one copy of the editor needs to be kept in physical memory. Each user's page table maps onto the same physical copy of the editor, but data pages are mapped onto different frames. Thus, to support 40 users, we need only one copy of the editor (150K), plus 40 copies of the 50K of data space per user. The total space required is now 2150K, instead of 8000K — a significant savings.

Other heavily used programs also can be shared: compilers, window systems, database systems, and so on. To be sharable, the code must be reentrant. The read-only nature of shared code should not be left to the correctness of the code; the operating system should enforce this property.

7.6.5 Protection

Memory protection in a paged environment is accomplished by protection bits that are associated with each frame. Normally, these bits are kept in the page table. One bit can define a page to be read and write or read-only. Every reference to memory goes through the page table to find the correct frame number. At the same time that the physical address is being computed, the protection bits can be checked to verify that no writes are being made to a read-only page. An attempt to write to a read-only page causes a hardware trap to the operating system (memory-protection violation).

This approach to protection can be expanded easily to provide a finer level of protection. We can create hardware to provide read-only, read-write, or execute-only protection. Or, by providing separate protection bits for each kind of access, any combination of these accesses can be allowed, and illegal attempts will be trapped to the operating system.

It is rare for a process to use all of its address range. In fact, many processes only use a small fraction of the address space available to them. It would be wasteful in these cases to create a page table with entries for every page in the address range. Most of this table would be unused, but would take up valuable memory space. Some systems provide hardware, in the form of a *page-table length register* (PTLR), to indicate the size of the page table. This value is checked against every logical address to verify that the address is in the valid range for the process. Failure of this test causes an error trap to the operating system.

7.6.6 Two Views of Memory

An important aspect of paging is the clear separation between the user's view of memory and the actual physical memory. The user program believes that memory is one contiguous space, containing only this one program. In fact, the user program is scattered throughout physical memory, which also holds other programs. The difference between the user's view of memory and the actual physical memory is reconciled by the address-translation hardware. The logical addresses are translated into physical addresses. This mapping is hidden from the user and is controlled by the operating system.

One result of the separation of logical and physical addresses is that they may in fact not be the same. This separation was particularly useful for the minicomputer manufacturers. Many minicomputers were designed in the 1960s, when memory was expensive and programs had to be small. Thus, most addresses were limited to 15 or 16 bits. With the availability of less expensive semiconductor memory, it became feasible to add more physical memory to these minicomputers. But increasing the address size, to allow the larger 17-bit or 18-bit addresses needed for the increased physical memory, meant either redesigning the instruction set or extending the word size to accommodate the extra bits. Either solution would involve a major change, invalidating all existing programs and documentation. The solution that most manufacturers adopted was memory mapping. Logical addresses (15 or 16 bits) are mapped onto larger (17-bit or 18-bit) physical addresses. With multiprogramming, the system can use all the memory. Individual users, however, cannot use more memory than they could before, since the logical address space has not been increased.

The operating system controls this mapping and can turn it on for the user and off for the operating system. Since the operating system is managing physical memory, it must be aware of the allocation details of physical memory: which frames are allocated, which frames are available, how many total frames there are, and so on. This information is generally kept in a data structure called a *frame table*. The frame table has one entry for each physical page frame, indicating whether the latter is free or allocated and, if it is allocated, to which page of which process or processes.

In addition, the operating system must be aware that user processes operate in user space, and all logical addresses must be mapped to produce physical addresses. If a user makes a system call (to do I/O, for example) and provides an address as a parameter (a buffer, for instance), that address must be mapped to produce the correct physical address. The operating system maintains a copy of the page table for each user, just as it maintains a copy of the instruction counter and register contents. This copy is used to translate logical addresses to physical addresses whenever the operating system must map a logical address to a physical address manually. It is also used by the CPU dispatcher to define the hardware page table when a process is to be allocated the CPU.

7.7 Segmentation

An important aspect of memory management that became unavoidable with paging is the separation of the user's view of memory and the actual physical memory. The user's view of memory is not the same as the actual physical memory. The user's view is mapped onto physical memory. The mapping allows the difference between logical memory and physical memory.

7.7.1 User's View of Memory

What is the real user's view of memory? Does the user think of memory as a linear array of words, some containing instructions and others containing data, or is there some other preferred memory view? There is general agreement that the user or programmer of a system does not think of memory as a linear array of words. Rather, the user prefers to view memory as a collection of variable-sized segments, with no necessary ordering among segments (Figure 7.18).

Consider how you think of a program when you are writing it. You think of it as a main program with a set of subroutines, procedures, functions, or modules. There may also be various data structures: tables, arrays, stacks, variables, and so on. Each of these modules or data elements is referred to by name. You talk about "the symbol table," "function *Sqrt*," "the main program," without caring what addresses in memory these elements occupy. You are not concerned with whether the symbol table is stored before or after the *Sqrt* function. Each of these segments is of variable length; the length is intrinsically defined by the purpose of the segment in the program. Elements within a segment are identified by their offset from the beginning of the segment: the first statement of the program, the seventeenth entry in the symbol table, the fifth instruction of the *Sqrt* function, and so on.

Segmentation is a memory-management scheme that supports this user's view of memory. A logical address space is a collection of segments. Each segment has a name and a length. Addresses specify both the segment name and the offset within the segment. The user therefore specifies each address by two quantities: a segment name and an offset. (Contrast this scheme with paging, where the user specified only a single address, which was partitioned by the hardware into a page number and an offset, all invisible to the programmer.)

For simplicity of implementation, segments are numbered and are referred to by a segment number, rather than by a segment name. Normally, the user program is assembled (or compiled), and the assembler (or compiler) automatically constructs segments reflecting the input program. A Pascal compiler might create separate segments for (1)

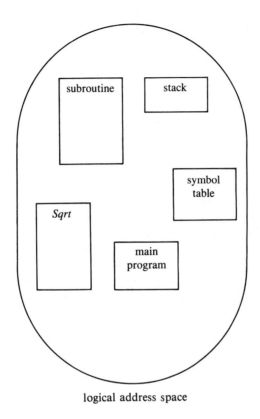

logical address space

Figure 7.18 User's view of a program.

the global variables; (2) the procedure call stack, to store parameters and return addresses; (3) the code portion of each procedure or function; and (4) the local variables of each procedure and function. A FORTRAN compiler might create a separate segment for each common block. Arrays might be assigned separate segments. The loader would take all of these segments and assign them segment numbers.

The Intel 8086 supports segmentation as its only memory-management scheme. Programs in this environment are commonly separated into CODE, DATA, and STACK segments.

7.7.2 Hardware

Although the user can now refer to objects in the program by a two-dimensional address, the actual physical memory is still, of course, a one-dimensional sequence of words. Thus, we must define an implementation to map two-dimensional user-defined addresses into one-dimensional physical addresses. This mapping is effected by a *segment table*.

The use of a segment table is illustrated in Figure 7.19. A logical address consists of two parts: a segment number, s, and an offset into that segment, d. The segment number is used as an index into the segment table. Each entry of the segment table has a segment *base* and a segment *limit*. The offset d of the logical address must be between 0 and the segment limit. If it is not, we trap to the operating system (logical addressing attempt beyond end of segment). If this offset is legal, it is added to the segment base to produce the address in physical memory of the desired word. The segment table is thus essentially an array of base-limit register pairs.

As an example, consider the situation shown in Figure 7.20. We have five segments numbered from 0 through 4. The segments are actually stored in physical memory as shown. The segment table has a separate entry for each segment, giving the beginning address of the segment in physical memory (the base) and the length of that segment (the limit). For example, segment 2 is 400 bytes long, and begins at location 4300. Thus, a reference to byte 53 of segment 2 is mapped onto location 4300 + 53 = 4353. A reference to segment 3, byte 852, is mapped to 3200 (the base of segment 3) + 852 = 4052. A reference to

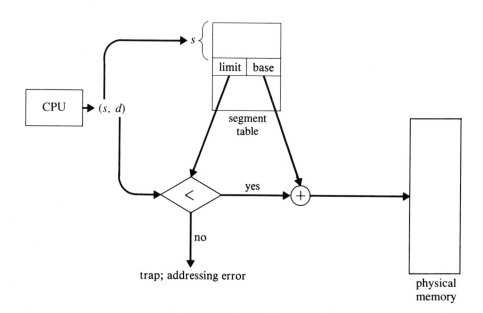

Figure 7.19   Segmentation hardware.

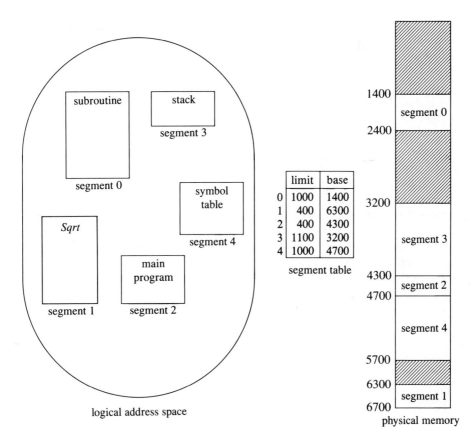

Figure 7.20   Example of segmentation.

byte 1222 of segment 0 would result in a trap to the operating system, since this segment is only 1000 bytes long.

7.7.3 Implementation of Segment Tables

Segmentation is closely related to the partition models of memory management presented earlier, the main difference being that one program may consist of several segments. Segmentation is a more complex concept, however, which is why we are describing it after discussing paging. Like the page table, the segment table can be put either in fast registers or in memory. A segment table kept in registers can be referenced quickly; the addition to the base and comparison with the limit can be done simultaneously to save time.

In the case where a program may consist of a large number of segments, it is not feasible to keep the segment table in registers, so we must keep it in memory. A *segment table base register* (STBR) points to the segment table. Also, since the number of segments used by a program may vary widely, a *segment table length register* (STLR) is used. For a logical address (s,d), we first check that the segment number s is legal (that is, $s <$ STLR). Then, we add the segment number to the STBR, resulting in the address (STBR $+ s$) in memory of the segment-table entry. This entry is read from memory and we proceed as before: Check the offset against the segment length and compute the physical address of the desired word as the sum of the segment base and offset.

As occurs with paging, this mapping requires two memory references per logical address, effectively slowing the computer system by a factor of 2, unless something is done. The normal solution is to use a set of associative registers to hold the most recently used segment-table entries. Again, a relatively small set of associative registers can generally reduce the time required for memory accesses to no more than 10 or 15 percent slower than unmapped memory accesses.

7.7.4 Protection and Sharing

A particular advantage of segmentation is the association of protection with the segments. Since the segments represent a semantically defined portion of the program, it is likely that all entries in the segment will be used the same way. Hence, we have some segments that are instructions, whereas other segments are data. In a modern architecture, instructions are non-self-modifying, so instruction segments can be defined as read-only or execute-only. The memory-mapping hardware will check the protection bits associated with each segment-table entry to prevent illegal accesses to memory, such as attempts to write into a read-only segment or to use an execute-only segment as data. By placing an array in its own segment, the memory-management hardware will automatically check that array indexes are legal and do not stray outside the array boundaries. Thus, many common program errors will be detected by the hardware before they can cause serious damage.

Another advantage of segmentation involves the *sharing* of code or data. Each process has a segment table associated with its process control block, which the dispatcher uses to define the hardware segment table when this process is given the CPU. Segments are shared when entries in the segment tables of two different processes point to the same physical locations. (Figure 7.21).

The sharing occurs at the segment level. Thus, any information can be shared if it is defined to be a segment. Several segments can be shared, so a program composed of several segments can be shared.

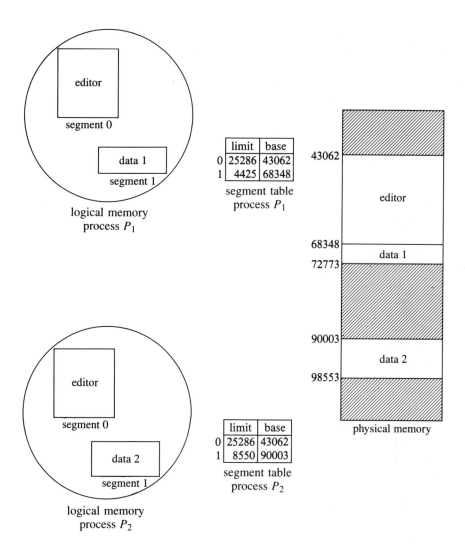

Figure 7.21 Sharing of segments in a segmented memory system.

For example, consider the use of a text editor in a time-sharing system. A complete editor might be quite large, composed of many segments. These segments can be shared among all users, limiting the physical memory needed to support editing tasks. Rather than n copies of the editor, we need only one copy. For each user, we still need separate, unique segments to store local variables. These segments, of course, would not be shared.

It is also possible to share only parts of programs. For example, common subroutine packages can be shared among many users if they are defined as sharable, read-only segments. Two FORTRAN programs, for instance, may use the same *Sqrt* subroutine, but only one physical copy of the *Sqrt* routine would be needed.

Although this sharing appears simple, there are subtle considerations. Code segments typically contain references to themselves. For example, a conditional jump normally has a transfer address. The transfer address is a segment number and offset. The segment number of the transfer address will be the segment number of the code segment. If we try to share this segment, all sharing processes must define the shared code segment to have the same segment number.

For instance, if we want to share the *Sqrt* routine, and one process wants to make it segment 4 and another wants to make it segment 17, how should the *Sqrt* routine refer to itself? Since there is only one physical copy of *Sqrt*, it must refer to itself in the same way for both users — it must have a unique segment number. As the number of users sharing the segment increases, so does the difficulty of finding an acceptable segment number.

Read-only data segments (without pointers) may be shared as different segment numbers, as may code segments that do not refer to themselves directly, but do so only indirectly. For example, conditional branches that specify the branch address as an offset from the current program counter or relative to a register containing the current segment number would allow code to avoid direct reference to the current segment number.

7.7.5 Fragmentation

The long-term scheduler must find and allocate memory for all the segments of a user program. This situation is similar to paging *except* that the segments are of *variable* length; pages are all the same size. Thus, as with the variable-sized partition scheme, memory allocation is a dynamic storage-allocation problem, usually solved with a best-fit or first-fit algorithm.

Segmentation may then cause external fragmentation, when all blocks of free memory are too small to accommodate a segment. In this case, the process may simply have to wait until more memory (or at least a larger hole) becomes available, or compaction may be used to create a larger hole. Since segmentation is by its nature a dynamic relocation algorithm, we can compact memory whenever we want. If the CPU scheduler must wait for one process, due to a memory-allocation problem, it may (or may not) skip through the CPU queue looking for a smaller, lower-priority process to run.

How serious a problem is external fragmentation for a segmentation scheme? Would long-term scheduling with compaction help? The answers to these questions depend mainly on the average segment size. At one extreme, we could define each process to be one segment. This approach reduces to the variable size partition scheme. At the other extreme, every word could be put in its own segment and relocated separately. This arrangement eliminates external fragmentation altogether; however, every word would need a base register for its relocation, doubling memory use! Of course, the next logical step — fixed-size, small segments — is paging. Generally, if the average segment size is small, external fragmentation will also be small. (By analogy, consider putting suitcases in the trunk of a car; they never quite seem to fit. However, if you open the suitcases and put the individual items in the trunk, everything fits.) Since the individual segments are smaller than the overall process, they are more likely to fit in the available memory blocks.

7.8 Paged Segmentation

Both paging and segmentation have their advantages and disadvantages. In fact, of the two most popular microprocessors now being used, the Motorola 68000 line is designed based on a flat address space, whereas the Intel 8086 family is based on segmentation. Both are merging memory models toward a mixture of paging and segmentation. It is possible to combine these two schemes to improve on each. This combination is best illustrated by the innovative but not widely used MULTICS system.

In the MULTICS system, logical addresses are formed from an 18-bit segment number and a 16-bit offset. Although this scheme creates a 34-bit address space, the table overhead is tolerable since the variable number of segments naturally implies an STLR. We need only as many segment-table entries as we have segments; there need be no empty segment-table entries.

However, with segments of 64K words, the average segment size could be large and external fragmentation could be a problem. Even if external fragmentation is not a problem, the search time to allocate a segment, using first-fit or best-fit, could be long. Thus, we may waste memory due to external fragmentation, or waste time due to lengthy searches, or both.

The solution adopted was to *page* the *segments*. Paging eliminates external fragmentation and makes the allocation problem trivial: any empty frame can be used for a desired page. The result is shown in Figure 7.22. Notice that the difference between this solution and pure segmentation is that the segment-table entry contains not the base address of the segment, but rather the base address of a *page table* for this segment. The segment offset is then broken into a 6-bit page number and a 10-bit page offset. The page number indexes into the page table to give the frame number. Finally, the frame number is combined with the page offset to form a physical address.

We must now have a separate page table for each segment. However, since each segment is limited in length by its segment-table entry, the page table does not need to be full sized. It requires only as many entries as are actually needed. In addition, the last page of each

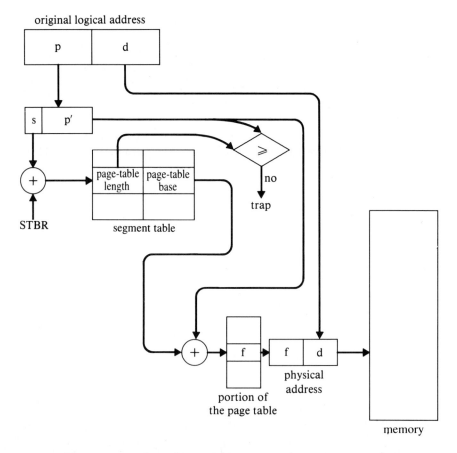

Figure 7.22   Paged segmentation on the GE 645 (MULTICS).

segment generally will not be completely full. Thus, we will have, on the average, one-half page of *internal* fragmentation per segment. Consequently, although we have eliminated external fragmentation, we have introduced internal fragmentation and increased table space overhead.

In truth, even the paged-segmentation view of MULTICS just presented is simplistic. Since the segment number is an 18-bit quantity, we could have up to 262,144 segments, requiring a very large segment table. To ease this problem, MULTICS pages the segment table! Thus, in general, an address in MULTICS uses the segment number to define a page index into a page table for the segment table. From this entry, it locates the part of the segment-table with the entry for this segment. The segment table entry points to a page table for this segment, which specifies the frame containing the desired word.

7.9 Summary

Memory-management algorithms for multiprogrammed operating systems range from the simple single-user system approach to paged segmentation. The greatest determinant of the method used in a particular system is the hardware provided. Every memory address generated by the CPU must be checked for legality and possibly mapped to a physical address. The checking cannot be implemented (efficiently) in software. Hence, we are constrained by the hardware available.

The memory-management algorithms discussed (single and multiple partitions, paging, segmentation, and combinations of paging and segmentation) differ in many aspects. The following list indicates some important considerations in comparing different memory-management strategies:

- **Hardware support**. A simple base register or a pair of base and limit registers is sufficient for the single and multiple partition schemes, whereas paging and segmentation need mapping tables to define the address map.

- **Performance**. As the algorithm becomes more complex, the time required to map a logical address to a physical address increases. For the simple systems, we need only to compare or add to the logical address — operations that are fast. Paging and segmentation can be as fast if the table is implemented in fast registers. If the table is in memory, however, user memory accesses can be substantially degraded. A set of associative registers can reduce the performance degradation to an acceptable level.

- **Fragmentation**. A multiprogrammed system will generally perform better with a higher level of multiprogramming. For a given set of processes, we can increase the multiprogramming level only by packing more processes into memory. To accomplish this task, we must reduce memory waste or fragmentation. Systems with fixed-sized allocation units, such as the single-partition scheme and paging, suffer from internal fragmentation. Systems with variable-sized allocation units, such as the multiple-partition scheme and segmentation, suffer from external fragmentation.

- **Relocation**. One solution to the external-fragmentation problem is compaction. Compaction involves shifting a program in memory without the program noticing the change. This consideration requires that logical addresses be relocated dynamically, at execution time. If addresses are relocated only at load time, we cannot compact storage.

- **Swapping**. Any algorithm can have swapping added to it. At intervals determined by the operating system, usually dictated by CPU-scheduling policies, processes are copied from main memory to a backing store, and later are copied back to main memory. This scheme allows more processes to be run than can be fit into memory at one time.

- **Sharing**. Another means of increasing the multiprogramming level is to share code and data among different users. Sharing generally requires that either paging or segmentation be used, to provide small packets of information (pages or segments) that can be shared. Sharing is a means of running many processes with a limited amount of memory, but shared programs and data must be designed carefully.

- **Protection**. If paging or segmentation is provided, different sections of a user program can be declared execute-only, read-only, or read-write. This restriction is necessary with shared code or data, and is generally useful in any case to provide simple run-time checks for common programming errors.

Exercises

7.1 Explain the difference between logical and physical addresses.

7.2 Consider a logical address space of eight pages of 1024 words each, mapped onto a physical memory of 32 frames.

    a. How many bits are there in the logical address?

    b. How many bits are there in the physical address?

7.3 Explain the following allocation algorithms:

    a. First-fit

    b. Best-fit

    c. Worst-fit

    d. Given memory partitions of 100K, 500K, 200K, 300K, and 600K (in order), how would each of these algorithms in parts a, b, and c place processes of 212K, 417K, 112K, and 426K (in order)? Which algorithm makes the best use of memory?

7.4 Explain the difference between internal and external fragmentation.

7.5 When a process is rolled out, it loses its ability to use the CPU (at least for a while). Describe another situation where a process loses its ability to use the CPU, but where the process does not get rolled out.

7.6 Consider a machine with a relocation register and a limit register. We would like to write an operating system that provides many users with a time-shared BASIC interpreter and editor. No user programs will be compiled; BASIC programs will be only interpreted. No other languages will be provided. Users will be able only to input from and output to their terminals, and to disk files. We have 100K memory, and the BASIC interpreter code takes about 15K. We also have four moving head disks.

    The BASIC program being interpreted will be stored in memory as compressed text and may declare vector and matrix data structures, so the amount of memory for each user is 15K plus program text storage plus data storage. Discuss how the system should allocate memory.

7.7 What is the effect of allowing two entries in a page table to point to the same page frame in memory? Explain how this effect could be used to decrease the amount of time needed to copy a large amount of memory from one place to another. What would the effect of updating some byte in the one page be on the other page?

7.8 Describe the hardware that is required to support paging with an acceptable amount of overhead.

7.9 Consider a paging system with the page table stored in memory.

  a. If a memory reference takes 200 nanoseconds, how long does a paged memory reference take?

  b. If we add associative registers, and 75 percent of all page-table references are found in the associative registers, what is the effective memory reference time? (Assume that finding a page-table entry in the associative registers takes zero time, if the entry is there.)

7.10 Consider the following segment table:

Segment	Base	Length
0	219	600
1	2300	14
2	90	100
3	1327	580
4	1952	96

What are the physical addresses for the following logical addresses?

  a. 0,430

  b. 1,10

  c. 1,11

  d. 2,500

  e. 3,400

  f. 4,112

7.11 Sharing segments among processes without requiring the same segment number is possible in a dynamically linked segmentation system.

  a. Define a system that allows static linking and sharing of segments without requiring that the segment numbers be the same.

  b. Describe a paging scheme that allows pages to be shared without requiring that the page numbers be the same.

Describe a mechanism by which one segment could belong to the address space of two different processes.

7.12 Why are segmentation and paging sometimes combined into one scheme?

7.13 Explain why it is easier to share a reentrant module using segmentation than it is to do so when pure paging is used.

7.14 Describe a mechanism by which one segment could belong to the address space of two different processes.

7.15 Consider a time-shared swapping system with one swapping disk and three fixed partitions in memory. Average latency time for the disk is 4 milliseconds; transfer time for one partition is 6 milliseconds. The idea is to be swapping in and out of one partition while executing the processes in the other two. A process is swapped out to the disk only when it waits for input from its user; it is swapped in when there is a free partition and an input line from its user.

  a. If this is the best of all possible worlds, we would hope to achieve 100-percent utilization of CPU and disk (both busy all the time). For utilization to be 100-percent, how long does a process execute while processing an input line, before waiting for the next line?

  b. If users submit one line every second to be processed, what is the maximum number of users that can be serviced?

7.16 In the IBM/370, memory protection is provided through the use of *keys*. A key is a 4-bit quantity. Each 2048K block of memory has a key (the storage key) associated with it. The CPU also has a key (the protection key) associated with it. A store operation is allowed only if both keys are equal, or if either is zero. Which of the following memory-management schemes could be used successfully with this hardware?

  a. Bare machine

  b. Single-user system

  c. Multiprogramming with a fixed number of processes

  d. Multiprogramming with a variable number of processes

  e. Paging

  f. Segmentation

7.17 Assume that we have a paged memory system with associative registers to hold the most active page-table entries. If the page-table is normally held in memory, and memory access time is 1 microsecond, what is the effective access time if 85 percent of all memory references find their entries in the associative registers?

What is the effective access time if the hit ratio to the associative registers is only 50 percent?

Bibliographic Notes

The fixed-sized partition allocation scheme was used in the IBM OS/360 MFT (multiprogramming with a fixed number of tasks), and in the IBM OS/360 MVT (multiprogramming with a variable number of tasks). Discussions of both systems are presented by Hoare and McKeag [1972]. External and internal fragmentation are discussed by Randell [1969].

Dynamic storage allocation is discussed by Knuth [1973, Section 2.5], who found through simulation results that first-fit is generally superior to best-fit. Additional discussions are offered by Shore [1975], Bays [1977], Stephenson [1983], Bozman et al. [1984], and Olderhoeft et al. [1985]. Discussions concerning the 50-percent rule are offered by Knuth [1973].

The concept of paging can be credited to the designers of the Atlas system, which is described by Kilburn et al. [1961, 1962]. An early paging system is the XDS-940, which is described by Lichtenberger and Pirtle [1965] and Lampson et al. [1966].

Cache memories, including associative memory, are described and analyzed by Smith [1982]. This paper also includes an extensive bibliography on the subject.

The concept of segmentation was first discussed by Dennis [1965]. Systems that employ contiguous allocation per segment include the Burroughs B5700, B6500, and B7600 computer systems, in which address mapping is done in hardware [Organick 1973], and the PDP-11/45 computer system.

Systems that employ paged segmentation include the GE 645, on which MULTICS was originally implemented [Organick 1972], and the RCA Spectra 70/46. The IBM 360/67 system uses a specialized paging scheme to deal with its very large page-table size.

The Motorola 68000 microprocessor family is described in [Motorola 1989a]. The Intel 8086 is shown in [Intel 1985a]; the new Intel 80486 hardware is covered in [Intel 1989].

8

Virtual Memory

In Chapter 7, we discussed various memory-management strategies that have been used in computer systems. All these strategies have the same goal: to keep many processes in memory simultaneously to allow multiprogramming. However, they all require the entire process to be in memory before the process can execute.

Virtual memory is a technique that allows the execution of processes that may not be completely in memory. The main visible advantage of this scheme is that programs can be larger than physical memory. Further, it abstracts main memory into a very large, uniform array of storage, separating logical memory as viewed by the user from physical memory. This frees programmers from concern over memory storage limitations. Virtual memory is not easy to implement, however, and may substantially decrease performance if it is used carelessly. In this chapter, we discuss virtual memory in the form of demand paging, and examine its complexity and cost.

8.1 Motivation

The memory-management algorithms of Chapter 7 are necessary because of one basic requirement: The entire logical address space of a process must be in physical memory before the process can execute. This restriction seems both necessary and reasonable, but it is also unfortunate, since it limits the size of a program to the size of physical memory.

In fact, an examination of real programs shows us that, in many cases, the entire program is not needed. For instance,

- Programs often have code to handle unusual error conditions. Since these errors seldom, if ever, occur in practice, this code is almost never executed.

- Arrays, lists, and tables are often allocated more memory than they actually need. An array may be declared 100 by 100 elements, even though it is seldom larger than 10 by 10 elements. An assembler symbol table may have room for 3000 symbols, although the average program has less than 200 symbols.

- Certain options and features of a program may be used rarely, such as a text-editor command to convert all characters in a range of lines to upper-case characters.

Even in those cases where the entire program is needed, it may not all be needed at the same time. (This was the case with overlays, for example.)

The ability to execute a program that is only partially in memory would have many benefits:

- A program would no longer be constrained by the amount of physical memory that is available. Users would be able to write programs for a very large *virtual* address space, simplifying the programming task.

- Since each user program could take less physical memory, more programs could be run at the same time, with a corresponding increase in CPU utilization and throughput, but with no increase in response time or turnaround time.

- Less I/O would be needed to load or swap each user program into memory, so each user program would run faster.

Thus, running a program that is not entirely in memory would benefit both the system and the user.

Virtual memory is the separation of user logical memory from physical memory. This separation allows a very large virtual memory to be provided for programmers when only a smaller physical memory is available (Figure 8.1). Virtual memory makes the task of programming much easier, since the programmer no longer needs to worry about the amount of physical memory available, but can concentrate instead on the problem to be programmed. One result of virtual memory has been the near disappearance of overlays.

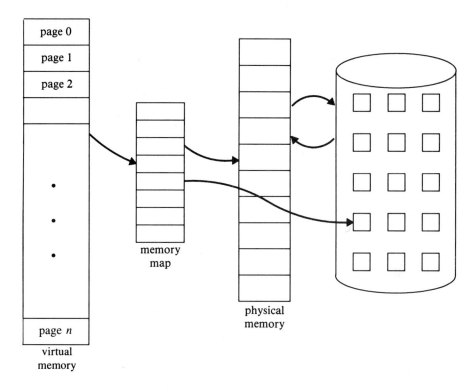

Figure 8.1 Virtual memory can be much larger than physical memory.

Virtual memory is commonly implemented by *demand paging*. It can also be implemented in a segmentation system. Several systems provide a paged segmentation scheme, where segments are broken into pages. Thus, the user view is segmentation, but the operating system can implement this view with demand paging. *Demand segmentation* can also be used to provide virtual memory. Burroughs' computer systems have used demand segmentation. The IBM OS/2 operating system also uses demand segmentation. However, segment-replacement algorithms are more complex than are page-replacement algorithms because the segments have variable sizes.

8.2 Demand Paging

A demand-paging system is similar to a paging system with swapping (Figure 8.2). Processes reside on secondary memory (which is usually a disk). When we want to execute a process, we swap it into memory.

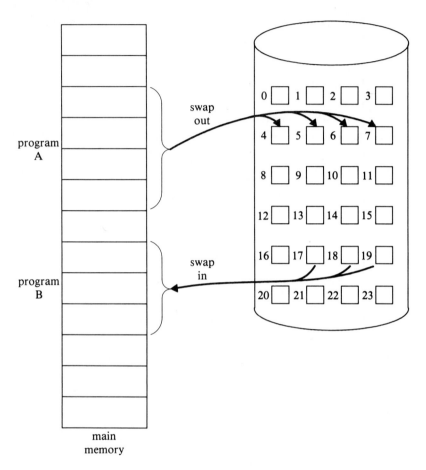

program
A

swap
out

swap
in

program
B

main
memory

0 1 2 3
4 5 6 7
8 9 10 11
12 13 14 15
16 17 18 19
20 21 22 23

Figure 8.2   Transfer of a paged memory to contiguous disk space.

Rather than swapping the entire process into memory, however, we use a "lazy" swapper. A lazy swapper never swaps a page into memory unless that page will be needed. Since we are now viewing a process as a sequence of pages, rather than one large contiguous address space, the use of the term *swap* is technically incorrect. A swapper manipulates entire processes, whereas a *pager* is concerned with the individual pages of a process. We shall thus use the term *pager* rather than *swapper* in connection with demand paging.

When a process is to be swapped in, the pager guesses which pages will be used (before the process is swapped out again). Instead of swapping in a whole process, the pager brings only those necessary pages into memory. Thus, it avoids reading into memory pages that will not be used anyway, decreasing the swap time and the amount of physical memory needed.

This scheme requires hardware support. One more bit is generally attached to each entry in the page table: a *valid-invalid* bit. When this bit is set to "valid," this value indicates that the associated page is in memory. If the bit is set to "invalid," this value indicates that the page is on disk. The page-table entry for a page that is brought in is set as usual, but the page-table entry for a page that is not loaded in is simply marked invalid. This situation is depicted in Figure 8.3.

Notice that marking a page invalid will have no effect if the process never attempts to access that page. Hence, if we guess right and page in

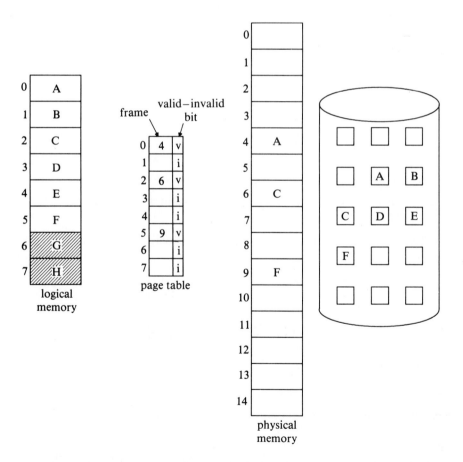

Figure 8.3 Page table when some pages are not in main memory.

all and only those pages that are actually needed, the process will run exactly as though we had brought in all pages. While the process executes and accesses pages that are *memory resident*, execution proceeds normally.

But what happens if the process tries to use a page that was not brought into memory? If we guess wrong and the process tries to access a page that was not brought into memory, then a *page-fault* trap will occur. The paging hardware, in translating the address through the page table, will notice that the invalid bit is set, causing a trap to the operating system (invalid address error). Normally, an invalid address error is the result of an attempt to use an illegal memory address (such as an incorrect array subscript). In such a case, the process should be terminated. In this case, however, the trap is the result of the operating system's failure to bring a valid part of the process into memory, in an attempt to minimize disk transfer overhead and memory requirements. We must therefore correct this oversight. The procedure is quite simple (Figure 8.4):

1. We check an internal table (usually kept with the process control block) for this process, to determine whether the reference was a valid or invalid memory access.

2. If it was invalid, we terminate the process. If it was a valid reference, but we have not yet brought in that page, we now page in the latter.

3. We find a free frame (by taking one from the free-frame list, for example).

4. We schedule a disk operation to read the desired page into the newly allocated frame.

5. When the disk read is complete, we modify the internal table kept with the process and the page table to indicate that the page is now in memory.

6. We restart the instruction that was interrupted by the illegal address trap. The process can now access the page as though it had always been in memory.

It is important to realize that, because we save the state (registers, condition code, instruction counter) of the interrupted process when the page fault occurs, we can restart the process in *exactly* the same place and state, except that the desired page is now in memory and is accessible. In this way, we are able to execute a process, even though portions of it are not (yet) in memory. When the process tries to access

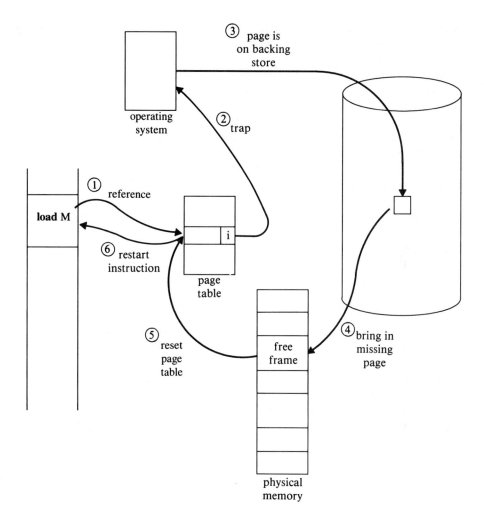

Figure 8.4 Steps in handling a page fault.

locations that are not in memory, the hardware traps to the operating system (page fault). The operating system reads the desired page into memory and restarts the process as though the page had always been in memory.

In the extreme case, we could start executing a process with *no* pages in memory. The process would immediately fault for the page with the first instruction. After this page was brought into memory, the process would continue to execute, faulting as necessary until every page that it needed was actually in memory. At that point, it could execute with no more faults. This is *pure demand paging*: Never bring a page into memory until it is required.

Theoretically, some programs may access a new page of memory with each instruction execution, possibly causing one page fault per instruction. This situation would result in unacceptable system performance. Fortunately, analysis of running processes show that this behavior is a very unlikely. Programs tend to have *locality of reference*, described in Section 8.7, which results in reasonable performance from demand paging.

The hardware to support demand paging is the same as the hardware for paging and swapping:

- **Page table**. This table has the ability to mark an entry invalid through a valid-invalid bit or special value of protection bits.

- **Secondary memory**. This memory holds those pages not in main memory. The secondary memory is usually a high-speed disk.   It is known as the swap device, and the section of disk used for this purpose is known as *swap space* or *backing store*.

In addition to this hardware support, considerable software is needed, as we shall see.

Some additional architectural constraints must be imposed. A crucial issue is the need to be able to restart any instruction after a page fault. In most cases, this requirement is easy to meet. A page fault could occur at any memory reference. If the page fault occurs on the instruction fetch, we can restart by fetching the instruction again. If a page fault occurs while we are fetching an operand, we must refetch the instruction, decode it again, and then fetch the operand.

As a worst case, consider a three-address instruction such as *ADD A* to *B* placing the result in *C*. The steps to execute this instruction would be

1. Fetch and decode the instruction (*ADD*).

2. Fetch *A*.

3. Fetch *B*.

4. Add *A* and *B*.

5. Store the sum in *C*.

If we faulted when we tried to store in *C* (because *C* is in a page not currently in memory), we would have to get the desired page, bring it in, correct the page table, and restart the instruction. The restart would require fetching the instruction again, decoding it again, fetching the two operands again, and then adding again. However, there is really not much repeated work (less than one complete instruction), and the repetition is necessary only when a page fault occurs.

The major difficulty occurs when one instruction may modify several different locations. For example, consider the IBM System 360/370 MVC (move character) instruction, which can move up to 256 bytes from one location to another (possibly overlapping) location. If either block (source or destination) straddles a page boundary, a page fault might occur after the move is partially done. In addition, if the source and destination blocks overlap, the source block may have been modified, in which case we cannot simply restart the instruction.

This problem is solved in two different ways, depending on the model. In one solution, the microcode computes and attempts to access both ends of both blocks. If a page fault is going to occur, it will happen at this step, before anything is modified. The move can then take place, as we know that no page fault can occur, since all the relevant pages are in memory. The other solution uses temporary registers to hold the values of overwritten locations. If there is a page fault, all the old values are written back into memory before the trap occurs. This action restores memory to its state before the instruction was started, so that the instruction can be repeated.

A similar architectural problem occurs in machines that use special addressing modes including autodecrement and autoincrement modes (for example, the PDP-11). These addressing modes use a register as a pointer and automatically decrement or increment the register as indicated. Autodecrement automatically decrements the register *before* using its contents as the operand address; autoincrement automatically increments the register *after* using its contents as the operand address. Thus, the instruction

$$MOV\ (R2)+,-(R3)$$

copies the contents of the location pointed to by register 2 into the location pointed to by register 3. Register 2 is incremented (by 2 for a word, since the PDP-11 is a byte-addressable computer) after it is used as a pointer; register 3 is decremented (by 2) before it is used as a pointer. Now consider what will happen if we get a fault when trying to store into the location pointed to by register 3. To restart the instruction, we must reset the two registers to the values they had before we started the execution of the instruction. One solution is to create a new special status register to record the register number and amount modified for any register that is changed during the execution of an instruction. This status register allows the operating system to "undo" the effects of a partially executed instruction that causes a page fault.

These are by no means the only architectural problems resulting from adding paging to an existing architecture to allow demand paging, but they illustrate some of the difficulties. Paging is added between the CPU and the memory in a computer system. It should be entirely transparent to the user process. Thus, people often assume that paging could be added to any system. Although this assumption is true for paging for relocation, where a page fault represents a fatal error, it is not correct when a page fault means only that an additional page must be brought into memory and the process restarted.

8.3 Performance of Demand Paging

Demand paging can have a significant effect on the performance of a computer system. To see why, let us compute the *effective access time* for a demand-paged memory. The memory access time, *ma*, for most computer systems now ranges from 10 to 200 nanoseconds. As long as we have no page faults, the effective access time is equal to the memory access time. If, however, a page fault occurs, we must first read the relevant page from disk, and then access the desired word.

Let p be the probability of a page fault ($0 \leq p \leq 1$). We would expect p to be very close to zero; that is, there will be only a few page faults. The *effective* access time is then

$$\text{effective access time} = (1-p) \times ma + p \times \text{page fault time}$$

To compute the effective access time, we must know how much time is needed to service a page fault. A page fault causes the following sequence to occur:

1. Trap to the operating system.

2. Save the user registers and process state.

3. Determine that the interrupt was a page fault.

4. Check that the page reference was legal and determine the location of the page on the disk.

5. Issue a read from the disk to a free frame:

   a. Wait in a queue for this device until the read request is serviced.

   b. Wait for the device seek and/or latency time.

   c. Begin the transfer of the page to a free frame.

6. While waiting, allocate the CPU to some other user (CPU scheduling; optional).

7. Interrupt from the disk (I/O completed).

8. Save the registers and process state for the other user.

9. Determine that the interrupt was from the disk.

10. Correct the page table and other tables to show that the desired page is now in memory.

11. Wait for the CPU to be allocated to this process again.

12. Restore the user registers, process state, and new page table, then resume the interrupted instruction.

Not all of these steps may be necessary in every case. For example, we are assuming that, in step 5, the CPU is allocated to another process while the I/O occurs. This arrangement allows multiprogramming to maintain CPU utilization, but requires additional time to resume the page-fault service routine when the I/O transfer is complete.

In any case, we are faced with three major components of the page-fault service time:

- Service the page-fault interrupt.

- Read in the page.

- Restart the process.

The first and third tasks may be reduced, with careful coding, to several hundred instructions. These tasks may take from 1 to 100 microseconds each. The page-switch time, on the other hand, will probably be close to 24 milliseconds. A typical moving-head disk has a latency of 8 milliseconds, a seek of 15 milliseconds and a transfer time of 1 millisecond. Thus, the total paging time would be close to 25 milliseconds, including hardware and software time. Remember also that we are looking at only the device service time. If a queue of processes is waiting for the device (other processes that have caused page faults), we have to add device queueing time as we wait for the paging device to be free to service our request, increasing the time to swap even more.

If we take an average page-fault service time of 25 milliseconds and a memory access time of 100 nanoseconds, then the effective access time in nanoseconds is

$$
\begin{aligned}
\text{effective access time} &= (1-p) \times (100) + p \times (25 \text{ milliseconds}) \\
&= (1-p) \times 100 + p \times 25{,}000{,}000 \\
&= 100 + 24{,}999{,}900 \times p.
\end{aligned}
$$

We see then that the effective access time is directly proportional to the page-fault rate. If one access out of 1000 causes a page fault, the effective access time is 25 microseconds. The computer would be slowed down by a factor of 250 because of demand paging. If we want less than 10-percent degradation, we need

$$110 > 100 + 25{,}000{,}000 \times p,$$
$$10 > 25{,}000{,}000 \times p,$$
$$p < 0.0000004.$$

That is, to keep the slowdown due to paging to a reasonable level, we can allow only less than 1 memory access out of 2,500,000 to page fault.

It is very important to keep the page-fault rate low in a demand-paging system. Otherwise, the effective access time increases, slowing process execution dramatically.

One additional aspect of demand paging is the handling and overall use of swap space. Disk I/O to swap space is generally faster than that to the file system. It is faster because swap space is allocated in much larger blocks, and file lookups and indirect allocation methods are not used. It is therefore possible for the system to gain better paging throughput, by copying an entire file image into the swap space at process startup, and then to perform demand paging from the swap space. Systems with limited swap space can still employ such a scheme when binary files are used. Demand pages for such files are brought directly from the file system. However, when page replacement is called for, these pages can simply be overwritten (since they are never modified) and read in from the file system again if needed. Yet another option is initially to demand pages from the file system, but to write the pages to swap space as they are replaced. This approach will ensure that only needed pages are ever read from the file system, but all subsequent paging is done from swap space. This method appears to be the optimum one; it is used in BSD UNIX.

8.4 Page Replacement

In our presentation so far, the page-fault rate is not a serious problem, since each page is faulted for at most once, when it is first referenced. This representation is not strictly accurate. Consider that, if a process of 10 pages actually uses only one-half of them, then demand paging saves the I/O necessary to load the five pages that are never used. We could also increase our degree of multiprogramming by running twice as many processes. Thus, if we had 40 frames, we could run eight processes, rather than the four that could run if each required 10 frames (five of which were never used).

If we increase our degree of multiprogramming, we are *overallocating* memory. If we run six processes, each of which is 10 pages in size, but actually uses only five pages, we have higher CPU utilization and throughput, with 10 frames to spare. It is possible, however, that each of these processes, for a particular data set, may suddenly try to use all 10 of its pages, resulting in a need for 60 frames, when only 40 are available. Although this situation may be unlikely, it becomes much more likely as we increase the multiprogramming level, so that the average memory usage is close to the available physical memory. (In our example, why stop at a multiprogramming level of six, when we can move to a level of seven or eight?)

Overallocation will show up in the following way. While a user process is executing, a page fault occurs. The hardware traps to the operating system, which checks its internal tables to see that this is a page fault and not an illegal memory access. The operating system determines where the desired page is residing on the disk, but then finds there are *no* free-frames on the free-frame list; all of memory is in use (Figure 8.5).

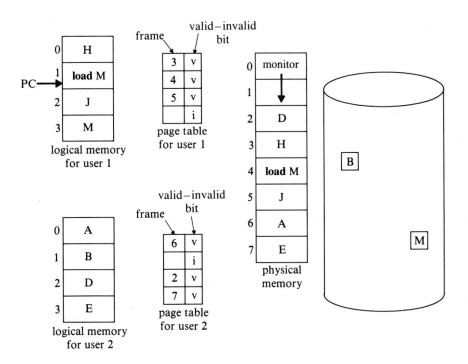

Figure 8.5 Need for page replacement.

The operating system has several options at this point. It could terminate the user process. However, demand paging is something that the *operating system* is doing to improve the computer system's utilization and throughput. Users should not be aware that their processes are running on a paged system. Paging should be logically transparent to the user. So this option is not the best choice.

We could swap out a process, freeing all its frames, and reducing the level of multiprogramming. This is a good idea at times, and we consider it further in Section 8.7, but first we shall discuss a more intriguing possibility: *page replacement*.

Page replacement takes the following approach. If no frame is free, we find one that is not currently being used and free it. We can free a frame by writing its contents to the disk, and changing the page table (and all other tables) to indicate that the page is no longer in memory (Figure 8.6). The freed frame can now be used to hold the page for

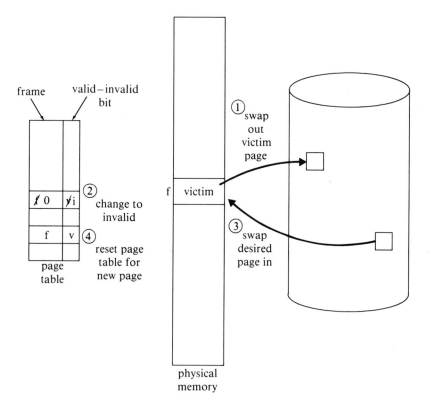

Figure 8.6 Page replacement.

which the process faulted. The page-fault service routine is now modified to include page replacement:

1. Find the location of the desired page on the disk.

2. Find a free frame:

    a. If there is a free frame, use it.

    b. Otherwise, use a page-replacement algorithm to select a *victim* frame.

    c. Write the victim page to the disk; change the page and frame tables accordingly.

3. Read the desired page into the (newly) free frame; change the page and frame tables.

4. Restart the user process.

Notice that, if no frames are free, *two* page transfers (one out and one in) are required. This situation effectively doubles the page-fault service time and will increase the effective access time accordingly.

This overhead can be reduced by the use of a *modify* (*dirty*) *bit*. Each page or frame may have a modify bit associated with it in the hardware. The modify bit for a page is set by the hardware whenever any word or byte in the page is written into, indicating that the page has been modified. When we select a page for replacement, we examine its modify bit (each page has its own modify bit). If the bit is set, we know that the page has been modified since it was read in from the disk. In this case, we must write that page to the disk. If the modify bit is not set, however, the page has *not* been modified since it was read into memory. Therefore, if the copy of the page on the disk has not been overwritten (by some other page, for example), we can avoid writing the memory page to the disk; it is already there. This technique also applies to read-only pages (for example, pages of binary code). Such pages cannot be modified; thus, they may be discarded when desired. This scheme can significantly reduce the time to service a page fault, since it reduces I/O time by one-half *if* the page is not modified.

Page replacement is basic to demand paging. It completes the separation between logical memory and physical memory. With this mechanism, a very large virtual memory can be provided for programmers on a smaller physical memory. With nondemand paging, user addresses were mapped into physical addresses, allowing the two sets of addresses to be quite different. With demand paging, the size of the logical address space is no longer constrained by physical memory. If we have a user process of 20 pages, we can execute it in 10 frames simply by using demand paging, and using a replacement algorithm to find a free frame whenever necessary. If a page is to be replaced, its contents are copied to the disk. A later reference to that page will cause a page fault. At that time, the page will be brought back into memory, perhaps replacing some other page in the process.

We must solve two major problems to implement demand paging: We must develop a *frame-allocation algorithm* and a *page-replacement algorithm*. If we have multiple processes in memory, we must decide how many frames to allocate to each process. Further, when page replacement is required, we must select the frames that are to be replaced. Designing appropriate algorithms to solve these problems is an important task, since disk I/O is so expensive. Even slight improvements in demand-paging methods yield large gains in system performance.

8.5 Page-Replacement Algorithms

There are many different page-replacement algorithms. Probably every operating system has its own unique replacement scheme. How do we select a particular replacement algorithm? In general, we want the one with the lowest *page-fault rate*.

We evaluate an algorithm by running it on a particular string of memory references and computing the number of page faults. The string of memory references is called a *reference string*. We can generate reference strings artificially (by a random-number generator, for example) or by tracing a given system and recording the address of each memory reference. The latter choice produces a very large number of data (on the order of a million addresses per second). To reduce the number of data, we note two things.

First, for a given page size (and the page size is generally fixed by the hardware or system), we need to consider only the page number, not the entire address. Second, if we have a reference to a page p, then any *immediately* following references to page p will never cause a page fault. Page p will be in memory after the first reference; the immediately following references will not fault.

For example, if we trace a particular process, we might record the following address sequence:

0100, 0432, 0101, 0612, 0102, 0103, 0104, 0101, 0611, 0102, 0103, 0104, 0101, 0610, 0102, 0103, 0104, 0101, 0609, 0102, 0105, which, at 100 bytes per page, is reduced to the following reference string

$$1, 4, 1, 6, 1, 6, 1, 6, 1, 6, 1.$$

To determine the number of page faults for a particular reference string and page-replacement algorithm, we also need to know the number of page frames available. Obviously, as the number of frames available increases, the number of page faults will decrease. For the reference string considered previously, for example, if we had three or more frames, we would have only three faults, one fault for the first reference to each page. On the other hand, with only one frame available, we would have a replacement with every reference, resulting in 11 faults. In general, we expect a curve such as that in Figure 8.7. As the number of frames increases, the number of page faults drops to some minimal level.

To illustrate the page-replacement algorithms, we shall use the reference string

$$7, 0, 1, 2, 0, 3, 0, 4, 2, 3, 0, 3, 2, 1, 2, 0, 1, 7, 0, 1$$

for a memory with three frames.

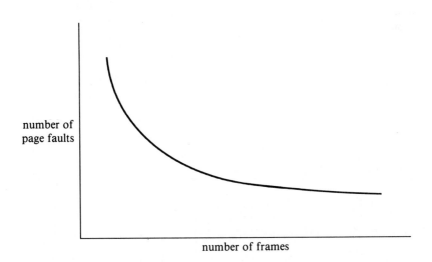

Figure 8.7 Graph of page faults versus the number of frames.

8.5.1 FIFO Algorithm

The simplest page-replacement algorithm is a *first-in, first-out* (FIFO) algorithm. A FIFO replacement algorithm associates with each page the time when that page was brought into memory. When a page must be replaced, the oldest page is chosen. Notice that it is not strictly necessary to record the time when a page is brought in. We can create a FIFO queue to hold all pages in memory. We replace the page at the head of the queue. When a page is brought into memory, we insert it at the tail of the queue.

For our example reference string, our three frames are initially empty. The first three references (7, 0, 1) cause page faults, and are brought into these empty frames. The next reference (2) replaces page 7, since page 7 was brought in first. Since 0 is the next reference and 0 is already in memory, we have no fault for this reference. The first reference to 3 results in page 0 being replaced, since it was the first of the three pages in memory (0, 1, and 2) to be brought in. This replacement means that the next reference, to 0, will fault. Page 1 is then replaced by page 0. This process continues as shown in Figure 8.8. Every time a fault occurs, we show which pages are in our three frames. There are 15 faults altogether.

The FIFO page-replacement algorithm is easy to understand and program. However, its performance is not always good. The page replaced may be an initialization module that was used a long time ago and is no longer needed. On the other hand, it could contain a heavily used variable that was initialized early and is in constant use.

Notice that, even if we select for replacement a page that is in active use, everything still works correctly. After we page out an active page to bring in a new one, we almost immediately fault for the active page. Some other page will need to be replaced in order to bring the active page back into memory. Thus, a bad replacement choice increases the page-fault rate and slows process execution, but does not cause incorrect execution.

reference string

7 0 1 2 0 3 0 4 2 3 0 3 2 1 2 0 1 7 0 1

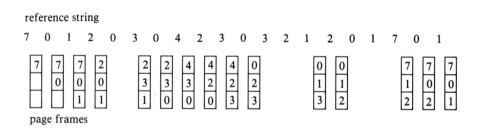

page frames

Figure 8.8   FIFO page-replacement algorithm.

To illustrate the problems that are possible with a FIFO page-replacement algorithm, we consider the reference string

$$1, 2, 3, 4, 1, 2, 5, 1, 2, 3, 4, 5.$$

Figure 8.9 shows the curve of page faults versus the number of available frames. We notice that the number of faults for four frames (10) is *greater* than the number of faults for three frames (nine)! This result is most unexpected and is known as *Belady's anomaly*. Belady's anomaly reflects the fact that, for some page-replacement algorithms, the page-fault rate may *increase* as the number of allocated frames increases. We would expect that giving more memory to a process would improve its performance. In some early research, investigators noticed that this assumption was not always true. Belady's anomaly was discovered as a result.

8.5.2 Optimal Algorithm

One result of the discovery of Belady's anomaly was the search for an *optimal* page-replacement algorithm. An optimal page-replacement algorithm has the lowest page-fault rate of all algorithms. An optimal

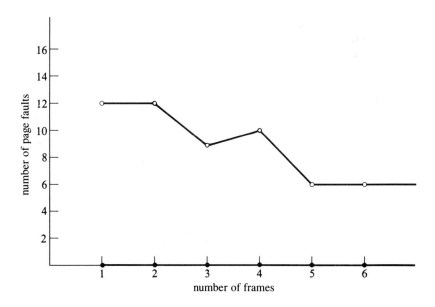

Figure 8.9   Page-fault curve for FIFO replacement on a reference string.

algorithm will never suffer from Belady's anomaly. An optimal page-replacement algorithm exists, and has been called OPT or MIN. It is simply

> Replace the page that will not be used
> for the longest period of time.

Use of this page-replacement algorithm guarantees the lowest possible page-fault rate for a fixed number of frames.

For example, on our sample reference string, the optimal page-replacement algorithm would yield nine page faults, as shown in Figure 8.10. The first three references cause faults that fill the three empty frames. The reference to page 2 replaces page 7, because 7 will not be used until reference 18, whereas page 0 will be used at 5, and page 1 at 14. The reference to page 3 replaces page 1, since page 1 will be the last of the three pages in memory to be referenced again. With only nine page faults, optimal replacement is much better than is a FIFO algorithm, which had 15 faults. (If we ignore the first three, which all algorithms must suffer, then optimal replacement is twice as good as FIFO replacement.) In fact, no replacement algorithm can process this reference string in three frames with less than nine faults.

Unfortunately, the optimal page-replacement algorithm is difficult to implement, since it requires future knowledge of the reference string. (We encountered a similar situation with the SJF CPU-scheduling algorithm in Section 4.5.2.) As a result, the optimal algorithm is used mainly for comparison studies. It may be quite useful to know that although a new algorithm is not optimal, it is within 12.3 percent of optimal at worst and within 4.7 percent on average.

8.5.3 LRU Algorithm

If the optimal algorithm is not feasible, perhaps an approximation to the optimal algorithm is possible. The key distinction between the FIFO and

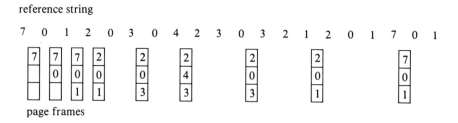

Figure 8.10 Optimal page-replacement algorithm.

OPT algorithms (other than looking backward or forward in time) is that the FIFO algorithm uses the time when a page was brought into memory; the OPT algorithm uses the time when a page is to be *used*. If we use the recent past as an approximation of the near future, then we will replace the page that *has not been used* for the longest period of time (Figure 8.11). This is the *least recently used* (LRU) algorithm.

LRU replacement associates with each page the time of that page's last use. When a page must be replaced, LRU chooses that page that has not been used for the longest period of time. This is the optimal page-replacement algorithm looking backward in time, rather than forward. (In fact, if we let S^R be the reverse of a reference string S, we can show that the page-fault rate for the OPT algorithm on S is the same as the page-fault rate for the LRU algorithm on S^R. Thus, the page-fault rate for the LRU and OPT algorithms can be computed in one pass over the reference string.)

The result of applying LRU replacement to our example reference string is shown in Figure 8.11. The LRU algorithm produces 12 faults. Notice that the first five faults are the same as the optimal replacement. When the reference to page 4 occurs, however, LRU replacement sees that of the three frames in memory, page 2 was used least recently. The most recently used page is page 0, and just before that page 3 was used. Thus, the LRU algorithm replaces page 2, not knowing that it is about to be used. When it then faults for page 2, the LRU algorithm replaces page 3 since of the three pages in memory {0, 3, 4}, page 3 is the least recently used. Despite these problems, LRU replacement with 12 faults is still much better than FIFO replacement with 15.

The LRU policy is often used as a page-replacement algorithm and is considered to be quite good. The major problem is *how* to implement LRU replacement. An LRU page-replacement algorithm may require substantial hardware assistance. The problem is to determine an order for the frames defined by the time of last use. Two implementations are feasible:

reference string

7   0   1   2   0   3   0   4   2   3   0   3   2   1   2   0   1   7   0   1

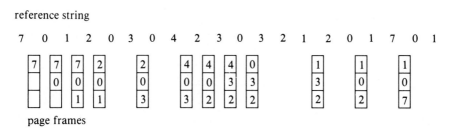

page frames

Figure 8.11   LRU page-replacement algorithm.

- **Counters**. In the simplest case, we associate with each page-table entry a time-of-use register and add to the CPU a logical clock or counter. The clock is incremented for every memory reference. Whenever a reference to a page is made, the contents of the clock register are copied to the time-of-use register in the page table for that page. In this way, we always have the "time" of the last reference to each page. We replace the page with the smallest time value. This scheme requires a search of the page table to find the LRU page. The times must also be maintained when page tables are changed (due to CPU scheduling). Overflow of the clock must be considered.

- **Stack**. Another approach to implementing LRU replacement is to keep a *stack* of page numbers. Whenever a page is referenced, it is removed from the stack and put on the top. In this way, the top of the stack is always the most recently used page and the bottom is the LRU page (Figure 8.12). Since entries must be removed from the middle of the stack, it is best implemented by a doubly linked list, with a head and tail pointer. Removing a page and putting it on the top of the stack then requires changing six pointers at worst. Each update is a little more expensive, but there is no search for a replacement; the tail pointer points to the bottom of the stack, which is the LRU page. This approach is particularly appropriate for software or microcode implementations of LRU replacement.

Neither optimal replacement nor LRU replacement suffers from Belady's anomaly. There is a class of page-replacement algorithms,

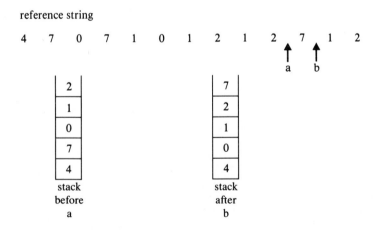

Figure 8.12 Use of a stack to record the most recent page references.

called *stack algorithms*, that can never exhibit Belady's anomaly. A stack algorithm is an algorithm for which it can be shown that the set of pages in memory for n frames is always a *subset* of the set of pages that would be in memory with $n + 1$ frames. For LRU replacement, the set of pages in memory would be the n most recently referenced pages. If the number of frames is increased, these n pages will still be the most recently referenced and so will still be in memory.

Note that neither implementation of LRU would be conceivable without hardware assistance. The updating of the clock registers or stack must be done for *every* memory reference. If we were to use an interrupt for every reference, to allow software to update such data structures, it would slow every memory reference by a factor of at least 10, hence slowing every user process by a factor of 10. Few systems could tolerate that level of overhead for memory management.

8.5.4 LRU Approximation Algorithms

Few systems provide sufficient hardware support for true LRU page replacement. Some systems provide no hardware support, and other page-replacement algorithms (such as a FIFO algorithm) must be used. Many systems provide some help, however, in the form of a *reference bit*. The reference bit for a page is set, by the hardware, whenever that page is referenced (either a read or a write to any byte in the page). Reference bits are associated with each entry in the page table.

Initially, all bits are cleared (to 0) by the operating system. As a user process executes, the bit associated with each page referenced is set (to 1) by the hardware. After some time, we can determine which pages have been used and which have not been used by examining the reference bits. We do not know the *order* of use, but we know which pages were used and which were not used. This partial ordering information leads to many page-replacement algorithms that approximate LRU replacement.

Additional-Reference-Bits Algorithm

We can gain additional ordering information by recording the reference bits at regular intervals. We can keep an 8-bit byte for each page in a table in memory. At regular intervals (say every 100 milliseconds), a timer interrupt transfers control to the operating system. The operating system shifts the reference bit for each page into the high-order bit of its 8-bit byte, shifting the other bits right 1 bit, discarding the low-order bit. These 8-bit shift registers contain the history of page use for the last eight time periods. If the shift register contains 00000000, then the page has not been used for eight time periods; a page that is used at least once each period would have a shift register value of 11111111.

A page with a history register value of 11000100 has been used more recently than has one with 01110111. If we interpret these 8-bit bytes as unsigned integers, the page with the lowest number is the LRU page, and it can be replaced. Notice that the numbers are not guaranteed to be unique, however. We can either replace (swap out) all pages with the smallest value, or use a FIFO selection among them.

The number of bits of history can be varied, of course, and would be selected (depending on the hardware available) to make the updating as fast as possible. In the extreme case, the number can be reduced to zero, leaving only the reference bit itself. This algorithm is called the *second-chance* page-replacement algorithm.

Second-Chance Algorithm

The basic algorithm of second-chance replacement is a FIFO replacement algorithm. When a page has been selected, however, we inspect its reference bit. If the value is 0, we proceed to replace this page. If the reference bit is 1, however, we give that page a second chance and move on to select the next FIFO page. When a page gets a second chance, its reference bit is cleared and its arrival time is reset to the current time. Thus, a page that is given a second chance will not be replaced until all other pages are replaced (or given second chances). In addition, if a page is used often enough to keep its reference bit set, it will never be replaced.

One way to implement the second-chance (sometimes referred to as the clock) algorithm is as a circular queue. A pointer indicates which page is to be replaced next. When a frame is needed, the pointer advances until it finds a page with a 0 reference bit. As it advances, it clears the reference bits (Figure 8.13). In the worst case, when all bits are set, the pointer cycles through the whole queue, giving each page a second chance. It clears all the reference bits before selecting the next page for replacement. Second-chance replacement degenerates to FIFO replacement if all bits are set.

LFU Algorithm

A *least frequently used* (LFU) page-replacement algorithm keeps a counter of the number of references that have been made to each page. The page with the smallest count is replaced. The reason for this selection is that an actively used page should have a large reference count. This algorithm suffers from the situation in which a page is used very heavily during the initial phase of a process, but then is never again used. Since

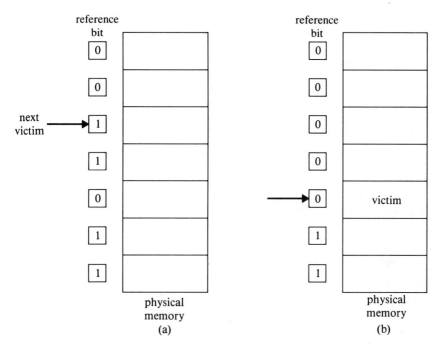

Figure 8.13 Second-chance page-replacement algorithm.

it was heavily used, it has a large count and remains in memory even though it is no longer needed. One solution is to shift the counts right by 1 bit at regular intervals, forming an exponentially decaying average usage count.

MFU Algorithm

Another page-replacement algorithm is *most frequently used* (MFU) replacement, which is based on the argument that the page with the smallest count was probably just brought in and has yet to be used. As you might expect, neither MFU or LFU replacement is common. The implementation of these algorithms is fairly expensive, and they do not approximate OPT replacement very well.

Additional Algorithms

There are many other algorithms that can be used for page replacement. For example, if we consider both the reference bit and the modify bit

(Section 8.4) as an ordered pair, we have the following four possible classes:

- (0,0) neither used nor modified
- (0,1) not used (recently) but modified
- (1,0) used but clean
- (1,1) used and modified

When page replacement is necessary, each page is in one of these four classes. We replace any page in the lowest nonempty class. If there are multiple pages in the lowest class, we can use FIFO replacement or choose randomly among them.

8.5.5 Ad Hoc Algorithms

Other procedures are often used in addition to a specific page-replacement algorithm. For example, systems commonly keep a *pool* of free frames. When a page fault occurs, a victim frame is chosen as before. However, the desired page is read into a free frame from the pool before the victim is written out. This procedure allows the process to restart as soon as possible, without waiting for the victim page to be written out. When the victim is later written out, its frame is added to the free-frame pool.

An expansion of this idea is to maintain a list of modified pages. Whenever the paging device is idle, a modified page is selected and is written to the disk. Its modify bit is then reset. This scheme increases the probability that a page will be clean when it is selected for replacement, and will not need to be written out.

Another modification is to keep a pool of free frames but to remember which page was in each frame. Since the frame contents are not modified by writing the frame to the disk, the old page can be reused directly from the free-frame pool if it is needed before that frame is reused. No I/O is needed in this case. When a page fault occurs, we first check whether the desired page is in the free-frame pool. If it is not, we must select a free frame and read into it.

This technique is used in the VAX/VMS system, along with a FIFO replacement algorithm. When the FIFO replacement algorithm mistakenly replaces a page that is still in active use, that page is quickly retrieved from the free-frame buffer and no I/O is necessary. The free-frame buffer provides protection against the relatively poor, but simple, FIFO replacement algorithm.

8.6 Allocation of Frames

How do we allocate the fixed amount of free memory among the various processes? If we have 93 free frames and two processes, how many frames does each process get?

The simplest case of virtual memory is the single-user system. Consider a single-user microcomputer system with 128K memory composed of pages of size 1K. Thus, there are 128 frames. The operating system may take 35K, leaving 93 frames for the user process. Under pure demand paging, all 93 frames would initially be put on the free-frame list. When a user process started execution, it would generate a sequence of page faults. The first 93 page faults would all get free frames from the free-frame list. When the free-frame list was exhausted, a page-replacement algorithm would be used to select one of the 93 in-memory pages to be replaced with the ninety-fourth, and so on. When the process terminated, the 93 frames would once again be placed on the free-frame list.

There are many variations on this simple strategy. We can require that the operating system allocate all of its buffer and table space from the free-frame list. When this space is not in use by the operating system, it can be used to support user paging. We could try to keep three free frames reserved on the free-frame list at all times. Thus, when a page fault occurs, there is a free frame available to page into. While the page swap is taking place, a replacement can be selected, which is then written to the disk as the user process continues to execute.

Other variants are also possible, but the basic strategy is clear: The user process is allocated any free frame.

A different problem arises when demand paging is combined with multiprogramming. Multiprogramming puts two (or more) processes in memory at the same time.

8.6.1 Minimum Number of Frames

There are, of course, various constraints on our strategies for the allocations of frames. We cannot allocate more than the total number of available frames (unless there is page sharing). There is also a minimum number of frames that can be allocated. Obviously, as the number of frames allocated to each process decreases, the page fault-rate increases, slowing process execution.

Besides the undesirable performance properties of allocating only a few frames, there is a minimum number of frames that must be allocated. This minimum number is defined by the instruction-set architecture. Remember that when a page fault occurs before an executing instruction is complete, the instruction must be restarted. Consequently, we must have enough frames to hold all the different pages that any single instruction can reference.

For example, consider a machine in which all memory-reference instructions have only one memory address. Thus, we need at least one frame for the instruction and one frame for the memory reference. In addition, if one-level indirect addressing is allowed (for example, a load instruction on page 16 can refer to an address on page 0, which is an indirect reference to page 23), then paging requires at least three frames per process. Think about what might happen if a process had only two frames.

The minimal number of frames is defined by the computer architecture. For example, the move instruction for the PDP-11 is more than one word for some addressing modes, and thus the instruction itself may straddle two pages. In addition, each of its two operands may be indirect references, for a total of six frames. The worst case for the IBM 370 is probably the Move Character instruction. Since the instruction is storage to storage, it takes 6 bytes and can straddle two pages. The block of characters to move and the area to be moved to can each also straddle two pages. This situation would require six frames. (Actually, the worst case is if the Move Character instruction is the operand of an Execute instruction that straddles a page boundary; in this case, we need eight frames.)

The worst-case scenario occurs in architectures that allow multiple levels of indirection (for example, each 16-bit word could contain a 15-bit address plus a 1-bit indirect indicator). Theoretically, a simple load instruction could reference an indirect address that could reference an indirect address (on another page) that could also reference an indirect address (on yet another page), and so on, until every page in virtual memory had been touched. Thus, in the worst case, the entire virtual memory must be in physical memory. To overcome this difficulty, we must place a limit on the levels of indirection (for example, limit an instruction to at most 16 levels of indirection). When the first indirection occurs, a counter is set to 16; the counter is then decremented for each successive indirection for this instruction. If the counter is decremented to 0, a trap occurs (excessive indirection). This limitation reduces the maximum number of memory references per instruction to 17, requiring the same number of frames.

The minimum number of frames per process is defined by the architecture, whereas the maximum number is defined by the amount of available physical memory. In between, we are still left with significant choice in frame allocation.

8.6.2 Allocation Algorithms

The easiest way to split m frames among n processes is to give everyone an equal share, m/n frames. For instance, if there are 93 frames and five processes, each process will get 18 frames. The leftover three frames could be used as a free-frame buffer pool. This scheme is called *equal allocation*.

An alternative is to recognize that various processes will need differing amounts of memory. If a small student process of 10K and an interactive database of 127K are the only two processes running in a system with 62 free frames, it does not make much sense to give each process 31 frames. The student process does not need more than 10 frames, so the other 21 are strictly wasted.

To solve this problem, we can use *proportional allocation*. We allocate available memory to each process according to the latter's size. Let the size of the virtual memory for process p_i be s_i, and define

$$S = \Sigma \, s_i.$$

Then, if the total number of available frames is m, we allocate a_i frames to process p_i, where a_i is approximately

$$a_i = s_i/S \times m.$$

Of course, we must adjust the a_is to be integers, greater than the minimum number of frames required by the instruction set, with a sum not exceeding m.

For proportional allocation, we would split 62 frames between two processes, one of 10 pages and one of 127 pages, by allocating four frames and 57 frames, respectively, since

$$10/137 \times 62 \approx 4,$$
$$127/137 \times 62 \approx 57.$$

In this way, both processes share the available frames according to their "needs," rather than equally.

In both equal and proportional allocation, of course, the allocation to each process may vary according to the multiprogramming level. If the multiprogramming level is increased, each process will lose some frames to provide the memory needed for the new process. On the other hand, if the multiprogramming level decreases, the frames that had been allocated to the departed process can now be spread over the remaining processes.

Notice that, with either equal or proportional allocation, a high-priority process is treated the same as is a low-priority process. By its definition, however, we may want to give the high-priority process more memory to speed its execution, to the detriment of low-priority processes.

One approach is to use a proportional allocation scheme where the ratio of frames depends not on the relative sizes of processes, but rather on the processes' priorities, or on a combination of size and priority.

Another approach is to allow high-priority processes to select frames from low-priority processes for replacement. A process can select a replacement from among its own frames or the frames of any lower-priority process. This approach allows a high-priority process to increase its frame allocation at the expense of the low-priority process.

8.7 Thrashing

If the number of frames allocated to a low-priority process falls below the minimum number required by the computer architecture, we must suspend that process's execution. We should then page out its remaining pages, freeing all its allocated frames. This provision introduces a swap-in, swap-out level of intermediate CPU scheduling.

In fact, look at any process that does not have "enough" frames. Although it is technically possible to reduce the number of allocated frames to the minimum, there is some (larger) number of pages that are in active use. If the process does not have this number of frames, it will very quickly page fault. At this point, it must replace some page. However, since all its pages are in active use, it must replace a page that will be needed again right away. Consequently, it very quickly faults again, and again, and again. The process continues to fault, replacing pages for which it will then fault and bring back in right away.

This very high paging activity is called *thrashing*. A process is thrashing if it is spending more time paging than executing.

8.7.1 Cause of Thrashing

Thrashing causes severe performance problems. Consider the following scenario, which is based on the actual behavior of early paging systems.

The operating system monitors CPU utilization. If CPU utilization is too low, we increase the degree of multiprogramming by introducing a new process to the system. A *global page-replacement algorithm* is used, replacing pages with no regard to the process to which they belong. Global and local replacement methods are described in Section 8.8.1. Now suppose a process enters a new phase in its execution and needs more frames. It starts faulting and taking pages away from other processes. These processes need those pages, however, and so they also fault, taking pages from other processes. These faulting processes must use the paging device to swap pages in and out. As they queue up for the paging device, the ready queue empties. As processes wait for the paging device, CPU utilization decreases.

The CPU scheduler sees the decreasing CPU utilization, and *increases* the degree of multiprogramming as a result. The new process tries to get started by taking pages from running processes, causing more page faults, and a longer queue for the paging device. As a result, CPU utilization drops even further, and the CPU scheduler tries to increase the degree of multiprogramming even more. Thrashing has occurred and system throughput plunges. The page-fault rate increases tremendously. As a result, the effective memory access time increases. No work is getting done because the processes are spending all their time paging.

This phenomenon is illustrated in Figure 8.14. CPU utilization is plotted against the degree of multiprogramming. As the degree of multiprogramming increases, CPU utilization also increases, although more slowly, until a maximum is reached. If the degree of multiprogramming is increased even further, thrashing sets in and CPU utilization drops sharply. At this point, to increase CPU utilization and stop thrashing, we must *decrease* the degree of multiprogramming.

The effects of thrashing can be limited by using a *local (or priority) replacement algorithm*. With local replacement, if one process starts thrashing, it cannot steal frames from another process and cause the latter to thrash also. Pages are replaced with regard to the process of

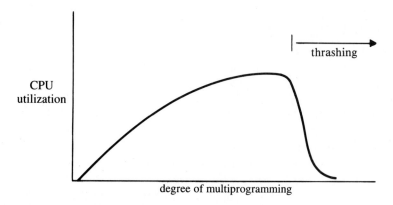

Figure 8.14   Thrashing.

which they are a part. However, if processes are thrashing, they will be in the queue for the paging device most of the time. The average service time for a page fault will increase, due to the longer average queue for the paging device. Thus, the effective access time will increase even for a process that is not thrashing.

To prevent thrashing, we must provide a process as many frames as it needs. But how do we know how many frames it "needs"? There are several techniques. The working-set strategy (discussed in Section 8.7.2) starts by looking at how many frames a process is actually using. This approach defines the *locality model* of process execution.

The locality model states that, as a process executes, it moves from locality to locality. A locality is a set of pages that are actively used together (Figure 8.15). A program is generally composed of several different localities, which may overlap.

For example, when a subroutine is called, it defines a new locality. In this locality, memory references are made to the instructions of the subroutine, its local variables, and a subset of the global variables. When the subroutine is exited, the process leaves this locality, since the local variables and instructions of the subroutine are no longer in active use. We may return to this locality later. Thus, we see that localities are defined by the program structure and its data structures. The locality model states that all programs will exhibit this basic memory reference structure.

Suppose we allocate enough frames to a process to accommodate its current locality. It will fault for the pages in its locality until all these pages are in memory; then, it will not fault again until it changes localities. If we allocate fewer frames than the size of the current locality, the process will thrash, since it cannot keep in memory all the pages that it is actively using.

8.7.2 Working-Set Model

The *working-set model* is based on the assumption of locality. This model uses a parameter, Δ, to define the *working-set window*. The idea is to examine the most recent Δ page references. The set of pages in the most recent Δ page references is the *working set* (Figure 8.16). If a page is in active use, it will be in the working set. If it is no longer being used, it will drop from the working set Δ time units after its last reference. Thus, the working set is an approximation of the program's locality.

For example, given the sequence of memory references shown in Figure 8.16, if $\Delta = 10$ memory references, then the working set at time t_1 is $\{1, 2, 5, 6, 7\}$. By time t_2, the working set has changed to $\{3, 4\}$.

The accuracy of the working set depends on the selection of Δ. If Δ is too small, it will not encompass the entire working set; if Δ is too

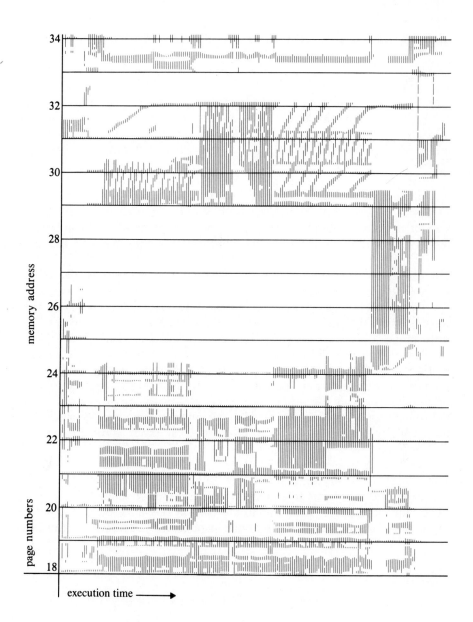

Figure 8.15 Locality in a memory reference pattern.

large, it may overlap several localities. In the extreme, if Δ is infinite, the working set is the entire program.

The most important property of the workings set is its size. If we compute the working-set size, WSS_i, for each process in the system, we can then consider

$$D = \Sigma \; WSS_i,$$

where D is the total demand for frames. Each process is actively using the pages in its working set. Thus, process i needs WSS_i frames. If the total demand is greater than the total number of available frames ($D > m$), thrashing will occur, since some processes will not have enough frames.

The use of the working-set model is then quite simple. The operating system monitors the working set of each process and allocates to that working set enough frames to provide it with its working-set size. If there are enough extra frames, another process can be initiated. If the sum of the working-set sizes increases, exceeding the total number of available frames, the operating system selects a process to suspend. The process's pages are written out and its frames are relocated to other processes. The suspended process can be restarted later.

This working-set strategy prevents thrashing while keeping the degree of multiprogramming as high as possible. Thus, it optimizes CPU utilization.

The difficulty with the working-set model is keeping track of the working set. The working-set window is a moving window. At each memory reference, a new reference appears at one end and the oldest reference drops off the other end. A page is in the working set if it is referenced anywhere in the working-set window. We can approximate the working-set model with a fixed interval timer interrupt and a reference bit.

For example, assume Δ is 10,000 references and we can cause a timer interrupt every 5000 references. When we get a timer interrupt, we copy and clear the reference-bit values for each page. Thus, if a page fault occurs, we can examine the current reference bit and the two in-memory bits to determine whether a page was used within the last

page reference trace

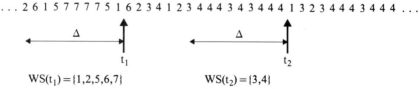

Figure 8.16   Working-set model.

10,000 to 15,000 references. If it was used, at least 1 of these bits will be on. If it has not been used, these bits will be off. Those pages with at least 1 bit on will be considered to be in the working set. Note that this arrangement is not entirely accurate, since we cannot tell where, within an interval of 5000, a reference occurred. We can reduce the uncertainty by increasing the number of our history bits and the number of interrupts (for example, 10 bits and interrupts every 1000 references). However, the cost to service these more frequent interrupts will be correspondingly higher.

8.7.3 Page-Fault Frequency

The working-set model is quite successful, and knowledge of the working set can be useful for prepaging (Section 8.8.2), but it seems a rather clumsy way to control thrashing. The *page-fault frequency* (PFF) strategy takes a more direct approach.

The specific problem is how to prevent thrashing. Thrashing has a high page-fault rate. Thus, we want to control the page-fault rate. When it is too high, we know that the process needs more frames. Similarly, if the page-fault rate is too low, then the process may have too many frames. We can establish upper and lower bounds on the desired page-fault rate (Figure 8.17). If the actual page-fault rate exceeds the upper limit, we allocate that process another frame; if the page-fault rate falls below the lower limit, we remove a frame from that process. Thus, we can directly measure and control the page-fault rate to prevent thrashing.

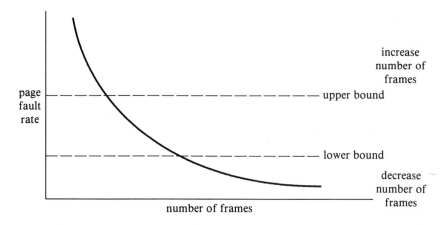

Figure 8.17 Page-fault frequency.

As with the working-set strategy, we may have to suspend a process. If the page-fault rate increases and no free frames are available, we must select some process and suspend it. The freed frames are then distributed to processes with high page-fault rates.

8.8 Other Considerations

The selections of a replacement algorithm and allocation policy are the major decisions to make for a paging system. There are many other considerations as well.

8.8.1 Global Versus Local Allocation

With multiple processes competing for frames, we can classify page-replacement algorithms into two broad categories: *global replacement* and *local replacement*. Global replacement allows a process to select a replacement frame from the set of all frames, even if that frame is currently allocated to some other process; one process can take a frame from another. Local replacement requires that each process select from only its own set of allocated frames.

With a local replacement strategy, the number of frames allocated to a process does not change. With global replacement, a process may happen to select only frames allocated to other processes, thus increasing the number of frames allocated to it (assuming that other processes do not choose *its* frames for replacement).

One problem with a global replacement algorithm is that a process cannot control its own page-fault rate. The set of pages in memory for a process depends not only on the paging behavior of that process, but also on the paging behavior of other processes. Therefore, the same process may perform quite differently (taking 0.5 seconds for one execution and 10.3 seconds for the next execution) due to totally external circumstances. This is not the case with a local replacement algorithm. Under local replacement, the set of pages in memory for a process is affected by the paging behavior of only that process. For its part, local replacement might hinder a process by not making available to it other, less used pages of memory. Thus, global replacement generally results in greater system throughput.

8.8.2 Prepaging

An obvious property of a pure demand-paging system is the large number of page faults that occur when a process is started. This situation is a result of trying to get the initial locality into memory. The same thing may happen at other times. For instance, when a swapped-out process is restarted, all of its pages are on the disk and each must be brought in by its own page fault. *Prepaging* is an attempt to prevent this high level of initial paging. The strategy is to bring into memory at one time all the pages that will be needed.

In a system using the working-set model, for example, we keep with each process a list of the pages in its working set. If we must suspend a process (due to an I/O wait or a lack of free frames), we remember the working set for that process. When the process is to be resumed (I/O completion or enough free frames), we automatically bring its entire working set back into memory before restarting the process.

Prepaging may be an advantage in some cases. The question is simply whether the cost of prepaging is less than the cost of servicing the corresponding page faults. It may well be the case that many of the pages brought back into memory by prepaging are not used. Assume that s pages are prepaged and a fraction α of these s pages are actually used ($0 \le \alpha \le 1$). The question is whether the cost of the αs saved page faults is greater or less than the cost of prepaging $(1 - \alpha)s$ unnecessary pages. If α is close to zero, prepaging loses; if α is close to one, prepaging wins.

8.8.3 Page Size

The designers of an operating system for an existing machine seldom have a choice concerning the page size. However, when new machines are being designed, a decision regarding the best page size must be made. As you might expect, there is no single best page size. Rather, there is a set of factors that support various sizes. Page sizes are invariably powers of 2, generally ranging from 512 (2^9) to 16,384 (2^{14}) bytes.

How do we select a page size? One concern is the size of the page table. For a given virtual memory space, decreasing the page size increases the number of pages, and hence the size of the page table. For a virtual memory of 4 megabytes (2^{22}), there would be 4096 pages of 1024 bytes but only 512 pages of 8192 bytes. Since each active process must have its own copy of the page table, we see that a large page size is desirable.

On the other hand, memory is better utilized with smaller pages. If a process is allocated memory starting at location 00000, continuing until it has as much as it needs, the process probably will not end exactly on a page boundary. Thus, a part of the last page must be allocated (since pages are the units of allocation) but is unused (internal fragmentation). Assuming independence of process size and page size, we would expect that, on the average, one-half of the last page of each process will be wasted. This loss would be only 256 bytes for a page of 512 bytes, but would be 4096 bytes for a page of 8192 bytes. To minimize internal fragmentation, we need a small page size.

Another problem is the time required to read or write a page. I/O time is composed of seek, latency, and transfer times. Transfer time is proportional to the amount transferred (that is, the page size), a fact that would seem to argue for a small page size. Remember, however, that latency and seek time normally dwarf transfer time. At a transfer rate of 2 megabytes per second, it takes only 0.2 milliseconds to transfer 512 bytes. Latency, on the other hand, is perhaps 8 milliseconds and seek time 20 milliseconds. Of the total I/O time (28.2 milliseconds), therefore, 1 percent is attributable to the actual transfer. Doubling the page size increases I/O time to only 28.4 milliseconds. It takes 28.4 milliseconds to read a single page of 1024 bytes, but 56.4 milliseconds to read the same amount as two pages of 512 bytes each. Thus, a desire to minimize I/O time argues for a larger page size.

With a smaller page size however, total I/O should be reduced, since locality will be improved. A smaller page size allows each page to match program locality more accurately. For example, consider a process of size 200K, of which only one-half (100K) are actually used in an execution. If we have only one large page, we must bring in the entire page, a total of 200K transferred and allocated. If we had pages of only 1 byte, then we could bring in only the 100K that are actually used, resulting in only 100K being transferred and allocated. With a smaller page size, we have better *resolution*, allowing us to isolate only the memory that is actually needed. With a larger page size we must allocate and transfer not only what is needed but also anything else that happens to be in the page, whether it is needed or not. Thus, a smaller page size should result in less I/O and less total allocated memory.

On the other hand, did you notice that with a page size of 1 byte, we would have a page fault for *each* byte? A process of 200K, using only one-half of that memory, would generate only one page fault with a page size of 200K, but 102,400 page faults for a page size of 1 byte. Each page fault generates the large amount of overhead needed for saving registers, replacing a page, queueing for the paging device, and updating tables. To minimize the number of page faults, we need to have a large page size.

The historical trend is toward larger page sizes. Indeed, the first edition of this book (1983) used 4096 bytes as the upper bound on page sizes, and this value was the most common page size in 1990. The Intel 80386 has a page size of 4K; the Motorola 68030 allows page sizes to vary from 256 bytes to 32K. The evolution to larger page sizes is probably the result of CPU speeds and main memory capacity increasing faster than have disk speeds. Page faults are more costly today, in overall system performance, than previously. It is therefore advantageous to increase page sizes to reduce their frequency. Of course, there is more internal fragmentation as a result.

There are other factors to consider (such as the relationship between page size and sector size on the paging device). The problem has no best answer. Some factors (internal fragmentation, locality) argue for a small page size, whereas others (table size, I/O time) argue for a large page size. Two systems allow two different page sizes. The MULTICS hardware (GE 645) allows pages of either 64 words or 1024 words. The IBM/370 allows pages of either 2K or 4K. The difficulty of picking a page size is illustrated by the fact that MVS on the IBM/370 selected 4K pages, whereas VS/1 selected 2K pages.

8.8.4 Program Structure

Demand paging is designed to be transparent to the user program. In many cases, the user is completely unaware of the paged nature of memory. In other cases, however, system performance can be improved by an awareness of the underlying demand paging.

As a contrived but informative example, assume pages are 128 words in size. Consider a Pascal program whose function is to initialize to 0 each element of a 128 by 128 array. The following code is typical:

```
var A: array [1..128] of array [1..128] of integer;
    for j := 1 to 128
      do for i := 1 to 128
        do A[i][j] := 0;
```

Notice that the array is stored row major. That is, the array is stored $A[1][1]$, $A[1][2]$, ..., $A[1][128]$, $A[2][1]$, $A[2][2]$, ..., $A[128][128]$. For pages of 128 words, each row takes one page. Thus, the proceeding code zeros one word in each page, then another word in each page, and so on. If the operating system allocates less than 128 frames to the entire program, then its execution will result in $128 \times 128 = 16{,}384$ page faults. Changing the code to

```
var A: array [1..128] of array [1..128] of integer;
    for i := 1 to 128
      do for j := 1 to 128
        do A[i][j] := 0;
```

on the other hand, zeros all the words on one page before starting the next page, reducing the number of page faults to 128.

Careful selection of data structures and programming structures can increase locality and hence lower the page-fault rate and the number of pages in the working set. A stack has good locality since access is always made to the top. A hash table, on the other hand, is designed to scatter references, producing bad locality. Of course, locality of reference is just one measure of the efficiency of the use of a data structure. Other heavily weighed factors include search speed, total number of memory references, and the total number of pages touched.

At a later stage, the compiler and loader can have a significant effect on paging. Separating code and data and generating reentrant code means that code pages can be read-only and hence will never be modified. Clean pages do not have to be paged out to be replaced. The loader can avoid placing routines across page boundaries, keeping each routine completely in one page. Routines that call each other many times can be packed into the same page. This is a variant of the bin-packing problem of operations research: Try to pack the variable-sized load segments into the fixed-sized pages so that interpage references are minimized. Such an approach is particularly useful for large page sizes.

8.8.5 I/O Interlock

When demand paging is used, we sometimes need to allow some of the pages to be *locked* in memory. One such situation occurs when I/O is done to or from user (virtual) memory. I/O is often implemented by a separate I/O processor. For example, a magnetic-tape controller is generally given the number of words (or bytes) to transfer and a memory address for the buffer (Figure 8.18). When the transfer is complete, the CPU is interrupted.

We must be sure the following sequence of events does not occur: A process issues an I/O request, and is put in a queue for that I/O device. Meanwhile, the CPU is given to other processes. These processes cause page faults, and, using a global replacement algorithm, one of them replaces the page containing the memory buffer for the waiting process. The pages are paged out. Some time later, when the I/O request advances to the head of the device queue, the I/O occurs to the specified address. However, this frame is now being used for a different page belonging to another process.

There are two common solutions to this problem. One solution is never to execute I/O to user memory. Instead, data are always copied between system memory and user memory. I/O takes place only between system memory and the I/O device. To write a block on tape, we first copy the block to system memory, and then write it to tape.

This extra copying may result in unacceptably high overhead. Another solution is to allow pages to be *locked* into memory. A lock bit is

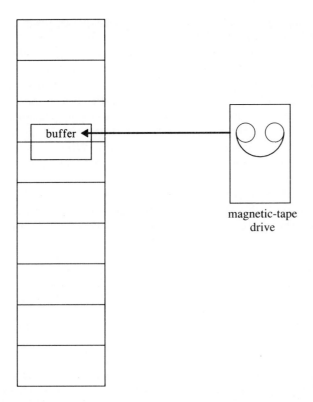

Figure 8.18 Frames used for I/O must be kept in memory.

associated with every frame. If the frame is locked, it cannot be selected for replacement. Under this approach, to write a block on tape, we lock into memory the pages containing the block. The system can then continue as usual. Locked pages cannot be replaced. When the I/O is complete, the pages are unlocked.

Another use for a lock bit involves normal page replacement. Consider the following sequence of events. A low-priority process faults. Selecting a replacement frame, the paging system reads the necessary page into memory. Ready to continue, the low-priority process enters the ready queue and waits for the CPU. Since it is a low-priority process, it may not be selected by the CPU scheduler for a while. While the low-priority process waits, a high-priority process faults. Looking for a replacement, the paging system sees a page that is in memory but has not been referenced or modified: the page the low-priority process just brought in. This page looks like a perfect replacement; it is clean and will not need to be written out, and it apparently has not been used for a long time.

Deciding whether the high-priority process should be able to replace the low-priority process is a policy decision. After all, we are simply delaying the low-priority process for the benefit of the high-priority process. On the other hand, we are wasting the effort spent to bring in the page of the low-priority process. If we decide to prevent replacing a newly brought-in page until it can be used at least once, then we can use the lock bit to implement this mechanism. When a page is selected for replacement, its lock bit is turned on and remains on until the faulting process is again dispatched.

Using a lock bit can be dangerous, however, if it gets turned on but never gets turned off. Should this situation occur (due to a bug in the operating system, for example), the locked frame becomes unusable.

8.8.6 Inverted Page Table

Usually, each process has a page table associated with it. The page table has one entry for each virtual page that the process is using (or one slot for each virtual address, regardless of its validity). This is a natural table representation since processes reference pages through the pages' virtual addresses. The operating system must then translate this reference into a physical memory address. Since the table is sorted by virtual address, the operating system is able to calculate where in the table the associated physical-address entry is, and uses that value directly. One of the drawbacks of virtual memory is the size of the page tables. Virtual-memory address spaces may be gigabytes large, resulting in tables with millions of entries. These tables may consume large amounts of physical memory, which is required just to keep track of how the other physical memory is being used.

To solve this problem, some operating systems use *inverted page tables*. The IBM System/38 computer, as well as the IBM RT and Hewlett-Packard Spectrum workstations, are examples of systems using such a scheme. An inverted page table has one entry for each real page of memory. Each entry then has associated with it the virtual address of the page stored in that real memory location. Thus, there is only one page table in the system, and it has only one entry for each page of physical memory.

To illustrate this, we shall describe a simplified version of the implementation of the inverted page table used in the IBM RT. Each virtual address consists of a triple

<process-id, page-number, offset>

Each inverted page-table entry is a pair <process-id, page-number>. When a memory reference occurs, part of the virtual address, consisting of <process-id, page-number>, is presented to the memory subsystem. The inverted page table is then searched for a match. If a match is found — say, at entry i — then the physical address <i, offset> is generated. If no match is found, then a page fault occurs, implying that either an illegal address has been generated or the page in question is not in memory.

By keeping information about which virtual-memory page is stored in each physical frame, inverted page tables reduce the amount of physical memory needed to store this information. However, this page table no longer contains complete information about virtual memory. For instance, if a virtual page is not currently in memory, this table does not show where on the backing store the page can be found. For this information to be available, external page tables must be kept. They look like the traditional per-process page tables, containing information on where each virtual page is located. But doesn't external page tables negate the utility of inverted page tables? Since these tables are referenced only when a page fault is occurring, they do not need to be available quickly. Instead, these tables are themselves paged in and out of memory as necessary. Unfortunately, a page fault may now result in the virtual-memory manager causing another page fault as it pages in the external page table it needs to locate the virtual page on the backing store. This special case requires careful handling in the kernel and a delay in the page-lookup processing.

Although this scheme decreases the amount of memory needed to store each page table, it increases the amount of time needed to search the table when a page reference occurs. Since the inverted page table is sorted by a physical address, but lookups occur on virtual addresses, the whole table would need to be searched for a match. This search would take far too long. To alleviate this problem, we use a hash table to limit the search to one — or at most a few — page-table entries. Of course, each access to the hash table adds a memory reference to the procedure, so one virtual-memory reference requires at least two real-memory reads: one for the hash table entry and one for the page table. To improve performance, we use associative memory registers to hold recently located entries. These registers are searched first, before the hash table is consulted.

Implementing shared memory on systems that use inverted page table also causes difficulties. Shared memory is usually implemented as two virtual addresses that are mapped to one physical address. This standard method cannot be used, however, since there is only one virtual page entry for every physical page, so one physical page can not have the two (or more) shared virtual addresses.

8.9 Demand Segmentation

Although demand paging is generally considered the most efficient virtual-memory system, a significant amount of hardware is required to implement it. When this hardware is lacking, less efficient means are sometimes devised to provide virtual memory. A case in point is *demand segmentation*. The Intel 80286 does not include paging features, but does have segments. The OS/2 operating system, which runs on this CPU, uses the segmentation hardware to implement demand segmentation as the only possible approximation of demand paging.

OS/2 allocates memory in segments rather than in pages. It keeps track of these segments through *segment descriptors*, which include information about the segment's size, protections, and location. A process does need to have all its segments in memory to execute. Instead, the segment descriptor contains a valid bit for each segment to indicate whether the segment is currently in memory. When a process addresses a segment containing either code or data, the hardware checks this valid bit. If the segment is in main memory, the access continues unhindered. If the segment is not in memory, a trap to the operating system occurs (segment fault), just as in demand-paging implementations. OS/2 then swaps out a segment to secondary storage, and brings in the entire requested segment. The interrupted instruction (the one causing the segment fault) then continues.

To determine which segment to replace in case of a segment fault, OS/2 uses another bit in the segment descriptor called *accessed bit*. An accessed bit serves the same purpose as does a reference bit in a demand-paging environment. It is set whenever any byte in the segment is either read or written. A queue is kept containing an entry for each segment in memory. After every time-slice, the operating system places at the head of the queue any segments with a set access bit. It then clears all access bits. In this way, the queue stays ordered with the most recently used segments at the head. In addition, OS/2 provides system calls that processes can use to inform the system of those segments that can either be discarded, or must always remain in memory. This information is used to rearrange the entries in the queue. When an invalid-segment trap occurs, the memory-management routines first determine whether there is sufficient free memory space to accommodate the segment. Memory compaction may be done to get rid of external fragmentation. If, after compaction, there is still not sufficient free memory, segment replacement is performed. The segment at the end of the queue is chosen for replacement and is written to swap space. If the newly freed space is large enough to accommodate the requested segment, then the requested segment is read into the vacated segment, the segment descriptor is updated, and the segment is placed at the head of the queue. Otherwise, memory compaction is performed, and the procedure is repeated.

It should be clear that demand segmentation requires considerable overhead. Thus, demand segmentation is not an optimal means for making best use of the resources of a computer system. The alternative on less sophisticated hardware is, however, no virtual memory at all. Given the problems entailed in systems lacking virtual memory, such as those described in Chapter 7, that solution is also lacking. Demand segmentation is therefore a reasonable compromise of functionality given hardware constraints that make demand paging impossible.

8.10 Summary

It is desirable to be able to execute a process whose logical address space is larger than the available physical address space. The programmer can make such a process executable by restructuring it using overlays, but this is generally a difficult programming task. Virtual memory is a technique to allow a large logical address space to be mapped onto a smaller physical memory. Virtual memory allows very large processes to be run, and also allows the degree of multiprogramming to be raised, increasing CPU utilization. Further, it frees application programmers from worrying about memory availability.

Pure demand paging never brings in a page until that page is actually referenced. The first reference causes a page fault to the operating-system resident monitor. The operating system consults an internal table to determine where the page is located on the backing store. It then finds a free frame and reads the page in from the backing store. The page table is updated to reflect this change, and the instruction that caused the page fault is restarted. This approach allows a process to run even though its entire memory image is not in main memory at once. As long as the page-fault rate is reasonably low, performance is acceptable.

Demand paging can be used to reduce the number of frames allocated to a process. This arrangement can raise the degree of multiprogramming (allowing more processes to be available for execution at one time) and — in theory, at least — the CPU utilization of the system. It also allows processes to be run even though their memory requirements exceed the total available physical memory. Such processes run in virtual memory.

If total memory requirements exceed the physical memory, then it may be necessary to replace pages from memory, in order to free frames for new pages. Various page-replacement algorithms are used. FIFO page replacement is easy to program, but suffers from Belady's anomaly. Optimal page replacement requires future knowledge. LRU replacement is an approximation of optimal, but even it may be difficult to implement. Most page-replacement algorithms, such as the second-chance algorithm, are approximations of LRU replacement.

In addition to a page-replacement algorithm, a frame-allocation policy is needed. Allocation can be fixed, suggesting local page replacement, or dynamic, suggesting global replacement. The working-set model assumes that processes execute in localities. The working set is the set of pages in the current locality. Accordingly, each process should be allocated enough frames for its current working set.

If a process does not have enough memory for its working set, it will thrash. Providing enough frames to each process to avoid thrashing may require process swapping and scheduling.

In addition to requiring that we solve the major problems of page replacement and frame allocation, the proper design of a paging system requires that we consider page size, I/O, locking, prepaging, program structure, and other topics. Virtual memory can be thought of as one level of a hierarchy of storage levels in a computer system. Each level has its own access time, size, and cost parameters. A full example of a hybrid, functional virtual-memory system is presented in Chapter 15.

Exercises

8.1 When do page faults occur? Describe the actions taken by the operating system when a page fault occurs.

8.2 Assume you have a page reference string for a process with m frames (initially all empty). The page reference string has length p with n distinct page numbers occurring in it. For any page-replacement algorithms,

    a. What is a lower bound on the number of page faults?

    b. What is an upper bound on the number of page faults?

8.3 Just as paging can be demand paging, so segmentation can be demand segmentation. We need a segment-replacement algorithm (similar to a page-replacement algorithm). Describe a reasonable segment-replacement algorithm. What problems occur with segment replacement that do not occur with page replacement?

8.4 A certain computer provides its users with a virtual-memory space of 2^{32} bytes. The computer has 2^{18} bytes of physical memory. The virtual memory is implemented by paging, and the page size is 4096 bytes. A user process generates the virtual address 11123456. Explain how the system establishes the corresponding physical location. Distinguish between software and hardware operations.

8.5 Which of the following programming techniques and structures are "good" for a demand-paged environment. Which are "not good"?

   a. Stack

   b. Hashed symbol table

   c. Sequential search

   d. Binary search

   e. Pure code

   f. Vector operations

   g. Indirection

8.6 Suppose we have a demand-paged memory. The page table is held in registers. It takes 8 milliseconds to service a page fault if an empty page is available or the replaced page is not modified, and 20 milliseconds if the replaced page is modified. Memory access time is 100 nanoseconds.

   Assume that the page to be replaced is modified 70 percent of the time. What is the maximum acceptable page-fault rate for an effective access time of no more than 200 nanoseconds?

8.7 Consider the following page-replacement algorithms. Rank these algorithms from "bad" to "perfect" according to their page-fault rate. Separate those algorithms that suffer from Belady's anomaly from those that do not.

   a. LRU replacement

   b. FIFO replacement

   c. Optimal replacement

   d. Second-chance replacement

8.8 Consider a paging system with a secondary-storage disk of 4 megabytes, with an average access and transfer time of 25 milliseconds, and a paged main memory of 262,144 bytes with a 200 nanosecond access time. If we want our paging system to look to the user like a memory of 4 megabytes with a 400-

nanosecond (average) access time, what percentage of accesses must occur without a page fault?

8.9 Consider the following sequence of memory references from a 460-byte program:

> 10, 11, 104, 170, 73, 309, 185, 245, 246, 434, 458, 364.

a. Give the reference string, assuming a page size of 100 bytes.

b. Find the page-fault rate for the reference string in part a, assuming 200 bytes of primary memory available to the program and a FIFO replacement algorithm.

c. Calculate what the page-fault rate would be if you used an LRU replacement algorithm.

d. Determine what the page-fault rate would be for the optimal replacement algorithm.

8.10 When virtual memory is implemented in a computing system, there are certain costs associated with the technique, and certain benefits. List the costs and the benefits. Is it possible for the costs to exceed the benefits? If it is, what measures can be taken to ensure that this does not happen?

8.11 Consider a demand-paging system with the following time-measured utilizations:

CPU utilization	20%
Paging disk	97.7%
Other I/O devices	5%

Which (if any) of the following will (probably) improve CPU utilization? Explain your answer.

a. Install a faster CPU.

b. Install a bigger paging disk.

c. Increase the degree of multiprogramming.

d. Decrease the degree of multiprogramming.

e. Install faster, other I/O devices.

8.12 An operating system supports a paged virtual memory, using a central processor with a cycle time of 1 microsecond. Pages have 1000 words, and the paging device is a drum that rotates at 3000 revolutions per minute, and transfers 1 million words per second. The following statistical measurements were obtained from the system:

- 0.1 percent of all instructions executed accessed a page other than the current page.

- Of the instructions that accessed another page, 80 percent accessed a page already in memory.

- When a new page was required, the replaced page was modified 50 percent of the time.

Calculate the effective instruction time (the average time required to execute an instruction) on this system, assuming that the system is running one process only, and that the processor is idle during drum transfers.

8.13 Consider the two-dimensional array A:

> **var** A: **array** [1..100] **of array** [1..100] **of** *integer*;

where $A[1][1]$ is at location 200, in a paged memory system with pages of size 200. A small process is in page 0 (locations 0 to 199) for manipulating the matrix; thus, every instruction fetch will be from page 0.

For three page frames, how many page faults are generated by the following array-initialization loops, using LRU replacement, and assuming page frame 1 has the process in it, and the other two are initially empty:

a. **for** j:= 1 **to** 100 **do**
       for i := 1 **to** 100 **do**
          $A[i][j]$:= 0;

b. **for** i := 1 **to** 100 **do**
       for j:= 1 **to** 100 **do**
          $A[i][j]$:= 0;

8.14 Consider the following page reference string:

> 1, 2, 3, 4, 2, 1, 5, 6, 2, 1, 2, 3, 7, 6, 3, 2, 1, 2, 3, 6.

How many page faults would occur for the following replacement algorithms, assuming one, two, three, four, five, six, or seven frames? Remember all frames are initially empty, so your first unique pages will all cost one fault each.

- LRU replacement

- FIFO replacement

- Optimal replacement

8.15 Suppose we want to use a paging algorithm that requires a reference bit (such as second-chance replacement or working-set model), but the hardware does not provide one. Sketch how we could simulate a reference bit even if one were not provided by the hardware, or explain why it is not possible to do so. If it is possible, calculate what the cost would be.

8.16 We have devised a new page-replacement algorithm that is rather complex, but we think that it may be optimal. In some consorted test cases, Belady's anomaly occurs. Is the new algorithm optimal?

8.17 Suppose your replacement policy (in a paged system) consists of regularly examining each page and discarding that page if it has not been used since the last examination. What would you gain and what would you lose by using this policy rather than LRU or second-chance replacement?

8.18 Segmentation is similar to paging, but uses variable-sized "pages." Define two segment-replacement algorithms based on FIFO and LRU page-replacement schemes. Remember that, since segments are not the same size, the segment that is chosen to be replaced may not be big enough to leave enough consecutive locations for the needed segment. Consider strategies for systems where segments cannot be relocated, and those for systems where they can.

8.19 Consider a system with 1 microsecond main memory and a drum secondary-storage system that has an average latency time of 5 microseconds and a transfer rate of 1 million words per second.

a. For a page size p and page-fault rate x ($0 \leq x \leq 1$), what is the effective access time?

b. Assume that the page-fault rate varies inversely exponentially with page size, $x = e^{-p/500}$. Thus, the larger the page size, the smaller the page-fault rate. What page size gives the minimal effective access time?

8.20 A page-replacement algorithm should minimize the number of page faults. We can do this minimization by distributing heavily used pages evenly over all of memory, rather than having them compete for a small number of page frames. We can associate with each page frame a counter of the number of pages that are associated with that frame. Then, to replace a page, we search for the page frame with the smallest counter.

a. Define a page-replacement algorithm using this basic idea. Specifically address the problems of (1) What the initial value of the counters is, (2) when counters are increased, (3) when counters are decreased, and (4) how the page to be replaced is selected.

b. How many page faults occur for your algorithm for the following reference string, for four page frames?

1, 2, 3, 4, 5, 3, 4, 1, 6, 7, 8, 7, 8, 9, 7, 8, 9, 5, 4, 5, 4, 2.

c. What is the minimal number of page faults for an optimal page-replacement strategy for the reference string in part b with four page frames?

8.21 Consider a demand-paging system with a paging drum that has an average access and transfer time of 5 milliseconds. Addresses are translated through a page table in main memory, with an access time of 1 microsecond per memory access. Thus, each memory reference through the page table takes two accesses. To improve this time, we have added an associative memory that reduces access time to one memory reference, if the page-table entry is in the associative memory.

Assume that 80 percent of the accesses are in the associative memory, and that, of the remaining, 10 percent (or 2 percent of the total) cause page faults. What is the effective memory access time?

8.22 Is it necessary always to put a page of a process back in the same place on the disk each time that page is written out? If it is not, explain the circumstances under which it is unnecessary.

8.23 What is the cause of thrashing? How does the system detect thrashing? Once it detects thrashing, what can the system do to eliminate this problem?

8.24 A Large Core Storage (LCS) is a large, relatively inexpensive, relatively slow memory available on some IBM machines. Unlike in CDC's ECS, processes can be executed directly out of LCS. Direct access of a single word takes about 4 microseconds, as opposed to 1 microsecond for primary memory. Assume that memory could be paged into pages of size 256 words. Although random access to LCS gives a 4-microsecond access time, a page of consecutive memory can be transferred to main memory in only 259 microseconds (4 microseconds for the first and then 1 microsecond for each additional location). Two memory-management schemes are under consideration: (1) paging into primary memory from LCS, and (2) executing directly from LCS. Calculate the effective memory access time for both schemes for the following types of processes. For what page-fault rates should which scheme be used?

a. A program with good locality and a page-fault rate of 1 percent

b. A program with bad locality and a page-fault rate of 37 percent

8.25 As a normal consumer, you have begun to acquire lots of stuff. Having a small house, you store some of your stuff in the attic, but the attic becomes rather crowded, so you have rented a storage locker. This would give you three places to keep things: the house (active use), the attic (easily accessed storage), and the storage locker (hard-to-access storage). Suggest a scheme to decide what should be kept in the attic and what should be in the storage locker.

8.26 We have an operating system for a machine that uses base and limit registers, but we have modified the machine to provide a page table. Can the page tables be set up to simulate base and limit registers? How can they be, or why can they not be?

8.27 Consider a demand-paged computer system that uses a paging drum, global LRU replacement, and an allocation policy that shares frames equally among processes (that is, if there are *m* frames and *n* processes, then each process gets *m/n* frames). The degree of multiprogramming is currently fixed at four. The system was recently measured to determine utilization of CPU and the paging drum. The results are one of the following alternatives. For each case, what is happening? Can the degree of multiprogramming be increased to increase the CPU utilization? Is the paging helping?

a. CPU utilization 13 percent; disk utilization 97 percent

b. CPU utilization 87 percent; disk utilization 3 percent

c. CPU utilization 13 percent; disk utilization 3 percent

8.28 Consider a machine with the following paging hardware: There are 32 page frames for pages of 512 words. Page tables have 32 entries and are kept in memory, starting at addresses that are multiples of 32 (so that the low order 5 bits are 0). Two special registers, UPT and SPT, point to the user page table and the supervisor page table, respectively. In user mode, the UPT is used for address translation until a page fault or other interrupt occurs, then the instruction counter is stored in the address contained in the IA (interrupt address) register, and execution continues at IA + 1 in supervisor mode using the page tables pointed at by SPT. If an interrupt occurs in supervisor mode, the same procedure is followed. Each page-table entry uses the sign bit as the valid-invalid bit (0 = in memory, 1 = not in memory), and the low-order 15 bits (16-bit words) specify the starting address of the page. The low-order 9 bits must be 0 (all pages start at multiples of the page size, 512). Every memory access is translated by one of the tables, UPT or SPT, depending on the mode of the CPU — user or supervisor.

a. What happens if the page for the address in IA is not in memory?

b. How can the operating system address memory absolutely (that is, without page-table translation)?

Bibliographic Notes

Demand paging was first used in the Atlas system, implemented on the Manchester University MUSE computer around 1960 [Kilburn et al. 1961, 1962]. Another early demand-paging system was MULTICS, implemented on the GE 645 system [Daley and Dennis 1968; Bensoussan et al. 1972; Organick 1972]. Other early demand-paging systems include the THE operating system (where the paging was implemented in software) [Bron 1972] and the TENEX operating system [Bobrow et al. 1972].

Belady et al. [1969] was the first person to observe that the FIFO replacement strategy may have the anomaly that bears his name. Mattson et al. [1970] demonstrated that stack algorithms are not subject to Belady's anomaly.

The optimal replacement algorithm is due to Belady [1966]. It was proved to be optimal by Mattson et al. [1970]. Belady's optimal algorithm is for a fixed allocation; Prieve and Fabry [1976] have an optimal algorithm for situations where the allocation can vary.

Gustavson [1968], Denning [1970], Aho et al. [1971], and Carr and Hennessy [1981] discussed various page-replacement algorithms. Belady [1966], Mattson et al. [1970], Coffman and Varian [1968], and Belady and Kuehner [1969] compared page-replacement algorithms. Comeau [1967], Brawn and Gustavson [1968], McKellar and Coffman [1969], Winograd et al. [1971], and Chu and Opderbeck [1974] were particularly concerned with performance issues.

Thrashing is discussed by Denning [1968] and Alderson et al. [1972]. The working-set model was developed by Denning [1968]. Discussion concerning the working set model are presented by Denning [1970, 1980a], Denning and Schwartz [1972], Coffman and Ryan [1972], Ferrari [1974], Bryant [1975], Easton and Bennett [1977], Masuda [1977], Denning and Slutz [1978], and Abu-Sufah and Padua [1983]. An analysis of demand paging policies with swapped working sets is presented by Potier [1977]. A modified working-set paging algorithm is presented by Smith [1976]. Characteristics of program localities are discussed by Madison and Batson [1976].

The page-fault-rate monitoring scheme is due to Wulf [1969], who successfully applied this technique to the Burroughs B5500 computer system. Chu and Opderbeck [1976] discussed program behavior and the page-fault-frequency Replacement Algorithm. Gupta and Franklin [1978] provide a performance comparison between the working set scheme and the and page-fault-frequency replacement scheme.

Belady [1966], Fine et al. [1966], Coffman and Varian [1968], Freibergs [1968], Brawn and Gustavson [1968], Hatfield [1972], and Baer and Sager [1976] conducted experiments to study the dynamic behavior of programs under paging. Denning [1968], DeMeis and Weizer [1969], and Alderson et al. [1972] considered various load-control strategies to prevent thrashing. Budzinski [1981] presented a comparison of dynamic and static virtual memory allocation algorithms. Budzinski et al. [1981] presented an algorithm for computing the optimal dynamic allocation in a virtual memory system.

Randell [1969], Arden and Boettner [1969], Batson et al. [1970], Denning [1970], and Hatfield and Gerald [1971] discussed page and segment sizes. The Intel 80386 paging hardware is described in [Intel 1986]; the Motorola 68030 hardware is covered in [Motorola 1989b]. Virtual memory management in the VAX/VMS operating system is discussed by Levy and Lipman [1982].

Vareha et al. [1969], and Mattson et al. [1970] discussed multilevel main storage. Such schemes were implemented in several large machines, including the IBM 370/168 and IBM 370/195 [Liptay 1968]. Program restructuring in a multilevel virtual memory is discussed by Lua and Ferrari [1983].

Randell and Kuehner [1968], Denning [1970], Doran [1976], and Hoare and McKeag [1972] presented survey papers on paging.

Inverted page tables are discussed in an article about the IBM RT storage manager by Chang [1988].

Demand segmentation is described by Iacobucci [1988], as are the details of OS/2. Further information about OS/2 can be found in [Microsoft 1989].

9

Secondary Storage Management

Most computer systems provide *secondary storage* as an extension of *primary storage* (which we call main memory). In this chapter, we discuss various methods for storing information on secondary storage, and some of the different algorithms used for accessing such storage. We assume that the stored information is in the form of files, which were briefly discussed in Chapter 3, and will be expanded on in Chapter 10.

9.1 Background

The main purpose of a computer system is to execute programs. These programs, together with the data they access, must be in main memory during execution. Ideally, we would want the programs and data to reside in main memory permanently. This is not possible for two reasons:

- Main memory is usually too **small** to store all needed programs and data permanently, as we saw in Chapter 7.

- Main memory is a **volatile** storage device that loses its contents when power is turned off or lost.

The main requirement of secondary storage is thus to be able to hold very large numbers of data permanently.

Magnetic tape was used as an early secondary-storage media. Although it is relatively permanent, and can hold large numbers of data, magnetic tape is quite slow in comparison to the access line of main memory. Even more important, magnetic tape is limited to sequential access. Thus, it is quite unsuitable for providing the random access needed for virtual memory. Tapes are currently used mainly for backup, for storage of infrequently used information, and as a medium for transferring information from one system to another.

Disks provide the bulk of secondary storage for modern computer systems. Most of this chapter is concerned with magnetic disks. We note, however, that read-writable optical disks are functionally similar. There are few alternatives to a good disk system.

The remainder of this chapter explores ways to allocate disk space and to recover freed space. These techniques are similar to those introduced in Chapter 7, where we discussed memory management. Secondary-storage algorithms are even more sensitive to time constraints, however, since secondary-storage access times are orders of magnitude longer than are those of main memory. The details of managing the logical contents of the disk are covered in Chapter 10.

9.2 Disk Structure

Physically, disks are relatively simple (Figure 9.1). Each disk has a flat circular shape, like a phonograph record. Its two surfaces are covered with a magnetic material, similar to magnetic tape. Information is recorded on the surfaces.

9.2.1 Physical Structure

When the disk is in use, a drive motor spins it at high speed (for example, 60 revolutions per second). There is a read-write head positioned just above the surface of the disk. The disk surface is logically divided into *tracks*. We store information by recording it magnetically on the track under the read-write head. There may be hundreds of tracks on a disk surface.

A *fixed-head disk* has a separate head for each track. This arrangement allows the computer to switch from track to track quickly, but it requires a large number of heads, making the device very expensive. More commonly, there is only one head, which moves in and out to access different tracks. This *moving-head disk* requires hardware to move the head, but only a single head is needed, resulting in a much less expensive system. In situations that demand high performance, a high-speed disk or a large memory device (random-

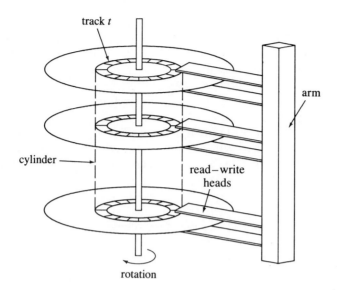

Figure 9.1 Moving-head disk mechanism.

access memory (RAM) disk) can be used to obtain a higher access and transfer speed than a conventional moving-head disk with a single head can supply.

Disks were originally designed for file storage, so the primary design criteria were cost, size, and speed. To provide additional storage capacity, developers took several approaches. They made the primary gain by improving the recording density, allowing more bits to be put on a surface. The density is reflected by the number of tracks per inch, and hence the total number of tracks on a surface. In addition, with separate heads on each side of the platter, disk capacity can be doubled at minimal cost. We can extend this approach by stacking several disks, each with two recording surfaces, on one spindle. Since all the disks rotate together, only one drive motor is needed, although each surface still needs its own read-write head.

Finally, the disk can be *removable*, allowing different disks to be mounted as needed. Removable disk packs may consist of one or several platters. Generally, they are held in hard plastic cases to prevent damage while they are not in the disk drive.

Such large disks are rigid aluminum platters covered with magnetic recording material. The read-write heads are kept as close as possible to the disk surface. Often, the head floats or flies only microns from the disk surface, supported by a cushion of air. Because the head floats so close to the surface, platters must be machined carefully to be flat.

Head crashes can be a problem. If the head contacts the disk surface (due to a power failure, for example), the head will scrape the recording medium off the disk, destroying the data that had been there. Usually, the head touching the surface causes the removed medium to become airborne and to come between the other heads and their platters, causing more crashes. Under normal circumstances, a head crash results in the entire disk being replaced.

Floppy disks take a different approach. The disks are coated with a hard surface, so the read-write head can sit directly on the disk surface without destroying the data. Thus, the disk itself is much less expensive to produce and use. The coating (and the read-write head) will wear with use, however, and need to be replaced over time.

Floppies are usually much smaller than hard disks, and hold from 100K bytes to a few megabytes per disk. They come in many variations (single-sided, double-sided, single-density, and double-density) and sizes ($5\frac{1}{4}$ inch, $3\frac{1}{2}$ inch, and so on). Generally, they are formatted and used in the same way as hard disks, except that all floppies are removable and may therefore be used conveniently to transfer data between computers. Hard disks vary from 10 megabytes to over 2 gigabytes per drive. Hard disks are also faster and more expensive.

The hardware for a disk system can be divided into two parts. The *disk drive* is the mechanical part, including the device motor, the read-write heads, and associated logic. The other part, called the *disk controller*, determines the logical interaction with the computer. The controller takes instructions from the CPU and orders the disk drive to carry out the instruction. This division allows many disk drives to be attached to the same disk controller. If an initial system has one disk controller and one disk drive, we can double the disk storage of the system for less than twice the cost simply by attaching a second drive to the existing controller. Some disk controllers contain caches of memory that are used for interaction among the system, the controller, and the disk. The cache holds data recently read to or written from the disk. If data are currently in the cache, the need for a disk transfer is obviated.

Information on the disk is referenced by a multipart address, which includes the drive number, the surface, and the track. All the tracks on one drive that can be accessed without the heads being moved (basically the tracks on the different surfaces) are called a *cylinder*.

Within a track, information is written in blocks. The blocks may be a fixed size, specified by the hardware. These are called *sectors*. Each sector can be separately read or written. Alternatively, the information on a track may be composed of variable-length blocks, separated by record gaps. This scheme is more flexible, but is more difficult to use. Many systems, even with hardware-variable disk blocks, will fix a block size in software. In either case, information is read from and written in blocks. Blocking and unblocking of records in software can easily hide the fixed or variable nature of the physical block size.

A sector is the smallest unit of information that can be read from or written to the disk. Depending on the disk drive, sectors vary from 32 bytes to 4096 bytes; there are 4 to 32 sectors per track, and from 20 to 1500 tracks per disk surface. To access a sector, we must specify the surface, track, and sector. To help the disk drive to locate its sector location, the drive records sector marks between the sectors. The read-write heads are moved to the correct track (seek time) and are electronically switched to the correct surface; then, we wait (latency time) for the requested sector to rotate below the heads. Seek time is dependent on the time it takes for the disk heads to move, so the farther apart the tracks are, the longer the seek time is.

I/O transfers between memory and disk are performed in units of one or more sectors. Addressing a particular sector requires a track (or cylinder) number, a surface number, and a sector number. Thus, the disk can be viewed as a three-dimensional array of sectors. Commonly, this array is treated by the operating system as a one-dimensional array of *disk blocks*. Each block is a sector. Typically, block addresses increase through all sectors on a track, then through all the tracks in a cylinder, and finally from cylinder 0 to the last cylinder on the disk. We use s to denote the number of sectors per track and t to denote the number of tracks per cylinder; clearly, we can convert from a disk address of cylinder i, surface j, sector k to a one-dimensional block number b, by

$$b = k + s \times (j + i \times t).$$

Notice that, with this mapping, accessing block $b + 1$ when the last block accessed was b requires a seek only when b was the last block of one cylinder and $b + 1$ is the first block of the next cylinder. Even in this case, the head is moved only one track.

A drum is effectively a one-cylinder disk. Since each track has its own read-write head, there is no seek time. The primary differences between disks and drums are performance, cost, and storage capacity, not logical structure, so we do not distinguish between them in this book — we refer to them both as disks.

Disks have two important characteristics that make them a convenient medium for storing multiple files:

- They can be rewritten in place; it is possible to read a block from the disk, to modify the block, and to write it back into the same place.

- We can access directly any given block of information on the disk. Thus, it is simple to access any file either sequentially or randomly, and switching from one file to another requires only moving the read-write heads and waiting for the disk to revolve.

9.2.2 Device Directory

A disk normally has a device directory indicating which files are on the disk. The directory lists the file by name, and includes such information as where on the disk the file is, and what are its length, type, owner, time of creation, time of last use, protections, and so on. Since blocks from disk can be rewritten in place, we can read, update, and rewrite the directory whenever it needs to be changed, without having to copy the rest of the disk.

Each physical disk unit, be it a disk pack or floppy, has its own device directory. The device directory is stored on the device, often at some fixed disk address, such as disk address 00001. (Address 00000 is generally a system boot loader.) This arrangement is particularly desirable for removable media devices, such as floppy-disk drives or removable disk packs. If the medium is dismounted, stored, and then remounted, perhaps on a different drive, we still want to be able to find the files on that device.

9.3 Free-Space Management

Since there is only a limited amount of disk space, it is necessary to reuse the space from deleted files for new files (some optical disks only allow one write to any given sector and thus such reuse is not physically possible). To keep track of free disk space, the system maintains a *free-space list*. The free-space list records all disk blocks that are *free* (that is, are not allocated to some file). To create a file, we search the free-space list for the required amount of space, and allocate that space to the new file. This space is then removed from the free-space list. When a file is deleted, its disk space is added to the free-space list. The free-space list, despite its name, might not be implemented as a list, as we shall discuss.

9.3.1 Bit Vector

Frequently, the free-space list is implemented as a *bit map* or *bit vector*. Each block is represented by 1 bit. If the block is free, the bit is 0; if the block is allocated, the bit is 1.

For example, consider a disk where blocks 2, 3, 4, 5, 8, 9, 10, 11, 12, 13, 17, 18, 25, 26, and 27 are free, and the rest of the blocks are allocated. The free-space bit map would be

110000110000001110011111100011111 ...

The main advantage of this approach is that it is relatively simple and efficient to find n consecutive free blocks on the disk. Indeed, many computers supplied bit-manipulation instructions that can effectively be used for that purpose. For example, the Intel 80386 and Motorola 68020 and 68030 have instructions that return the position of the first bit with the value 1 in a register. The Apple Macintosh operating system, running on the 68020, uses the bit-vector method to allocate disk space. Again, we see hardware features driving software functionality. Unfortunately, bit vectors are inefficient unless the entire vector is kept in main memory for most accesses (and is written to disk occasionally for recovery needs). Keeping it in main memory is possible for smaller disks, such as on microcomputers, but not for larger ones.

9.3.2 Linked List

Another approach is to link all the free disk blocks together, keeping a pointer to the first free block. This block contains a pointer to the next free disk block, and so on. In our example, we would keep a pointer to block 2, as the first free block. Block 2 would contain a pointer to block 3, which would point to block 4, which would point to block 5, which would point to block 8, and so on (Figure 9.2). This scheme is not efficient; to traverse the list, we must read each block, which requires substantial I/O time.

9.3.3 Grouping

A modification of the free-list approach is to store the addresses of n free blocks in the first free block. The first $n-1$ of these are actually free. The last one is the disk address of another block containing the addresses of another n free blocks. The importance of this implementation is that the addresses of a large number of free blocks can be found quickly.

9.3.4 Counting

Another approach is to take advantage of the fact that, generally, several contiguous blocks may be allocated or freed simultaneously, particularly when contiguous allocation (Section 9.4.1) is used. Thus, rather than keeping a list of n free disk addresses, we can keep the address of the first free block and the number n of free contiguous blocks that follow

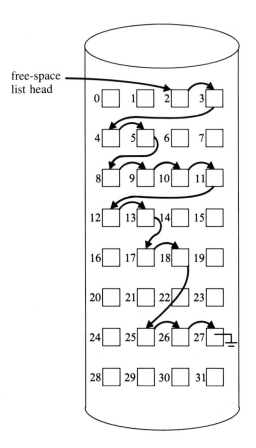

Figure 9.2   Linked free-space list on disk.

the first block. Each entry in the free-space list then consists of a disk
address and a count. Although each entry requires more space than
would a simple disk address, the overall list will be shorter, as long as
the count is generally greater than 1.

9.4 Allocation Methods

The direct-access nature of disks allows us flexibility in the
implementation of files. In almost every case, many files will be stored
on the same disk. The main problem is how to allocate space to these
files so that disk space is utilized effectively and files can be accessed
quickly. Three major methods of allocating disk space are in wide use:
contiguous, *linked*, and *indexed*.   Each method has its advantages and

disadvantages. Accordingly, some systems (such as Data General's RDOS for its Nova line of computers) support all three. More commonly, a system will use one particular method for all files.

For the purpose of our discussion, a file may be considered to be a sequence of blocks. All the basic I/O functions operate in terms of blocks. The conversion from logical records to physical blocks is a relatively simple software problem.

9.4.1 Contiguous Allocation

The *contiguous* allocation method requires each file to occupy a set of contiguous addresses on the disk. Disk addresses define a linear ordering on the disk. Notice that, with this ordering, accessing block $b + 1$ after block b normally requires no head movement. When head movement is needed (from the last sector of one cylinder to the first sector of the next cylinder), it is only one track. Thus, the number of disk seeks required for accessing contiguously allocated files is minimal, as is seek time when a seek is finally needed.

Contiguous allocation of a file is defined by the disk address and length of the first block. If the file is n blocks long, and starts at location b, then it occupies blocks $b, b + 1, b + 2, ..., b + n - 1$. The directory entry for each file indicates the address of the starting block and the length of the area allocated for this file (Figure 9.3).

Accessing a file that has been contiguously allocated is fairly easy. For sequential access, the file system remembers the disk address of the last block referenced and, when necessary, reads the next block. For direct access to block i of a file that starts at block b, we can immediately access block $b + i$. Thus, both sequential and direct access can be supported by contiguous allocation.

The difficulty with contiguous allocation is finding space for a new file. Once the implementation of the free-space list is defined, we can decide how to find space for a contiguously allocated file. If the file to be created is n blocks long, we must search the free-space list for n free contiguous blocks. For a bit map, we need to find n 0 bits in a row; for a list of addresses and counts, we need a count of at least n.

The contiguous disk-space-allocation problem can be seen to be a particular application of the general *dynamic storage-allocation* problem discussed in Section 7.4, which is how to satisfy a request of size n from a list of free holes. *First-fit*, *best-fit*, and *worst-fit* are the most common strategies used to select a free hole from the set of available holes. Simulations have shown that both first-fit and best-fit are better than worst-fit in terms of both time and storage utilization. Neither first-fit nor best-fit is clearly best in terms of storage utilization, but first-fit is generally faster.

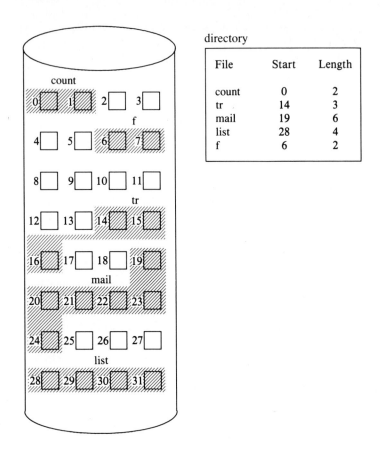

Figure 9.3   Contiguous allocation of disk space.

These algorithms suffer from *external fragmentation*. As files are allocated and deleted, the free disk space is broken into little pieces. External fragmentation exists when enough total disk space exists to satisfy a request, but this space is not contiguous; storage is fragmented into a large number of small holes. Depending on the total amount of disk storage and the average file size, external fragmentation may be either a minor or a major problem.

Some older microcomputer systems used contiguous allocation on floppy disks. To prevent loss of significant amounts of disk space to external fragmentation, the user had to run a repacking routine that copied the entire file system onto another floppy disk or onto a tape. The original floppy was then completely freed, creating one large contiguous free hole. The routine then copied the files back onto the floppy by allocating contiguous space from this one large hole.   This scheme effectively *compacted* all free space into one hole, solving the fragmentation problem. The cost of this compaction is time. Copying all the files from a disk to compact space may take hours and may be necessary on a weekly basis.

There are other problems with contiguous allocation. A major problem is determining how much space is needed for a file. When the file is created, the total amount of space it will need must be found and allocated. How does the creator (program or person) know the size of the file to be created? In some cases, this determination may be fairly simple (copying an existing file, for example), but in general the size of an output file may be difficult to estimate.

If we allocate too little space to a file, we may find that that file cannot be extended. Especially with a best-fit allocation strategy, the space on both sides of the file may be in use. We simply cannot make the file larger. Two possibilities then exist. First, the user program can be terminated, with an appropriate error message. The user must then allocate more space and run the program again. These repeated runs may be costly. To prevent them, the user will normally overestimate the amount of space needed, resulting in considerable wasted space.

The other possibility is to find a larger hole, to copy the contents of the file to the new space, and to release the previous space. This series of actions may be repeated as long as space exists, although it can also be time-consuming. Notice, however, that in this case the user never needs to be informed explicitly about what is happening; the system continues despite the problem, although more and more slowly.

Even if the total amount of space needed for a file is known in advance, preallocation may be inefficient. A file that grows slowly over a long period (months or years) must be allocated enough space for its final size, even though much of that space may be unused for a long time.

9.4.2 Linked Allocation

The problems discussed in Section 9.4.1 can be traced directly to the requirement that space be allocated contiguously. *Linked allocation* solves these problems. With linked allocation, each file is a linked list of disk blocks; the disk blocks may be scattered anywhere on the disk. The directory contains a pointer to the first and last blocks of the file. For example, a file of five blocks might start at block 9, continue at block 16, then block 1, block 10, and finally block 25 (Figure 9.4). Each block contains a pointer to the next block. These pointers are not made available to the user. Thus, if each sector is 512 words, and a disk address (the pointer) requires two words, then the user sees blocks of 510 words.

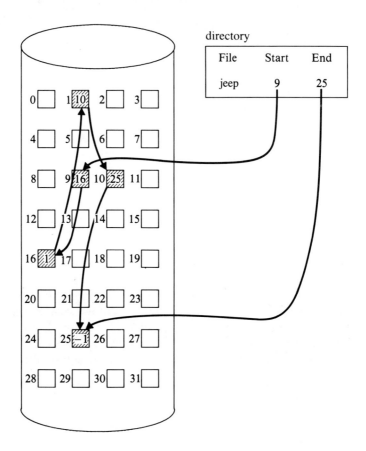

Figure 9.4   Linked allocation of disk space.

Creating a file is easy: We simply create a new entry in the device directory. With linked allocation, each directory entry has a pointer to the first disk block of the file. This pointer is initialized to *nil* (the end-of-list pointer value) to signify an empty file. The size field is also set to zero. A write to a file removes the first free block from the free-space list, and writes to that block. This new block is then linked to the end of the file. To read a file, we simply read blocks by following the pointers from block to block.

There is no external fragmentation with linked allocation. Any free block on the free-space list can be used to satisfy a request, since all blocks are linked together. Notice also that there is no need to declare the size of a file when that file is created. A file can continue to grow as long as there are free blocks. Consequently, it is never necessary to compact disk space.

Linked allocation does have disadvantages, however. The major problem is that it can be used effectively for only sequential-access files. To find the ith block of a file, we must start at the beginning of that file and follow the pointers until we get to the ith block. Each access to a pointer requires a disk read. Hence, it is inefficient to support a direct-access capability for linked allocation files.

Another disadvantage to linked allocation is the space required for the pointers. If a pointer requires two words out of a 512-words block, then 0.39 percent of the disk is being used for pointers, not for information. Each file requires slightly more space.

A more severe problem is reliability. Since the files are linked together by pointers scattered all over the disk, consider what would happen if a pointer were lost or damaged. A bug in the operating-system software or a disk hardware failure might result in picking up the wrong pointer. This error could result in linking into the free-space list or into another file. One partial solution is to use doubly linked lists or to store the file name and relative block number in each block; these schemes require even more overhead for each file.

An important variation on the linked allocation method is the use of a *file-allocation table* (FAT). A section of disk that contains a table is set aside. The table has one entry for each disk block, and is indexed by block number. The table is used much as is a linked list. The directory contains the block number of the first block of the file. The table entry indexed by that block number then contains the block number of the next block in the file. This chain continues until the last block, which has a special end-of-file value in the table entry. Unused blocks are indicated by a zero table value. Allocating a new block to a file is a simple matter of finding the first zero-valued table entry, and replacing the previous end-of-file value with the address of the new block. The zero is then replaced with the end-of-file value. This simple but efficient method of disk-space allocation is used by the MS-DOS and OS/2 operating systems. An illustrative example is the FAT structure of Figure 9.5 for a file consisting of disk blocks 217, 618, and 339.

9.4.3 Indexed Allocation

Linked allocation solves the external-fragmentation and size-declaration problems of contiguous allocation. However, linked allocation cannot support direct access, since the blocks are scattered all over the disk. Equally detrimental, the pointers to the blocks are scattered all over the disk. Indexed allocation solves this problem by bringing all the pointers together into one location: the *index block*.

Each file has its own index block, which is an array of disk-block addresses. The ith entry in the index block points to the ith block of the

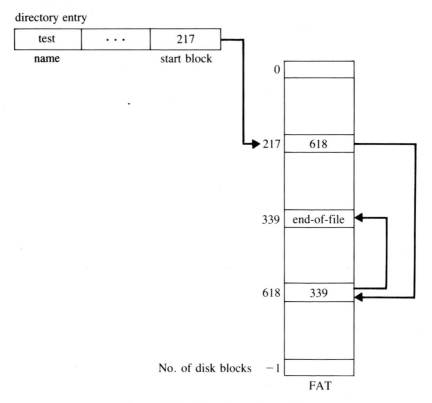

Figure 9.5   File-allocation table.

file. The directory contains the address of the index block (Figure 9.6). To read the ith block, we use the pointer in the ith index-block entry to find and read the desired block. This scheme is similar to the paging scheme described in Chapter 7.

When the file is created, all pointers in the index block are set to *nil*. When the ith block is first written, a block is removed from the free-space list, and its address is put in the ith index-block entry.

Indexed allocation supports direct access, without suffering from external fragmentation. Any free block anywhere on the disk may satisfy a request for more space.

Indexed allocation does suffer from wasted space. The pointer overhead of the index block is generally greater than the pointer overhead of linked allocation. Most files are small. Assume that we have a file of only one or two blocks. With linked allocation, we lose the space of only one pointer per block (one or two pointers). With indexed

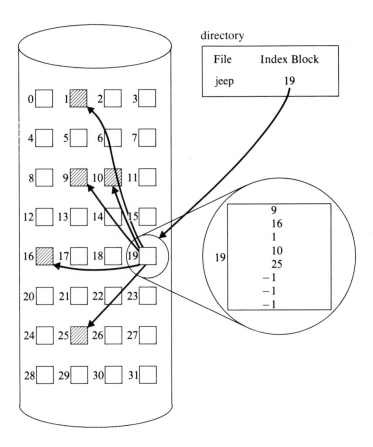

Figure 9.6 Indexed allocation of disk space.

allocation, an entire index block must be allocated, even if only one or two pointers will be non-*nil*.

This point raises the question of how large the index block should be. Every file must have an index block, so we want the index block to be as small as possible. If the index block is too small, however, it will not be able to hold enough pointers for a large file, and a mechanism will have to be available to deal with this issue:

- **Linked scheme**. An index block is normally one disk block. Thus, it can be read and written directly by itself. To allow for large files, we may link together several index blocks. For example, an index block might contain a small header giving the name of the file, and a set of the first 100 disk-block addresses. The next address (the last word in the index block) is *nil* (for a small file) or is a pointer to another index block (for a large file).

- **Multilevel index**. A variant of the linked representation is to use a separate index block to point to the index blocks, which point to the file blocks themselves. To access a block, the operating system uses the first level index to find the second-level index to find the desired data block. This approach could be continued to a third or fourth level, but two levels of indexes are generally sufficient. If we can get 256 pointers into an index block, then two levels of indexes allows 65,536 data blocks, which (at 1024 bytes each) allows a file of up to 67,108,864 bytes — a size that exceeds the physical capacity of many devices.

- **Combined scheme**. Another alternative, used in the BSD UNIX system, is to keep the first, say, 15 pointers of the index block in the device directory. The first 12 of these pointers point to *direct blocks*; that is, they directly contain addresses of blocks that contain data of the file. Thus, the data for small (no more than 12 blocks) files do not need a separate index block. If the block size is 4096 bytes, then up to 48K bytes of data may be accessed directly. The next three pointers point to *indirect blocks*. The first indirect-block pointer is the address of a *single indirect block*. The single indirect block is an index block, containing not data, but rather the addresses of blocks that do contain data. Then there is a *double-indirect-block* pointer, which contains the address of a block that contains the addresses of blocks that contain pointers to the actual data blocks. The last pointer would contain the address of a *triple indirect block*.

9.4.4 Performance

Storage efficiency is different in the various allocation methods. The latter also differ in the time required to access a block on disk. This second factor is particularly important for small, slow disk systems.

One difficulty in comparing the performance of the various systems is in determining how the systems will be used. For any type of access, contiguous allocation requires only one access to get a disk block. Since we can easily keep the initial address of the file in core, we can immediately calculate the disk address of the ith block (or the next block) and read it directly.

For linked allocation, we can also keep the address of the next block in memory and read it directly. This method is fine for sequential access; for direct access, however, an access to the ith block might require i disk reads. This problem indicates why linked allocation should not be used for an application requiring direct access.

As a result, some systems support direct access files by using contiguous allocation and sequential access by linked allocation. For these systems, the type of access to be made must be declared when the file is created. A file created for sequential access will be linked and cannot be used for direct access. A file created for direct access will be contiguous and can support both direct access and sequential access, but its maximum length must be declared when it is created. Notice that, in this case, the operating system must have appropriate data structures and algorithms to support *both* allocation methods. Files can be converted from one type to another by the creation of a new file of the desired type, into which the contents of the old file are copied. The old file may then be deleted, and the new file renamed.

Indexed allocation is more complex. If the index block is already in memory, then the access can be made directly. However, keeping the index block in memory requires considerable space. If this memory space is not available, then we may have to read first the index block and then the desired data block. For a two-level index, two index-block reads might be necessary. For a very large file, accessing a block near the end of the file would require reading in all the index blocks to follow the pointer chain before the data block finally could be read. Thus, the performance of indexed allocation depends on the index structure, on the size of the file, and on the position of the block desired.

Some systems combine contiguous allocation with indexed allocation by using contiguous allocation for small files (up to three or four blocks), and automatically switching to an indexed allocation if the file grows large. Since most files are small, and contiguous allocation is efficient for small files, average performance can be quite good.

Many other optimizations are possible and are in use. Given the disparity between CPU and disk speed, it is not unreasonable to add thousands of extra instructions to the operating system to save just a few disk head movements.

9.5 Disk Scheduling

Since most jobs depend heavily on the disk for loading and input and output files, it is important that disk service be as fast as possible. The operating system can improve on the average disk service time by scheduling the requests for disk access.

Disk speed is composed of three parts. To access a block on the disk, the system must first move the head to the appropriate track or cylinder. This head movement is called a *seek*, and the time to complete it is *seek time*. Once the head is at the right track, it must wait until the desired block rotates under the read-write head. This delay is *latency* time. Finally, the actual transfer of data between the disk and main memory can take place. This last part is *transfer* time. The total time to service a disk request is the sum of the seek time, latency time, and transfer time.

As we discussed in Chapter 2, every I/O device, including each disk drive, has a queue of pending requests. Whenever a process needs I/O to or from the disk, it issues a system call to the operating system. The request specifies several pieces of necessary information:

- Whether this is an input or output operation

- What the disk address is (drive, cylinder, surface, block)

- What the memory address is

- What amount of information is to be transferred (a byte or word count)

If the desired disk drive and controller are available, the request can be serviced immediately. However, while the drive or controller is serving one request, any additional requests, normally from other processes, will need to be queued.

For a multiprogramming system with many processes, the disk queue may often be nonempty. Thus, when a request is complete, we must pick a new request from the queue and service it. A disk service requires that the head be moved to the desired track, then a wait for latency, and finally the transfer of data.

9.5.1 FCFS Scheduling

The simplest form of disk scheduling is, of course, *first-come, first-served* (FCFS) scheduling. This algorithm is easy to program and is intrinsically fair. However, it may not provide the best (average) service. Consider, for example, an ordered disk queue with requests involving tracks

98, 183, 37, 122, 14, 124, 65, and 67,

listed first (98) to last (67). If the read-write head is initially at track 53, it will first move from 53 to 98, then to 183, 37, 122, 14, 124, 65, and finally to 67, for a total head movement of 640 tracks. This schedule is diagrammed in Figure 9.7.

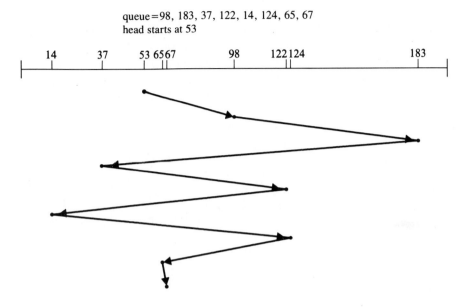

queue=98, 183, 37, 122, 14, 124, 65, 67
head starts at 53

Figure 9.7   FCFS disk scheduling.

The problem with this schedule is illustrated by the wild swing from 122 to 14 and then back to 124. If the requests for tracks 37 and 14 could be serviced together, before or after the requests at 122 and 124, the total head movement could be decreased substantially and the average time to service each request would decrease, improving disk throughput.

9.5.2 SSTF Scheduling

It seems reasonable to service together all requests close to the current head position, before moving the head far away to service another request. This assumption is the basis for the *shortest-seek-time-first* (SSTF) disk-scheduling algorithm. The SSTF algorithm selects the request with the minimum seek time from the current head position. Since seek time is generally proportional to the track difference between the requests, we implement this approach by moving the head to the closest track in the request queue.

For our example request queue, the closest request to the initial head position (53) is at track 65. Once we are at track 65, the next closest request is at track 67. At this point, the distance to track 37 is 30, whereas the distance to 98 is 31. Therefore, the request at track 37 is closer and is served next. Continuing, we service the request at track 14, then 98, 122, 124, and finally at 183 (Figure 9.8). This scheduling method results in a total head movement of only 236 tracks, little more than one-third of the distance needed for FCFS scheduling. This algorithm would result in a substantial improvement in average disk service.

SSTF scheduling is essentially a form of shortest-job-first (SJF) scheduling, and, like SJF scheduling, it may cause *starvation* of some requests. Remember that, in a real system, requests may arrive at any time. Assume that we have two requests in the queue, for 14 and 186. If a request near 14 arrives while we are servicing that request, it will be serviced next, making the request at 186 wait. While this request is being serviced, another request close to 14 could arrive. In theory, a continual stream of requests near one another could arrive, causing the request for track 186 to wait indefinitely.

The SSTF algorithm, although a substantial improvement over the FCFS algorithm, is not optimal. For example, if we move the head from 53 to 37, even though the latter is not closest, and then to 14, before turning around to service 65, 67, 98, 122, 124, and 183, we can reduce the total head movement to 208 tracks.

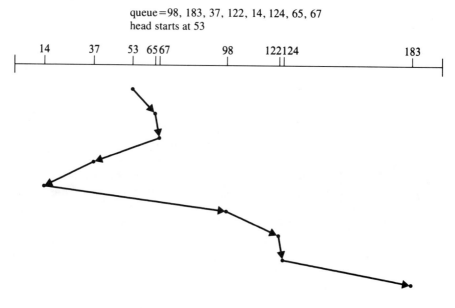

Figure 9.8   SSTF disk scheduling.

9.5.3 SCAN Scheduling

Recognition of the dynamic nature of the request queue leads to the SCAN algorithm. The read-write head starts at one end of the disk, and moves toward the other end, servicing requests as it reaches each track, until it gets to the other end of the disk. At the other end, the direction of head movement is reversed and servicing continues. The head continuously scans the disk from end to end. We again use our example.

Before applying SCAN to scheduling,

$$98, 183, 37, 122, 14, 124, 65, \text{ and } 67$$

we need to know the direction of head movement, in addition to the head's last position. If the head was moving toward 0, the head movement would service 37 and 14 as it moved to 0. At track 0, the head would reverse and move to the other end of the disk, servicing the requests at 65, 67, 98, 122, 124, and 183 as it moves (Figure 9.9). If a request arrives in the queue just in front of the head, it will be serviced almost immediately, whereas a request arriving just behind the head

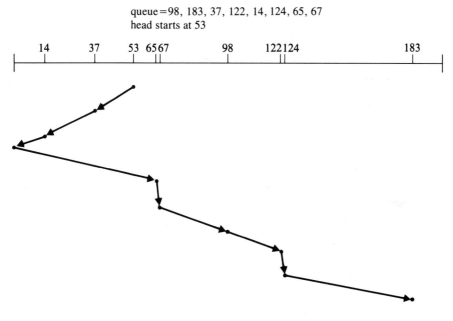

queue=98, 183, 37, 122, 14, 124, 65, 67
head starts at 53

14   37   53 65 67   98   122 124   183

Figure 9.9 SCAN disk scheduling.

will have to wait until the head moves to the end of the disk, reverses direction, and returns, before being serviced.

The SCAN algorithm is sometimes called the elevator algorithm, since it is similar to the behavior of elevators as they service requests to move from floor to floor in a building. Another analogy is that of shoveling snow from a sidewalk during a snowstorm. Starting from one end, we remove snow as we move toward the other end. As we move, new snow falls behind us. At the far end, we reverse direction and remove the newly fallen snow behind us.

Assuming a uniform distribution of requests for tracks, consider the density of requests when the head reaches one end and reverses direction. At this point, there are relatively few requests immediately behind the head, since these tracks have recently been serviced. The heaviest density of requests is at the other end of the disk. These requests have also waited the longest.

9.5.4 C-SCAN Scheduling

A variant of SCAN scheduling that is designed to provide a more uniform wait time is C-SCAN (circular SCAN) scheduling. As does SCAN scheduling, C-SCAN scheduling moves the head from one end of the disk to the other, servicing requests as it goes. When it reaches the other end, however, it immediately returns to the beginning of the disk, without servicing any requests on the return trip. C-SCAN scheduling essentially treats the disk as though it were circular, with the last track adjacent to the first one.

9.5.5 LOOK Scheduling

Notice that, as we described them, both SCAN and C-SCAN scheduling always move the head from one end of the disk to the other. In practice, neither algorithm is implemented in this way. More commonly, the head is only moved as far as the last request in each direction. As soon as there are no requests in the current direction, the head movement is reversed. These versions of SCAN and C-SCAN scheduling are called LOOK scheduling ("look" for a request before moving in that direction) and C-LOOK scheduling (Figure 9.10).

9.6 Selecting a Disk-Scheduling Algorithm

Given so many disk-scheduling algorithms, how do we choose a particular algorithm? SSTF scheduling is quite common and has a natural appeal. SCAN and C-SCAN scheduling are more appropriate for systems

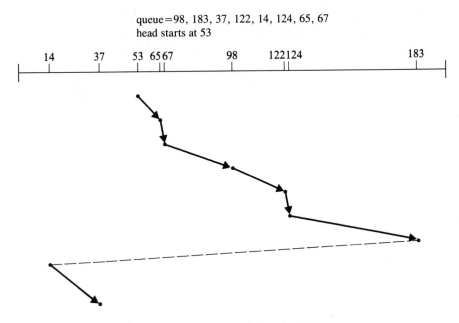

queue = 98, 183, 37, 122, 14, 124, 65, 67
head starts at 53

Figure 9.10   C-LOOK disk scheduling.

that place a heavy load on the disk. It is possible to define an optimal algorithm, but the computation needed for an optimal schedule may not justify the savings over SSTF or SCAN scheduling.

With any scheduling algorithm, however, performance depends heavily on the number and types of requests. In particular, if the queue seldom has more than one outstanding request, then all scheduling algorithms are effectively equivalent. In this case, FCFS scheduling is also a reasonable algorithm.

Notice also that the requests for disk service can be greatly influenced by the file-allocation method. A program reading a contiguously allocated file will generate several requests that are close together on the disk, resulting in limited head movement. A linked or indexed file, on the other hand, may include blocks that are widely scattered on the disk, resulting in better disk-space utilization at the expense of head movement.

The location of directories and index blocks also is important. Since every file must be opened to be used, and opening a file requires searching the directory structure, the directories will be accessed frequently. Placing the directories halfway between the inner and outer edge of the disk, rather than at either end, can significantly reduce disk-head movement. For instance, if a directory entry is in the first sector and a file's data are in the last sector, then the disk head needs to move the entire width of the disk. If the directory entry is more toward the middle, the head will have to move at most one-half the width.

It should be clear that, as a result of these considerations, the disk-scheduling algorithm, like all others, should be written as a separate module of the operating system, allowing it to be removed and to be replaced with a different algorithm if necessary. Either FCFS or SSTF scheduling is a reasonable initial choice.

9.7 Sector Queueing

The disk-scheduling algorithms we have just discussed (FCFS, SSTF, SCAN, and C-SCAN scheduling) are all aimed at minimizing disk-head movement, in order to minimize total service time and wait time. Fixed-head devices, such as drums, do not have this problem, however, since there is no head movement and no significant time to select a track. Thus, different algorithms are used for these devices.

Sector queueing is an algorithm for scheduling fixed-head devices. It is based on the division of each track into a fixed number of blocks, called *sectors*. The disk address in each request specifies the track and sector. Since seek time is zero for fixed-head devices, the main service time is latency time. For FCFS scheduling, assuming that requests are uniformly distributed over all sectors, the expected latency is one-half of a revolution.

Consider, however, the following example. Assume the head is currently over sector 2 and the first request in the queue is for sector 12. To service this request, we must wait until sector 12 revolves under the read-write heads. If there is a request in the queue for sector 5, it could be serviced before the request for sector 12, without causing the request for sector 12 to be delayed. Thus, we can improve our throughput greatly by servicing a request for each sector as that sector passes under the head, even if the request is not at the head of the waiting queue.

Sector queueing defines a separate queue for each sector of the drum. When a request arrives for sector i, it is placed in the queue for sector i. As sector i rotates beneath the read-write heads, the first request in its queue is serviced.

Sector queueing is used primarily with fixed-head devices. It can also be used with moving-head devices, if there is more than one request for service within a particular track or cylinder. Once the head is moved to a particular cylinder, all requests for this cylinder can be serviced without further head movement. Hence, sector queueing can be used to order multiple requests within the same cylinder. Like other scheduling algorithms, of course, sector queueing will have an effect only if the operating system must choose from a set of more than one request.

As noted in Section 9.2, some disk controllers include enough local memory to create a disk cache, which may be sufficiently large to store an entire track at a time. On such systems, sector queueing is not useful. Once a seek is performed, the track is read into the disk cache starting at the sector under the disk head (alleviating latency time). The disk controller then transfers any sector requests to the operating system.

9.8 Performance and Reliability Improvements

Disks tend to be a major bottleneck in system performance and reliability. They are the slowest main computer component, as we have shown. Although techniques such as memory and controller caches help to improve performance, overall system performance still depends on the speed and reliability of the disks. In addition, a disk crash is one of the most catastrophic computer hardware failures. Not only must the disk be replaced, but restoration of the disk's data also is usually required. This may take hours, as backup copies of the data on tape are transferred to the disk. Under normal circumstances, these restored data are not a precise image of the disk when it crashed. Backups are usually performed daily or weekly, meaning that any changes to the data since the last backup are lost if a disk crashes. Improving disk speed and reliability is therefore an important topic in current research.

Recently, several improvements in disk-use techniques have been put forward. These methods involve the use of multiple disks working cooperatively. To improve speed, researchers have proposed *disk stripping* (or interleaving), a technique now in use on a few systems. A group of disks is treated as one storage unit, with each block broken into several subblocks. Each subblock is stored on a separate disk. The time required to transfer one block into memory decreases drastically, since the disks transfer their subblocks in parallel, fully utilizing their *I/O bandwidth*, or transfer capacity. This decrease is especially notable if the disks are *synchronized* such that there is no latency between the subblock access on each drive. This advantage is also magnified if many small, inexpensive disks are used in place of few, large, expensive disks. The access rate improves since the number of small random accesses per second increases.

This idea was the basis for the development of redundant arrays of inexpensive disks (*RAID*), which improves performance, especially the price:performance ratio and provides for the duplication of data to improve reliability. Redundancy can be organized in various ways, with differing performance and cost efficiencies. The simplest RAID organization, called *mirroring* or *shadowing*, consists of keeping a duplicate copy of each disk. This solution is, of course, costly. In the most complex RAID organization, *block interleaved parity*, data are written to each disk in the array in a block unit, just as in more normal configurations. However, an extra block of parity data is written. This parity block is the parity of all the equivalent blocks on each disk in the array. For instance, if there are eight disks in the array, then sectors 0 of disks 1 through 7 have their parity computed and stored on disk 8. The computation takes place on a bit level for each byte, just as memory parity is computed. If one disk crashes, one of the data bits is essentially erased (an *erasure error*), but can be recomputed from the other data bits plus the parity. Thus, a single disk crash no longer results in loss of data (although multiple simultaneous crashes do). Of course, use of RAID improves speed by virtue of the use of multiple disks and controllers. This gain is less than that realized from pure disk stripping, however, since the parity block must also be read or written for each block access, and the parity computation must be performed. We can decrease this overhead by distributing the parity over all disks, rather than setting aside one parity disk. Since the tradeoff between speed and reliability is a reasonable one, RAID use is becoming more common, with many vendors either researching or producing RAID hardware and software. It has been shown that, with an array of 100 inexpensive disks and 10 parity disks, the mean time to data loss (MTDL) of the array is 90 years, compared to the 2 or 3 years of standard, large, expensive disks.

9.9 Storage Hierarchy

In this chapter, we have been concerned with secondary-storage management — in particular, disk management. Disk-based systems provide the primary on-line storage of information for both programs and data. Most programs (compilers, assemblers, sort routines, editors, formatters, and so on) are stored on a disk until loaded into memory, and then use the disk as both the source and destination of the information for their processing. Hence, the proper management of disk storage is of central importance to a computer system.

In a larger sense, however, disk systems are only one of many possible storage systems: There are also registers, main memory, drums, disks, tapes, and so on. Each storage system provides the basic functions of storing datum, holding that datum data until it is retrieved at a later time. The main differences among the various storage systems are in speed, cost, size, and volatility.

The wide variety of storage in a computer system can be organized in a hierarchy (Figure 9.11) according to either speed or their cost. The higher levels are expensive, but are fast. As we move down the hierarchy, the cost per bit decreases, whereas the access time increases, and the amount of storage at each level increases. This tradeoff is reasonable; if a given storage system were both faster and less expensive than another — other properties being the same — then there would be no reason to use the slower, more expensive memory.

The design of a complete memory system attempts to balance these factors: It uses only as much expensive memory as necessary, while providing as much inexpensive memory as possible. Demand paging is an example of such a system design: A limited amount of expensive, fast main memory is used to provide fast access to a much larger virtual memory, which is actually stored on less expensive, slower secondary

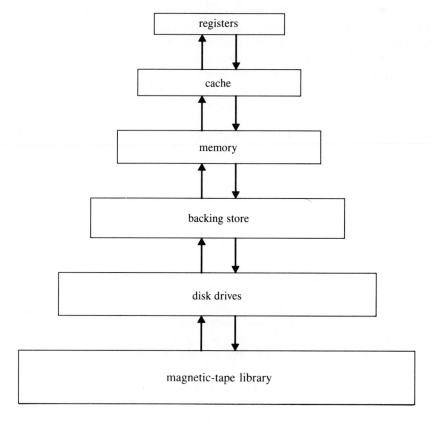

Figure 9.11 Storage hierarchies.

memory. Main memory can be viewed as a fast *cache* for secondary memory.

Caching is an important principle of computer systems, both in hardware and software. Information is normally kept in some storage system (such as main memory). As it is used, it is copied into a faster storage system (the cache) on a temporary basis. When we need a particular piece of information, we first check whether it is in the cache. If it is, we use the information directly from the cache; if it is not, we use the information from the main storage system, putting a copy in the cache in the hope that it will be needed again.

Since caches have limited size, *cache management* is an important design problem. Careful selection of the cache size and of a replacement policy can result in 80 to 99 percent of all accesses being in the cache, resulting in very high performance.

Extending this view, internal programmable registers, such as index registers and accumulators, are a high-speed cache for main memory. The programmer (or compiler) implements the register-allocation and register-replacement algorithms to decide which information to keep in registers and which to keep in main memory.

Virtual memory also can be viewed as a cache for an on-line file system. The file system itself may have several levels of storage. The faster, but more limited, disk storage can be backed up by the larger, but slower, tape storage. Optical disks are also efficient high-capacity but low-cost storage media. When compared to magnetic tape, they have the drawback of higher cost, but offer much greater speed and convenience. Transfers between these two storage levels are generally requested explicitly, but many systems now automatically archive a file that has not been used for a long time (1 month) and then automatically fetch back the file to disk when it is next referenced. The movement of information between levels of a storage hierarchy may be either explicit or implicit.

9.10 Summary

Disk systems are the major secondary I/O device on most computers. Requests for disk I/O are generated both by the file system and by virtual-memory systems. Each request specifies the address on the disk to be referenced. This address includes a track or cylinder number.

A disk normally has a device directory indicating which files are on the disk. The directory lists the file by name, and includes such information as the file location on the disk, its length, type, owner, time of creation, time of last use, and so on.

Files can be allocated space on the disk in three ways: through contiguous, linked, or indexed allocation. Contiguous allocation can suffer from external fragmentation. Direct-access files cannot be supported with linked allocation. Indexed allocation may require substantial overhead for its index block.

Moving-head disk-scheduling algorithms are designed to minimize total head movement; they include the FCFS, SSTF, SCAN, and C-SCAN algorithms. Sector queueing is a scheduling algorithm for fixed-head devices, such as drums.

Exercises

9.1 Consider a file currently consisting of 100 blocks. Assume that the file-control block (and index block in case of indexed allocation) is already in memory. Calculate how many disk I/O operations are required for contiguous, linked, and indexed (single-level) allocation strategies, if, for one block, the following hold. In the contiguous-allocation case, assume that there is no room to grow in the beginning, but there is room to grow in the end. Assume that the block information to be added is stored in memory.

   a. The block is added at the beginning.

   b. The block is added in the middle.

   c. The block is added at the end.

   d. The block is removed from the beginning.

   e. The block is removed from the middle.

   f. The block is removed from the end.

9.2 Consider a system where free space is kept in a free-space list.

   a. Suppose that the pointer to the free-space list is lost. Can the system reconstruct the free-space list?

   b. Suggest a scheme to ensure that the pointer is never lost as a result of memory failure.

9.3 Why must the bit map for file allocation be kept on mass storage, rather than in main memory?

9.4 Consider a system that supports the strategies of contiguous, linked, and indexed allocation. What criteria should be used in deciding which strategy should be utilized for a particular file?

9.5 Consider a file system on a disk that has both logical and physical block sizes of 512 bytes. Assume the information about each file is already in memory. For each of the three allocation strategies (contiguous, linked, and indexed), answer these questions:

a. How is the logical-to-physical address mapping accomplished in this system? (For the indexed allocation, assume that a file is always less than 512 blocks long.)

b. If we are currently at logical block 10 (the last block accessed was block 10) and want to access logical block 4, how many physical blocks must be read from the disk?

9.6 One problem with contiguous allocation is that the user must preallocate enough space for each file. If the file grows to be larger than the space allocated for it, special actions must be taken. One solution to this problem is to define a file structure consisting of an initial contiguous area (of a specified size). If this area is filled, the operating system automatically defines an overflow area that is linked to the initial contiguous area. If the overflow area is filled, another overflow area is allocated. Compare this implementation of a file with the standard contiguous and linked implementations.

9.7 Fragmentation on a storage device could be eliminated by recompaction of the information. Typical disk and drum devices do not have relocation or base registers (such as are used when memory is to be compacted), so how can we relocate files? Why are recompacting and relocation of files often avoided?

9.8 Why would a drum be used in preference to a disk for a paging device?

9.9 All the disk-scheduling disciplines, except FCFS scheduling, are not truly fair (starvation may occur).

a. Explain why this assertion is true.

b. Describe a scheme to ensure fairness.

c. Explain why fairness is an important goal in a time-sharing system.

9.10 Suppose the head of a moving-head disk with 200 tracks, numbered 0 to 199, is currently serving a request at track 143 and has just finished a request at track 125. The queue of requests is kept in the FIFO order:

86, 147, 91, 177, 94, 150, 102, 175, 130.

What is the total head movement needed to satisfy these requests for the following disk-scheduling algorithms?

a. FCFS scheduling

b. SSTF scheduling

c. SCAN scheduling

d. LOOK scheduling

e. C-SCAN scheduling

9.11 When the average queue length is small, all the disk-scheduling algorithms reduce to FCFS scheduling. Explain why this is true.

9.12 What is the major conceptual difference between disk scheduling and elevator scheduling? (Hint: Consider whether we are we trying to minimize elevator movement.)

9.13 Compare the throughput of C-SCAN and SCAN scheduling, assuming a uniform distribution of requests.

9.14 SSTF scheduling tends to favor mid-range cylinders over the innermost and outermost cylinders. Explain why this is true.

9.15 Requests are not usually uniformly distributed. For example, the cylinders on which the file-directory structures reside are accessed more frequently than are most files. Suppose that you know that 50 percent of the requests are for a small fixed number of cylinders.

a. Which of the scheduling algorithms in this chapter would be best?

b. Can you suggest a new scheduling algorithm for this case? If you can, describe your algorithm.

9.16 Is disk scheduling, other than FCFS scheduling, useful in a single-user environment?

9.17 Why is latency optimization usually not employed in disk scheduling? How would the standard algorithms (FCFS, SSTF, SCAN, and C-SCAN scheduling) be modified to include latency optimization?

9.18 With the decline in semiconductor-memory prices, several companies have begun to make semiconductor RAM "disks." These devices use memory chips rather than disks for storage. As a result, these disks have no moving parts, and hence are both faster and more reliable than are normal mechanical disks. These new devices are designed to be *plug-compatible* with existing disks, so programming and addressing is identical to that in normal disks. However, the new disks are much faster. How would their use affect your selection of a disk-scheduling algorithm? What factors would you need to consider?

9.19 While job hunting, a student hears a potential employer mention that her company's system uses sector queueing to minimize head movement on their moving-head disks. What comment should the student make during the interview?

9.20 Write a program-type monitor (Chapter 5) for disk-scheduling using the SCAN and C-SCAN disk-scheduling algorithms.

Bibliographic Notes

Discussions concerning magnetic disk technology is presented by Freedman [1983], and Harker et al. [1981]. Optical disks are covered by Kenville [1982], Fujitani [1984], O'Leary and Kitts [1985], Gait [1988], and Olsen and Kenly [1989]. A high-speed, large-capacity "jukebox" optical disk system is discussed by Ammon et al. [1985]. Discussions concerning floppy disks are offered by Pechura and Schoeffler [1983] and Sarisky [1983]. Discussions concerning redundant arrays of inexpensive disks (RAID) are presented by Patterson et al. [1988].

The Apple Macintosh disk-space management scheme is discussed in Apple [1987]. The MS-DOS FAT system is explained in [Norton and Wilton 1988], and the OS/2 description is found in [Iacobucci 1988]. These operating systems use the Motorola MC68000 family [Motorola 1989a] and the Intel 8086 [Intel 1985a, 1985b, 1986, 1990] CPUs, respectively.

Dynamic storage allocation was discussed by Knuth [1973, Section 2.5], who found, through simulation results, that first-fit is generally superior to best-fit. Additional discussions are offered by Shore [1975] and Bays [1977]. An adaptive exact-fit storage management scheme is presented by Oldehoeft and Allan [1985]. Disk file allocation based on the buddy system is discussed by Koch [1987]. A file organization scheme that guarantees retrieval in one access is discussed by Larson and Kajla 1984].

Denning [1967] described the FCFS, SSTF, and SCAN disk-scheduling algorithms. A complete survey of all the various disk-scheduling algorithms was presented by Teorey [1972] and Teorey and Pinkerton [1972]. Teorey and Pinkerton [1972] compared the various algorithms using simulations, and recommended use of either SCAN or C-SCAN scheduling, depending on the load.

Wilhelm [1976] and Hofri [1980] compared the FCFS and the SSTF seek disk-scheduling algorithms. Frank [1969], Gotlieb and MacEwen [1973], Fuller [1974], and Perros [1980] computed various performance aspects of disk-scheduling algorithms. Lynch [1972b] and Wilhelm [1976] discussed the consequences of nonuniform request distributions.

Denning [1967] presented various drum-scheduling algorithms, including FCFS and SATF (shortest-access-time-first) scheduling. Analysis of a paging drum can be found in the articles by Weingarten [1966], Coffman [1969], and Fuller [1972]. Abate and Dubner [1969], Stone and Fuller [1973], and Fuller [1974] discussed rotational optimization for fixed-head devices such as drums.

Disk caching is discussed by McKeon [1985] and Smith [1985]. General discussions concerning mass storage technology are offered by Chi [1982], Copeland [1982], and Hoagland [1985]. Analysis of memory hierarchies for sequential data access is given by Welch [1979].

PART 4

Files and Protection

File management is one of the most visible services of an operating system. A file is a collection of related information defined by its creator. Files are mapped, by the operating system, onto physical devices. Files are normally organized into directories to ease their use.

The operating system is responsible for the following activities in connection with file management: the creation and deletion of files and directories, the support of primitives for manipulating files and directories, the mapping of files onto disk storage, and backup of files on stable (nonvolatile) storage.

Protection mechanisms provide controlled access by limiting the types of file access that can be made by the various users. Protection must also be available to ensure that besides the files, memory segments, CPU, and other resources can be operated on by only those processes that have gained proper authorization from the operating system.

Protection is provided by a mechanism that controls the access of programs, processes, or users to the resources defined by a computer system. This mechanism must provide a means for specification of the controls to be imposed, together with a means of enforcement.

10

File Systems

For most users, the file system is the most visible aspect of an operating system. Files store data and programs. The operating system implements the abstract concept of a file by managing mass storage devices, such as tapes and disks. In this chapter, we consider the various ways to map files onto devices. Also, files are normally organized into directories to ease their use, so we look at a variety of directory structures. Finally, when multiple users have access to files, it may be desirable to control by whom and in what ways files may be accessed. This control is known as *file protection*.

10.1 File-System Organization

File management is one of the most visible services of an operating system. Computers can store information in several different physical forms; magnetic disk and tape are the most common storage media. Each storage device has its own characteristics and physical organization.

So that the computer system will be convenient to use, the operating system provides a uniform logical view of information storage. The operating system abstracts from the physical properties of its storage devices to define a logical storage unit, the *file*. Files are mapped, by the operating system, onto physical devices.

The file system consists of two distinct parts: the collection of the actual *files*, each containing related information, and the *directory structure*, which provides information about all the files in the system.

10.1.1 File Concept

What is a *file*? A file is a collection of related information defined by its creator. Commonly, files represent programs (both source and object forms) and data. Data files may be numeric, alphabetic, alphanumeric, or binary. Files may be free-form, such as text files, or may be formatted rigidly. In general, a file is a sequence of bits, bytes, lines, or records whose meaning is defined by the file's creator and user. The concept of a file is thus very general.

A file is named, and is referred to by its name. It has certain other properties, such as its type, the time of its creation, the name (or account number) of its creator, its length, and so on.

The information in a file is defined by its creator. Many different types of information may be stored in a file: source programs, object programs, numeric data, text, payroll records, graphic images, sound recordings, and so on. A file has a certain defined *structure* according to its type. A *text* file is a sequence of characters organized into lines (and possibly pages); a *source* file is a sequence of subroutines and functions, each of which is further organized as declarations followed by executable statements; an *object* file is a sequence of bytes organized into loader record blocks.

One major consideration is whether the operating system should know and support file types. If an operating system knows the type of a file, it can then operate on the file in reasonable ways. For example, a common mistake occurs when a user tries to print the binary object form of a program. This attempt normally produces garbage, but can be prevented *if* the operating system has been told that the file is a binary object program.

Another example comes from the TOPS-20 operating system. If the user tries to execute an object program whose source file has been modified (edited) since the object file was produced, the source file will be recompiled automatically. This function ensures that the user always runs an up-to-date object file. Otherwise, the user could waste a significant amount of time executing the old object file. Notice that, for this function to be possible, the operating system must be able to discriminate the source file from the object file, to check the time that each file was last modified or created, and to determine the language of the source program (in order to use the correct compiler).

There are disadvantages to having the operating system know the type of a file. One problem is the resulting size of the operating system.

If the operating system defines 14 different file types, it must then contain the code to support these file types correctly. In addition, every file must be definable as one of the file types supported by the operating system. Severe problems may result from new applications that require information structured in ways not supported by the operating system.

For example, assume that a system supports two types of files: text files (composed of ASCII characters separated by a carriage return and line feed) and executable binary files. Now if we (as users) want to define an encrypted file to protect our files from being read by unauthorized people, we may find neither file type to be appropriate. The encrypted file is not ASCII text lines, but rather is (apparently) random bits. Although it may appear to be a binary file, however, it is not executable. As a result, we may have to circumvent or misuse the operating system's file-types mechanism, or to modify or abandon our encryption scheme.

The other extreme is to impose (and support) no file type in the operating system. This approach has been adopted in UNIX, among others. UNIX considers each file to be a sequence of 8-bit bytes; no interpretation of these bits is made by the operating system. This scheme provides maximum flexibility, but minimal support. Each application program must include its own code to interpret an input file into the appropriate structure.

Files are usually kept on disks. Disk systems typically have a well-defined block size determined by the size of a sector. All disk I/O is in units of one block (physical record), and all blocks are the same size. It is unlikely that the physical record size will exactly match the length of the desired logical record. Logical records may even vary in length. *Packing* a number of logical records into physical blocks is a common solution to this problem.

For example, the UNIX operating system defines all files to be simply a stream of bytes. Each byte is individually addressable by its offset from the beginning (or end) of the file. In this case, the logical record is 1 byte. The file system automatically packs and unpacks bytes into physical disk blocks (say, 512 bytes per block) as necessary.

The logical record size, physical block size, and packing technique determine how many logical records are in each physical block. The packing can be done either by the user's application program or by the operating system.

In either case, the file may be considered to be a sequence of blocks. All the basic I/O functions operate in terms of blocks. The conversion from logical records to physical blocks is a relatively simple software problem.

Notice that disk space being always allocated in blocks has the result that, in general, some portion of the last block of each file may be wasted. If each block is 512 bytes, then a file of 1949 bytes would be allocated four blocks (2048 bytes); the last 99 bytes would be wasted. The wasted bytes allocated to keep everything in units of blocks (instead of bytes) is *internal fragmentation*. All file systems suffer from internal fragmentation; the larger the block size, the greater the internal fragmentation.

10.1.2 Directory Structure

The files in a computer system are represented by entries in a *device directory* or *volume table* of contents. The device directory records information — such as name, location, size, and type — for all files on that device.

A device directory may be sufficient for a single-user system with limited storage space. As the amount of storage and the number of users increase, however, it becomes increasingly difficult for the users to organize and keep track of all the files. The solution to this problem is the imposition of a directory *structure* on the file system. A directory structure provides a mechanism for organizing the many files in the file system. It may span device boundaries and include several different disk units, or even span disks on different computers. In this way, the user needs to be concerned with only the logical directory and file structure, and can completely ignore the problems of physically allocating space for files.

In fact, many systems actually have two separate directory structures: the device directory and the file directories. The device directory is stored on each physical device and describes all files on that device. The device-directory entry mainly describes the physical properties of each file: where the file is, how long it is, how it is allocated, and so on. The file directories are a logical organization of the files on all devices. The file-directory entry concentrates on logical properties of each file: name, file type, owning user, accounting information, protection access codes, and so on. A file-directory entry may simply point to the device-directory entry to provide information on physical properties, or may duplicate this information. Our main interest now is with the file-directory structure; device directories should be well understood.

The particular information kept for each file in the directory varies from operating system to operating system. The following information may be kept in a directory entry; not all systems keep all this information:

- **File name**. The symbolic file name is the only information kept in human-readable form.

- **File type**. This information is need for those systems that support different types.

- **Location**. This is a pointer to the device and location on that device of the file.

- **Size**. The current size of the file (in bytes, words or blocks), and possibly the maximum allowed size are included.

- **Current position**. This is a pointer to the current read or write position in the file.

- **Protection**. Access-control information controls who can do reading, writing, executing, and so on.

- **Usage count**. This value indicates the number of processes that are currently using (have opened) this file.

- **Time, date, and process identification**. This information may be kept for (1) creation, (2) last modification, and (3) last use. These data can be useful for protection and for usage monitoring.

It may take from 16 to over 1000 bytes to record this information for each file. In a system with a large number of files, the size of the directory itself may be hundreds of thousands of bytes. Thus, the device directory may need to be stored on the device and brought into memory piecemeal, as needed.

The directory system can be viewed as a symbol table that translates file names into their directory entries. If we take such a view, then it becomes apparent that the directory itself can be organized in many ways. We want to be able to insert entries, to delete entries, to search for a named entry, and to list all the entries in the directory. We discuss the appropriate data structures that can be used in the implementation of the directory structure. In Section 10.5, we discuss logical organization of the directory structure.

A linear list of directory entries requires a linear search to find a particular entry. This is simple to program but is time-consuming in execution. To create a new file, we must first search the directory to be sure that no existing file has the same name. Then, we add a new entry at the end of the directory. To delete a file, we search the directory for the named file, then release the space allocated to it. To reuse the directory entry, we can do one of several things. We can mark the entry as unused (a special name, such as an all-blank name, or a used/unused bit in each entry), or we can attach it to a list of free directory entries. A third alternative is to copy the last entry in the directory in the freed location and to decrease the length of the directory. A linked list can also be used to decrease the time to delete a file.

The real disadvantage of a linear list of directory entries is the linear search to find a file. A sorted list allows a binary search and decreases the average search time. However, the search algorithm is more complex to program. In addition, the list must be kept sorted. This requirement may complicate creating and deleting files, since we may have to move substantial amounts of directory information to maintain a sorted directory. (Notice, however, that if we want to be able to produce a list of all files in a directory sorted by file name, we do not have to sort separately before listing.) A linked binary tree might help here.

Another data structure that has been used for a file directory is a *hash table*. A hash-table data structure can greatly improve the directory search time. Insertion and deletion are also fairly straightforward, although some provision must be made for *collisions* — situations where two file names hash to the same location. The major difficulties with a hash table are the generally fixed size of the hash table and the dependence of the hash function on the size of the hash table.

For example, assume we establish a hash table of 64 entries. The hash function converts file names into integers from 0 to 63, probably by a final operation that uses the remainder of a division by 64. If we later try to create a sixty-fifth file, we must enlarge the directory hash table — say, to 100 entries. As a result, we need a new hash function, which must map file names to the range 0 to 99, and we must reorganize the existing directory entries to reflect their new hash-function values.

10.2 File Operations

A file is an *abstract data type*. To define a file properly, we need to consider the operations that can be performed on files. The operating system provides system calls to create, write, read, reset, and delete files. Let us consider what the operating system must do for each of the five basic file operations. It should then be easy to see how similar operations, such as renaming a file, would be implemented.

- **Creating a file**. Two steps are necessary to create a file. First, space in the file system must be found for the file. We shall discuss how to allocate space for the file in Section 10.4. Second, an entry for the new file must be made in the directory. The directory entry records the name of the file and the location in the file system.

- **Writing a file**. To write a file, we make a system call specifying both the name of the file and the information to be written to the file. Given the name of the file, the system searches the directory to find the location of the file. The directory entry will need to store a pointer to the current block of the file (usually the beginning of the file). Using this pointer, we can compute the address of the next block and write the information. The write pointer must be updated. In this way, successive writes can be used to write a sequence of blocks to the file.

- **Reading a file**. To read from a file, we use a system call that specifies the name of the file and where (in memory) the next block of the file should be put. Again, the directory is searched for the associated directory entry, and the directory will need a pointer to the next block to be read. Once that block is read, the pointer is updated.

  In general, a file is either being read or written, thus, although it would be possible to have two pointers, a read pointer and a write pointer, most systems have only one, a *current file position*. Both the read and write operations use this same pointer, saving space in the directory entry, and reducing the system complexity.

- **Resetting a file**. The directory is searched for the appropriate entry, and the current file position is reset to the beginning of the file. Resetting a file need not involve any actual I/O.

- **Deleting a file**. To delete a file, we search the directory for the named file. Having found the associated directory entry, we release all file space (so it can be reused by other files) and invalidate the directory entry.

You may have noticed that all the operations mentioned involve searching the directory for the entry associated with the named file. The directory entry contains all the important information needed to operate on the file. To avoid this constant searching, many systems will *open* a file when that file first is used actively. The operating system keeps a small table containing information about all open files. When a file operation is requested, an index into this table is used, so no searching is required. When the file is no longer actively used, it is *closed* and is removed from the table of open files.

Some systems implicitly open a file when the first reference is made to it. The file is automatically closed when the job or program that opened the file terminates. Most systems, however, require that a file be opened explicitly by the programmer with a system call (open) before that file can be used. The open operation takes a file name and searches the directory, copying the directory entry into the table of open files, assuming the file protections allow such access. Then, the open system call will typically return a pointer to the entry in the table of open files. This pointer, not the actual file name, is used in all I/O operations, avoiding any further searching.

The five operations we described certainly comprise the minimal set of required file operations. More commonly, we shall also want to *edit* the file and to modify its contents. A common modification is *appending* new information to the end of an existing file. We may want to create a *copy* of a file, or copy the file to an I/O device, such as a printer or a display. Since files are named objects, we may want to *rename* an existing file. We certainly want to execute a file if it is object format. Also of use are facilities to lock sections of an open file for multiprocess access, to share sections, and even to map sections into memory on virtual-memory systems. This last function allows a part of the virtual address space to be logically associated with a section of a file. Reads and writes to that memory region are then treated as reads and writes to the file, greatly simplifying file use.

10.3 Access Methods

Files store information. When it is used, this information must be accessed and read into computer memory. There are several ways that the information in the file can be accessed. Some systems provide only one access method for files. On other systems, such as those of IBM, many different access methods are supported, and choosing the right one for a particular application is a major design problem.

10.3.1 Sequential Access

Information in the file is processed in order, one record after the other. This is by far the most common mode of access of files. For example, computer editors usually access files in this fashion.

The bulk of the operations on a file are reads and writes. A read operation reads the *next* portion of the file and automatically advances the file pointer. Similarly, a write appends to the end of the file and advances to the end of the newly written material (the new end of file). Such a file can be reset to the beginning, and, on some systems, a program may be able to skip forward or backward n records, for some integer n (perhaps only for $n = 1$). This scheme is known as *sequential access* to a file (Figure 10.1). Sequential access is based on a tape model of a file.

10.3.2 Direct Access

An alternative access method is *direct access*, which is based on a disk model of a file. For direct access, the file is viewed as a numbered

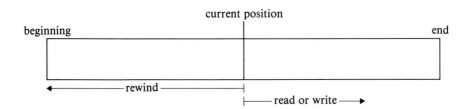

Figure 10.1   Sequential-access file.

sequence of blocks or records. A direct-access file allows arbitrary blocks to be read or written. Thus, we may read block 14, then read block 53, and then write block 7. There are no restrictions on the order of reading or writing for a direct-access file.

Direct-access files are of great use for immediate access to large amounts of information. Large databases are often of this type. When a query concerning a particular subject arrives, we compute which block contains the answer, and then read that block directly to provide the desired information.

For example, on an airline-reservation system, we might store all the information about a particular flight (for example, flight 713) in the block identified by the flight number. Thus, the number of available seats for flight 713 is stored in block 713 of the reservation file. To store information about a larger set, such as people, we might compute a hash function on the people's names, or search a small in-core index to determine a block to read and search.

The file operations must be modified to include the block number as a parameter. Thus, we have *read n*, where *n* is the block number, rather than *read next*, and *write n*, rather than *write next*. An alternative approach is to retain *read next* and *write next*, as with sequential access, and to add an operation, *position file to n*, where *n* is the block number. Then, to effect a *read n*, we would *position to n* and then *read next*.

The block number provided by the user to the operating system is normally a *relative block number*. A relative block number is an index relative to the beginning of the file. Thus, the first relative block of the file is 0, the next is 1, and so on, even though the actual absolute disk address of the block may be 14703 for the first block, and 3192 for the second. The use of relative block numbers allows the operating system to decide where the file should be placed (the allocation problem as discussed in Section 10.5), and helps to prevent the user from accessing portions of the file system that may not be part of his file. Some systems start their relative block numbers at 0; others start at 1.

Not all operating systems support both sequential and direct access for files. Some systems allow only sequential file access; others allow only direct access. Some systems require that a file be defined as sequential or direct when it is created; such a file can be accessed only in a manner consistent with its declaration. Notice, however, that it is easy to simulate sequential access on a direct-access file. If we simply keep a variable *cp*, which defines our current position, then we can simulate sequential file operations, as shown in Figure 10.2. On the other hand, it is extremely inefficient and clumsy to simulate a direct-access file on a sequential-access file.

10.3.3 Other Access Methods

Other access methods can be built on top of a direct-access method. These additional methods generally involve the construction of an *index* for the file. The index, like an index in the back of a book, contains pointers to the various blocks. To find an entry in the file, we first search the index and then use the pointer to access the file directly and to find the desired entry.

For example, a retail-price file might list the universal product codes (UPCs) for items, with the associated prices. Each entry consists of a 10-digit UPC code and a six-digit price, for a 16-byte entry. If our disk has 1024 bytes per block, we can store 64 entries per block. A file of 120,000 entries would occupy about 2000 blocks (2 million bytes). By keeping the file sorted by UPC code, we can define an index consisting of the first UPC code in each block. This index would have 2000 entries of 10 digits each, or 20,000 bytes, and thus could be kept in memory. To find the price of a particular item, we can (binary) search the index. From this search, we would know exactly which block contains the desired entry and access that block. This structure allows us to search a large file with very little I/O.

Sequential access	Implementation for direct access
reset	$cp := 0$;
read next	*read cp*;
	$cp := cp+1$;
write next	*write cp*;
	$cp := cp+1$;

Figure 10.2   Simulation of sequential access on a direct-access file.

With large files, the index file itself may become too large to be kept in memory. One solution is to create an index for the index file. The primary index file would contain pointers to secondary index files, which would point to the actual data items.

For example, IBM's indexed sequential access method (ISAM) uses a small master index that points to disk blocks of a secondary index The secondary index blocks point to the actual file blocks. The file is kept sorted on a defined key. To find a particular item, we first make a binary search of the master index, which provides the block number of the secondary index. This block is read in, and again a binary search is used to find the block containing the desired record. Finally, this block is searched sequentially. In this way, any record can be located from its key by at most two direct access reads.

10.4 Consistency Semantics

Consistency semantics is an important criterion for evaluation of any file system that supports sharing of files. It is a characterization of the system that specifies the semantics of multiple users accessing a shared file simultaneously. In particular, these semantics should specify when modifications of data by one user are observable by other users.

For the following discussion, we assume that a series of file accesses (that is, Reads and Writes) attempted by a user to the same file, is always enclosed between the Open and Close operations. We call the series of accesses between an Open and Close operation a *file session*. To illustrate the concept, we sketch several prominent examples of consistency semantics.

10.4.1 UNIX Semantics

The UNIX file system (Chapter 15) uses the following consistency semantics.

- Writes to an open file by a user are visible immediately to other users that have this file open at the same time.

- There is a mode of sharing where users share the pointer of current location into the file. Thus, the advancing of the pointer by one user affects all sharing users. Here, a file has a single image that interleaves all accesses, regardless of their origin.

These semantics lend themselves to an implementation where a file is associated with a single physical image that is accessed as an exclusive resource. Contention for this single image results in users being delayed.

10.4.2 Session Semantics

The Andrew file system (Chapter 14) uses the following consistency semantics.

- Writes to an open file by a user are not visible immediately to other users that have the same file open simultaneously.

- Once a file is closed, the changes made to it are visible only in sessions starting later. Already-open instances of the file do not reflect these changes.

According to these semantics, a file may be temporarily associated with several (possibly different) images at the same time. Consequently, multiple users are allowed to perform both Read and Write accesses concurrently on their image of the file, without being delayed. Notice that almost no constraints are enforced on scheduling accesses.

10.4.3 Immutable-Shared-Files Semantics

A different, quite unique approach is that of *immutable shared files*. Once a file is declared as shared by its creator, it cannot be modified any more. An immutable file has two important properties: Its name may not be reused and its contents may not be altered. Thus, the name of an immutable file signifies the fixed contents of the file, not the file as a container for variable information. The implementation of these semantics in a distributed system (Chapter 14) is very simple, since the sharing is very disciplined (read-only).

10.5 Directory-Structure Organization

Many different file directory structures have been proposed and are in use. The directory is essentially a *symbol table*. The operating system takes the symbolic file name and finds the named file. In this section, we examine several alternative schemes for defining the logical structure of the directory system.   When considering a particular directory structure, we need to keep in mind the operations that are to be performed on a directory:

- **Search**. We need to be able to search a directory structure to find the entry for a particular file. Since files have symbolic names and similar names may indicate a relationship between files, we may want to be able to find all files that match a particular pattern.

- **Create file**. New files need to be created and added to the directory.

- **Delete file**. When a file is no longer needed, we want to remove it from the directory.

- **List directory**. We need to be able to list the files in a directory and the contents of the directory entry for each file in the list.

- **Backup**. For reliability, it is generally a good idea to save the contents and structure of the file system at regular intervals. This saving often consists of copying all files to magnetic tape. This technique provides a backup copy in case of system failure or if the file is simply no longer in use. In this case, the file can be copied to tape, and the disk space of that file released for reuse by another file.

10.5.1 Single-Level Directory

The simplest directory structure is the single-level directory. The device directory is an example of a single-level directory. All files are contained in the same directory, which is easy to support and understand (Figure 10.3).

A single-level directory has significant limitations, however, when the number of files increases or when there is more than one user. Since all files are in the same directory, they must have unique names. If we have two users who call their data file *test*, then the unique-name rule is

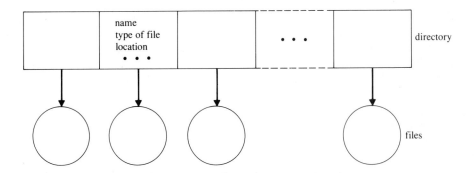

Figure 10.3 Single-level directory.

violated. (For example, in one programming class, 23 students called the program for their second assignment *prog2*; another 11 called it *assign2*.) Although file names are generally selected to reflect the content of the file, they are often quite limited in length. (MS-DOS allows only 11-character file names; UNIX allows 255 characters.)

Even with a single user, as the number of files increases, it becomes difficult to remember the names of all the files in order to create only files with unique names. (It is not uncommon for a user to have hundreds of files on one computer system and an equal number of additional files on another system.)

10.5.2 Two-Level Directory

The major disadvantage to a single-level directory is the confusion of file names between different users. The standard solution is to create a *separate* directory for each user. Especially on a large system, this user directory is a *logical*, rather than physical, organization, since all the files are still physically on the same device.

In the two-level directory structure, each user has her own user file directory (UFD). Each UFD has a similar structure (linear, binary, or hashed), but lists only the files of a single user. When a user job starts or a user logs in, the system's master file directory (MFD) is searched. The master file directory is indexed by user name or account number, and each entry points to the user directory for that user (Figure 10.4).

When a user refers to a particular file, only his own user file directory is searched. Thus, different users may have files with the same name, as long as all the file names within each UFD are unique.

To create a file for a user, the operating system searches only that user's directory to ascertain whether another file of that name already

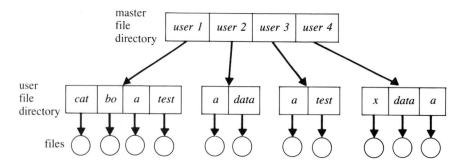

Figure 10.4   Two-level directory structure.

exists. To delete a file, the operating system confines its search to the local UFD; thus, it cannot accidentally delete another user's file with the same name.

The user directories themselves must be created and deleted as necessary. A special system program is run with the appropriate user name and account information. The program creates a new user file directory and adds an entry for it to the master file directory. The execution of this program might, of course, be restricted. The allocation of disk space for user directories can be handled using the techniques discussed in Section 10.5 for files themselves.

There are still problems with the two-level directory structure. This structure effectively isolates one user from another. This is an advantage when the users are completely independent, but a disadvantage when the users *want* to cooperate on some task and to access files of other users. Some systems simply do not allow local user files to be accessed by other users.

If access is to be permitted, one user must have the ability to name a file in another user's directory. To name a particular file uniquely in a two-level directory, we must give both the user name and the file name. A two-level directory can be thought of as a tree of height 2. The root of the tree is the master file directory. Its direct descendants are the user file directories. The descendants of the user file directories are the files themselves. The files are the leaves of the tree. Specifying a user name and a file name defines a path in the tree from the root (the master file directory) to a leaf (the specified file). Thus, a user name and a file name define a *path name*. Every file in the system has a path name. To name a file uniquely, a user must know the path name of the file desired.

For example, if user A wishes to access her own test file named *test*, she can simply refer to *test*. To access the test file of user B (with directory-entry name *userb*), however, she might have to refer to */userb/test*. Every system has its own syntax for naming files in directories other than the user's own.

A special case of this situation occurs in regard to the system files. Those programs provided as a part of the system (loaders, assemblers, compilers, utility routines, libraries, and so on) are generally defined as files. When the appropriate commands are given to the operating system, these files are read by the loader and are executed. Many command interpreters act by simply treating the command as the name of a file to load and execute. As the directory system is presently defined, this file name would be searched for in the current user file directory. One solution would be to copy the system files into each user file directory. However, copying all the system files would be enormously wasteful of space. (If the system files require 5 megabytes, then supporting 12 users would require sixty (5 × 12 = 60) megabytes just for copies of the system files.)

The standard solution is to complicate the search procedure slightly. A special user directory is defined to contain the system files (for example, user 0). Whenever a file name is given to be loaded, the operating system first searches the local user file directory. If the file is found, it is used. If it is not found, the system automatically searches the special user directory that contains the system files. The sequence of directories searched when a file is named is called the *search path*.

10.5.3 Tree-Structured Directories

Once we have seen how to view a two-level directory as a two-level tree, the natural generalization is to extend the directory structure to a tree of arbitrary height (Figure 10.5). This generalization allows users to create their own subdirectories and to organize their files accordingly. The MS-DOS file system, for instance, is structured as a tree. The tree has a root directory. Every file in the system has a unique path name. A

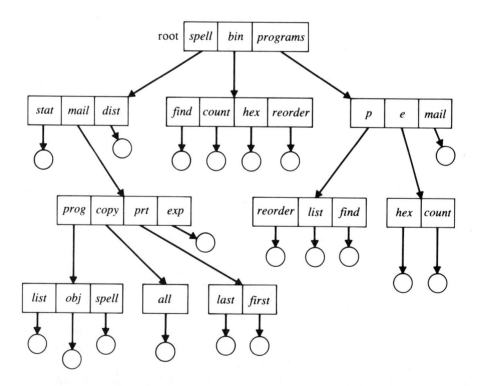

Figure 10.5   Tree-structured directory structure.

path name is the path from the root, through all the subdirectories, to a specified file.

A directory (or subdirectory) contains a set of files and/or subdirectories. All directories have the same internal format. One bit in each directory entry defines the entry as a file (0) or a subdirectory (1). Special system calls are used to create and delete directories.

In normal use, each user has a *current directory*. The current directory should contain most of the files that are of current interest to the user. When reference is made to a file, the current directory is searched. If a file is needed that is not in the current directory, then the user must either specify a path name or change the current directory. A system call will take a directory name as a parameter and use it to redefine the current directory. Thus, the user can change his current directory whenever he desires. When the user job starts, or the user logs in, the operating system searches the accounting file to find an entry for this user (for accounting purposes). Also stored in the accounting file is a pointer to (or the name of) the user's initial directory. A local variable for this user is defined, to specify the user's current directory.

Path names can be of two types: *absolute* path names or *relative* path names. An absolute path name begins at the root and follows a path down to the specified file, giving the directory names on the path. A relative path name defines a path from the current directory. For example, in the tree structured file system of Figure 10.5, if the current directory is *root/spell/mail*, then the relative path name *prt/first* refers to the same file as does the absolute path name *root/spell/mail/prt/first*.

Allowing the user to define his own subdirectories permits him to impose a structure on his files. This structure might result in separate directories for files associated with different topics (for example, a subdirectory was created to hold the text of this book) or different forms of information (for example, the directory *programs* may contain source programs; the directory *bin* may store all the binaries).

An interesting policy decision in a tree-structured directory structure is how to handle the deletion of a directory. If a directory is empty, its entry in its containing directory can simply be deleted. However, suppose the directory to be deleted is not empty, but contains several files, or possibly subdirectories. One of two approaches can be taken. Some systems will not delete a directory unless it is empty. Thus, to delete a directory, someone must first delete all the files in that directory. If there are any subdirectories, this procedure must be applied recursively to them, so that they can be deleted also. This approach may result in a substantial amount of work.

An alternative approach is just to assume that, when a request is made to delete a directory, all of that directory's files and subdirectories are also to be deleted. Note that either approach is fairly easy to implement; the choice is one of policy. There are systems that have been implemented each way.

Files of other users can be accessed easily. For example, user B can access files of user A by specifying their path names. User B can specify either an absolute or a relative path name. Alternatively, user B could change her current directory to be user A's directory, and access the files by their file names. Some systems also allow users to define their own search paths. In this case, user B could define her search path to be (1) her local directory, (2) the system file directory, and (3) user A's directory, in that order. As long as the name of a file of user A did not conflict with the name of a local file or system file, it could be referred to simply by its name.

10.5.4 Acyclic-Graph Directories

Consider two programmers who are working on a joint project. The files associated with that project can be stored in a subdirectory, separating them from other projects and files of the two programmers. But since both programmers are equally responsible for the project, both want the subdirectory to be in their own directories. The common subdirectory should be *shared*. A shared directory or file will exist in the file system in two (or more) places at once. Notice that a shared file (or directory) is not the same as two copies of the file. With two copies, each programmer can view the copy rather than the original, but if one programmer changes the file, the changes will not appear in the other's copy. With a shared file, there is only *one* actual file, so any changes made by one person would be immediately visible to the other. This is particularly important for shared subdirectories; a new file created by one person will automatically appear in all the shared subdirectories.

A tree structure prohibits the sharing of files or directories. An *acyclic graph* allows directories to have shared subdirectories and files (Figure 10.6). The *same* file or subdirectory may be in two different directories. An acyclic graph (that is, a graph with no cycles) is a natural generalization of the tree-structured directory scheme.

In a situation where several people are working as a team, all the files to be shared may be put together into one directory. The user file directories of all the team members would each contain this directory of shared files as a subdirectory. Even when there is a single user, his file organization may require that some files be put into several different subdirectories. For example, a program written for a particular project should be both in the directory of all programs and in the directory for that project.

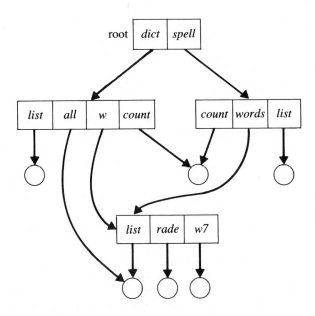

Figure 10.6   Acyclic-graph directory structure.

Shared files and subdirectories can be implemented in several ways. A common way, exemplified by BSD UNIX, is to create a new directory entry called a *link*. A link is effectively a pointer to another file or subdirectory. For example, a link may be implemented as an absolute or relative path name (a *symbolic link*). When a reference to a file is made, we search the directory. The directory entry is marked as a link and the name of the real file (or directory) is given. We *resolve* the link by using the path name to locate the real file. Links are easily identified by their format in the directory entry, and are effectively named indirect pointers. The operating system ignores these links when traversing directory trees to preserve the acyclic structure of the system.

The other approach to implementing shared files is simply to duplicate all information about them in both sharing directories. Thus, both entries are identical and equal. A link is clearly different from the original directory entry; thus, the two are not equal. Duplicate directory entries, however, make the original and the copy indistinguishable. A major problem with duplicate directory entries is maintaining consistency if the file is modified.

An acyclic-graph directory structure is more flexible than a simple tree structure, but is also more complex. Several problems must be considered carefully. Notice that a file may now have multiple absolute path names. Consequently, distinct file names may refer to the same file. This is similar to the aliasing problem for programming languages. If we are trying to traverse the entire file system (to find a file, to accumulate statistics on all files, or to copy all files to backup storage), this problem becomes significant, since we do not want to traverse shared structures more than once.

Another problem involves deletion. When can the space allocated to a shared file be deallocated and reused? One possibility is to remove the file whenever anyone deletes it, but this action may leave dangling pointers to the now-nonexistent file. Worse, if the remaining file pointers contain actual disk addresses, and the space is subsequently reused for other files, these dangling pointers may point into the middle of other files.

In a system where sharing is implemented by symbolic links, this situation is somewhat easier to handle. The deletion of a link need not affect the original file; only the link is removed. If the file entry itself is deleted, the space for the file is deallocated, leaving the links dangling. We can search for these links and remove them also, but unless a list of the associated links is kept with each file, this search can be quite expensive. Alternatively, we can leave the links until an attempt is made to use them. At that time, we can determine that the file of the name given by the link does not exist, and can fail to resolve the link name; the access is treated just like any other illegal file name. (In this case, the system designer should consider carefully what to do when a file is deleted and another file of the same name is created, before a symbolic link to the original file is used.)

Another approach to deletion is to preserve the file until all references to it are deleted. To implement this approach, we must have some mechanism for determining that the last reference to the file has been deleted. We could keep a list of all references to a file (directory entries or symbolic links). When a link or a copy of the directory entry is established, a new entry is added to the file-reference list. When a link or directory entry is deleted, we remove its entry on the list. The file is deleted when its file-reference list is empty.

The trouble with this approach is the variable and potentially large size of the file-reference list. However, we really do not need to keep the entire list — we need to keep only a count of the *number* of references. A new link or directory entry increments the reference count; deleting a link or entry decrements the count. When the count is 0, the file can be deleted; there are no remaining references to it.   UNIX uses this approach, keeping a reference count in the file information block (i-node). By effectively prohibiting multiple references to directories, we maintain an acyclic-graph structure. A description of the UNIX file system is provided in Chapter 15.

10.5.5 General Graph Directory

One serious problem with using an acyclic graph structure is ensuring that there are no cycles. If we start with a two-level directory and allow users to create subdirectories, a tree-structured directory results. It should be fairly easy to see that simply adding new files and subdirectories to an existing tree-structured directory preserves its tree-structured nature. However, when we add links to an existing tree-structured directory, the tree structure is destroyed, resulting in a simple graph structure (Figure 10.7).

The primary advantage of an acyclic graph is the relative simplicity of the algorithms to traverse it and to determine when there are no more references to a file. We want to avoid traversing shared sections of an acyclic graph twice, mainly for performance reasons. If we have just searched a major shared subdirectory for a particular file, without finding that file, we want to avoid searching that subdirectory again; the second search would be a waste of time.

If cycles are allowed to exist in the directory, we likewise want to avoid searching any component twice, for reasons of correctness as well as performance. A poorly designed algorithm might result in an infinite loop continually searching through the cycle and never terminating.

A similar problem exists when we are trying to determine when a file can be deleted. As with acyclic-graph directory structures, a 0 in the

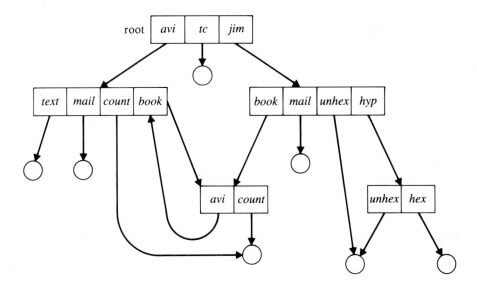

Figure 10.7 General graph directory.

reference count means that there are no more references to the file or directory, and the file can be deleted. However, it is also possible, when cycles exist, that the reference count may be nonzero, even when it is no longer possible to refer to a directory or file. This anomaly results from the possibility of self-referencing (a cycle) in the directory structure. In this case, it is generally necessary to use *garbage collection* to determine when the last reference has been deleted and the disk space can be reallocated. Garbage collection involves traversing the file system, marking everything that can be accessed. Then, a second pass collects everything that is not marked onto a list of free space. (A similar marking procedure can be used to ensure that a traversal or search will cover everything in the file system once and only once.) Garbage collection for a disk-based file system, however, is extremely time-consuming and is thus seldom attempted.

Garbage collection is necessary only because of possible cycles in the graph. Thus, an acyclic-graph structure is much easier to work with. The difficulty is to avoid cycles, as new links are added to the structure. How do we know when a new link will complete a cycle? There are algorithms to detect cycles in graphs; however, they are computationally expensive, especially when the graph is on disk storage. Generally, tree directory structures are more common than are acyclic-graph structures.

10.6 File Protection

When information is kept in a computer system, a major concern is its protection from both physical damage (*reliability*) and improper access (*protection*).

Reliability is generally provided by duplicate copies of files. Many computers have systems programs that automatically (or through computer-operator intervention) copy disk files to tape at regular intervals (once per day or week or month) to maintain a copy should a file system be accidentally destroyed. File systems can be damaged by hardware problems (such as errors in reading or writing), power surges or failures, head crashes, dirt, temperature, and vandalism. Files may be deleted accidentally. Bugs in the file system software can also cause file contents to be lost.

Protection can be provided in many ways. For a small single-user system, we might provide protection by physically removing the floppy disks and locking them in a desk drawer or file cabinet. In a multiuser system, however, other mechanisms are needed.

The need for protecting files is a direct result of the ability to access files. On systems that do not permit access to the files of other users, protection is not needed. Thus, one extreme would be to provide complete protection by prohibiting access. The other extreme is to provide free access with no protection. Both of these approaches are too extreme for general use. What is needed is *controlled access*.

Protection mechanisms provide controlled access by limiting the types of file access that can be made. Access is permitted or denied depending on several factors, one of which is the type of access requested. Several different types of operations may be controlled:

- **Read**. Read from the file.

- **Write**. Write or rewrite the file.

- **Execute**. Load the file into memory and execute it.

- **Append**. Write new information at the end of the file.

- **Delete**. Delete the file and free its space for possible reuse.

Other operations, such as renaming, copying, or editing the file, may also be controlled. For many systems, however, these higher-level functions (such as copying) may be implemented by a system program that makes lower-level system calls. Protection is provided at only the lower level. For instance, copying a file may be implemented simply by a sequence of read requests. In this case, a user with read access can also cause the file to be copied, printed, and so on.

The directory operations that must be protected are somewhat different. We want to control the creation and deletion of files in a directory. In addition, we probably want to control whether a user can determine the existence of a file in a directory. Sometimes, knowledge of the existence and name of a file may be significant in itself. Thus, listing the contents of a directory must be a protected operation.

Many different protection mechanisms have been proposed. Chapter 11 fully addresses protection issues; we shall discuss only a few pertinent ones. As always, each has its advantages and disadvantages and must be selected as appropriate for its intended application. A small computer system that is used by only a few members of a research group may not need the same types of protection as will a large corporate computer that is used for research, finance, and personnel operations.

Protection can be associated either with the file itself or with the path used to specify the file. The more common scheme provides protection on the path. Thus, if a path name refers to a file in a directory, the user must be allowed access to both the directory and the file. In systems where files may have numerous path names (such as acyclic or general graphs), a given user may have different access rights to a file depending on the path name used.

10.6.1 Naming

The protection schemes of several systems depend on the inability of a user to access a file that he cannot name. If the user cannot name a file, then he cannot operate on it. This scheme assumes that there is no mechanism for obtaining the names of other user's files and that the names cannot be guessed easily. In fact, since file names are generally picked to be mnemonic, they can often be guessed easily.

10.6.2 Passwords

Another approach is to associate a password with each file. Just as access to the computer system itself is often controlled by a password, access to each file can be controlled by a password. If the passwords are chosen randomly and changed often, this scheme may be effective in limiting access to a file to only those users who know the password.

There are, however, several disadvantages to this scheme:

- If we associate a separate password with each file, the number of passwords that need to be remembered may become large, making the scheme impractical. If only one password is used for all the files, then, once it is discovered, all files are accessible. Some systems (for example, TOPS-20) allow a user to associate a password with a subdirectory rather than with an individual file, to deal with this problem.

- Commonly, only one password is associated with each file. Thus, protection is on an all-or-nothing basis. To provide protection on a more detailed level, we must use multiple passwords.

10.6.3 Access Lists

Another approach is to make access dependent on the identity of the user. Various users may need different types of access to a file or directory. An *access list* can be associated with each file and directory, specifying the user name and the types of access allowed for each user. When a user requests access to a particular file, the operating system checks the access list associated with that file. If that user is listed for the requested access, the access is allowed. Otherwise, a protection violation occurs and the user job is denied access to the file.

10.6.4 Access Groups

The main problem with access lists can be their length. If we want to allow everyone to read a file, we must list all users with read access.

This technique has two undesirable consequences:

- Constructing such a list may be a tedious and unrewarding task, especially if we do not know in advance the list of users in the system.

- The directory entry that previously was of fixed size needs now to be of variable size, resulting in space management being more complicated.

These problems can be resolved by use of a condensed version of the access list.

To condense the length of the access list, many systems recognize three classifications of users in connection with each file:

- **Owner**. The user who created the file is the owner.

- **Group**. A set of users who are sharing the file and need similar access is a group, or workgroup.

- **Universe**. All other users in the system comprise the universe.

As an example, consider a person, Sara, who is designing a new computer game. She has hired three graduate students (Jim, Dawn, and Jill) to work on the project. The game program is kept in a file named *game*. The protection associated with this file is as follows:

- Sara should be able to invoke all operations on the file.

- Jim, Dawn, and Jill should be able only to read, write, and execute the file; they should not be allowed to delete the file.

- All others users should be able to execute the file. (Sara is interested in letting as many people as possible play the game in order to obtain appropriate feedback.)

To achieve such a protection, we must create a new group with members Jim, Dawn, and Jill. The name of the group must be then associated with the file *game*, and the access-right must be set in accordance with the policy we have outlined.

Note that, for this scheme to work properly, group membership must be tightly controlled. This control can be accomplished in a number of different ways. For example, in the UNIX system, groups can be created and modified by only the manager of the facility (or by any superuser). Thus, this control is achieved through human interaction. In the VMS system, groups can be created and controlled just as files are, with appropriate control.

With this classification, only three fields are needed to define protection. Each field is often a collection of bits, each of which either allows or prevents the access associated with it. For example, the UNIX system defines three fields of 3 bits each: **rwx**, where **r** controls read access, **w** controls write access, and **x** controls execution. A separate field is kept for the file owner, for the owner's group and for all other users. In this scheme, 9 bits per file are needed to record protection information.

10.7   Implementation Issues

A file system poses two quite different design problems. The first problem is defining how the file system should look to the user. This task involves the definition of a file and its attributes, operations allowed on a file, and the directory structure. Next, algorithms and data structures must be created to map the logical file system onto the physical devices that exist for use with the file system.

The file system itself is generally composed of many different levels, as shown in Figure 10.8. This is an example of a layered design. Each level in the design uses the features of lower levels to create new features for use by higher levels.

The lowest level, *I/O control*, consists of device drivers and interrupt handlers to transfer information between memory and the disk system. The *basic file system* uses this information to read and write particular blocks to and from the disk. Each disk block is identified by its numeric disk address (for example, drive 1, cylinder 73, surface 2, sector 10).

The *file organization module* knows about both files and disk blocks. By knowing the type of file allocation used and the location of the file, the file organization module can generate the addresses of the blocks for the basic file system to read. Finally, the *logical file system* uses the directory structure to provide the file-organization module with the values the latter needs from a symbolic file name.

To create a new file, an application program calls the logical file system. The logical file system knows the format of the directory structures. To create a new file, we read the appropriate directory into memory, update it with the new entry, and write it back to the disk. The directories can be treated exactly as files are — files with a type field indicating that they are directories. Thus, the logical file system can call the file-organization module to map the directory I/O into disk-block numbers, which are passed on to the basic file system and I/O control system.

Once the directory has been updated, the logical file system can use it to perform I/O. When a file is opened, the directory structure is

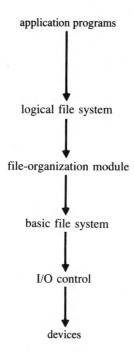

application programs

logical file system

file-organization module

basic file system

I/O control

devices

Figure 10.8 Layered file system.

searched for the desired file entry. It would be possible to search the directory structure for every I/O operation, but that would be inefficient. To speed the search, the operating system generally keeps a table of opened files in memory. The first reference to a file (normally an open) causes the directory structure to be searched and the directory entry for this file to be copied into the table of opened files. The index into this table is returned to the user program and all further references are made through the index (a file descriptor) rather than with a symbolic name. All changes to the directory entry are made to the copy in the table of opened files. When the file is closed, the updated entry is copied back to the disk-based directory structure.

While this approach is much faster than are constant references to the disk copy of the directory entry, it can cause problems. If the operating system fails, the table of opened files is generally lost, and with it any changes in the directories of opened files. This can leave the file system in an inconsistent state, where the actual state of some files is not as described in the directory structure. Frequently, a special program is run at reboot time to check for and correct disk inconsistencies.

Another aspect of file use that must be defined carefully is access control (protection). Every access to a file or directory must be checked for correctness. Systems have been designed that check file protection only when the file is opened. Separate system calls are used for **open for read** and **open for write**. Although the operating system can certainly check protection at this point, it must continue to check that a file that is **open for read** is never written to. Thus, *every* access must be checked for validity.

10.8 Summary

A file is an abstract data type defined and implemented by the operating system. A file is a sequence of logical records. A logical record may be a byte, a line (fixed or variable length), or a more complex data item. The operating system may specifically support various record types or may leave that support to the application program.

The major task for the operating system is to map the logical file concept onto physical storage devices such as magnetic tape or disk. Since the physical record size of the device may not be the same as the logical record size, it may be necessary to block logical records into physical records. Again, this task may be supported by the operating system or left for the application program.

Tape-based file systems are quite constrained; most file systems are disk-based. Tapes are commonly used for data transport between machines, or for backup or archival storage.

Each device in a file system keeps a volume table of contents or device directory listing the location of the files on the device. In addition, it is useful to create directories to allow files to be organized. A single-level directory in a multiuser system causes naming problems, since each file must have a unique name. A two-level directory solves this problem by creating a separate directory for each user. Each user has her own directory, containing her own files.

The natural generalization of a two-level directory is a tree-structured directory. A tree-structured directory allows a user to create subdirectories to organize his files. Acyclic-graph directory structures allow subdirectories and files to be shared, but complicate searching and deletion. A general graph structure allows complete flexibility in the sharing of files and directories, but sometimes requires garbage collection to recover unused disk space.

Since files are the main information-storage mechanism in most computer systems, file protection is needed. Access to files can be controlled separately for each type of access: read, write, execute, append, list directory, and so on. File protection can be provided by passwords, by access lists, or by special ad hoc techniques.

File systems are often implemented in a layered or modular structure. The lower levels deal with the physical properties of storage devices. Upper levels deal with symbolic file names and logical properties of files. Intermediate levels map the logical file concepts into physical device properties.

Exercises

10.1 Consider a file system where a file can be deleted and its disk space reclaimed while links to that file still exist. What problems may occur if a new file is created in the same storage area? How can these problems be avoided?

10.2 Some systems automatically delete all user files when a user logs off or a job terminates, unless the user explicitly requests that they be kept; other systems keep all files unless the user explicitly deletes them. Discuss the relative merits of each approach.

10.3 Could you simulate a multilevel directory structure with a single-level directory structure in which arbitrarily long names can be used? If your answer is yes, explain how you can do so, and contrast this scheme with the multilevel directory scheme. If your answer is no, explain what prevents your simulation's success. How would your answer change if file names were limited to seven characters?

10.4 Explain the purpose of the *open* and *close* operations.

10.5 Some systems automatically open a file when it is referenced for the first time, and close the file when the job terminates. Discuss the advantages and disadvantages of this scheme as compared to the more traditional one, where the user has to open and close the file explicitly.

10.6 Give an example of an application in which data in a file should be accessed in the following order:

a. Sequentially

b. Randomly

10.7 Some systems provide file sharing by maintaining a single copy of a file; other systems maintain several copies, one for each of the users sharing the file. Discuss the relative merits of each approach.

10.8 In some systems, a subdirectory can be read and written by an authorized user, just as ordinary files can be.

a. Describe what protection problems that could arise.

b. Suggest a scheme for dealing with each of the protection problems you named in part a.

10.9 Consider a system that supports 5000 users. Suppose that you want to allow 4990 of these users to be able to access one file.

a. How would you specify this protection scheme in UNIX?

b. Could you suggest another protection scheme that can be used more effectively for this purpose than the scheme provided by UNIX?

10.10 Researchers have suggested that, instead of having an access list associated with each file (which users can access the file, and how), we should have a *user control list* list associated with each user (which files a user can access, and how). Discuss the relative merits of these two schemes.

Bibliographic Notes

General discussions concerning file systems are offered by Mullender and Tanenbaum [1984], Golden and Pechura [1986], and Grosshans [1986].

The issue of file size is discussed by Powell [1977] in connection to the Demos file system, and by Satyanarayanan [1981] in connection with the TOP-10 system.

A multilevel directory structure was first implemented on the MULTICS system [Organick 1972]. Other systems using a multilevel directory structure include Atlas [Wilkes 1975], TENEX [Bobrow et al. 1972], and UNIX [Ritchie and Thompson 1974]. A flat directory structure for the Pilot, a personal-computer operating system, is described by Redell et al. [1980]. Watson [1970] and Organick [1972] discussed the implementation of directory structures.

File-system integrity was discussed by Wilkes [1975] for the Cambridge multiple-access system and by Organick [1972] for the MULTICS system. The BSD UNIX operating system uses the FSCK program to recover from disk inconsistencies caused by a crash. The process is described in [CSRG 1986]. MS-DOS uses the CHKDSK program, as documented in [Microsoft 1986]. Anyanwu and Marshall [1986] present a crash resistant UNIX file system. A fast file system for UNIX is presented by McKusick et al. [1984].

The MS-DOS file system is described in [Norton and Wilton 1988]. The Networked File System (NFS) was designed by Sun Microsystems, and allows directory structures to be spread across networked computer systems. Discussions concerning NFS are presented in [Sandberg et al. 1985], [Sandberg 1987], and [Sun Microsystems 1990]. NFS is fully described in Chapter 14. The immutable shared files semantics is described by Schroeder et al. [1985].

Protection

The various processes in an operating system must be protected from one another's activities. For that purpose, various mechanisms exist that can be used to ensure that the files, memory segments, CPU, and other resources can be operated on by only those processes that have gained proper authorization from the operating system.

For example, the access-control facility in a file system allows a user to dictate how and by whom his files can be accessed. Memory-addressing hardware ensures that a process can execute only within its own address space. The timer ensures that no process can gain control of the CPU without relinquishing that control. Finally, users are not allowed to do their own I/O, to protect the integrity of the various peripheral devices.

In this chapter, we examine the problem of protection in greater detail, and develop a unifying model for implementing protection.

11.1 Goals of Protection

As computer systems have become more sophisticated and pervasive in their applications, the need to protect their integrity has also grown. Protection was originally conceived as an adjunct to multiprogramming operating systems, so that untrustworthy users might safely share a common logical name space, such as a directory of files, or share a common physical name space, such as memory. Modern protection concepts have evolved to increase the reliability of any complex system that makes use of shared resources.

Protection refers to a mechanism for controlling the access of programs, processes, or users to the resources defined by a computer system. This mechanism must provide a means for specification of the controls to be imposed, together with some means of enforcement. We distinguish between protection and *security*, which is a measure of confidence that the integrity of a system and its data will be preserved. Security assurance is a much broader topic than is protection, and we address it only briefly in this text (Section 11.8).

There are several reasons for providing protection. Most obvious is the need to prevent mischievous, intentional violation of an access restriction by a user. Of more general importance, however, is the need to ensure that each program component active in a system uses system resources only in ways consistent with the stated policies for the uses of these resources. This is an absolute requirement for a reliable system.

Protection can improve reliability by detecting latent errors at the interfaces between component subsystems. Early detection of interface errors can often prevent contamination of a healthy subsystem by a subsystem that is malfunctioning. An unprotected resource cannot defend against use (or misuse) by an unauthorized or incompetent user. A protection-oriented system provides means to distinguish between authorized and unauthorized usage.

11.1.1 Mechanism and Policy

The role of protection in a computer system is to provide a *mechanism* for the enforcement of the *policies* governing resource use. These policies can be established in a variety of ways. Some are fixed in the design of the system, whereas others are formulated by the management of a system. Still others are defined by the individual users to protect their own files and programs. A protection system must have the flexibility to enforce a variety of policies that can be declared to it.

Policies for resource use may vary, depending on the application, and they may be subject to change over time. For these reasons, protection can no longer be considered solely as a matter of concern to the designer of an operating system. It should also be available as a tool for the applications programmer, so that resources created and supported by an applications subsystem can be guarded against misuse. In this chapter, we describe the protection mechanisms the operating system should provide, so that an application designer can use them in designing her own protection software.

One important principle is the separation of *policy* from *mechanism*. Mechanisms determine how something will be done. In contrast, policies decide *what* will be done. The separation of policy and mechanism is important for flexibility. Policies are likely to change from place to place or time to time. In the worst case, every change in policy would require a change in the underlying mechanism. General mechanisms would be more desirable, since a change in a policy would then require the modification of only some system parameters or tables.

11.1.2 Domain of Protection

A computer system is a collection of processes and objects. By *objects*, we mean both hardware objects (such as the CPU, memory segments, printers, disks, and tape drives), and software objects (such as files, programs, and semaphores). Each object has a unique name that differentiates it from all other objects in the system, and each can be accessed only through well-defined and meaningful operations. Objects are essentially *abstract data types*.

The operations that are possible may depend on the object. For example, a CPU can only be executed on. Memory segments can be read and written, whereas a card reader can only be read. Tape drives can be read, written, and rewound. Data files can be created, opened, read, written, closed, and deleted; program files can be read, written, executed, and deleted.

Obviously, a process should be allowed to access only those resources it has been authorized to access. Furthermore, at any time, it should be able to access only those resources that it currently requires to complete its task. This requirement, commonly referred to as the *need-to-know* principle, is useful in limiting the amount of damage a faulty process can cause in the system. For example, when process p invokes procedure A, the procedure should only be allowed to access its own variables and the formal parameters passed to it; it should not be able to access all the variables of process p. Similarly, consider the case where process p invokes a compiler to compile a particular file. The compiler should not be able to access any arbitrary files, but only a well-defined subset of files (such as the source file, listing file, and so on) related to the file to be compiled. Conversely, the compiler may have private files used for accounting or optimization purposes, which process p should not be able to access.

To facilitate this scheme, we introduce the concept of a *protection domain*. A process operates within a protection domain, which specifies the resources that the process may access. Each domain defines a set of objects and the types of operations that may be invoked on each object. The ability to execute an operation on an object is an *access right*. A *domain* is a collection of access rights, each of which is an ordered pair <*object-name, rights-set*>. For example, if domain D has the access right

<file F, {read,write}>, then a process executing in domain D can both read and write file F; it cannot, however, perform any other operation on that object.

Domains need not be disjoint; they may share access rights. For example, in Figure 11.1, we have three domains: D_1, D_2, and D_3. The access right <O_4, {print}> is shared by both D_2 and D_3, implying that a process executing in either one of these two domains can print object O_4. Note that a process must be executing in domain D_1 to read and write object O_1. On the other hand, only processes in domain D_3 may execute object O_1.

Consider the standard dual-mode (monitor-user mode) model of operating-system execution. When a process executes in the monitor mode, it can execute privileged instructions and thus gain complete control of the computer system. On the other hand, if the process executes in user mode, it can invoke only nonprivileged instructions. Consequently, it can execute only within its predefined memory space. These two modes protect the operating system (executing in monitor domain) from the user processes (executing in user domain). In a multiprogrammed operating system, two protection domains are insufficient, since users also want to be protected from one another. Therefore, a more elaborate scheme is needed.

11.2 Access Matrix

Our model of protection can be viewed abstractly as a matrix, called an *access matrix*. The rows of the access matrix represent domains, and the columns represent objects. Each entry in the matrix consists of a set of access rights. Since objects are defined explicitly by the column, we can omit the object name from the access right. The entry **access**(i,j) defines the set of operations that a process, executing in domain D_i, can invoke on object O_j.

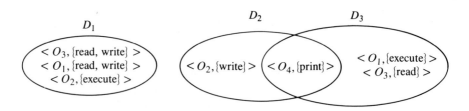

Figure 11.1   System with three protection domains.

object domain	F_1	F_2	F_3	card reader	printer
D_1	read		read		
D_2				read	print
D_3		read	execute		
D_4	read write		read write		

Figure 11.2   Access matrix.

To illustrate these concepts, we consider the access matrix shown in Figure 11.2. There are four domains and five objects: three files (F_1, F_2, F_3), one card reader, and one printer. When a process executes in domain D_1, it can read files F_1 and F_3. A process executing in domain D_4 has the same privileges as it does in domain D_1, but in addition, it can also write onto files F_1 and F_3. Note that the card reader and printer can be accessed only by a process executing in domain D_2.

How can the access matrix be implemented effectively? In general, the matrix will be sparse; that is, most of the entries will be empty. Although there are data-structure techniques available for representing sparse matrices, they are not particularly useful for this application, because of the way in which the protection facility is used.

11.2.1 Global Table

The simplest implementation of the access matrix is a global table consisting of a set of ordered triples <domain, object, rights-set>. Whenever an operation M is executed on an object O_j within domain D_i, the global table is searched for a triple $<D_i, O_j, R_k>$, where $M \in R_k$. If this triple is found, the operation is allowed to continue; otherwise, an exception (error) condition is raised. This implementation suffers from several drawbacks. The table is usually large and thus cannot be kept in main memory, so additional I/O is needed. Virtual-memory techniques are often used for managing this table. In addition, it is difficult to take advantage of special groupings of objects or domains. For example, if a particular object can be read by everyone, it must have a separate entry in every domain.

11.2.2 Access Lists

Each column in the access matrix can be implemented as an access list for one object, as described in Section 10.6.3. Obviously, the empty entries can be discarded. The resulting list for each object consists of ordered pairs <domain, rights-set>, which define all domains with a nonempty set of access rights for that object.

This approach can be extended easily to define a list plus a *default* set of access rights. When an operation M on an object O_j is attempted in domain D_j, we search the access list for object O_j, looking for an entry $<D_j, R_k>$ with $M \in R_k$. If the entry is found, we allow the operation; if it is not, we check the default set. If M is in the default set, we allow the access. Otherwise, access is denied and an exception condition occurs. Note that, for efficiency, we may check the default set first, and then search the access list.

11.2.3 Capability Lists

Rather than associating the columns of the access matrix with the objects as access lists, we associate each row with its domain. A *capability list* for a domain is a list of objects and the operations allowed on those objects. An object is often represented by its physical name or address, called a *capability*. To execute operation M on object O_j, the process executes the operation M, specifying the capability (pointer) for object O_j as a parameter. Simple *possession* of the capability means that access is allowed.

The capability list is associated with a domain, but is never directly accessible to a process executing in that domain. Rather, the capability list is itself a protected object, maintained by the operating system and accessed by the user only indirectly. Capability-based protection relies on the fact that the capabilities are never allowed to migrate into any address space directly accessible by a user process (where they could be modified). If all capabilities are secure, the object they protect is also secure against unauthorized access.

Capabilities were originally proposed as a kind of secure pointer, to meet the need for resource protection that was foreseen as multiprogrammed computer systems came of age. The idea of an inherently protected pointer (from the point of view of a user of a system) provides a foundation for protection that can be extended up to the applications level.

To provide inherent protection, we must distinguish capabilities from other kinds of objects, and must interpret them by an abstract machine on which higher-level programs run. Capabilities are usually distinguished from other data in one of two ways:

- Each object has a *tag* to denote its type as either a capability or as accessible data. The tags themselves must not be directly accessible by an applications program. Hardware or firmware support may be used to enforce this restriction. Although only 1 bit is necessary to distinguish between capabilities and other objects, more bits are often used. This extension allows all objects to be tagged with their types by the hardware. Thus, the hardware can distinguish integers, floating-point numbers, pointers, Booleans, characters, instructions, capabilities, and uninitialized values by their tags.

- Alternatively, the address space associated with a program can be split into two parts. One part is accessible to the program and contains the program's normal data and instructions. The other part, containing the capability list, is accessible only by the operating system. A segmented memory space (Section 7.7) is useful to support this approach.

Several capability-based protection systems have been developed; we describe them briefly in Section 11.5.

11.2.4 A Lock-Key Mechanism

The *lock-key scheme* is a compromise between access lists and capability lists. Each object has a list of unique bit patterns, called *locks*. Similarly, each domain has a list of unique bit patterns, called *keys*. A process executing in a domain can access an object only if that domain has a key that matches one of the locks of the object.

As capability lists must be, the list of keys for a domain must be managed by the operating system on behalf of the domain. Users are not allowed to examine or modify the list of keys (or locks) directly.

11.2.5 Comparison

Access lists correspond directly to the needs of the users. When a user creates an object, she can specify which domains can access the object, as well as the operations allowed. However, since access-rights information for a particular domain is not localized, determining the set of access rights for each domain is difficult. In addition, every access to the object must be checked, requiring a search of the access list. In a large system with long access lists, this search can be time-consuming.

Capability lists do not correspond directly to the needs of the users; they are useful, however, for localizing information for a particular process. The process attempting access must present a capability for that access. Then, the protection system needs only to verify that the capability is valid. Revocation of capabilities, however, may be inefficient (Section 11.4).

The lock-key mechanism is a compromise between these two schemes. The mechanism can be both effective and flexible, depending on the length of the keys. The keys can be passed freely from domain to domain. In addition, access privileges may be effectively revoked by the simple technique of changing some of the keys associated with the object (Section 11.4).

Most systems use a combination of access lists and capabilities. When a process first tries to access an object, the access list is searched. If access is denied, an exception condition occurs. Otherwise, a capability is created and is attached to the process. Additional references use the capability to demonstrate swiftly that access is allowed. After the last access, the capability is destroyed. This strategy is used in the MULTICS system and in the CAL system; these systems use both access lists and capability lists.

As an example, consider a file system. Each file has an associated access list. When a process opens a file, the directory structure is searched to find the file, access permission is checked, and buffers are allocated. All this information is recorded in a new entry in a file table associated with the process. The operation returns an index into this table for the newly opened file. All operations on the file are made by specifying the index into the file table. The entry in the file table then points to the file and its buffers. When the file is closed, the file-table entry is deleted. Since the file table is maintained by the operating system, it cannot be corrupted by the user. Thus, the only files that the user can access are those that have been opened. Since access is checked when the file is opened, protection is ensured. This strategy is used in the UNIX system.

Note that the right to access *must* still be checked on each access, and the file-table entry has a capability only for the allowed operations. If a file is opened for reading, then a capability for read access is placed in the file-table entry. If an attempt is made to write onto the file, this protection violation is determined by comparing the requested operation with the capability in the file-table entry.

11.2.6 Policies

The access-matrix scheme provides us with the mechanism for specifying a variety of policies. The mechanism consists of implementing the access matrix and ensuring that the semantic properties we have outlined indeed hold. More specifically, we must ensure that a process executing in domain D_i can access only those objects specified in row i, and then only as allowed by the access-matrix entries.

Policy decisions concerning protection can be implemented by the access matrix. The policy decisions involve which rights should be included in the (i,j)th entry. We must also decide the domain in which each process executes. This last policy is usually decided by the operating system.

The users normally decide the contents of the access-matrix entries. When a user creates a new object O_j, the column O_j is added to the access matrix with the appropriate initialization entries, as dictated by the creator. The user may decide to enter some rights in some entries in column j and other rights in other entries, as needed.

11.3 Dynamic Protection Structures

The association between a process and a domain may be either static (if the set of resources available to a process is fixed throughout the latter's lifetime) or dynamic. As might be expected, the problems inherent in establishing dynamic protection domains require more careful solution than do the simpler problems of the static case.

If the association between processes and domains is fixed, and we want to adhere to the need-to-know principle, then a mechanism must be available to change the content of a domain. A process may execute in two different phases. For example, it may need read access in one phase and write access in another. If the access matrix is static, we must define the domain to include both read and write access. However, this arrangement provides more rights than are needed in each of the two phases, since we have read access in the phase where we need only write access, and vice versa. Thus, the need-to-know principle is violated. We must allow the contents of the access matrix to be modified, so that the matrix always reflects the minimum necessary access rights for the process and its domain.

If the association is dynamic, a mechanism is available to allow a process to switch from one domain to another. We may also want to allow the content of a domain to be changed. If we cannot change the content of a domain, we can provide the same effect by creating a new domain with the changed content, and switching to that new domain when we want to change the domain content.

Clearly, both the static and dynamic schemes require strict control. Otherwise, protection policies could be violated. Fortunately, we already have a mechanism for defining and implementing that control: the access matrix. When we switch a process from one domain to another, we are executing an operation (switch) on an object (the domain). We can control domain switching by including domains among the objects of the access matrix. Similarly, when we change the content of the access matrix, we are performing an operation on an object: the access matrix. Again, we can control these changes by including the access matrix itself as an object. Actually, since each entry in the access matrix may be modified individually, we must consider each entry in the access matrix as an object to be protected.

Now, we need to consider only the operations that are possible on these new objects (domains and the access matrix), and to decide how we want processes to be able to execute these operations.

Processes should be able to switch from one domain to another. Domain switching from domain D_i to domain D_j is allowed to occur if and only if the access right *switch* $\in$ **access**(i, j). Thus, in Figure 11.3, a process executing in domain D_2 can switch to domain D_3 or to domain D_4. A process in domain D_4 can switch to D_1, and one in domain D_1 can switch to domain D_2.

Allowing controlled change to the contents of the access-matrix entries requires three additional operations: **copy**, **owner**, and **control**.

The ability to copy an access right from one domain (row) of the access matrix to another is denoted by an asterisk (*) appended to the access right. The *copy* right allows the copying of the access right only within the column (that is, for the object) for which the right is defined. For example, in Figure 11.4(a), a process executing in domain D_2 can copy the read operation into any entry associated with file F_2. Hence, the access matrix of Figure 11.4(a) can be modified to the access matrix shown in Figure 11.4(b).

There are two variants to this scheme:

1. A right is copied from **access**(i, j) to **access**(k, j); it is then removed from **access**(i, j); this is a *transfer* of a right, rather than a copy.

object domain	F_1	F_2	F_3	card reader	printer	D_1	D_2	D_3	D_4
D_1	read		read				switch		
D_2				read	print			switch	switch
D_3		read	execute						
D_4	read write		read write			switch			

Figure 11.3   Access matrix of Figure 11.2 with domains as objects.

object \ domain	F_1	F_2	F_3
D_1	execute		write*
D_2	execute	read*	execute
D_3	execute		

(a)

object \ domain	F_1	F_2	F_3
D_1	execute		write*
D_2	execute	read*	execute
D_3	execute	read	

(b)

Figure 11.4   Access matrix with copy rights.

2. Propagation of the *copy* right may be limited. That is, when the right R^* is copied from **access**(*i, j*) to **access**(*k, j*), only the right R (not R^*) is created. A process executing in domain D_k cannot further copy the right R.

A system may select only one of these three *copy* rights, or it may provide all three by identifying them as separate rights: *copy, transfer,* and *limited copy.*

The *copy* right allows a process to copy some rights from an entry in one column to another entry in the same column. We also need a mechanism to allow adding new rights and removing some rights. The *owner* right controls these operations. If **access**(*i, j*) includes the *owner* right, then a process executing in domain D_i, can add and remove any right in any entry in column *j*. For example, in Figure 11.5(a), domain D_1 is the owner of F_1, and thus can add and delete any valid right in column F_1. Similarly, domain D_2 is the owner of F_2 and F_3, and thus can add and remove any valid right within these two columns. Thus, the

object domain	F_1	F_2	F_3
D_1	owner execute		write
D_2		read* owner	read* owner write*
D_3	execute		

(a)

object domain	F_1	F_2	F_3
D_1	owner execute		
D_2		owner read* write*	read* owner write*
D_3		write	write

(b)

Figure 11.5   Access matrix with owner rights.

access matrix of Figure 11.5(a) can be modified to the access matrix shown in Figure 11.5(b).

The *copy* and *owner* rights allow a process to change the entries in a column. A mechanism is also needed to change the entries in a row. The *control* right is applicable to only domain objects. If **access**(*i, j*) includes the *control* right, then a process executing in domain D_i can remove any access right from row *j*. For example, suppose that, in Figure 11.3, we include the *control* right in **access**(D_2, D_4). Then, a process executing in domain D_2 could modify domain D_4, as shown in Figure 11.6.

These operations on the domains and the access matrix are not in themselves particularly important. What is more important is that they illustrate the ability of the access-matrix model to allow the implementation and control of dynamic protection requirements. New objects and new domains can be created dynamically and included in

object\domain	F_1	F_2	F_3	card reader	printer	D_1	D_2	D_3	D_4
D_1	read		read				switch		
D_2				read	print			switch	switch control
D_3		read	execute						
D_4	write		write			switch			

Figure 11.6 Modified access matrix of Figure 11.3.

the access-matrix model. However, we have shown only that the basic mechanism is here; the policy decisions concerning which domains are to have access to which objects in which ways must be made by the system designers and users.

The dynamic protection model provides a mechanism to solve the access-control problem of Section 5.6. We saw that monitors were insufficient to allow the user to create his own resources and to control their use. If the resources were embedded in a monitor, their use would be controlled by the built-in monitor-scheduling policy; the user could not enforce his own scheduling policy. In addition, the fact that only one process at a time can execute in a monitor prevents simultaneous access to the resources, which is needed for the readers in the readers-writers problem.

To solve these problems, we must make the resources external to the monitor. Now, however, we have no control over the use of the resources. To provide this control, we create a monitor, called a *manager*, for each resource. This manager schedules and controls access to the resources. To use a resource, a process first calls the manager, which returns to the user process a capability for the resource. The process must present the capability when it accesses the resource. When the process finishes, it returns the capability to the manager, which may then allocate that capability to other waiting processes, according to its own scheduling algorithm. Thus, capabilities provide a solution to the access-control problem of Section 5.6. A malfunctioning user process can cause only limited mischief that will affect other processes; it may acquire a capability to the shared resource and refuse to release it. We can remedy this circumstance, at the cost of additional execution overhead, by providing for preemptive revocation of capabilities.

11.4 Revocation

In a dynamic protection system, it may sometimes be necessary to revoke access rights to objects that are shared by different users. Various questions about revocation may arise:

- **Immediate versus delayed**. Does revocation occur immediately, or is it delayed? If revocation is delayed, can we find out when it will take place?

- **Selective versus general**. When an access right to an object is revoked, does it affect *all* the users who have an access right to that object, or can we specify a select group of users whose access rights should be revoked?

- **Partial versus total**. Can a subset of the rights associated with an object be revoked, or must we revoke all access rights for this object?

- **Temporary versus permanent**. Can access be revoked permanently (that is, the revoked access right will never again be available), or can access be revoked and later be obtained again?

With an access-list scheme, revocation is quite easy. The access list is searched for the access right(s) to be revoked, and they are deleted from the list. Revocation is immediate, and can be general or selective, total or partial, and permanent or temporary.

Capabilities, however, present a much more difficult revocation problem. Since the capabilities are distributed throughout the system, we must find them before we can revoke them. There are a number of different schemes for implementing revocation for capabilities, including the following:

- **Reacquisition**. Periodically, capabilities are deleted from each domain. If a process wants to use a capability, it may find that that capability has been deleted. The process may then try to reacquire the capability. If access has been revoked, the process will not be able to reacquire the capability.

- **Back-pointers**. A list of pointers is maintained with each object, pointing to all capabilities associated with that object. When revocation is required, we can follow these pointers, changing the capabilities as necessary. This scheme has been adopted in the MULTICS system. It is quite general, although it is a costly implementation.

- **Indirection**. The capabilities do not point to the objects directly, but instead point indirectly. Each capability points to a unique entry in a global table, which in turn points to the object. We implement revocation by searching the global table for the desired entry and deleting it. When an access is attempted, the capability is found to point to an illegal table entry. Table entries can be reused for other capabilities without difficulty, since both the capability and the table entry contain the unique name of the object. The object for a capability and its table entry must match. This scheme was adopted in the CAL system. It does not allow selective revocation.

- **Keys**. A key is a unique bit pattern that can be associated with each capability. This key is defined when the capability is created, and it can be neither modified nor inspected by the process owning that capability. A *master key* associated with each object can be defined or replaced with the **set-key** operation. When a capability is created, the current value of the master key is associated with the capability. When the capability is exercised, its key is compared to the master key. If the keys match, the operation is allowed to continue; otherwise, an exception condition is raised. Revocation replaces the master key with a new value by the **set-key** operation, invalidating all previous capabilities for this object.

  Note that this scheme does not allow selective revocation, since only one master key is associated with each object. If we associate a list of keys with each object, then selective revocation can be implemented. Finally, we can group all keys into one global table of keys. A capability is valid only if its key matches some key in the global table. We implement revocation by removing the matching key from the table. With this scheme, a key can be associated with several objects, and several keys can be associated with each object, providing maximum flexibility.

  In key-based schemes, the operations of defining keys, inserting them into lists, and deleting them from lists should not be available to all users. In particular, it would be reasonable to allow only the owner of an object to set the keys for that object. This choice, however, is a policy decision that the protection system can implement, but should not define.

11.5 Existing Systems

So far, we have avoided pinpointing exactly what a *domain* is. A domain is an abstract concept that can be realized in a variety of ways:

- A domain may be defined for each *user*. The set of objects that can be accessed depends on the identity of the user. Domain switching occurs when the user is changed — generally when one user logs out and another user logs in.

- Each *process* may be a domain. In this case, each row in the access matrix describes which objects can be accessed by that process, as well as which operations are allowed. Domain switching corresponds to one process sending a message to another process, and then waiting for a response.

- Each *procedure* may be a domain. Each row in the access matrix then describes which objects can be accessed by that procedure. In this situation, procedure calls cause domain switching.

In this section, we briefly survey some of the most widely known protection systems. These systems vary in their complexity and in the type of policies that can be implemented on them.

11.5.1 UNIX

In the UNIX system, the protection scheme is basically designed around the file system. Three protection fields are associated with each file, corresponding to owner, group, and universal classification. Each field consists of three bits, r, w, and x. The r bit controls read access, w controls write access, and x controls execute access. A domain in UNIX is associated with the user.

Switching the domain corresponds to changing the user identification temporarily. This change is accomplished through the file system as follows. An owner identification and a domain bit (known as the "set-uid bit") are associated with each file. When a user (with *user-id* = A) starts executing a file owned by B, whose associated domain bit is *on*, the *user-id* is set to B. When the computation exits the file, the *user-id* is reset to A. This mechanism is further discussed in Chapter 15.

There are other common methods used to change domains in operating systems in which user-ids are used for domain definition, since almost all systems need to provide such a mechanism. This mechanism is used when an otherwise privileged facility needs to be made available to the general user population. For instance, it might be desirable to allow users to access a network without letting them write their own networking programs. In such a case, on a UNIX system, the set-uid bit on a networking program would be set, causing the user-id to change when the program is run. The user-id would change to that of a user with network access privilege (such as "root," the most powerful user-id). An alternative to this method is to place privileged programs in a special directory. The operating system would be designed to change the user-id of any program run from this directory.

Some systems simply do not allow a change of user-id. In these instances, special techniques must be used to allow users access to privileged facilities. For instance, a *daemon* process might be started at boot time and run as a special user-id. Users then run a separate program, which sends requests to this process whenever they need to use the facility.

11.5.2 MULTICS

In the MULTICS system, the protection scheme is designed around the file system and a *ring* structure. The protection facility associated with the file system was described in Section 10.6. Briefly, an access list, as well as owner and universal access fields, is associated with each file.

The protection domains in MULTICS are organized hierarchically into a ring structure. Each ring corresponds to a single domain (Figure 11.7). The rings are numbered from 0 to 7. Let D_i and D_j be any two domain rings. If $j < i$, then D_i is a subset of D_j. That is, a process executing in domain D_i has more privileges than does a process executing in domain D_j

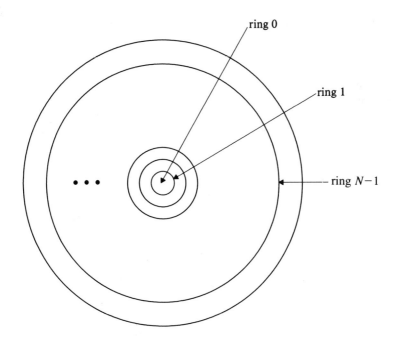

Figure 11.7 MULTICS ring structure.

D_i. A process executing in domain D_0 has the most privileges. If there are only two rings, this scheme is equivalent to the monitor-user mode of execution, where monitor mode corresponds to D_0 and user mode corresponds to D_1.

MULTICS has a segmented address space; each segment is a file. Each segment is associated with one of the rings. A segment description includes an entry that identifies the ring number. In addition, it includes three access bits to control reading, writing, and execution. The association between segments and rings is a policy decision with which we are not concerned in this book. With each process, a *current-ring-number* counter is associated, identifying the ring in which the process is executing currently. When a process is executing in ring i, it cannot access a segment associated with ring j, $j < i$. It can, however, access a segment associated with ring k, $k \geq i$. The type of access, however, is restricted, according to the access bits associated with that segment.

Domain switching in MULTICS occurs when a process crosses from one ring to another by calling a procedure in a different ring. Obviously, this switch must be done in a controlled manner; otherwise, a process can start executing in ring 0, and no protection will be provided. To allow controlled domain switching, we modify the ring field of the segment descriptor to include the following:

- **Access bracket**. This consists of a pair of integers, $b1$ and $b2$, such that $b1 \leq b2$.

- **Limit**. This is an integer $b3$, such that $b3 > b2$.

- **List of gates**. This identifies the entry points (gates) at which the segments may be called.

If a process executing in ring i calls a procedure (segment) with access bracket $(b1,b2)$, then the call is allowed if $b1 \leq i \leq b2$, and the current ring number of the process remains i. Otherwise, a trap to the operating system occurs, and the situation is handled as follows:

- If $i < b1$, then the call is allowed to occur, since we have a transfer to a ring (domain) with fewer privileges. However, if parameters are passed that refer to segments in a lower ring (that is, segments that are not accessible to the called procedure), then these segments must be copied into an area that can be accessed by the called procedure.

- If $i > b2$, then the call is allowed to occur only if $b3$ is less than or equal to i, and the call has been directed to one of the designated entry points in the list of gates. This scheme allows processes with limited access rights to call procedures in lower rings that have more access rights, but only in a carefully controlled manner.

The main disadvantage of the ring (hierarchical) structure is that it does not allow us to enforce the need-to-know principle. In particular, if an object must be accessible in domain D_j but not accessible in domain D_i, then we must have $j < i$. But this means that every segment accessible in D_i is also accessible in D_j.

11.5.3 Hydra

Hydra is a capability-based protection system that provides considerable flexibility. The system provides a fixed set of possible access rights that are known to and interpreted by the system. These rights include such basic forms of access as the right to read, write, or execute a memory segment. In addition, however, the system provides the means for a user (of the protection system) to declare additional rights. The interpretation of user-defined rights is performed solely by the user's program, but the system provides access protection for the use of these rights, as well as for the use of system-defined rights. The facilities provided by this system are quite interesting, and constitute a significant development in protection technology.

Operations on objects are defined procedurally. The procedures that implement such operations are themselves a form of object, and are accessed indirectly by capabilities. The names of user-defined procedures must be identified to the protection system if it is to deal with objects of the user-defined type. When the definition of an object is made known to Hydra, the names of operations on the type become *auxiliary rights*. Auxiliary rights can be described in a capability for an instance of the type. For a process to perform an operation on a typed object, the capability it holds for that object must contain the name of the operation being invoked among its auxiliary rights. This restriction enables discrimination of access rights to be made on an instance-by-instance and process-by-process basis.

Another interesting concept is *rights amplification*. This scheme allows certification of a procedure as "trustworthy" to act on a formal parameter of a specified type, on behalf of any process that holds a right to execute the procedure. The rights held by a trustworthy procedure are independent of, and may exceed, the rights held by the calling process. However, it is necessary neither to regard such a procedure as universally trustworthy (the procedure is not allowed to act on other types, for instance), nor to extend trustworthiness to any other procedures or program segments that might be executed by a process.

Amplification is useful in allowing implementation procedures access to the representation variables of an abstract data type. If a process holds a capability to a typed object A, for instance, this capability may include an auxiliary right to invoke some operation P, but would not include any of the so-called kernel rights, such as read, write, or execute, on the segment that represents A. Such a capability gives a process a means of indirect access (through the operation P) to the representation of A, but only for specific purposes.

On the other hand, when a process invokes the operation P on an object A, the capability for access to A may be amplified as control passes to the code body of P. This amplification may be necessary, to allow P the right to access the storage segment representing A, to implement the operation that P defines on the abstract data type. The code body of P may be allowed to read or to write to the segment of A directly, even though the calling process cannot. On return from P, the capability for A is restored to its original, unamplified state. This is a typical case in which the rights held by a process for access to a protected segment must change dynamically, depending on the task to be performed. The dynamic adjustment of rights is performed to guarantee consistency of a programmer-defined abstraction. Amplification of rights can be stated explicitly in the declaration of an abstract type to the Hydra system.

A Hydra subsystem is built on top of its protection kernel and may require protection of its own components. A subsystem interacts with the kernel through calls on a set of kernel-defined primitives that defines access rights to resources defined by the subsystem. Policies for use of these resources by user processes can be defined by the subsystem designer, but are enforceable by use of the standard access protection afforded by the capability system.

A programmer can make direct use of the protection system, after acquainting himself with its features in the appropriate reference manual. Hydra provides a large library of system-defined procedures that can be called by user programs. A user of the Hydra system would explicitly incorporate calls on these system procedures into the code of his programs, or would use a program translator that had been interfaced to Hydra.

11.5.4 Cambridge CAP System

A different approach to capability-based protection has been taken in the design of the Cambridge CAP system. CAP's capability system is simpler and superficially less powerful than that of Hydra. However, closer examination shows that it too can be used to provide secure protection of user-defined objects. In CAP, there are two kinds of capabilities. The ordinary kind is called a *data capability*. It can be used to provide access to objects, but the only rights provided are the standard read, write, or execute of the individual storage segments associated with the object. Data capabilities are interpreted by microcode in the CAP machine.

A so-called *software capability* is protected by, but not interpreted by, the CAP microcode. It is interpreted by a *protected* (that is, a privileged) procedure, which may be written by an applications programmer as part of a subsystem. A particular kind of rights amplification is associated with a protected procedure. When executing the code body of such a procedure, a process temporarily acquires the rights to read or write the contents of a software capability itself. This specific kind of rights amplification corresponds to an implementation of the **seal** and **unseal** primitives on capabilities (see Bibliographic Notes for references). Of course, this privilege is still subject to type verification to ensure that only software capabilities for a specified abstract type are allowed to be passed to any such procedure. Universal trust is not placed in any code other than the CAP machine's microcode.

The interpretation of a software capability is left completely to the subsystem, through the protected procedures it contains. This scheme allows a variety of protection policies to be implemented. Although a programmer can define her own protected procedures (any of which might be incorrect), the security of the overall system cannot be compromised. The basic protection system will not allow an unverified, user-defined, protected procedure access to any storage segments (or capabilities) that do not belong to the protection environment in which it resides. The most serious consequence of an insecure protected procedure is a protection breakdown of the subsystem for which that procedure has responsibility.

The designers of the CAP system have noted that the use of software capabilities has allowed them to realize considerable economies in formulating and implementing protection policies commensurate with the requirements of abstract resources. However, a subsystem designer who wants to make use of this facility cannot simply study a reference manual, as is the case with Hydra. Instead, he must learn the principles and techniques of protection, since the system provides him with no library of procedures to be used.

11.6   Language-Based Protection

To the degree that protection is provided in existing computer systems, it has usually been achieved through the device of an operating-system kernel, which acts as a security agent to inspect and validate each attempt to access a protected resource. Since comprehensive access validation is potentially a source of considerable overhead, either we must give it hardware support to reduce the cost of each validation, or we must accept that the system designer may be inclined to compromise the goals of protection. It is difficult to satisfy all these goals if the flexibility to implement various protection policies is restricted by the support mechanisms provided or if protection environments are made larger than necessary to secure greater operational efficiency.

As operating systems have become more complex, and particularly as they have attempted to provide higher-level user interfaces, the goals of protection have become much more refined. In this refinement, we find that the designers of protection systems have drawn heavily on ideas that originated in programming languages and especially on the concept of abstract data types. Protection systems are now concerned not only with the identity of a resource to which access is attempted but also with the functional nature of that access. In the newest protection systems, concern for the function to be invoked extends beyond a set of system-defined functions, such as standard file access methods, to include functions that may be user-defined as well.

Policies for resource use may also vary, depending on the application, and they may be subject to change over time. For these reasons, protection can no longer be considered as a matter of concern to only the designer of an operating system. It should also be available as a tool for use by the applications designer, so that resources of an applications subsystem can be guarded against tampering or the influence of an error.

At this point, programming languages enter the picture. Specifying the desired control of access to a shared resource in a system is making a declarative statement about the resource. This kind of statement can be integrated into a language by an extension of its typing facility. When protection is declared along with data typing, the designer of each subsystem can specify its requirements for protection, as well as its need for use of other resources in a system. Such a specification should be given directly as a program is composed, and in the language in which the program itself is stated. There are several significant advantages to this approach:

1. Protection needs are simply declared, rather than programmed as a sequence of calls on procedures of an operating system.

2. Protection requirements may be stated independently of the facilities provided by a particular operating system.

3. The means for enforcement does not need to be provided by the designer of a subsystem.

4. A declarative notation is natural because access privileges are closely related to the linguistic concept of data type.

How can a protection mechanism be implemented by the translator of a programming language? The conventional responsibility of a language implementation is the translation of algorithm statements in the programming language into a sequence of machine code that will carry out the algorithm on a target machine. If protection domains can also be specified, then an implementation must ensure that any translation it provides cannot enable a process to gain access to resources outside of its prescribed domain, regardless of the correctness of the algorithm statement given by the programmer. There is a significant difference between providing an implementation of program statements and providing one of protection specifications. Statements are procedural and can be translated directly on a line-by-line basis into a sequence of machine code. Protection specifications, however, are nonprocedural. They must be interpreted by an agent provided by an implementation.

Perhaps the greatest obstacle to embedding protection specifications in programming languages has been the lack of standard, or even roughly equivalent, means of protection-enforcement mechanisms across a variety of computer systems. Although most computer systems provide sufficient hardware and operating-system support to perform a straightforward translation of programs written in any of the statement-oriented programming languages, such as FORTRAN, COBOL, PL/1, and Pascal, relatively few systems provide support for the protection of individual storage segments within the workspace of a user.

There is a variety of techniques that can be provided by a programming language implementation to enforce protection, but any of these must depend for security on some degree of support from an underlying machine and its operating system. For example, suppose a language were used to generate code to run on the Cambridge CAP system. On this system, every storage reference made on the underlying hardware occurs indirectly through a capability. This restriction prevents any process from accessing a resource outside of its protection environment at any time. However, a program may impose arbitrary restrictions on how a resource may be used during execution of a particular code segment by any process. We can implement such restrictions most readily by using the software capabilities provided by CAP. A language implementation might provide standard, protected procedures to interpret software capabilities that would realize the protection policies that could be specified in the language. This scheme puts policy specification at the disposal of the programmer, while freeing her from the details of implementing its enforcement.

Even if a system does not provide a protection kernel as powerful as those of Hydra, CAP, or MULTICS, there are still mechanisms available for implementing protection specifications given in a programming language. The principal distinction will be that the *security* of this protection will not be as great as that supported by a protection kernel, because the mechanism must rely on more assumptions about the operational state of the system. A compiler can separate references for which it can certify that no protection violation could occur from those for which a violation might be possible, and can treat them differently. The security provided by this form of protection rests on the assumption that the code generated by the compiler will not be modified prior to or during its execution.

What, then, are the relative merits of enforcement based solely on a kernel, as opposed to enforcement provided largely by a compiler?

- **Security**. Enforcement by a kernel provides a greater degree of security of the protection system itself than does the generation of protection-checking code by a compiler. In a compiler supported scheme, security rests on correctness of the translator, on some underlying mechanism of storage management that protects the segments from which compiled code is executed, and, ultimately, on the security of files from which a program is loaded. Some of these same considerations also apply to a software-supported protection kernel, but to a lesser degree, since the kernel may reside in fixed physical storage segments and may be loaded from only a designated file. With a tagged capability system, in which all address computation is performed either by hardware or by a fixed microprogram, even greater security is possible. Hardware-supported protection is also relatively immune to protection violations that might occur as a result of either hardware or system software malfunction.

- **Flexibility**. There are limits to the flexibility of a protection kernel in implementing a user-defined policy, although it may supply adequate facilities for the system to provide enforcement for its own policies. With a programming language, protection policy can be declared and enforcement provided as needed by an implementation. If a language does not provide sufficient flexibility, it can be extended or replaced, with less perturbation of a system in service than would be caused by the modification of an operating-system kernel.

- **Efficiency**. The best efficiency is obtained when enforcement of protection is supported directly by hardware (or microcode). Insofar as software support is required, language-based enforcement has the advantage that static access enforcement can be verified off-line at compile time. Also, since the enforcement mechanism can be tailored by an intelligent compiler to meet the specified need, the fixed overhead of kernel calls can often be avoided.

In summary, the specification of protection in a programming language allows the high-level description of policies for the allocation and use of resources. A language implementation can provide software for protection enforcement when automatic hardware-supported checking is unavailable. In addition, it can interpret protection specifications to generate calls on whatever protection system is provided by the hardware and the operating system.

One way of making protection available to the application program is through the use of *software capability* that could be used as an object of computation. Inherent in this concept is the idea that certain program components might have the privilege of creating or examining these software capabilities. A capability-creating program would be able to execute a primitive operation that would seal a data structure, rendering the latter's contents inaccessible to any program components that did not hold either the seal or the unseal privileges. They might copy the data structure, or pass its address to other program components, but they could not gain access to its contents. The reason for introducing such software capabilities is to bring a protection mechanism into the programming language. The only problem with the concept as proposed is that the use of the **seal** and **unseal** operations takes a procedural approach to specifying protection. A nonprocedural or declarative notation seems a preferable way to make protection available to the applications programmer.

What is needed is a safe, dynamic access-control mechanism for distributing capabilities to system resources among user processes. If it is to contribute to the overall reliability of a system, the access-control mechanism should be safe to use. If it is to be useful in practice, it should also be reasonably efficient. This requirement has led to the development of a number of new language constructs that provide a mechanism for the safe and efficient distribution of capabilities among customer processes (see the Bibliographic Notes for appropriate references). These mechanisms ensure that a user process will use the managed resource only if it was granted a capability. However, they do not ensure that the user process will use the shared resources correctly. A mechanism is needed to allow the programmer to declare various restrictions:

- On the specific operations that a particular process may invoke on an allocated resource (for example, a reader of a file should only be allowed to read the file, whereas a writer should be able both to read and to write). It should not be necessary to grant the same set of rights to every user process, and it should be impossible for a process to enlarge its set of access rights, except with the authorization of the access control mechanism.

- On the order in which a particular process may invoke the various operations of a resource (for example, a file must be opened before it can be read). It should be possible to give two processes different restrictions on the order in which they can invoke the operations of the allocated resource.

A specification notation for allowing such restrictions to be declared is *access-right expressions*. Access-right expressions ensure that a process can use only specified operations and that the process invokes the operations in only a sequence anticipated by the designer of the resource. The notation is based on regular expressions, which provide a familiar framework and seem to have sufficient expressive power to describe most of the sequencing constraints of practical interest.

The incorporation of protection concepts into programming languages, as a practical tool for system design, is at present only in its infancy. It is likely that protection will become a matter of greater concern to the designers of new systems with distributed architectures and increasingly stringent requirements on data security. As this comes to pass, the importance of suitable language notations in which to express protection requirements will be recognized more widely.

11.7 Protection Problems

The mechanisms we have outlined so far provide an operating system with powerful tools for the construction of arbitrary protection policies. The task of protecting information in an operating system has received significant attention in recent years. Several important problems have been defined, not all of which have easy (or possible) solutions.

- **Modification**. When a user passes an object as an argument to a procedure, it may be necessary to ensure that the procedure cannot modify the object. We can implement this restriction readily by passing an access right that does not have the modification (write) right. However, if amplification may occur (such as in Hydra), the right to modify may be reinstated. Thus, the user-protection requirement can be circumvented. In general, of course, a user may trust that a procedure indeed performs its task correctly. This assumption, however, is not always correct, because of hardware or software errors. Hydra solves this problem by restricting amplifications.

- **Limitation of propagation of access rights**. When the owner of an object wants to allow some users to share access to that object, the owner may also want to ensure that those users cannot in turn propagate the access rights to other unauthorized users. The owner can accomplish this protection by associating the *copy* and *owner* rights with only the owner of the object. Note that this restriction does not completely solve the problem, since user A (who has access permission to an object) may allow user B (who does not have access permission to that object) to log in under user A's name and thus to access the object.

- **Revocation**. A user or a system may want to revoke a previously granted access right to an object for a number of different reasons. We discussed how revocation can be accomplished in Section 11.4.

- **Trojan horse**. Many systems have mechanisms for allowing programs written by users to be used by other users. If these programs are executed in a domain that provides the access rights of the executing user, they may misuse these rights. Inside a text-editor program, for example, there may be code to search the file to be edited for certain keywords. If any are found, the entire file may be copied to a special area accessible to the creator of the text editor. A code segment that misuses its environment is called a *Trojan horse*. The trojan-horse problem is exacerbated by long search paths (such as are common on UNIX systems). All the directories in the search path must be secure, or a Trojan horse could be slipped into the user's path and executed accidentally.

- **Mutual suspicion**. Consider the case where a program is provided that can be invoked as a service by a number of different users. This service program may be a subroutine to sort an array, a compiler, an auditor, or a game. When users invoke this service program, they take the risk that the program will malfunction and will either damage the given data, or will retain some access right to the data to be used (without authority) later. Similarly, the service program may have some private files (for accounting purposes, for example) that should not be accessed directly by the calling user program. This problem is called the *mutually suspicious subsystem problem*. The procedure call mechanism of Hydra was designed as a direct solution to this problem.

- **Confinement**. The *copy* and *owner* rights provide us with a mechanism to limit the propagation of access rights. They do not, however, provide us with the appropriate tools for preventing the propagation of information (that is, disclosure of information). The problem of guaranteeing that no information initially held in an object can migrate outside of its execution environment is called the *confinement problem*. This problem is in general unsolvable (see Bibliographic Notes for references).

- **Trap door**. The designer of a program or system might leave a hole in the software that only he is capable of using. For instance, the code might check for a specific user identifier or password and circumvent normal security procedures. A very clever trap door could be included in a compiler. The compiler could generate standard object code as well as a trap door, regardless of the source code being compiled. This is a particularly nefarious activity, since a search of the source code of the program would not reveal any problems. Only the source code of the compiler would contain the information. Trap doors pose a difficult problem because, to detect them, we would have to analyze all the source code for all components of a system. Given that software systems may consist of millions of lines of code, this analysis is not done frequently.

- **Worm and virus**. Most operating systems provide a means for processes to spawn other processes. A *worm* is a process that uses this mechanism to clobber system performance. The worm spawns copies of itself, using up system resources and perhaps locking out system use by all other processes. On computer networks, worms are particularly potent, since they may reproduce themselves among systems and thus shut down the entire network. Such an event occurred in 1988 to UNIX systems on the worldwide Internet, causing millions of dollars of lost system and programmer time.

  A *virus* is similar to a worm, the main difference being that a virus is not a complete program, but rather is a piece of code attached to another program. It is triggered by a specific event (the execution of the program at a certain date, for instance). A virus replicates by adding itself to other programs. Viruses are most commonly spread on microcomputers, via users exchanging floppy disks and using disks in new systems. Both worms and viruses may be malevolent with file deletion and disk erasure being common results. Since they usually work among systems, worms and viruses are generally considered to pose security rather than protection problems.

11.8 Security

Protection, as we have discussed it, is strictly an *internal* problem: How do we provide controlled access to programs and data stored in a computer system? Security, on the other hand, requires not only an adequate protection system, but also consideration of the *external* environment within which the system operates. Internal protection is not useful if the operator's console is exposed to unauthorized personnel, or if files (stored, for example, on tapes and disks) can simply be removed from the computer system and taken to a system with no protection. These security problems are essentially management, not operating-system, problems.

The major security problem for operating systems is the *authentication* problem. The protection system depends on an ability to identify the programs and processes that are executing. This ability, in turn, eventually rests on our power to identify each user of the system. A user normally identifies himself. How do we determine if a user's identity is authentic? Generally, authentication is based on some combination of three sets of items: user possession (a key or card), user knowledge (a user identifier and password), and a user attribute (fingerprint, retina pattern, or signature).

The most common approach to authenticating a user identity is the use of user *passwords*. When the user identifies herself, she is asked for a password. If the user-supplied password matches the password stored in the system, the system assumes that the user is legitimate.

Passwords are often used to protect objects in the computer system, in the absence of more complete protection schemes. They can be considered a special case of either keys or capabilities. Associated with each resource (such as a file) is a password. Whenever a request is made to use the resource, the password must be given. If the password is correct, access is granted. Different passwords may be associated with different access rights. For example, different passwords may be used for reading, appending, and updating a file.

Passwords have problems associated with them, but passwords are extremely common because they are easy to understand and use. The problems with passwords are related to the difficulty of keeping a password secret. Passwords can be compromised by being guessed or accidentally exposed. Exposure is a particularly severe problem if the password is written down where it can be read or lost. Short passwords do not leave enough choices to prevent a password from being guessed by repeated trials. For example, a four-decimal password provides only 10,000 variations. On the average, only 5000 would need to be tried before the correct one would be guessed. If a program could be written that would try a password every 1 millisecond, it would then take only about 5 seconds to guess a password. Longer passwords are less susceptible to being guessed by enumeration.

Passwords can be either system-generated or user-selected. System-generated passwords may be difficult to remember, and thus may be commonly written down. User-selected passwords, however, are often easy to guess (the user's name or favorite car, for example). At some sites, administrators occasionally check user passwords and notify the users if the password is too short or easy to guess. Some systems also *age* passwords, forcing users to change them at regular intervals (every month, for instance). This method is not foolproof either, since users may easily toggle between two passwords.

Several variants on the simple password scheme can be used. For example, the password can be changed frequently. In the extreme, the password is changed for each session. A new password is selected (either by the system or by the user) at the end of *each* session, and that password must be used for the next session. Note that, even if a password is misused, it can be used only once, and its use prevents the legitimate user from using it. Consequently, the legitimate user discovers the security violation at the next session, when she uses a now-invalid password. Steps can then be taken to repair the broached security.

Another approach is to have a set of paired passwords. When a session begins, the system randomly selects and presents one part of a password pair; the user must supply the other part. This approach can be generalized to the use of an algorithm as a password. The algorithm might be an integer function, for example. The system selects a random integer and presents it to the user. The user applies the function and replies with the result of the function. The system also applies the function. If the two results match, access is allowed.

One problem with all these approaches is the difficulty of keeping the password (or list of password pairs, or algorithms) secret. The UNIX system uses a variant of the algorithmic password to avoid the necessity of keeping its password list secret. Each user has a password. The system contains a function that is very difficult (the designers hope impossible) to invert, but simple to compute. That is, given a value x, it is easy to compute the function value $f(x)$. Given a function value $f(x)$, however, it is impossible to compute x. This function is used to encode all passwords. Only the encoded passwords are stored. When a user presents a password, it is encoded and compared against the stored encoded password. Even if the stored encoded password is seen, it cannot be decoded, so the password cannot be determined. Thus, the password file does not need to be kept secret. The flaw in this method is that the operating system no longer has control over the passwords. Although the passwords are encrypted, anyone with a copy of the password file may run fast encryption routines against it, comparing an on-line dictionary, for instance, against each password. On sufficiently fast computers, such a comparison may only take a few hours. For this reason, new versions of UNIX hide the password entries. On current UNIX systems, it is a good idea for users to use combination passwords, such as two dictionary words separated by a punctuation character. Such passwords do not easily succumb to algorithmic guessing techniques.

Two management techniques can be used to improve the security of a system. One is *threat monitoring*. The system can check for suspicious patterns of activity in an attempt to detect a security violation. A common example of this scheme is a time-sharing system that counts the number of incorrect passwords given when a user is trying to log in. More than a few incorrect attempts may signal an attempt to guess a password. Another common technique is an *audit log*. An audit log simply records the time, user, and type of all accesses to an object. After security has been violated, the audit log can be used to determine how and when the problem occurred and perhaps the amount of damage done. This information can be useful, both for recovery from the violation and, possibly, in the development of better security measures to prevent future problems.

Networked computers are much more susceptible to security attacks than are standalone systems. Rather than the risk of attacks from a known set of access points, such as directly connected terminals, we face attacks from an unknown and very large set of access points — a potentially severe security problem. To a lesser extent, systems connected to telephone lines via modems are also more exposed. In fact, the U.S. federal government considers systems to be only as secure as is their most far-reaching connection. For instance, a top-security system may be accessed only from within a building also considered top-secure. The system loses the top-secure rating if any form of communication can occur outside that environment.

11.9 Encryption

As computer networks gain popularity, more and more sensitive (classified) information is being transmitted over channels where eavesdropping and message interception are possible. For example, bank accounts, medical records, and criminal records are now routinely transferred between various sites, generally in separate, special-purpose networks. To keep such sensitive information secure, we need mechanisms to allow a user to protect data transferred over the network.

Encryption is one common method of protecting information transmitted over unreliable links. The basic mechanism works as follows:

1. The information (text) is *encrypted* (encoded) from its initial readable form (called *clear text*), to an internal form (called *cipher text*). This internal text form, although readable, does not make any sense.

2. The cipher text can be stored in a readable file, or transmitted over unprotected channels.

3. To make sense of the cipher text, the receiver must *decrypt* (decode) it back into clear text.

Even if the encrypted information is accessed by an unauthorized person, it will be useless unless it can be decoded. The main issue is the development of encryption schemes that are impossible (or at least very difficult) to break.

There is a variety of methods to accomplish this task. The most common ones provide a general encryption algorithm E, a general decryption algorithm D, and a secret key (or keys) to be supplied for each application. Let E_k and D_k denote the encryption and decryption algorithms, respectively, for a particular application with a key k. Then the encryption algorithm must satisfy the following properties for any message m:

1. $D_k(E_k(m)) = m$.

2. Both E_k and D_k can be computed efficiently.

3. The security of the system depends only on the secrecy of the key, and not on the secrecy of the algorithms E and D.

One such scheme, called the *Data Encryption Standard*, was recently adopted by the National Bureau of Standards. This scheme suffers from the *key-distribution* problem: before communication can take place, the secret keys must be sent securely to both the sender and receiver. This task cannot be done effectively in a communication-network environment. A solution to this problem is to use a *public key-encryption* scheme. Each user has both a public and a private key, and two users can communicate knowing only each other's public key.

An algorithm based on this concept follows. This algorithm is believed to be almost unbreakable. The public encryption key is a pair (e,n); the private key is a pair (d,n), where e, d, and n are positive integers. Each message is represented as an integer between 0 and $n - 1$. (A long message is broken into a series of smaller messages, each of which can be represented as such an integer.) The functions E and D are defined as

$$E(m) = m^e \textbf{ mod } n = C,$$
$$D(C) = C^d \textbf{ mod } n.$$

The main problem is choosing the encryption and decryption keys. The integer n is computed as the product of two large (100 or more digits) randomly chosen prime numbers p and q with

$$n = p \times q.$$

The value of d is chosen to be a large, randomly chosen integer relatively prime to $(p - 1) \times (q - 1)$. That is, d satisfies

greatest common divisor$[d, (p - 1) \times (q - 1)] = 1.$

Finally, the integer e is computed from p, q, and d to be the *multiplicative inverse* of d modulo $(p - 1) \times (q - 1)$. That is, e satisfies

$$e \times d \textbf{ mod } (p - 1) \times (q - 1) = 1.$$

We should point out that, although n is publicly known, p and q are not. This condition is allowed because of the well-known fact that it is very difficult to factor n. Consequently, the integers d and e cannot be guessed easily.

Let us illustrate this scheme with an example. Let $p = 5$ and $q = 7$. Then, $n = 35$ and $(p - 1) \times (q - 1) = 24$. Since 11 is relatively prime to 24, we can choose $d = 11$; and since $11 \times 11 \textbf{ mod } 24 = 121 \textbf{ mod } 24 = 1$, $e = 11$. Suppose now that $m = 3$. Then,

$$C = m^e \textbf{ mod } n = 3^{11} \textbf{ mod } 35 = 12,$$

and

$$C^d \textbf{ mod } n = 12^{11} \textbf{ mod } 35 = 3 = m.$$

Thus, if we encode m using e, we can decode m using d.

11.10 Summary

Computer systems contain many objects. These objects need to be protected from misuse. Objects may be hardware (such as memory, CPU time, or I/O devices) or software (such as files, programs, and abstract data types). An access right is permission to perform an operation on an object. A domain is a set of access rights. Processes execute in domains and may use any of the access rights in the domain to access and manipulate objects.

The access matrix is a general model of protection. The access matrix provides a mechanism for protection without imposing a particular protection policy on the system or its users. The separation of policy and mechanism is an important design property.

The access matrix is sparse. It is normally implemented either as access lists associated with each object, or as capability lists associated with each domain. We can include dynamic protection in the access-matrix model by considering domains and the access matrix itself as objects.

Real systems are much more limited, and tend to provide protection only for files. UNIX is representative, providing read, write, and execution protection separately for the owner, group, and general public for each file. MULTICS uses a ring structure in addition to file access. Hydra and the Cambridge CAP system are capability systems that extend protection to user-defined software objects.

Protection is an internal problem. Security must consider both the computer system and the environment (people, buildings, businesses, valuable objects, and threats) within which the system is used. Passwords are commonly used to solve the authentication problem.

Exercises

11.1 What are the main differences between capability lists and access lists?

11.2 A Burroughs B7000/B6000 MCP file can be tagged as sensitive data. When such a file is deleted, its storage area is overwritten by some random bits. For what purpose would such a scheme be useful?

11.3 In a ring-protection system, level 0 has the greatest access to objects and level n (greater than zero) has fewer access rights. The access rights of a program at a particular level in the ring structure are considered as a set of capabilities. What is the relationship between the capabilities of a domain at level j and a domain at level i to an object (for $j > i$)?

11.4 Consider a system in which "computer games" can be played by students only between 10 P.M. and 6 A.M., by faculty members between 5 P.M. and 8 A.M., and by the computer center staff at all times. Suggest a scheme for implementing this policy efficiently.

11.5 The RC 4000 system (and other systems) have defined a tree of processes (called a process tree) such that all the descendants of a process are given resources (objects) and access rights by their ancestors only. Thus, a descendant can never have the ability to do anything that its ancestors cannot do. The root of the tree is the operating system, which has the ability to do anything. Assume the set of access rights was represented by an access matrix, A. $A(x,y)$ defines the access rights of process x to object y. If x is a descendant of z, what is the relationship between $A(x,y)$ and $A(z,y)$ for an arbitrary object y?

11.6 A password may become known to other users in a variety of ways. Is there a simple method for detecting that such an event has occurred? Explain your answer.

11.7 The list of all passwords is kept within the operating system. Thus, if a user manages to read this list, password protection is no longer provided. Suggest a scheme that will avoid this problem. (Hint: Use different internal and external representations.)

11.8 What hardware features are needed for efficient capability manipulation? Can these be used for memory protection?

11.9 Consider an environment where a number is associated with each process and object in the system. Suppose that we allow a process with number n to access an object with number m only if $n > m$. What type of protection structure do we have?

11.10 What protection problems may arise if a shared stack is used for parameter passing?

11.11 Suppose a process is given the privilege of accessing an object only n times. Suggest a scheme for implementing this policy.

11.12 If all the access rights to an object are deleted, the object can no longer be accessed. At this point, the object should also be deleted, and the space it occupies should be returned to the system. Suggest an efficient implementation of this scheme.

11.13 What is the need-to-know principle? Why is it important for a protection system to adhere to this principle?

11.14 Why is it difficult to protect a system in which users are allowed to do their own I/O?

11.15 Capability lists are usually kept within the address space of the user. How does the system ensure that the user cannot modify the contents of the list?

11.16 An experimental addition to UNIX allows a user to connect a "watchdog" program to a file such that the watchdog is invoked whenever a program requests access to the file. The watchdog then either grants or denies access to the file. Discuss the pros and cons of using watchdogs for security.

Bibliographic Notes

The access-matrix model of protection between domains and objects was developed from the work of Lampson [1969, 1971], and Graham and Denning [1972]. Popek [1974], Saltzer and Schroeder [1975], and Jones [1978] provide excellent surveys on the subject of protection. Harrison et al. [1976] used a formal version of this model to enable them to prove mathematically properties of a protection system.

The principle of separation of policy and mechanism has been advocated by the designer of Hydra [Levin et al. 1975].

The concept of a capability has evolved from Iliffe's and Jodeit's *codewords*, which were implemented in the Rice University computer [Iliffe and Jodeit 1962]. The term *capability* was introduced by Dennis and Van Horn [1966]. The capability concept was further developed by Lampson [1969, 1971] and Jones [1973].

The Hydra system is described by Wulf et al. [1974], Cohen and Jefferson [1975], Levin et al. [1975], and Wulf et al. [1981]. The CAP system is described by Needham and Walker [1974, 1977]. A general discussion concerning capability machines has been written by Lampson and Sturgis [1976].

Discussions concerning the MULTICS ring protection system have been written by Graham [1968], Organick [1972], Schroeder and Saltzer [1972], and Saltzer [1974].

Revocation has been discussed by Redell [1974], Redell and Fabry [1974], Cohen and Jefferson [1975], and Ekanadham and Bernstein [1979].

The confinement problem was first discussed by Lampson [1973]. Additional discussion has been offered by Lipner [1975]. The Trojan-

The confinement problem was first discussed by Lampson [1973]. Additional discussion has been offered by Lipner [1975]. The Trojan-horse problem was discussed by Branstad [1973].

The use of higher-level languages for specifying access control was first suggested by Morris [1973], who has proposed the use of the *seal* and *unseal* operation discussed in Section 11.7. Silberschatz et al. [1977], Kieburtz and Silberschatz [1978], and McGraw and Andrews [1979] have proposed various language constructs for dealing with general dynamic resource-management schemes. The access-right expression scheme of Section 11.7 was developed by Kieburtz and Silberschatz [1983]. Jones and Liskov [1976, 1978] considered the problem of how a static access-control scheme can be incorporated in a programming language that supports abstract data types, and how compile time checking can be used effectively to check access control.

The issue of security was discussed by Comber [1969], Weissman [1969], Conway et al. [1972], Popek [1974], Saltzer [1974], Saltzer and Schroeder [1975], Hsiao et al. [1979], Landwehr [1981], and Denning [1982b]. The U.S. federal government is, of course, concerned about security. It publishes the *Orange Book*, which describes a set of security levels and the features an operating system must have to qualify for each security rating. Reading it is a good starting point for understanding security concerns. Also of general interest is the collection of papers in Abrams and Podell [1987], and the text by Lobel [1986]. UNIX-specific security issues (although somewhat outdated) are discussed by Wood and Kockan [1985]. The watchdogs extension to BSD UNIX is presented by Bershad and Pinkerton [1988].

Issues concerning the design and verification of secure systems are discussed by Rushby [1981] and Silverman [1983]. A security kernel for a multiprocessor microcomputer is described by Schell [1983]. A distributed secure system is described by Rushby and Randell [1983].

Password security is discussed by Morris and Thompson [1979]. Methods to fight password pirates are discussed by Morshedian [1986]. Password authentication with insecure communications is discussed by Lamport [1981]. The issue of computer break-ins is discussed by Lehmann [1987] and Reid [1987].

Diffie and Hellman [1976, 1979] were the first researchers to propose the use of the public key-encryption scheme. The algorithm presented in Section 11.9, which is based on the public key-encryption scheme, was developed by Rivest et al. [1978]. Lempel [1979], Simmons [1979], Davies [1980], Gifford [1982], Denning [1982b], and Ahituv et al. [1987] are concerned with the use of cryptography in computer systems. Discussions concerning protection of digital signatures are offered by Akl [1983], Davies [1983], Denning [1983, 1984].

Discussions concerning UNIX security are offered by Grampp and Morris [1984], Wood and Kochan [1985], Farrow [1986a, 1986b], Filipski and Hanko [1986], Fernandez and Allen [1988], Hecht et al. [1988], Kramer [1988], and Fischer [1989].

Survey papers have been written by Popek [1974], Denning [1976], and Linden [1976].

PART 5

Distributed Systems

A distributed system is a collection of processors that do not share memory or a clock. Instead, each processor has its own local memory, and the processors communicate with each other through various communication lines. The processors in a distributed system vary in size and function. They may include small microprocessors, workstations, minicomputers, and large general-purpose computer systems.

A distributed system provides the user with access to the various resources that the system maintains. Access to a shared resource allows computation speedup, and improved data availability and reliability. A distributed system must also provide various mechanisms for process synchronization and communication, for dealing with the deadlock problem, and for dealing with a variety of failures that are not encountered in a centralized system.

A *distributed file system* is a file-service system whose users, servers, and storage devices are dispersed among the various sites of a distributed system. Accordingly, service activity has to be carried out across the network; instead of a single centralized data repository, there are multiple and independent storage devices.

CHAPTER

12

Distributed System Structures

A recent trend in computer systems is to distribute computation among several physical processors. There are basically two schemes for building such systems. In a *tightly coupled* system, the processors share memory and a clock. In these *multiprocessor* systems, communication usually takes place through the shared memory (Chapter 5).

In a *loosely coupled* system, the processors do not share memory or a clock. Instead, each processor has its own local memory. The processors communicate with each other through various communication lines, such as high-speed buses or telephone lines. These systems are usually referred to as *distributed* systems.

In this chapter, we discuss the general structure of distributed systems. We contrast the main differences in operating system design between these types of systems and the centralized systems with which we were concerned previously.

12.1 Motivation

A distributed system is a collection of loosely coupled processors interconnected by communication network. From the point of view of a specific processor in a distributed system, the rest of the processors and their respective resources are *remote*, whereas its own resources are *local*.

The processors in a distributed system may vary in size and function. They may include small microprocessors, workstations, minicomputers, and large general-purpose computer systems. These processors are referred to by a number of different names, such as *sites*, *nodes*, *computers*, *machines*, and so on, depending on the context in which they are mentioned. We mainly use the term *site*, to emphasize the physical distribution of these systems. Generally, one site, the *server*, has a resource that another site, the *client* (or user), would like to use. It is the purpose of the distributed system to provide an efficient and convenient environment for this type of sharing of resources.

There are four major reasons for building distributed systems: *resource sharing, computation speedup, reliability, and communication*. In this section, we briefly elaborate on each of them.

12.1.1 Resource Sharing

If a number of different sites (with different capabilities) are connected to one another, then a user at one site may be able to use the resources available at another. For example, a user at site *A* may be using a laser printer available only at site *B*. Meanwhile, a user at *B* may access a file that resides at *A*. In general, resource sharing in a distributed system provides mechanisms for sharing files at remote sites, processing information in a distributed database, printing files at remote sites, using remote specialized hardware devices (such as a high-speed array processor), and other operations.

12.1.2 Computation Speedup

If a particular computation can be partitioned into a number of subcomputations that can run concurrently, then the availability of a distributed system may allow us to distribute the computation among the various sites, to run it concurrently. In addition, if a particular site is currently overloaded with jobs, some of them may be moved to other, lightly loaded, sites. This movement of jobs is called *load sharing*.

12.1.3 Reliability

If one site fails in a distributed system, the remaining sites can potentially continue operating. If the system is composed of a number of large autonomous installations (that is, general-purpose computers), the failure of one of them should not affect the rest. If, on the other hand, the system is composed of a number of small machines, each of which is responsible for some crucial system function (such as terminal character I/O or the file system), then a single failure may halt the operation of the whole system. In general, if enough redundancy exists in the system (in both hardware and data), the system can continue with its operation, even if some of its sites have failed.

The failure of a site must be detected by the system, and appropriate action may be needed to recover from the failure. The system must no longer use the services of that site. In addition, if the function of the failed site can be taken over by another site, the system must ensure that the transfer of function occurs correctly. Finally, when the failed site recovers or is repaired, mechanisms must be available to integrate it back into the system smoothly.

12.1.4 Communication

When a number of sites are connected to one another by a communication network, the users at different sites have the opportunity to exchange information. At a low level, *messages* are passed between systems. This is quite similar to the single-computer message system discussed in Section 5.6. Given message passing, all the higher-level functionality found in standalone systems can be expanded to encompass the distributed system. These include file transfer, login, and mail.

The advantage of a distributed system is that these functions can be carried out over great distances. A project can be performed by two people at geographically separate sites. By transferring the files of the project, logging in to each other's remote systems to run programs, and exchanging mail to coordinate the work, the users are able to minimize the limitations inherent in long-distance work.

Obviously, an operating system that was designed as a collection of processes that communicate through a message system (such as the Accent system) can be easily extended to a distributed system.

12.2 Topology

The sites in the system can be physically connected in a variety of ways. Each configuration has advantages and disadvantages. We briefly describe the most common configurations implemented, and compare them with respect to the following criteria:

- **Basic cost**. How expensive is it to link the various sites in the system?

- **Communication cost**. How long does it take to send a message from site A to site B?

- **Reliability**. If a link or a site in the system fails, can the remaining sites still communicate with each other?

The various topologies are depicted as graphs whose nodes correspond to sites. An edge from node *A* to node *B* corresponds to a direct connection between the two sites.

12.2.1 Fully Connected

In a *fully connected* network, each site is directly linked with all other sites in the system (Figure 12.1). The basic cost of this configuration is very high, since a direct communication line must be available between every two sites. The basic cost grows as the square of the number of sites. In this environment, however, messages between the sites can be sent very fast; a message needs to use only one link to travel between any two sites. In addition, such systems are very reliable, since many links must fail for the system to become partitioned. A system is *partitioned* if it has been split into two (or more) subsystems that lack any connection between them.

12.2.2 Partially Connected

In a *partially connected* network, direct links exist between some, but not all, pairs of sites (Figure 12.2). Hence, the basic cost of this configuration is lower than that of the fully connected network. However, a message from one site to another may have to be sent through several intermediate sites, resulting in slower communication. For example, in the system depicted in Figure 12.2, a message from site *A* to site *D* must be sent through sites *B* and *C*.

In addition, a partially connected system is not as reliable as is a fully connected network. The failure of one link may partition the network. For the example in Figure 12.2, if the link from *B* to *C* fails, then the network is partitioned into two subsystems. One subsystem includes sites *A*, *B*, and *E*; the second subsystem includes sites *C* and *D*.

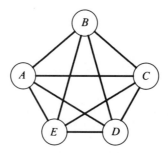

Figure 12.1   Fully connected network.

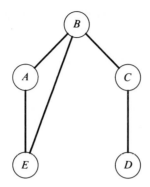

Figure 12.2 Partially connected network.

The sites in one partition cannot communicate with the sites in the other. So that this possibility is minimized, each site is usually linked to at least two other sites. For example, if we add a link from A to D, the failure of a single link cannot result in the partition of the network.

12.2.3 Hierarchy

In a *hierarchical* network, the sites are organized as a tree (Figure 12.3). This is a common organization for corporate networks. Individual offices are linked to the local main office. Main offices are linked to regional offices; regional offices are linked to corporate headquarters.

Each site (except the root) has a unique parent, and some number of children. The basic cost of this configuration is generally less than that of the partially connected scheme. In this environment, a parent and

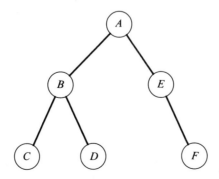

Figure 12.3 Tree-structured network.

child communicate directly. Siblings may communicate with each other only through their common parent. A message from one sibling to another must be sent up to the parent, and then down to the sibling. Similarly, cousins can communicate with each other only through their common grandparent.

If a parent site fails, then its children can no longer communicate with each other or with other processors. In general, the failure of any node (except a leaf) partitions the network into several disjoint subtrees.

12.2.4 Star

In a *star* network, one of the sites in the system is connected to all other sites (Figure 12.4). None of the other sites are connected to any other. The basic cost of this system is linear in the number of sites. The communication cost is also low, since a message from process A to B requires at most two transfers (from A to the central site, and then from the central site to B). This simple transfer scheme, however, may not ensure speed, since the central site may become a bottleneck. Consequently, even though the number of message transfers needed is low, the time required to send these messages may be high. In many star systems, therefore, the central site is completely dedicated to the message-switching task.

If the central site fails, the network is completely partitioned.

12.2.5 Ring

In a *ring* network, each site is physically connected to exactly two other sites (Figure 12.5a). The ring can be either unidirectional or bidirec-

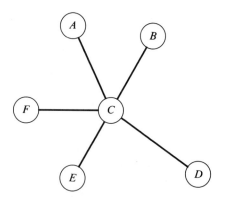

Figure 12.4   Star network.

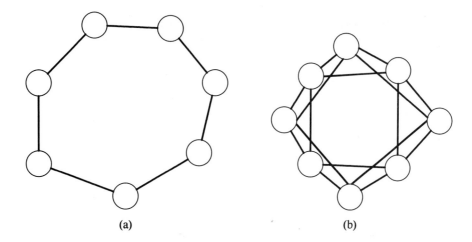

Figure 12.5   Ring networks. (a) Single links. (b) Double links.

tional. In a unidirectional architecture, a site can transmit information to only one of its neighbors. All sites must send information in the same direction. In a bidirectional architecture, a site can transmit information to both of its neighbors. The basic cost of a ring is linear in the number of sites. However, the communication cost can be high. A message from one site to another travels around the ring until it reaches its destination. In a unidirectional ring, this process could require $n - 1$ transfers. In a bidirectional ring, at most $n/2$ transfers are needed.

In a bidirectional ring, two links must fail before the network will be partitioned. In a unidirectional ring, a single site failure (or link failure) would partition the network. One remedy is to extend the architecture by providing double links, as depicted in Figure 12.5(b).

12.2.6 Multiaccess Bus

In a *multiaccess bus* network, there is a single shared link (the bus). All the sites in the system are directly connected to that link, which may be organized as a straight line (Figure 12.6a) or as a ring (Figure 12.6b). The sites can communicate with each other directly through this link. The basic cost of the network is linear in the number of sites. The communication cost is quite low, unless the link becomes a bottleneck. Notice that this network topology is similar to that of the star network with a dedicated central site. The failure of one site does not affect communication among the rest of the sites. However, if the link fails, the network is completely partitioned.

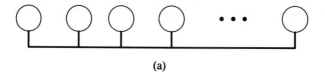

(a)

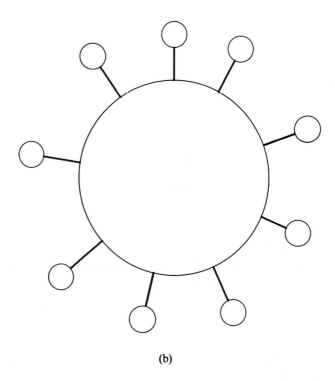

(b)

Figure 12.6   Bus network. (a) Linear bus. (b) Ring bus.

12.3 Communication

The designer of a *communication* network must address four basic issues:

- **Routing strategies**. How are the messages sent through the network?

- **Connection strategies**. How do two processes send a sequence of messages?

- **Contention**. Since the network is a shared resource, how do we resolve conflicting demands for its use?

- **Design strategies.** What is the overall design for communication between applications?

In Sections 12.3.1 through 12.3.4, we elaborate on each of these.

12.3.1 Routing Strategies

When a process at site A wants to communicate with a process at site B, how is the message sent? If there is only one physical path from A to B (such as in a star or hierarchical network), the message must be sent through that path. However, if there are multiple physical paths from A to B, then several routing options exist. Each site has a *routing table*, indicating the alternative paths that can be used to send a message to other sites. The table may include information about the speed and cost of the various communication paths, and it may be updated as necessary, either manually or via programs that exchange routing information. The three most common routing schemes are *fixed routing*, *virtual routing*, and *dynamic routing*:

- **Fixed routing.** A path from A to B is specified in advance and does not change unless a hardware failure disables this path. Usually, the shortest path is chosen, so that communication costs are minimized.

- **Virtual circuit.** A path from A to B is fixed for the duration of one *session*. Different sessions involving messages from A to B may have different paths.

- **Dynamic routing.** The path used to send a message from site A to site B is chosen only when a message is sent. Since the decision is made dynamically, separate messages may be assigned different paths. Site A will make a decision to send the message to site C; C, in turn, will decide to send it to site D, and so on. Eventually, a site will deliver the message to B. Usually a site sends a message to another site on that link that is the least used at that particular time.

There are tradeoffs among these three schemes. Fixed routing cannot adapt to load changes. In other words, if a path has been established between A and B, the messages must be sent along this path, even if the path is heavily used while another possible path is lightly used. We can partially remedy this problem by using virtual circuits, and can avoid it completely avoided by using dynamic routing. Fixed routing and virtual circuits ensure that messages from A to B will be delivered in the order in which they were sent. In dynamic routing, messages may arrive out of order. We can remedy this problem by appending a sequence number to each message.

12.3.2 Connection Strategies

Once messages are able to reach their destinations, processes may institute communications "sessions" to exchange information. There are a number of different ways to connect pairs of processes that want to communicate over the network. The three most common schemes are *circuit switching, message switching,* and *packet switching:*

- **Circuit switching**. If two processes want to communicate, a permanent physical link is established between them. This link is allocated for the duration of the communication, and no other process can use that link during this period (even if the two processes are not actively communicating for a while). This scheme is similar to that used in the telephone system. Once a communication line has been opened between two parties (that is, party *A* calls party *B*), no one else can use this circuit, until the communication is terminated explicitly (for example, when one of the parties hangs up).

- **Message switching**. If two processes want to communicate, a temporary link is established for the duration of one message transfer. Physical links are allocated dynamically among correspondents as needed, and are allocated for only short periods of time. Each message is a block of data, together with some system information (such as the source, the destination, and error-correction codes) that allow the communication network to deliver the message to the destination correctly. This scheme is similar to the post-office mailing system. Each letter is considered a message that contains both the destination address and source (return) address. Note that many messages (from different users) can be shipped over the same link.

- **Packet switching**. Messages are generally of variable length. To simplify the system design, we commonly implement communication with fixed-length messages called *packets.* One logical message may have to be divided into a number of packets. Each packet may be sent to its destination separately, and each may take a different path through the network. The packets must be reassembled into messages as they arrive.

There are obvious tradeoffs among these schemes. Circuit switching requires set-up time, but incurs less overhead for shipping each message, and may waste network bandwidth. Message and packet switching, on the other hand, require less set-up time, but incur more overhead per message. Also, in packet switching, each message must be divided into packets and later reassembled.

12.3.3 Contention

Since a link may connect multiple sites, it is possible that several sites will want to transmit information over a link simultaneously. This difficulty occurs mainly in a ring or multiaccess bus network. In this case, the transmitted information may become scrambled and must be discarded. The sites must be notified about the problem, so that they can retransmit the information. If no special provisions are made, this situation may be repeated, resulting in degraded performance. Several techniques have been developed to avoid repeated collisions, including *collision detection*, *token passing*, and *message slots*.

- **CSMA/CD.** Before transmitting a message over a link, a site must listen to determine whether another message is currently being transmitted over that link; this technique is called *carrier sense with multiple access* (CSMA). If the link is free, the site can start transmitting. Otherwise, it must wait (and continue to listen) until the link is free. If two or more sites begin transmitting at exactly the same time (each thinking that no other site is using the link), then they will register a *collision detection* (CD) and will stop transmitting. Each site will try again after some random time interval. Note that, when site *A* starts transmitting over a link, it must listen continuously to detect collisions with messages from other sites. The main problem with this approach is that, when the system is very busy, many collisions may occur, and thus performance may be degraded. Nevertheless, CSMA/CD has been used successfully in the Ethernet system, the most common network system.

- **Token passing**. A unique message type, known as a *token*, continuously circulates in the system (usually a ring structure). A site that wants to transmit information must wait until the token arrives. It removes the token from the ring and begins to transmit its messages. When the site completes its round of message passing, it retransmits the token. This action, in turn, allows another site to receive and remove the token, and to start its message transmission. If the token gets lost, then the system must detect the loss and generate a new token. It usually does that by declaring an *election*, to elect a unique site where a new token will be generated. Later, in Section 13.7, we present one election algorithm. A token-passing scheme has been adopted by the IBM and Apollo systems.

- **Message slots**. A number of fixed-length message slots continuously circulate in the system (usually a ring structure). Each slot can hold a fixed-sized message and control information (such as what the source and destination are, and whether the slot is empty or full). A site that is ready to transmit must wait until an empty slot arrives. It then inserts its message into the slot, setting the appropriate control information. The slot with its message then continues in the network. When it arrives at a site, that site inspects the control information to determine whether the slot contains a message for this site. If not, that site recirculates the slot and message. Otherwise, it removes the message, resetting the control information to indicate that the slot is empty. The site can then either use the slot to send its own message or release the slot. Since a slot can contain only fixed-sized messages, a single logical message may have to be broken down into a number of smaller packets, each of which is sent in a separate slot. This scheme has been adopted in the experimental Cambridge Digital Communication Ring.

12.3.4 Design Strategies

When designing a communication network, we must deal with the inherent complexity of coordinating asynchronous operations communicating in a potentially slow and error-prone environment. We can simplify the design problem (and related implementation) by partitioning the problem into multiple layers. Following the International Standards Organization (ISO), we refer to the layers with the following descriptions:

1. **Physical layer.** The physical layer is responsible for handling both the mechanical and electrical details of the physical transmission of a bit stream.

2. **Data-link layer.** The data-link layer is responsible for handling the *frames*, or fixed-length parts of packets, including any error detection and recovery that occurred in the physical layer.

3. **Network layer.** The network layer is responsible for providing connections and for routing packets in the communication network, including handling the address of outgoing packets, decoding the address of incoming packets, and maintaining routing information for proper response to changing load levels.

4. **Transport layer.** The transport layer is responsible for low-level access to the network and for transfer of messages between the clients, including partitioning messages into packets, maintaining packet order, controlling-flow, and generating physical addresses.

5. **Session layer.** The session layer is responsible for implementing sessions, or process-to-process communications protocols. Typically,

these are the actual communications for remote logins, and file and mail transfers.

6. **Presentation layer**. The presentation layer is responsible for resolving the differences in formats among the various sites in the network, including character conversions, and half duplex/full duplex (echoing).

7. **Application layer**. The application layer is responsible for interacting directly with the users. This layer deals with file transfer, remote-login protocols and electronic mail, as well as schemas for distributed databases.

12.4 Network Types

There are basically two types of networks: *local-area networks* and *wide-area networks*. The main difference between the two is the way in which they are geographically distributed. Local-area networks are composed of processors that are distributed over small geographical areas, such as a single building or a number of adjacent buildings. Wide-area networks, on the other hand, are composed of a number of autonomous processors that are distributed over a large geographical area (such as the United States). These differences imply major variations in the speed and reliability of the communications network, and are reflected in the operating-system design.

12.4.1 Local-Area Networks

Local-area networks (LANs) emerged in the early 1970s, as a substitute for large mainframe computer systems. It had become apparent that, for many enterprises, it is more economical to have a number of small computers, each with its own self-contained applications, rather than a single large system. Since each small computer is likely to need a full complement of peripheral devices (such as disks and printers), and since some form of data sharing is likely to occur in a single enterprise, it was a natural step to connect these small systems into a network.

LANs are usually designed to cover a small geographical area (such as a single building, or a few adjacent buildings) and are generally used in an office environment. Since all the sites in such systems are close to one another, the communication links have a higher speed and lower error rate than do their counterparts in wide-area networks. The most common links are twisted pair, baseband coaxial cable, broadband coaxial cable, and fiber optics. The most common configurations are multiaccess bus, ring, and star networks. Communication speeds range from 1 megabyte per second to 1 gigabyte per second, with 10 megabytes per second being the norm.

A typical LAN may consist of a number of different minicomputers, various shared peripheral devices (such as laser printers or magnetic-tape units), workstations, and one or more gateways (specialized processors) that provide access to other networks (Figure 12.7). An Ethernet scheme is commonly used to construct LANs. The communication medium is a multiaccess coaxial cable with the collision-detection scheme described in Section 12.3. Messages between the various nodes in the network are sent in packets. Since there is no central controller, new sites can be added easily to the network.

12.4.2 Wide-Area Networks

Wide-area networks (WANs) emerged in the late 1960s, mainly as an academic research project to provide efficient communication between sites, allowing hardware and software to be conveniently and economically shared by a wide community of users. The first network to

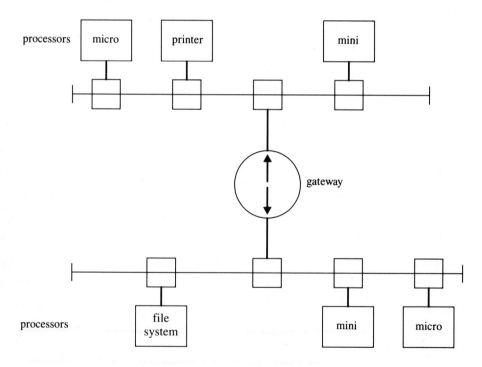

Figure 12.7   Local-area network.

be designed and developed was the Arpanet. Work on the Arpanet began in 1968. The Apranet has grown from a four-site experimental network to a worldwide network of networks, the Internet, comprising thousands of computer systems. Recently, a number of commercial networks have also appeared on the market. The Telenet system is available within the continental United States; the Datapac system is available in Canada. These networks provide their customers with the ability to access a wide range of hardware and software computing resources.

Since the sites in a WAN are physically distributed over a large geographical area, the communication links are by default relatively slow and unreliable. Typical links are telephone lines, microwave links, and satellite channels. These communication links are controlled by special *communication processors* (Figure 12.8), which are responsible for defining the interface through which the sites communicate over the network, as well as for transferring information among the various sites.

As a specific example, let us consider the Internet WAN. The system provides an ability for geographically separated sites, called *hosts*, to communicate with one another. The host computers typically differ from one another in type, speed, word length, operating system, and so on. Hosts are generally on LANs, which are in turn connected to the Internet via regional networks. The regional networks, such as NSFnet in the Northeast United States, are interlinked with *routers* to form the worldwide network. Connections between networks frequently use a telephone-system service called T1, which provides a transfer rate of 1.544 megabit per second. The routers connect networks at the ISO network layer, and control the paths each packet takes through the net. This routing may be either dynamic, to increase communications efficiency, or static, to reduce security risks or to allow communications charges to be computed. Most hosts are logically addressed with a multipart host name using the *domain name system*. Names progress from the most specific to the most general part of the address, with periods separating the fields. For instance, "bob.cs.brown.edu" refers to host "bob" in the Brown University Department of Computer Science.

Other WANs in operation use standard telephone lines as their primary means of communication. The UNIX news network, UUCP, allows systems to communicate with each other at predetermined times, via modems, to exchange messages. The messages are then routed to other nearby systems and in this way either are propagated to all hosts on the network (if it is a public message) or are transferred to their destination (for private messages). WANs are generally slower than LANs; their transmission rates range from 1200 bytes per second to over 1 megabyte per second.

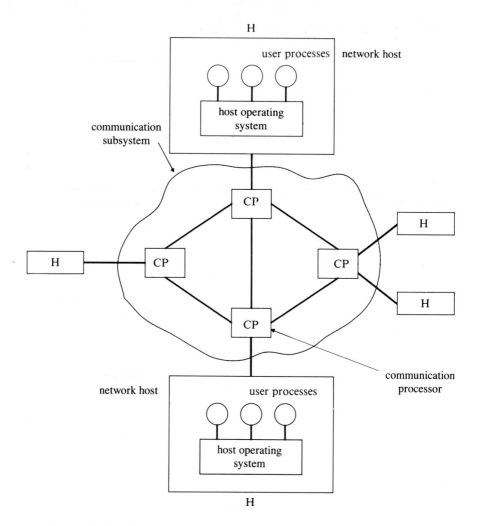

Figure 12.8   Communication processors in a wide-area network.

12.5 Types of Operating Systems

A distributed operating system provides the users with access to the various resources that the system provides. By _resources,_ we mean both hardware (such as printers and tape drives) and software (such as files and programs). Access to these resources is controlled by the operating system. There are basically two complementary schemes for providing such a service:

- **Network operating systems**. The users are aware of the multiplicity of machines, and need to access these resources by either logging into the appropriate remote machine, or transferring data from the remote machine to their own machines.

- **Distributed operating systems**. The users do not need to be aware of the multiplicity of machines. They access remote resources in the same manner as they do local resources.

We discuss these two schemes in Sections 12.5.1 and 12.5.2.

12.5.1 Network Operating Systems

A major function of a network operating system is to provide a mechanism for file transfer from one machine to another. In such an environment, each site maintains its own local file system. If a user at site A wants to access a file at site B, the file must be copied explicitly from one site to another.

The Internet provides a mechanism for such a transfer with the File Transfer Protocol (FTP) program. Suppose that a user wants to copy a file F_1 residing at site B into a local (site A) file F_2. The user must first invoke the FTP program. The program then asks the user for the following information:

a. The name of the site from which the file transfer is to take place (that is, site B).

b. The access information, which verifies that the user has the appropriate access privileges at site B.

Once this checking has been done, the user can copy file F_1 from B to F_2 on A by executing

$$\textbf{get } F_1 \textbf{ to } F_2.$$

In this scheme, the file location is not transparent to the user; users must know exactly where each file is. Moreover, there is no real file sharing, since a user can only copy a file from one site to another. Thus, several copies of the same file may exist, resulting in a waste of space. In addition, if these copies are modified, the various copies will be inconsistent.

12.5.2 Distributed Operating Systems

In a distributed operating system, the users access remote resources in the same manner they do as local resources. Data and process migration from one site to another is under the control of the distributed operating system.

Data Migration

Suppose that a user on site A wants to access data (such as a file) that resides at site B. There are two basic methods for the system to transfer the data. One approach is to transfer the entire file to site A. From that point on, all access to the file is local. When the user no longer needs access to the file, a copy of it (if it has been modified) is sent back to site B. Of course, even if only a modest change has been made to a large file, all the data must be transferred. This approach is used in the Andrew file system, as discussed in Chapter 14.

The other approach is to transfer to site A only those portions of the file that are actually *necessary* for the immediate task. If another portion is required later, another transfer will take place. When the user no longer wants to access the file, any part of it that has been modified must be sent back to site B. (Note the similarity to demand paging.) The Sun Microsystems' Network File System (NFS) protocol uses this method (see Chapter 14).

Clearly, if only a small part of a large file is being accessed, the latter approach is preferable. If significant portions of the file are being accessed, it is more efficient to copy the entire file.

Note that it is not sufficient merely to transfer data from one site to another. The system must also perform various data translations if the two sites involved are not directly compatible (for instance, if they use different character-code representations or represent integers with a different number of bits).

Computation Migration

In some circumstances, it may be more efficient to transfer the computation, rather than the data, across the system. For example, consider a job that needs to access various large files that reside at different sites, to obtain a summary of those files. It would be more efficient to access the files at the sites where they reside and then to return the desired results to the site that initiated the computation.

Such a computation can be carried out in a number of different ways. Suppose that process p wants to access a file at site A. Access to the file is carried out at site A, and could be initiated by a remote procedure call. Process p invokes a predefined procedure at site A. The procedure executes appropriately, and then returns the needed parameters to p.

Alternatively, process p can send a message to site A. The operating system at site A creates a new process q whose function is to carry out the designated task. When process q completes its execution, it sends the needed result back to p by the message system. Note that, in this scheme, process p may execute concurrently with process q and in fact may have several processes running concurrently on several sites.

Both schemes could be used to access several files residing at various sites. One remote procedure call might result in the invocation of another remote procedure call, or even in the transfer of messages to another site. Similarly, process q could, during the course of its execution, send a message to another site, which in turn would create another process. This process might either send a message back to q or repeat the cycle.

Process Migration

When a process is submitted for execution, it is not always executed at the site in which it is initiated. It may be advantageous to execute the entire process, or parts of it, at different sites. This scheme may be used for several reasons:

- **Load balancing**. The processes (or subprocesses) may be distributed across the network to even the workload.

- **Computation speedup**. If a single process can be divided into a number of subprocesses that may run concurrently on different sites, then the total process turnaround time can be reduced.

- **Hardware preference**. The process may have characteristics that make it more suitable for execution on some specialized processor (such as matrix inversion on an array processor, rather than on a microprocessor).

- **Software preference**. The process may require software that is available at only a particular site, and either the software cannot be moved, or it is less expensive to move the process.

There are basically two complementary techniques used to move processes in a network. The system can attempt to hide the fact that the process has migrated from the client. This scheme has the advantage that the user does not need to code his program explicitly to accomplish the migration. This method is usually employed for achieving load balancing and computation speedup among homogeneous systems.

The other approach is to allow (or require) the user to specify explicitly how the process should migrate. This method is usually employed when the process must be moved to satisfy a hardware or software preference.

12.6 Design Issues

It has been the challenge of many designers to make the multiplicity of processors and storage devices transparent to the users. Ideally, a distributed system should look to its users like a conventional, centralized system. The user interface of a transparent distributed system should not distinguish between local and remote resources. That is, users should be able to access remote distributed systems as though the latter were local, and it should be the responsibility of the distributed system to locate the resources and to arrange for the appropriate interaction.

Another aspect of transparency is user mobility. It would be convenient to allow users to log in any machine in the system, and not to force them to use a specific machine. A transparent distributed system facilitates user mobility by bringing over the user's environment (for example, home directory) to wherever she logs in. Both the Andrew file system and Project Athena provide this functionality on a large scale.

We use the term *fault tolerance* in a very broad sense. Communication faults, machine failures (of type fail-stop), storage-device crashes, and decays of storage media are all considered to be faults that should be tolerated to some extent. A fault-tolerant system should continue functioning, perhaps in a degraded form, when faced with these failures. The degradation can be in performance, in functionality, or in both. It should be, however, proportional, in some sense, to the failures that cause it. A system that grinds to a halt when only a few of its components fail is certainly not fault tolerant. Unfortunately, fault tolerance is difficult to implement. Most commercial systems provide only limited tolerance. For instance, the DEC VAXcluster allows multiple computers to share a set of disks. If a system crashes, users may still access their information from another system. Of course, if a disk fails, all the systems will halt.

The capability of a system to adapt to increased service load is called *scalability*. Systems have bounded resources and can become completely saturated under increased load. For example, regarding a file system, saturation occurs either when a server's CPU runs at a very high utilization rate, or when disks are almost full. Scalability is a relative property, but it can be measured accurately. A scalable system should react more gracefully to increased load than does a nonscalable one. First, its performance should degrade more moderately than that of a nonscalable system. Second, its resources should reach a saturated state later, when compared with a nonscalable system. Even perfect design cannot accommodate evergrowing load. Adding new resources might solve the problem, but it might generate additional indirect load on other resources (for example, adding machines to a distributed system can clog the network and increase service loads). Even worse, expanding the system can incur expensive design modifications. A scalable system should have the potential to grow without these problems. In a distributed system, the ability to scale up gracefully is of special importance, since expanding the network by adding new machines or interconnecting two networks is commonplace. In short, a scalable design should withstand high service load, accommodate growth of the user community, and enable simple integration of added resources.

Fault tolerance and scalability are related to each other. A heavily loaded component can become paralyzed and behave like a faulty component. Also, shifting load from a faulty component to that component's backup can saturate the latter. Generally, having spare resources is essential for ensuring reliability as well as for handling peak loads gracefully. An inherent advantage that a distributed system has is a potential for fault tolerance and scalability because of the multiplicity of resources. However, inappropriate design can obscure this potential. Fault-tolerance and scalability considerations call for a design demonstrating distribution of control and data.

Very large-scale distributed systems, to a great extent, are still only theoretical. There are no magic guidelines to ensure the scalability of a system. It is easier to point out why current designs are not scalable. We shall discuss several designs that pose problems, and shall propose possible solutions, all in the context of scalability.

One principle for designing very large-scale systems is the principle that the service demand from any component of the system should be bounded by a constant that is independent of the number of nodes in the system. Any service mechanism whose load demand is proportional to the size of the system is destined to become clogged once the system grows beyond a certain size. Adding more resources would not alleviate such a problem. The capacity of this mechanism simply limits the growth of the system.

Central control schemes and central resources should not be used to build scalable (and fault-tolerant) systems. Examples of centralized entities are central authentication servers, central naming servers, and central file servers. Centralization is a form of functional asymmetry among machines constituting the system. The ideal alternative is a configuration that is functionally symmetric; that is, all the component machines have an equal role in the operation of the system, and hence each machine has some degree of autonomy. Practically, it is virtually impossible to comply with such a principle. For instance, incorporating diskless machines violates functional symmetry, since the workstations depend on a central disk. However, autonomy and symmetry are important goals to which we should aspire.

The practical approximation to symmetric and autonomous configuration is *clustering.* The system is partitioned into a collection of semiautonomous clusters. A cluster consists of a set of machines and a dedicated cluster server. So that cross-cluster resource references will be relatively infrequent, each machine's requests should be satisfied by its own cluster server most of the time. Of course, this scheme depends on the ability to localize resource references and to place the component units appropriately. If the cluster is well balanced — that is, if the server in charge suffices to satisfy all the cluster demands — it can be used as a modular building block to scale up the system.

A major problem in the design of any service is the process structure of the server. Servers are supposed to operate efficiently in peak periods, when hundreds of active clients need to be served simultaneously. A single-processor server is certainly not a good choice, since whenever a request necessitates disk I/O the whole service will be blocked. Assigning a process for each client is a better choice; however, the expense of frequent context switches between the processes must be considered. A related problem has to do with the fact that all the server processes need to share information. It appears that one of the best solutions for the server architecture is the use of lightweight processes or threads, which we discussed in Section 4.4. The abstraction presented by a group of lightweight processes is that of multiple threads of control associated with some shared resources. Usually, a lightweight process is not bound to a particular client. Instead, it serves single requests of different clients. Scheduling threads can be preemptive or nonpreemptive. If threads are allowed to run to completion, then their shared data do not need to be protected explicitly. Otherwise, some explicit locking mechanism must be used. It is clear that some form of lightweight-processes scheme is essential for servers to be scalable.

12.7 Summary

A distributed system is a collection of processors that do not share memory or a clock. Instead, each processor has its own local memory, and the processors communicate with each other through various communication lines, such as high-speed buses or telephone lines. The processors in a distributed system vary in size and function. They may include small microprocessors, workstations, minicomputers, and large general-purpose computer systems.

Principally, there are two types of distributed systems: local-area networks (LANs) and wide-area networks (WANs). The main difference between the two is in the way they are distributed geographically. LANs are composed of processors that are distributed over small geographical areas, such as a single building or a few adjacent buildings. WANs are composed of autonomous processors that are distributed over a large geographical area (such as the United States).

The processors in the system are connected through a communication network, which can be configured in a number of different ways. The network may be fully or partially connected. It may be a tree, a star, a ring, or a multiaccess bus. The communication-network design must include routing and connection strategies, and must solve the problems of contention and security.

A distributed system provides the user with access to the various resources the system provides. Access to a shared resource can be provided by data migration, computation migration, or job migration. A distributed file system must address two major issues: transparency (does a user access all files in the same manner regardless of where they are in the network?) and locality (where do files reside in the system?).

Exercises

12.1 What are the main differences between a wide-area network and a local-area network?

12.2 Contrast the various network topologies in terms of reliability.

12.3 What network configuration would best suit the following environments?

    a. A dormitory floor

    b. A campus

    c. A state

    d. A nation

12.4 Why do most wide-area networks employ only a partially connected topology?

12.5 What are the advantages and disadvantages of making the computer network transparent to the user?

12.6 What are the formidable problems that designers must solve to implement a network transparent system?

12.7 Process migration within a heterogeneous network is usually impossible, given the differences in architectures and operating systems. Describe a method for process migration across different architectures running

   a. The same operating system

   b. Different operating systems

12.8 Even though the ISO model of networking specifies seven layers of functionality, most computer systems use fewer layers to implement a network. Why do they use fewer layers? What problems could this cause?

Bibliographic Notes

Kahn [1972], Pyke [1973], Enslow [1973], Doll [1974], Crowther et al. [1975], and Tanenbaum [1988] have provided general overviews of computer networks. A detailed discussion of networking hardware and software can be found in Fortier [1989]. The Internet and several other networks are discussed in Quarterman and Hoskins [1986]. Forsdick et al. [1978] and Donnelley [1979] discussed operating systems for computer networks.

Discussions concerning LANs have been written by Metcalfe and Boggs [1976] and Clark et al. [1978]. A special issue of *Computer Networks*, December [1979], included nine papers on LANs covering such subjects as hardware, software, simulation, and examples. A taxonomy and extensive list of LANs were presented by Thurber and Freeman [1980]. Clark et al. [1978], Needham [1979], Wilkes and Wheeler [1979], and Stallings [1984] discussed various types of ring-structured LANs.

Feng [1981] surveyed the various network topologies. Boorstyn and Frank [1977] and Gerla and Kleinrock [1977] discussed topology design problems.

Discussions concerning distributed operating-system structures are offered by Jones et al. [1979] (the StarOS system), Kepecs and Solomon [1984] (the SODA system), Ousterhout et al. [1980] (the Medusa system), Popek et al. [1981] and Walker et al. [1983] (the Locus system), and Cheriton and Zwaenepoel [1983] (the V kernel). A survey of various distributed operating systems is presented by Tanenbaum and Van Renesse [1985]. The design of a capability-based distributed operating system is presented by Mullender and Tanenbaum [1986].

The Andrew File System is introduced in Satyanarayanan et al. [1985]; Athena is described by Balkovich et al. [1985] and Treese [1988]. Apollo's Domain operating system has become more UNIX-like with time;

its original functionality is described by Leach et al. [1982]. VAXclusters allow a small number of DEC VAX systems to be connected together to share disk storage, as is shown in Digital [1989]. Sun's Network File System is discussed further in Chapter 14.

Reliable communication in the presense of failures is discussed by Birman and Joseph [1987]. The principle that the service demand from any component of the system should be bounded by a constant that is independent of the number of nodes in the system was first advanced by Barak and Kornatzky [1987].

Discussions concerning distributed file systems are offered by Gien [1978] (the File Transfer Protocol scheme).

13

Distributed Coordination

In Chapters 5 and 6, we described various mechanisms for process synchronization and communication, as well as methods for dealing with the deadlock problem. In this chapter, we examine how these issues can be dealt with in a distributed environment. In addition, since a distributed system may suffer from a variety of failures that are not encountered in a centralized system, we also discuss here the issue of failure in a distributed system.

13.1 Event Ordering

In a centralized system, it is always possible to determine the order in which two events have occurred, since there is a single common memory and clock. In many applications, it is of utmost importance to be able to determine order. For example, in a resource-allocation scheme, we specify that a resource can be used only *after* the resource has been granted. In a distributed system, however, there is no common memory and no common clock. Therefore, it is sometimes impossible to say which of two events occurred first. The *happened-before* relation is only a partial ordering of the events in distributed systems. Since the ability to define a total ordering is crucial in many applications, we present a distributed algorithm for extending the *happened-before* relation to a consistent total ordering of all the events in the system.

13.1.1 The Happened-Before Relation

Since we are considering only sequential processes, all events executed in a single process are totally ordered. Also, by the law of causality, a message can be received only after it has been sent. Therefore, we can define the *happened-before* relation (denoted by →) on a set of events as follows (assuming that sending and receiving a message constitutes an event):

1. If A and B are events in the same process, and A was executed before B, then $A \to B$.

2. If A is the event of sending a message by one process and B is the event of receiving that message by another process, then $A \to B$.

3. If $A \to B$ and $B \to C$ then $A \to C$.

Since an event cannot happen before itself, the → relation is an irreflexive partial ordering.

If two events, A and B, are not related by the → relation (that is, A did not happen before B, and B did not happen before A), then we say that these two events were executed *concurrently*. In this case, neither event can causally affect the other. If, however, $A \to B$, then it is possible for event A to affect event B causally.

The definitions of concurrency and of happened-before can best be illustrated by a space-time diagram, such as that in Figure 13.1. The horizontal direction represents space (that is, different processes), and the vertical direction represents time. The labeled vertical lines denote processes (or processors). The labeled dots denote events. A wavy line denotes a message sent from one process to another. From this diagram, it is clear that events A and B are concurrent if and only if no path exists either from A to B or from B to A.

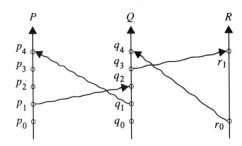

Figure 13.1   Relative time for three concurrent processes.

For example, consider Figure 13.1. Some of the events related by the *happened-before* relation are

$$p_1 \rightarrow q_2,$$
$$r_0 \rightarrow q_4,$$
$$q_3 \rightarrow r_1,$$
$$p_1 \rightarrow q_4 \quad \text{(since } p_1 \rightarrow q_2 \text{ and } q_2 \rightarrow q_4\text{)}.$$

Some of the concurrent events in the system are

$$q_0 \text{ and } p_2,$$
$$r_0 \text{ and } q_3,$$
$$r_0 \text{ and } p_3,$$
$$q_3 \text{ and } p_3.$$

We cannot know which of two concurrent events, such as q_0 and p_2, happened first. However, since neither event can affect the other (there is no way for one of them to know whether the other has occurred yet), it is not important which of them actually happens first. It is only important that any processes that care about the order of two concurrent events agree on some order.

13.1.2 Implementation

To be able to determine that an event A happened before an event B, we need either a common clock or a set of perfectly synchronized clocks. Since in a distributed system neither of these is available, we must define the *happened-before* relation without the use of physical clocks.

We associate with each system event a *time-stamp*. We can then define the *global ordering* requirement: For every pair of events A and B, if $A \rightarrow B$, then the time-stamp of A is less than the time-stamp of B. (Note that the converse need not be true.)

How do we enforce the global ordering requirement in a distributed environment? We define within *each* process P_i a *logical clock*, LC_i. The logical clock can be implemented as a simple counter that is incremented between any two successive events executed within a process. Since the logical clock has a monotonically increasing value, it assigns a unique number to every event, and if an event A occurs before event B in process P_i, then $LC_i(A) < LC_i(B)$. The time-stamp for an event is the value of the logical clock for that event. Clearly, this scheme ensures that, for any two events in the same process, the global ordering requirement is met.

Unfortunately, this scheme does not ensure that the global ordering requirement is met across processes. To illustrate the problem, we consider two processes P_1 and P_2 that communicate with each other. Suppose that P_1 sends a message to P_2 (event A) with $LC_1(A) = 200$, and P_2 receives the message (event B) with $LC_2(B) = 195$ (because the processor for P_2 is slower than the processor for P_1 and so its logical clock ticks slower). This situation violates our requirement, since $A \rightarrow B$, but the time-stamp of A is greater than the time-stamp of B.

To resolve this difficulty, we require a process to advance its logical clock when it receives a message whose time-stamp is greater than the current value of its logical clock. In particular, if process P_i receives a message (event B) with time-stamp t and $LC_i(B) < t$, then it should advance its clock such that $LC_i(B) = t+1$. Thus, in our example, when P_2 receives the message from P_1, it will advance its logical clock such that $LC_2(B) = 201$.

Finally, to realize a total ordering, we need only to observe that, with our time-stamp ordering scheme, if the time-stamps of two events A and B are the same, then the events are concurrent. In this case, we may use process identity numbers to break ties and to create a total ordering. The use of time-stamps is discussed later in this chapter and in Chapter 13.

13.2 Mutual Exclusion

In this section, we present a number of different algorithms for implementing mutual exclusion in a distributed environment. We assume that the system consists of n processes, each of which resides at a different processor. To simplify our discussion, we assume that processes are numbered uniquely from 1 to n, and that there is a one-to-one mapping between processes and processors (that is, each process has its own processor).

13.2.1 Centralized Approach

In a centralized approach to providing mutual exclusion, one of the processes in the system is chosen to coordinate the entry to the critical section. Each process that wants to invoke mutual exclusion sends a *request* message to the coordinator. When the process receives a *reply* message from the coordinator, it can proceed to enter its critical section. After exiting its critical section, the process sends a *release* message to the coordinator and proceeds with its execution.

On receiving a *request* message, the coordinator checks to see whether some other process is in its critical section. If no process is in its critical section, the coordinator immediately sends back a *reply* message. Otherwise, the request is queued. When the coordinator receives a *release* message, it removes one of the request messages from the queue (in accordance with some scheduling algorithm) and sends a *reply* message to the requesting process.

It should be clear that this algorithm ensures mutual exclusion. In addition, if the scheduling policy within the coordinator is fair (such as first-come, first-served scheduling), no starvation can occur. This scheme requires three messages per critical-section entry: a request, a reply, and a release.

If the coordinator process fails, then a new process must take its place. In Section 13.5, we discuss how such a failure can be detected. In Section 13.7, we describe various algorithms for electing a unique new coordinator. Once a new coordinator has been elected, it must poll all the processes in the system, to reconstruct its request queue. Once the queue has been constructed, the computation may resume.

13.2.2 Fully Distributed Approach

If we want to distribute the decision making across the entire system, then the solution is far more complicated. We present an algorithm that is based on the event-ordering scheme described in Section 13.1.

When a process P_i wants to enter its critical section, it generates a new time-stamp, TS, and sends the message $request(P_i, TS)$ to all other processes in the system (including itself). On receiving a *request* message, a process may reply immediately (that is, send a *reply* message back to P_i), or it may defer sending a reply back (because it is already in its critical section, for example). A process that has received a *reply* message from all other processes in the system can enter its critical section, queueing incoming requests and deferring them. After exiting its critical section, the process sends *reply* messages to all its deferred requests.

The decision whether process P_i replies immediately to a $request(P_j, TS)$ message or defers its reply is based on three factors:

1. If process P_i is in its critical section, then it defers its reply to P_j.

2. If process P_i does *not* want to enter its critical section, then it sends a *reply* immediately to P_j.

3. If process P_i wants to enter its critical section but has not yet entered it, then it compares its own request time-stamp with the time-stamp TS of the incoming request made by process P_j. If its own request time-stamp is less than TS, then it sends a *reply* immediately to P_j (P_j asked first). Otherwise, the reply is deferred.

This algorithm exhibits the following desirable behavior:

- Mutual exclusion is obtained.

- Freedom from deadlock is ensured.

- Freedom from starvation is ensured, since entry to the critical section is scheduled according to the time-stamp ordering. The time-stamp ordering ensures that processes are served in a first-come, first-served order.

- The number of messages per critical-section entry is $2 \times (n - 1)$. This is the minimum number of required messages per critical-section entry when processes act independently and concurrently.

To illustrate how the algorithm functions, we consider a system consisting of processes P_1, P_2, and P_3. Suppose that processes P_1 and P_3 want to enter their critical sections. Process P_1 then sends a message *request* (P_1, time-stamp = 10) to processes P_2 and P_3, while process P_3 sends a message *request* (P_3, time-stamp = 4) to processes P_1 and P_2. The time-stamps 4 and 10 were obtained from the logical clocks described in Section 13.1. When process P_2 receives these *request* messages, it replies immediately. When process P_1 receives the *request* from process P_3 it replies immediately, since the time-stamp (10) on its own request message is greater than the time-stamp (4) for process P_3. When process P_3 receives the *request* from process P_1, it defers its reply, since the time-stamp (4) on its request message is less than the time-stamp (10) for the message of process P_1. On receiving replies from both process P_1 and process P_2, process P_3 can enter its critical section. After exiting its critical section, process P_3 sends a *reply* to process P_1, which can then enter its critical section.

Note that this scheme requires the participation of all the processes in the system. This approach has three undesirable consequences:

1. The processes need to know the identity of all other processes in the system. When a new process joins the group of processes participating in the mutual-exclusion algorithm, the following actions need to be taken:

   a. The process must receive the names of all the other processes in the group.

   b. The name of the new process must be distributed to all the other processes in the group.

   This task is not as trivial as it may seem, since some *request* and *reply* messages may be circulating in the system when the new process joins the group. The interested reader is referred to the Bibliographic Notes for more details.

2. If one of the processes fails, then the entire scheme collapses. We can resolve this difficulty by continuously monitoring the state of all the processes in the system. If one process fails, then all other processes are notified, so that they will no longer send *request* messages to the failed process. When a process recovers, it must initiate the procedure that allows it to rejoin the group.

3. Processes that have not entered their critical section must pause frequently to assure other processes that they intend to enter the critical section. This protocol is therefore suited for small, stable sets of cooperating processes.

13.2.3 Token-Passing Approach

Another method of providing mutual exclusion is to circulate a token among the processes in the system. A *token* is a special type of message that is passed around the system. Possession of the token entitles the holder to enter the critical section. Since there is only a single token in the system, only one process can be in its critical section at a time.

We assume that the processes in the system are *logically* organized in a ring structure. The physical communication network need not be a ring. As long as the processes are connected to each other, it is possible to implement a logical ring. To implement mutual exclusion, we pass the token around the ring. When a process receives the token, it may enter its critical section, keeping the token. After the process exits its critical section, the token is passed around again. If the process receiving the token does not want to enter its critical section, it passes the token to its neighbor. This scheme is similar to algorithm 1 in Chapter 5, but a token is substituted for a shared variable.

Since there is only a single token, only one process can be in its critical section at a time. In addition, if the ring is unidirectional, freedom from starvation is ensured. The number of messages required to implement mutual exclusion may vary from one message per entry, in the case of high contention (that is, every process wants to enter its critical section), to an infinite number of messages, in the case of low contention (that is, no process wants to enter its critical section).

Two types of failure must be considered. First, if the token is lost, an election must be called to generate a new token. Second, if a process fails, a new logical ring must be established. There are a number of different algorithms for election and for reconstructing a logical ring. In Section 13.7, we present an election algorithm. We leave it to you to develop an algorithm for reconstructing the ring, in Exercise 13.3.

13.3 Deadlock Prevention

The deadlock-prevention and deadlock-avoidance algorithms presented in Chapter 6 can also be used in a distributed system, provided that appropriate modifications are made. For example, we can use the resource-ordering deadlock-prevention technique by simply defining a *global* ordering among the system events. That is, all resources in the entire system are assigned unique numbers, and a process may request a resource (at any processor) with unique number i only if it is not holding a resource with a unique number less than or equal to i. Similarly, we can use the banker's algorithm in a distributed system by designating one of the processes in the system (the *banker*) as the process that maintains the information necessary to carry out the banker's algorithm. Every resource request must be channeled through the banker.

These two schemes can be used in dealing with the deadlock problem in a distributed environment. The first scheme is simple to implement and requires very little overhead. The second scheme can also be implemented easily, but it may require too much overhead. The banker may become a bottleneck, since the number of messages to and from the banker may be large. Thus, the banker's scheme does not seem to be of practical use in a distributed system.

In this section, we present a new deadlock-prevention scheme that is based on a time-stamp-ordering approach with resource preemption. For simplicity, we consider only the case of a single instance of each resource type.

To control the preemption, we assign a unique priority number to each process. These numbers are used to decide whether a process P_i should wait for a process P_j. For example, we can let P_i wait for P_j if P_i has a higher priority than P_j; otherwise P_i is rolled back. This scheme prevents deadlocks because, for every edge $P_i \rightarrow P_j$ in the wait-for graph, P_i has a higher priority than P_j. Thus, a cycle cannot exist.

One difficulty with this scheme is the possibility of starvation. Some processes with very low priority may always be rolled back. This difficulty can be avoided through the use of time-stamps. Each process in the system is assigned a unique time-stamp when it is created. Two complementary deadlock-prevention schemes using time-stamps have been proposed:

- **The wait-die scheme.**   This approach is based on a nonpreemptive technique. When process P_i requests a resource currently held by P_j, P_i is allowed to wait only if it has a smaller time-stamp than does P_j (that is, P_i is older than P_j). Otherwise, P_i is rolled back (dies). For example, suppose that processes P_1, P_2, and P_3 have time-stamps 5,

10, and 15, respectively. If P_1 requests a resource held by P_2, P_1 will wait. If P_3 requests a resource held by P_2, P_3 will be rolled back.

- **The wound-wait scheme.** This approach is based on a preemptive technique and is a counterpart to the wait-die system. When process P_i requests a resource currently held by P_j, P_i is allowed to wait only if it has a larger time-stamp than does P_j (that is, P_i is younger than P_j). Otherwise, P_j is rolled back (P_j is *wounded* by P_i). Returning to our previous example, with processes P_1, P_2, and P_3, if P_1 requests a resource held by P_2, then the resource will be preempted from P_2 and P_2 will be rolled back. If P_3 requests a resource held by P_2, then P_3 will wait.

Both schemes can avoid starvation, provided that, when a process is rolled back, it is *not* assigned a new time-stamp. Since time-stamps always increase, a process that is rolled back will eventually have the smallest time-stamp. Thus, it will not be rolled back again. There are, however, significant differences in the way the two schemes operate.

- In the wait-die scheme, an older process must wait for a younger one to release its resource. Thus, the older the process gets, the more it tends to wait. By contrast, in the wound-wait scheme, an older process never waits for a younger process.

- In the wait-die scheme, if a process P_i dies and is rolled back because it requested a resource held by process P_j, then P_i may reissue the same sequence of requests when it is restarted. If the resource is still held by P_j, then P_i will die again. Thus, P_i may die several times before acquiring the needed resource. Contrast this series of events with what happens in the wound-wait scheme. Process P_i is wounded and rolled back because P_j requested a resource it holds. When P_i is restarted and requests the resource now being held by P_j, P_i waits. Thus, there are fewer rollbacks in the wound-wait scheme.

The major problem with these two schemes is that unnecessary rollbacks may occur.

13.4 Deadlock Detection

The deadlock-prevention algorithm may preempt resources even if no deadlock has occurred. To prevent unnecessary preemptions, we can use a deadlock-detection algorithm. We construct a wait-for graph describing the resource-allocation state. Since we are assuming only a single resource of each type, a cycle in the wait-for graph represents a deadlock.

The main problem in a distributed system is deciding how to maintain the wait-for graph. We elaborate on this problem by describing several common techniques to deal with this issue. These schemes require that each site keep a local wait-for graph. The nodes of the graph correspond to all the processes (local as well as nonlocal) that are currently either holding or requesting any of the resources local to that site. For example, in Figure 13.2 we have a system consisting of two sites, each maintaining its local wait-for graph. Note that processes P_2 and P_3 appear in both graphs, indicating that the processes have requested resources at both sites.

These local wait-for graphs are constructed in the usual manner for local processes and resources. When a process P_i in site A needs a resource held by process P_j in site B, a request message is sent by P_i to site B. The edge $P_i \rightarrow P_j$ is then inserted in the local wait-for graph of site B.

Clearly, if any local wait-for graph has a cycle, deadlock has occurred. On the other hand, the fact that there are no cycles in any of the local wait-for graphs does not mean that there are no deadlocks. To illustrate this problem, we consider the system depicted in Figure 13.2. Each wait-for graph is acyclic; nevertheless, a deadlock exists in the system. To prove that a deadlock has not occurred, we must show that the union of all local graphs is acyclic. The graph (shown in Figure 13.3) obtained by taking the union of the two wait-for graphs of Figure 13.2 does indeed contain a cycle, implying that the system is in a deadlock state.

There are a number of different methods for organizing the wait-for graph in a distributed system. We shall describe several common schemes.

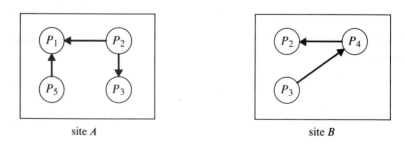

site A site B

Figure 13.2   Local wait-for graphs.

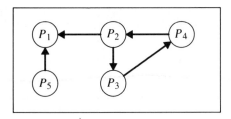

Figure 13.3   Global wait-for graph for Figure 13.2.

13.4.1 Centralized Approach

In the centralized approach, a global wait-for graph is constructed as the union of all the local wait-for graphs. It is maintained in a *single* process: The *deadlock-detection coordinator*. Since there is communication delay in the system, we must distinguish between two types of wait-for graphs. The *real* graph describes the real but unknown state of the system at any instance in time, as would be seen by an omniscient observer. The *constructed* graph is an approximation generated by the coordinator during the execution of its algorithm. Obviously, the constructed graph must be generated such that, whenever the detection algorithm is invoked, the reported results are correct in a sense that, if a deadlock exists, it is reported properly, and if a deadlock is reported, then the system is indeed in a deadlock state. As we shall show, it is not easy to construct such correct algorithms.

There are three different options (points is time) when the wait-for graph may be constructed:

1. Whenever a new edge is inserted or removed in one of the local wait-for graphs

2. Periodically, when a number of changes have occurred in a wait-for graph

3. Whenever the coordinator needs to invoke the cycle-detection algorithm

Let us consider option 1. Whenever an edge is either inserted or removed in a local graph, the local site must also send a message to the coordinator to notify the latter of this modification. On receiving such a message, the coordinator updates its global graph. Alternatively, a site can send a number of such changes in a single message periodically. Returning to our previous example, the coordinator process will maintain the wait-for graph as depicted in Figure 13.3. When site *B* inserts the edge $P_3 \rightarrow P_4$ in its local wait-for graph, it also sends a message to the coordinator. Similarly, when site A deletes the edge $P_5 \rightarrow P_1$, because P_1 has released a resource that was requested by P_5, an appropriate message is sent to the coordinator.

When the deadlock-detection algorithm is invoked, the coordinator searches its global graph. If a cycle is found, a victim is selected to be rolled back. The coordinator must notify all the sites that a particular process has been selected as victim. The sites, in turn, roll back the victim process.

Note that, in this scheme (option 1), unnecessary rollbacks may occur, as a result of two situations:

- *False cycles* may exist in the global wait-for graph. To illustrate this point, we consider a snapshot of the system as depicted in Figure 13.4. Suppose that P_2 releases the resource it is holding in site A, resulting in the deletion of the edge $P_1 \rightarrow P_2$ in A. Process P_2 then requests a resource held by P_3 at site B, resulting in the addition of the edge $P_2 \rightarrow P_3$ in B. If the *insert* $P_2 \rightarrow P_3$ message from B arrives before the *delete* $P_1 \rightarrow P_2$ message from A, the coordinator may discover the false cycle $P_1 \rightarrow P_2 \rightarrow P_3 \rightarrow P_1$ after the *insert* (but before the *delete*). Deadlock recovery may be initiated, although no deadlock has occurred.

- Unnecessary rollbacks may also result when a *deadlock* has indeed occurred and a victim has been picked, but at the same time one of the processes was aborted for reasons unrelated to the deadlock (such as the process exceeding its allocated time). For example, suppose that site A in Figure 13.2 decides to abort P_2. At the same time, the coordinator has discovered a cycle and picked P_3 as a victim. Both P_2 and P_3 are now rolled back, although only P_2 needed to be rolled back.

Note that the same problems are inherited in solutions employing the other two options. (that is, options 2 and 3).

Let us now present a centralized deadlock-detection algorithm, using option 3, which detects all deadlocks that actually occur, and does not detect false deadlocks. To avoid the report of false deadlocks, we require that requests from different sites be appended with unique identifiers (time-stamps). When process P_i, at site A, requests a resource from P_j, at site B, a request message with time-stamp TS is sent. The edge $P_i \rightarrow P_j$ with the label TS is inserted in the local wait-for of A. This edge is inserted in the local wait-for graph of B only if B has received the request message and cannot immediately grant the requested

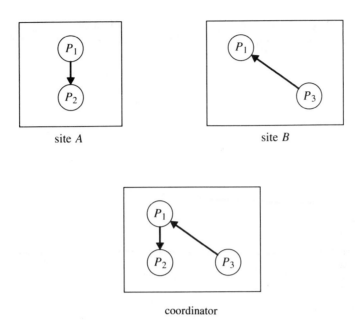

site *A*   site *B*

coordinator

Figure 13.4 Local and global wait-for graphs.

resource. A request from P_i to P_j in the same site is handled in the usual manner; no time-stamps are associated with the edge $P_i \rightarrow P_j$. The detection algorithm is then as follows:

1. The controller sends an initiating message to each site in the system.

2. On receiving this message, a site sends its local wait-for graph to the coordinator. Note that each of these wait-for graphs contains all the local information the site has about the state of the real graph. The graph reflects an instantaneous state of the site, but it is not synchronized with respect to any other site.

3. When the controller has received a reply from each site, it constructs a graph as follows:

   a. The constructed graph contains a vertex for every process in the system.

   b. The graph has an edge $P_i \rightarrow P_j$ if and only if (1) there is an edge $P_i \rightarrow P_j$ in one of the wait-for graphs, or (2) an edge $P_i \rightarrow P_j$ with some label *TS* appears in more than one wait-for graph.

We assert that, if there is a cycle in the constructed graph, then the system is in a deadlock state. If there is no cycle in the constructed graph, then the system was not in a deadlock state when the detection algorithm was invoked as result of the initiating messages sent by the coordinator (in step 1).

13.4.2 Hierarchical Approach

The centralized deadlock-detection algorithm requires all information to reside in one process. An alternative is to distribute the information among the various processes. The *hierarchical* deadlock-detection algorithm is a distributed algorithm.

As in the case of the centralized approach, each site maintains its own local graph. In contrast to the centralized scheme, however, the global wait-for graph is distributed over a number of different *controllers*. These controllers are organized in a tree, where each leaf contains the local wait-for graph of a single site. Each nonleaf controller maintains a wait-for graph that contains relevant information from the graphs of the controllers in the subtree below it.

In particular, let A, B, and C be controllers such that C is the lowest common ancestor of A and B (C is unique, since we are dealing with a tree). Suppose that node P_i appears in the local wait-for graph of A and B. Then P_i must also appear in the local wait-for graph of

1. Controller C

2. Every controller in the path from C to A

3. Every controller in the path from C to B

In addition, if P_i and P_j appear in the wait-for graph of controller D and there exists a path from P_i to P_j in the wait-for graph of one of the children of D, then an edge $P_i \rightarrow P_j$ must be in the wait-for graph of D.

If a cycle exists in any of the wait-for graphs, then the system is deadlocked, and appropriate recovery steps must be taken.

To illustrate this algorithm, we consider the system of Figure 13.2. A tree for this system is depicted in Figure 13.5. Since P_2 and P_3 appear in A and B, they also appear in C. Since there exists a path from P_2 to P_3 in A, the edge $P_2 \rightarrow P_3$ is included in C. Similarly, since there exists a path from P_3 to P_2 in B, the edge $P_3 \rightarrow P_2$ is included in C. Note that the wait-for graph in C contains a cycle, implying the presence of a deadlock.

We have not presented an algorithm for constructing and maintaining this hierarchy of controllers; that is left for you to do in Exercise 13.5.

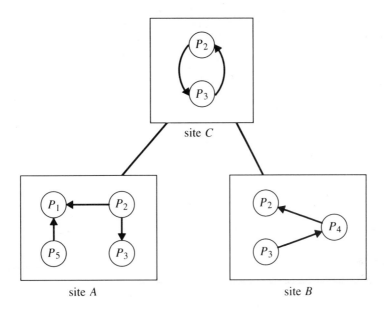

Figure 13.5   Hierarchical wait-for graph.

13.4.3 Fully Distributed Approach

In the *fully distributed* deadlock-detection algorithm, all controllers share equally the responsibility for detecting deadlock. In this scheme, every site constructs a wait-for graph that represents a part of the total graph, depending on the dynamic behavior of the system. The idea is that, if a deadlock exists, a cycle will appear in (at least) one of the partial graphs. We present one such algorithm, which involves construction of partial graphs in every site.

Each site maintains its own local wait-for graph. A local wait-for graph differs from the one described in Section 13.4.2 in that we add one additional node P_{ex} to the graph. An arc $P_i \rightarrow P_{ex}$ exists in the graph if P_i is waiting for a data item in another site being held by *any* process. Similarly, an arc $P_{ex} \rightarrow P_j$ exists in the graph if there exists a process at another site that is waiting to acquire a resource currently being held by P_j in this local site.

To illustrate this situation, we consider the two local wait-for graphs of Figure 13.2. The addition of the node P_{ex} in both graphs results in the local wait-for graphs shown in Figure 13.6.

If a local wait-for graph contains a cycle that does not involve node P_{ex}, then the system is in a deadlock state. If, however, there exists a cycle involving P_{ex}, then this implies that there is a *possibility* of a

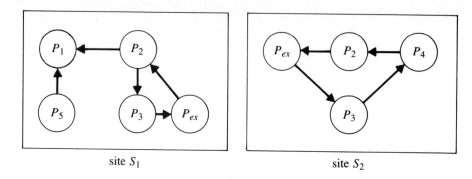

site S_1 site S_2

Figure 13.6   Local wait-for graphs.

deadlock.   To ascertain whether a deadlock does exist, a distributed deadlock-detection algorithm must be invoked.

Suppose that, at site S_i, the local wait-for graph contains a cycle involving node P_{ex}. This cycle must be of the form

$$P_{ex} \to P_{k_1} \to P_{k_2} \to \cdots \to P_{k_n} \to P_{ex},$$

which indicates that transaction P_{k_n} in S_i is waiting to acquire a data item in some other site — say, S_j. On discovering this cycle, site S_i sends to site S_j a deadlock-detection message containing information about that cycle.

When site S_j receives this deadlock-detection message, it updates its local wait-for graph with the new information. Then, it searches the newly constructed wait-for graph for a cycle not involving P_{ex}. If one exists, a deadlock is found and an appropriate recovery scheme is invoked. If a cycle involving P_{ex} is discovered, then S_j transmits a deadlock-detection message to the appropriate site — say, S_k. Site S_k, in return, repeats the procedure. Thus, after a finite number of rounds, either a deadlock is discovered, or the deadlock-detection computation halts.

To illustrate this procedure, we consider the local wait-for graphs of Figure 13.6. Suppose that site S_1 discovers the cycle

$$P_{ex} \to P_2 \to P_3 \to P_{ex}.$$

Since P_3 is waiting to acquire a data item in site S_2, a deadlock-detection message describing that cycle is transmitted from site S_1 to site S_2. When site S_2 receives this message, it updates its local wait-for graph, obtaining the wait-for graph of Figure 13.7. This graph contains the cycle

$$P_2 \rightarrow P_3 \rightarrow P_4 \rightarrow P_2,$$

which does not include node P_{ex}. Therefore, the system is in a deadlock state and an appropriate recovery scheme must be invoked.

Note that the outcome would be the same if site S_2 discovered the cycle first in its local wait-for graph and sent the deadlock-detection message to site S_1. In the worst case, both sites discover the cycle at about the same time, and two deadlock-detection messages will be sent: one by S_1 to S_2 and another by S_2 to S_1. This situation results in unnecessary message transfer and overhead in updating the two local wait-for graphs and searching for cycles in both graphs.

To reduce message traffic, we assign to each transaction P_i a unique identifier, which we denote by $ID(P_i)$. When site S_k discovers that its local wait-for graph contains a cycle involving node P_{ex} of the form

$$P_{ex} \rightarrow P_{K_1} \rightarrow P_{K_2} \rightarrow \cdots \rightarrow P_{K_n} \rightarrow P_{ex},$$

it sends a deadlock-detection message to another site only if

$$ID(P_{K_n}) < ID(P_{K_1}).$$

Otherwise, site S_k continues its normal execution, leaving the burden of initiating the deadlock-detection algorithm to some other site.

To illustrate this scheme, we consider again the wait-for graphs maintained at sites S_1 and S_2 of Figure 13.6. Suppose that

$$ID(P_1) < ID(P_2) < ID(P_3) < ID(P_4).$$

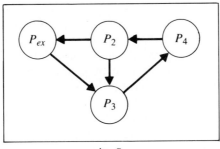

site S_2

Figure 13.7 Local wait-for graph.

Let both sites discover these local cycles at about the same time. The cycle in site S_1 is of the form

$$P_{ex} \rightarrow P_2 \rightarrow P_3 \rightarrow P_{ex}.$$

Since $ID(P_3) > ID(P_2)$, site S_1 does not send a deadlock-detection message to site S_2.

The cycle in site S_2 is of the form

$$P_{ex} \rightarrow P_3 \rightarrow P_4 \rightarrow P_2 \rightarrow P_{ex}.$$

Since $ID(P_2) < ID(P_3)$, site S_2 does send a deadlock-detection message to site S_1, which, on receiving the message, updates its local wait-for graph. Site S_1 then searches for a cycle in the graph and discovers that the system is in a deadlock state.

13.5 Robustness

A distributed system may suffer from various types of hardware failure. The failure of a link, the failure of a site, and the loss of a message are the most common failures. To ensure that the system is robust, we must *detect* any of these failures, *reconfigure* the system so that computation may continue, and *recover* when a site or a link is repaired.

13.5.1 Failure Detection

In an environment with no shared memory, it is generally not possible to differentiate among link failure, site failure, and message loss. We can usually detect that one of these failures has occurred, but we may not be able to identify what kind of failure it is. Once a failure has been detected, appropriate action must be taken, depending on the particular application.

To detect link and site failure, we use a *handshaking* procedure. Suppose that sites A and B have a direct physical link between them. At fixed intervals, both sites send each other an *I-am-up* message. If site A does not receive this message within a predetermined time period, it can assume that site B has failed, that the link between A and B has failed, or that the message from B has been lost. At this point, site A has two choices. It can wait for another time period to receive an *I-am-up* message from B, or it can send an *Are-you-up?* message to B.

If site A does not receive an *I-am-up* message or a reply to its inquiry, the procedure can be repeated. The only conclusion that site A can draw safely is that some type of failure has occurred.

Site *A* can try to differentiate between link failure and site failure by sending an *Are-you-up?* message to *B* by another route (if one exists). If and when *B* receives this message, it immediately replies positively. This positive reply tells *A* that *B* is up, and that the failure is in the direct link between them. Since it is not known in advance how long it will take the message to travel from *A* to *B* and back, a *time-out* scheme must be used. At the time *A* sends the *Are-you-up?* message, it specifies a time interval during which it is willing to wait for the reply from *B*. If *A* receives the reply message within that time interval, then it can safely conclude that *B* is up. If, however, it does not receive the reply message within the time interval (that is, a time-out occurs), then *A* may conclude only that one or more of the following situations has occurred:

1. Site *B* is down.

2. The direct link (if one exists) from *A* to *B* is down.

3. The alternative path from *A* to *B* is down.

4. The message has been lost.

Site *A* cannot, however, decide which of these has indeed occurred.

13.5.2 Reconfiguration

Suppose that site *A* has discovered, through the mechanism described in the previous section, that a failure has occurred. It must then initiate a procedure that will allow the system to reconfigure and to continue its normal mode of operation.

- If a direct link from *A* to *B* has failed, this information must be broadcast to every site in the system, so that the various routing tables can be updated accordingly.

- If it is believed that a site has failed (because it can no longer be reached), then every site in the system must be so notified, so that they will no longer attempt to use the services of the failed site. The failure of a site that serves as a central coordinator for some activity (such as deadlock detection) requires the election of a new coordinator. Similarly, if the failed site is part of a logical ring, then a new logical ring must be constructed. Note that, if the site has not failed (that is, if it is up but cannot be reached), then we may have the undesirable situation where two sites serve as the coordinator. When the network is partitioned, the two coordinators (each for its own partition) may initiate conflicting actions. For example, if the coordinators are responsible for implementing mutual exclusion, we may have a situation where two processes may be executing simultaneously in their critical sections.

13.5.3 Recovery from Failure

When a failed link or site is repaired, it must be integrated into the system gracefully and smoothly.

- Suppose that a link between A and B has failed. When it is repaired, both A and B must be notified. We can accomplish this notification by continuously repeating the handshaking procedure, described in Section 13.5.1.

- Suppose that site B has failed. When it recovers, it must notify all other sites that it is up again. Site B then may have to receive from the other sites various information to update its local tables; for example, it may need routing table information, a list of sites that are down, or undelivered messages and mail. Note that, if the site has not failed, but simply could not be reached, then this information is still required.

13.6 Reaching Agreement

For a system to be reliable we need a mechanism that allows a set of processes to agree on a common "value." There are several reasons why such an agreement may not take place. First, the communication medium may be faulty, resulting in lost or garbled messages. Second, the processes themselves may be faulty, resulting in unpredictable process behavior. The best we can hope for, in this case, is that processes fail in a clean way, stopping their execution without deviating from their normal execution pattern. In the worst case, processes may send garbled or incorrect messages to other processes, or even collaborate with other failed processes in an attempt to destroy the integrity of the system.

This problem has been expressed as the *Byzantine generals problem*. Several divisions of the Byzantine army, each commanded by its own general, surround an enemy camp. The Byzantine generals must reach a common agreement on whether or not to attack the enemy at dawn. It is crucial that all generals agree, since an attack by only some of the divisions would result in defeat. The various divisions are geographically dispersed and the generals can communicate with each other only via messengers who run from camp to camp. There are at least two major reasons why the generals may not be able to reach an agreement:

- Messengers may get caught by the enemy and thus may be unable to deliver their messages. This situation corresponds to unreliable communication in a computer system, and is discussed further in Section 13.6.1.

- Generals may be *traitors*, trying to prevent the *loyal* generals from reaching an agreement. This situation corresponds to faulty processes in a computer system, and is discussed further in Section 13.6.2.

13.6.1 Unreliable Communications

Let us assume that, if processes fail, they do so in a clean way, and that the communication medium is unreliable. Suppose that process P_i at site A, which has sent a message to process P_j at site B, needs to know whether P_j has received the message in order to decide how to proceed with its computation. For example, P_i may decide to compute a function S if P_j has received its message, or to compute a function F if P_j has not received the message (because of some hardware failure).

To detect failures, we can use a *time-out* scheme similar to the one described in Section 13.5.1. When P_i sends out a message, it also specifies a time interval during which it is willing to wait for an acknowledgment message from P_j. When P_j receives the message, it immediately sends an acknowledgment to P_i. If P_i receives the acknowledgment message within the specified time interval, it can safely conclude that P_j has received its message. If, however, a time-out occurs, then P_i needs to retransmit its message and to wait for an acknowledgment. This procedure continues until P_i either gets the acknowledgment message back, or is notified by the system that site B is down. In the first case, it will compute S', in the latter case, it will compute F. Note that, if these are the only two viable alternatives, P_i must wait until it has been notified that one of the situations has occurred.

Suppose now that P_j also needs to know that P_i has received its acknowledgment message, in order to decide on how to proceed with its computation. For example, P_j may want to compute S only if it is assured that P_i got its acknowledgment. In other words, P_i and P_j will compute S if and only if both have agreed on it. It turns out that, in the presence of failure, it is not possible to accomplish this task. More precisely, it is not possible in a distributed environment for processes P_i and P_j to agree completely on their respective states.

Let us prove this claim. Suppose that there exists a minimal sequence of message transfers such that, after the messages have been delivered, both processes agree to compute S. Let m' be the last message sent by P_i to P_j. Since P_i does not know whether its message will arrive at P_j (since the message may be lost due to a failure), P_i will execute S regardless of the outcome of the message delivery. Thus, m' could be removed from the sequence without affecting the decision procedure. Hence, the original sequence was not minimal, contradicting our assumption and showing that there is no sequence. The processes can never be sure that both will compute S.

13.6.2 Faulty Processes

Let us assume that the communication medium is reliable but that processes can fail in unpredicatable ways. Consider a system of n processes, of which no more that m are faulty. Suppose that each process P_i has some private value of V_i. We wish to devise an algorithm that allows each nonfaulty process P_i to construct a vector $X_i = (A_{i,1}, A_{i,2}, ..., A_{i,n})$ such that

1. If P_j is a nonfaulty process, then $A_{i,j} = V_j$.
2. If P_i and P_j are both nonfaulty processes, then $X_i = X_j$.

There are many solutions to this problem, which is the Byzantine generals problem; all share the following properties.

1. A correct algorithm can be devised only if $n \geq 3 \times m + 1$.
2. The worst-case delay for reaching agreement is proportionate to $m + 1$ message-passing delays.
3. The number of messages required for reaching agreement is very large. No single process is trustworthy, so all processes must collect all information and make their own decisions.

Rather than presenting a general solution, which would be quite complicated, we present an algorithm for the simple case where $m = 1$ and $n = 4$. The algorithm requires two rounds of information exchange:

1. Each process sends its private value to the other three processes.
2. Each process sends the information it has obtained in the first round to all other processes.

A faulty process obviously may refuse to send messages. In this case, a nonfaulty process can choose an arbitrary value and pretend that that value was sent by that process.

Once these two rounds are completed, a nonfaulty process P_i can construct its vector $X_i = (A_{i,1}, A_{i,2}, A_{i,3}, A_{i,4})$ as follows:

1. $A_{i,i} = V_i$.

2. For $j \neq i$, if at least two of the three values reported for process P_j (in the two rounds of exchange) agree, then the majority value is used to set the value of $A_{i,j}$. Otherwise, a default value, say Nil, is used to set the value of $A_{i,j}$.

13.7 Election Algorithms

As we pointed out in Section 13.4.1, many distributed algorithms employ a coordinator process that performs functions needed by the other processes in the system. These functions include enforcing mutual exclusion, maintaining a global wait-for graph for deadlock detection, replacing a lost token, or controlling an input or output device in the system. If the coordinator process fails due to the failure of the site at which it resides, the system can continue execution only by restarting a new copy of the coordinator on some other site. The algorithms that determine where a new copy of the coordinator should be restarted are called *election* algorithms.

Election algorithms assume that a unique priority number is associated with each active process in the system. For ease of notation, we assume that the priority number of process P_i is i. To simplify our discussion, we assume a one-to-one correspondence between processes and sites, and thus refer to both as processes. The coordinator is always the process with the largest priority number. Hence, when a coordinator fails, the algorithm must elect that active process with the largest priority number. This number must be sent to each active process in the system. In addition, the algorithm must provide a mechanism for a recovered process to identify the current coordinator.

In this section, we present two interesting examples of election algorithms for two different configurations of distributed systems. The first algorithm is applicable to systems where every process can send a message to every other process in the system. The second algorithm is applicable to systems organized as a ring (logically or physically). Both algorithms require n^2 messages for an election, where n is the number of processes in the system. We assume that a process that has failed knows on recovery that it indeed has failed and thus takes appropriate actions (as described later) to rejoin the set of active processes.

13.7.1 The Bully Algorithm

Suppose that process P_i sends a request that is not answered by the coordinator within a time interval T. In this situation, it is assumed that the coordinator has failed, and P_i tries to elect itself as the new coordinator. This task is completed through the following algorithm.

Process P_i sends an election message to every process with a higher priority number. Process P_i then waits for a time interval T for an answer from any one of these processes.

If no response is received within time T, it is assumed that all processes with numbers greater than i have failed, and P_i elects itself the new coordinator. Process P_i restarts a new copy of the coordinator and sends a message to inform all active processes with priority numbers less than i that P_i is the new coordinator.

However, if an answer is received, P_i begins a time interval T', waiting to receive a message informing it that a process with a higher priority number has been elected. (Some other process is electing itself coordinator, and should report the results within time T'.) If no message is sent within T', then the process with a higher number is assumed to have failed, and process P_i should restart the algorithm.

If P_i is not the coordinator, then, at any time during execution, P_i may receive one of the following two messages from process P_j:

1. P_j is the new coordinator ($j > i$). Process P_i, in turn, records this information.

2. P_j started an election ($j < i$). Process P_i sends a response to P_j and begins its own election algorithm, provided that P_i has not already initiated such an election.

The process that completes its algorithm has the highest number and is elected as the coordinator. It has sent its number to all active processes with smaller numbers. After a failed process recovers, it immediately begins execution of the same algorithm. If there are no active processes with higher numbers, the recovered process forces all processes with lower numbers to let it become the coordinator process, even if there is a currently active coordinator with a lower number. For this reason, the algorithm is termed the *bully* algorithm.

Let us demonstrate the operation of the algorithm with a simple example of a system consisting of processes P_1 through P_4. The operations are as follows:

1. All processes are active; P_4 is the coordinator process.

2. P_1 and P_4 fail. P_2 determines P_4 has failed by sending a request that is not answered within time T. P_2 then begins its election algorithm by sending a request to P_3.

3. P_3 receives the request, responds to P_2, and begins its own algorithm by sending an election request to P_4.

4. P_2 receives P_3's response, and begins waiting for an interval T'.

5. P_4 does not respond within an interval T, so P_3 elects itself the new coordinator, and sends the number 3 to P_2 and P_1 (which P_1 does not receive, since it has failed).

6. Later, when P_1 recovers, it sends an election request to P_2, P_3, and P_4.

7. P_2 and P_3 respond to P_1 and begin their own election algorithms. P_3 will again be elected, using the same events as before.

8. Finally, P_4 recovers and notifies P_1, P_2, and P_3 that it is the current coordinator. (P_4 sends no election requests, since it is the process with the highest number in the system.)

13.7.2 A Ring Algorithm

The *ring* algorithm assumes that the links are unidirectional, and that processes send their messages to their right neighbors. The main data structure used by the algorithm is the *active list*, a list that contains the priority numbers of all active processes in the system when the algorithm ends; each process maintains its own active list. The algorithm works as follows:

1. If process P_i detects a coordinator failure, it creates a new active list that is initially empty. It then sends a message *elect(i)* to its right neighbor, and adds the number i to its active list.

2. If P_i receives a message *elect(j)* from the process on the left, it must respond in one of three ways:

   a. If this is the first *elect* message it has seen or sent, P_i creates a new active list with the numbers i and j. It then sends the message *elect(i)*, followed by the message *elect(j)*.

   b. If $i \neq j$ (that is, the message received does not contain P_i's number), then P_i adds j to its active list and forwards the message to its right neighbor.

c. If $i = j$ (that is, P_i receives the message *elect(i)*), then the active list for P_i now contains the numbers of all the active processes in the system. Process P_i can now determine the largest number in the active list to identify the new coordinator process.

This algorithm does not specify how a recovering process determines the number of the current coordinator process. One solution would be to require a recovering process to send an inquiry message. This message is forwarded around the ring to the current coordinator, which in turn sends a reply containing its number.

13.8 Summary

In a distributed system with no common memory and no common clock, it is sometimes impossible to determine the exact order in which two events occur. The happened-before relation is only a partial ordering of the events in distributed systems. Time-stamps can be used to provide a consistent event ordering in a distributed system.

A centralized scheme can be used for implementing mutual exclusion and deadlock detection. Alternative distributed algorithms include the token-passing algorithm for synchronization of a ring-structured network, and a hierarchical deadlock-detection algorithm.

A distributed system may suffer from various types of hardware failure. For the system to be fault tolerant, it must detect failures and reconfigure the system. When the failure is repaired, the system must be reconfigured again. Two algorithms, the bully algorithm and a ring algorithm, can be used to elect a new coordinator in case of failures.

Exercises

13.1 Is it always crucial to know that the message you have sent has arrived at its destination safely? If your answer is "yes," explain why. If your answer is "no," give appropriate examples.

13.2 Your company is building a computer network and you are asked to write an algorithm for achieving distributed mutual exclusion. Which scheme will you use? Explain your choice.

13.3 Present an algorithm for reconstructing a logical ring in case a process in the ring fails.

13.4 Your company is building a computer network and you are asked to develop a scheme for dealing with the deadlock problem.

a. Would you use a deadlock-detection scheme, or a deadlock-prevention scheme?

b. If you must use a deadlock-prevention scheme, which one will you use? Explain your choice.

c. If you must use a deadlock-detection scheme, which one would you use? Explain your choice.

13.5 Write an algorithm for maintaining the hierarchical deadlock-detection scheme presented in Section 13.4.2.

13.6 Why is deadlock detection much more expensive in a distributed environment than it is in a centralized environment?

13.7 Derive a more efficient election algorithm for bidirectional rings. How many messages are needed for n processes?

Bibliographic Notes

The distributed algorithm for extending the happened-before relation to a consistent total ordering of all the events in the system (Section 13.1) was developed by Lamport [1978a].

The first general algorithm for implementing mutual exclusion in a distributed environment also was developed by Lamport [1978a]. Lamport's scheme requires $3 \times (n - 1)$ messages per critical-section entry. Subsequently, Ricart and Agrawala [1981] proposed a distributed algorithm that requires only $2 \times (n - 1)$ messages. Their algorithm was presented in Section 13.2. The token-passing algorithm for ring-structured systems presented in Section 13.2.3 was developed by Le Lann [1977]. Discussions concerning mutual exclusion in computer networks are presented by Carvalho and Roucairol [1983].

The issue of distributed synchronization was discussed by Reed and Kanodia [1979] (shared-memory environment), Lamport [1978a, 1978b], and Schneider [1982] (totally disjoint processes). A distributed solution to the dining philosophers problem is presented by Chang [1980].

The time-stamp distributed deadlock-detection algorithm was published by Rosenkrantz, et al. [1978]. The centralized deadlock-detection algorithm that does not detect false deadlocks was developed by Stuart, et al. [1984]. The hierarchical scheme was presented by Menasce and Muntz [1979]. A deadlock-detection scheme in which the wait-for graph is distributed over the network was proposed by Menasce and Muntz [1979]. This algorithm was shown to be incorrect by Gligor and Shattuck [1980], who also proposed a modification to the algorithm. Obermarck [1982] has further modified this basic algorithm to get better performance. His algorithm was presented in Section 13.4.3. An extension of the banker's algorithm for resource allocation in a distributed operating system is presented by Madduri and Finkel [1984].

The Byzantine generals problem is discussed by Lamport, et al. [1982] and Pease, et al. [1980]. The bully algorithm was presented by Garcia-Molina [1982]. The election algorithm for a ring-structured system was written by Le Lann [1977].

The problem of deadlock prevention and avoidance in a packet-switched data-transport system has been discussed by Merlin and Schweitzer [1980a, 1980b] and Gelernter [1981]. Toueg and Ullman [1979] and Toueg [1980] discussed deadlock-free packet-switching networks.

CHAPTER
14

Distributed File Systems

A *distributed file system* (DFS) is a distributed implementation of the classical time-sharing model of a file system, where multiple users share files and storage resources (Chapter 10). The purpose of a DFS is to support the same kind of sharing when the files are physically dispersed among the various sites of a distributed system.

In this chapter, we discuss the various ways a distributed file system can be designed and implemented. First, we discuss common concepts on which distributed file systems are based. Then, we illustrate our concepts by examining the UNIX United, NFS, Andrew, Sprite, and Locus distributed file systems. We take this approach to the presentation since distributed systems is an active research area, and the many design tradeoffs we shall illuminate are still being examined. By exploring these example systems, we hope to provide a sense of the considerations involved in designing an operating system, and also to indicate current areas of operating-system research.

14.1 Background

A distributed system is a collection of loosely coupled machines interconnected by a communication network. We use the term *machine* to denote either a mainframe or a workstation. From the point of view of a specific machine in a distributed system, the rest of the machines and their respective resources are *remote*, whereas the machine's own resources are referred to as *local*.

To explain the structure of a DFS, we need to define the terms *service*, *server*, and *client*. A *service* is a software entity running on one or more machines and providing a particular type of function to a priori unknown clients. A *server* is the service software running on a single machine. A *client* is a process that can invoke a service using a set of operations that forms its *client interface*. Sometimes, a lower-level interface is defined for the actual cross-machine interaction. When the need arises, we refer to this interface as the *intermachine interface*.

Using this terminology, we say that a file system provides file services to clients. A client interface for a file service is formed by a set of primitive *file operations*, such as create a file, delete a file, read from a file, and write to a file. The primary hardware component that a file server controls is a set of secondary-storage devices (that is, magnetic disks), on which files are stored, and from which they are retrieved according to the clients requests.

A DFS is a file system whose clients, servers, and storage devices are dispersed among the machines of a distributed system. Accordingly, service activity has to be carried out across the network, and instead of a single centralized data repository there are multiple and independent storage devices. As will become evident, the concrete configuration and implementation of a DFS may vary. There are configurations where servers run on dedicated machines, as well as configurations where a machine can be both a server and a client. A DFS can be implemented as part of a distributed operating system, or alternatively by a software layer whose task is to manage the communication between conventional operating systems and file systems. The distinctive features of a DFS are the multiplicity and autonomy of clients and servers in the system.

Ideally, a DFS should look to its clients like a conventional, centralized file system. The multiplicity and dispersion of its servers and storage devices should be made transparent. That is, the client interface of a DFS should not distinguish between local and remote files. It is up to the DFS to locate the files and to arrange for the transport of the data. A transparent DFS facilitates user mobility by bringing over the user's environment (that is, home directory) to wherever a user logs in.

The most important *performance* measurement of a DFS is the amount of time needed to satisfy various service requests. In conventional systems, this time consists of disk access time and a small amount of CPU processing time. In a DFS, however, a remote access has the additional overhead attributed to the distributed structure. This overhead includes the time needed to deliver the request to a server, as well as the time for getting the response across the network back to the client. For each direction, in addition to the actual transfer of the information, there is the CPU overhead of running the communication protocol software. The performance of a DFS can be viewed as another dimension of the DFS's transparency. That is, the performance of an ideal DFS would be comparable to that a conventional file system.

The fact that a DFS manages a set of dispersed storage devices is the DFS's key distinguishing feature. The overall storage space managed by a DFS is composed of different, and remotely located, smaller storage spaces. Usually, there is correspondence between these constituent storage spaces and sets of files. We use the term *component unit* to denote the smallest set of files that can be stored on a single machine, independently from other units. All files belonging to the same component unit must reside in the same location.

14.2 Naming and Transparency

Naming is a mapping between logical and physical objects. For instance, users deal with logical data objects represented by file names, whereas the system manipulates physical blocks of data, stored on disk tracks. Usually, a user refers to a file by a textual name. The latter is mapped to a lower-level numerical identifier that in turn is mapped to disk blocks. This multilevel mapping provides users with an abstraction of a file that hides the details of how and where on the disk the file is actually stored.

In a *transparent* DFS, a new dimension is added to the abstraction: that of hiding where in the network the file is located. In a conventional file system, the range of the naming mapping is an address within a disk. In a DFS, this range is augmented to include the specific machine on whose disk the file is stored. Going one step further with the concept of treating files as abstractions leads to the possibility of *file replication.* Given a file name, the mapping returns a set of the locations of this file's replicas. In this abstraction, both the existence of multiple copies and their location are hidden.

14.2.1 Naming Structures

There are two related notions regarding name mappings in a DFS that need to be differentiated:

- **Location transparency**. The name of a file does not reveal any hint of the file's physical storage location.

- **Location independence**. The name of a file does not need to be changed when the file's physical storage location changes.

Both definitions are relative to the level of naming discussed previously, since files have different names at different levels (that is, user-level textual names, and system-level numerical identifiers). A location-independent naming scheme is a dynamic mapping, since it can map the same file name to different locations at two different times. Therefore, location independence is a stronger property than is location transparency.

In practice, most of the current DFSs provide a static, location-transparent mapping for user-level names. These systems, however, do not support file *migration*; that is, changing the location of a file automatically is impossible. Hence, the notion of location independence is quite irrelevant for these systems. Files are permanently associated with a specific set of disk blocks. Disks can be moved between machines manually, but file migration implies an automatic, operating-system initiated action. Only Andrew (Section 14.7.3) and some experimental file systems support location independence and file mobility. Andrew supports file mobility mainly for administrative purposes. A protocol provides migration of Andrew's component units to satisfy high-level user requests, without changing either the user-level names, or the low-level names of the corresponding files.

There are a few aspects that can further differentiate location independence and static location transparency:

- Divorcing data from location, as exhibited by location independence, provides better abstraction for files. A file name should denote the file's most significant attributes, which are its contents, not its location. Location-independent files can be viewed as logical data containers that are not attached to a specific storage location. If only static location transparency is supported, the file name still denotes a specific, although hidden, set of physical disk blocks.

- Static location transparency provides users with a convenient way to share data. Users can share remote files by simply naming the files in a location-transparent manner, as though the files were local. Nevertheless, sharing the storage space is cumbersome, since logical names are still statically attached to physical storage devices. Location independence promotes sharing the storage space itself, as well as the data objects. When files can be mobilized, the overall, systemwide storage space looks like a single, virtual resource. A possible benefit of such a view is the ability to balance the utilization of disks across the system.

- Location independence separates the naming hierarchy from the storage-devices hierarchy and from the intercomputer structure. By contrast, if static location transparency is used (although names are transparent), we can easily expose the correspondence between component units and machines. The machines are configured in a pattern similar to the naming structure. This may restrict the architecture of the system unnecessarily and conflict with other considerations. A server in charge of a root directory is an example of a structure that is dictated by the naming hierarchy and contradicts decentralization guidelines.

Once the separation of name and location has been completed, files residing on remote server systems may be accessed by various clients. In fact, these clients may be *diskless* and rely on servers to provide all files, including the operating-system kernel. Special protocols are needed for the boot sequence, however. Consider the problem of getting the kernel to a diskless workstation. Since the diskless workstation has no kernel, it cannot use the DFS code to retrieve the kernel. Instead, a special boot protocol, stored in read-only memory (ROM) on the client, is invoked. It is able to retrieve only one special file (the kernel or boot code) from a fixed destination. Once the kernel is copied over the network and loaded, its DFS code is able to make all the other operating-system files available. The advantages of diskless clients are many, including lower cost (since no disk is needed on each machine) and greater convenience (when an operating-system upgrade occurs, only the server copy needs to be modified, not all the clients as well). The disadvantage is the added complexity of the boot protocols and the performance loss resulting from the use of a network rather than of a local disk.

14.2.2 Naming Schemes

There are three main approaches to naming schemes in a DFS. In the simplest approach, files are named by some combination of their host name and local name, which guarantees a unique systemwide name. In Ibis, for instance, a file is identified uniquely by the name *host:local-name*, where *local-name* is a UNIX-like path. This naming scheme is neither location transparent nor location independent. Nevertheless, the same file operations can be used for both local and remote files. The structure of the DFS is a collection of isolated component units that are entire conventional file systems. In this first approach, component units remained isolated, although means are provided to refer to a remote file. We do not consider this scheme any further in this text.

The second approach, popularized by Sun's Network File System (NFS), provides means to attach remote directories to local directories, thus giving the appearance of a coherent directory tree. Only previously mounted remote directories can be accessed transparently. There is some integration of components to support transparent sharing. This integration, however, is limited and is not uniform, since each machine may attach different remote directories to its tree. The resulting structure is versatile. Usually, it is a forest of UNIX trees with shared subtrees.

Total integration of the component file systems is achieved using the third approach. A single global name structure spans all the files in the system. Ideally, the composed file-system structure should be isomorphic to the structure of a conventional file system. However, in practice, there are many special files (for example, UNIX device files and binary directories) that makes this goal difficult to attain. We shall examine different variations of this approach in our discussions of UNIX United, Locus, Sprite, and Andrew in Section 14.7.

An important criterion for evaluation of the naming structures is their administrative complexity. The most complex and most difficult structure to maintain is the NFS structure. Since any remote directory can be attached anywhere onto the local directory tree, the resulting hierarchy can be very unstructured. The effect of a server becoming unavailable is that some arbitrary set of directories on different machines becomes unavailable. In addition, a separate accreditation mechanism is used to control which machine is allowed to attach which directory to its tree.

14.2.3   Implementation Techniques

Implementation of transparent naming requires a provision for the mapping of a file name to the associated location. Keeping this mapping manageable calls for aggregating sets of files into component units, and providing the mapping on a component unit basis rather than on a single-file basis. This aggregation serves administrative purposes as well. UNIX-like systems use the hierarchical directory tree to provide name-to-location mapping, and to aggregate files recursively into directories.

To enhance the availability of the crucial mapping information, we can use methods such as replication, local caching, or both. As we already noted, location independence means that the mapping changes over time; hence, replicating the mapping renders a simple yet consistent update of this information impossible. A technique to overcome this obstacle is to introduce low-level, *location-independent file identifiers*. Textual file names are mapped to lower-level file identifiers that indicate to which component unit the file belongs, but that are still location independent. These identifiers can be replicated and cached freely without being invalidated by migration of component units. A second level of mapping, which maps component units to locations and needs a simple yet consistent update mechanism, is the inevitable price. Implementing UNIX-like directory trees using these low-level, location-independent identifiers makes the whole hierarchy invariant under component unit migration. The only thing that does change is the component unit-location mapping.

A common way to implement these low-level identifiers is to use structured names. These are bit strings that usually have two parts. The first part identifies the component unit to which the file belongs; the second part identifies the particular file within the unit. Variants with more parts are possible. The invariant of structured names, however, is that individual parts of the name are unique at all times only within the context of the rest of the parts. We can obtain uniqueness at all times either by taking care not to reuse a name that is still used, or by adding sufficiently more bits (this method is used in Andrew), or by using a time-stamp as one of the parts of the name (as done in Apollo Domain). Another way to view this is that we are taking a location-transparent system, such as Ibis, and adding another level of abstraction to produce a location-independent naming scheme.

The use of the techniques of aggregation of files into component units, and the use of lower-level location-independent file identifiers, are exemplified in Andrew and Locus.

14.3 Remote Services

Consider a user who requests access to a remote file. Assuming that the server storing the file was located by the appropriate naming scheme, the actual data transfer to satisfy the user request for the remote access must take place.

One way to achieve this transfer is through the _remote-service_ method. Requests for accesses are delivered to the server. The server machine performs the accesses, and their results are forwarded back to the user. There is a direct correspondence between accesses and traffic to and from the server. Access requests are translated to messages for the servers, and server replies are packed as messages sent back to the users. Every access is handled by the server and results in network traffic. For example, a read results in a request message being sent to the server, and a reply to the user with the requested data.

You should realize that there is a direct analogy between disk-access methods in conventional file systems and the remote-service method in DFSs. The remote-service method is analogous to performing a disk access for each access request.

One of the most common forms of remote service is the _remote procedure call_ (RPC) paradigm, which we briefly discussed in Section 5.7. The RPC was designed as a way to abstract the procedure-call mechanism for use between systems with network connections. It is similar in many respects to the interprocess communication scheme (IPC) described in Section 5.7, and is usually built on top of such a system. Since we are dealing with an environment where the processes are executing on separate systems, we must use a *message-based* communication scheme to provide remote service. In contrast to the IPC facility, the messages exchanged for RPC communication are well structured, and are thus no longer just packets of data. They are addressed to an RPC daemon listening to a *port* on the remote system, and contain the name of a process to run and the parameters to pass to that process. The process is then executed as requested, and any output is sent back to the requester in a separate message.

A *port* is simply a number included at the start of a message packet. Whereas a system normally has one network address, it can have many ports within that address to differentiate the many network services it supports. If a remote process needs a service, it addresses its messages to the proper port. For instance, if a system wished to allow other systems to be able to list the current users on it, it would have a daemon supporting such an RPC attached to a port, say port 3027. Any remote system can obtain the needed information (that is, the list of current users) by sending an RPC message to port 3027 on the server; the data would be received in a reply message.

There are several issues that we should discuss in regard to the operation of the RPC mechanism. One important issue is that of semantics. Since we are dealing with message transfer over unreliable communication links, it is much easier for an operating system to ensure that a message was acted on at least once, than it is to ensure that the message was acted on exactly once. Since normal procedure calls have the latter meaning, most systems attempt to duplicate that functionality. They do so by attaching to each message a time-stamp. The server must keep a history of all the time-stamps of messages it has already processed. Incoming messages that have a time-stamp already in the history are ignored.

Another important issue concerns the communication between server and client. With standard procedure calls, some form of binding takes place during link, load, or execution time (see Chapter 7), such that a procedure call's name is replaced by the address of the procedure call. The RPC scheme requires a similar binding of client and the server port, but how does a client know the port numbers on the server? Neither system has full information about the other. Two approaches are common. First, the binding information may be predecided, in the form of fixed port addresses. At compile time, an RPC call has a fixed port number associated with it. Once a program is compiled, the server cannot change the port number of the requested service. Second, binding can be done dynamically by a rendezvous mechanism.

Typically, an operating system provides a rendezvous (also called a matchmaker) daemon on a fixed RPC port. A client then sends a message to the rendezvous daemon requesting the port address of the RPC it needs to execute. The port number is returned, and the RPC calls may be sent to that port until the process terminates (or the server crashes). This method requires the extra overhead of the initial request, but is more flexible than the first approach. A sample interaction is shown in Figure 14.1.

A distributed file system can be implemented easily as a set of RPC daemons and clients. The messages are addressed to the DFS port on a server on which a file operation is to take place. The message contains the disk operation to be performed. Disk operations might be **read**, **write**, **rename**, **delete**, or **status**, corresponding to the usual file-related system calls. The return message contains any data resulting from that call, which is executed by the DFS daemon on behalf of the client. For instance, a message might contain a request to transfer a whole file to a client, or be limited to simple block requests. In the latter case, several such requests might be needed if a whole file is to be transferred.

14.4 Caching

To ensure reasonable performance of the remote service scheme discussed in Section 14.3, we use a form of *caching*. In conventional file systems, the rationale for caching is to reduce disk I/O (thereby increasing performance), whereas in DFSs the goal is to reduce network traffic.

14.4.1 Basic Scheme

The concept of caching is simple. If the data needed to satisfy the access request are not already cached, then a copy of those data is brought from the server to the user. Accesses are performed on the cached copy. The idea is to retain recently accessed disk blocks in the cache, so that repeated accesses to the same information can be handled locally, without additional network traffic. A replacement policy (for example, least recently used) is used to keep the cache size bounded. There is no direct correspondence between accesses and traffic to the server. Files are still identified with one master copy residing at the server machine, but copies of (parts of) the file are scattered in different caches. When a cached copy is modified, the changes need to be reflected on the master copy to preserve the relevant consistency semantics. The problem of keeping the cached copies consistent with the master file is the *cache-consistency problem*, which will be discussed in Section 14.4.3. Observant

client   messages   server

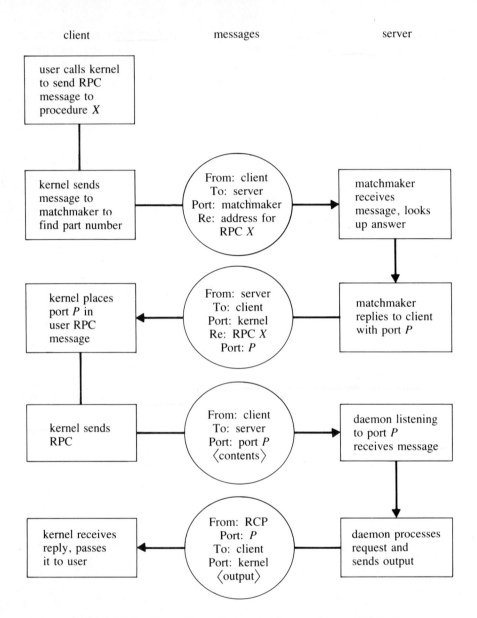

Figure 14.1   Execution of a remote procedure call (RPC).

readers will realize that DFS caching could just as easily be called network virtual memory. It acts similarly to demand-paged virtual memory except that the backing store is not a local disk, but rather is a remote server.

Caching is a much more complex topic than is remote service since there are many more variations of functionality and implementation. The granularity of the cached data can vary from blocks of a file to an entire file. Usually, more data are cached than are needed to satisfy a single access, so that many accesses can be served by the cached data. The Andrew system caches entire files, but it is not intended to handle very large files, since files are required to fit on the user's local disk. The other systems discussed in this chapter support caching of individual blocks driven by clients' demand. Increasing the caching unit increases the hit ratio, but delays the actual data transfer and increases the potential for consistency problems. Selecting the unit of caching involves considering parameters such as the network transfer unit and the *remote procedure call* (RPC) protocol service unit (in case an RPC protocol is used). The network transfer unit (for Ethernet, a packet) is about 1.5K, so larger units of cached data need to be disassembled for delivery and reassembled on reception.

Block size and the total cache size are obviously of importance for block-caching schemes. In UNIX-like systems, common block sizes are 4K or 8K. For large caches (over 1 megabyte) large block sizes (over 8K) are beneficial. For smaller caches, large block sizes are less beneficial because they result in fewer blocks in the cache.

Disk caches have one clear advantage over main memory cache — reliability. Modifications to cached data are lost in a crash if the cache is kept in volatile memory. Moreover, if the cached data are kept on disk, they are still there during recovery and there is no need to fetch them again. On the other hand, main-memory caches have several advantages of their own:

- Main memory caches permit workstations to be diskless.

- Data can be accessed more quickly from a cache in main memory than from one on a disk.

- The current technology trend is toward bigger and less expensive memories. The achieved performance speedup is predicted to outweigh the advantages of disk caches.

- The server caches (the ones used to speed up disk I/O) will be in main memory regardless of where user caches are located; by using main-memory caches on the user machine too, we can build a single caching mechanism for use by both servers and users (as is done in Sprite).

Many remote-access implementations can be thought of as a hybrid of caching and remote service. In NFS and Locus, for instance, the implementation is based on remote service but is augmented with caching for performance. On the other hand, Sprite's implementation is based on caching, but under certain circumstances a remote service method is adopted. Thus, when we evaluate the two methods, we actually evaluate to what degree one method should be emphasized over the other.

14.4.2 Update Policy

The policy used to write modified data blocks back to the server's master copy has critical effect on the system's performance and reliability. The simplest policy is to write data through to disk as soon as they are placed on any cache. The advantage of *write-through* is its reliability. Little information is lost when a client system crashes. However, this policy requires each write access to wait until the information is sent to the server, which results in poor write performance. Caching with write-through is equivalent to using remote service for write accesses and exploiting caching only for read accesses. NFS provides write-through access.

An alternate write policy is to delay updates to the master copy. Modifications are written to the cache and then are written through to the server sometime later. This policy has two advantages over write-through. First, since writes are to the cache, write accesses complete much more quickly. Second, data may be overwritten before they are written back, in which case they need never be written at all. Unfortunately, *delayed-write* schemes introduce reliability problems, since unwritten data will be lost whenever a user machine crashes.

There are several variations of the delayed-write policy that differ in when modified data blocks are flushed to the server. One alternative is to flush a block when it is about to be ejected from the client's cache. This option can result in good performance, but some blocks can reside in the client's cache a long time before they are written back to the server. A compromise between this alternative and the write-through policy is to scan the cache at regular intervals and to flush blocks that have been modified since the last scan. Sprite uses this policy with a 30-second interval.

Yet another variation on delayed-write is to write data back to the server when the file is closed. This policy, *write-on-close*, is used in the Andrew system. In case of files that are open for very short periods or are modified rarely, this policy does not significantly reduce network traffic. In addition, the write-on-close policy requires the closing process to delay while the file is written through, which reduces the performance advantages of delayed writes. The performance advantages of this policy over delayed-write with more frequent flushing are apparent for files that are open for long periods and are modified frequently.

14.4.3 Consistency

A client machine is faced with the problem of deciding whether or not a locally cached copy of the data is consistent with the master copy (and hence can be used). If the client machine determines that its cached data are out of date, accesses can no longer be served by those cached data. An up-to-date copy of the data needs to be cached. There are two approaches to verify the validity of cached data:

- **Client-initiated approach**. The client initiates a validity check in which it contacts the server and checks whether the local data are consistent with the master copy. The frequency of the validity check is the crux of this approach and determines the resulting consistency semantics. It can range from a check before every access, to a check on only first access to a file (on file open, basically). Every access that is coupled with a validity check is delayed, compared with an access served immediately by the cache. Alternatively, a check can be initiated every fixed interval of time. Depending on its frequency, the validity check can load both the network and the server.

- **Server-initiated approach**. The server records, for each client, the (parts of) files it caches. When the server detects a potential inconsistency, it must react. A potential for inconsistency occurs when a file is cached by two different clients in conflicting modes. If session semantics (Section 10.4.2) are implemented, then, whenever a server receives a request to close a file that has been modified, it should react by notifying the clients to consider the cached data invalid and discard that data. Clients having this file open at that time discard their copy when the current session is over. Other clients discard their copy at once. Under session semantics, the server does not need to be informed about opens of already cached files. The server's reaction is triggered only by the close of a writing session, and hence only this kind of session is delayed. In Andrew, session semantics are implemented, and a server-initiated method, called *callback*, is employed.

  On the other hand, if a more restrictive consistency semantics such as UNIX semantics (Section 10.4.1) is implemented, the server must play a more active role. The server must be notified whenever a file is opened and the intended mode (read or write mode) must be indicated for every open. Assuming such notification, the server can act when it detects a file that is opened simultaneously in conflicting modes by disabling caching for that particular file (as done in Sprite). Actually, disabling caching results in switching to a remote-service mode of operation.

14.4.4 A Comparison of Caching and Remote Service

Essentially, the choice between caching and remote service trades off a potentially increased performance with decreased simplicity. We evaluate this tradeoff by listing the advantages and disadvantages of the two methods:

- A substantial number of the remote accesses can be handled efficiently by the local cache when caching is used. Capitalizing on locality in file-access patterns makes caching even more attractive. Thus, most of the remote accesses will be served as fast as will local ones. Moreover, servers are contacted only occasionally, rather than for each access. Consequently, server load and network traffic are reduced, and the potential for scalability is enhanced. By contrast, every remote access is handled across the network when the remote-service method is used. The penalty in network traffic, server load, and performance is obvious.

- Total network overhead in transmitting big chunks of data (as done in caching) is lower than when series of responses to specific requests are transmitted (as in the remote-service method).

- Disk-access routines on the server may be better optimized if it is known that requests are always for large, contiguous segments of data, rather than for random disk blocks.

- The cache-consistency problem is the major drawback of caching. In access patterns that exhibit infrequent writes, caching is superior. However, when writes are frequent, the mechanisms employed to overcome the consistency problem incur substantial overhead in terms of performance, network traffic, and server load.

- To benefit from caching, execution should be carried out on machines that have either local disks or large main memories. Remote access on diskless, small-memory-capacity machines should be done through the remote-service method.

- In caching, since data are transferred en masse between the server and client, rather than in response to the specific needs of a file operation, the lower intermachine interface is quite different from the upper user interface. The remote-service paradigm, on the other hand, is just an extension of the local file-system interface across the network. Thus, the intermachine interface mirrors the local user-file-system interface.

14.5 Stateful versus Stateless Service

There are two approaches to server-side information. Either the server tracks each file being accessed by each client, or it simply provides blocks as they are requested by the client without knowledge of the blocks use.

The typical scenario of a *stateful file service* is as follows. A client must perform an open on a file before accessing that file. The server fetches some information about the file from its disk, stores it in its memory, and gives the client a connection identifier that is unique to the client and the open file. (In UNIX terms, the server fetches the inode and gives the client a file descriptor, which serves as an index to an in-core table of inodes.) This identifier is used for subsequent accesses until the session ends. A stateful service is characterized as a connection between the client and the server during a session. Either on closing the file, or by garbage-collection mechanism, the server must reclaim the main-memory space used by clients who are no longer active.

The advantage of stateful service is increased performance. File information is cached in main memory and can be accessed easily via the connection identifier, thereby saving disk accesses. In addition, a stateful server would know whether a file were open for sequential access and could therefore read ahead the next blocks. Stateless servers cannot do so, since they have no knowledge of the purpose of the client's requests. The key point regarding fault tolerance in a stateful service approach is that main-memory information is kept by the server about its clients.

A *stateless file server* avoids this state information by making each request self-contained. That is, each request identifies the file and position in the file (for read and write accesses) in full. The server need not keep a table of open files in main memory, although this is usually done for efficiency reasons. Moreover, there is no need to establish and terminate a connection by open and close operations. They are totally redundant, since each file operation stands on its own and is not considered as part of a session. A client process would open a file, and that open would not result in a remote message being sent. Reads and writes would of course take place as remote messages (or cache lookups). The final close by the client would again result in only a local operation.

The distinction between stateful and stateless service becomes evident when we consider the effects of a crash occurring during a service activity. A stateful server loses all its volatile state in a crash. Ensuring the graceful recovery of such a server involves restoring this state — usually by a recovery protocol based on a dialog with clients. Less graceful recovery requires that the operations that were underway when the crash occurred, be aborted. A different problem is caused by client failures. The server needs to become aware of such failures, in order to reclaim space allocated to record the state of crashed client processes. This phenomenon is sometimes referred to as *orphan detection and elimination*.

A stateless server avoids these problems, since a newly reincarnated server can respond to a self-contained request without any difficulty. Therefore, the effects of server failures and recovery are almost unnoticeable. There is no difference between a slow server and a recovering server from a client's point of view. The client keeps retransmitting its request if it receives no response.

The penalty for using the robust stateless service is longer request messages, and slower processing of requests, since there is no in-core information to speed the processing. In addition, stateless service imposes additional constraints on the design of the DFS. First, since each request identifies the target file, a uniform, systemwide, low-level naming scheme should be used. Translating remote to local names for each request would cause even slower processing of the requests. Second, since clients retransmit requests for file operations, these operations must be idempotent; that is, each operation must have the same effect and return the same output if executed several times consecutively. Self-contained read and write accesses are idempotent, as long as they use an absolute byte count to indicate the position within the file they access and do not rely on an incremental offset (as done in UNIX read and write system calls). However, we must be careful when implementing destructive operations (such as delete a file) to make them idempotent too.

In some environments, a stateful service is a necessity. If the server employs the server-initiated method for cache validation, it cannot provide stateless service, since it maintains a record of which files are cached by which clients.

The way UNIX uses file descriptors and implicit offsets is inherently stateful. Servers must maintain tables to map the file descriptors to inodes, and store the current offset within a file. This is why NFS, which employs a stateless service, does not use file descriptors, and does include an explicit offset in every access.

14.6 File Replication

Replication of files on different machines is a useful redundancy for improving availability. Multimachine replication can benefit performance too, since selecting a nearby replica to serve an access request results in shorter service time.

The very basic requirement of a replication scheme is that different replicas of the same file reside on failure-independent machines. That is, the availability of one replica is not affected by the availability of the rest of the replicas. This obvious requirement implies that replication management is inherently a location-opaque activity. Provisions for placing a replica on a particular machine must be available.

It is desirable to hide the details of replication from users. It is the task of the naming scheme to map a replicated file name to a particular replica. The existence of replicas should be invisible to higher levels. However, the replicas must be distinguished from one another by different lower-level names. Another transparency issue is providing replication control at higher levels. Replication control includes determining the degree of replication and the placement of replicas. Under certain circumstances, it is desirable to expose these details to users. Locus, for instance, provides users and system administrators with mechanisms to control the replication scheme.

The main problem associated with replicas is their update. From a user's point of view, replicas of a file denote the same logical entity, and thus an update to any replica must be reflected on all other replicas. More precisely, the relevant consistency semantics must be preserved when accesses to replicas are viewed as virtual accesses to the replicas' logical files. If consistency is not of primary importance, it can be sacrificed for availability and performance. This is an incarnation of a fundamental tradeoff in the area of fault tolerance. The choice is between preserving consistency at all costs, thereby creating a potential for indefinite blocking, and sacrificing consistency under some (we hope rare) circumstance of catastrophic failures for the sake of guaranteed progress. Among the surveyed systems, Locus employs replication extensively and sacrifices consistency in the case of network partition, for the sake of availability of files for both read and write accesses (see Section 14.7.5 for details).

As an illustration of these concepts, we describe the replication scheme of Ibis, which uses a variation of the primary-copy approach. The domain of the name mapping is a pair <primary-replica-identifier, local-replica-identifier>. Since there maybe no replica locally, a special value is used in that case. Thus, the mapping is relative to a machine. If the local replica is the primary one, the pair contains two identical identifiers. Ibis supports demand replication, which is an automatic replication control policy (similar to whole-file caching). Demand replication means that reading a nonlocal replica causes it to be cached locally, thereby generating a new nonprimary replica. Updates are performed on only the primary copy and cause all other replicas to be invalidated by sending appropriate messages. Atomic and serialized invalidation of all nonprimary replicas is not guaranteed. Hence, a stale replica may be considered valid. To satisfy remote write accesses, we migrate the primary copy to the requesting machine.

14.7 Example Systems

In this section, we illustrate the common concepts on which distributed file systems are based by examining five different and interesting distributed file systems: UNIX United, NFS, Andrew, Sprite, and Locus.

14.7.1 UNIX United

The *UNIX United* project from the University of Newcastle upon Tyne, England, is one of the earliest attempts to scale up the UNIX file system to a distributed one without modifying the UNIX kernel. In UNIX United, a software subsystem is added to each of a set of interconnected UNIX systems (referred to as *component* or *constituent* systems), so as to construct a distributed system that is functionally indistinguishable from a conventional centralized UNIX system. The system is presented in two levels of detail. First, an overview of UNIX United is given. Then, the implementation, the Newcastle Connection layer, is examined and some issues regarding networking and internetworking are discussed.

Overview

Any number of interlinked UNIX systems can be joined to compose a UNIX United system. Their naming structures (for files, devices, directories, and commands) are joined together into a single naming structure, in which each component system is, for all intents and purposes, just a directory. Ignoring for the moment questions regarding accreditation and access control, the resulting system is one where each user can read or write any file, use any device, execute any command, or inspect any directory, regardless of the system to which it belongs.

The component unit is a complete UNIX directory tree belonging to a certain machine. The position of these component units in the naming hierarchy is arbitrary. They can appear in the naming structure in positions subservient to other component units (directly or through intermediary directories).

Roots of component units are assigned names so that they become accessible and distinguishable externally. A file system's own root is still referred to as "/" and still serves as the starting point of all path names starting with a "/". However, a subservient file system can access its superior system by referring to its own root parent (that is, "/.."). Therefore, there is only one root that is its own parent and that is not assigned a string name — namely, the root of the composite name structure, which is just a virtual node needed to make the whole structure a single tree. Under this convention, there is no notion of absolute path name. Each path name is relative to some context, either to the current working directory or to the current component unit.

In Figure 14.2, *unix1*, *unix2*, *unix3*, and *unix4* are names of component systems. As an illustration of the relative path names, note that within the *unix1* system, file *f2* on the system *unix2* is referred to as */../unix2/f2*. Within the *unix3* system, this file is referred to as */../../unix2/f2*. Now, suppose that the current root ("/") is as shown by the arrow. Then, file *f3* is referred to as */f3*, file *f1* is referred to as */../f1*, file *f2* is referred to as */../../unix2/f2*, and finally file *f4* is referred to as */../../unix2/dir/unix4/f4*.

Observe that users are aware of the upward boundaries of their current component unit, since they must use the "../" syntax whenever they wish to ascend outside of their current machine. Hence, UNIX United does not provide complete location transparency.

The traditional root directories (for example, */dev*, */temp*) are maintained for each machine separately. Because of the relative naming

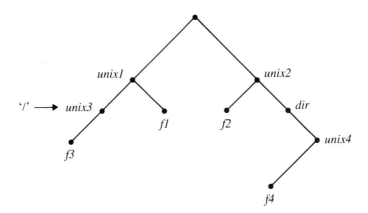

Figure 14.2 Example of a UNIX United directory structure.

scheme they are named, from within a component system, in exactly the same manner as in a conventional UNIX.

Each component system has its own set of named users and its own administrator (superuser). The latter is responsible for the accreditation for users of his own system, as well as for that of remote users. A remote user's identifier is prefixed with the name of the user's original system for uniqueness. Accesses are governed by the standard UNIX file-protection mechanisms, even if they cross components boundaries. That is, there is no need for users to log in separately, or to provide passwords, when they access remote files. However, users wishing to access files in a remote system must arrange with the specific system administrator separately.

It is often convenient to set the naming structure so as to reflect organizational hierarchy of the environment in which the system exists.

The Newcastle Connection

The Newcastle Connection is a (user-level) software layer incorporated in each component system. This connection layer separates the UNIX kernel on one hand, and the user-level programs on the other hand (see Figure 14.3). It intercepts all system calls concerning files, and filters out those that have to be redirected to remote systems. Also, the connection layer accepts system calls that have been directed to it from other systems. Remote layers communicate by the means of an RPC protocol.

The connection layer preserves the same UNIX system-call interface as that of the UNIX kernel, in spite of the extensive remote activity that the system carries out. The penalty of preserving the kernel intact is that the service is implemented as user-level daemon processes, which slow down remote operation.

Each connection layer stores a partial skeleton of the overall naming structure. Obviously, each system stores locally its own file system. In addition, each system stores fragments of the overall name structure

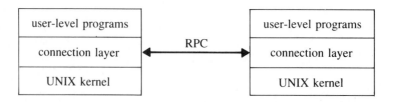

Figure 14.3   Schematic view of UNIX United architecture.

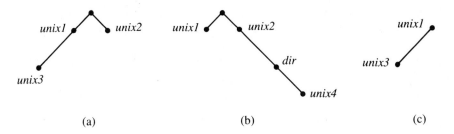

Figure 14.4   The file system of (a) *unix1*, (b) *unix2*, and (c) *unix3*.

that relate it to its neighboring systems in the naming structure (that is, systems that can be reached via traversal of the naming tree without passing through another system). In Figure 14.4, we show the partial skeletons of the hierarchy of the file systems of Figure 14.2 as maintained by the systems *unix1*, *unix2*, and *unix3*, respectively (only the relevant parts are shown).

The fragments maintained by different systems overlap and hence must remain consistent, a requirement that makes changing the overall structure an infrequent event. Some leaves of the partial structure stored locally correspond to remote roots of other parts of the global file system. These leaves are specially marked, and contain addresses of the appropriate storage sites of the descending file systems. Path name traversals have to be continued remotely when such marked leaves are encountered, and, in fact, can span several systems until the target file is located. Once a name is resolved and the file is opened, that file is accessed using file descriptors. The connection layer marks descriptors that refer to remote files and keeps network addresses and routing information for them in a per-process table.

The actual remote file accesses are carried out by a set of file-server processes on the target system. Each client has its own file server process with which it communicates directly. The initial connection is established with the aid of a *spawner* process that has a standard fixed name that makes it callable from any external process. This spawner process performs the remote access-rights checks according to a machine-user identification pair. Also, it converts this identification to a valid local name. So that UNIX semantics will be preserved, once a client process forks, its file service process forks as well. This service scheme does not excel in terms of robustness. Special recovery actions have to be taken in case of simultaneous server and client failures. However, the connection layer attempts to mask and isolate failures resulting from the fact that the system is a distributed one.

Networking Issues

UNIX United is well suited for a diverse internetwork topology, spanning local-area networks (LANs) as well as direct links and even wide-area networks (WANs). The logical name space needs to be mapped onto routing information properly. An important design principle is that the naming hierarchy need bear no relationship to the topology. The approach taken is that each machine routes remote requests to an appropriate one of its physically adjacent machines, which can then pass on the request further. Therefore, each system has to be aware of hardware addresses only of machines that are directly connected to it (by the same LAN, or by a hard-wired link). UNIX United takes advantage of its own systemwide unique naming scheme to guide addressing and routing. Within each machine, routing tables translate these logical names to the next hop en route to the destination.

When path-name traversal is performed, the path name is followed as an intermachine route, so that all authentication and protection demands are satisfied. However, it may not be necessary to repeat the same route when a file has been opened successfully, if some shorter route is available.

As a message travels along the physical links, the addressing information it contains (which is described in terms of paths) sometimes will have to be adjusted to reflect the fact that movement around the physical topology causes movement around the naming structure (recall that there is no relationship between the two). To illustrate this, we consider the name structure and partial topology of the UNIX United scheme depicted in Figure 14.5. In this environment, a message from *U1* to *U2* would include the path /../U2. Passing through *M1*, this message would need this path to be changed to /../M2/U2.

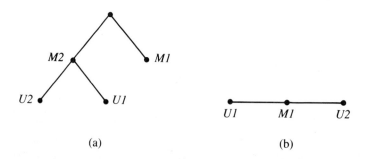

(a)   (b)

Figure 14.5   (a) UNIX United name structure and (b) partial topology.

14.7.2 The Sun Network File System

The Network File System (NFS) is both an implementation and a specification of a software system for accessing remote files across LANs (or even WANs). The implementation is part of the SunOS operating system, which is a modified version of 4.2BSD UNIX, running on a Sun workstation using an unreliable datagram protocol (UDP/IP protocol) and Ethernet (or another networking system). The specification and the implementation are intertwined in our description of NFS. Whenever a level of detail is needed, we refer to the SunOS implementation; whenever the description is general enough, it applies to the specification also.

Overview

NFS views a set of interconnected workstations as a set of independent machines with independent file systems. The goal is to allow some degree of sharing among these file systems (on explicit request) in a transparent manner. Sharing is based on server-client relationship. A machine may be, and often is, both a client and a server. Sharing is allowed between any pair of machines, rather than with only dedicated server machines. To ensure machine independence, sharing of a remote file system affects only the client machine and no other machine.

To make a remote directory accessible in a transparent manner from a particular machine, say from *M1*, a client of that machine has to carry out a mount operation first. The semantics of the operation are that a remote directory is mounted over a directory of a local file system. Once the mount operation is completed, the mounted directory looks like an integral subtree of the local file system, replacing the subtree descending from the local directory. The local directory becomes the name of the root of the newly mounted directory. Specification of the remote directory as an argument for the mount operation is done in a nontransparent manner; the location (that is, host name) of the remote directory has to be provided. However, from then on, users on machine *M1* can access files in the remote directory in a totally transparent manner.

To illustrate file mounting, we consider the file system depicted in Figure 14.6, where the triangles represent subtrees of directories that are of interest. In this figure, three independent file systems of machines named *U*, *S1* and *S2* are shown. At this point, at each machine, only the local files can be accessed. In Figure 14.7(a), the effects of the mounting of *S1:/usr/shared* over *U:/usr/local* are shown. This figure depicts the view users on *U* have of their file system. Observe that they can access any file within the *dir1* directory, for instance, using the prefix */usr/local/dir1*

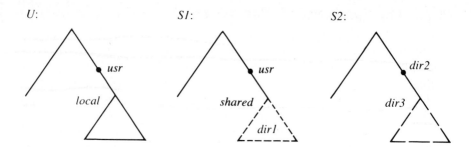

Figure 14.6   Three independent file systems.

on *U* after the mount is complete. The original directory */usr/local* on that machine is no longer visible.

Subject to access-rights accreditation, potentially any file system, or a directory within a file system, can be mounted remotely on top of any local directory. In SunOS 4.0, diskless workstations can even mount their own roots from servers.

Cascading mounts are also permitted. That is, a file system can be mounted over another file system that is not a local one, but rather is a remotely mounted one. However, a machine is affected by only the mounts it has itself invoked.

By mounting a remote file system, the client does not gain access to other file systems that were, by chance, mounted over the former file system. Thus, the mount mechanism does not exhibit a transitivity property. In Figure 14.7(b), we illustrate cascading mounts by continuing with our previous example. The figure shows the result of

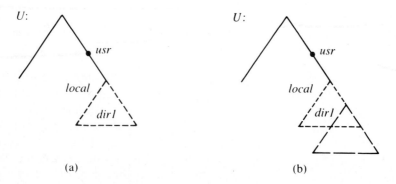

Figure 14.7   NFS file system (a) mounts and (b) cascading mounts.

mounting *S2:/dir2/dir3* over *U:/usr/local/dir1*, which is already remotely mounted from *S1*. Users can access files within *dir3* on *U* using the prefix */usr/local/dir1*. If a shared file system is mounted over a user's home directories on all machines in a network, a user can log in to any workstation and get his home environment. This property is referred to as *user mobility*.

One of the design goals of NFS was to operate in a heterogeneous environment of different machines, operating systems, and network architectures. The NFS specification is independent of these media and thus encourages other implementations. This independence is achieved through the use of RPC primitives built on top of an External Date Representation (XDR) protocol used between two implementation-independent interfaces. Hence, if the system consists of heterogeneous machines and file systems that are properly interfaced to NFS, file systems of different types can be mounted both locally and remotely.

The NFS specification distinguishes between the services provided by a mount mechanism and the actual remote-file-access services. Accordingly, two separate protocols are specified for these services; a *mount protocol*, and a protocol for remote file accesses called the *NFS protocol*. The protocols are specified as sets of RPCs. These RPCs are the building blocks used to implement transparent remote file access.

The Mount Protocol

The mount protocol is used to establish the initial logical connection between a server and a client. In Sun's implementation, each machine has a server process, outside the kernel, performing the protocol functions.

A mount operation includes the name of the remote directory to be mounted and the name of the server machine storing it. The mount request is mapped to the corresponding RPC and is forwarded to the mount server running on the specific server machine. The server maintains an *export list* (the */etc/exports* in UNIX, which can be edited by only a superuser), which specifies local file systems that it exports for mounting, along with names of machines that are permitted to mount them. Recall that any directory within an exported file system can be mounted remotely by an accredited machine. Hence, a component unit is such a directory. When the server receives a mount request that conforms to its export list, it returns to the client a *file handle* that serves as the key for further accesses to files within the mounted file system. The file handle contains all the information that the server needs to distinguish an individual file it stores. In UNIX terms, the file handle consists of a file-system identifier, and an inode number to identify the exact mounted directory within the exported file system.

The server also maintains a list of the client machines and the corresponding currently mounted directories. This list is mainly for administrative purposes — for instance, for notifying all clients that the server is going down. Adding and deleting an entry in this list is the only way that the server state can be affected by the mount protocol.

Usually, a system has a static mounting preconfiguration that is established at boot time (*/etc/fstab* in UNIX); however, this layout can be modified. Besides the actual mount procedure, the mount protocol includes several other procedures such as unmount, return export list, and so on.

The exact details of how a mount operation changes the user's view of the file system are explained later; however, it is crucial to note that this operation changes only the user's view and does not affect the server side.

The NFS Protocol

The NFS protocol provides a set of remote procedure calls for remote file operations. The procedures support the following operations:

- Searching for a file within a directory

- Reading a set of directory entries

- Manipulating links and directories

- Accessing file attributes

- Reading and writing files

These procedures can be invoked only after a file handle for the remotely mounted directory has been established.

The omission of open and close operations is intentional. A prominent feature of NFS servers is that they are *stateless*. Servers do not maintain information about their clients from one access to another access. There are no parallels to UNIX's open-files table or file structures on the server side. Consequently, each request has to provide a full set of arguments, including a unique file identifier and an absolute offset inside the file for the appropriate operations. The resulting design is robust, since no special measures need to be taken to recover a server after a crash. File operations need to be idempotent for this end.

Maintaining the list of clients mentioned in the mount protocol subsection seems to violate the statelessness of the server. However, it is not essential for the correct operation of the client or the server, and hence this list does not need to be restored after a server crash.

Consequently, it might include inconsistent data and should be treated only as a hint.

A further implication of the stateless-server philosophy and a result of the synchrony of a RPC is that modified data (including indirection and status blocks) must be committed to the server's disk before results are returned to the client. The consequent performance penalty can be quite large, since the advantages of caching are lost. In fact, there are several products now on the market that specifically address this NFS problem.

A single NFS write procedure call is guaranteed to be atomic, and also is not intermixed with other write calls to the same file. The NFS protocol, however, does not provide concurrency-control mechanisms. Since a write system call may be broken up into several RPC writes (because each NFS write or read call can contain up to 8K of data), two users writing to the same remote file may get their data intermixed. The claim is that, since locks management is inherently stateful, a service outside the NFS should provide locking (and SunOS does). Users are advised to coordinate access to shared files using mechanisms outside the scope of NFS.

NFS Architecture

The NFS architecture consists of three major layers; it is depicted schematically in Figure 14.8. The first layer is the UNIX file-system interface, based on the open, read, write, and close calls, and file descriptors.

The second layer is called *Virtual File System* (VFS) layer; it serves two important functions:

- It separates file-system generic operations from their implementation by defining a clean VFS interface. Several implementations for the VFS interface may coexist on the same machine, allowing transparent access to different types of file systems mounted locally.

- The VFS is based on a file representation structure called a *vnode* that contains a numerical designator for a file that is networkwide unique. (Recall that UNIX inodes are unique within only a single file system.) The kernel maintains one vnode structure for each active node (file or directory).

Thus, the VFS distinguishes local files from remote ones, and local files are further distinguished according to their file-system types.

Similarly to standard UNIX, the kernel maintains a table (*/etc/mtab* in UNIX) recording the details of the mounts in which it took part as a

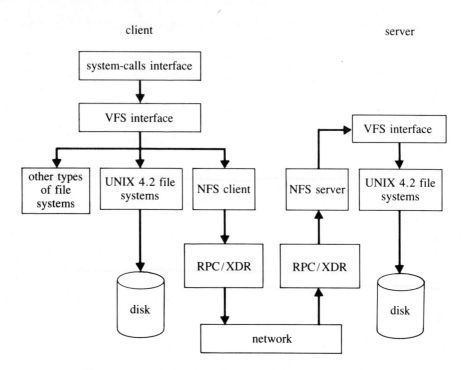

Figure 14.8   Schematic view of the NFS architecture.

client. Further, the vnodes for each directory that is mounted over are kept in memory at all times and are marked, so that requests concerning such directories will be redirected to the corresponding mounted file systems via the mount table. Essentially, the vnode structures, complemented by the mount table, provide a pointer for every file to its parent file system, as well as to the file system over which it is mounted.

The VFS activates file-system-specific operations to handle local requests according to their file-system types, and calls the NFS protocol procedures for remote requests. File handles are constructed from the relevant vnodes and are passed as arguments to these procedures. The layer implementing the NFS protocol is the bottom layer of the architecture and is called the NFS service layer.

As an illustration of the architecture, let us trace how an operation on an already-open remote file is handled (follow the example on Figure 14.8). The client initiates the operation by a regular system call. The operating-system layer maps this call to a VFS operation on the appropriate vnode. The VFS layer identifies the file as a remote one and invokes the appropriate NFS procedure. An RPC call is made to the NFS service layer at the remote server. This call is reinjected to the VFS layer on the remote system, which finds that it is local and invokes the appropriate file-system operation. This path is retraced to return the result. An advantage of this architecture is that the client and the server are identical; thus, it is possible for a machine to be a client, or a server, or both.

The actual service on each server is performed by several kernel processes that provide a temporary substitute to a lightweight process (threads) facility.

Path-Name Translation

We do path-name translation by breaking the path into component names and performing a separate NFS *lookup call* for every pair of component name and directory vnode. Once a mount point is crossed, every component lookup causes a separate RPC to the server (see Figure 14.9). This expensive path-name-traversal scheme is needed, since each client has a unique layout of its logical name space, dictated by the mounts it performed. It would have been much more efficient to hand a server a path name and to receive a target vnode once a mount point was encountered. But at any point there can be another mount point for the particular client of which the stateless server is unaware.

To make lookup faster, a directory name lookup cache on the client's side holds the vnodes for remote directory names. This cache speeds up references to files with the same initial path name. The directory cache is discarded when attributes returned from the server do not match the attributes of the cached vnode.

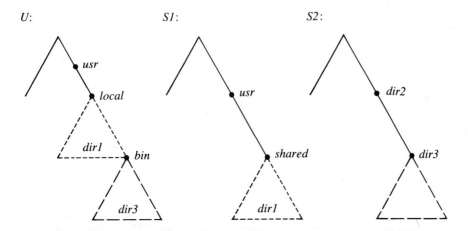

Figure 14.9 Path-name translation.

Recall that mounting a remote file system on top of another already-mounted remote file system (cascading mount) is allowed in NFS. However, a server cannot act as an intermediary between a client and another server. Instead, a client must establish a direct server-client connection with the second server by directly mounting the desired directory. When a client has a cascading mount, more than one server can be involved in a path-name traversal. However, each component lookup is performed between the original client and some server. Therefore, when a client does a lookup on a directory on which the server has mounted a file system, the client sees the underlying directory instead of the mounted directory.

Remote Operations

With the exception of opening and closing files, there is almost one-to-one correspondence between the regular UNIX system calls for file operations and the NFS protocol RPCs. Thus, a remote file operation can be translated directly to the corresponding RPC. Conceptually, NFS adheres to the remote-service paradigm, but in practice buffering and caching techniques are employed for the sake of performance. There is no direct correspondence between a remote operation and an RPC. Instead, file blocks and file attributes are fetched by the RPCs and are cached locally. Future remote operations use the cached data, subject to some consistency constraints.

There are two caches: file-blocks cache and file-attribute (inode-information) cache. On a file open, the kernel checks with the remote server whether to fetch or revalidate the cached attributes. The cached file blocks are used only if the corresponding cached attributes are up to date. The attribute cache is updated whenever new attributes arrive from the server. Cached attributes are discarded after 3 seconds for files or 30 seconds for directories. Both read-ahead and delayed-write techniques are used between the server and the client. Clients do not free delayed-write blocks until the server confirms that the data have been written to disk. In contrast to the system used in Sprite, delayed-write is retained even when a file is opened concurrently, in conflicting modes. Hence, UNIX semantics are not preserved.

Tuning the system for performance makes it difficult to characterize the consistency semantics of NFS. New files created on a machine may not be visible elsewhere for 30 seconds. It is indeterminate whether writes to a file at one site are visible to other sites that have this file open for reading. New opens of that file observe only the changes that have already been flushed to the server. Thus, NFS provides neither strict emulation of UNIX semantics, nor the session semantics of Andrew. In spite of these drawbacks, the utility and high performance of the mechanism makes it the most widely used, multivendor distributed system in operation.

14.7.3 Andrew

Andrew is a distributed computing environment that has been under development since 1983 at Carnegie-Mellon University. As such, it is one of the newest distributed file systems. The Andrew file system constitutes the underlying information-sharing mechanism among clients of the environment. One of the most formidable attributes of Andrew is its scalability. The system is targeted to span over 5000 workstations.

Overview

Andrew distinguishes between client machines (sometimes referred to as workstations) and dedicated *server machines*. Servers and clients alike run the 4.2BSD UNIX operating system and are interconnected by an internet of LANs.

Clients are presented with a partitioned space of file names: a *local name space and a shared name space*. Dedicated servers, collectively called *Vice*, after the name of the software they run, present the shared name space to the clients as an homogeneous, identical, and location transparent file hierarchy. The local name space is the root file system of a workstation, from which the shared name space descends. Workstations run the *Virtue* protocol to communicate with Vice, and are required to have local disks where they store their local name space. Servers collectively are responsible for the storage and management of the shared name space. The local name space is small, is distinct for each workstation, and contains system programs essential for autonomous operation and better performance. Also local are temporary files and files that the workstation owner explicitly wants, for privacy reasons, to store locally.

Viewed at a finer granularity, clients and servers are structured in clusters interconnected by a backbone LAN. Each cluster consists of a collection of workstations and a representative of Vice called a *cluster server* and is connected to the backbone by a *router*. The decomposition into clusters is done primarily to address the problem of scale. For optimal performance, workstations should use the server on their own cluster most of the time, thereby making cross-cluster file references relatively infrequent.

The file-system architecture was based on consideration of scale, too. The basic heuristic was to offload work from the servers to the clients, in light of experience indicating that server CPU speed is the system's bottleneck. Following this heuristic, the key mechanism selected for remote file operations is *whole file caching*. Opening a file causes it to be cached, in its entirety, on the local disk. Reads and writes are directed to the cached copy without involving the servers at all. Under certain circumstances, the cached copy can be further used for forthcoming opens.

We note that this design cannot accommodate remote access to very large files (that is, files larger than local disk size). Thus, a separate design is needed to address the issue of use of large databases or programs in the Andrew environment.

There are additional issues in Andrew's design that we will not discuss here; briefly, they are these:

- **Client mobility**. Clients are able to access any file in the shared name space from any workstation. The only effect clients may notice when accessing files not from their usual workstations is some initial performance degradation due to the caching of files.

- **Security**. The Vice interface is considered as the boundary of trustworthiness, since no client programs are executed on Vice machines. Authentication and secure-transmission functions are provided as part of a connection-based communication package, based on the RPC paradigm. After mutual authentication, a Vice server and a client communicate via encrypted messages. Encryption is performed by hardware devices. Information about clients and groups is stored in a protection database that is replicated at each server.

- **Protection**. Andrew provides *access lists* for protecting directories and the regular UNIX bits for file protection. The access-list mechanism is based on a recursive group structure.

- **Heterogeneity**. Defining a clear interface to Vice is a key for integration of diverse workstation hardware and operating system. So that heterogeneity is facilitated, some files in the local */bin* directory are symbolic links pointing to machine-specific executable files residing in Vice.

The Shared Name Space

Andrew's shared name space is constituted of component units called *volumes*. Andrew's volumes are unusually small component units. Typically, they are associated with the files of a single client. Few volumes reside within a single disk partition, and they may grow (up to a quota) and shrink in size. Conceptually, volumes are glued together by a mechanism similar to the UNIX mount mechanism. However, the granularity difference is significant, since in UNIX only an entire disk partition (containing a file system) can be mounted. Volumes are a key administrative unit and play a vital role in identifying and locating an individual file.

A Vice file or directory is identified by a low-level identifier called a *fid*. Each Andrew directory entry maps a path-name component to a fid. A fid is 96 bits long and has three equal-length components: a *volume number*, a *vnode number*, and a *uniquifier*. The vnode number is used as an index into an array containing the inodes of files in a single volume. The uniquifier allows reuse of vnode numbers, thereby keeping certain data structures compact. Fids are location transparent; therefore, file movements from server to server do not invalidate cached directory contents.

Location information is kept on a volume basis in a *volume-location database* replicated on each server. A client can identify the location of every volume in the system by querying this database. It is the aggregation of files into volumes that makes it possible to keep the location database at a manageable size.

To balance the available disk space and utilization of servers, volumes need to be migrated among disk partitions and servers. When a volume is shipped to its new location, its original server is left with temporary forwarding information, so that the location database does not need to be updated synchronously. While the volume is being transferred, the original server still may handle updates, which are shipped later to the new server. At some point, the volume is briefly disabled so that the recent modifications can be processed; then, the new volume becomes available again at the new site. The volume-movement operation is atomic; if either server crashes, the operation is aborted.

Read-only replication at the granularity of an entire volume is supported for system-executable files and for seldom-updated files in the upper levels of the Vice name space. The volume-location database specifies the server containing the only read-write copy of a volume and a list of read-only replication sites.

File Operations and Consistency Semantics

The fundamental architectural principle in Andrew is the caching of entire files from servers. Accordingly, a client workstation interacts with Vice servers only during opening and closing of files, and even this is not always necessary. No remote interaction is caused by reading or writing files (in contrast to the remote-service method). This key distinction has far-reaching ramifications for performance as well as for semantics of file operations.

The operating system on each workstation intercepts file-system calls and forwards them to a client-level process on that workstation. This process, called *Venus*, caches files from Vice when they are opened, and stores modified copies of files back on the servers from which they came when they are closed. Venus may contact Vice only when a file is opened or closed; reading and writing of individual bytes of a file are performed directly on the cached copy and bypass Venus. As a result, writes at some sites are not visible immediately at other sites.

Caching is further exploited for future opens of the cached file. Venus assumes that cached entries (files or directories) are valid unless notified otherwise. Therefore, Venus does not need to contact Vice on a file open in order to validate the cached copy. The mechanism to support this policy, called *callback*, dramatically reduces the number of cache validation requests received by servers. It works as follows. When a client caches a file or a directory, the server updates its state information recording this caching. We say that the client has a callback on that file. The server notifies the client before allowing a modification to the file by another client. In such a case, we say that the server removes the callback on the file for the former client. A client can use a cached file for open purposes only when the file has a callback. If a client closes a file after modifying it, all other clients caching this file lose their callbacks. Therefore, when these clients open the file later, they have to get the new version from the server.

Reading and writing bytes of a file are done directly by the kernel without Venus intervention on the cached copy. Venus regains control when the file is closed and, if the file has been modified locally, Venus updates the file on the appropriate server. Thus, the only occasions in which Venus contacts Vice servers are on opens of files that either are not in the cache or have had their callback revoked, and on closes of locally modified files.

Basically, Andrew implements session semantics. The only exceptions are file operations other than the primitive read and write (such as protection changes at the directory level), which are visible everywhere on the network immediately after the operation completes.

In spite of the callback mechanism, a small amount of cached validation traffic is still present, usually to replace callbacks lost because of machine or network failures. When a workstation is rebooted, Venus considers all cached files and directories suspect, and generates a cache-validation request for the first use of each such entry.

The callback mechanism forces each server to maintain callback information and each client to maintain validity information. If the amount of callback information maintained by a server is excessive, the server can break callbacks and reclaim some storage by unilaterally notifying clients and revoking the validity of their cached files. There is a potential for inconsistency if the callback state maintained by Venus gets out of sync with the corresponding state maintained by the servers.

Venus also caches contents of directories and symbolic links, for path-name translation. Each component in the path name is fetched, and a callback is established for it if it is not already cached, or if the client does not have a callback on it. Lookups are done locally by Venus on the fetched directories using fids. There is no forwarding of requests from one server to another. At the end of a path-name traversal, all the intermediate directories and the target file are in the cache with callbacks on them. Future open calls to this file will involve no network communication at all, unless a callback is broken on a component of the path name.

The only exceptions to the caching policy are modifications to directories that are made directly on the server responsible for that directory for reasons of integrity. There are well-defined operations in the Vice interface for such purposes. Venus reflects the changes in its cached copy to avoid refetching the directory.

Implementation

Client processes are interfaced to a UNIX kernel with the usual set of system calls. The kernel is modified slightly to detect references to Vice files in the relevant operations and to forward the requests to the client-level Venus process at the workstation.

Venus carries out path-name translation component by component, as was described earlier. It has a mapping cache that associates volumes to server locations in order to avoid server interrogation for an already-known volume location. If a volume is not present in this cache, Venus contacts any server to which it has already a connection, requests the location information, and enters that information into the mapping cache. Unless Venus already has a connection to the server, it establishes a new connection. It then uses this connection to fetch the file or directory. Connection establishment is needed for authentication and security purposes. When a target file is found and cached, a copy is created on the local disk. Venus then returns to the kernel, which opens the cached copy and returns its handle to the client process.

The UNIX file system is used as a low-level storage system for both servers and clients. The client cache is a local directory on the workstation's disk. Within this directory are files whose names are placeholders for cache entries. Both Venus and server processes access UNIX files directly by their inodes to avoid the expensive path name-to-inode translation routine (*namei*). Since the internal inode interface is not visible to client-level processes (both Venus and server processes are client-level processes), an appropriate set of additional system calls was added.

Venus manages two separate caches: one for status and the other for data. It uses a simple least recently used (LRU) algorithm to keep each of them bounded in size. When a file is flushed from the cache, Venus notifies the appropriate server to remove the callback for this file. The status cache is kept in virtual memory to allow rapid servicing of *stat* (file status returning) system calls. The data cache is resident on the local disk, but the UNIX I/O buffering mechanism does some caching of disk blocks in memory that is transparent to Venus.

A single client-level process on each file server services all file requests from clients. This process uses a lightweight-process package with nonpreemptable scheduling to service many client requests concurrently. The RPC package is integrated with the lightweight-process package, thereby allowing the file server to be concurrently making or servicing one RPC per lightweight process. RPC is built on top of a low-level datagram abstraction. Whole file transfer is implemented as a side effect of these RPC calls. There is one RPC connection per client, but there is no a priori binding of lightweight processes to these connections. Instead, a pool of lightweight processes services client requests on all connections. The use of a single multithreaded server process allows the caching of data structures needed to service requests. On the other hand, a crash of a single server process has the disastrous effect of paralyzing this particular server.

14.7.4 Sprite

Sprite is an experimental distributed operating system under development at the University of California at Berkeley. It is part of the Spur project, whose goal is the design and construction of a high-performance multiprocessor workstation. A preliminary version of Sprite is currently operational on interconnected Sun workstations.

Overview

Sprite designers envision the next generation of workstations as powerful machines with vast physical memory. The configuration for which Sprite is targeted is large and fast disks concentrated on a few server machines servicing the storage needs of hundreds of diskless workstations. The workstations are interconnected by several LANs. Because file caching is used, the large physical memories will compensate for the lack of local disks.

The interface that Sprite provides in general, and to the file system in particular, is much like the one provided by UNIX. The file system appears as a single UNIX tree encompassing all files and devices in the network, making them equally and transparently accessible from every workstation. The location transparency in Sprite is complete; there is no way to discern a file's network location from that file's name.

Unlike NFS, Sprite enforces consistency of shared files. Each read system call is guaranteed to return the most up-to-date data for a file, even if it is being opened concurrently by several remote processes. Thus, Sprite emulates a single time-sharing UNIX system in a distributed environment.

A unique feature of the Sprite file system is its interplay with the virtual-memory system. Most versions of UNIX use a special disk partition as a swapping area for virtual-memory purposes. In contrast, Sprite uses ordinary files, called *backing files*, to store the data and stacks of running processes. The basis for this design is that it simplifies process migration and enables flexibility and sharing of the space allocated for swapping. Backing files are cached in the main memories of servers, just like any other file. The designers claim that clients should be able to read random pages from server's (physical) cache faster than they can from local disks, which means that a server with a large cache may provide better paging performance than will local disk.

The virtual memory and file system share the same cache and negotiate on how to divide it according to their conflicting needs. Sprite allows the file cache on each machine to grow and shrink in response to changing demands of the machine's virtual memory and file system. This scheme is similar to Apollo's Domain operating system, which has a dynamically sized swap space.

We briefly mention some other features of Sprite. In contrast to UNIX, where only code can be shared among processes, Sprite provides a mechanism for sharing an address space between client processes on a single workstation. A process migration facility, which is transparent both to clients as well as the migrated process, is also provided.

Prefix Tables

Sprite presents its client with a single file-system hierarchy. The hierarchy is composed of several subtrees called *domains* (the Sprite term for component units), with each server providing storage for one or more domains. Each machine maintains a server map called a *prefix table*, whose function is to map domains to servers. The mapping is built and updated dynamically by a broadcast protocol that places a message on the network for all other network members to read. We first describe how the tables are used during name lookups, and later describe how the tables change dynamically.

Each entry in a prefix table corresponds to one of the domains. It contains the name of the topmost directory in the domain (called the prefix for the domain), the network address of the server storing the domain, and a numeric designator identifying the domain's root directory for the storing server. Typically, this designator is an index into the server table of open files; it saves repeating expensive name translation.

Every lookup operation for an absolute path name starts with the client searching its prefix table for the longest prefix matching the given file name. The client strips the matching prefix from the file name and sends the remainder of the name to the selected server along with the designator from the prefix-table entry. The server uses this designator to locate the root directory of the domain, and then proceeds by usual UNIX path-name translation for the remainder of the file name. If the server succeeds in completing the translation, it replies with a designator for the open file.

There are several cases where the server does not complete the lookup:

- When the server encounters an absolute path name in a symbolic link, it immediately returns to the client the absolute path name. The client looks up the new name in its prefix table and initiates another lookup with a new server.

- A path name can ascend past the root of a domain (because of a parent ".." component). In such a case, the server returns the remainder of the path name to the client. The latter combines the remainder with the prefix of the domain that was just exited to form a new absolute path name.

- A path name can also descend into a new domain. This can happen when an entry for a domain is absent from the table, and as a result the prefix of the domain above the missing domain is the longest matching prefix. The selected server cannot complete the path-name traversal since the latter descends outside its domain. Alternatively, when a root of a domain is beneath a working directory and a file in that domain is referred to with a relative path name, the server also cannot complete the translation. The solution to these situations is to place a marker to indicate domain boundaries (a mount point, in NFS terms). The marker is a special kind of file called a *remote link*. Similar to a symbolic link, its content is a file name — its own name in this case. When a server encounters a remote link, it returns the file name to the client.

Relative path names are treated much as they are in conventional UNIX. When a process specifies a new working directory, the prefix mechanism is used to open the working directory and both its server address and designator are saved in the process's state. When a lookup operation detects a relative path name, it sends the path name directly to the server for the current working directory, along with the latter's designator. Hence, from the server's point of view, there is no difference between relative and absolute name lookups.

So far, the key difference from mappings based on the UNIX mount mechanism was the initial step of matching the file name against the prefix table, instead of looking it up component by component. Systems (such as NFS and conventional UNIX) that employ a name-lookup cache create a similar effect of avoiding the component-by-component lookup once the cache holds the appropriate information.

Prefix tables are a unique mechanism mainly because of the way they evolve and change. When a remote link is encountered by the server, it indicates that the client lacks an entry for a domain — the domain whose remote link was encountered. To obtain the missing prefix information, a client broadcasts a file name. A *broadcast* is a network message that is seen by all systems on the network. The server storing that file responds with the prefix-table entry for this file, including the string to use as a prefix, the server's address, and the descriptor corresponding to the domain's root. The client then can fill in the details in its prefix table.

Initially each client starts with an empty prefix table. The broadcast protocol is invoked to find the entry for the root domain. More entries are added gradually as needed; a domain that has never been accessed will not appear in the table.

The server locations kept in the prefix table are hints that are corrected when found to be wrong. Hence, if a client tries to open a file and gets no response from the server, it invalidates the prefix-table entry and attempts a broadcast query. If the server has become available again, it responds to the broadcast and the prefix-table entry is reestablished. This same mechanism also works if the server reboots at a different network address, or if its domains are moved to other servers.

The prefix mechanism ensures that, whenever a server storing a domain is functioning, the domain's files can be opened and accessed from any machine regardless of the status of the servers of domains above the particular domain. Essentially, the built-in broadcast protocol enables dynamic configuration and a certain degree of robustness. Also, when a prefix for a domain exists in a client's table, a direct client-server connection is established as soon as the client attempts to open a file in that domain (in contrast to path name traversal schemes).

A machine with a local disk that wishes to keep private some local files can place an entry for the private domain in its prefix table and refusing to respond to broadcast queries about that domain. One of the uses of this provision can be for the directory /usr/tmp, which holds temporary files generated by many UNIX programs. Every workstation needs access to /usr/tmp. But workstations with local disks would probably prefer to use their own disk for the temporary space. Recall that the designers of Sprite expect reads from a server cache to be faster than those from a local disk, but do not predict this relationship for writes. They can set up their /usr/tmp domains for private use, with a network file server providing a public version of the domain for diskless clients. All broadcast queries for /usr/tmp would be handled by the public server.

A primitive form of read-only replication can also be provided. It can be arranged that servers storing a replicated domain give different clients different prefix entries (standing for different replicas) for the same domain. The same technique can be used for sharing binary files by different hardware types of machines.

Since the prefix tables bypass part of the directory-lookup mechanism, the permission checking done during lookup is bypassed too. The effect is that all programs implicitly have search permission along all the paths denoting prefixes of domains. If access to a domain is to be restricted, it must be restricted at or below the root of the domain.

Caching and Consistency

An important aspect of the Sprite file-system design is the extent of the use of caching techniques. Capitalizing on the large main memories and advocating diskless workstations, file caches are stored in memory, instead of on local disks (as in Andrew). Caching is used by both client and server workstations. The caches are organized on a block basis, rather than on a file basis (as in Andrew). The size of the blocks is currently 4K. Each block in the cache is virtually addressed by the file designator and a block location within the file. Using virtual addresses instead of physical disk addresses enables clients to create new blocks in the cache and to locate any block without the file inode being brought from the server.

When a read kernel call is invoked to read a block of a file, the kernel first checks its cache and returns the information from the cache, if it is present. If the block is not in the cache, the kernel reads it from disk (if the file is locally stored), or requests it from the server; in either case, the block is added to the cache, replacing the least recently used block. If the block is requested from the server, the server checks its own cache before issuing a disk I/O request, and adds the block to its cache, if the block was not already there. Currently, Sprite does not use read-ahead to speed up sequential read (in contrast to NFS).

A delayed-write approach is used to handle file modification. When an application issues a write kernel call, the kernel simply writes the block into its cache and returns to the application. The block is not written through to the server's cache or the disk until it is ejected from the cache, or 30 seconds have elapsed since the block was last modified. Hence, a block written on a client machine will be written to the server's cache in at most 30 seconds, and will be written to the server's disk after an additional 30 seconds. This policy results in better performance in exchange for the possibility of recent changes being lost in a crash.

Sprite employs a version-number scheme to enforce consistency of shared files. The version number of a file is incremented whenever a file is opened in write mode. When a client opens a file, it obtains from the server the file's current version number, which the client compares to the version number associated with the cached blocks for that file. If they are different, the client discards all cached blocks for the file and reloads its cache from the server when the blocks are needed. Because of the delayed-write policy, the server does not always have the current file data. Servers handle this situation by keeping track of the last writer for each file. When a client other than the last writer opens the file, the server forces the last writer to write all its modified data blocks back to the server's cache.

When a server detects (during an open operation) that a file is open on two or more workstations and at least one of them is writing the file, it disables client caching for that file. All subsequent reads and writes go through the server, which serializes the accesses. Caching is disabled on a file basis, resulting in only clients with open files being affected. Obviously, a substantial degradation of performance occurs when caching is disabled. A noncachable file becomes cachable again when it has been closed by all clients. A file may be cached simultaneously by several active readers.

This approach depends on the fact that the server is notified whenever a file is opened or closed. This prohibits performance optimizations such as name caching in which clients open files without contacting the file servers. Essentially, the servers are used as centralized control points for cache consistency. To fulfill this function, they must maintain state information about open files.

14.7.5   Locus

Locus is a project at the University of California at Los Angeles to build a full-scale distributed operating system. The system is upward-compatible with UNIX, but unlike NFS, UNIX United, and other UNIX-based distributed systems, the extensions are major and necessitate an entirely new kernel, rather than a modified one.

Overview

The Locus file system presents to clients and applications a single tree-structure naming hierarchy. This structure covers all objects (files, directories, executable files, and devices) of all the machines in the system. Locus names are fully transparent; it is not possible to discern from a name of an object the latter's location in the network. To a first approximation, there is almost no way to distinguish the Locus name structure from a standard UNIX tree.

A Locus file may correspond to a set of copies distributed on different sites. An additional transparency dimension is introduced since it is the system's responsibility to keep all copies up to date and ensure that access requests are served by the most recent available version. Clients may have control over both the number and location of replicated files. Conversely, clients may prefer to be totally unaware of the replication scheme. In Locus, file replication serves mainly to increase availability for reading purposes in the event of failures and partitions. A primary-copy approach is adopted for modifications.

Locus adheres to the same file-access semantics with which standard UNIX presents clients. Locus strives to provide these semantics in the distributed and replicated environment in which it operates. Alternate mechanisms of advisory and enforced locking of files and parts of files are also offered. Moreover, atomic updates of files are supported by *commit* and *abort* system calls.

Operation during failures and network partitions is emphasized in Locus's design. As long as a copy of a file is available, read requests can be served, and it is still guaranteed that the version read is the most recent available one. Automatic mechanisms take care to update stale copies of files at the time of the merge of their storage site to a partition.

Emphasis on high performance in the design of Locus led to the incorporation of networking functions (such as formatting, queuing, transmitting, and retransmitting messages) into the operating system. Specialized remote operations protocols were devised for kernel-to-kernel communication, in contrast to the prevalent approach of using the RPC protocol, or some other existing protocol. The reduction of the number of network layers has achieved high performance for remote operations. On the other hand, this specialized protocol hampers the portability of Locus to different networks and file systems.

An efficient but limited process facility called *server processes* (lightweight processes) was created for serving remote requests. These are processes that have no nonprivileged address space. All their code and stacks are resident in the operating system nucleus; they can call internal system routines directly, and can share some data. These processes are assigned to serve network requests that accumulate in a system queue. The system is configured with some number of these processes, but that number is automatically and dynamically altered during system operation.

The Name Structure

The logical name structure disguises both location and replication details from clients and applications. In effect, logical filegroups are joined together to form this unified structure. Physically, a logical filegroup is mapped to multiple *physical containers* (called also *packs*) that reside at various sites and that store replicas of the files of that filegroup. The pair <logical-filegroup-number, inode number>, which will be referred to as a file's *designator*, serves as a globally unique low-level name for a file. Observe that the designator itself hides both location and replication details.

Each site has a consistent and complete view of the logical name structure. A logical mount table is replicated globally and contains an entry for each logical filegroup. An entry records the file designator of the directory over which the filegroup is logically mounted, and indication of which site is currently responsible for access synchronization within the filegroup. The function of this site is explained subsequently. In addition, each site that stores a copy of the directory over which a subtree is mounted must keep that directory's inode in memory with an indication that it is mounted over. This is done so that any access from any site to that directory will be caught, allowing the standard UNIX mount indirection to function (via the logical mount table). A protocol, implemented within the mount and unmount Locus system calls, performs update of the logical mount tables on all sites, when necessary.

On the physical level, physical containers correspond to disk partitions and are assigned pack numbers that, together with a logical filegroup number, identify an individual pack. One of the packs is designated as the *primary copy*. A file must be stored at the site of the primary copy, and in addition can be stored at any subset of the other sites where there exists a pack corresponding to its filegroup. Thus, the primary copy stores the filegroup completely, whereas the rest of the packs might be partial.

Replication is especially useful for directories in the high levels of the name hierarchy. Such directories exhibit mostly read-only characteristics and are crucial for path-name translation of most files.

The various copies of a file are assigned the same inode number on all the filegroup's packs. Consequently, a pack has an empty inode slot for all files that it does not store. Data-page numbers may be different on different packs; hence, reference over the network to data pages use logical page numbers rather than physical ones. Each pack has a mapping of these logical numbers to its physical numbers. So that automatic replication management will be facilitated, each inode of a file copy contains a version number, determining which copy dominates other copies.

Each site has a container table, which maps logical filegroup numbers to disk locations for the filegroups that have packs locally on this site. When requests for accesses to files stored locally arrive at a site, this table is consulted to map the file designator to a local disk address.

Although globally unique file naming is very important most of the time, there are certain files and directories that are hardware and site specific (that is, /bin, which is hardware specific, and /dev, which is site specific). Locus provides transparent means for translating references to these traditional file names to a hardware- and site-specific files.

File Operations

Locus' approach to file operations is certainly a departure from the prevalent client-server model. Providing replicated files with synchronous access necessitates an additional function. Locus distinguishes three logical roles in file accesses, each one potentially performed by a different site:

- **Using site** (US). The US issues the requests to open and access a remote file.

- **Storage site** (SS). The SS is the site selected to serve the requests.

- **Current synchronization site** (CSS). The CSS enforces global synchronization policy for a filegroup, and selects an SS for each open request referring to a file in the filegroup. There is at most one CSS for each filegroup in any set of communicating sites (that is, a partition). The CSS maintains the version number and a list of physical containers for every file in the filegroup.

In the following subsections, we describe the open, read, write, close, commit, and abort operations, as they are carried out by the US, SS, and CSS entities. Related synchronization issues are described separately in the next subsection.

Opening a file commences as follows. The US determines the relevant CSS by looking up the filegroup in the logical mount table, and then forwards the open request to the CSS. The CSS polls potential SSs for that file to decide which one of them will act as the real SS. In its polling messages, the CSS includes the version number for the particular file, so that the potential SSs can, by comparing this number to their own, decide whether or not their copy is up to date. The CSS selects a SS by considering the responses it received from the candidate sites, and sends the selected SS identity to the US. Both the CSS and the SS allocate in-core inode structures for the opened file. The CSS needs this information to make future synchronization decisions, and the SS maintains the inode in order to serve forthcoming accesses efficiently.

After a file is open, read requests are sent directly to the SS without the CSS intervention. A read request contains the designator of the file, the logical number of the needed page within that file, and a guess as to where the in-core inode is stored in the SS. Once the inode is found, the SS translates the logical page number to a physical number, and a standard low-level routine is called to allocate a buffer and to obtain the appropriate page from disk. The buffer is queued on the network queue for transmission as a response to the US, where it is stored in a kernel buffer. Once a page is fetched to the US, further read calls are serviced from the kernel buffer. As in the case of local disk reads, read-ahead is useful to speed up sequential reads, both at the US and the SS.

If a process loses its connection with a file it is reading remotely, the system attempts to reopen a different copy of the same version of the file.

Translating a path name into a file designator proceeds by a seemingly conventional path-name traversal mechanism, since path names are regular UNIX path names, with no exceptions (unlike UNIX United). Every lookup of a component of the path name within a directory involves opening the latter and reading from it. Observe that there is no parallel to NFS's remote lookup operation and that the actual directory searching is performed by the client rather than by the server.

A directory opened for path-name searching is open not for normal read, but instead for an internal unsynchronized read. The distinction is that no global synchronization is needed, and no locking is done while the reading is performed; that is, updates to the directory can occur while the search is ongoing. When the directory is local, the CSS is not even informed of such access.

In Locus, a primary-copy policy is employed for file modification. The CSS has to select the primary-copy pack site as the SS for an open for a write. The act of modifying data takes on two forms. If the modification does not include the entire page, the old page is read from the SS using the read protocol. If the change involves the entire page, a buffer is set up at the US without any reads. In either case, after changes are made, possibly by delayed-write, the page is sent back to the SS. All modified pages must be flushed to the SS before a modified file can be closed.

If a file is closed by the last client process at a US, the SS and CSS must be informed so that they can deallocate in-core inode structures, and so that the CSS can alter state data that might affect its next synchronization decision.

Commit and abort system calls are provided, and closing a file commits it. If a file is open for modification by more that one process, the changes are not made permanent until one of the processes issues a commit system call or until all the processes close the file.

When a file is modified, shadow pages are allocated at the SS. The in-core copy of the disk inode is updated to point to these new shadow pages. The disk inode is kept intact, pointing to the original pages. The atomic commit operation consists of replacing the disk inode with the in-core inode. After that point, the file contains the new information. To abort a set of changes, we merely discard the in-core inode information and free up the disk space used to record the changes. The US function never deals with actual disk pages, but rather deals with logical pages. Thus, the entire shadow-page mechanism is implemented at the SS and is transparent to the US.

Locus deals with file modification by first committing the change to the primary copy. Later, messages are sent to all other SSs of the modified file as well as the CSS. At minimum, these messages identify the modified file and contain the new version number (to prevent attempts to read the old versions). At this point, it is the responsibility of these additional SSs to bring their up to date by propagating the entire file or just the changes. A queue of propagation requests is kept within the kernel at each site, and a kernel process services the queue efficiently by issuing appropriate read requests. This propagation procedure uses the standard commit mechanism. Thus, if contact with the file containing the newer version is lost, the local file is left with a coherent copy, albeit still out of date.

Given this commit mechanism, we are always left with either the original file or a completely changed file, but never with a partially made change, even in the face of site failures.

Synchronized Accesses to Files

Locus tries to emulate conventional UNIX semantics on file accesses in a distributed environment. In standard UNIX, multiple processes are permitted to have the same file open concurrently. These processes issue read and write system calls, and the system guarantees that each successive operation sees the effects of the ones that precede it. We can implement this scheme fairly easily by having the processes share the same operating-system data structures and caches, and by using locks on data structures to serialize requests. Since remote tasking is supported in Locus, such situations can arise when the sharing processes do not co-reside on the same machine and hence complicate the implementation significantly.

There are two sharing modes to consider. First, in UNIX, several processes descending from the same ancestor process can share the same current position (offset) in a file. A single token scheme is devised to preserve this special mode of sharing. A site can proceed to execute system calls that need the offset only when the token is present.

Second, in UNIX, the same in-core inode for a file can be shared by several processes. In Locus, the situation is much more complicated, since the inode of the file can be cached at several sites. Also, data pages are cached at multiple sites. A multiple-data-tokens scheme is used to synchronize sharing of the file's inode and data. A single exclusive-writer, multiple-readers policy is enforced. Only a site with the write token for a file may modify the file, and any site with a read token can read the file. Both token schemes are coordinated by token managers operating at the corresponding storage sites.

The cached data pages are guaranteed to contain valid data only when the file's data token is present. When the write data token is taken from that site, the inode is copied back to the SS, as are all modified pages. Since arbitrary changes may have occurred to the file when the token was not present, all cached buffers are invalidated when the token is released. When a data token is granted to a site, both the inode and data pages need to be fetched from the SS. There are some exceptions to this policy. Some attribute reading and writing calls (for example, *stat*), as well as directory reading and modifying (for example, *lookup*) calls are not subject to the synchronization constraints. These calls are sent directly to the SS, where the changes are made, committed, and propagated to all storage and using sites.

This mechanism guarantees consistency; each access sees the most recent data. A different issue regarding access synchronization is serializability of accesses. To this end, Locus offers facilities for locking entire files or parts of them. Locking can be advisory (checked only as a result of a locking attempt), or enforced (checked on all reads and writes). A process can choose either to fail if it cannot immediately get a lock or to wait for the lock to be released.

Operation in a Faulty Environment

The basic approach in Locus is to maintain, within a single partition, strict synchronization among copies of a file, so that all clients of that file within that partition see the most recent version.

The primary-copy approach eliminates the possibility of conflicting updates, since the primary copy must be in the client's partition to allow an update. However, the problem of detecting updates and propagating them to all the copies remains, especially since updates are allowed in a partitioned network. During normal operation, the commit protocol ascertains proper detection and propagation of updates, as was described earlier. However, a more elaborate scheme has to be employed by recovering sites that wish to bring their packs up to date. To this end, the system maintains a *commit count* for each filegroup, enumerating each commit of every file in the filegroup. Each pack has a *lower-water mark* (*lwm*) that is a commit-count value, up to which the system guarantees that all prior commits are reflected in the pack. Also, the primary copy pack keeps a complete list of all the recent commits in secondary storage. When a pack joins a partition, it contacts the primary copy site, and checks whether its lwm is within the recent commit-list bounds. If it is, the pack site schedules a kernel process, which brings the pack to a consistent state by performing the missing updates. If the primary pack is not available, writing is disallowed in this partition, but reading is possible after a new CSS is chosen. The new CSS communicates with the partition members so that it will be informed of the most recent available (in the partition) version of each file in the filegroup. Once the new CSS accomplishes this objective, other pack sites can reconcile themselves with it. As a result, all communicating sites see the same view of the filegroup, and this view is as complete as possible, given a particular partition. Note that, since updates are allowed within the partition with the primary copy, and reads are allowed in the rest of the partitions, it possible to read out-of-date replicas of a file. Thus, Locus sacrifices consistency for the ability to continue and both to update and to read files in a partitioned environment.

When a pack is too far out of date (that is, its *lwm* indicates a value prior to the earliest commit-count value in the primary-copy commit list), the system invokes an application-level process to bring the filegroup up to date. At this point, the system lacks sufficient knowledge of the most recent commits to redo the changes. Instead, the site must inspect the entire inode space to determine which files in its pack are out of date.

When a site is lost from an operational Locus network, a clean-up procedure is necessary. Essentially, once a site has decided that a particular site is unavailable, it must invoke failure handling for all resources that local processes were using at that site and for all local resources that processes were using at that site. This substantial cleaning procedure is the penalty of the state information kept by all three sites participating in file access.

Since directory updates are not restricted to being applied to the primary copy, conflicts among updates in different partitions may arise. However, because of the simple nature of directory-entry modification, an automatic reconciliation procedure is devised. This procedure is based on comparing the inodes and string-name pairs of replicas of the same directory. The most extreme action taken is when the same name string corresponds to two different inodes. The file's name is altered slightly, and the file's owner is notified by electronic mail.

14.8 Summary

A distributed file system (DFS) is a file-service system whose clients, servers, and storage devices are dispersed among the various sites of a distributed system. Accordingly, service activity has to be carried out across the network, and instead of a single centralized data repository there are multiple and independent storage devices.

Ideally, a DFS should look to its clients like a conventional, centralized file system. The multiplicity and dispersion of its servers and storage devices should be made transparent. That is, the client interface of a DFS should not distinguish between local and remote files. It is up to the DFS to locate the files and to arrange for the transport of the data. A transparent DFS facilitates client mobility by bringing over the client's environment to the site where a client logs in.

There are several approaches to naming schemes in a DFS. In the simplest approach, files are named by some combination of their host name and local name, which guarantees a unique systemwide name. Another approach, popularized by NFS, provides means to attach remote directories to local directories, thus giving the appearance of a coherent directory tree.

Requests to access a remote file are usually handled by two complementary methods. With remote service, requests for accesses are delivered to the server. The server machine performs the accesses, and their results are forwarded back to the client. With *caching*, if the data needed to satisfy the access request are not already cached, then a copy of those data is brought from the server to the client. Accesses are performed on the cached copy. The idea is to retain recently accessed disk blocks in the cache, so that repeated accesses to the same information can be handled locally, without additional network traffic. A replacement policy is used to keep the cache size bounded. The problem of keeping the cached copies consistent with the master file is the *cache-consistency problem*.

There are two approaches to server-side information. Either the server tracks each file being accessed by each client, or it simply provides blocks as they are requested by the client without knowledge of their use. This is is the stateful versus stateless service paradigm.

Replication of files on different machines is a useful redundancy for improving availability. Multimachine replication can benefit performance too, since selecting a nearby replica to serve an access request results in shorter service time.

Exercises

14.1 What are the benefits of a DFS when compared to a file system in a centralized system?

14.2 Which of the example DFSs would efficiently handle a large, multiclient database application most efficiently?   Explain your answer.

14.3 Under what circumstances would a client prefer a location-transparent DFS?   Under which would she prefer a location-independent DFS?   Discuss the reasons for these preferences.

14.4 What aspects of a distributed system would you select for a system running on a totally reliable network?

14.5 Compare and contrast the techniques of caching disk blocks locally, on a client system, and remotely, on a server.

14.6 What are the benefits of mapping objects into virtual memory, as Apollo Domain does?   What are the detriments?

Bibliographic Notes

Discussions concerning distributed file systems are offered by Gien [1978] (the File Transfer Protocol Scheme), Israel et al. [1978], and Sturgis et al. [1980] (general discussions concerning the design and use of distributed file systems), Swinehart et al. [1979] (the Woodstock file system), Birrell and Needham [1980] (a universal file server), Dion [1980] (the Cambridge file server), Fridrich and Older [1981] (the FELIX file server), and Chu [1969] (file allocation in a distributed environment). A comparison of two network-based file servers is presented by Mitchell and Dion [1982]. A distributed file service based on optimistic concurrency control is described by Mullender and Tanenbaum [1985].

Discussions concerning consistency and recovery control for replicated files are offered by Davcev and Burkhard [1985]. Wah [1984] discussed the issue of file placement on distributed computer systems.

UNIX United is described by Brownbridge et al. [1982] and Randell [1983]. The Locus system is discussed by Walker et al. [1983] and Popek and Walker [1985]. The Sprite system is described by Ousterhout et al. [1988], and Nelson et al. [1988]. Sun's Network File System (NFS) is presented in [Sandberg et al. 1985], [Sandberg 1987], and [Sun Microsystems 1990]. The Andrew system is discussed by Satyanarayanan et al. [1985], Morris et al. [1986], and Howard et al. [1988].

A detailed survey of mainly centralized file servers is found in Svobodova [1984]. The emphasis there is on support of atomic transactions and not on location transparency and naming.

The Roe system is discussed by Ellis and Floyd [1983]. The Eden system is described in Jessop et al. [1982], Almes et al. [1983], and Black [1985]. The system is based on the object-oriented and capability-based approaches [Levy 1984]. The Stork system is presented by Paris and Tichy [1983]. The Apollo Domain system is discussed by Leach et al. [1982].

PART 6

Case Studies

━━━━━━━━━━

We can now draw together the various concepts described in this book by describing real operating systems. Two UNIX-based operating systems are covered in detail — Berkeley 4.3BSD and Mach. These operating systems were chosen in part because UNIX at one time was almost small enough to understand and yet is not a ``toy'' operating system. Most of its internal algorithms were selected for *simplicity*, not for speed or sophistication. UNIX is readily available to departments of computer science, so many students may have access to it. Mach gives us an opportunity to study a modern operating system that provides compatibility with 4.3BSD but has a vastly different design and implementation.

In addition to Berkeley 4.3BSD and Mach, we briefly discuss several other highly influential operating systems. The order of presentation has been chosen to highlight the similarities and differences of the systems; it is not strictly chronological, and does not reflect the relative importance of the system.

15

The UNIX Operating System

Although operating system concepts can be considered in purely theoretical terms, it is often useful to see how they are implemented in practice. This chapter presents an in-depth examination of the 4.3BSD operating system, a version of UNIX, as an example of the various concepts presented in this book. By examining a complete, real system, we can see how the various concepts discussed in this book relate both to one another and to practice. We consider first a brief history of UNIX, and present its user and programmer interfaces. Then, we discuss the internal data structures and algorithms used by the UNIX kernel to support the user-programmer interface.

15.1 History

The first version of UNIX was developed in 1969 by Ken Thompson of the Research Group at Bell Laboratories to use an otherwise idle PDP-7. He was soon joined by Dennis Ritchie. Thompson, Ritchie, and other members of the Research Group produced the early versions of UNIX.

Ritchie had previously worked on the MULTICS project, and MULTICS had a strong influence on the newer operating system. Even the name UNIX is merely a pun on MULTICS. The basic organization of the file system, the idea of the command interpreter (the shell) as a user process, the use of a separate process for each command, the original line-editing characters (# to erase the last character and @ to erase the entire line), and numerous other features came directly from MULTICS. Ideas from various other operating systems, such as MIT's CTSS and the XDS-940 system, were also used.

Ritchie and Thompson worked quietly on UNIX for many years. Their work on the first version allowed them to move it to a PDP-11/20, for a second version. A third version resulted from rewriting most of the operating system in the systems programming language C, instead of the previously used assembly language. C was developed at Bell Laboratory to support UNIX. UNIX was also moved to larger PDP-11 models, such as the 11/45 and 11/70. Multiprogramming and other enhancements were added when it was rewritten in C and moved to systems (such as the 11/45) that had hardware support for multiprogramming.

As UNIX developed, it became widely used within Bell Laboratory and gradually spread to a few universities. The first version widely available outside Bell Laboratory was Version 6, released in 1976. (The version number for early UNIX systems corresponds to the edition number of the UNIX *Programmer's Manual* that was current when the distribution was made; the code and the manuals were revised independently.)

In 1978, Version 7 was distributed. This UNIX system ran on the PDP-11/70 and the Interdata 8/32, and is the ancestor of most modern UNIX systems. In particular, it was soon ported to other PDP-11 models and to the VAX computer line. The version available on the VAX was known as 32V. Research has continued since then.

After the distribution of Version 7 in 1978, the UNIX Support Group (USG) assumed administrative control and responsibility from the Research Group for distributions of UNIX within AT&T, the parent organization for Bell Laboratory. UNIX was becoming a product, not simply a research tool. The Research Group has continued to develop their own version of UNIX to support their own internal computing, however. Next came version 8, which included a facility called the *stream I/O system* that allows flexible configuration of kernel IPC modules. It also contained RFS, a remote file system similar to Sun's NFS. Next came versions 9 and 10 (the latter version released in 1989, which is available only within Bell Laboratory).

USG mainly provided support for UNIX within AT&T. The first external distribution from USG was System III, in 1982. System III incorporated features of Version 7, and 32V, and also of several UNIX systems developed by groups other than Research. Features of UNIX/RT, a real-time UNIX system, as well as numerous portions of the Programmer's Work Bench (PWB) software tools package were included in System III.

USG released System V in 1983; it is largely derived from System III. The divestiture of the various Bell operating companies from AT&T has left AT&T in a position to market System V aggressively. USG was restructured as the UNIX System Development Laboratory (USDL), which released UNIX System V Release 2 (V.2) in 1984. UNIX System V Release 2, Version 4 (V.2.4) added a new implementation of virtual memory with copy-on-write paging and shared memory. USDL was in turn replaced by AT&T Information Systems (ATTIS), which distributed System V Release 3 (V.3) in 1987. V.3 adapts the version V8 implementation of the stream I/O system and makes it available as STREAMS. It also includes RFS.

The small size, modularity, and clean design of early UNIX systems led to UNIX-based work at numerous other computer-science organizations, such as Rand, BBN, the University of Illinois, Harvard, Purdue, and even DEC. The most influential of the non-Bell Laboratory and non-AT&T UNIX development groups, however, has been the University of California at Berkeley.

The first Berkeley VAX UNIX work was the addition in 1978 of virtual memory, demand paging, and page replacement to 32V by Bill Joy and Ozalp Babaoglu to produce 3BSD UNIX. This was the first implementation of any of these facilities on any UNIX system. The large virtual memory space of 3BSD allowed the development of very large programs, such as Berkeley's own Franz LISP. The memory-management work convinced the Defense Advanced Research Projects Agency (DARPA) to fund Berkeley for the development of a standard UNIX system for government use; 4BSD UNIX was the result.

The 4BSD work for DARPA was guided by a steering committee that included many notable people from the UNIX and networking communities. One of the goals of this project was to provide support for the DARPA Internet networking protocols (TCP/IP). This support was provided in a general manner. It is possible in 4.2BSD to communicate uniformly among diverse network facilities, including local-area networks (such as Ethernets and token rings) and wide-area networks (such as NSFNET). This implementation was the most important reason for the current popularity of these protocols. It was used as the basis for the implementations of many vendors of UNIX computer systems, and even other operating systems. It permitted the Internet to grow from 60 connected networks in 1984 to more than 1000 in 1989.

In addition, Berkeley adapted many features from contemporary operating systems to improve the design and implementation of UNIX. Many of the terminal line-editing functions of the TENEX (TOPS-20) operating system were provided by a new terminal driver. A new user interface (the C Shell), a new text editor (ex/vi), compilers for Pascal and LISP, and many new systems programs were written at Berkeley. For 4.2BSD, certain efficiency improvements were inspired by the VMS operating system.

UNIX software from Berkeley is released in *Berkeley Software Distributions*. It is convenient to refer to the Berkeley VAX UNIX systems following 3BSD as 4BSD, although there were actually several specific releases, most notably 4.1BSD and 4.2BSD. The generic numbers 2BSD and 4BSD are used for the PDP-11 and VAX distributions of Berkeley UNIX. 4.2BSD, first distributed in 1983, was the culmination of the original Berkeley DARPA UNIX project, although further research continues at Berkeley. 2.9BSD is the equivalent version for PDP-11 systems.

In 1986, 4.3BSD was released. It was so similar to 4.2BSD that its manuals described 4.2BSD better than the 4.2BSD manuals did. It did include numerous internal changes, however, including bug fixes and performance improvements. Some new facilities were also added, including support for the Xerox Network System protocols.

4.3BSD Tahoe is the latest version, released in 1988. It includes various new developments, such as improved networking congestion control and TCP/IP performance. Also, disk configurations were separated from the device drivers, and are now read off of the disks themselves. Expanded time-zone support is also included. 4.3BSD Tahoe was actually developed on and for the CCI Tahoe system (Computer Console, Inc., Power 6 computer), rather than for the usual VAX base. The corresponding PDP-11 release is 2.10.1BSD, which is distributed by the USENIX Association, which also publishes the 4.3BSD manuals.

4BSD was the operating system of choice for VAXes from its initial release (1979) until the release of System III (1982). 4BSD is still the best choice for many research and networking installations. Many organizations would buy a 32V license and order 4BSD from Berkeley without even bothering to get a 32V tape.

The current set of UNIX systems is not limited to those by Bell Laboratory, AT&T, and Berkeley, however. As UNIX has grown in popularity, it has been moved to many different computers and computer systems. A wide variety of UNIX, and UNIX-like, operating systems have been created. DEC supports its UNIX (called Ultrix) for VAXes; Microsoft rewrote UNIX for the Intel 8088 family and called it XENIX; IBM has UNIX (AIX) on its PCs, workstations, and mainframes. In fact, UNIX is available on almost all general-purpose computers; it runs on personal computers, workstations, minicomputers, mainframes, and supercomputers, from Apple Macintosh IIs to Cray IIs. Because of its wide availability, it is used in environments ranging from academic to military to manufacturing process control. Most of these systems are based on Version 7, System III, 4.2BSD, or System V.

The wide popularity of UNIX with computer vendors has made UNIX the most portable of operating systems, and has made it possible for users to expect a UNIX environment independent of any specific computer manufacturer. But the large number of implentations of the system has led to remarkable variation in the programming and user interfaces distributed by the vendors. For true vendor independence, application-program developers need consistent interfaces. This would allow all "UNIX" applications to run on all UNIX systems, which is certainly not the current situation. This issue has become important as UNIX has become the preferred program-development platform for applications ranging from databases to graphics and networking, and has led to a strong market demand for UNIX standards.

There are several standardization projects underway, starting with the *lusr/group 1984 Standard* sponsored by the UniForum industry user's group. Since then, many official standards bodies have continued the effort, including IEEE and ISO (the POSIX standard). The X/Open Group international consortium is also working on a Common Application Environment, which subsumes the IEEE interface standard. Finally, the ANSI standards body is even standardizing the C programming language. If these projects succeed, one flavor on UNIX (and C) will prevail, allowing UNIX to become even more popular. There are in fact two separate sets of powerful UNIX vendors working on this problem: the AT&T-guided UNIX International (UI) and the Open Software Foundation(OSF) have both agreed to follow the POSIX standard while going their own way in other areas.

AT&T replaced its ATTIS group in 1989 with the UNIX Software Organization (USO), which recently shipped the first merged UNIX, System V Release 4. This system combines features from System V, 4.3BSD, and Sun's SunOS, including long file names, the Berkeley file system, symbolic links, multiple access groups, job control, and reliable signals; it also conforms to the published POSIX standards.

Figure 15.1 summarizes the relationships among the various versions of UNIX.

Meanwhile, CSRG continues work on the next BSD release. This probably will be a testing ground for new features, which will be incorporated in other, nonexperimental UNIX implementations. Currently planned are POSIX compatibility, the POSIX terminal driver, and ISO-OSI networking.

The UNIX system has grown from a personal project of two Bell Laboratory employees to an operating system being defined by multinational standardization bodies. Yet this system is still of interest to academia. We believe that UNIX has become and will remain an important part of operating-system theory and practice. UNIX is an excellent vehicle for academic study. For example, the Tunis operating system, the Xinu operating system, and the Minix operating system are based on the concepts of UNIX, but were developed explicitly for classroom study. There is a plethora of ongoing UNIX-related research systems, including Mach, Chorus, Comandos, and Roisin. The original

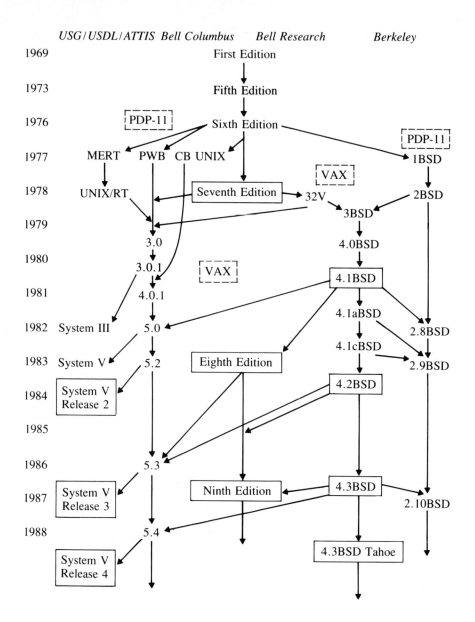

Figure 15.1   History of UNIX versions.

developers, Ritchie and Thompson, were honored in 1983 by the Association for Computing Machinery Turing award for their work on UNIX.

The specific UNIX version used in this chapter is the VAX version of 4.3BSD. This system is used because it implements many interesting operating-system concepts, such as demand paging and networking. It has also been influential in other UNIX systems, in standards, and in networking developments. The VAX implementation is used because 4.3BSD was developed on the VAX and that machine still represents a convenient point of reference, despite the recent proliferation of implementations on other hardware (such as the Motorola 68000 and 88000, the National 32032, the Intel i286, i386, and i486, the Sun SPARC, and the MIPS RISC CPUs).

15.2 Design Principles

UNIX was designed to be a time-sharing system. The standard user interface (the shell) is simple and may be replaced by another, if desired. The file system is a multilevel tree, which allows users to create their own subdirectories. All user data files are simply a sequence of bytes.

Disk files and I/O devices are treated as similarly as possible. Thus, device dependencies and peculiarities are kept in the kernel as much as possible, and even in the kernel most of them are confined to the device drivers.

UNIX supports multiple processes. A process can easily create new processes. CPU scheduling is a simple priority algorithm. Memory management is a variable-region algorithm with swapping. 4.3BSD uses demand paging as a mechanism to support memory-management and CPU-scheduling decisions.

Because UNIX was originated first by one programmer, Ken Thompson, and then by another, Dennis Ritchie, as a system for their own convenience, it was small enough to understand. Most of the algorithms were selected for *simplicity*, not for speed or sophistication. The intent was to have the kernel and libraries provide a small set of facilities that was sufficiently powerful to allow one to build a more complex system if one were needed. UNIX's clean design has resulted in many imitations and modifications.

Although the designers of UNIX had a significant amount of knowledge about other operating systems, UNIX had no elaborate design spelled out before its implementation. This flexibility appears to have been one of the key factors in the development of the system. Some design principles were involved, however, even though they were not spelled out at the outset.

UNIX was designed by programmers for programmers. Thus, it has always been interactive, and facilities for program development have always been a high priority. Such facilities include the program *make* (which can be used to check to see which of a collection of source files for a program need to be compiled, and then to do the compiling) and the *Source Code Control System (SCCS)* (which is used to keep successive versions of files available without having to store the entire contents of each step).

The operating system is written mostly in C, which was developed to support UNIX, since neither Thompson nor Ritchie enjoyed programming in assembly language. The avoidance of assembly language was also necessary because of the uncertainty about the machine or machines on which UNIX would be run. It has greatly simplified the problems of moving UNIX from one hardware system to another.

From the beginning, UNIX development systems have had all the UNIX sources available on-line, and the developers have used the systems under development as their primary systems. This has greatly facilitated the discovery of deficiencies and their fixes, as well as of new possibilities and their implementations. It has also encouraged the plethora of UNIX variants existing today, but the benefits have outweighed the disadvantages: if something is broken, it can be fixed at a local site, rather than having to wait for the next release of the system. Such fixes, as well as new facilities, may be incorporated into later distributions.

The size constraints of the PDP-11 (and earlier computers used for UNIX) have forced a certain elegance. Where other systems have elaborate algorithms for dealing with pathological conditions, UNIX just does a controlled crash called *panic*. Instead of attempting to cure such conditions, UNIX tries to prevent them. Where other systems would use brute force or macro expansion, UNIX mostly has had to develop more subtle, or at least simpler, approaches.

These early strengths of UNIX produced much of its popularity, which in turn produced new demands that challenged those strengths. UNIX was used for tasks such as networking, graphics, and real-time operation, which did not always fit into its original text-oriented model. Thus, changes were made to some internal facilities and new programming interfaces were added. These new facilities, and others — particularly window interfaces — required large amounts of code to support them, radically increasing the size of the system. For instance, networking and windowing both doubled the size of the system. This in turn pointed out the continued strength of UNIX — whenever a new development occurred in the industry, UNIX could usually absorb it, but still remain UNIX.

15.3 Programmer Interface

As do most computer systems, UNIX consists of two separable parts: the kernel and the systems programs. We can view the UNIX operating system as being layered, as shown in Figure 15.2. Everything below the system-call interface and above the physical hardware is the *kernel*. The kernel provides the file system, CPU scheduling, memory management, and other operating-system functions through system calls. Systems programs use the kernel-supported system calls to provide useful functions, such as compilation and file manipulation.

System calls define the *programmer interface* to UNIX; the set of systems programs commonly available defines the *user interface*. The programmer and user interface define the context that the kernel must support.

System calls in VAX 4.2BSD are made by a trap to location 40 of the VAX interrupt vectors. Parameters are passed to the kernel on the hardware stack; the kernel returns values in registers R0 and R1. Register R0 may also return an error code. The carry bit distinguishes a normal return from an error return.

This level of detail is seldom seen by the UNIX programmer, fortunately. Most systems programs are written in C, and the *UNIX Programmer's Manual* presents all system calls as C functions. A system program written in C for 4.3BSD on the VAX can generally be moved to

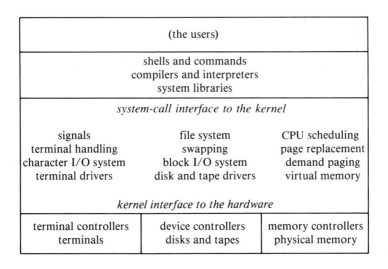

(the users)		
shells and commands compilers and interpreters system libraries		
system-call interface to the kernel		
signals terminal handling character I/O system terminal drivers	file system swapping block I/O system disk and tape drivers	CPU scheduling page replacement demand paging virtual memory
kernel interface to the hardware		
terminal controllers terminals	device controllers disks and tapes	memory controllers physical memory

Figure 15.2   4.3BSD layer structure.

another 4.3BSD system and simply recompiled, even though hardware details may be quite different. The details of system calls are known only to the compiler. This is a major reason for the portability of UNIX programs.

System calls for UNIX can be roughly grouped into three categories: file manipulation, process control, and information manipulation. In Chapter 3, we listed a fourth, device manipulation, but since devices in UNIX are treated as (special) files, the same system calls support both files and devices (although there is an extra system call for setting device parameters).

15.3.1 File Manipulation

A *file* in UNIX is a sequence of bytes. Different programs expect various levels of structure, but the kernel does not impose a structure on files. For instance, the convention for text files is lines of ASCII characters separated by a single newline character (which is the linefeed character in ASCII), but the kernel knows nothing of this convention.

Files are organized in tree-structured *directories*. Directories are themselves files that contain information on how to find other files. A *path name* to a file is a text string that identifies a file by specifying a path through the directory structure to the file. Syntactically, it consists of individual file-name elements separated by the slash character. For example, in */usr/local/font*, the first slash indicates the root of the directory tree, called the *root* directory. The next element, *usr*, is a subdirectory of the root, *local* is a subdirectory of *usr*, and *font* is a file or directory in the directory *local*. Whether *font* is an ordinary file or a directory cannot be determined from the path-name syntax.

UNIX has both *absolute path names* and *relative path names*. Absolute path names start at the root of the file system and are distinguished by a slash at the beginning of the path name; */usr/local/font* is an absolute path name. Relative path names start at the *current directory*, which is an attribute of the process accessing the path name. Thus, *local/font* indicates a file or directory named *font* in the directory *local* in the current directory, which might or might not be */usr*.

A file may be known by more than one name in one or more directories. Such multiple names are known as *links*, and all links are treated equally by the operating system. 4.3BSD also supports *symbolic links*, which are files containing the absolute path name of another file. The two kinds of links are also known as *hard links* and *soft links*. Soft (symbolic) links, unlike hard links, may point to directories and may cross file-system boundaries.

The file name "." in a directory is a hard link to the directory itself. The file name ".." is a hard link to the parent directory. Thus, if the current directory is */user/jlp/programs*, then *../bin/wdf* refers to */user/jlp/bin/wdf*.

Hardware devices have names in the file system. These *device special files* or *special files* are known to the kernel as device interfaces, but are nonetheless accessed by the user by much the same system calls as are other files.

Figure 15.3 shows a typical UNIX file system. The root (/) normally contains a small number of directories as well as */vmunix*, the binary boot image of the operating system; */dev* contains the device special files, such as */dev/console*, */dev/lp0*, */dev/mt0*, and so on; */bin* contains the binaries of the essential UNIX systems programs. Other binaries may be in */usr/bin* (for "applications" systems programs such as text formatters), */usr/ucb* (for systems programs written by Berkeley rather than AT&T), or */usr/local/bin* (for systems programs written at the local site). Library files — such as the C, Pascal, and FORTRAN subroutine libraries — are kept in */lib* (or */usr/lib* or */usr/local/lib*).

The files of users themselves are stored in a separate directory for each user, typically in */user*. Thus, the user directory for *carol* would normally be in */user/carol*. For a large system, these directories may be further grouped to ease administration, creating a file structure with */user/prof/avi* and */user/staff/carol*. Administrative files and programs, such as the password file, are kept in */etc*. Temporary files can be put in */tmp*, which is normally erased once a day, or */usr/tmp*.

Each of these directories may have considerably more structure. For example, the font-description tables for the troff formatter for the Merganthaler 202 typesetter are kept in */usr/lib/troff/dev202*. All the conventions concerning the location of specific files and directories have been defined by programmers and their programs; the operating-system kernel needs only */etc/init*, which is used to initialize terminal processes, to be operable.

System calls for basic file manipulation are *creat, open, read, write, close, unlink*, and *trunc*. The *creat* system call, given a path name, creates an (empty) file (or truncates an existing one). An existing file is opened by the *open* system call, which takes a path name and a mode (such as read, write, or read/write) and returns a small integer, called a *file descriptor*. A file descriptor may then be passed to a *read* or *write* system call (along with a buffer address and the number of bytes to transfer) to perform data transfers to or from the file. A file is closed when its file descriptor is passed to the *close* system call. The *trunc* call reduces the length of a file to zero.

A file descriptor is an index into a small table of open files for this process. Descriptors start at 0 and seldom get higher than 6 or 7 for typical programs, depending on the maximum number of simultaneously open files.

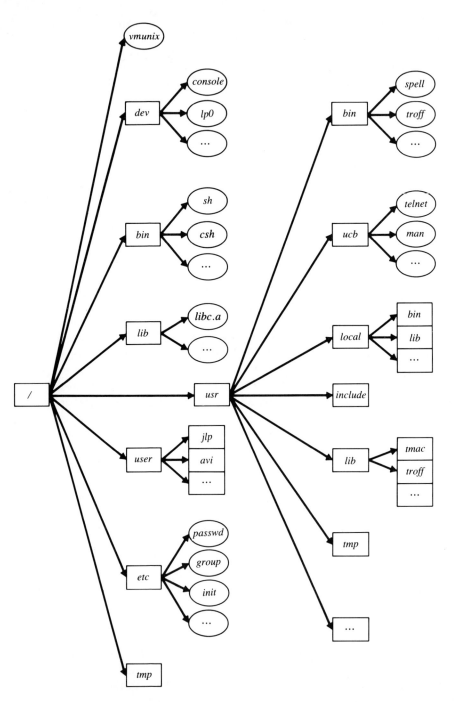

Figure 15.3   Typical UNIX directory structure.

Each *read* or *write* updates the current offset into the file, which is associated with the file-table entry and is used to determine the position in the file for the next *read* or *write*. The *lseek* system call allows the position to be reset explicitly. The *dup* and *dup2* system calls can be used to produce a new file descriptor that is a copy of an existing one. The *fcntl* system call can also do that, and in addition can examine or set various parameters of an open file. For example, it can make each succeeding write to an open file append to the end of that file. There is an additional system call, *ioctl*, for manipulating device parameters.

Information about the file (such as its size, protection modes, owner, and so on) can be obtained by the *stat* system call. Several system calls allow some of this information to be changed: *rename* (change file name), *chmod* (change the protection modes), and *chown* (change the owner and group). Many of these system calls have variants that apply to file descriptors instead of file names. The *link* system call makes a hard link for an existing file, creating a new name for an existing file. A link is removed by the *unlink* system call; if it is the last link, the file is deleted. The *symlink* system call makes a symbolic link.

Directories are made by the *mkdir* system call and are deleted by *rmdir*. The current directory is changed by *cd*.

Although it is possible to use the standard file calls (*open* and others) on directories, it is inadvisable to do so, since directories have an internal structure that must be preserved. Instead, another set of system calls is provided to open a directory, to step through each file entry within the directory, to close the directory, and to perform other functions; these are *opendir*, *readdir*, *closedir*, and others.

15.3.2 Process Control

A *process* is a program in execution. Processes are identified by their *process identifier*, which is an integer. A new process is created by the *fork* system call. The new process consists of a copy of the address space of the original process (the same program and the same variables with the same values). Both processes (the parent and the child) continue execution at the instruction after the *fork* with one difference: The return code for the *fork* is zero for the new (child) process, whereas the (nonzero) process identifier of the child is returned to the parent.

Typically, the *execve* system call is used after a fork by one of the two processes to replace its virtual memory space with a new program. The *execve* system call loads a binary file into memory (destroying the memory image of the program containing the *execve* system call) and starts its execution.

A process may terminate by using the *exit* system call, and its parent process may wait for that event by using the *wait* system call. If the child process crashes, the system simulates the exit call. The *wait* system call provides the process id of a terminated child so that the parent can tell which of possibly many children terminated. A second system call, *wait3*, is similar to *wait* but also allows the parent to collect performance statistics about the child. Between the time the child exits, and the time the parent completes one of the *wait* system calls, the child is a *zombie*. A zombie process can do nothing, but exists merely so the parent can collect its status information. If the parent process of a zombie exits before a child, the zombie is inherited by the init process (which in turn *wait*s on it). A typical use of these facilities is shown in Figure 15.4.

The simplest form of communication between processes is by *pipes*, which may be created before the *fork*, and whose endpoints are then set up between the *fork* and the *execve*. A pipe is essentially a queue of bytes between two processes. The pipe is accessed by a file descriptor, like an ordinary file. One process writes into the pipe and the other reads from the pipe. The size of the original pipe system was fixed by the system. With 4.3BSD, pipes are implemented on top of the socket system, which has variable-sized buffers. Reading from an empty pipe or writing into a full pipe causes the process to be blocked until the state of the pipe changes. Special arrangements are needed for a pipe to be placed between a parent and child (so only one is reading and one is writing).

All user processes are descendants of one original process, called *init* (which has process identifier 1). Each terminal port available for interactive use has a *getty* process forked for it by *init*. The *getty* process initializes terminal line parameters and waits for a user's *login name*, which it passes through an *execve* as an argument to a *login* process. The *login* process collects the user's password, encrypts the password, and compares the result to an encrypted string taken from the file

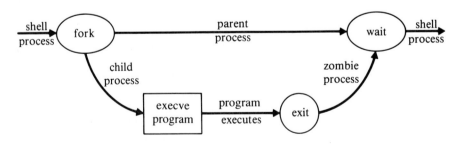

Figure 15.4 A shell forks a subprocess to execute a program.

/etc/passwd. If the comparison is successful, the user is allowed to log in. The *login* process executes a *shell*, or command interpreter, after setting the numeric *user identifier* of the process to that of the user logging in. (The shell and the user identifier are found in /etc/passwd by the user's login name.)   It is with this shell that the user ordinarily communicates for the rest of the login session; the shell itself forks subprocesses for the commands the user tells it to execute.

The user identifier is used by the kernel to determine the user's permissions for certain system calls, especially those involving file accesses. There is also a *group identifier*, which is used to provide similar privileges to a collection of users. In 4.3BSD a process may be in several groups simultaneously. The *login* process puts the shell in all the groups permitted to the user by the files /etc/passwd and /etc/group.

There are actually two user identifiers used by the kernel: the *effective user identifier* is the identifier used to determine file access permissions. If the file of a program being loaded by an *execve* has the *setuid* bit set in its inode, the effective user identifier of the process is set to the user identifier of the owner of the file, while the *real user identifier* is left as it was.   This allows certain processes to have more than ordinary privileges while still being executable by ordinary users. The setuid idea was patented by Dennis Ritchie (U.S. Patent 4,135,240) and is one of the distinctive features of UNIX. There is a similar *setgid* bit for groups.   A process may determine its real and effective user identifier with the *getuid* and *geteuid* calls, respectively. The *getgid* and *getegid* calls determine the process identifier and group identifier, respectively.   The rest of a process's groups may be found with the *getgroups* system call.

15.3.3 Signals

Signals are a facility for handling exceptional conditions similar to software interrupts. There are 20 different signals, each corresponding to a distinct condition. A signal may be generated by a keyboard interrupt, by an error in a process (such as a bad memory reference), or by a number of asynchronous events (such as timers or job-control signals from the shell). Almost any signal may also be generated by the *kill* system call.

The *interrupt* signal, SIGINT, is used to stop a command before it completes. It is usually produced by the ^C character (ASCII 3) or, in the more traditional configuration, the *delete* character (ASCII 127). In 4.2BSD, the important keyboard characters are defined by a table for each terminal and can be redefined easily. The *quit* signal, SIGQUIT, is usually produced by the \ character (ASCII 28). The *quit* signal both stops the currently executing program and dumps the latter's current memory image to a file named *core* in the current directory. The core file can be used by debuggers. SIGILL is produced by an illegal instruction and SIGSEGV by an attempt to address memory outside of the legal virtual memory space of a process.

Arrangements can be made either for most signals to be ignored (to have no effect), or for a routine in the user process (a signal handler) to be called. A signal handler may safely do one of two things before returning from catching a signal — call the *exit* system call, or modify a global variable. There is one signal (the *kill* signal, number 9, SIGKILL) that cannot be ignored or caught by a signal handler. SIGKILL is used, for example, to kill a runaway process that is ignoring other signals such as SIGINT or SIGQUIT.

Signals can be lost: If another signal of the same kind is sent before a previous signal has been accepted by the process to which it is directed, the first signal will be overwritten and only the last signal will be seen by the process. Also, there is no relative priority among UNIX signals. If two different signals are sent to the same process at the same time, it is indeterminate which one the process will receive first.

Signals were originally intended to deal with exceptional events. As is true of the use of most other features in UNIX, however, signal use has steadily expanded. 4.1BSD introduced job control, which uses signals to start and stop subprocesses on demand. This facility allows one shell to control multiple processes: starting, stopping, and backgrounding them as the user wishes. 4.3BSD added the SIGWINCH signal, invented by Sun Microsystems, for informing a process that the window in which output is being displayed has changed size. Signals are also used to deliver urgent data from network connections.

Users also wanted more reliable signals, and a bug fix in an inherent race condition in the old signals implementation. Thus, 4.2BSD also brought with it a race-free, reliable, separately implemented signal capability. It allows individual signals to be blocked during critical sections, and has a new system call to let a process sleep until interrupted. It is similar to hardware-interrupt functionality. It is now part of the POSIX standard.

15.3.4 Process Groups

Groups of related processes frequently cooperate to accomplish a common task. For instance, processes may create, and communicate over, pipes. Such a set of processes is termed a *process group*, or a *job*. Signals may be sent to all processes in a group. A process usually inherits its process group from its parent, but the *setpgrp* system call allows a process to change its group.

Process groups are used by the C shell to control the operation of multiple jobs. Any one process group may have its I/O attached to a terminal at one time. This *foreground* job has the attention of the user on that terminal while all other nonattached jobs (*background* jobs) perform their function without user interaction. Access to the terminal is controlled by process group signals. Each job has a *controlling terminal* (again, inherited from its parent). If the process group of the controlling terminal matches the group of a process, that process is in the foreground, and is allowed to perform I/O. If a nonmatching (background) process attempts the same, a SIGTTIN or SIGTTOU signal is sent to its process group. This usually results in the process group freezing until it is foregrounded by the user, at which point it receives a SIGCONT signal, indicating they may perform the I/O. Similarly, a SIGSTOP may be sent to the foreground process group to freeze it.

15.3.5 Information Manipulation

System calls exist to set and return both an interval timer (*getitimer/setitimer*) and the current time (*gettimeofday/settimeofday*) in microseconds. In addition, processes can ask for their process identifier (*getpid*), their group identifier (*getgid*), the name of the machine on which they are executing (*gethostname*), and many other values.

15.3.6 Library Routines

The system-call interface to UNIX is supported and augmented by a large collection of library routines and header files. The header files provide the definition of complex data structures used in system calls. In addition, a large library of functions provides additional program support.

For example, the UNIX I/O system calls provide for the reading and writing of blocks of bytes. Some applications may want to read and write only 1 byte at a time. Although it would be possible to read and write 1 byte at a time, this would require a system call for each byte — a very high overhead. Instead, a set of standard library routines (the standard I/O package accessed through the header file *<stdio.h>*) provides another interface, which reads and writes several thousand bytes at a time using local buffers, and transfers between these buffers (in user memory) when I/O is desired. Formatted I/O is also supported by the standard I/O package.

Additional library support is provided for mathematical functions, network access, data conversion, and so on. The 4.3BSD kernel supports over 150 system calls; the C program library has over 300 library functions. Although the library functions eventually result in system calls where necessary (for example, the *getchar* library routine will result in a *read* system call if the file buffer is empty), it is generally unnecessary for the programmer to distinguish between the basic set of kernel system calls and the additional functions provided by library functions.

15.4 User Interface

Both the programmer and the user of a UNIX system deal mainly with the set of systems programs that have been written and are available for execution. These programs make the necessary system calls to support their function, but the system calls themselves are contained within the program and do not need to be obvious to the user.

The common systems programs can be grouped into several categories; most of them are file or directory oriented. For example, the system programs to manipulate directories are: *mkdir* to create a new directory, *rmdir* to remove a directory, *cd* to change the current directory to another, and *pwd* to print the absolute path name of the current (working) directory.

The *ls* program lists the names of the files in the current directory. Any of 18 options can ask that properties of the files be displayed also. For example, the *-l* option asks for a long listing, showing the file name, owner, protection, date and time of creation, and size. The *cp* program creates a new file that is a copy of an existing file. The *mv* program moves a file from one place to another in the directory tree. In most cases, this move simply requires a renaming of the file; if necessary, however, the file is copied to the new location and the old copy is deleted. A file is deleted by the *rm* program (which makes an *unlink* system call).

To display a file on the terminal, a user can run *cat*. The *cat* program takes a list of files and concatenates them, copying the result to the standard output, commonly the terminal. On a high-speed cathode-ray tube (CRT) display of course, the file may speed by too fast to be read. The *more* program displays the file one screen at a time, pausing until the user types a character to continue to the next screen. The *head* program displays just the first few lines of a file; *tail* shows the last few lines.

These are the basic systems programs widely used in UNIX. In addition, there are a number of editors (*ed, sed, emacs, vi,* and so on), compilers (C, Pascal, FORTRAN, and so on), and text formatters (TROFF, TEX, SCRIBE, and so on). There are also programs for sorting (*sort*) and comparing files (*cmp, diff*), looking for patterns (*grep, awk*), sending mail to other users (*mail*), and many other activities.

15.4.1 Shells and Commands

Both user-written and systems programs are normally executed by a command interpreter. The command interpreter in UNIX is a user process like any other. It is called a *shell*, as it surrounds the kernel of the operating system. Users can write their own shell, and there are in fact several shells in general use. The *Bourne shell*, written by Steve Bourne, is probably the most widely used — or at least is the most widely available. The *C shell*, mostly the work of Bill Joy, a founder of Sun Microsystems, is the most popular on BSD systems. The Korn shell, by Dave Korn, has been quite popular in recent years.

The common shells share much of their command-language syntax. UNIX is normally an interactive system. The shell indicates its readiness to accept another command by typing a prompt, and the user types a command on a single line. For instance, in the line

$$\% \; ls \; -l$$

the percent sign is the usual C shell prompt and the *ls -l* (typed by the user) is the (long) list-directory command. Commands may take arguments, which the user types after the command name on the same line, separated by white space (spaces or tabs).

Although there are a few commands built into the shells (such as *cd*), a typical command is an executable binary object file. A list of several directories, the *search path*, is kept by the shell. For each command, each of the directories in the search path is searched, in order, for a file of the same name. If a file is found, it is loaded and executed. The search path can be set by the user. The directories */bin* and */usr/bin* are almost always in the search path, and a typical search path on a BSD system might be

$$(\; . \; /home/prof/avi/bin \; /usr/local/bin \; /usr/ucb \; /bin \; /usr/bin \;)$$

The *ls* command's object file is */bin/ls* and the shell itself is */bin/sh* (the Bourne shell) or */bin/csh* (the C shell).

Execution of a command is done by a *fork* system call followed by an *execve* of the object file. The shell usually then does a *wait* to suspend its own execution until the command completes (Figure 15.4). There is a simple syntax (an ampersand [&] at the end of the command line) to indicate that the shell should *not* wait for the completion of the command. A command left running in this manner while the shell continues to interpret further commands is said to be a *background* command, or to be running in the background. Processes for which the shell *does* wait are said to run in the *foreground*.

The C shell in 4.3BSD systems provides a facility called *job control* (partially implemented in the kernel), as mentioned previously. Job control allows processes to be moved between the foreground and the background. The processes can be stopped and restarted on various conditions, such as a background job wanting input from the user's terminal. This scheme allows most of the control of processes provided by windowing or layering interfaces, but requires no special hardware. Job control is also very useful in window systems, such as the X Window System developed at MIT. Each window is treated as a terminal, allowing multiple processes to be in the foreground (one per window) at any one time. Of course, background processes may exist on any of the windows. The Korn shell also supports job control, and it is likely that job control (and process groups) will be standard in future versions of UNIX.

15.4.2 Standard I/O

Processes may open files as they like, but most processes expect three file descriptors (numbers 0, 1, and 2) to be open when they start. These file descriptors are inherited across the *execve* (and possibly the *fork*) that created the process. They are known as *standard input* (0), *standard output* (1), and *standard error* (2). All three are frequently open to the user's terminal. Thus, the program can read what the user types by reading standard input, and the program can send output to the user's screen by writing to standard output. The standard error file descriptor is also open for writing and is used for error output; standard output is used for ordinary output. Most programs can also accept a file (rather than a terminal) for standard input and standard output.

The common shells have a simple syntax for changing what files are open for the standard I/O streams of a process. Changing a standard file is called *I/O redirection*. The syntax for I/O redirection is shown in Figure 15.5. In this example, the *ls* command produces a listing of the names of files in the current directory, the *pr* command formats that list into pages suitable for a printer, and the *lpr* command spools the formatted output to a printer, such as */dev/lp0*. The next command forces all output and all error messages to be redirected to a file. Without the ampersand, errors appear on the terminal.

15.4.3 Pipelines, Filters, and Shell Scripts

The first three commands of Figure 15.5 could have been done in the one command

% *ls | pr | lpr*

Command	Meaning of command
% ls > filea	direct output of *ls* to file *filea*
% pr < filea > fileb	input from *filea* and output to *fileb*
% lpr < fileb	input from *fileb*
%	
% make program >& errs	save both standard output and standard error in a file

Figure 15.5 Standard I/O redirection.

Each vertical bar tells the shell to arrange for the output of the preceding command to be passed as input to the following command. A pipe is used to carry the data from one process to the other. One process writes into one end of the pipe, and another process reads from the other end. In the example, the write end of one pipe would be set up by the shell to be the standard output of *ls*, and the read end of the pipe would be the standard input of *pr*; there would be another pipe between *pr* and *lpr*.

A command such such as *pr* that passes its standard input to its standard output, performing some processing on it, is called a *filter*. Many UNIX commands can be used as filters. Complicated functions can be pieced together as pipelines of common commands. Also, common functions, such as output formatting, do not need to be built into numerous commands, since the output of almost any program can be piped through *pr* (or some other appropriate filter).

Both of the common UNIX shells are also programming languages, with shell variables and the usual higher-level programming-language control constructs (loops, conditionals). The execution of a command is analogous to a subroutine call. A file of shell commands, a *shell script*, can be executed like any other command, with the appropriate shell being invoked automatically to read it. *Shell programming* thus can be used to combine ordinary programs conveniently for sophisticated applications without the necessity of any programming in conventional languages.

This external user view is commonly thought of as the definition of UNIX, yet it is the most easily changed definition. Writing a new shell with a quite different syntax and semantics would greatly change the user view while not changing the kernel or even the programmer interface. Several menu-driven and iconic interfaces for UNIX now exist, and the X Window System is rapidly is becoming a standard. The heart of UNIX is, of course, the kernel. This kernel is much more difficult to change than is the user interface, since all programs depend on the system calls it provides to remain consistent. Of course, new system calls can be added to increase functionality, but programs must then be modified to use the new calls.

15.5 Process Management

A major design problem for operating systems is the representation of processes. One substantial difference between UNIX and many other systems is the ease with which multiple processes can be created and manipulated. These processes are represented in UNIX by various control blocks. There are no system control blocks accessible in the virtual address space of a user process; control blocks associated with a process are stored in the kernel. The information in these control blocks is used by the kernel for process control and CPU scheduling.

15.5.1 Process Control Blocks

The most basic data structure associated with processes is the *process structure*. A process structure contains everything that is necessary to know about a process when the latter is swapped out, such as its unique process identifier, scheduling information (such as the priority of the process), and pointers to other control blocks. There is an array of process structures whose length is defined at system linking time. The process structures of ready processes are kept linked together by the scheduler in a doubly linked list (the ready queue), and there are pointers from each process structure to the process's parent, its youngest living child, and various other relatives of interest, such as a list of processes sharing the same program code (text).

The *virtual address space* of a user process is divided into text (program code), data, and stack segments. The data and stack segments are always in the same address space, but may grow separately, and usually in opposite directions: most frequently the stack grows down as the data grows up toward it. The text segment is sometimes (as on an Intel 8086 with separate instruction and data space) in a different address space from the data and stack and is usually read-only.

Every process with sharable text (almost all, under 4.3BSD) has a pointer from its process structure to a *text structure*. The text structure records how many processes are using the text segment, including a pointer into a list of their process structures, and where the page table for the text segment can be found on disk when it is swapped. The text structure itself is always resident in main memory: an array of such structures is allocated at system link time. The text, data, and stack segments for the processes may be swapped. When the segments are swapped in, they are paged.

The *page tables* record information on the mapping from the process's virtual memory to physical memory. The process structure contains pointers to the page table, for use when the process is resident in main memory, or the address of the process on the swap device, when the process is swapped. There is no special separate page table for a shared text segment; every process sharing the text segment has entries for its pages in the process's page table.

Information about the process that is needed only when the process is resident (that is, not swapped out) is kept in the *user structure* (or *u structure*), rather than in the process structure. The *u* structure is mapped into kernel virtual data space. A copy of the VAX process control block is kept here for saving the process's general registers, stack pointer, program counter, and page-table base registers when the process is not running. There is space to keep system-call parameters and to return values. All user and group identifiers associated with the process (not just the effective user identifier kept in the process structure) are kept here. Signals, timers, and quotas have data structures here. Of more obvious relevance to the ordinary user, the current directory and the table of open files are maintained in the user structure.

Every process has both a user and a system phase. Most ordinary work is done by the *user process*, but, when a system call is made, it is the *system process* that performs the system call. The system and user phases of a process never execute simultaneously. The system process has a different stack from that of the user process. The *kernel stack* for the process immediately follows the user structure: The kernel stack and the user structure together compose the *system data segment* for the process.

Figure 15.6 illustrates how the process structure is used to find the various parts of a process.

The *fork* system call allocates a new process structure (with a new process identifier) for the child process and copies the user structure. There is ordinarily no need for a new text structure, as the processes share their text; the appropriate counters and lists are merely updated. A new page table is constructed, and new main memory is allocated for the data and stack segments of the child process. The copying of the user structure preserves open file descriptors, user and group identifiers, signal handling, and most similar properties of a process.

The *vfork* system call does *not* copy the data and stack to the new process; rather, the new process simply shares the page table of the old one. A new user structure and a new process structure are still created.

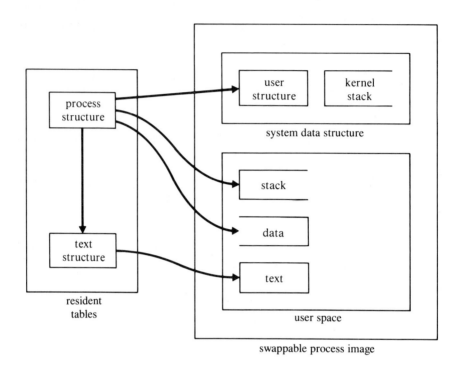

Figure 15.6   CPU-scheduling components.

A common use of this system call is by a shell to execute a command and to wait for its completion. The parent process uses *vfork* to produce the child process. Since the child process wishes to use an *execve* immediately to change its virtual address space completely, there is no need for a complete copy of the parent process. Such data structures as are necessary for manipulating pipes may be kept in registers between the *vfork* and the *execve*. Files may be closed in one process without affecting the other process, since the kernel data structures involved depend on the user structure, which is not shared. The parent is suspended when it calls *vfork* until the child either calls *execve* or terminates, so that the parent will not change memory the child needs.

When the parent process is large, *vfork* can produce substantial savings in system CPU time. However, it is a fairly dangerous system call, since any memory change occurs in both processes until the *execve* occurs. An alternative is to share all pages by duplicating the page table, but to mark the entries of both page tables as *copy-on-write*. The hardware protection bits are set to trap any attempt to write in these shared pages. If such a trap occurs, a new frame is allocated and the shared page is copied to the new frame. The page tables are adjusted to show that this page is no longer shared (and therefore no longer needs to be write-protected), and execution can resume.

An *execve* system call creates no new process or user structure; rather, the text and data of the process are replaced. Open files are preserved (although there is a way to specify that certain file descriptors are to be closed on an *execve*). Most signal-handling properties are preserved, but arrangements to call a specific user routine on a signal are canceled, for obvious reasons. The process identifier and most other properties of the process are unchanged.

15.5.2 CPU Scheduling

CPU scheduling in UNIX is designed to benefit interactive processes. Processes are given small CPU time slices by a priority algorithm that reduces to round-robin scheduling for CPU-bound jobs.

Every process has a *scheduling priority* associated with it; larger numbers indicate lower priority. Processes doing disk I/O or other important tasks have negative priorities and cannot be killed by signals. Ordinary user processes have positive priorities and thus are all less likely to be run than are any system process, although user processes may set precedence over one another through the *nice* command.

The more CPU time a process accumulates, the lower (more positive) its priority becomes, and vice versa, so there is negative feedback in CPU scheduling and it is difficult for a single process to take all the CPU time. Process aging is employed to prevent starvation.

Older UNIX systems used a 1-second quantum for the round-robin scheduling. 4.3BSD reschedules processes every 0.1 second and recomputes priorities every second. The round-robin scheduling is accomplished by the *timeout* mechanism, which tells the clock interrupt driver to call a kernel subroutine after a specified interval; the subroutine to be called in this case causes the rescheduling and then resubmits a *timeout* to call itself again. The priority recomputation is also timed by a subroutine that resubmits a *timeout* for itself.

There is no preemption of one process by another in the kernel. A process may relinquish the CPU because it is waiting on I/O or because its time slice has expired. When a process chooses to relinquish the CPU, it goes to sleep on an *event*. The kernel primitive used for this purpose is called *sleep* (not to be confused with the user-level library routine of the same name). It takes an argument, which is by convention the address of a kernel data structure related to an *event* the process wants to occur before it is awakened. When the event occurs, the system process that knows about it calls *wakeup* with the address corresponding to the event, and *all* processes that had done a *sleep* on the same address are put in the ready queue to be run.

For example, a process waiting for disk I/O to complete will *sleep* on the address of the buffer header corresponding to the data being transferred. When the interrupt routine for the disk driver notes the transfer is complete, it calls *wakeup* on the buffer header. The interrupt uses the kernel stack for whatever process happened to be running at the time, and the *wakeup* is done from that system process.

The process that actually does run is chosen by the scheduler. *Sleep* takes a second argument, which is the scheduling priority to be used for this purpose. This priority argument, if negative, also prevents the process from being awakened prematurely by some exceptional event, such as a *signal*.

When a signal is generated, it is queued until the system half of the affected process next runs. This usually happens soon, since the signal normally causes the process to be awakened if the latter has been waiting for some other condition.

There is no memory associated with events and the caller of the routine that does a *sleep* on an event must be prepared to deal with a premature return, including the possibility that the reason for waiting has vanished.

There are *race conditions* involved in the event mechanism. If a process decides (because of checking a flag in memory, for instance) to sleep on an event and the event occurs before the process can execute the primitive that does the actual sleep on the event, the process sleeping may then sleep forever. We prevent this situation by raising the hardware processor priority during the critical section so that no interrupts can occur, and thus only the process desiring the event can run until it is sleeping. Hardware processor priority is used in this manner to protect critical regions throughout the kernel, and is the greatest obstacle to porting UNIX to multiple processor machines. However, this problem has not stopped such ports from being done repeatedly.

Many processes such as text editors are I/O bound and usually will be scheduled mainly on the basis of waiting for I/O. Experience suggests that the UNIX scheduler performs best with I/O-bound jobs, as can be observed when there are several CPU-bound jobs, such as text formatters or language interpreters, running.

What has been referred to here as CPU *scheduling* corresponds closely to the *short-term scheduling* of Chapter 4, although the negative-feedback property of the priority scheme provides some long-term scheduling in that it largely determines the long-term *job mix*. Medium-term scheduling is done by the swapping mechanism described in Section 15.6.

15.6 Memory Management

Much of UNIX's early development was done on a PDP-11. The PDP-11 has only eight segments in its virtual address space, and each of these are at most 8192 bytes. The larger machines, such as the PDP-11/70, allow separate instruction and address spaces, which effectively double the address space and number of segments, but this is still a relatively small address space. In addition, the kernel was even more severely constrained due to dedicating one data segment to interrupt vectors, another to point at the per-process system data segment, and yet another for the UNIBUS registers. Further, on the smaller PDP-11s, total physical memory was limited to 256K. The total memory resources were insufficient to justify or support complex memory-management algorithms. Thus, UNIX swapped the entire process memory image.

15.6.1 Swapping

Pre-3BSD UNIX systems use swapping exclusively to handle memory contention among processes: If there is too much contention, processes are swapped out until enough memory is available. Also, a few large processes can force many small processes out of memory, and a process larger than nonkernel main memory cannot be run at all. The system data segment (the *u* structure and kernel stack) and the user data segment (text [if nonsharable], data, and stack) are kept in contiguous main memory for swap-transfer efficiency, so external fragmentation of memory can be a serious problem.

Allocation of both main memory and swap space is done first-fit. When the size of a process's memory image increases (due to either stack expansion or data expansion), a new piece of memory big enough for the whole image is allocated. The memory image is copied, the old memory is freed, and the appropriate tables are updated. (An attempt is made in some systems to find memory contiguous to the end of the current piece to avoid some copying.) If no single piece of main memory is large enough, the process is swapped out such that it will be swapped back in with the new size.

There is no need to swap out a sharable text segment, because it is read-only, and there is no need to read in a sharable text segment for a process when another instance is already in core. This is one of the main reasons for keeping track of sharable text segments: less swap traffic. The other reason is the reduced amount of main memory required for multiple processes using the same text segment.

Decisions regarding which processes to swap in or out are made by the *scheduler process* (also known as the *swapper*). The *scheduler* wakes up at least once every 4 seconds to check for processes to be swapped in or out. A process is more likely to be swapped out if it is idle, has been in main memory a long time, or is large; if no obvious candidates are found, other processes are picked by age. A process is more likely to be swapped in if it has been swapped out a long time, or is small. There are checks to prevent thrashing, basically by not letting a process be swapped out if it has not been in memory for a certain amount of time.

If jobs do not need to be swapped out, the process table is searched for a process deserving to be brought in (determined by how small the process is and how long it has been swapped). If there is not enough memory available, processes are swapped out until there is.

In 4.3BSD, swap space is allocated in pieces that are multiples of a power of 2 and a minimum size (for example, 32 pages), up to a maximum that is determined by the size of the swap-space partition on the disk. If several logical disk partitions may be used for swapping, they should be the same size, for this reason. The several logical disk partitions should also be on separate disk arms to minimize disk seeks.

Many UNIX systems still use the swapping scheme just described. All Berkeley UNIX systems, on the other hand, depend primarily on paging for memory-contention management, and depend only secondarily on swapping. A scheme similar in outline to the traditional one is used to determine which processes get swapped in or out, but the details differ and the influence of swapping is less.

15.6.2 Paging

Berkeley introduced paging to UNIX with 3BSD. VAX 4.2BSD is a demand-paged virtual-memory system. External fragmentation of memory is eliminated by paging. (There is, of course, internal fragmentation, but it is negligible with a reasonably small page size.) Swapping can be kept to a minimum because more jobs can be kept in main memory, since not all of any of them has to be resident.

Demand paging is done in a straightforward manner. When a process needs a page and the page is not there, a page fault to the kernel occurs, a frame of main memory is allocated, and the proper disk page is read into the frame.

There are a few optimizations. If the page needed is still in the page table for the process, but has been marked invalid by the page-replacement process, it can be marked valid and used without any I/O transfer. Pages can similarly be retrieved from the list of free frames. When most processes are started, many of their pages are prepaged and are put on the free list for recovery by this mechanism. Arrangements may also be made for a process to have no prepaging on startup, but this is seldom done, as it results in more page-fault overhead, being closer to pure demand paging.

If the page has to be fetched from disk, it must be locked in memory for the duration of the transfer. This locking ensures that the page will not be selected for page replacement. Once the page is fetched and mapped properly, it must remain locked if raw physical I/O is being done on it.

The *page-replacement* algorithm is more interesting. The VAX has no hardware memory page-reference bit. This makes many memory-management algorithms, such as page-fault frequency, unusable. 4.2BSD uses a modified *global clock least recently used* (LRU) algorithm. The map of all nonkernel main memory (the *core map* or *cmap*) is swept linearly and repeatedly by a software *clock hand*. When the clock hand reaches a given frame, if the frame is marked as in use by some software condition (for example, physical I/O is in progress using it), or the frame is already free, the frame is left untouched and the clock hand sweeps to the next frame. Otherwise, the corresponding text or process page-table entry for this frame is located. If the entry is already invalid, the frame is added to the free list; otherwise, the page-table entry is made invalid but reclaimable (that is, if it does not get paged out by the next time it is wanted, it can just be made valid again). Of course, if the page is dirty (the VAX *does* have a dirty bit), it must first be written to disk before being added to the free list.

There are checks to make sure the number of valid data pages for a process does not fall too low, and to keep the paging device from being flooded with requests. There is also a mechanism by which a process may limit the amount of main memory it uses.

The LRU clock hand is implemented in the *pagedaemon*, which is process 2 (remember the *scheduler* is process 0 and *init* is process 1). This process spends most of its time sleeping, but a check is done several times per second (scheduled by a *timeout*) to see if action is necessary; if it is, process 2 is awakened. Whenever the number of free frames falls below a threshold, *lotsfree*, the *pagedaemon* is awakened; thus, if there is always a lot of free memory, the *pagedaemon* imposes no load on the system because it never runs.

The sweep of the clock hand each time the *pagedaemon* process is awakened (that is, the number of frames scanned, which is usually more than the number paged out), is determined both by the number of frames lacking to reach *lotsfree* and by the number of frames the *scheduler* has determined are needed for various reasons (the more frames needed, the longer the sweep). If the number of frames free rises to *lotsfree* before the expected sweep is completed, the hand stops and the *pagedaemon* process sleeps. The parameters that determine the range of the clock-hand sweep are determined at system startup according to the amount of main memory such that *pagedaemon* does not use more than 10 per cent of all CPU time.

If the *scheduler* decides that the paging system is overloaded, processes will be swapped out whole until the overload is relieved. This usually happens only if several conditions are met: load average is high, free memory has fallen below a very low limit, *minfree*; and the average memory available over recent time is less than a desirable amount, *desfree*, where *lotsfree* > *desfree* > *minfree*. In other words, only a chronic shortage of memory with several processes trying to run will cause swapping, and even then free memory has to be *very* low at the moment. (An excessive paging rate or a need for memory by the kernel itself may also enter into the calculations in rare cases.) Processes may be swapped by the *scheduler*, of course, for other reasons (such as just not running for a long time).

The parameter *lotsfree* is usually one-quarter of the memory in the map the clock hand sweeps, and *desfree* and *minfree* are usually the same across different systems, but are limited to fractions of available memory.

Every process's text segment is by default shared and read-only. This scheme is practical with paging, since there is no external fragmentation, and the swap space gained by sharing more than offsets the negligible amount of overhead involved, since the kernel virtual space is large.

CPU scheduling, swapping, and paging interact: the lower the priority of a process, the more likely that its pages will be paged out and the more likely that it will be swapped in its entirety.

The age preferences in choosing processes to swap guard against thrashing, but paging does so more effectively. Ideally, processes will not be swapped out unless they are idle, since each process will need only a small working set of pages in main memory at any one time, and the *pagedaemon* will reclaim unused pages for use by other processes.

The amount of memory the process will need is some fraction of that process's total virtual size, up to one-half if that process has been swapped a long time.

The VAX 512-byte hardware pages are too small for I/O efficiency, so they are clustered in groups of two so that all paging I/O is actually done in 1024-byte chunks. In other words, the effective page size is not tied to the hardware page size of the machine, although it must be a multiple of the hardware page size.

15.7 File System

The UNIX file system supports two main objects: files and directories. Directories are just files with a special format, so the representation of a file is the basic UNIX concept.

15.7.1 Blocks and Fragments

Most of the file system is taken up by *data blocks*, which contain whatever the users have put in their files. Let us consider how these data blocks are stored on the disk.

The hardware disk sector is usually 512 bytes. A block size larger than 512 bytes is desirable for speed. However, since UNIX file systems usually contain a very large number of small files, much larger blocks would cause excessive internal fragmentation. This is why the earlier 4.1BSD file system was limited to a 1024-byte (1K) block.

The 4.2BSD solution is to use *two* block sizes: all the blocks of a file are of a large *block* size (such as 8K), except the last. The last block is an appropriate multiple of a smaller *fragment* size (for example, 1024) to fill out the file. Thus, a file of size 18,000 bytes would have two 8K blocks and one 2K fragment (which would not be filled completely).

The *block* and *fragment* sizes are set during file-system creation according to the intended use of the file system: If many small files are expected, the fragment size should be small; if repeated transfers of large files are expected, the basic block size should be large. Implementation details force a maximum block-to-fragment ratio of 8 : 1, and a minimum block size of 4K, so typical choices are 4096 : 512 for the former case and 8192 : 1024 for the latter.

Suppose data are written to a file in transfer sizes of 1K bytes, and the block and fragment sizes of the file system are 4K and 512 bytes. The file system will allocate a 1K fragment to contain the data from the first transfer. The next transfer will cause a new 2K fragment to be allocated. The data from the original fragment must be copied into this new fragment, followed by the second 1K transfer. The allocation routines do attempt to find space on the disk immediately following the existing fragment so that no copying is necessary, but, if this is not possible, up to seven copies may be required before the fragment becomes a block. Provisions have been made for programs to discover the block size for a file so that transfers of that size may be made, to avoid fragment recopying.

15.7.2 Inodes

A file is represented by an *inode*. An inode is a record that stores most of the information about a specific file on the disk. The name *inode* (pronounced *EYE node*) is derived from "index node" and was originally spelled "i-node"; the hyphen fell out of use over the years. The term is sometimes spelled *I node*.

The inode contains the user and group identifiers of the file, the times of the last file modification and access, a count of the number of hard links (directory entries) to the file, and the type of the file (plain file, directory, symbolic link, character device, block device, or socket). In addition, the inode contains 15 pointers to the disk blocks containing the data contents of the file. The first 12 of these pointers point to *direct blocks*; that is, they contain addresses of blocks that contain data of the file. Thus, the data for small files (no more than 12 blocks) can be referenced immediately, since a copy of the inode is kept in main memory while a file is open. If the block size is 4K, then up to 48K of data may be accessed directly from the inode.

The next three pointers in the inode point to *indirect blocks*. If the file is large enough to use indirect blocks, the indirect blocks are each of the major block size; the fragment size applies to only data blocks. The first indirect block pointer is the address of a *single indirect block*. The single indirect block is an index block, containing not data, but rather the addresses of blocks that do contain data. Then, there is a *double indirect block* pointer, the address of a block that contains the addresses of blocks that contain pointers to the actual data blocks. The last pointer would contain the address of a *triple indirect block*; however, there is no need for it. The minimum block size for a file system in 4.2BSD is 4K, so files with as many as 2^{32} bytes will use only double, not triple, indirection. That is, since each block pointer takes 4 bytes, we have 49,152 bytes accessible in direct blocks, 4,194,304 bytes accessible by a single indirection, and 4,294,967,296 bytes reachable through double indirection, for a total of 4,299,210,752 bytes, which is larger than 2^{32} bytes. The number 2^{32} is significant because the file offset in the file structure in main memory is kept in a 32-bit word. Files therefore cannot be larger than 2^{32} bytes. Four gigabytes is large enough for most purposes.

15.7.3 Directories

There is no distinction between plain files and directories at this level of implementation; directory contents are kept in data blocks and directories are represented by an inode in the same way as plain files. Only the inode type field distinguishes between plain files and directories. Plain files are not assumed to have a structure, however, whereas directories have a specific structure. In Version 7, file names were limited to 14 characters, so directories were a list of 16-byte entries: 2 bytes for an inumber and 14 bytes for a file name.

In 4.2BSD, file names are of variable length, up to 255 bytes, so directory entries are also of variable length. Each entry contains first the length of the entry, then the file name and the inumber. This variable-length entry makes the directory management and search routines more complex, but greatly improves the ability of users to choose meaningful names for their files and directories, with no practical limit on the length of the name.

The first two names in every directory are "." and "..". New directory entries are added to the directory in the first space available, generally after the existing files. A linear search is used.

The user refers to a file by a path name, whereas the file system uses the inode as its definition of a file. Thus, the kernel has to map the supplied user path name to an inode. The directories are used for this mapping.

First, a starting directory is determined. If the first character of the path name is "/", the starting directory is the root directory. If the path name starts with any character other than a slash, the starting directory is the current directory of the current process. The starting directory is checked for existence, proper file type, and access permissions, and an error is returned if necessary. The inode of the starting directory is always available.

The next element of the path name, up to the next "/", or to the end of the path name, is a file name. The starting directory is searched for this name, and an error is returned if the name is not found. If there is yet another element in the path name, the current inode must refer to a directory, and an error is returned if it does not, or if access is denied. This directory is searched as was the previous one. This process continues until the end of the path name is reached and the desired inode is returned.

Hard links are simply directory entries like any other. Symbolic links are handled for the most part by starting the search over with the path name taken from the contents of the symbolic link. We prevent infinite loops by counting the number of symbolic links encountered during a path-name search and returning an error when a limit (eight) is exceeded.

Nondisk files (such as devices) do not have data blocks allocated on the disk. The kernel notices these file types (as indicated in the inode) and calls appropriate drivers to handle I/O for them.

Once the inode is found by, for instance, the *open* system call, a *file structure* is allocated to point to the inode. The file descriptor given to the user refers to this file structure.

15.7.4 Mapping of a File Descriptor to an Inode

System calls that refer to open files indicate the file by passing a file descriptor as an argument. The file descriptor is used by the kernel to index a table of open files for the current process. Each entry of the table contains a pointer to a *file structure*. This file structure in turn points to the inode; see Figure 15.7.

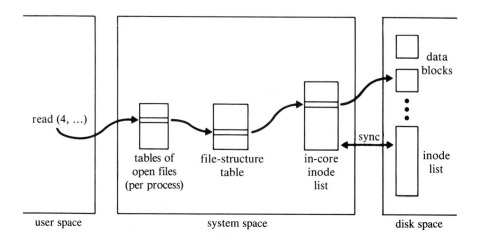

Figure 15.7   File-system control blocks.

The *read* and *write* system calls do not take a position in the file as an argument. Rather, the kernel keeps a *file offset*, which is updated by an appropriate amount after each *read* or *write* according to the number of data actually transferred. The offset can be set directly by the *lseek* system call. If the file descriptor indexed an array of inode pointers instead of file pointers, this offset would have to be kept in the inode. Since more than one process may open the same file, and each such process needs its own offset for the file, keeping the offset in the inode is inappropriate. Thus, the file structure is used to contain the offset.

File structures are inherited by the child process after a *fork*, so several processes may also have the *same* offset into a file.

The *inode structure* pointed to by the file structure is an in-core copy of the inode on the disk and is allocated out of a fixed-length table. The in-core inode has a few extra fields, such as a reference count of how many file structures are pointing at it, and the file structure has a similar reference count for how many file descriptors refer to it.

15.7.5 Disk Structures

The file system that the user sees is supported by data on a mass storage device, usually a disk. The user ordinarily knows of only one file system, but this one logical file system may actually consist of several *physical* file systems, each on a different device. Since device characteristics differ, each separate hardware device defines its own physical file system. In fact, it is generally desirable to partition large

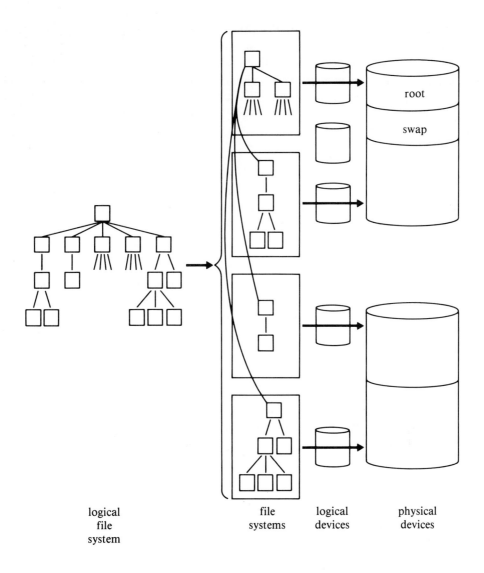

Figure 15.8 Mapping of a logical file system to physical devices.

physical devices, such as disks, into multiple *logical* devices. Each logical device defines a physical file system. Figure 15.8 illustrates how a directory structure is partitioned into file systems, which are mapped onto logical devices, which are partitions of physical devices. The sizes and locations of these partitions were coded into device drivers in earlier systems, but are maintained on the disk by 4.3BSD.

Partitioning a physical device into multiple file systems has several benefits. Different file systems can support different uses. Although most partitions would be used by the file system, at least one will be necessary for a swap area for the virtual-memory software. Reliability is improved, since software damage is generally limited to only one file system. We can improve efficiency by varying the file system parameters (such as the block and fragment sizes) for each partition. Also, separate file systems prevent one program from using all available space for a large file, since files cannot be split across file systems.

The actual number of file systems on a drive varies according to the size of the disk and the purpose of the computer system as a whole. One file system, the *root file system*, is always available. Others may be *mounted* — that is, integrated into the directory hierarchy of the root file system.

A bit in the inode structure indicates that the inode has a file system mounted on it. A reference to this file causes the *mount table* to be searched to find the device number of the mounted device. The device number is used to find the inode of the root directory of the mounted file system, and that inode is used. Conversely, if a path-name element is ".." and the directory being searched is the root directory of a file system that is mounted, the mount table is searched to find the inode it is mounted on, and that inode is used.

Each file system is a separate system resource and represents a set of files. The first sector on the logical device is the *boot block*, containing a primary bootstrap program, which may be used to call a secondary bootstrap program residing in the next 7.5K. The *superblock* contains static parameters of the file system. These include the total size of the file system, the block and fragment sizes of the data blocks, and assorted parameters that affect allocation policies.

15.7.6 Implementations

The user interface to the file system is simple and well defined. This has allowed the implementation of the file system itself to be changed without significant effect on the user. The file system was changed between Version 6 and Version 7, and again between Version 7 and 4BSD. For Version 7, the size of inodes doubled, the maximum file and file-system sizes increased, and the details of free-list handling and superblock information changed. At that time also, *seek* (with a 16-bit offset) became *lseek* (with a 32-bit offset) to allow specification of offsets properly in the larger files than permitted, but few other changes were visible outside the kernel.

In 4.0BSD, the size of blocks used in the file system was increased from 512 bytes to 1024 bytes. Although this increased size produced increased internal fragmentation on the disk, it doubled throughput, due mainly to the greater number of data accessed on each disk transfer. This idea was later adopted by System V, along with a number of other ideas, device drivers, and programs.

4.2BSD added the Berkeley Fast File System, which increased speed, and was accompanied by new features. Symbolic links required new system calls. Long file names necessitated the new directory system calls to traverse the now-complex internal directory structure. Finally, the *truncate* calls were added. The Fast File System was a complete success, and is now being added to most types of UNIX. Its performance is made possible by its layout and allocation policies, which we discuss next.

15.7.7 Layout and Allocation Policies

The kernel uses a *logical device number-inode number* pair to identify a file. The logical device number defines the file system involved. The inodes in the file system are numbered in sequence. In the Version 7 file system, all inodes are in an array immediately following a single superblock at the beginning of the logical device, with the data blocks following the inodes. The *inumber* is effectively just an index into this array.

With the Version 7 file system, a block of a file can be anywhere on the disk between the end of the inode array and the end of the file system. Free blocks are kept in a linked list in the superblock. Blocks are pushed onto the front of the free list, and are removed from the front as needed to serve new files or to extend existing files. Thus, the blocks of a file may be arbitrarily far from both the inode and each other. Furthermore, the more a file system of this kind is used, the more disorganized the blocks in a file become. We can reverse this process only by reinitializing and restoring the entire file system, which is not a convenient thing to do.

Another difficulty is that the reliability of the file system is suspect. For speed, the superblock of each mounted file system is kept in memory. This allows the kernel to access a superblock quickly, especially for using the free list. Every 30 seconds, the superblock is written to the disk, to keep the in-core and disk copies synchronized (by the update program, using the *sync* system call). However, it is not uncommon for system bugs or hardware failures to destroy the in-core superblock during a system crash. The free list is then lost, and must be constructed by a lengthy examination of all blocks in the file system.

The 4.2BSD file-system implementation is radically different from that of Version 7. This reimplementation was done primarily to improve efficiency and robustness, and most such changes are invisible outside the kernel. There were some other changes introduced at the same time, such as symbolic links and long file names (up to 255 characters), that are visible at both the system-call and the user levels. Most of the changes required for these features were not in the kernel, however, but rather were in the programs that use them.

Space allocation is especially different. The major new concept in 4.2BSD is the *cylinder group*. The cylinder group was introduced to allow localization of the blocks in a file. Each cylinder group occupies one or more consecutive cylinders of the disk, so that disk accesses within the cylinder group require minimal disk head movement. Every cylinder group has a superblock, a cylinder block, an array of inodes, and some data blocks (Figure 15.9).

The superblock is identical in each cylinder group, so that it can be recovered from any one of them in the event of disk corruption. The *cylinder block* contains dynamic parameters of the particular cylinder group. These include a bit map of free data blocks and fragments and a bit map of free inodes. Statistics on recent progress of the allocation strategies are also kept here.

The header information in a cylinder group (the superblock, the cylinder block, and the inodes) is not always at the beginning of the cylinder group. If it were, the header information for every cylinder group might be on the same disk platter; a single disk head crash could wipe out all of them. Therefore, each cylinder group has its header information at a different offset from the beginning of the group.

It is common for the directory-listing command *ls* to read all the inodes of every file in a directory, making it desirable for all such inodes to be close together. For this reason, the inode for a file is usually allocated from the same cylinder group as is the inode of the file's parent directory. Not everything can be localized, however, so an inode for a new directory is put in a *different* cylinder group from that of its

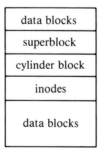

Figure 15.9   4.3BSD cylinder group.

parent directory. The cylinder group chosen for such a new directory inode is that with the greatest number of unused inodes.

To reduce disk head seeks involved in accessing the data blocks of a file, we allocate blocks from the same cylinder group as often as possible. Since a single file cannot be allowed to take up all the blocks in a cylinder group, a file exceeding a certain size (such as 32K) has further block allocation redirected to a different cylinder group, the new group being chosen from among those having more than average free space. If the file continues to grow, allocation is again redirected (at each megabyte) to yet another cylinder group. Thus, all the blocks of a small file are likely to be in the same cylinder group, and the number of long seeks involved in accessing a large file is kept small.

There are two levels of disk-block-allocation routines. The global policy routines select a desired disk block according to the considerations already discussed. The local policy routines use the specific information recorded in the cylinder blocks to choose a block near the one requested. If the requested block is not in use, it is returned. Otherwise, the block rotationally closest to the one requested in the same cylinder, or a block in a different cylinder but in the same cylinder group, is returned. If there are no more blocks in the cylinder group, a quadratic rehash is done among all the other cylinder groups to find a block; if that fails, an exhaustive search is done. If enough free space (typically 10 percent), is left in the file system, blocks usually are found where desired, the quadratic rehash and exhaustive search are not used, and performance of the file system does not degrade with use.

Because of the increased efficiency of the Fast File System, typical disks are now utilized at 30 percent of their raw transfer capacity. This percentage is a marked improvement over that realized with the Version 7 file system, which used about 3 percent of the bandwidth.

4.3BSD Tahoe introduced the Fat Fast File System, which allows the number of inodes per cylinder group, the number of cylinders per cylinder group, and the number of distinguished rotational positions to be set when the file system is created. 4.3BSD used to set these parameters according to the disk hardware type.

15.8 I/O System

One of the purposes of an operating system is to hide the peculiarities of specific hardware devices from the user. For example, the file system presents a simple consistent storage facility (the file) independent of the underlying disk hardware. In UNIX, the peculiarities of I/O devices are also hidden from the bulk of the kernel itself by the *I/O system*. The I/O system consists of a buffer caching system, general device driver code, and drivers for specific hardware devices. Only the device driver knows the peculiarities of a specific device. The major parts of the I/O system are diagrammed in Figure 15.10.

There are three main kinds of I/O in 4.3BSD: block devices, character devices, and the *socket* interface. The socket interface, together with its protocols and network interfaces, will be treated in Section 15.9.1.

Block devices include disks and tapes. Their distinguishing characteristic is that they are directly addressable in a fixed block size, usually 512 bytes. A block-device driver is required to isolate details of tracks, cylinders, and so on, from the rest of the kernel. Block devices are accessible directly through appropriate device special files (such as */dev/rp0*), but are more commonly accessed indirectly through the file system. In either case, transfers are buffered through the *block buffer cache*, which has a profound effect on efficiency.

Character devices include terminals and line printers, but also almost everything else (except network interfaces) that does not use the block buffer cache. For instance, */dev/mem* is an interface to physical main memory, and */dev/null* is a bottomless sink for data and an endless source of end-of-file markers. Some devices, such as high-speed graphics interfaces, may have their own buffers or may always do I/O directly into the user's data space; since they do not use the block buffer cache, they are classed as character devices.

Terminals and terminal-like devices use *C-lists*, which are buffers smaller than those of the block buffer cache.

Block devices and *character* devices are the two main device classes. Device drivers are accessed by one of two arrays of entry points. One array is for block devices; the other is for character devices. A device is distinguished by a class (block or character) and a *device number*. The device number consists of two parts. The *major device number* is used to index the array for character or block devices to find entries into the

system-call interface to the kernel					
socket	plain file	cooked block interface	raw block interface	raw tty interface	cooked tty
protocols	file system				line discipline
network interface	block-device driver			character-device driver	
the hardware					

Figure 15.10   4.3BSD kernel I/O structure.

appropriate device driver. The *minor device number* is interpreted by the device driver as, for example, a logical disk partition or a terminal line.

A device driver is connected to the rest of the kernel only by the entry points recorded in the array for its class, and by its use of common buffering systems. This segregation is important for portability, and also for system configuration.

15.8.1 Block Buffer Cache

The block devices use a block buffer cache. The buffer cache consists of a number of buffer headers, each of which points to a piece of physical memory as well as a device number and a block number on the device. The buffer headers are kept in several linked lists, one each for

- Information that is never written out, such as super-blocks of file systems

- Blocks in use (the cache) in LRU order

- Empty buffers with no memory or disk blocks associated with them

The buffers in these lists are also hashed by device and block number for search efficiency.

When a block is wanted from a device (a read), the cache is searched. If the block is found, it is used, and no I/O transfer is necessary. If it is not found, a buffer is chosen from the list of empty buffers, the device number and block number associated with it are updated, memory is found for it, and the new data are transferred into it from the device. If there are no empty buffers, the LRU buffer is written to its device (if it is modified) and the buffer is reused.

On a write, if the block in question is already in the buffer cache, the new data are put in the buffer (overwriting any previous data), the buffer header is marked to indicate the buffer has been modified, and no I/O is immediately necessary. The data will be written when the buffer is needed for other data. If the block is not found in the buffer cache, an empty buffer is chosen (as with a read) and a transfer is done to this buffer.

Writes are periodically forced for dirty buffer blocks to minimize potential file-system inconsistencies after a crash.

The number of data in a buffer in 4.3BSD is variable, up to a maximum over all file systems, usually 8K. The minimum size is the paging-cluster size, usually 1024 bytes. Buffers are page-cluster aligned and any page cluster may be mapped into only one buffer at a time, just as any disk block may be mapped into only one buffer at a time.

The number of data in a buffer may grow as a user process writes more data following those already in the buffer. When this happens, a new buffer large enough to hold all the data is allocated, and the original data are copied into it, followed by the new data. If a buffer shrinks, a buffer is taken off the empty queue, excess pages are put in it, and that buffer is released to be written to disk.

Some devices, such as magnetic tapes, require blocks to be written in a certain order, so facilities are provided to force synchronous writes of buffers to these devices. Blocks of directories are also written synchronously, to forstall crash inconsistencies.

The size of the buffer cache can have a profound effect on the performance of a system, since, if it is large enough, the percentage of cache hits can be quite high and the number of actual I/O transfers low.

There are some interesting interactions among the buffer cache, the file system, and the disk drivers. When data are written to a disk file, they are buffered in the cache, and the disk driver sorts its output queue according to disk address. These two things allow the disk driver to minimize disk head seeks and to write data at times optimized for disk rotation. When data are read from a disk file, the block I/O system does some read-ahead; however, reads are much nearer to asynchronous than writes. Thus, output to the disk through the file system is often faster than is input for large transfers, counter to intuition.

15.8.2 Raw Device Interfaces

Almost every block device also has a character interface, and these are called *raw device interfaces*. Such an interface differs from the *block interface* in that the block buffer cache is bypassed.

Each disk driver maintains a queue of pending transfers. Each record in the queue specifies whether it is a read or a write, a main memory address for the transfer, a device address for the transfer (usually the 512-byte block number), and a transfer size (in bytes). It is simple to map the information from a block buffer to what is required for this queue.

It is almost as simple to map a piece of main memory corresponding to part of a user process's virtual address space. This mapping is what a raw disk interface, for instance, does. Unbuffered transfers directly to or from a user's virtual address space are thus allowed. The size of the transfer is limited by the physical devices, some of which require an even number of bytes. The software restricts the size of a single transfer to what will fit in a 16-bit word; this limitation is an artifact of the system's PDP-11 history and of the PDP-11 derivation of many of the devices themselves.

The kernel accomplishes transfers for swapping and paging simply by putting the appropriate request on the queue for the appropriate device. No special swapping or paging device driver is needed.

The 4.2BSD file-system implementation was actually written and largely tested as a user process that used a raw disk interface, before the code was moved into the kernel. In an interesting about-face, in the Mach operating system (Chapter 16) the file system is moved out of the kernel.

15.8.3 C-Lists

Terminal drivers use a character buffering system. This system involves keeping small blocks of characters (usually 28 bytes) in linked lists. There are routines to enqueue and dequeue characters for such lists. Although all free character buffers are kept in a single free list, most device drivers that use them limit the number of characters that may be queued at one time for any given terminal line.

A write system call to a terminal enqueues characters on a list for the device. An initial transfer is started, and interrupts cause dequeuing of characters and further transfers.

Input is similarly interrupt driven. Terminal drivers typically support *two* input queues, however, and conversion from the first (raw queue) to the other (canonical queue) is triggered by the interrupt routine putting an end-of-line character on the raw queue. The process doing a read on the device is then awakened, and its system phase does the conversion; the characters thus put on the canonical queue are then available to be returned to the user process by the read.

It is also possible to have the device driver bypass the canonical queue and return characters directly from the raw queue. This is known as *raw mode*. Full-screen editors, and other programs that need to react to every keystroke, use this mode.

15.9 Interprocess Communication

Many tasks can be accomplished in isolated processes, but many others require interprocess communication. Isolated computing systems have long served for many applications, but networking is increasingly important. With the increasing use of personal workstations, resource sharing is becoming more common. Interprocess communication has not traditionally been one of UNIX's strong points.

Most UNIX systems have not permitted *shared memory* because the PDP-11 hardware did not encourage it. System V does support a shared memory facility, and one was planned for 4.2BSD but was not implemented due to time constraints. In any case, shared memory presents a problem in a networked environment, since network accesses can never be as fast as memory accesses on the local machine. Although we could, of course, pretend that memory was shared between two separate machines by copying data across a network transparently, the major benefit of shared memory (speed) would be lost.

15.9.1 Sockets

The *pipe* (discussed in Section 15.4.3) is the IPC mechanism most characteristic of UNIX. A pipe permits a reliable unidirectional byte stream between two processes. It is traditionally implemented as an ordinary file, with a few exceptions. It has no name in the file system, being created instead by the *pipe* system call. Its size is fixed, and when a process attempts to write to a full pipe, the process is suspended. Once all data previously written into the pipe have been read out, writing continues at the beginning of the file (pipes are not true circular buffers). One benefit of the small size (usually 4096 bytes) of pipes is that pipe data are seldom actually written to disk; they usually are kept in memory by the normal block buffer cache.

In 4.3BSD, pipes are implemented as a special case of the *socket* mechanism. The *socket* mechanism provides a general interface not only to facilities such as pipes, which are local to one machine, but also to networking facilities. Even on the same machine, a pipe can be used only by two processes related through use of the *fork* system call. The socket mechanism can be used by unrelated processes.

A *socket* is an endpoint of communication. A socket in use usually has an *address* bound to it. The nature of the address depends on the *communication domain* of the socket. A characteristic property of a domain is that processes communicating in the same domain use the same *address format*. A single socket can communicate in only one domain.

The three domains currently implemented in 4.3BSD Tahoe are the UNIX domain (AF_UNIX), the Internet domain (AF_INET), and the XEROX Network Services (NS) domain (AF_NS). The address format of the UNIX domain is ordinary file-system path names, such as */alpha/beta/gamma*. Processes communicating in the Internet domain use DARPA Internet communications protocols (such as TCP/IP) and Internet addresses, which consist of a 32-bit host number and a 32-bit port number.

There are several *socket types*, which represent classes of services. Each type may or may not be implemented in any communication domain. If a type is implemented in a given domain, it may be implemented by one or more protocols, which may be selected by the user:

- **Stream sockets**. These sockets provide reliable, duplex, sequenced data streams. No data are lost or duplicated in delivery, and there are no record boundaries. This type is supported in the Internet domain by the TCP protocol. In the UNIX domain, pipes are implemented as a pair of communicating stream sockets.

- **Sequenced packet sockets**. These sockets provide data streams like those of stream sockets, except that record boundaries are provided. This type is used in the XEROX AF_NS protocol.

- **Datagram sockets**. These sockets transfer messages of variable size in either direction. There is no guarantee that such messages will arrive in the same order they were sent, or that they will be unduplicated, or that they will arrive at all, but the original message (record) size is preserved in any datagram that does arrive. This type is supported in the Internet domain by the UDP protocol.

- **Reliably delivered message sockets**. These sockets transfer messages that are guaranteed to arrive, and that otherwise are like the messages transferred using datagram sockets. This type is currently unsupported.

- **Raw sockets**. These sockets allow direct access by processes to the protocols that support the other socket types. The protocols accessible include not only the uppermost ones, but also lower-level protocols. For example, in the Internet domain, it is possible to reach TCP, IP beneath that, or an Ethernet protocol beneath that. This capability is useful for developing new protocols.

The socket facility has a set of system calls specific to it. The *socket* system call creates a socket. It takes as arguments specifications of the communication domain, the socket type, and the protocol to be used to support that type. The value returned is a small integer called a *socket descriptor*, which is in the same name space as file descriptors. The socket descriptor indexes the array of open "files" in the *u* structure in the kernel, and has a file structure allocated for it. The 4.3BSD file structure may point to a *socket* structure instead of to an inode. In this case, certain socket information (such as a the socket's type, message count, and the data in its input and output queues) is kept directly in the socket structure.

For another process to address a socket, the socket must have a name. A name is bound to a socket by the *bind* system call, which takes the socket descriptor, a pointer to the name, and the length of the name as a byte string. The contents and length of the byte string depend on the address format. The *connect* system call is used to initiate a connection. The arguments are syntactically the same as those for *bind*;

the socket descriptor represents the local socket and the address is that of the foreign socket to which the attempt to connect is made.

Many processes that communicate using the socket IPC follow the *client-server model*. In this model, the *server* process provides a *service* to the *client* process. When the service is available, the server process listens on a well-known address, and the client process uses *connect*, as described previously, to reach the server.

A server process uses *socket* to create a socket and *bind* to bind the well-known address of its service to that socket. Then, it uses the *listen* system call to tell the kernel that it is ready to accept connections from clients, and to specify how many pending connections the kernel should queue until the server can service them. Finally, the server uses the *accept* system call to accept individual connections. Both *listen* and *accept* take as an argument the socket descriptor of the original socket. *Accept* returns a new socket descriptor corresponding to the new connection; the original socket descriptor is still open for further connections. The server usually uses *fork* to produce a new process after the *accept* to service the client while the original server process continues to listen for more connections.

There are also system calls for setting parameters of a connection and for returning the address of the foreign socket after an *accept*.

When a connection for a socket type such as a stream socket is established, the addresses of both endpoints are known and no further addressing information is needed to transfer data. The ordinary *read* and *write* system calls may then be used to transfer data.

The simplest way to terminate a connection and to destroy the associated socket is to use the *close* system call on its socket descriptor. We may also wish to terminate only one direction of communication of a duplex connection; the *shutdown* system call may be used for this.

Some socket types, such as datagram sockets, do not support connections; instead, their sockets exchange datagrams that must be addressed individually. The system calls *sendto* and *recvfrom* are used for such connections. Both take as arguments a socket descriptor, a buffer pointer and the length, and an address-buffer pointer and length. The address buffer contains the address to send to for *sendto* and is filled in with the address of the datagram just received by *recvfrom*. The number of data actually transferred is returned by both system calls.

The *select* system call may be used to multiplex data transfers on several file descriptors and/or socket descriptors. It may even be used to allow one server process to listen for client connections for many services and to *fork* a process for each connection as the latter is made. It does a *socket*, *bind*, and *listen* for each service, and then does a *select* on all the socket descriptors. When *select* indicates activity on a descriptor, the server does an *accept* on it and forks a process on the new descriptor returned by *accept*, leaving the parent process to do a *select* again.

15.9.2 Network Support

Almost all current UNIX systems support the UUCP network facilities, which are mostly used over dial-up telephone lines to support the UUCP mail network and the USENET news network. These are, however, rudimentary networking facilities, as they do not support even remote login, much less remote procedure call or distributed file systems. These facilities are also almost completely implemented as user processes, and are not part of the operating system proper.

4.3BSD supports the DARPA Internet protocols UDP, TCP, IP, and ICMP on a wide range of Ethernet, token-ring, and ARPANET interfaces. The framework in the kernel to support this is intended to facilitate the implementation of further protocols, and all protocols are accessible via the socket interface. The first version of the code was written by Rob Gurwitz of BBN as an add-on package for 4.1BSD.

The International Standards Organization's (ISO) Open System Interconnection (OSI) Reference Model for networking prescribes seven layers of network protocols and strict methods of communication between them. An implementation of a protocol may communicate only with a peer entity speaking the same protocol at the same layer, or with the protocol-protocol interface of a protocol in the layer immediately above or below in the same system.

The 4.3BSD networking implementation, and to a certain extent the *socket* facility, is more oriented toward the ARPANET Reference Model (ARM). The ARPANET in its original form served as a proof of concept for many networking concepts, such as packet switching and protocol layering. The ARPANET was retired in 1988 because the hardware that supported it was no longer state of the art. Its successors, such as the NSFNET and the Internet, are even larger, and serve as a communications utility for researchers and as a testbed for internet gateway research. The ARM predates the ISO model; the latter was in large part inspired by the ARPANET research.

Although the ISO model is often interpreted as requiring a limit of one protocol communicating per layer, the ARM allows several protocols in the same layer. There are only four protocol layers in the ARM, plus

- **Process/Applications**. This layer subsumes the Application, Presentation, and Session layers of the ISO model. Such user-level programs as the File Transfer Protocol (FTP) and Telnet (remote login) exist at this level.

- **Host-Host**. This layer corresponds to ISO's Transport and the top part of its Network layers. Both the Transmission Control Protocol (TCP) and the Internet Protocol (IP) are in this layer, with TCP on top of IP. TCP corresponds to an ISO Transport protocol, and IP performs the addressing functions of the ISO network layer.

- **Network Interface**. This layer spans the lower part of the ISO network layer and all of the Data Link layer. The protocols involved here depend on the physical network type. The ARPANET uses the IMP-Host protocols, whereas an Ethernet uses Ethernet protocols.

- **Network Hardware**. The ARM is primarily concerned with software, so there is no explicit network hardware layer; however, any actual network will have hardware corresponding to the ISO hardware layer.

The networking framework in 4.3BSD is more generalized than either the ISO model or the ARM, although it is most closely related to the latter; see Figure 15.11.

User processes communicate with network protocols (and thus with other processes on other machines) via the *socket* facility, which corresponds to the ISO Session layer, as it is responsible for setting up and controlling communications.

Sockets are supported by *protocols* — possibly by several, layered one on another. A protocol may provide services such as reliable

ISO reference model	Arpanet reference model	4.2BSD layers	Example layering
application	process/ applications	user programs and libraries	telnet
presentation			
session		sockets	SOCK_STREAM
transport	host–host	protocols	TCP
network			IP
	network interface	network interfaces	Ethernet driver
data link			
hardware	network hardware	network hardware	interlan controller

Figure 15.11   Network reference models and layering.

delivery, suppression of duplicate transmissions, flow control, or addressing, depending on the socket type being supported and the services required by any higher protocols.

A protocol may communicate with another protocol or with the network interface that is appropriate for the network hardware. There is little restriction in the general framework on what protocols may communicate with what other protocols, or on how many protocols may be layered on top of one another. The user process may, by means of the raw socket type, directly access any layer of protocol from the uppermost used to support one of the other socket types, such as streams, down to a raw network interface. This capability is used by routing processes and also for new protocol development.

There tends to be one *network-interface* driver per network controller type. The network interface is responsible for handling characteristics specific to the local network being addressed, such that the protocols using the interface do not need to be concerned with these characteristics.

The functions of the network interface depend largely on the *network hardware*, which is whatever is necessary for the network to which it is connected. Some networks may support reliable transmission at this level, but most do not. Some provide broadcast addressing, but many do not.

There are projects in progress at various organizations to implement protocols other than the Internet ones, including the protocols ISO has thus far adopted to fit the OSI model. Such an implementation is expected from Berkeley in the near future. 4.3BSD already contains an implementation of the XEROX XNS protocols, in addition to TCP/IP.

The socket facility and the networking framework use a common set of memory buffers, or *mbuf*s. These are intermediate in size between the large buffers used by the block I/O system and the C-lists used by character devices. An *mbuf* is 128 bytes long, 112 bytes of which may be used for data; the rest is used for pointers to link the *mbuf* into queues and for indicators of how much of the data area is actually in use.

Data are ordinarily passed between layers (socket-protocol, protocol-protocol, or protocol-network interface) in *mbuf*s. This ability to pass the buffers containing the data eliminates some data copying, but there is still frequently a need to remove or add protocol headers. It is also convenient and efficient for many purposes to be able to hold data that occupy an area the size of the memory-management page. Thus, it is possible for the data of an *mbuf* to reside not in the *mbuf* itself, but rather elsewhere in memory. There is an *mbuf* page table for this purpose, as well as a pool of pages dedicated to *mbuf* use.

15.10 Summary

The early advantages of UNIX were that this system was written in a high-level language, was distributed in source form, and had provided powerful operating-system primitives on an inexpensive platform. These advantages led to UNIX's popularity at educational, research, and government institutions, and eventually in the commercial world. This popularity first produced many strains of UNIX with variant and improved facilities, and later produced market pressures that are currently leading to the consolidation of these versions. One of the most influential versions is 4.3BSD, developed at Berkeley for the VAX, and later ported to many other platforms.

UNIX provides a file system with tree-structured directories. Files are supported by the kernel as unstructured sequences of bytes. Direct access and sequential access are supported through system calls and library routines.

Files are stored as an array of fixed-size data blocks with perhaps a trailing fragment. The data blocks are found by pointers in the inode. Directory entries point to inodes. Disk space is allocated from cylinder groups to minimize head movement and to improve performance.

UNIX is a multiprogrammed system. Processes can easily create new processes with the *fork* system call. Processes can communicate with pipes or, more generally, sockets. They may be grouped into jobs that may be controlled with signals.

Processes are represented by two structures: the process structure and the user structure. CPU scheduling is a priority algorithm with dynamically computed priorities that reduces to round-robin scheduling in the extreme case.

4.3BSD memory management is swapping supported by paging. A pagedaemon process uses a modified second-chance page-replacement algorithm to keep enough free frames to support the executing processes.

Page and file I/O uses a block buffer cache to minimize the amount of actual I/O. Terminal devices use a separate character buffering system.

Networking support is one of the most important features in 4.3BSD. The socket concept provides the programming mechanism to access other processes, even across a network. Sockets provide an interface to several sets of protocols.

Exercises

15.1 What are the major differences between 4.3BSD UNIX and SYSVR3? Is one "better" than the other?

15.2 Why are there many different versions of UNIX currently available? In what ways is this an advantage to UNIX? Why is it a disadvantage?

15.3 How were the design goals of UNIX different from those of other operating systems during the early stages of its development?

15.4 What are the advantages and disadvantages of writing an operating system in a high-level language, such as C?

15.5 In what circumstances is the system call sequence *fork execve* most appropriate? When is *vfork* preferable?

15.6 Does 4.3BSD UNIX give scheduling priority to I/O or CPU-bound processes? For what reason does it differentiate between these categories, and why is one given priority over the other? How does it know which of these categories fits a given process?

15.7 Early UNIX systems (and even some current ones) used swapping for memory management, while 4.3BSD used paging and swapping. Discuss the advantages and disadvantages of the two memory methods.

15.8 Describe the modifications to a file system that the 4.3BSD kernel makes when a process requests the creation of a new file */tmp/foo* and writes to it sequentially until its size reaches 20K.

15.9 What socket type should be used to implement an inter-computer file transfer program? Why? What type should be used for a program that periodically tests to see if another computer is up on the network?

Bibliographic Notes

The best general description of the distinctive features of UNIX is still that presented by Ritchie and Thompson [1974]. Much of the history of UNIX is given in Ritchie [1979]. A critique of UNIX is offered by Blair et al. [1985]. The most influential ancestor of UNIX is MULTICS, which is thoroughly examined in Organick [1975]. Early differences between the two main modern versions of UNIX, 4.2BSD and System V, are given in [Chambers and Quarterman 1983]. System V internals are described at length in [Bach 1987]. The authoritative treatment of the design and implementation of 4.3BSD is that by Leffler et al. [1989].

Possibly the best book on general programming under UNIX, especially on the use of the shell and facilities such as *yacc* and *sed*, is

Kernighan and Pike [1984]. Two others of interest are Bourne [1983] and McGilton and Morgan [1983]. The best-supported language under UNIX is C [Kernighan and Ritchie 1978]. C is also the system's implementation language. The ANSI X3.159 standard for C is defined in [X3J11 1989], and is described in [Kernighan and Ritchie 1988]. The Korn shell is described in [Korn 83].

The set of documentation that comes with UNIX systems is called the *UNIX Programmer's Manual* (UPM) and is traditionally organized in two volumes. Volume 1 contains short entries for every command, system call, and subroutine package in the system and is also available on-line via the *man* command. Volume 2, *Supplementary Documents* (usually divided into Volumes 2A and 2B for convenience of binding) contains assorted papers relevant to the system and manuals for those commands or packages too complex to describe in one or two pages. Berkeley systems add Volume 2C to contain documents concerning Berkeley-specific features.

The Version 7 file system is described in [Thompson 1978] and the 4.2BSD file system is described in [McKusick et al. 1984]. A crash-resistant UNIX file system is described by Anyanwu and Marshall [1986]. The basic reference for processes is Thompson [1978]. The 3BSD memory-management system is described in [Babaoglu and Joy 1981], and some 4.3BSD memory-management developments are described in [McKusick and Karels 1988]. The I/O system is described in Thompson [1978].

A description of the UNIX operating-system security is given by Grampp and Morris [1984] and by Wood and Kochan [1985].

Two useful papers on communications under 4.2BSD are Leffler et al. [1978, 1983], both in UPM Volume 2C.

The *ISO Reference Model* is given in [ISO 1981]. The *ARPANET Reference Model* is set forth in [Cerf and Cain 1983]. The Internet and its protocols are described in [Comer 1988], and the general state of networks is given in [Quarterman 1990].

There are many useful papers in the two special issues of *The Bell System Technical Journal* on UNIX [BSTJ 1978, BSTJ 1984]. Other papers of interest have appeared at various USENIX conferences and are available in the proceedings of those conferences, as well as in the USENIX refereed journal, *Computer Systems*.

Several textbooks describing variants of the UNIX system are [Holt 1983] discussing the Tunis operating system, [Comer 1984, 1987] discussing the Xinu operating system, and [Tanenbaum 1987] describing the Minix operating system.

16

The Mach Operating System

The Mach operating system is designed to incorporate the many recent innovations in operating-system research to produce a fully functional, technically advanced operating system. Unlike UNIX, which was developed without regard for multiprocessing, Mach incorporates multiprocessing support throughout. Its multiprocessing support is also very flexible, ranging from shared memory systems to systems with no memory shared between processors. Mach is designed to run on computer systems ranging from one to thousands of processors. In addition, Mach is easily ported to many varied computer architectures. A key goal of Mach is to be a distributed operating system capable of functioning on heterogeneous hardware.

Although many experimental operating systems are being designed, built, and used, Mach is better able to satisfy the needs of the masses than the others are because it offers full compatibility with UNIX 4.3BSD. As such, it provides a unique opportunity for us to compare two functionally similar, but internally dissimilar, operating systems. The order and contents of the presentation of Mach is different from that of UNIX to reflect the differing emphasis of the two systems. There is no section on the user interface, since the latter is similar to that of 4.3BSD.

16.1 History

Mach was designed and implemented at Carnegie-Mellon University (CMU) with the support of the Defense Advanced Research Projects

Agency (DARPA). DARPA was responsible for the development of recent BSD UNIX releases, as was described in Chapter 15. BSD was becoming unwieldy due to the sheer number of features it supported in its kernel. DARPA therefore shifted its interest to work being done at CMU, especially in the areas of reducing kernel size. DARPA funded CMU's development of Mach as a more structured and smaller alternative to BSD.

Mach is based on the Accent operating system, previously developed at CMU. Accent was not the type of operating system DARPA was seeking, since it lacked the support for 4.3BSD, was difficult to port, and did not have a general-purpose integration of message passing and virtual memory. Many of the basic concepts in Mach are based on Accent work but have been changed substantially.

In 1986, the first Mach release became available for the DEC VAX computer family, including multiprocessor versions of the VAX. Versions for the IBM RT PC and for SUN 3 workstations followed shortly. 1987 saw the release of the Encore Multimax and Sequent versions, with full support for multiprocessing, and the first official versions, Release 0 and Release 1. To that point, all the machines running Mach had *Uniform Memory Access* (UMA) design. That is, supported multiprocessor systems had processors with uniform access to the system's memory.

Release 2 went a step further. Mach was ported to *Non-Uniform Memory Access* (NUMA) systems in which processors share memory, but each processor has limited access, or no access at all, to some of the memory on the system. Release 2 also began the effort to "kernelize" UNIX, although that work will not be evident until Release 3 in 1990. Release 2 provides compatibility with 4.3BSD by including most of the latter in the kernel. The lower levels of BSD are replaced with the Mach concepts and implementations (as discussed throughout the rest of this chapter). Thus, Release 2.5 is actually larger than the BSD kernel. As of Release 2.5, Mach is available on a wide variety of systems, including single-processor SUN, Intel, IBM, and DEC machines, and multiprocessor DEC, Sequent, and Encore systems.

Mach was propelled into the forefront of industry action when the Open Software Foundation (OSF) announced in 1989 that it would use Mach as the basis for its new operating system. This operating system is to compete with the System V, Release 4, the operating system of choice among *UI* (UNIX International) members. OSF has such important companies as IBM, DEC, and HP as its members. Mach is also the operating system on the *NeXT* workstation, the brainchild of Steve Jobs, of Apple Computer fame.

Of course, development of Mach at CMU still continues. With the forthcoming Release 3 of Mach, the kernelization process may reduce the size of the kernel to less than one-tenth of the BSD kernel's size (Figure 16.1). All the BSD code will be moved out of the kernel and into one or more user-level processes. The Mach kernel will contain only the new low-level features required to support BSD and other operating systems. It will be possible, for instance, to have multiple operating-system environments (which are rewritten to use Machs features) running in user level on top of Mach. This approach is similar to the *virtual-machine* concept described in Chapter 3.

16.2 Design Principles

The Mach operating system was designed to provide some basic mechanisms that most current operating systems lack. The goal was to design an operating system that is BSD compatible and, in addition, excels in the following areas:

- Support for diverse architectures, including UMA, NUMA, and NORMA (*No Remote Memory Access*) multiprocessors

- Ability to function with varying intercomputer network speeds, from wide-area networks to high-speed local-area networks and tightly coupled multiprocessors

- Simplified kernel structure, with a small number of abstractions; the abstractions are supposed to be sufficiently general that they can be used to implement other operating systems on top of Mach

- Distributed operation, providing network transparency to clients and an object-oriented organization both internally and externally

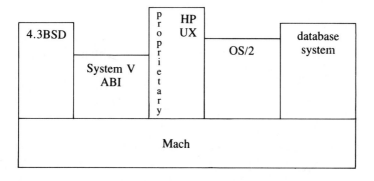

Figure 16.1 Mach Release 3 structure.

- Integrated memory management and interprocess communication, to provide a straightforward and efficient communication and memory mechanism with a single construct

- Heterogeneous system support, to make Mach widely available and interoperable among computer systems from multiple vendors

The designers of Mach have been heavily influenced by BSD (and by UNIX in general), whose benefits include:

- A simple programmer interface, with a good set of *primitives*, or basic services, and a consistent set of interfaces to system facilities

- Easy portability to a wide class of uniprocessors

- An extensive library of utilities and applications

- The ability to easily combine utilities via pipes

Of course, BSD was seen as having several drawbacks that need to be redressed:

- A kernel that had become the repository of many frequently redundant features — and that consequently is difficult to manage and modify

- Original design goals that made it difficult to provide support for multiprocessors, distributed systems, and shared program libraries; for instance, since the kernel was designed for uniprocessors, it has no provisions for locking code or data that other processors might be using

- Too many fundamental abstractions, providing too many similar, competing means to accomplish the same task

It should be clear that the development of Mach continues to be a huge undertaking. The benefits of such a system are equally large, however. The operating system runs on many existing uni- and multiprocessor architectures, and should be easily ported to future ones. It enables computer scientists to experiment in many system areas conveniently, without having to write their own tailor-made operating system. These areas include operating systems, databases, reliable distributed systems, multiprocessor languages, security, and distributed artificial intelligence. In its current instantiation, Mach is at least as efficient as other major versions of UNIX when performing similar tasks, and it frequently is faster — a bonus its designers had not envisioned.

16.3 System Components

For Mach to achieve the goals set for it, the operating-system functionality must be reduced to a small set of basic abstractions. (This was also an original goal of UNIX, but it has since expanded in functionality.) From these abstractions, all other functionality must be derivable; otherwise, the kernel would be incomplete. Recall that a kernel must provide a means for users to accomplish their work. This is usually transformed into the requirement that basic services be provided: program execution, I/O operations, file system-manipulation, resource allocation, and protection. Of course, each operating system has its own approach to making this functionality available. The Mach approach is to place as little as possible within the kernel, but to make what is there powerful enough that all other features can be derived.

Mach's design philosophy is to have a simple, extensible kernel, centered on communication facilities. For instance, all requests to the kernel, and all data movement among processes, are handled through one communication mechanism. By limiting all data operations to one mechanism, Mach is able to provide protection to its users by protecting the communications mechanism. It is extensible, since many traditionally kernel-based functions can be implemented as user-level servers. For instance, although there is a default pager, other pagers may be implemented externally and called by the kernel for the user.

Mach is based on an *object-oriented* paradigm for ease of design and modification. Traditional systems have data, and operations that manipulate these data. Object-oriented systems bundle these two components into an abstract object, where only the operations of the object are able to act on the entities defined in it. The details of how these operations are implemented are hidden, as are the internal data structures. Thus, we can use an object only by invoking its defined, exported, operations. We can make changes to the internal operations without changing the interface definition, freeing the programmer to make any optimizations needed without affecting other aspects of system operation. The object-oriented approach supported by Mach allows objects to reside anywhere in a network of Mach systems, transparent to the user. We shall discuss these techniques when we discuss the *port* mechanism.

The primitive abstractions supported by Mach are as follows:

- **Task**. This is an execution environment. It is the basic unit of resource allocation, and has a virtual address space, and protected access to system resources. A task usually has processors, ports, and virtual memory associated with it.

- **Thread**. This is the basic unit of execution. It is the smallest object of work, and runs in the context of a task. It shares the tasks' resources with other threads in the task. There is no notion of a "process" in Mach. Rather, a traditional process would be implemented as a task with a single thread of control.

- **Port**. This is the basic object reference mechanism in Mach. All communication is done through ports, which are one-way communication channels and are managed and protected by the kernel. Functionally, they are message queues. We invoke an operation on an object by *sending* a message to a port associated with that object. The object being represented by a port *receives* the messages. The sender and receiver must have *port rights* to access the port. For instance, a sender must have a send *capability* to send a message to a port, just as a receiver needs a receive capability to retrieve messages from the queue.

- **Port set**. This is a group of ports sharing a common message queue. A thread may receive messages for a port set, and thus service multiple ports. Such a thread would use the destination port's identity to differentiate the function being requested.

- **Message**. This is the basic method of communication between threads in Mach. It is a typed collection of data objects, and may contain the data themselves, pointers to the data, or port capabilities (to pass port access rights to another thread).

- **Memory object**. This is an item on secondary storage that is mapped into a task's address space. One example is a file managed by a file server, but a memory object can be any object for which data read and write requests can be handled, such as a UNIX pipe.

We shall elaborate on these abstractions in the remainder of this chapter.

An unusual feature of Mach, and a key to its efficiency, is its blending of memory and interprocess-communication features. Whereas some other distributed systems (such as SunOS with its NFS features) have special-purpose extensions to the file system to extend it over a network, Mach provides a general-purpose, extensible blending of memory and messages at the heart of its kernel. This feature not only allows Mach to be used for distributed and parallel programming, but also helps in the implementation of the kernel itself.

But how are memory management and IPC related? Memory management is done through the use of *memory objects*. A memory object is represented by a port (or ports), and IPC messages are sent to this port to request operations on the object. Because IPC is used, memory objects may reside on remote systems and be accessed transparently. The kernel caches memory object's contents in local memory. Conversely, memory-management techniques are used in the implementation of message passing. We have already seen that messages tend to involve much system overhead and are generally less efficient than is, for instance, shared memory. Since Mach is a message-based kernel, it is important that message handling be carried out efficiently. Most of the inefficiency of messages is due to either the copying of messages from one process to another (if the message is intracomputer) or the low network processing speed (for intercomputer messages). Additional inefficiency on UNIX systems results from the file-system analogy on which UNIX message passing is based.

To solve these problems, Mach uses virtual-memory remapping to transfer large messages. That is, to transfer a message between two tasks, Mach changes the receiving task's memory map to include the memory containing the message in the sending process' address space. This technique saves the copying of data; it is further discussed in Section 16.5. In the case of messages between separate hosts, data must be transferred over the network. However, the data are copied only when they are referenced. This technique is also known as *copy on reference* (or *lazy evaluation*). Since messages may be as large as the virtual address space, this optimization may save the copying of billions of bytes of data in just one message. Although this optimization is not currently used in Mach, it should be available in future versions.

There are several advantages to the Mach approach:

- Mach allows increased flexibility in memory management to user programs.

- The model has great generality, which allows its use in tightly and loosely coupled computers.

- Ports are used for referencing objects, adding a level of abstraction that may be used to implement task migration. That is, all objects are location independent, since the only data a referencer has about the object is the port name and Mach allows objects to be on systems remote from the message sender. Task migration is not implemented currently (and would be outside the Mach kernel), but would be efficient since the task would be transferred not all at once, but rather in a copy-on-reference manner.

- Performance is improved.

16.4 Process Management

A *task* can be thought of as a traditional process that does not have an instruction pointer or a register set. A task contains a virtual address space, a set of port rights, and accounting information. A task may be created or destroyed, just as in UNIX. A task does nothing unless it has one or more *thread*s executing in it.

16.4.1 Basic Structure

A task containing one thread is similar to a UNIX process. Just as a *fork* system call produces a new UNIX process, Mach creates a new task to emulate this behavior. The new task's memory is a duplicate of the parent's address space, as dictated by the *inheritance attributes* of the parent's memory. The new task contains one thread, which is started at the same point as the fork call in the parent. Threads and tasks may also be suspended and resumed.

Threads are especially useful in server applications, which are common in UNIX. They also allow efficient use of parallel computing resources. Rather than needing one process on each processor (with the corresponding performance penalty and operating-system overhead), a task may have its threads spread among parallel processors. Threads also add efficiency to user-level programs. For instance, in UNIX, an entire process must wait when a page fault occurs, or when a system call is executed. In a task with multiple threads, only the thread that causes the page fault or executes a system call is delayed; all other threads continue executing. Of course, threads have some cost associated with them, since they must have supporting data structures in the kernel, and more complex kernel-scheduling algorithms must be provided.

Just as processes have states associated with them, so do threads. A thread may be in one of the following states:

- **Running**. The thread is either executing or in the run queue waiting to be allocated a processor. A thread is considered to be running even if it is blocked within the kernel (waiting for a page fault to be satisfied, for instance).

- **Suspended**. The thread is not executing on a processor or in the run queue. It will not continue with its execution until returned to the run state.

A task may be considered to be in one of these states. An operation on a task affects all threads in a task, so suspending a task involves suspending all the threads in it. Task and thread suspensions are separate, independent mechanisms, however, so resuming a thread in a suspended task does not resume the task.

Mach provides primitives from which synchronization tools can be built. This is consistent with Mach's philosophy of providing minimum yet sufficient functionality in the kernel. The Mach IPC facility can be used for synchronization, with processes exchanging messages at rendezvous points. Thread-level synchronization uses the primitives *thread_suspend* and *thread_resume* to start and stop threads at appropriate times. A *suspend count* is kept for each thread. This count allows multiple suspend calls to be executed on a thread, and only when an equal number of resume calls occurs is the thread resumed. Unfortunately, this feature results in its own limitation. Since it is an error for a *thread_resume* to be executed before a *thread_suspend* (because the suspend count would become negative), these routines cannot be used to synchronize shared data access. For instance, these routines cannot be used to solve the readers and writers problem (from Chapter 5). However, the *wait* and *signal* operations associated with semaphores, and used for synchronization, can be implemented via the IPC calls, as will be discussed in Section 16.5.

16.4.2 The C-Threads Package

It is a common theme that Mach provides low-level but flexible routines instead of polished, large, and more restrictive functions. Rather than making programmers work at this low level, Mach provides many higher-level interfaces for programming in C and other languages. For instance, the *C Threads* package provides multiple threads of control, shared variables, mutual exclusion for critical sections, and condition variables for synchronization to the programmer. The thread-control routines include these:

- The routine *cthread_fork* creates a new thread within a task; it is given a function to execute and a parameter (or pointer to parameters) as input. The thread then executes concurrently with the creating thread, which receives a thread identifier when the call returns.

- The routine *cthread_exit* destroys a calling thread, and, if not detached, returns a value to the creating thread.

- The routine *cthread_join* waits for a thread to terminate and then continue (similar to the UNIX *wait* system calls).

- The routine *cthread_detach* indicates that a thread will never be *cthread_join*ed.

- The routine *cthread_yield* indicates to the scheduler that another thread could be run at this point. This routine is also useful in the presence of a preemptive scheduler, since it may be used to relinquish the CPU voluntarily before the quantum expires if a thread has no use for the CPU.

Mutual exclusion is achieved through the use of spin locks, as was discussed in Chapter 5. The routines associated with mutual exclusion are these:

- The routine *mutex_alloc* dynamically creates a mutex variable.

- The routine *mutex_free* deallocates a dynamically created mutex variable.

- The routine *mutex_lock* locks a mutex variable. The executing thread loops in a spin lock until the lock is attained. A deadlock results if a thread with a lock tries to lock the same mutex variable. Bounded waiting is not guaranteed by the C Threads package. Rather, it is dependent on the hardware instructions used to implement the mutex routines.

- The routine *mutex_unlock* unlocks a mutex variable, much like the typical *signal* operation of a semaphore.

General synchronization can be achieved through the use of *condition variables*, which can be used to implement a *condition critical region* or a *monitor*, as was described in Chapter 5. A condition variable is associated with a mutex variable, and reflects a Boolean state of that variable. The routines associated with general synchronization are these:

- The routine *condition_alloc* dynamically allocates a condition variable. This routine results in a macro expansion to execute a version of the UNIX *malloc* function that has been enhanced to support multiple threads.

- The routine *condition_free* deletes a dynamically created condition variable allocated as result of *condition_alloc*. This routine results in a macro expansion to execute a version of the UNIX *free* function that has been enhanced to support multiple threads.

- The routine *condition_wait* unlocks the associated mutex variable, and blocks the thread until a *condition_signal* is executed on the condition variable, indicating that the event being waited for may have occurred. The mutex variable is then locked, and the thread continues. A *condition_signal* does not guarantee that the condition still holds when the unblocked thread finally returns from its condition_wait call, so the awakened thread must loop, executing the *condition_wait* routine until it is unblocked and the condition holds.

As an example of the C Threads routines, consider the bounded-buffer synchronization problem of Chapter 5. The producer and consumer are represented as threads that access the common bounded-buffer pool. We use a mutex variable to protect the buffer while it is being updated. Once we have exclusive access to the buffer, we use condition variables to block the producer thread if the buffer is full, and to block the consumer thread if the buffer is empty. Although this program normally would be written in the C language on a Mach system, we shall use the familiar Pascal-like syntax of previous chapters for clarity. As in Chapter 5, we assume that the buffer consists of n slots, each capable of holding one item. The *mutex* semaphore provides mutual exclusion for accesses to the buffer pool and is initialized to the value 1. The *empty* and *full* semaphores count the number of empty and full buffers, respectively. The semaphore *empty* is initialized to the value n; the semaphore *full* is initialized to the value 0. The condition variable *nonempty* is true while the buffer has items in it, and *nonfull* is true if the buffer has an empty slot.

The first step includes the allocation of the mutex and condition variables:

> **mutex_alloc**(*mutex*);
> **condition_alloc**(*nonempty, nonfull*);

The code for the producer thread is shown in Figure 16.2; the code for the consumer thread is shown in Figure 16.3. When the program terminates, the mutex and condition variables need to be deallocated:

> **mutex_free**(*mutex*);
> **condition_free**(*nonempty, nonfull*);

16.4.3 The CPU Scheduler

The CPU scheduler for a thread-based multiprocessor operating system is more complex than are its process-based relatives. There are generally more threads in a multithreaded system than there are processes in a multitasking system. Keeping track of multiple processors is also difficult, and is a relatively new area of research. Mach uses a simple policy to keep the scheduler manageable. Only threads are scheduled,

```
repeat
    ...
    produce an item into nextp
    ...
    mutex_lock(mutex);
    while(full)
        condition_wait(nonfull, mutex);
    ...
    add nextp to buffer
    ...
    condition_signal(nonempty);
    mutex_unlock(mutex);
until false;
```

Figure 16.2   The structure of the producer process.

so no knowledge of tasks is needed in the scheduler. All threads compete equally for resources, including time quanta.

Each thread has an associated priority from 0 through 127, based on the exponential average of its usage of the CPU. That is, a thread that used the CPU for a large amount of time, recently, has the lowest priority. Mach uses the priority to place the thread in one of the 32 global run queues. These queues are searched in priority order for waiting threads when a processor becomes idle. Mach also has per-processor, or local, run queues it must manage along with the global run queues. A local run queue is used for threads that are bound to an

```
repeat
    mutex_lock(mutex);
    while(empty)
        condition_wait(nonempty, mutex);
    ...
    remove an item from the buffer to nextc
    ...
    condition_signal(nonfull);
    mutex_unlock(mutex);
    ...
    consume the item in nextc
    ...
until false;
```

Figure 16.3   The structure of the consumer process.

individual processor. For instance, a device driver for a device connected to an individual CPU must run only on that CPU.

Instead of there being a central dispatcher that assigns threads to processors, each processor consults the local and global run queues to select the appropriate next thread to run. Threads in the local run queue have absolute priority over those in the global queues, since it is assumed that they are performing some chore for the kernel. The run queues (like most other objects in Mach) are locked when they are modified to avoid simultaneous changes by multiple processors. To speed dispatching of threads on the global run queue, Mach maintains a list of idle processors. More details of the CPU scheduler are provided in Section 16.8

Additional scheduling difficulties arise from the multiprocessor nature of Mach. A fixed time quantum is not appropriate because there may be fewer runable threads than there are available processors, for instance. It would be wasteful to interrupt a thread with a context switch to the kernel when its quantum runs out, only to have it be placed right back in the running state. Instead of using a fixed-length quantum, Mach varies the size of the time quantum inversely with the total number of threads in the system. It keeps the time quantum over the entire system constant, however. For example, in a system with 10 processors, 11 threads, and a 10-millisecond quantum, a context switch needs to occur on each processor only once per second to maintain the desired quantum.

Of course, there are still complications to be considered. Even relinquishing the CPU while waiting for a resource is more difficult than it is on traditional operating systems. First, an *assert_wait* must be issued by a thread to alert the kernel that the thread is about to block. This avoids race conditions and deadlocks, which could occur when running in a multiprocessor environment. The system call *thread_block* actually causes the thread to be moved off the run queue until the appropriate event occurs. There are many other internal thread states that are used by the scheduler to control thread execution.

16.4.4 Exception Handling

Mach implements the standard *Signal* package of UNIX (as discussed in Section 15.3.3). Recall that signals provide software generated interrupts and exceptions. Interrupts are externally generated disruptions of a thread or task, whereas exceptions are caused by the occurrence of unusual conditions during a thread's execution. Unfortunately, signals are of limited functionality in multithreaded operating systems. The first problem is that, in UNIX, a signal's handler must be a routine in the process receiving the signal. If the signal is caused by a problem in the process itself (for example, a division by zero), the problem cannot be remedied, since a process has limited access to its own context. A second, more troublesome aspect of signals is that they were designed for only single-threaded applications, and this is a severe limitation for their use in Mach. Because the signal system must work correctly with multithreaded applications for Mach to run 4.3BSD programs, signals could not be abandoned. Producing a functionally correct signal package required several rewrites of the code, however! A final problem with signals is that they can be lost. This occurs when another signal of the same type occurs before the first is handled. Mach exceptions are queued as a result of their RPC (remote procedure call) implementation, as described later.

The UNIX signal package is used for both internally generated interrupts (exceptions) and external interrupts. *Exceptions* are used not only to detect errors in a program, but also to support debugging. The signal facility is obviously not sufficient for Mach to be able to support debuggers of multithreaded applications. For this reason, Mach includes a general-purpose exception-handling facility. This facility is also useful for other reasons, such as the recording of the entire state of a task in the presence of a fatal error (a BSD core dump), allowing tasks to handle their own errors (mostly arithmetic), and the emulation of instructions not implemented in hardware. The two categories into which these uses of exceptions fall — error handling and debugging — are encompassed by the Mach exception-handling facility.

The Mach facility was designed to provide a single, simple, consistent exception-handling system, with support for standard, as well as user-defined, exceptions. To avoid redundancy in the kernel, Mach uses kernel primitives whenever possible. For instance, a handler is just another thread in the task in which the exception occurs. RPC messages are used to synchronize the execution of the thread causing the exception (the "victim") and the handler, and to communicate information about the exception between the victim and handler.

The two classes of exceptions are handled in slightly separate ways. Error handling is done on a per-thread basis, whereas debugging causes all exceptions within the task to be forwarded to the same handler. It makes little sense to try to debug only one thread, or to have exceptions from multiple threads invoking multiple debuggers. Aside from this distinction, the only other difference between the two types of exceptions is their inheritance from a parent process. Taskwide exception-handling facilities are passed from the parent to child tasks, so debuggers are able to manipulate an entire tree of tasks. Error handlers are not inherited, and default to no handler at thread- and task-creation time. Finally, error handlers take precedence over debuggers if the exceptions occur simultaneously. The reason for this approach is that error handlers are normally part of the task, and therefore should execute normally even in the presense of a debugger.

Exception handling proceeds as follows:

- The victim thread causes notification of an exception's occurrence via a *raise* RPC message being sent to the handler.

- The victim then *waits* until the exception is handled.

- The handler receives notification of the exception, usually including information about the exception, the thread, and the task causing the exception.

- The handler performs its function according to the type of exception. This involves either *clearing* the exception, causing the victim to resume, or *terminating* the victim thread.

To support the execution of BSD programs on Mach, Mach needs to support BSD-style signals. Externally-generated signals, including those sent from one BSD process to another, are currently processed by the BSD section of the Mach kernel. Their behavior is therefore the same as it is under BSD. Hardware exceptions are a different matter, because BSD programs expect to receive hardware exceptions as signals. Therefore, a hardware exception caused by a thread must arrive at the thread as a signal. To produce this result, hardware exceptions are converted to exception RPCs. For tasks and threads that do not make explicit use of the Mach exception handling facility, the destination of this RPC defaults to an in-kernel task. This task has only one purpose: Its thread runs in a continuous loop receiving these exception RPCs. For each RPC, it converts the exception into the appropriate signal that is sent to the thread that caused the hardware exception. It then completes the RPC, clearing the original exception condition. With the completion of the RPC, the initiating thread reenters run state. It immediately sees the signal and executes its signal handling code. In this manner, all hardware exceptions begin in a uniform way — as exception RPCs — but threads not designed to handle such exceptions receive them as they would on a standard BSD system — as signals.

16.5 Interprocess Communication

Recall that, in 4.3BSD, communication may take the form of pipes, signals, ptys, and sockets. Generally, network communication occurs between hosts with fixed, global names (internet addresses). There is no location independence of facilities, because any remote system needing to use a facility must know the name of the system providing that facility.   The data in the messages are untyped streams of bytes. Mach simplifies this picture by sending messages between location-independent ports.   The messages contain typed data for ease of interpretation.   All BSD communication methods may be implemented using this simplified system.

The two components of Mach IPC are *ports* and *messages*.   Almost everything in Mach is an object, and all objects are addressed via their communications ports.   Messages are sent to these ports to initiate operations on the objects by the routines that implement the objects. By depending on only ports and messages for all communication, Mach delivers   location   independence   of   objects   and   security   of communication.   Data independence is provided by the NetMsgServer task, as discussed later.   Security is ensured by message senders and receivers being required to have *rights*.   A right consists of a port name and a capability (send or receive) on that port, and is very much like a capability in object-oriented systems. There can be only one task with receive rights to any given port, but many tasks may have send rights. When an object is created, its creator also allocates a port to represent the object, and obtains the access rights to that port. Rights can be given out by the creator of the object (including the kernel), and are passed in messages. If the holder of a receive right sends that right in a message, the receiver of the message gains the right and the sender loses it.   A task may allocate ports to allow access to any objects it owns, or for communication. The destruction of either a port or the holder of the receive right causes the revocation of all rights to that port, and the tasks holding send rights can be notified if desired.

16.5.1 Ports

A port is implemented as a protected, bounded queue within the kernel of the system on which the object resides.   If a queue is full, a sender may abort the send, wait for a slot to become available in the queue, or have the kernel deliver the message for it. In the latter case, the kernel is acting as a one-message queue, and will accept no more messages from the sender until it has delivered the sender's message.

The system call *port_allocate* allocates a new port in a specified task and gives that task all access rights to the new port.   The port name is returned to the caller. The related call *port_deallocate* removes a given task's access rights to a port. If the task holds the receive right, the port is destroyed and all other tasks with send rights are notified.   Finally, the *port_status* system call returns the current status of a task's port.   In addition,   a   backup   port   may   be   declared   with   the   system   call *port_set_backup*.   A backup port is given the receive right for a port if the task containing the receive right requests its deallocation (or terminates).

When a task is created, the kernel also creates several ports for it. The function *task_self* returns the name of the port that represents the task in calls to the kernel. For instance, for a task to allocate a new port, it would call *port_allocate* with *task_self* as the name of the task that will own the port. Thread creation results in a similar *thread_self* thread kernel port. This is similar to the standard process-id concept found in UNIX. Another port created for a task is returned by *task_notify*, and is the name of the port to which the kernel may send event-notification messages.

Ports may also be collected into *port set*s. This facility is useful if one thread is to service requests coming in on multiple ports (for example, for multiple objects). A port may be a member of at most one port set at a time, and, if a port is in a set, it may not be used directly to receive messages. Instead, the message will be routed to the port set's queue. A port set may not be passed in messages, unlike a port. The *port_set_allocate* call creates a new port set, and *port_set_add* adds a port to a port set; *port_set_remove* undoes this operation; *port_set_deallocate* destroys a port set; *port_set_status* returns the status of a port set. Port sets are objects that serve a purpose similar to the 4.3BSD *select* system call, but are more efficient.

16.5.2 Messages

A message consists of a fixed-length header and a variable number of typed data objects. The header contains the destination's port name, the name of the reply port to which return messages should be sent, and the length of the message. The data in the message (*in-line* data) are currently limited to less than 8K. Any data exceeding that limit must be sent in multiple messages, or more likely via reference by a pointer in a message (*out-of-line* data, as will be described). Each data section may be a simple type (numbers or characters), port rights, or pointers to out-of-line data. Each section has an associated type, so that the receiver can unpack the data correctly. The use of pointers in a message provides the means to transfer the entire address space of a task in one single message. The kernel also inspects the message for certain types of data. The kernel must process port information within a message, either by translating the port name into an internal port-data structure address, or by forwarding it for processing to the NetMsgServer, as we shall explain.

The kernel also must process pointers to out-of-line data, since a pointer to data in the sender's address space would be invalid in the receiver's — especially if the sender and receiver reside on different systems! Generally, systems send messages by copying the data from the sender to the receiver. Since this technique can be inefficient, especially in the case of large messages, Mach optimizes this procedure. The data referenced by a pointer in a message being sent to a port on the same system are not copied between the sender and the receiver. Instead, the page table of the receiving task is modified to include a copy-on-write copy of the pages of the message. This operation is *much* faster than a data copy, and makes message passing very efficient. In essence, message passing is implemented via virtual-memory management.

This operation is actually implemented in two phases. A pointer to a region of memory causes the kernel to map that region of memory into its own space temporarily, setting the sender's memory map to copy-on-write mode to ensure that any modifications do not affect the original version of the data. When a message is received, the kernel moves its mapping to the receiver's address space, using a newly allocated region of virtual memory within that task. Thus, Mach virtual memory is said to be *sparse*, consisting of regions of data separated by unallocated addresses. This scheme is shown in Figure 16.4. Messages are sent via the *msg_send* system call, and are received with *msg_receive*. An RPC mechanism is implemented via *msg_RPC*, which sends a message and waits for a reply.

Intersystem messages with out-of-line data are slightly more complicated. Mach is designed to allow them to be treated like local messages, in that the data do not need to be transferred, but instead

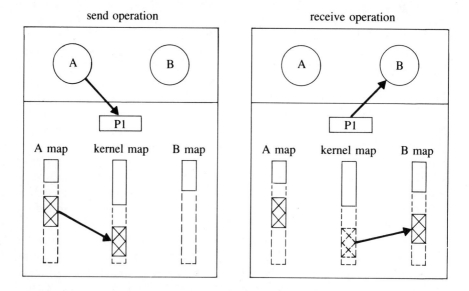

Figure 16.4   Mach message transfer.

could be mapped into the receiver's address space in copy-on-reference mode. Accesses by the receiving task's threads would cause page faults, as usual. What is unusual is that the page faults would be passed by the kernel to the appropriate memory manager, which may reside on the system of the sending task, or even on an unrelated system. This flexibility is made possible by the memory-management system's generality and position-independent functionality, as described in Section 16.6. Currently, Mach does not use this method for intersystem messages. There are associated difficulties that have not yet been addressed within Mach, leaving intersystem copy-on-write unimplemented. These problems include network failure or memory-manager failure, causing parts of a message to be unavailable when the receiving task page faults.

16.5.3 The NetMsgServer

For a message to be sent between computers, there must be a way for the network software to locate the destination port of a message. UNIX traditionally leaves this mechanism to the low-level network protocols, which require computers to have fixed addresses that are known to peer systems. One of Mach's tenets is that all objects within the system are location independent, and that the location is transparent to the user. This requires Mach to provide a higher-level networkwide naming system, the *Network Message Server* or NetMsgServer. The NetMsgServer is a user-level, capability-based networking daemon that allows tasks to register *network ports*. Network ports are ports that may receive messages from other computers. The NetMsgServer on a given computer has knowledge of the network ports on the system, and is able to contact the NetMsgServers on other computers to maintain a distributed database of network ports, which may be queried by tasks or kernels.

Now that the NetMsgServer has knowledge of all network ports, it is able to serve the crucial role of message forwarder. The kernel uses the NetMsgServer when a message needs to be sent to a port that is not on the computer on which the kernel is running. Generally, the NetMsgServer provides the same functions for network ports, such as protection and notification, as the Mach kernel does for local ports on an individual system. A user can gain send rights to a network port by asking the NetMsgServer to look up a name in its database, or by receiving a port right in a message. Tasks automatically inherit send rights to the NetMsgServer, so they may query it directly.

Since Mach is designed to work among heterogeneous systems on a network, it must be able to send between systems data that are formatted in a way that is understandable by both the sender and receiver. Unfortunately, computers vary the format in which they store types of data. For instance, an integer on one system might take 2 bytes to store, and the most significant byte might be stored before the least significant one. Another system might reverse this ordering. The NetMsgServer therefore has another aspect of its operation. It uses the type information stored in a message to translate the data from the sender's to the receiver's format. In this way, all data are represented correctly when they reach their destination.

As an example of the NetMsgServer's operation, consider a thread on node *A* sending a message to a port that happens to be in a task on node *B*. The program simply sends a message to a port to which it has a send right. The message first passes to the kernel, which determines that the destination port is nonlocal and thus forwards the message to the NetMsgServer on node *A*. The NetMsgServer then contacts (through its database information) the NetMsgServer on node *B* and sends the message. The NetMsgServer on node *B* then presents the message to the kernel after translating the network port to the equivalent local port for node *B*. The kernel finally provides the message to the receiving task when it executes a *msg_receive* call. This sequence of events is shown in Figure 16.5.

The NetMsgServer on a given computer accepts the remote procedure calls *netname_check_in*, *netname_look_up*, and *netname_check_out*.

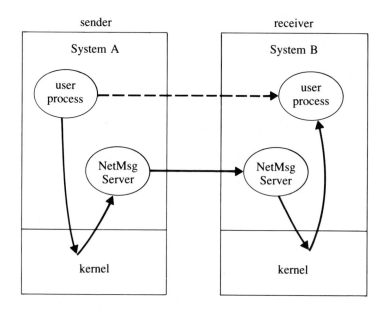

Figure 16.5   Network IPC forwarding by NetMsgServer.

They are used to add, look up, and remove network ports from the NetMsgServer database, respectively. As a security precaution, a port value provided in the *netname_check_in* remote procedure call must match that in the *netname_check_out* call for a thread to ask for a port name to be removed from the database.

16.5.4 Synchronization Through IPC

The IPC mechanism is very flexible, and is used throughout Mach. For example, it may be used for thread synchronization. A port may be used as a synchronization variable, and may have *n* messages sent to it for *n* resources. Any thread wishing to use a resource executes *msg_receive* call on that port. The thread will receive a message if the resource is available; otherwise, it will wait on the port until a message is available there. To return a resource after use, the thread can execute a *msg_send* system call. In this regard, *msg_receive* is equivalent to the *wait* operation, and *msg_send* is equivalent to the *signal* operation on a semaphore. This method can be used for synchronizing semaphore operations among threads in the same task, but cannot be used for synchronization among tasks since only one task may have receive rights to a port. For more general-purpose semaphores, a simple daemon may be written that implements the same method.

16.6 Memory Management

Given the object-oriented nature of Mach, it is not surprising that a principle abstraction in Mach is the *memory object*. Memory objects will be used (in Version 3) to manage secondary storage, and generally represent files, pipes, or other data that are mapped into virtual memory for reading and writing (Figure 16.6). Memory objects may be backed by user-level memory managers, which take the place of the more traditional kernel-incorporated virtual-memory pager found in other operating systems. In contrast to the traditional approach of having the kernel provide management of secondary storage, Mach will treat secondary-storage objects (usually files) as it does all other objects in the system. Each object will have a port associated with it, and may be manipulated by having messages sent to its port. The advantages of such a flexible approach are decreased kernel complexity, and increased experiment and implementation convenience, among others.

16.6.1 Basic Structure

The virtual address space of a task is generally *sparse*, consisting of many holes of unallocated space. For instance, a memory-mapped file is

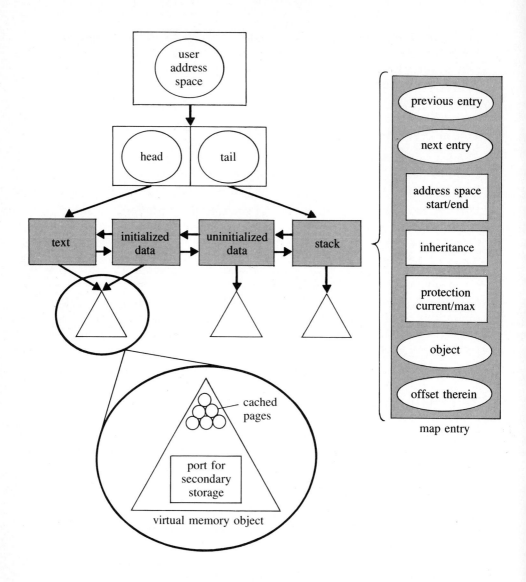

Figure 16.6   Mach virtual memory task address map.

placed in some set of addresses. Large messages are also transferred as shared memory segments. For each of these segments, a section of virtual-memory address is used to provide the threads with access to the message. As new items are mapped or removed from the address space, holes of unallocated memory appear in the address space. Mach makes no attempt to compress the address space, although a task may fail if it has no room for a requested region in its address space. Given that current address spaces are 4 gigabytes or more, this limitation is currently not a problem. Using normal page-table algorithms to maintain a 4 gigabyte address space for each task, especially one with holes in it, would use excessive amounts of memory. The key to sparse address spaces is that page-table space is used for only currently allocated regions. When a page fault occurs, the kernel must check to see whether the page is in a valid region, rather than simply indexing into the page table and checking the entry. Although the resulting lookup is more complex, the benefits of reduced memory-storage requirements and simpler address-space maintenance appear to make the approach worthwhile.

Mach also supports standard virtual-memory functionality, including the allocation, deallocation, and copying of virtual memory. To allocate a new region of virtual memory, a thread may call *vm_allocate*. The address may be given, or may be chosen by the kernel. Physical memory is not allocated until pages in this region are accessed. The kernel allocates a new memory object when *vm_allocate* is executed, and uses the default pager (discussed later) to manage this object. Virtual-memory regions are also allocated automatically when a task receives a message containing out-of-line data. The *vm_deallocate* call removes a region from a task's address space; it destroys the region only if no other threads are accessing it. The system calls *vm_read*, *vm_write*, and *vm_copy* allow the transfer of data between tasks (via the port mechanism). The call *vm_region* returns information about a region in a given task's address space. The *vm_protect* call changes the access protection of a region of memory, whereas *vm_inherit* is used to specify how a region of memory is to be passed to child tasks at the time of their creation (shared, copy-on-write, or not present).

16.6.2 User-Level Memory Managers

A secondary-storage object is usually mapped into the virtual address space of a task. Mach maintains a cache of memory-resident pages of all mapped objects, as in other virtual-memory implementations. However, a page fault occurring when a thread accesses a nonresident page is executed as a message to the object's port. The concept of a memory object being created and serviced by nonkernel tasks (unlike threads, for instance, which are created and maintained by only the kernel) is important. The end result of this is that, in the traditional sense, memory can be paged by user-written memory managers. When the object is destroyed, it is up to the memory manager to write back any changed pages to secondary storage. No assumptions are made by

Mach as to the content or importance of memory objects, so the latter are independent of the kernel.

There are several circumstances in which user-level memory managers are insufficient. For instance, a task allocating a new region of virtual memory might not have a memory manager assigned to that region, since it does not represent a secondary-storage object (but must be paged), or a memory manager could crash due to a bug. Mach itself also needs a memory manager to take care of its memory needs. For these cases, Mach provides a *default memory manager*. The default memory manager uses the standard file system to store data that must be written to disk, rather than requiring a separate swap space, as in 4.3BSD. The default memory manager has an interface identical to that of the user-level ones. A thread internal to the Mach kernel, the *pageout daemon*, uses a primitive FIFO paging algorithm to select victims for replacement. The default memory manager then implements the pageout daemon's policy decision. A user-level manager may be more intelligent than the default, and may implement any paging algorithm suitable to the object it is backing. If the manager fails to reduce the resident set of pages when asked to do so by the kernel, the default memory manager is invoked and actually pages out the user-level manager to reduce the latter's resident set size. If the user-level manager ever recovers from the problem that prevented it from completing the kernel's request, it will touch these pages (causing the kernel to page them in again), and then will page them out as it sees fit.

If a thread needs access to data in a memory object (for instance, a file), it invokes *vm_map* rather than *vm_allocate*. Included in this system call is a port, associated with a memory manager, which is responsible for the region. The kernel executes calls on this port when data are to be read or written in that region. An added complexity is that the kernel makes these calls asynchronously, since it would not be reasonable for the kernel to be waiting on a user-level thread. Unlike the situation with pageout, the kernel has no recourse if its request is not satisfied by the external memory manager. The kernel has no knowledge of the contents of an object or of how that object must be manipulated. If a memory object is mapped by multiple tasks on different machines, the memory manager is responsible for any consistency and functionality requirements of these tasks. For instance, two tasks on different machines may try to modify an object concurrently. If this situation was allowed by the memory manager, each of the computers would have a different version of the object — which usually would be undesirable. Multiple tasks on a single computer do not create this problem because the *vm_map* call places the object in each of the tasks' memory maps.

When the first *vm_map* call is made on a memory object, the kernel creates two ports and passes these to the associated memory manager via a *memory_manager_init* call. To be more precise, the kernel sends a message to the port passed in the *vm_map* call, invoking the *memory_manager_init* routine, which the memory manager must provide as part of its support of a memory object. The two ports passed to the memory manager are a *control port* and a *name port*. The control port is used by the memory manager to provide data to the kernel (for example, pages to be made resident). Name ports are used throughout Mach. They do not receive messages, but rather are simply used as a point of reference and comparison; they are discussed further in Section 16.8. Finally, the memory object must respond to a *memory_manager_init* call with a *memory_object_set_attributes* call to indicate that it is ready to accept requests. When all tasks with send rights to a memory object relinquish those rights, the kernel deallocates the object's ports, thus freeing the memory manager and memory object for destruction. This scheme is detailed in Section 16.8

There are several kernel calls that are needed to support external memory managers. The *vm_map* call has already been discussed. There are also commands to get and set attributes and to provide page-level locking when it is required (for instance, after a page fault has occurred but before the memory manager has returned the appropriate data). The *memory_object_data_provided* call is used by the memory manager to pass a page (or multiple pages, if read-ahead is being used) to the kernel in response to a page fault. This call is necessary since the kernel invokes the memory manager asynchronously. There are also several calls to allow the memory manager to report errors to the kernel.

The memory manager itself must provide support for several calls in order to support an object. We have already discussed *memory_object_init* and others. When a thread causes a page fault on a memory object's page, the kernel sends a *memory_object_data_request* to the memory object's port on behalf of the faulting thread. The thread is placed in wait state until the memory manager returns the page in a *memory_object_data_provided* call, or returns an appropriate error to the kernel. Any of the pages that have been modified that the kernel needs to remove from resident memory (due to page aging, for instance) are sent to the memory object via *memory_object_data_write*. Again, there are several other calls for locking, protection information and modification, and the other details with which all virtual memory systems must deal.

In the current version (2.5), Mach does not allow external memory managers to affect the page-replacement algorithm directly. Mach does not export the memory-access information that would be needed for an external task to select the least recently used page, for instance. Methods of providing such information are currently under investigation. External memory managers are still useful for a variety of reasons, however:

- They may reject the kernel's replacement victim if they know of a better candidate (for instance, MRU page replacement).

- They may monitor the memory object they are backing and request pages to be paged out before the memory usage invokes Mach's pageout daemon.

- They are especially important in maintaining consistency of secondary storage for threads on multiple processors, as we shall show in the next section.

- They may control the order of operations on secondary storage, to enforce consistency constraints demanded by database management systems. For example, in transaction logging, transactions must be written to a log file on disk before they modify the database data.

- They can control mapped file access.

16.6.3 Shared Memory

Mach uses shared memory to reduce the complexity of various system facilities, as well as to provide these features in an efficient manner. Shared memory generally provides very fast IPC, reduces overhead in file management, and helps to support multiprocessing and database management. Mach does not use shared memory for all these traditional shared-memory roles, however. For instance, all threads in a task share that task's memory, so no formal shared-memory facility is needed within a task. However, Mach must still provide traditional shared memory to support other operating-system constructs, such as the UNIX *fork* system call.

It is obviously difficult for tasks on multiple machines to share memory, and to maintain data consistency. Mach does not try to solve this problem directly; rather, it provides facilities to allow them to be solved. Mach supports consistent shared memory only when the memory is shared by tasks running on processors that share memory. A parent task is able to declare which regions of memory are to be *inherited* by its children, and which are to be read-writable. This is different from copy-on-write inheritance, in which each task maintains its own copy of any changed pages. A writable object is addressed from each task's address map, and all changes are made to the same copy. The threads within the tasks are responsible for coordinating changes to memory so that they do not interfere with one another (by writing to the same location concurrently). This may be done through normal synchronization methods, through either critical sections or mutual-exclusion locks on the data.

For the case of memory shared among separate machines, Mach allows the use of external memory managers. If a set of unrelated tasks wish to share a section of memory, they may use the same external memory manager and access the same secondary-storage areas through it. The implementor of this system would need to write the tasks and the external pager. This pager could be as simple or as complicated as needed. A simple implementation would allow no readers while a page was being written to. Any write attempt would cause the pager to invalidate the page in all tasks currently accessing it. The pager would then allow the write and would revalidate the readers with the new version of the page. The readers would simply wait on a page fault until the page again became available. Mach provides such a memory manager: the NetMemServer (network memory server).

16.7 Programmer Interface

There are several levels at which a programmer may work within Mach. There is, of course, the system-call level, which is equivalent to the 4.3BSD system-call interface. The current version of Mach actually includes most of 4.3BSD as one thread in the kernel. Any BSD system call traps to the kernel and is serviced by this thread on behalf of caller, much as standard BSD would handle it. Since the current emulation is not multithreaded, it has limited efficiency. The next version of Mach (3.0), however, will include a totally rewritten BSD emulation that contains less original BSD code. This version will be multithreaded and will no longer be part of the kernel. Rather, it will be in the user side of the operating system. Part of the code will actually be in the form of a library included in each task which uses BSD functionality. The remainder will be in a separate task, the BSD Server. System calls will then pass through the kernel before being redirected, if appropriate, to the library in the task's address space or to the BSD Server. Although this extra transfer of control will decrease the efficiency of Mach, this decrease should be somewhat ameliorated by the ability for multiple threads to be executing BSD-like code concurrently.

At the next higher level of programming is the C *Threads* package, which we introduced in Section 16.4.2. It is a run-time library that provides a C language interface to the basic Mach threads primitives. It provides convenient access to these primitives, including routines for the forking and joining of threads, mutual exclusion through mutex variables (Section 16.4), and synchronization through use of condition variables. Unfortunately, it is not appropriate for the C Threads package to be used between systems that share no memory (NORMA systems), since it depends on shared memory to implement its constructs.   There is currently no equivalent of C Threads for NORMA systems.   Other run-time libraries can and have been written for Mach, including threads support for other languages.

Although the use of primitives makes Mach flexible, it also makes many programming tasks repetitive.   For instance, sending and receiving messages has significant amounts of code associated with it in each task that uses messages (which in Mach is most of them). The designers of Mach therefore provide an interface generator called MIG. MIG is essentially a compiler that takes as input a definition of the interface to be used (declarations of variables, types and procedures), and generates the RPC interface code needed to send and receive the messages fitting this definition and to connect the messages to the sending and receiving threads.

The output of MIG includes three C language files: an *include* file, with definitions to be shared by the file program's components; and two *procedure* files, one for the user-side task and the other for the server side of the communication channel.   The user-side code is able to create and send messages to the server side, and to wait to receive a reply.   A programmer wishing to use the server needs only to link with the user-side routines and to have these routines called (with the proper message contents) by the program. The server side is able to accept messages, to unpack them, to dispatch them to the proper routine, and to reply after the routine finishes processing the data.   Of course, the server implementor must still write the main and message-processing routines, but the message interface is already complete.   The main routine must allocate ports and register them with the name service to allow other tasks to find it on the network (see Section 16.8).   Once a message is received by the server, it can call a routine (*mig_server*) that will unpack the message, call the server-side routine, and format and pack a reply message. A full server can be implemented using these facilities in less than 100 lines of C code.

16.8 Implementation Details

There are many innovative techniques used within Mach to support the system calls made available to application programs and servers.   In this section, we discuss the more interesting methods used internally in Mach.

We now have sufficient information concerning the various aspects of Mach to understand how Mach is able to support one of the key operations of UNIX: the *fork* system call.   This call is used by one process to create a new process that has a duplicate of the memory of its parent. The child may then continue execution (possibly modifying the memory) or may use *execve* to replace its memory with a new process image. Within Mach, *fork* creates a new task with one thread. The task has a copy-on-write copy of the parent's address space, and the thread is initialized to run starting at the instruction following the *fork* call, just as in BSD UNIX. Of course, the *fork* is more efficient than in standard UNIX since the memory of the parent is not really copied. A simple duplication of the parent's address map, with data pages set to copy-on-write (and a duplicated stack), is all that is needed.

Mach is implemented using object-oriented programming techniques. Most data structures are implemented as objects, with both a data section and a set of routines that read or modify the data. Since Mach was designed to be easily portable, it was not written in an object-oriented language, such as C++, which may not be found on all systems. Instead, the entire kernel is written in the C language. This object-oriented flavor is being expanded in Mach Version 3.0. A tool found on standard UNIX, the *cpp* C language preprocessor, is being used in the BSD-emulating server to allow the implementors to use object-oriented techniques. Although it does not have the advanced features found in object-oriented programming languages, it is powerful enough to support the basic facilities.

Each time an internal object is created, it is assigned an associated reference count to track the number of times it is referenced. This count is initialized to 1; it is incremented whenever some other objects or routines acquire use of it, and is decremented whenever they relinquish that use. When the count reaches 0, it is safe for Mach to delete that object. The use of reference counts allows objects to be created and destroyed dynamically. This avoids the more static allocation techniques found in other operating-system implementations. For instance, BSD UNIX has several arrays, including ones to store process information and network buffers, which are defined at compile time and are fixed during run time. If a system runs out of processes, the kernel needs to be recompiled and the system halted and rebooted. Mach's dynamic allocation mechanism allows the number of important resources to grow and shrink as needed. However, Mach currently has no way of recovering from its entire memory space filling.

Mach locks all objects while they are being written to. Contrast this with standard operating-system constructs, in which the sections of code that modify data (critical sections) protect themselves from multiple concurrent execution. Critical sections are not appropriate methods of control in multiprocessor operating systems. Consider, for example, the routines that change virtual-memory maps. They are common in Mach, and on multiprocessor systems may be invoked on several processors concurrently. With critical sections, the code would ensure that only one processor executes that code at any given time. This, however, would cause all other processors to have to wait while an individual processor executed in its critical section. With the data-locking model used in Mach, each data object is locked by its routines when they modify it. It is far less likely that one data object (say, process n's virtual address map) will need to be modified by multiple processors than it is that the virtual-address-map code will need to be concurrently executed. Therefore, Mach uses mutual exclusion locks on data structures themselves. Locking of individual objects allows all other computation to continue, including modifications to other instances of the data. This allows much more concurrency in the operating system and thus more efficiency. Since the locking is done automatically by the objects, the kernel code is also uncluttered with locking routines, keeping the code simpler and reducing the possibility of data corruption due to some code section not being protected properly.

Any thread executing in kernel mode is not preemptible. These include threads which execute in kernel state permanently, or even temporarily (for instance, a user application executing a system call). On first glance, it would seem that these kernel threads could be interruptible, just as user threads are, since all objects are locked during modification. Recall, however, that 4.3BSD emulation is done through inclusion of most of BSD as a kernel-level task. Since BSD is complicated, its native locking mechanism of critical sections was not modified. It does not use the data-locking method. Thus, Mach cannot afford to interrupt any threads that may be executing BSD kernel code. The locking is not sufficient to ensure that data structures will be uncorrupted if normal Mach thread scheduling occurs. Instead, Mach allows each kernel thread to run until the thread declares itself to be in a noncritical state and thus to be preemptible. The scheduler may then allow the thread to continue (and possibly to declare itself nonpreemptable) if there is nothing else waiting for the processor, or may move the thread to the wait queue and run some other thread. Of course, kernel threads cooperate, so there is no possibility of starvation. A thread makes itself available for preemption only when it is in a safe state: one in which is is not accessing any important kernel objects. Thus, no locking is needed. As mentioned, the 4.3BSD emulation of Mach is being rewritten to allow it to run in part as a user-level library and in part as kernel-level system calls. The server and library will use standard Mach locking and will be multithreaded.

Name ports are used on many objects in Mach. They never actually receive messages, but rather are used as a point of reference by threads that hold send rights to them. For instance, since we can compare ports within a task, two threads holding send rights to a name port can compare those ports to determine whether the latter refer to the same object. Name ports are generally used when an object does not wish to grant a right to a task but does want a thread in that task to be able to refer to it (in a system call, for instance). For example, the kernel provides a name port for a memory object so tasks may execute a *vm_region* call on that object to learn the source of the data in a given region.

16.9 Summary

The Mach operating system is designed to incorporate the many recent innovations in operating-system research to produce a fully functional, technically advanced operating system. Mach was designed with three critical goals in mind:

1. Emulate 4.3BSD UNIX so that the executable files from a UNIX system can run correctly under Mach

2. Have a modern operating system that supports many memory models, and parallel and distributed computing

3. Design a kernel that is simpler and easier to modify than is 4.3BSD

As we have shown in this chapter, Mach is well on its way to achieving these goals.

Mach currently includes 4.3BSD in its kernel, which provides the emulation needed but enlarges the kernel. This 4.3BSD code is being rewritten to provide the same 4.3 functionality, but to use the Mach primitives. This change will allow most of the 4.3BSD support code to run in user space, and to be multithreaded.

Mach uses lightweight processes, in the form of multiple threads of execution within one task (or address space), to support multiprocessing and parallel computation. Its extensive use of messages as the only communications method ensures that protection mechanisms are complete and efficient. By integrating messages with the virtual-memory system, Mach also ensures that messages can be handled efficiently. Finally, by having the virtual-memory system use messages to communicate with the daemons managing the backing store, Mach provides great flexibility in the design and implementation of these memory-object-managing tasks.

By providing low-level, or primitive, system calls from which more complex functions may be built, Mach reduces the size of the kernel while permitting operating-system emulation at the user level, much like IBM's virtual-machine systems.

Exercises

16.1 What *n* features of Mach make it appropriate for distributed processing?

16.2 Name two ways that port sets are useful in implementing parallel programs.

16.3 Consider an application that maintains a database of information, and provides facilities for other tasks to add, delete, and query the database. Give three configurations of ports, threads, and message types that could be used to implement this system. Which is the best? Explain your answer.

16.4 Give the outline of a task that would migrate subtasks (tasks it creates) to other systems. Include information about how it would decide when to migrate tasks, which tasks to migrate, and how the migration would take place.

16.5 Name two types of applications for which you would use the MIG package.

16.6 Why would someone use the low-level system calls instead of the C Threads package?

16.7 Why are external memory managers not able to replace the internal page-replacement algorithms? What information would need to be made available to the external managers for the latter to make page-replacement decisions? Why would providing this information violate the principle behind the external managers?

16.8 Why is it difficult to implement mutual exclusion and condition variables in an environment where like CPUs do not share any memory? What approach and mechanism could be used to make such features available on a NORMA system?

16.9 What are the advantages to rewriting the 4.3BSD code as an external, user-level library, rather than leaving it as part of the Mach kernel? Explain your answer. Are there any disadvantages?

Bibliographic Notes

The functional equivalence of message-based and procedure-based operating systems has been established by Lauer and Needham [1978]. Neither approach has an outright advantage over the other, but each is more applicable depending on the machine architecture on which it is used.

The Accent operating system is described by Rashid and Robertson [1981]. An historical overview of the progression from an even earlier system, RIG, through Accent to Mach is given by Rashid [1986].

An overview of the original design of Mach is given by Accetta et al. [1986]. The Mach scheduler is described in detail by Tevanian et al. [1987a] and Black [1990]. An early version of the Mach shared memory and memory-mapping system is presented by Tevanian et al. [1987b].

A current (as of this writing) description of the C Threads package is given by Cooper and Draves [1987]; MIG is described by Draves et al. [1989]. An overview of these packages' functionality and a general introduction to programming in Mach is presented by Walmer and Thompson [1989].

The Mach exception-handling facility is discussed in Black et al. [1988]. A multithreaded debugger based on this mechanism is described in Caswell and Black [1989].

A series of talks about Mach sponsored by the OSF UNIX consortium is available on videotape from OSF. Topics include an overview, threads, networking, memory management, many internal details, and some example implementations of Mach. The slides from these talks are in [OSF 1989].

On systems where USENET News is available (most educational institutions in the United States and some overseas), the news group *comp.sys.mach* is used to exchange information on the Mach project and its components.

CHAPTER
17

Historical Perspective

In Chapter 1, we presented a short historical survey of the development of operating systems. That survey was brief and without much detail, since the fundamental concepts of operating systems (CPU scheduling, memory management, processes, and so on) had not yet been presented. By the time we finished with Chapter 14, however, the basic concepts were well understood. We were thus in a position to examine how our concepts have been applied in a real operating system, UNIX.

In this chapter, we discuss briefly several other highly influential operating systems. Some of them (such as the XDS-940 or the THE system) were one-of-a-kind systems; others (such as OS/360) are widely used. The order of presentation has been chosen to highlight the similarities and differences of the systems, and is not strictly chronological or ordered by importance. The serious student of operating systems should be familiar with all these systems.

The treatment of each system is still very brief, but each section contains references to further reading. The papers, written by the designers of the systems, are important both for their technical content, and, perhaps more important, for their style and flavor. This chapter serves as a *Bibliographic Notes* for the entire book.

17.1 Atlas

The Atlas operating system [Kilburn et al. 1961, Howarth et al. 1961, Fotheringham 1961, Kilburn et al. 1962, Morris et al. 1967] was designed at the University of Manchester in England in the late 1950s and early 1960s. Many of its basic features, which were quite new and novel at the time, have become standard parts of modern operating systems. Device drivers were a major part of the system. In addition, system calls were added by a set of special instructions called *extra codes*.

Atlas was a batch operating system with spooling. Spooling allowed the system to schedule jobs according to the availability of peripheral devices, such as magnetic tape units, paper tape readers, paper tape punches, line printers, card readers, or card punches.

The most remarkable feature of Atlas, however, was its memory management. Core memory was quite new and very expensive at the time. Many computers, like the IBM 650, used a drum for primary memory. The Atlas system used a drum for its main memory, but had a small amount of core memory that was used as a cache for the drum. Demand paging was used to transfer information between core memory and the drum automatically.

The Atlas system used a Ferranti computer with 48-bit words. Addresses were 24 bits, but were encoded in decimal, which allowed only 1 million words to be addressed. At that time, this was a very large address space. The physical memory for Atlas was a 98K word drum and 16K words of core. Memory was divided into 512-word pages, providing 32 frames in physical memory. An associative memory of 32 registers implemented the mapping from a virtual address to a physical address.

If a page fault occurred, a page-replacement algorithm was invoked. One memory frame was always kept empty, so that a drum transfer could start immediately. The page-replacement algorithm attempted to predict the future memory-accessing behavior based on past behavior. A reference bit for each frame was set whenever the frame was accessed. The reference bits were read into memory every 1024 instructions. The last 32 values of the reference bit were used to define the time since the last reference (t_1) and the interval between the last two references (t_2). Pages were chosen for replacement in the following order:

1. Any page with $t_1 > t_2 + 1$. This page is considered to be no longer in use.

2. If $t_1 \leq t_2$ for all pages, then replace that page with the largest $t_2 - t_1$.

The page-replacement algorithm assumes that programs access memory in loops. If the time between the last two references is t_2, then another reference is expected t_2 time units later. If a reference does not occur ($t_1 > t_2$), it is assumed that the page is no longer being used, and the page is replaced. If all pages are still in use, then the page that will not be needed for the longest time is replaced. The time to the next reference is expected to be $t_2 - t_1$.

17.2 XDS-940

The XDS-940 operating system [Lichtenberger and Pirtle 1965, Lampson et al. 1966] was designed at the University of California at Berkeley. Like the Atlas system, it used paging for memory management. Unlike the Atlas system, the XDS-940 was a time-shared system.

The paging was used only for relocation, not for demand paging. The virtual memory of any user process was only 16K words, whereas the physical memory was 64K words. Pages were 2K words each. The page table was kept in registers. Since physical memory was larger than virtual memory, several user processes could be in memory at the same time. The number of users could be increased by sharing of pages when the latter contained read-only reentrant code. Processes were kept on a drum and were swapped in and out of memory as necessary.

The XDS-940 system was constructed from a modified XDS-930. The modifications were typical of the changes made to a basic computer to allow an operating system to be written properly. A user-monitor mode was added. Certain instructions, such as I/O and Halt, were defined to be privileged. An attempt to execute a privileged instruction in user mode would trap to the operating system.

A system-call instruction was added to the user-mode instruction set. This instruction was used to create new resources, such as files, allowing the operating system to manage the physical resources. Files, for example, were allocated in 256-word blocks on the drum. A bit map was used to manage free drum blocks. Each file had an index block with pointers to the actual data blocks. Index blocks were chained together.

The XDS-940 system also provided system calls to allow processes to create, start, suspend, and destroy subprocesses. A user programmer could construct a system of processes. Separate processes could share memory for communication and synchronization. Process creation defined a tree structure, where a process is the root and its subprocesses are nodes below it in the tree. Each of the subprocesses could, in turn, create more subprocesses.

17.3 THE

The THE operating system [Dijkstra 1968, Bron 1972, McKeag and Wilson 1976 (Chapter 3)] was designed at the Technische Hogeschool at

Eindhoven in the Netherlands. It is a batch system running on a Dutch computer, the EL X8, with 32K of 27-bit words. The system was mainly noted for its clean design, particularly its layer structure, and its use of a set of concurrent processes employing semaphores for synchronization.

Unlike the XDS-940 system, however, the set of processes in the THE system was static. The operating system itself was designed as a set of cooperating processes. In addition, five user processes were created, which served as the active agents to compile, execute, and print user programs. When one job was finished, the process would return to the input queue to select another job.

A priority CPU-scheduling algorithm was used. The priorities are recomputed every 2 seconds and were inversely proportional to the amount of CPU time used recently (in the last 8 to 10 seconds). This scheme gave higher priority to I/O-bound processes and to new processes.

Memory management was limited by the lack of hardware support. However, since the system was limited and user programs could be written only in Algol, a software paging scheme was used. The Algol compiler automatically generated calls to system routines, which made sure the requested information was in memory, swapping if necessary. The backing store was a 512K word drum. A 512-word page was used, with an LRU page-replacement strategy.

Another major concern of the THE system was deadlock control. The banker's algorithm was used to provide deadlock avoidance.

Closely related to the THE system is the Venus system [Liskov 1972]. The Venus system was also a layer-structure design, using semaphores to synchronize processes. The lower levels of the design were implemented in microcode, however, providing a much faster system. The memory management was changed to a paged-segmented memory. The system was also designed as a time-sharing system, rather than a batch system.

17.4 RC 4000

The RC 4000 system, like the THE system, was notable primarily for its design concepts. It was designed for the Danish RC 4000 computer by Regenecentralen, particularly by Brinch Hansen [1970, 1973a (Chapter 8)]. The objective was not to design a batch system, or a time-sharing system, or any other specific system. Rather, the goal was to create an operating-system nucleus, or kernel, on which a complete operating system could be built [Lauesen 1975]. Thus, the system structure was layered, and only the lower levels — the kernel — were provided.

The kernel supported a collection of concurrent processes. Processes were supported by a round-robin CPU scheduler. Although processes could share memory, the primary communication and synchronization mechanism was the *message system* provided by the kernel. Processes could communicate with each other by exchanging fixed-sized messages of eight words in length. All messages were stored in buffers from a common buffer pool. When a message buffer was no longer required, it was returned to the common pool.

A *message queue* was associated with each process. It contained all the messages that had been sent to that process, but had not yet been received. Messages were removed from the queue in FIFO order. The system supported four primitive operations, which were executed atomically:

- **send-message** (**in** *receiver*, **in** *message*, **out** *buffer*)

- **wait-message** (**out** *sender*, **out** *message*, **out** *buffer*)

- **send-answer** (**out** *result*, **in** *message*, **in** *buffer*)

- **wait-answer** (**out** *result*, **out** *message*, **in** *buffer*)

The last two operations allowed processes to exchange several messages at a time.

These primitives required that a process service its message queue in a FIFO order, and that it block itself while other processes were handling its messages. To remove these restrictions, the developers provided two additional communication primitives. They allowed a process to wait for the arrival of the next message or to answer and service its queue in any order:

- **wait-event** (**in** *previous-buffer*, **out** *next-buffer*, **out** *result*)

- **get-event** (**out** *buffer*)

I/O devices were also treated as processes. The device drivers were code that converted the device interrupts and registers into messages. Thus, a process would write to a terminal by sending that terminal a message. The device driver would receive the message and output the character to the terminal. An input character would interrupt the system and transfer to a device driver. The device driver would create a message from the input character and send it to a waiting process.

Brinch Hansen has continued his work on operating systems, and especially the principles of operating-system design. The language Concurrent Pascal [Brinch Hansen 1975] was defined to allow the writing of operating systems in a higher-level language. Concurrent Pascal has been used to define the Solo operating system [Brinch Hansen 1977].

Solo is a single-user multiprogrammed operating system for the PDP-11/45. It consists of a collection of concurrent processes. The most important aspect of the Solo system is that the use of a higher-level language allowed the entire system to be programmed by two people in less than 1 year. The system is sufficiently compact to be studied as an example in a course on operating systems.

17.5   CTSS

The CTSS (Compatible Time-Sharing System) system [Corbato et al. 1962] was designed at MIT as an experimental time-sharing system. It was implemented on an IBM 7090 and eventually supported up to 32 interactive users. The users were provided with a set of interactive commands, which allowed them to manipulate files and to compile and run programs through a terminal.

The 7090 had a 32K memory, made up of 36-bit words. The monitor used 5K words, leaving 27K for the users. User memory images were swapped between memory and a fast drum. CPU scheduling employed a multilevel-feedback-queue algorithm. The time quantum for level i was 2^i time units. If a program did not finish its CPU burst in one time quantum, it was moved down to the next level of the queue, giving it twice as much time. The program at the highest level (with the shortest quantum) was run first. The initial level of a program was determined by its size, so that its time quantum was at least as long as its swap time.

CTSS was extremely successful, and continued to be used as late as 1972. Although it was quite limited, it succeeded in demonstrating that time sharing was a convenient and practical mode of computing. One result of CTSS was increased development of time-sharing systems. Another result was the development of MULTICS.

17.6   MULTICS

MULTICS was designed at MIT [Corbato and Vyssotsky 1965, Daley and Dennis 1968, Organick 1972, Corbato et al. 1972] as a natural extension of CTSS. CTSS and other early time-sharing systems were so successful that there was an immediate desire to proceed quickly to bigger and better systems. As larger computers became available, the designers of CTSS set out to create a time-sharing *utility*. Computing service would be provided like electrical power. Large computer systems would be connected by telephone wires to terminals in offices and homes throughout a city. The operating system would be a time-shared system running continuously with a vast file system of shared programs and data.

MULTICS was designed by a team from MIT, GE (which later sold its computer department to Honeywell), and Bell Laboratory (which dropped out of the project in 1969). The basic GE 635 computer was modified to a new computer system called the GE 645, mainly by the addition of paged-segmentation memory hardware.

A virtual address was composed of an 18-bit segment number and a 16-bit word offset. The segments were then paged in 1K word pages. The second-chance page-replacement algorithm was used.

The segmented virtual address space was merged into the file system; each segment was a file. Segments were addressed by the name of the file. The file system itself was a multilevel tree structure, allowing users to create their own subdirectory structures.

Like CTSS, MULTICS used a multilevel feedback queue for CPU scheduling. Protection was accomplished by an access list associated with each file and a set of protection rings for executing processes. The system, which was written almost entirely in PL/1 [Corbato 1969], comprised about 300,000 lines of code. It was extended to a multiprocessor system, allowing a CPU to be taken out of service for maintenance while the system continued running.

17.7   OS/360

The longest line of operating-system development is undoubtedly that for IBM computers. The early IBM computers, such as the IBM 7090 and the IBM 7094, are prime examples of the development of common I/O subroutines, followed by a resident monitor, privileged instructions, memory protection, and simple batch processing. These systems were developed separately, often by each site independently. As a result, IBM was faced with many different computers, with different languages and different system software.

The IBM/360 was designed to alter this situation. The IBM/360 was designed as a family of computers spanning the complete range from small business machines to large scientific machines. Only one set of software would be needed for these systems, which all used the same operating system: OS/360 [Mealy et al. 1966]. This arrangement was supposed to reduce the maintenance problems for IBM and to allow users to move programs and applications freely from one IBM system to another.

Unfortunately, OS/360 tried to be all things for all people. As a result, it did none of its tasks especially well. The file system included a type field that defined the type of each file, and different file types were defined for fixed-length and variable-length records and for blocked and unblocked files. Contiguous allocation was used, so the user had to guess the size of each output file. The control-card language Job Control Language (JCL) added parameters for every possible option, making it incomprehensible to the average user.

The memory-management routines were hampered by the architecture. Although a base-register addressing mode was used, the program could access and modify the base register, so that absolute addresses were generated by the CPU. This arrangement prevented dynamic relocation; the program was bound to physical memory at load time. Two separate versions of the operating system were produced: OS/MFT used fixed regions and OS/MVT used variable regions.

The system was written in assembly language by thousands of programmers, resulting in millions of lines of code. The operating system itself required large amounts of memory for its code and tables. Operating-system overhead often consumed one-half of the total CPU cycles. Over the years, new versions were released to add new features and to fix errors. However, fixing one error often caused another in some remote part of the system, so that the number of known errors in the system was fairly constant.

Virtual memory was added to OS/360 with the change to the IBM 370 architecture. The underlying hardware provided a segmented-paged virtual memory. New versions of OS used this hardware in different ways. OS/VS1 created one large virtual address space, and ran OS/MFT in that virtual memory. Thus, the operating system itself was paged, as well as user programs. OS/VS2 Release 1 ran OS/MVT in virtual memory. Finally, OS/VS2 Release 2, which is now called MVS, provided each user with his own virtual memory.

MVS is still basically a batch operating system. The CTSS system was run on an IBM 7094, but MIT decided that the address space of the 360, IBM's successor to the 7094, was too small for MULTICS, so they switched vendors. IBM then decided to create its own time-sharing system, TSS/360 [Comfort 1965, Lett and Konigsford 1968]. Like MULTICS, TSS/360 was supposed to be a large time-shared utility. The basic 360 architecture was modified in the model 67 to provide virtual memory. Several sites purchased the 360/67 in anticipation of TSS/360.

TSS/360 was delayed [Schwemm 1972], however, so other time-sharing systems were developed as temporary systems until TSS/360 was available. A time-sharing option (TSO) was added to OS/360. IBM's Cambridge Scientific Center developed CMS as a single-user system and CP/67 to provide a virtual machine to run it on [Meyer and Seawright

1970, Parmelee et al. 1972]. The University of Michigan developed the Michigan Terminal System (MTS) [Alexander 1972]; Stanford developed Wylbur [Fajman 1973].

When TSS/360 was eventually delivered, it was a failure. It was too large and too slow. As a result, no site would switch from its temporary system to TSS/360. Today, time sharing on IBM systems is largely provided either by TSO under MVS or by CMS under CP/67 (renamed VM).

What went wrong with TSS/360 and MULTICS? Part of the problem was that these were really quite advanced systems, and were too large and too complex to be understood. Another problem was the assumption that computing power would be available from a large, remote computer by time sharing. It now appears that most computing will be done by small individual machines — personal computers — not by a large, remote time-shared systems that try to be all things to all users.

17.8 Other Systems

There are, of course, more operating systems, most of them with some interesting properties. The MCP operating system for the Burroughs computer family [McKeag and Wilson 1976] was the first to be written in a system programming language. It also supported segmentation and multiple CPUs. The SCOPE operating system for the CDC 6600 [McKeag and Wilson 1976] was also a multi-CPU system. The coordination and synchronization of the multiple processes were surprisingly well designed. Tenex [Bobrow et al. 1972] was an early demand-paging system for the PDP-10, which has had a great influence on subsequent time-sharing systems, such as TOPS-20 for the DEC-20. The VMS operating system for the VAX is based on the RSX operating system for the PDP-11. CP/M is the most common operating system for 8-bit microcomputer systems; MS-DOS is the most common system for 16-bit microcomputers.

BIBLIOGRAPHY

[Abate and Dubner 1969] J. Abate and H. Dubner, "Optimizing the Performance of a Drumlike Storage," *IEEE Transactions on Computers*, Volume C-18, Number 11 (November 1969), pages 992–996.

[Abbot 1984] C. Abbot, "Intervention Schedules for Reat-Time Programming," *IEEE Transactions on Software Engineering*, Volume SE-10, Number 3 (May 1984), pages 268–274.

[Abrams and Podell 1987] M. D. Abrams and H. J. Podell, *Tutorial: Computer and Network Security*, IEEE Computer Society #756, Los Angeles, CA (1987).

[Abu-Sufah and Padua 1982] W. Abu-Sufah and D. A. Padua, "Some Results on the Working Set Anomalies in Numerical Programs," *IEEE Transactions on Software Engineering*, Volume SE-8, Number 2 (March 1982), pages 97–106.

[Accetta et al. 1986] M. Accetta, R. Baron, W. Bolosky, D. B. Golub, R. Rashid, A. Tevanian, and M. Young, "Mach: A New Kernel Foundation for Unix Development," *Proceedings of the Summer 1986 USENIX Conference* (June 1986).

[Agrawal et al. 1986] D. P. Agrawal, V. K. Janakiram, and G. C. Pathak, "Evaluating the Performance of Multicomputer Configurations," *Communications of the ACM*, Volume 29, Number 5 (May 1986), pages 23–37.

[Ahituv et al. 1987] N. Ahituv, Y. Lapid and S. Neumann, "Processing Encrypted Data," *Communications of the ACM*, Volume 30, Number 9 (September 1987), pages 777–780.

[Aho et al. 1971] A. V. Aho, P. J. Denning, and J. D. Ullman, "Principles of Optimal Page Replacement," *Journal of the ACM*, Volume 18, Number 1 (January 1971), pages 80–93.

[Akl 1983] S. G. Akl, "Digital Signatures: A Tutorial Survey," *Computer*, Volume 16, Number 2 (February 1893), pages 15–24.

[Almes et al. 1983] G. T. Almes, A. P. Black, E. D. Lazowska, and J. D. Noe, "The Eden System: A Technical Review," *IEEE Transactions on Software Engineering*, Volume SE-11, Number 1 (January 1983), pages 43–59.

[Ammon et al. 1985] G. J. Ammon, J. A. Calabria, and D. T. Thomas, "A High-Speed, Large-Capacity, 'Jukebox' Optical Disk System," *Computer*, Volume 18, Number 7 (July 1985), pages 36–48.

[Anyanwu and Marshall 1986] J. A. Anyanwu and L. F. Marshall, "A Crash Resistant UNIX File System," *Software—Practice and Experience*, Volume 16 (February 1986), pages 107–118.

[Apple 1987] Apple Computer Inc., *Apple Technical Introduction to the Macintosh Family*, Addison-Wesley, Reading, MA (1987).

[Arden and Boettner 1969] B. Arden and D. Boettner, "Measurement and Performance of a Multiprogramming System," *Proceedings of the Second ACM Symposium on Operating System Principles* (October 1969), pages 130–146.

[AT&T 1986] AT&T, Steven V. Earhart, Ed., *UNIX Programmer's Manual*, Holt, Rinehart, and Winston, New York, NY (1986).

[Atwood 1976] J. W. Atwood, "Concurrency in Operating Systems," *Computer*, Volume 9, Number 10 (October 1976), pages 18–26.

[Babaoglu and Joy 1981] O. Babaoglu and W. Joy, "Converting a Swap-Based System To Do Paging in an Architecture Lacking Page-Referenced Bits," *Proceedings of the Eighth ACM Symposium on Operating System Principles* (December 1969), pages 78–86.

[Bach 1987] M. J. Bach, *The Design of the UNIX Operating System*, Prentice-Hall, Englewood Cliffs, NJ (1987).

[Baer 1980] J. L. Baer, *Computer System Architecture*, Computer Science Press, Rockville, MD (1980).

[Baer and Sager 1976] J. Baer and G. R. Sager, "Dynamic Improvement of Locality in Virtual Memory Systems," *IEEE Transaction on Software Engineering*, Volume SE-1, Number 1 (March 1976), pages 54–62.

[Balkovich et al. 1985] E. Balkovich, S. R. Lerman, and R. P. Parmelee, "Computing in Higher Education: The Athena Experience," *Communications of the ACM*, Volume 28, Number 11 (November 1985), pages 1214–1224.

[Barak and Kornatzky 1987] A. Barak and Y. Kornatzky, "Design Principles of Operating Systems for Large Scale Multicomputers," *Experience with Distributed Systems, Lecture Notes in Computer Science*, Volume 309, Springer-Verlag (September 1987), pages 104–123.

[Barron 1974] D. W. Barron, "Job Control Languages and Job Control Programs," *Computer Journal*, Volume 17, Number 3 (August 1974), pages 282–286.

[Baskett 1971] F. Baskett, "The Dependence of Computer System Queues upon Processing Time Distribution and Central Processor Scheduling," *Proceedings of the Third ACM Symposium on Operating System Principles* (October 1971), pages 109–113.

[Batson et al. 1970] A. P. Batson, S. Ju, and D. Wood, "Measurements of Segment Size," *Communications of the ACM*, Volume 13, Number 3 (March 1970), pages 155–159.

[Bayer et al. 1978] R. Bayer, R. M. Graham, and G. Seegmuller, Eds., *Operating Systems — An Advanced Course*, Springer-Verlag, Berlin (1978).

[Bays 1977] C. Bays, "A Comparison of Next-Fit, First-Fit, and Best-Fit," *Communications of the ACM*, Volume 20, Number 3 (March 1977), pages 191–192.

[Belady 1966] L. A. Belady, "A Study of Replacement Algorithms for a Virtual-Storage Computer," *IBM Systems Journal*, Volume 5, Number 2 (1966), pages 78–101.

[Belady and Kuehner 1969] L. A. Belady and C. J. Kuehner, "Dynamic Space Sharing in Computer Systems," *Communications of the ACM*, Volume 12, Number 5 (May 1969), pages 282–288.

[Belady et al. 1969] L. A. Belady, R. A. Nelson, and G. S. Shedler, "An Anomaly in Space-Time Characteristics of Certain Programs Running in a Paging Machine," *Communications of the ACM*, Volume 12, Number 6 (June 1969), pages 349–353.

[Bensoussan et al. 1972] A. Bensoussan, C. T. Clingen, and R. C. Daley, "The Multics Virtual Memory: Concepts and Design," *Communications of the ACM*, Volume 15, Number 5, (May 1972), pages 308–318.

[Bernstein and Siegel 1975] A. J. Bernstein and P. Siegel, "A Computer Architecture for Level Structured Operating Systems," *IEEE Transactions on Computers*, Volume C-24, Number 8 (August 1975), pages 785–793.

[Bershad and Pinkerton 1988] B. N. Bershad and C. B. Pinkerton, "Watchdogs: Extending the Unix File System," *Proceedings of the Winter 1988 USENIX Conference* (February 1988).

[Bhuyan et al. 1989] L. N. Bhuyan, Q. Yang, and D. P. Agrawal, "Performance of Multiprocessor Interconnection Networks," *Computer*, Volume 22, Number 2 (February 1989), pages 25–37.

[Bic and Shaw 1988] L. Bic and A. C. Shaw, *The Logical Design of Operating Systems*, Second Edition, Prentice-Hall, Englewood Cliffs, NJ (1988).

[Birman and Joseph 1987] K. Birman and T. Joseph, "Reliable Communication in the Presence of Failures," *ACM Transactions on Computer Systems*, Volume 5, Number 1 (February 1987).

[Birrell and Needham 1980] A. D. Birrell and R. M. Needham, "A Universal File Server," *IEEE Transactions on Software Engineering*, Volume SE-6, Number 5 (September 1980), pages 450–453.

[Birrell and Nelson 1984] A. D. Birrell and B. J. Nelson, "Implementing Remote Procedure Calls," *ACM Transactions on Computer Systems*, Volume 2, Number 1 (February 1984), pages 39–59.

[Black 1985] A. P. Black, "Supporting Distributed Applications: Experience with Eden," *Proceedings of the Tenth Symposium on Operating System Principles* (December 1985), pages 181–193.

[Black 1990] D. L. Black, "Scheduling Support for Concurrency and Parallelism in the Mach Operating System," *IEEE Computer* (May 1990), pages 35-43.

[Black et al. 1988] D. L. Black, D. B. Golub, R. F. Rashid, A. Tevanian Jr., and M. Young, "The Mach Exception Handling Facility," Technical Report, Carnegie Mellon University (April 1988).

[Blair et al. 1985] G. S. Blair, J. R. Malone, and J. A. Mariani, "A Critique of UNIX," *Software—Practice and Experience*, Volume 15, Number 6 (December 1985), pages 1125–1139.

[Bobrow et al. 1972] D. G. Bobrow, J. D. Burchfiel, D. L. Murphy, and R. S. Tomlinson, "TENEX, a Paged Time Sharing System for the PDP-10," *Communications of the ACM*, Volume 15, Number 3 (March 1972).

[Boorstyn and Frank 1977] R. R. Boorstyn and H. Frank, "Large-Scale Network Topological Optimization," *IEEE Transactions on Communications*, Volume COM-25, Number 1 (January 1977), pages 29–47.

[Bourne 1978] S. R. Bourne, "The UNIX Shell," *Bell System Technical Journal*, Volume 57, Number 6 (July-August 1978), pages 1971–1990.

[Bourne 1983] S. R. Bourne, *The UNIX System*, Addison-Wesley, Reading, MA (1983).

[Bozman et al. 1984] G. Bozman, W. Buco, T. P. Daly, and W. H. Tezlaff, "Analysis of Free-Storage Algorithms-Revisted," *IBM Systems Journal*, Volume 23, Number 1 (1984), pages 44–66.

[Branstad 1973] D. K. Branstad, "Privacy and Protection in Operating Systems," *Computer*, Volume 6, Number 1 (January 1973), pages 43−46.

[Bratman and Boldt 1959] H. Bratman and I. V. Boldt, "The SHARE 709 System: Supervisory Control," *Journal of the ACM*, Volume 6, Number 2 (April 1959), pages 152−155.

[Brawn and Gustavson 1968] B. Brawn and F. G. Gustavson, "Program Behavior in a Paging Environment," *Proceedings of the AFIPS Fall Joint Computer Conference* (1968), pages 1019−1032.

[Brinch Hansen 1970] P. Brinch Hansen, "The Nucleus of a Multiprogramming System," *Communications of the ACM*, Volume 13, Number 4 (April 1970), pages 238−241 and 250.

[Brinch Hansen 1972a] P. Brinch Hansen, "A Comparison of Two Synchronizing Concepts," *Acta Informatica*, Volume 1, Number 3 (1972), pages 190−199.

[Brinch Hansen 1972b] P. Brinch Hansen, "Structured Multiprogramming," *Communications of the ACM*, Volume 15, Number 7 (July 1972), pages 574−578.

[Brinch Hansen 1973a] P. Brinch Hansen, *Operating System Principles*, Prentice-Hall, Englewood Cliffs, NJ (1973).

[Brinch Hansen 1973b] P. Brinch Hansen, "Concurrent Programming Concepts," *Computing Surveys*, Volume 5, Number 4 (December 1973), pages 223−245.

[Brinch Hansen 1975] P. Brinch Hansen, "The Programming Language Concurrent Pascal," *IEEE Transactions on Software Engineering*, Volume SE-1, Number 2 (June 1975), pages 199−207.

[Brinch Hansen 1977] P. Brinch Hansen, *The Architecture of Concurrent Programs*, Prentice-Hall, Englewood Cliffs, NJ (1977).

[Brinch Hansen 1983] P. Brinch Hansen, *Programming a Personal Computer*, Prentice-Hall, Englewood Cliffs, NJ (1983).

[Bron 1972] C. Bron, "Allocation of Virtual Store in the THE Multiprogramming System," in [Hoare and Perrott 1972], pages 168−193.

[Brown 1970] G. D. Brown, *System/360 Job Control Language*, John Wiley and Sons, New York, NY (1970).

[Brown 1978] H. Brown, "Recent Developments in Command Languages," *Information Technology: Proceedings of the Third Jerusalem Conference on Information Technology*, North-Holland, Amsterdam (1978), pages 453−460.

[Brownbridge et al. 1982] D. R. Brownbridge, L. F. Marshall, and B. Randell, "The Newcastle Connection or UNIXes of the World Unite!," *Software—Practice and Experience*, Volume 12, Number 12 (December 1982), pages 1147−1162.

[Brumfield 1986] J. A. Brumfield, "A Guide to Operating Systems Literature," *Operating Systems Review*, Volume 20, Number 2 (April 1986), pages 38–42.

[Brunt and Tuffs 1976] R. F. Brunt and D. E. Tuffs, "A User-Oriented Approach to Control Languages," *Software—Practice and Experience*, Volume 6, Number 1 (January-March 1976), pages 93–108.

[Bryant 1975] P. Bryant, "Predicting Working Set Sizes," *IBM Journal of Research and Development*, Volume 19, Number 3 (May 1975), pages 221–229.

[BSTJ 1978] "UNIX Time-Sharing System," *The Bell System Technical Journal*, Volume 57, Number 6, Part 2 (July-August 1978).

[BSTJ 1984] "The UNIX System," *The Bell System Technical Journal*, Volume 63, Number 8, Part 2 (October 1984).

[Budzinski 1981] R. L. Budzinski, "A Comparison of Dynamic and Static Virtual Memory Allocation Algorithms," *IEEE Transactions on Software Engineering*, Volume SE-7, Number 1 (January 1981), pages 122–131.

[Budzinski et al. 1981] R. Budzinski, E. Davidson, W. Mayeda, and H. Stone, "DMIN: An Algorithm for Computing the Optimal Dynamic Allocation in a Virtual Memory Computer," *IEEE Transactions on Software Engineering*, Volume SE-7, Number 1 (January 1981), pages 113–121.

[Bunt 1976] R. B. Bunt, "Scheduling Techniques for Operating Systems," *Computer*, Volume 9, Number 10 (October 1976), pages 10–17.

[Burns 1978] J. E. Burns, "Mutual Exclusion with Linear Waiting Using Binary Shared Variables," *SIGACT News*, Volume 10, Number 2 (Summer 1978), pages 42–47.

[Burns and Lynch 1980] J. E. Burns and N. A. Lynch, "Mutual Exclusion Using Indivisible Reads and Writes," *Proceedings of the Eighteenth Annual Allerton Conference on Communication, Control, and Computing*, (1980), pages 833–842.

[Burns et al. 1982] J. E. Burns, P. Jackson, N. A. Lynch, M. J. Fischer, and G. L. Peterson, "Data Requirements for Implementation of N-Process Mutual Exclusion Using a Single Shared Variable," *Journal of the ACM*, Volume 29, Number 1 (January 1982), pages 183–205.

[Buzen 1973] J. P. Buzen, "Computational Algorithms for Closed Queuing Networks with Exponential Servers," *Communications of the ACM*, Volume 16, Number 9 (September 1973), pages 527–531.

[Carvalho and Roucairol 1983] O. S. Carvalho and G. Roucairol, "On Mutual Exclusion in Computer Networks," *Communications of the ACM*, Volume 26, Number 2 (February 1983), pages 146–147.

[Carr and Hennessy 1981] W. R. Carr and J. L. Hennessy, "WSClock — A Simple and Effective Algorithm for Virtual Memory Management," *Proceedings of the Eighth Symposium on Operating System Principles* (December 1981), pages 87–95.

[Caswell and Black 1989] D. Caswell and D. Black, "Implementing a Mach Debugger for Multithreaded Applications," Technical Report, Carnegie Mellon University, PA (November 1989).

[Cerf 1972] V. G. Cerf, "Multiprocessors, Semaphores, and a Graph Model of Computation," PhD. Thesis, University of California at Los Angeles, CA (1972).

[Cerf and Cain 1983] V. G. Cerf and E. Cain, "The DoD Internet Architecture Model," *Computer Networks*, Volume 7, Number 5 (October 1983), pages 307–318.

[Chambers and Quarterman 1983] J. Chambers and J. Quarterman, "UNIX System V and 4.1C BSD," *Proceedings of the Summer 1983 USENIX Conference* (July 1983).

[Chang 1980] E. Chang, "N-Philosophers: An Exercise in Distributed Control," *Computer Networks*, Volume 4, Number 2 (April 1980), pages 71–76.

[Chang and Mergen 1988] A. Chang and M. F. Mergen, "801 Storage: Architecture and Programming," ACM Transactions on Computer Systems, Volume 6, Number 1 (February, 1988), pages 28–50.

[Cheriton and Zwaenepoel 1983] D. R. Cheriton and W. Z. Zwaenepoel, "The Distributed V Kernel and Its Performance for Diskless Workstations," *Proceedings of the Ninth Symposium on Operating Systems Principles* (October 1983), pages 129–140.

[Cheriton et al. 1979] D. R. Cheriton, M. A. Malcolm, L. S. Melen, and G. R. Sager, "Thoth, a Portable Real-Time Operating System," *Communications of the ACM*, Volume 22, Number 2 (February 1979), pages 105–115.

[Chi 1982] C. S. Chi, "Advances in Computer Mass Storage Technology," *Computer*, Volume 15, Number 5 (May 1982), pages 60–74.

[Chu 1969] W. W. Chu, "Optimal File Allocation in a Multiple Computer System," *IEEE Transactions on Computers*, Volume C-18, Number 10 (October 1969), pages 885–889.

[Chu and Opderbeck 1974] W. W. Chu and H. Opderbeck, "Performance of Replacement Algorithms with Different Page Sizes," *Computer*, Volume 7, Number 11 (November 1974), pages 14−21.

[Chu and Opderbeck 1976] W. W. Chu and H. Opderbeck, "Program Behavior and the Page-Fault-Frequency Replacement Algorithm," *Computer*, Volume 9, Number 11 (November 1976), pages 29−38.

[Clark et al. 1978] D. D. Clark, K. T. Pogran, and D. P. Reed, "An Introduction to Local Area Networks," *Proceedings of the IEEE*, Volume 66, Number 11 (November 1978), pages 1497−1517.

[Coffman 1969] E. G. Coffman, "Analysis of a Drum Input/Output Queue Under Scheduling Operation in a Paged Computer System," *Journal of the ACM*, Volume 16, Number 1 (January 1969), pages 73−90.

[Coffman and Kleinrock 1968a] E. G. Coffman and L. Kleinrock, "Computer Scheduling Methods and their Countermeasures," *Proceedings of the AFIPS Spring Joint Computer Conference* (April 1968), pages 11−21.

[Coffman and Kleinrock 1968b] E. G. Coffman and L. Kleinrock, "Feedback Queuing Models for Time-Shared Systems," *Journal of the ACM*, Volume 15, Number 4 (October 1968), pages 549−576.

[Coffman and Varian 1968] E. G. Coffman and L. C. Varian, "Further Experimental Data on the Behavior of Programs in a Paging Environment," *Communications of the ACM*, Volume 11, Number 7 (July 1968), pages 471−474.

[Coffman and Ryan 1972] E. G. Coffman and T. A. Ryan, "A Study of Storage Partitioning using a Mathematical Model of Locality," *Communications of the ACM*, Volume 15, Number 3, (March 1972), pages 185−190.

[Coffman and Denning 1973] E. G. Coffman and P. J. Denning, *Operating Systems Theory*, Prentice-Hall, Englewood Cliffs, NJ (1973).

[Coffman et al. 1971] E. G. Coffman, M. J. Elphick, and A. Shoshani, "System Deadlocks," *Computing Surveys*, Volume 3, Number 2 (June 1971), pages 67−78.

[Cohen and Jefferson 1975] E. S. Cohen and D. Jefferson, "Protection in the Hydra Operating System," *Proceedings of the Fifth Symposium on Operating System Principles* (November 1975), pages 141−160.

[Comeau 1967] L. W. Comeau, "A Study of the Effect of User Program Optimization in a Paging System," *Proceedings of the First ACM Symposium on Operating System Principles* (October 1967).

[Comer 1984] D. Comer, *Operating System Design: the Xinu Approach*, Prentice-Hall, Englewood Cliffs, NJ (1984).

[Comer 1987] D. Comer, *Operating System Design — Volume II: Internetworking with Xinu*, Prentice-Hall, Englewood Cliffs, NJ (1987).

[Comer 1988] D. Comer, *Internetworking with TCP/IP Principles, Protocols, and Architecture*, Prentice-Hall, Englewood Cliffs, NJ (1988).

[Conway 1963] M. Conway, "A Multiprocessor System Design," *Proceedings of the AFIPS Fall Joint Computer Conference* (1963), pages 139–146.

[Conway et al. 1967] R. W. Conway, W. L. Maxwell, and L. W. Miller, *Theory of Scheduling*, Addison-Wesley, Reading, MA (1967).

[Conway et al. 1972] R. W. Conway, W. L. Maxwell, and H. L. Morgan, "On the Implementation of Security Measures in Information Systems," *Communications of the ACM*, Volume 15, Number 4 (April 1972), pages 211–220.

[Cooper and Draves 1987] E. C. Cooper and R. P. Draves, "C Threads," Technical Report, Carnegie Mellon University, PA (July 1987)

[Copeland 1982] G. Copeland, "What If Mass Storage Were Free," *Computer*, Volume 15, Number 7 (July 1982), pages 27–35.

[Corbato and Vyssotsky 1965] F. J. Corbato and V. A. Vyssotsky, "Introduction and Overview of the MULTICS System," *Proceedings of the AFIPS Fall Joint Computer Conference* (1965), pages 185–196; reprinted in [Rosen 1967], pages 714–730.

[Corbato et al. 1962] F. J. Corbato, M. Merwin-Daggett, and R. C. Daley, "An Experimental Time-Sharing System," *Proceedings of the AFIPS Fall Joint Computer Conference* (May 1962), pages 335–344.

[Corbato et al. 1972] F. J. Corbato, J. H. Saltzer, and C. T. Clingen, "MULTICS — The First Seven Years," *Proceedings of the AFIPS Spring Joint Computer Conference* (1972), pages 571–583.

[Courtois et al. 1971] P. J. Courtois, F. Heymans, and D. L. Parnas, "Concurrent Control with 'Readers' and 'Writers'," *Communications of the ACM*, Volume 14, Number 10 (October 1971), pages 667–668.

[Cox 1975] G. W. Cox, "Portability and Adaptability in Operating System Design," PhD. Thesis, Purdue University (1975).

[Creasy 1981] R. J. Creasy, "The Origin of the VM/370 Time-Sharing System," *IBM Journal of Research and Development*, Volume 25, Number 5 (September 1981), pages 483–490.

[Crowther et al. 1975] W. R. Crowther, F. E. Heart, A. A. McKenzie, J. M. McQuillan, and D. C. Walden, "Issues in Packet Switching Network Design," *Proceedings of the AFIPS National Computer Conference* (1975), pages 161–176.

[CSRG 1986] Computer Systems Research Group — University of California at Berkeley, *BSD UNIX Reference Manuals*, six volumes, USENIX Association (1986).

[Daley and Dennis 1968] R. C. Daley and J. B. Dennis, "Virtual Memory, Processes, and Sharing in MULTICS," *Communications of the ACM*, Volume 11, Number 5 (May 1968), pages 306–312.

[Davcev and Burkhard] D. Davcev and W. A. Burkhard, "Consistency and Recovery Control for Replicated Files," *Proceedings of the Tenth Symposium on Operating Systems Principles*, ACM, Volume 19, Number 5 (December 1985), pages 87–96.

[Davies 1980] D. W. Davies, "Protection," *Distributed Systems: An Advanced Course*, Springer-Verlag, Berlin (1980).

[Davies 1983] D. W. Davies, "Applying the RSA Digital Signature to Electronic Mail," *Computer*, Volume 16, Number 2 (February 1983), pages 55–62.

[deBruijn 1967] N. G. deBruijn, "Additional Comments on a Problem in Concurrent Programming and Control," *Communications of the ACM*, Volume 10, Number 3 (March 1967), pages 137–138.

[Deitel 1990] H. M. Deitel, *An Introduction to Operating Systems*, Second Edition, Addison-Wesley, Reading, MA (1990).

[Denning 1968] P. J. Denning, "The Working Set Model for Program Behavior," *Communications of the ACM*, Volume 11, Number 5 (May 1968), pages 323–333.

[Denning 1970] P. J. Denning, "Virtual Memory," *Computing Surveys*, Volume 2, Number 3 (September 1970), pages 153–189.

[Denning 1971] P. J. Denning, "Third Generation Computer System," *Computing Surveys*, Volume 3, Number 34 (December 1971), pages 175–216.

[Denning 1976] P. J. Denning, "Fault-Tolerant Operating Systems," *Computing Surveys*, Volume 8, Number 4 (December 1976), pages 359–389.

[Denning 1980a] P. J. Denning, "Working Sets Past and Present," *IEEE Transactions on Software Engineering*, Volume SE-6, Number 1 (January 1980), pages 64–84.

[Denning 1980b] P. J. Denning, "Another Look at Operating Systems," *Operating Systems Review*, Volume 14, Number 4 (October 1980), pages 78–82.

[Denning 1982a] P. J. Denning, "Are Operating Systems Obsolete?" *Communications of the ACM*, Volume 25, Number 4 (April 1982), pages 225–227.

[Denning 1982b] D. E. Denning, *Cryptography and Data Security*, Addison-Wesley, Reading, MA (1982).

[Denning 1983] D. E. Denning, "Protecting Public Keys and Signature Keys," *IEEE Computer*, Volume 16, Number 2 (February 1983), pages 27–35.

[Denning 1984] D. E. "Digital Signatures with RSA and Other Public-Key Cryptosystems," *Communications of the ACM*, Volume 27, Number 4 (April 1984), pages 388–392.

[Denning and Schwartz 1972] P. J. Denning and S. C. Schwartz, "Properties of the Working Set Model," *Communications of the ACM*, Volume 15, Number 3 (March 1972), pages 191–198.

[Denning and Slutz 1978] P. J. Denning and D. R. Slutz, "Generalized Working Sets for Segment Reference Strings," *Communications of the ACM*, Volume 21, Number 9 (September 1978), pages 750–759.

[Dennis 1965] J. B. Dennis, "Segmentation and the Design of Multiprogrammed Computer Systems," *Journal of the ACM*, Volume 12, Number 4 (October 1965), pages 589–602.

[Dennis and Van Horn 1966] J. B. Dennis and E. C. Van Horn, "Programming Semantics for Multiprogrammed Computations," *Communications of the ACM*, Volume 9, Number 3 (March 1966), pages 143–155.

[Devillers 1977] R. Devillers, "Game Interpretation of the Deadlock Avoidance Problem," *Communications of the ACM*, Volume 20, Number 10 (October 1977), pages 741–745.

[Diffie and Hellman 1976] W. Diffie and M. E. Hellman, "New Directions in Cryptography," *IEEE Transactions on Information Theory*, Volume 22, Number 6 (November 1976), pages 644–654.

[Diffie and Hellman 1979] W. Diffie and M. E. Hellman, "Privacy and Authentication," *Proceedings of the IEEE*, Volume 67, Number 3 (March 1979), pages 397–427.

[Digital 1989] Digital Equipment Corporation, *VMS System Software Handbook*, Maynard, MA (1989).

[Dijkstra 1965a] E. W. Dijkstra, "Cooperating Sequential Processes," Technical Report EWD-123, Technological University, Eindhoven, the Netherlands (1965); reprinted in [Genuys 1968], pages 43–112.

[Dijkstra 1965b] E. W. Dijkstra, "Solution of a Problem in Concurrent Programming Control," *Communications of the ACM*, Volume 8, Number 9 (September 1965), Page 569.

[Dijkstra 1968] E. W. Dijkstra, "The Structure of the THE Multiprogramming System," *Communications of the ACM*, Volume 11, Number 5 (May 1968), pages 341–346.

[Dijkstra 1971] E. W. Dijkstra, "Hierarchical Ordering of Sequential Processes," *Acta Informatica*, Volume 1, Number 2 (1971), pages 115−138; reprinted in [Hoare and Perrott 1972], pages 72−93.

[Dion 1980] J. Dion, "The Cambridge File Server," *Operating Systems Review*, Volume 14, Number 4 (October 1980), pages 26−35.

[Doll 1974] D. R. Doll, "Telecommunications Turbulence and the Computer Network Evolution," *Computer*, Volume 7, Number 2 (February 1974), pages 13−22.

[Donnelley 1979] J. E. Donnelley, "Components of a Network Operating System," *Computer Networks*, Volume 3, Number 6 (December 1979), pages 389−399.

[Doran 1976] R. W. Doran, "Virtual Memory," *Computer*, Volume 9, Number 10 (October 1976), pages 27−37.

[Doran and Thomas 1980] R. W. Doran and L. K. Thomas, "Variants of the Software to Mutual Exclusion," *Information Processing Letters*, Volume 10, Number 4/5 (1980), pages 206−208.

[Draves et al. 1989] R. P. Draves, M. B. Jones, and M. R. Thompson, "MIG - The MACH Interface Generator," Technical Report, Carnegie Mellon University, PA (November 1989).

[Easton and Bennett 1977] M. C. Easton and B. T. Bennett, "Transient-Free Working Set Statistics," *Communications of the ACM*, Volume 20, Number 2 (February 1977), pages 93−99.

[Eisenberg and McGuire 1972] M. A. Eisenberg and M. R. McGuire, "Further Comments on Dijkstra's Concurrent Programming Control Problem," *Communications of the ACM*, Volume 15, Number 11 (November 1972), page 999.

[Ekanadham and Bernstein 1979] K. Ekanadham and A. J. Bernstein, "Conditional Capabilities," *IEEE Transactions on Software Engineering*, Volume SE-5, Number 5 (September 1979), pages 458−464.

[Ellis and Floyd 1983] C. S. Ellis and R. A. Floyd, "The ROE File System," *Proceedings of the Third Symposium on Reliability in Distributed Software and Database Systems* (October 1983).

[Enslow 1977] P. H. Enslow, "Multiprocessor Organization — A Survey," *Computing Surveys*, Volume 9, Number 1 (March 1977), pages 103−129.

[Farrow 1986a] R. Farrow, "Security Issues and Strategies for Users," *UNIX World* (April 1986), pages 65−71.

[Farrow 1986b] R. Farrow, "Security for Superusers, or How to Break the UNIX System," *UNIX World* (May 1986), pages 65−70.

[Feng 1981] T. Feng, "A Survey of Interconnection Networks," *Computer*, Volume 14, Number 12 (1981), pages 12−27.

[Fernandez and Allen 1988] G. Fernandez and L. Allen, "Extending the UNIX Protection Model with Access Control Lists," *Proceedings of the Summer 1988 USENIX Conference* (June 1988), pages 119−132.

[Ferrari 1974] D. Ferrari, "Improving Locality by Critical Working Sets," *Communications of the ACM*, Volume 17, Number 11 (November 1974), pages 614−620.

[Filipski and Hanko 1986] A. Filipski and J. Hanko, "Making UNIX Secure," *Byte* (April 1986), pages 113−128.

[Fine et al. 1966] G. H. Fine, C. W. Jackson, and P. V. McIsaac, "Dynamic Program Behavior Under Paging," *Proceedings of the ACM National Meeting* (1966), pages 223−228.

[Finkel 1988] R. A. Finkel, *Operating Systems Vade Mecum*, Second Edition, Prentice-Hall, Englewood Cliffs, NJ (1988).

[Fontao 1971] R. O. Fontao, "A Concurrent Algorithm for Avoiding Deadlocks," *Proceedings of the Third ACM Symposium on Operating Systems Principles* (October 1971), pages 72−79.

[Forsdick et al. 1978] H. C. Forsdick, R. E. Schantz, and R. H. Thomas, "Operating Systems for Computer Networks," *Computer*, Volume 11, Number 1 (January 1978), pages 48−57.

[Fortier 1989] P. J. Fortier, *Handbook of LAN Technology*, McGraw Hill, New York, NY (1989).

[Fotheringham 1961] J. Fotheringham, "Dynamic Storage Allocation in the Atlas Computer Including an Automatic Use of a Backing Store," *Communications of the ACM*, Volume 4, Number 10 (October 1961), pages 435−436.

[Frailey 1973] D. J. Frailey, "A Practical Approach to Managing Resources and Avoiding Deadlock," *Communications of the ACM*, Volume 16, Number 5 (May 1973), pages 323−329.

[Frank 1976] G. R. Frank, "Job Control in the MU5 Operating System," *Computer Journal*, Volume 19, Number 2 (May 1976), pages 139−143.

[Freedman 1983] D. H. Freedman, "Searching for Denser Disks," *Infosystems* (September 1983), page 56.

[Freibergs 1968] I. F. Freibergs, "The Dynamic Behavior of Programs," *Proceedings of the AFIPS Fall Joint Computer Conference* (1968), pages 1163−1167.

[Fridrich and Older 1981] M. Fridrich and W. Older, "The Felix File Server," *Proceedings of the Eighth Symposium on Operating Systems Principles* (December 1981), pages 37–46.

[Fujitani 1984] L. Fujitani, "Laser Optical Disk: The Coming Revolution in On-Line Storage," *Communications of the ACM*, Volume 27, Number 6 (June 1984), pages 546–554.

[Fuller 1972] S. H. Fuller, "An Optimal Drum Scheduling Algorithm," *IEEE Transactions on Computers*, Volume C-21, Number 11 (November 1972), pages 1153–1165.

[Fuller 1974] S. H. Fuller, "Minimal-Total-Processing-Time Drum and Disk Scheduling Disciplines," *Communications of the ACM*, Volume 17, Number 7 (July 1974), pages 376–381.

[Gait 1988] J. Gait, "The Optical File Cabinet: A Random-Access File System for Write-On Optical Disks," *Computer*, Volume 21, Number 6 (June 1988).

[Garcia-Molina 1982] H. Garcia-Molina "Elections in Distributed Computing Systems," *IEEE Transactions on Computers*, Volume C-31, Number 1 (January 1982).

[Gelernter 1981] D. Gelernter, "A DAG Bàsed Algorithm for Prevention of Store-and-Forward Deadlock in Packet Networks," *IEEE Transactions on Computers*, Volume C-30, Number 10 (October 1981), pages 709–715.

[Gerla and Kleinrock 1977] M. Gerla and L. Kleinrock, "Topological Design of Distributed Computer Networks," *IEEE Transactions on Communications*, Volume COM-25, Number 1 (January 1977), pages 48–60.

[Gien 1978] M. Gien, "A File Transfer Protocol FTP," *Computer Networks*, Volume 2, Numbers 4/5 (September-October 1978), pages 312–319.

[Gifford 1982] D. K. Gifford, "Cryptographic Sealing for Information Secrecy and Authentication," *Communications of the ACM*, Volume 25, Number 4 (April 1982), pages 274–286.

[Gligor and Shattuck 1980] V. D. Gligor and S. H. Shattuck, "On Deadlock Detection in Distributed Systems," *IEEE Transactions on Software Engineering*, Volume SE-6, Number 5 (September 1980), pages 435–440.

[Gold 1978] E. M. Gold, "Deadlock Prediction: Easy and Difficult Cases," *SIAM Journal of Computing*, Volume 7, Number 3 (August 1978), pages 320–336.

[Goldberg 1974] R. P. Goldberg, "Survey of Virtual Machine Research," *Computer* (June 1974).

[Golden and Pechura 1986] D. Golden and M. Pechura, "The Structure of Microcomputer File Systems," *Communications of the ACM*, Volume 29, Number 3 (March 1986), pages 222–230.

[Gotlieb and MacEwen 1973] C. C. Gotlieb and G. H. MacEwen, "Performance of Movable-Head Disk Scheduling Disciplines," *Journal of the ACM*, Volume 20, Number 4 (October 1973), pages 604–623.

[Graham 1968] R. M. Graham, "Protection in an Information Processing Utility," *Communications of the ACM*, Volume 11, Number 5 (May 1968), pages 365–369.

[Graham and Denning 1972] G. S. Graham and P. J. Denning, "Protection — Principles and Practice," *Proceedings of the AFIPS Spring Joint Computer Conference* (1972), pages 417–429.

[Gram and Hertweck 1975] C. Gram and F. R. Hertweck, "Command Languages: Design Considerations and Basic Concepts," in [Unger 1975], pages 43–67.

[Grampp and Morris 1984] F. T. Grampp and R. H. Morris, "UNIX Operating System Security," *AT&T Bell Laboratories Technical Journal*, Volume 63 (October 1984), pages 1649–1672.

[Grosshans 1986] D. Grosshans, *File Systems Design and Implementation*, Prentice-Hall, Englewood Cliffs, NJ (1986).

[Gupta and Franklin 1978] R. K. Gupta and M. A. Franklin, "Working Set and Page Fault Frequency Replacement Algorithms: A Performance Comparison," *IEEE Transactions on Computers*, Volume C-27, Number 8 (August 1978), pages 706–712.

[Gustavson 1968] F. G. Gustavson, "Program Behavior in a Paging Environment," *Proceedings of the AFIPS Fall Joint Computer Conference* (1968), pages 1019–1032.

[Habermann 1969] A. N. Habermann, "Prevention of System Deadlocks," *Communications of the ACM*, Volume 12, Number 7 (July 1969), pages 373–377 and 385.

[Habermann 1972] A. N. Habermann, "Synchronization of Communicating Processes," *Communications of the ACM*, Volume 15, Number 3 (March 1972), pages 171–176.

[Habermann 1976] A. N. Habermann, *Introduction to Operating System Design*, Science Research Associates, Palo Alto, CA (1976).

[Habermann et al. 1976] A. N. Habermann, L. Flon, and L. Cooprider, "Modularization and Hierarchy in a Family of Operating Systems," *Communications of the ACM*, Volume 19, Number 5 (May 1976), pages 266–272.

[Hall et al. 1980] D. E. Hall, D. K. Scherrer, and J. S. Sventek, "A Virtual Operating System," *Communications of the ACM*, Volume 23, Number 9 (September 1980), pages 495–502.

[Harker et al. 1981] J. M. Harker, D. W. Brede, R. E. Pattison, G. R. Santana, and L. G. Taft, "A Quarter Century of Disk File Innovation," *IBM Journal of Research and Development*, Volume 25, Number 5 (September 1981), pages 677−689.

[Harrison et al. 1976] M. A. Harrison, W. L. Ruzzo, and J. D. Ullman, "Protection in Operating Systems," *Communications of the ACM*, Volume 19, Number 8 (August 1976), pages 461−471.

[Hatfield 1972] D. Hatfield, "Experiments on Page Size, Program Access Patterns, and Virtual Memory Performance," *IBM Journal of Research and Development*, Volume 16, Number 1 (January 1972), pages 58−62.

[Hatfield and Gerald 1971] D. Hatfield and J. Gerald, "Program Restructuring for Virtual Memory," *IBM Systems Journal*, Volume 10, Number 3 (1971), pages 168−192.

[Havender 1968] J. W. Havender, "Avoiding Deadlock in Multitasking Systems," *IBM Systems Journal*, Volume 7, Number 2 (1968), pages 74−84.

[Hecht et al. 1988] M. S. Hecht, A. Johri, R. Aditham, and T. J. Wei, "Experience Adding C2 Security Features to UNIX," *Proceedings of the Summer 1988 USENIX Conference* (June 1988), pages 133−146.

[Henderson and Zalcstein 1980] P. Henderson and Y. Zalcstein, "Synchronization Problems Solvable By Generalized PV Systems," *Journal of the ACM*, Volume 27, Number 1 (January 1980), pages 60−71.

[Hendricks and Hartmann 1979] E. C. Hendricks and T. C. Hartmann, "Evolution of a Virtual Machine Subsystem," *IBM Systems Journal*, Volume 18, Number 1 (1979), pages 111−142.

[Hoagland 1985] A. S. Hoagland, "Information Storage Technology — A Look at the Future," *Computer*, Volume 18, Number 7 (July 1985), pages 60−68.

[Hoare 1972a] C. A. R. Hoare, "Operating Systems: Their Purpose, Objectives, Functions, and Scope," in [Hoare and Perrott 1972], pages 11−19.

[Hoare 1972b] C. A. R. Hoare, "Towards a Theory of Parallel Programming," in [Hoare and Perrott 1972], pages 61−71.

[Hoare 1974] C. A. R. Hoare, "Monitors: An Operating System Structuring Concept," *Communications of the ACM*, Volume 17, Number 10 (October 1974), pages 549−557; Erratum in *Communications of the ACM*, Volume 18, Number 2 (February 1975), page 95.

[Hoare and McKeag 1972] C. A. R. Hoare and R. M. McKeag, "A Survey of Store Management Techniques," in [Hoare and Perrott 1972], pages 117−151.

[Hoare and Perrott 1972] C. A. R. Hoare and R. H. Perrott, Eds., *Operating Systems Techniques*, Academic Press, London (1972).

[Hofri 1980] M. Hofri, "Disk Scheduling: FCFS Versus SSTF Revisited," *Communications of the ACM*, Volume 23, Number 11 (November 1980), pages 645−653.

[Holley et al. 1979] L. H. Holley, R. P. Parmelee, C. A. Salisbury, and D. N. Saul, "VM/370 Asymmetric Multiprocessing," *IBM Systems Journal*, Volume 18, Number 1 (1979), pages 47−70.

[Holt 1971a] R. C. Holt, "Comments on Prevention of System Deadlocks," *Communications of the ACM*, Volume 14, Number 1 (January 1971), pages 36−38.

[Holt 1971b] R. C. Holt, "On Deadlock in Computer Systems," PhD. Thesis, Cornell University (1971).

[Holt 1972] R. C. Holt, "Some Deadlock Properties of Computer Systems," *Computing Surveys*, Volume 4, Number 3 (September 1972), pages 179−196.

[Horning and Randell 1973] J. J. Horning and B. Randell, "Process Structuring," *Computing Surveys*, Volume 5, Number 1 (March 1973), pages 5−30.

[Howard 1973] J. H. Howard, "Mixed Solutions for the Deadlock Problem," *Communications of the ACM*, Volume 16, Number 7 (July 1973), pages 427−430.

[Howard 1976] J. H. Howard, "Signaling in Monitors," *Proceedings of the Second International Conference on Software Engineering* (October 1976), pages 47−52.

[Howard et al. 1988] J. H. Howard, M. L. Kazar, S. G. Menees, D. A. Nichols, M. Satyanarayanan, and R. N. Sidebotham, "Scale and Performance in a Distributed File System," *ACM Transactions on Computer Systems*, Volume 6, Number 1 (February 1988), pages 55−81.

[Howarth et al. 1961] D. J. Howarth, R. B. Payne, and F. H. Sumner, "The Manchester University Atlas Operating System, Part II: User's Description," *Computer Journal*, Volume 4, Number 3 (October 1961), page 226−229.

[Hsiao et al. 1979] D. K. Hsiao, D. S. Kerr, and S. E. Madnick, *Computer Security*, Academic Press, New York, NY (1979).

[Hyman 1966] H. Hyman, "Comments on a Problem in Concurrent Programming Control," *Communications of the ACM*, Volume 9, Number 1 (January 1966), page 45.

[Iacobucci 1988] E. Iacobucci, *OS/2 Programmer's Guide*, Osborne McGraw-Hill, Berkeley, CA (1988).

[Iliffe and Jodeit 1962] J. K. Iliffe and J. G. Jodeit, "A Dynamic Storage Allocation System," *Computer Journal*, Volume 5, Number 3 (October 1962), pages 200–209.

[Intel 1985a] Intel Corporation, *iAPX 86/88, 186/188 User's Manual Programmer's Reference*, Intel Corp., Santa Clara, CA (1985).

[Intel 1985b] Intel Corporation, *iAPX 286 Programmer's Reference Manual*, Intel Corp., Santa Clara, CA (1985).

[Intel 1986] Intel Corporation, *iAPX 386 Programmer's Reference Manual*, Intel Corp., Santa Clara, CA (1986).

[Intel 1989] Intel Corporation, *i486 Microprocessor*, Intel Corp., Santa Clara, CA (1989).

[Intel 1990] Intel Corporation, *i486 Microprocessor Programmer's Reference Manual*, Intel Corp., Santa Clara, CA (1990).

[Isloor and Marsland 1980] S. S. Isloor and T. A. Marsland, "The Deadlock Problem: An Overview," *Computer*, Volume 13, Number 9 (September 1980), pages 58–78.

[ISO 1981] "ISO Open Systems Interconnection — Basic Reference Model," ISO/TC 97/SC 16 N 719, *International Organization for Standardization* (August 1981).

[Israel et al. 1978] J. Israel, J. G. Mitchell, and H. E. Sturgis, "Separating Data From Function in a Distributed File System," *Proceedings of the Second IRIA International Symposium on Operating Systems* (October 1978).

[Jensen et al. 1985] E. D. Jensen, C. D. Locke, and H. Tokuda, "A Time-Driven Scheduling Model for Real-Time Operating Systems," *Proceedings of the IEEE Real-Time Systems Symposium* (December 1985), pages 112–122.

[Jessop et al. 1982] W. H. Jessop, D. M. Jacobson, J. D. Noe, J. L. Baer, and C. Pu, "The Eden Transaction Based File System," *Proceedings of the Second Symposium on Reliability in Distributed Software and Databases Systems* (July 1982), pages 163–169.

[Jones 1973] A. K. Jones, "Protection in Programmed Systems," PhD. Thesis, Carnegie-Mellon University (June 1973).

[Jones 1978] A. K. Jones, "Protection Mechanisms and the Enforcement of Security Policies," in [Bayer et al. 1978], pages 228–250.

[Jones and Liskov 1978] A. K. Jones and B. H. Liskov, "A Language Extension for Expressing Constraints on Data Access," *Communications of the ACM*, Volume 21, Number 5 (May 1978), pages 358–367.

[Jones and Schwarz 1980] A. K. Jones and P. Schwarz, "Experience Using Multiprocessor Systems — A Status Report," *Computing Surveys*, Volume 12, Number 2 (June 1980), pages 121–165.

[Jones et al. 1979] A. K. Jones, R. J. Chansler Jr., I. Durham, K. Schwans, and S. R. Vegdahl, "StarOS: A Multiprocessor Operating System for the Support of Task Forces," *Proceedings of the Seventh Symposium on Operating Systems Principles* (December 1979), pages 117–127.

[Kahn 1972] R. Kahn, "Resource-Sharing Computer Communications Networks," *Proceedings of the IEEE*, Volume 60, Number 11 (November 1972), pages 1397–1407.

[Kameda 1980] T. Kameda, "Testing Deadlock-Freedom of Computer Systems," *Journal of the ACM*, Volume 27, Number 2 (April 1980), pages 270–280.

[Kay and Lauder 1988] J. Kay and P. Lauder, "A Fair Share Scheduler," *Communications of the ACM*, Volume 31, Number 1 (January 1988) pages 44–55.

[Kenville 1982] R. F. Kenville, "Optical Disk Data Storage," *Computer*, Volume 15, Number 7 (July 1982), pages 21–26.

[Kepecs and Solomon 1984] J. H. Kepecs and M. H. Solomon, "SODA: A Simplified Operating System for Distributed Applications," *Third Annual ACM SIGACT-SIGOPS Symposium on Principles of Distributed Computing* (August 1984), pages 27–29.

[Kernighan and Pike 1984] B. W. Kernighan and R. Pike, *The UNIX Programming Environment*, Prentice-Hall, Englewood Cliffs, NJ (1984).

[Kernighan and Ritchie 1978] B. W. Kernighan and D. M. Ritchie, *The C Programming Language*, Prentice-Hall, Englewood Cliffs, NJ (1978).

[Kernighan and Ritchie 1988] B. W. Kernighan and D. M. Ritchie, *The C Programming Language*, Prentice-Hall, Englewood Cliffs, NJ (1988).

[Kessels 1977] J. L. W. Kessels, "An Alternative to Event Queues for Synchronization in Monitors," *Communications of the ACM*, Volume 20, Number 7 (July 1977), pages 500–503.

[Kieburtz and Silberschatz 1978] R. B. Kieburtz and A. Silberschatz, "Capability Managers," *IEEE Transactions on Software Engineering*, Volume SE-4, Number 6 (November 1978), pages 467–477.

[Kieburtz and Silberschatz 1983] R. B. Kieburtz and A. Silberschatz, "Access Right Expressions," *ACM Transactions on Programming Languages and Systems*, Volume 5, Number 1 (January 1983), pages 78–96.

[Kilburn et al. 1961] T. Kilburn, D. J. Howarth, R. B. Payne, and F. H. Sumner, "The Manchester University Atlas Operating System, Part I: Internal Organization," *Computer Journal*, Volume 4, Number 3 (October 1961), pages 222–225.

[Kilburn et al. 1962] T. Kilburn, D. B. G. Edwards, M. J. Lanigan, and F. H. Sumner, "One-Level Storage System," *IEEE Transactions on Electronic Computers*, Volume EC-11, Number 2 (April 1962), pages 223–235; reprinted in [Bell and Newell 1971], pages 276–290.

[Kleinrock 1970] L. Kleinrock, "A Continuum of Time-Sharing Scheduling Algorithms," *Proceedings of the AFIPS Spring Joint Computer Conference* (1970), pages 453–458.

[Kleinrock 1975] L. Kleinrock, *Queueing Systems, Volume II: Computer Applications*, Wiley-Interscience, New York, NY (1975).

[Knuth 1966] D. E. Knuth, "Additional Comments on a Problem in Concurrent Programming Control," *Communications of the ACM*, Volume 9, Number 5 (May 1966), pages 321–322.

[Knuth 1973] D. E. Knuth, *The Art of Computer Programming, Volume 1: Fundamental Algorithms*, Second Edition, Addison-Wesley, Reading, MA (1973).

[Koch 1987] P. D. L. Koch, "Disk File Allocation Based on the Buddy System," *ACM Transactions on Computer Systems*, Volume 5, Number 4 (November 1987), pages 352–370.

[Korn 1983] D. Korn, "KSH, A Shell Programming Language," *Proceedings of the Summer 1983 USENIX Conference* (July 1983), pages 191–202.

[Kosaraju 1973] S. Kosaraju, "Limitations of Dijkstra's Semaphore Primitives and Petri Nets," *Operating Systems Review*, Volume 7, Number 4 (October 1973), pages 122–126.

[Krakowiak 1988] S. Krakowiak, *Principles of Operating Systems*, MIT Press, Cambridge, MA (1988).

[Kramer 1988] S. M. Kramer, "Retaining SUID Programs in a Secure UNIX," *Proceedings of the 1988 Summer USENIX Conference* (June 1988), pages 107–118.

[Lamport 1974] L. Lamport, "A New Solution of Dijkstra's Concurrent Programming Problem," *Communications of the ACM*, Volume 17, Number 8 (August 1974), pages 453–455.

[Lamport 1976] L. Lamport, "Synchronization of Independent Processes," *Acta Informatica*, Volume 7, Number 1 (1976), pages 15–34.

[Lamport 1977] L. Lamport, "Concurrent Reading and Writing," *Communications of the ACM*, Volume 20, Number 11 (November 1977), pages 806−811.

[Lamport 1978a] L. Lamport, "Time, Clocks, and the Ordering of Events in a Distributed System," *Communications of the ACM*, Volume 21, Number 7 (July 1978), pages 558−565.

[Lamport 1978b] L. Lamport, "The Implementation of Reliable Distributed Multiprocess Systems," *Computer Networks*, Volume 2, Number 2 (April 1978), pages 95−114.

[Lamport 1981] L. Lamport, "Password Authentication with Insecure Communications" *Communications of the ACM*, Volume 24, Number 11 (November 1981), pages 770−772.

[Lamport 1986a] L. Lamport, "The Mutual Exclusion Problem: Part I — A Theory of Interprocess Communication," *Journal of the ACM*, Volume 33, Number 2 (1986), pages 313−326.

[Lamport 1986b] L. Lamport, "The Mutual Exclusion Problem: Part II — Statement and Solutions," *Journal of the ACM*, Volume 33, Number 2 (1986), pages 327−348.

[Lamport et al. 1982] L. Lamport, R. Shostak, and M. Pease, "The Byzantine Generals Problem," *ACM Transactions on Programming Languages and Systems*, Volume 4, Number 3 (July 1982), pages 382−401.

[Lampson 1968] B. W. Lampson, "A Scheduling Philosophy for Multiprocessing Systems," *Communications of the ACM*, Volume 11, Number 5 (May 1968), pages 347−360.

[Lampson 1969] B. W. Lampson, "Dynamic Protection Structures," *Proceedings of the AFIPS Fall Joint Computer Conference* (1969), pages 27−38.

[Lampson 1971] B. W. Lampson, "Protection," *Proceedings of the Fifth Annual Princeton Conference on Information Science Systems* (1971), pages 437−443; reprinted in *Operating System Review*, Volume 8, Number 1 (January 1974), pages 18−24.

[Lampson 1973] B. W. Lampson, "A Note on the Confinement Problem," *Communications of the ACM*, Volume 10, Number 16 (October 1973), pages 613−615.

[Lampson and Sturgis 1976] B. W. Lampson and H. E. Sturgis, "Reflections on an Operating System Design," *Communications of the ACM*, Volume 19, Number 5 (May 1976), pages 251−265.

[Landwehr 1981] C. E. Landwehr, "Formal Models of Computer Security," *Computing Surveys*, Volume 13, Number 3 (September 1981), pages 247−278.

[Lang 1969] C. A. Lang, "SAL — Systems Assembly Languages," *Proceedings of the AFIPS Spring Joint Computer Conference* (1969), pages 543–555.

[Larson and Kajla 1984] P. Larson and A. Kajla, "File Organization: Implementation of a Method Guaranteering Retrieval in One Access," *Communications of the ACM*, Volume 27, Number 7 (July 1984), pages 670–677.

[Lauer and Needham 1978] H. C. Lauer and R. M. Needham, "On the Duality of Operating System Structures," *Proceedings of the Second International Symposium on Operating Systems* (October 1978); reprinted in *Operating Systems Review*, Volume 13, Number 2 (April 1979), pages 3–19.

[Lauesen 1973] S. Lauesen, "Job Scheduling Guaranteeing Reasonable Turnaround Times," *Acta Informatica*, Volume 2, Number 1 (1973), pages 1–11.

[Lauesen 1975] S. Lauesen, "A Large Semaphore Based Operating System," *Communications of the ACM*, Volume 18, Number 7 (July 1975), pages 377–389.

[Lazowska et al. 1984] E. D. Lazowska, J. Zahorjan, G. S. Graham, and K. C. Sevcik, *Quantitative System Performance*, Prentice-Hall, Englewood Cliffs, NJ (1984).

[Leach et al. 1982] P. J. Leach, B. L. Stump, J. A. Hamilton, and P. H. Levine, "UID's as Internal Names in a Distributed File System," *Proceedings of the First Symposium on Principles of Distributed Computing* (August 1982), pages 34–41.

[Leffler et al. 1978] S. J. Leffler, R. S. Fabry, and W. N. Joy, "A 4.2BSD Interprocess Communication Primer," *Unix Programmer's Manual*, Volume 2C, University of California at Berkeley, CA (1978).

[Leffler et al. 1983] S. J. Leffler, W. N. Joy, and R. S. Fabry, "4.2BSD Networking Implementation Notes," *Unix Programmer's Manual*, Volume 2C, University of California at Berkeley, CA (1983).

[Leffler et al. 1989] S. J. Leffler, M. K. McKusick, M. J. Karels, and J. S. Quarterman, *The Design and Implementation of the 4.3BSD UNIX Operating System*, Addison-Wesley, Reading, MA (1989).

[Lehmann 1987] F. Lehmann, "Computer Break-Ins," *Communications of the ACM*, Volume 30, Number 7 (July 1987), pages 584–585.

[Le Lann 1977] G. Le Lann, "Distributed Systems — Toward a Formal Approach," *Proceedings of the IFIP Congress 77* (1977), pages 155–160.

[Lempel 1979] A. Lempel, "Cryptology in Transition," *Computing Surveys*, Volume 11, Number 4 (December 1979), pages 286–303.

[Lett and Konigsford 1968] A. L. Lett and W. L. Konigsford, "TSS/360: A Time-Shared Operating System," *Proceedings of the AFIPS Fall Joint Computer Conference* (1968), pages 15−28.

[Levin et al. 1975] R. Levin, E. S. Cohen, W. M. Corwin, F. J. Pollack, and W. A. Wulf, "Policy/Mechanism Separation in Hydra," *Proceedings of the Fifth ACM Symposium on Operating System Principles* (1975), pages 132−140.

[Levy 1984] H. M. Levy, *Capability-Based Computer Systems*, Digital Press, Bedford, MA (1984).

[Levy and Lipman 1982] H. M. Levy and P. H. Lipman, "Virtual Memory Management in the VAX/VMS Operating System," *Computer*, Volume 15, Number 3 (March 1982), pages 35−41.

[Levy and Silberschatz 1990] E. Levy and A. Silberschatz, "Distributed File Systems: Concepts and Examples," *Computing Surveys*, Volume 22, Number 4 (December 1990), pages 321−374.

[Lichtenberger and Pirtle 1965] W. W. Lichtenberger and M. W. Pirtle, "A Facility for Experimentation in Man-Machine Interaction," *Proceedings of the AFIPS Fall Joint Computer Conference* (1965), pages 589−598.

[Linden 1976] T. A. Linden, "Operating System Structures to Support Security and Reliable Software," *Computing Surveys*, Volume 8, Number 4 (December 1976), pages 409−445.

[Lipner 1975] S. Lipner, "A Comment on the Confinement Problem," *Operating System Review*, Volume 9, Number 5 (November 1975), pages 192−196.

[Liptay 1968] J. S. Liptay, "Structural Aspects of the System/360 Model 85: The Cache," *IBM Systems Journal*, Volume 7, Number 1 (1968), pages 15−21.

[Lipton 1974] R. Lipton, "On Synchronization Primitive Systems," PhD. Thesis, Carnegie-Mellon University (1974).

[Liskov 1972] B. H. Liskov, "The Design of the Venus Operating System," *Communications of the ACM*, Volume 15, Number 3 (March 1972), pages 144−149.

[Lister and Maynard 1976] A. M. Lister and K. J. Maynard, "An Implementation of Monitors," *Software—Practice and Experience*, Volume 6, Number 3 (July 1976), pages 377−386.

[Little 1961] J. D. C. Little, "A Proof of the Queuing Formula L=λW," *Operations Research*, Number 9, Number 3 (1961), pages 383−387.

[Liu and Layland 1973] C. L. Liu and J. W. Layland, "Scheduling Algorithms for Multiprogramming in a Hard Real Time Environment," *Journal of the ACM*, Volume 20, Number 1 (January 1973), pages 46−61.

[Lobel 1986] J. Lobel, *Foiling the System Breakers: Computer Security and Access Control*, McGraw-Hill, New York, NY (1986).

[Lomet 1980] D. Lomet, "Subsystems of Processes with Deadlock Avoidance," *IEEE Transactions on Software Engineering*, Volume SE-6, Number 3 (May 1980), pages 297−303.

[Loucks and Sauer 1987] L. K. Loucks and C. H. Sauer, "Advanced Interactive Executive (AIX) Operating System Overview," *IBM Systems Journal*, Volume 26, Number 4 (1987), pages 326−345.

[Lua and Ferrari 1983] E. J. Lua and D. Ferrari, "Program Restructuring in a Multilevel Virtual Memory," *IEEE Transactions on Software Engineering*, Volume SE-9, Number 1 (January 1983), pages 66−79.

[Lucas 1971] H. C. Lucas, "Performance Evaluation and Monitoring," *Computing Surveys*, Volume 3, Number 3 (September 1971), pages 79−91.

[Lynch 1972a] W. C. Lynch, "An Operating System Design for the Computer Utility Environment," in [Hoare and Perrott 1972], pages 341−350.

[Lynch 1972b] W. C. Lynch, "Do Disk Arms Move?" *Performance Evaluation Review, ACM Sigmetrics Newsletter* Volume 1 (December 1972), pages 3−16.

[Lynch 1972c] W. C. Lynch, "Operating System Performance," *Communications of the ACM*, Volume 15, Number 7 (July 1972), pages 579−586.

[MacKinnon 1979] R. A. MacKinnon, "The Changing Virtual Machine Environment: Interfaces to Real Hardware, Virtual Hardware, and Other Virtual Machines," *IBM Systems Journal*, Volume 18, Number 1 (1979), pages 18−46.

[Madduri and Finkel 1984] H. Madduri and R. Finkel, "Extension of the Banker's Algorithm for Resource Allocation in a Distributed Operating System," *Information Processing Letters*, Volume 19, Number 1 (July 1984), pages 1−8.

[Madison and Batson 1976] A. W. Madison and A. P. Batson, "Characteristics of Program Localities," *Communications of the ACM*, Volume 19, Number 5 (May 1976), pages 285−294.

[Madnick and Donovan 1974] S. E. Madnick and J. J. Donovan, *Operating Systems*, McGraw-Hill, New York, NY (1974).

[Maekawa et al 1987] M. Maekawa, A. E. Oldehoeft, and R. R. Oldehoeft, *Operating Systems: Advanced Concepts*, Benjamin/Cummings, Menlo Park, CA (1987).

[Maples 1985] C. Maples, "Analyzing Software Performance in a Multiprocessor Environment," *IEEE Software*, Volume 2, Number 4 (July 1985), pages 50−64.

[Masuda 1977] T. Masuda, "Effect of Program Localities on Memory Management Strategies," *Proceedings of the Sixth Symposium on Operating Systems Principles* (November 1977), pages 117−124.

[Mattson et al. 1970] R. L. Mattson, J. Gecsei, D. R. Slutz, and I. L. Traiger, "Evaluation Techniques for Storage Hierarchies," *IBM Systems Journal*, Volume 9, Number 2 (1970), pages 78-117.

[McGilton and Morgan 1983] H. McGilton and R. Morgan, *Introducing the UNIX System*, McGraw-Hill, New York, NY (1983).

[McGraw and Andrews 1979] J. R. McGraw and G. R. Andrews, "Access Control in Parallel Programs," *IEEE Transactions on Software Engineering*, Volume SE-5, Number 1 (January 1979), pages 1−9.

[McKellar and Coffman 1969] A. McKellar and E. G. Coffman, "The Organization of Matrices and Matrix Operations in a Paged Multiprogramming Environment," *Communications of the ACM*, Volume 12, Number 3 (March 1969), pages 153−165.

[McKeon 1985] B. McKeon, "An Algorithm for Disk Caching with Limited Memory," *Byte*, Volume 10, Number 9 (September 1985), pages 129−138.

[McKinney 1969] J. M. McKinney, "A Survey of Analytical Time-Sharing Models," *Computing Surveys*, Volume 1, Number 2 (June 1969), pages 105−116.

[McKusick and Karels 1988] M. K. McKusick and K. J. Karels, "Design of a General Purpose Memory Allocator for the 4.3BSD UNIX Kernel," *Proceedings of the Summer 1988 USENIX Conference* (June 1988), pages 295−304.

[McKusick et al. 1984] M. K. McKusick, W. N. Joy, S. J. Leffler, and R. S. Fabry. "A Fast File System for UNIX," *ACM Transactions on Computer Systems*, Volume 2, Number 3 (August 1984), pages 181−197.

[Mealy et al. 1966] G. H. Mealy, B. I. Witt, and W. A. Clark, "The Functional Structure of OS/360," *IBM Systems Journal*, Volume 5, Number 1 (1966).

[Menasce and Muntz 1979] D. Menasce and R. R. Muntz, "Locking and Deadlock Detection in Distributed Data Bases," *IEEE Transactions on Software Engineering*, Volume SE-5, Number 3 (May 1979), pages 195−202.

[Merlin and Schweitzer 1980a] P. M. Merlin and P. J. Schweitzer, "Deadlock Avoidance in Store-and-Forward Networks — I: Store and Forward Deadlock," *IEEE Transactions on Communications*, Volume COM-28, Number 3 (March 1980), pages 345−354.

[Merlin and Schweitzer 1980b] P. M. Merlin and P. J. Schweitzer, "Deadlock Avoidance in Store-and-Forward Networks — II: Other Deadlock Types," *IEEE Transactions on Communications*, Volume COM-28, Number 3 (March 1980), pages 355–360.

[Metcalfe and Boggs 1976] R. M. Metcalfe and D. R. Boggs, "Ethernet: Distributed Packet Switching for Local Computer Networks," *Communications of the ACM*, Volume 19, Number 7 (July 1976), pages 395–404.

[Metzner 1982] J. R. Metzner, "Structuring Operating Systems Literature for the Graduate Course," *Operating Systems Review*, Volume 16, Number 4 (October 1982), pages 10–25.

[Meyer and Seawright 1970] R. A. Meyer and L. H. Seawright, "A Virtual Machine Time-Sharing System," *IBM Systems Journal*, Volume 9, Number 3 (1970), pages 199–218.

[Microsoft 1986] Microsoft Corporation, *Microsoft MS-DOS User's Reference* and *Microsoft MS-DOS Programmer's Reference*, Microsoft Press, Redmond, WA (1986).

[Microsoft 1989] Microsoft Corporation, *Microsoft Operating System/2 Programmer's Reference*, 3 Volumes, Microsoft Press, Redmond, WA (1989).

[Minoura 1982] T. Minoura, "Deadlock Avoidance Revisited," *Journal of the ACM*, Volume 24, Number 4 (October 1982), pages 1023–1048.

[Mitchell and Dion 1982] J. G. Mitchell and J. Dion, "A Comparison of Two Network-Based File Servers," *Communications of the ACM*, Volume 25, Number 4 (April 1982), pages 233–245.

[Morris et al. 1967] D. Morris, F. H. Sumner, and M. T. Wyld, "An Appraisal of the Atlas Supervisor," *Proceedings of the ACM National Meeting* (August 1967), pages 67–75.

[Morris 1973] J. H. Morris, "Protection in Programming Languages," *Communications of the ACM*, Volume 16, Number 1 (January 1973), pages 15–21.

[Morris et al. 1986] J. H. Morris, M. Satyanarayanan, M. H. Conner, J. H. Howard, D. S. H. Rosenthal, and F. D. Smith, "Andrew: A Distributed Personal Computing Environment," *Communications of the ACM*, Volume 29, Number 3 (March 1986), pages 184–201.

[Morris and Thompson 1979] R. Morris and K. Thompson, "Password Security: A Case History," *Communications of the ACM*, Volume 22, Number 11 (November 1979), pages 594–597.

[Morshedian 1986] D. Morshedian, "How to Fight Password Pirates," *Computer*, Volume 19, Number 1 (January 1986).

[Motorola 1989a] Motorola Inc., *MC68000 Family Reference*, Second Edition, Prentice Hall, Englewood Cliffs, NJ (1989).

[Motorola 1989b] Motorola Inc., *MC68030 Enhanced 32-Bit Microprocessor User's Manual*, Second Edition, Prentice Hall, Englewood Cliffs, NJ (1989).

[Mullender and Tanenbaum 1984] S. J. Mullender and A. S. Tanenbaum, "Immediate Files," *Software—Practice and Experience*, Volume 14 (April 1984), pages 365—368.

[Mullender and Tanenbaum 1985] S. J. Mullender and A. S. Tanenbaum, "A Distributed File Service Based on Optimistic Concurrency Control," *Proceedings of the Tenth Symposium on Operating Systems Principles* (December 1985), pages 51—62.

[Mullender and Tanenbaum 1986] S. J. Mullender and A. S. Tanenbaum, "The Design of a Capability-Based Distributed Operating System," *Computer Journal*, Volume 29, Number 4 (1986), pages 289—299.

[Needham 1979] R. M. Needham, "System Aspects of the Cambridge Ring," *Proceedings of the Seventh Symposium on Operating System Principles* (December 1979), pages 82—85.

[Needham and Walker 1974] R. M. Needham and R. D. H. Walker, "Protection and Process Management in the CAP Computer," *Proceedings of the IRIA International Workshop on Protection in Operating Systems* (1974), pages 155—160.

[Needham and Walker 1977] R. M. Needham and R. D. H. Walker, "The Cambridge CAP Computer and its Protection System," *Proceedings of the Sixth Symposium on Operating System Principles* (November 1977), pages 1—10.

[Nelson et al. 1988] M. Nelson, B. Welch, and J. K. Ousterhout, "Caching in the Sprite Network File System," *ACM Transactions on Computer Systems*, Volume 6, Number 1 (February 1988), pages 134—154.

[Newton 1979] G. Newton, "Deadlock Prevention, Detection, and Resolution: An Annotated Bibliography," *Operating Systems Review*, Volume 13, Number 2 (April 1979), pages 33—44.

[Norton 1986] P. Norton, *Inside the IBM PC*, Revised and Enlarged, Brady Books, New York, NY (1986).

[Norton and Wilton 1988] P. Norton and R. Wilton, *The New Peter Norton Programmer's Guide to the IBM PC & PS/2*, Microsoft Press, Redmond, WA (1988).

[Nutt 1977] G. J. Nutt, "A Parallel Processor Operating System Comparison," *IEEE Transactions on Software Engineering*, Volume SE-3, Number 6 (November 1977), pages 467—475.

[O'Leary and Kitts 1985] B. T. O'Leary and D. L. Kitts, "Optical Device for a Mass Storage System," *Computer*, Volume 18, Number 7 (July 1985), pages 24–35

[Obermarck 1982] R. Obermarck, "Distributed Deadlock Detection Algorithm," *ACM Transactions on Database Systems*, Volume 7, Number 2 (June 1982), pages 187–208.

[Oldehoeft and Allan 1985] R. R. Oldehoeft and S. J. Allan, "Adaptive Exact-Fit Storage Management," *Communications of the ACM*, Volume 28, Number 5 (May 1985), pages 506–511.

[Olsen and Kenley 1989] R. P. Olsen and G. Kenley, "Virtual Optical Disks Solve the On-Line Storage Crunch," *Computer Design*, Volume 28, Number 1 (January 1989), pages 93–96.

[Operdeck and Chu 1974] H. Operdeck and W. W. Chu, "Performance of the Page Fault Frequency Algorithm in a Multiprogramming Environment," *Proceedings of the IFIP Congress 74* (1974), pages 235–241.

[Organick 1972] E. I. Organick, *The Multics System: An Examination of its Structure*, MIT Press, Cambridge, MA (1972).

[Ousterhout et al. 1980] J. K. Ousterhout, D. A. Scelza, and S. S. Pradeep, "Medusa: An Experiment in Distributed Operating System Structure," *Communications of the ACM*, Volume 23, Number 2 (February 1980), pages 92–105.

[Ousterhout et al. 1988] J. K. Ousterhout, A. R. Cherenson, F. Douglis, M. N. Nelson, and B. B. Welch, "The Sprite Network Operating System," *IEEE Computer*, Volume 21, Number 2 (February 1988), pages 23–36.

[Paris and Tichy 1983] J. F. Paris and W. F. Tichy, "Stork: An Experimental Migrating File System for Computer Networks," *Proceedings of the IEEE INFCOM* (1983), pages 168–175.

[Parmelee et al. 1972] R. P. Parmelee, T. I. Peterson, C. C. Tillman, and D. Hatfield, "Virtual Storage and Virtual Machine Concepts," *IBM Systems Journal*, Volume 11, Number 2 (1972), pages 99–130.

[Parnas 1975] D. L. Parnas, "On a Solution to the Cigarette Smokers' Problem Without Conditional Statements," *Communications of the ACM*, Volume 18, Number 3 (March 1975), pages 181–183.

[Parnas and Habermann 1972] D. L. Parnas and A. N. Habermann, "Comment on Deadlock Prevention Method," *Communications of the ACM*, Volume 15, Number 9 (September 1972), pages 840–841.

[Patil 1971] S. Patil, "Limitations and Capabilities of Dijkstra's Semaphore Primitives for Coordination Among Processes," Technical Report, MIT (1971).

[Patterson et al. 1988] D. A. Patterson, G. Gibson, and R. H. Katz, "A Case for Redundant Arrays of Inexpensive Disks (RAID)," *Proceedings of the ACM SIGMOD International Conference on the Management of Data* (1988).

[Pease et al. 1980] M. Pease, R. Shostak, and L. Lamport, "Reaching Agreement in the Presence of Faults," *Journal of the ACM*, Volume 27, Number 2 (April 1980), pages 228−234.

[Pechura and Schoeffler 1983] M. A. Pechura and J. D. Schoeffler, "Estimating File Access Time of Floppy Disks," *Communications of the ACM*, Volume 26, Number 10 (October 1983), pages 754−763.

[Perros 1980] H. G. Perros, "A Regression Model for Predicting the Response Time of a Disc I/O System," *Computer Journal*, Volume 23, Number 1 (February 1980), pages 34−36.

[Peterson 1981] G. L. Peterson, "Myths About the Mutual Exclusion Problem," *Information Processing Letters*, Volume 12, Number 3 (June 1981).

[Popek 1974] G. J. Popek, "Protection Structures," *Computer*, Volume 7, Number 6 (June 1974), pages 22−23.

[Popek and Walker 1985] G. Popek and B. Walker, Eds., *The LOCUS Distributed System Architecture*, MIT Press, Cambridge, MA (1985).

[Popek et al. 1981] G. J. Popek, B. Walker, J. Chow, D. Edwards, C. Kline, G. Rudisin, and G. Theil, "LOCUS A Network Transparent, High Reliability Distributed System," *Proceedings of the Eighth Symposium on Operating System Principles* (December 1981), pages 160−168.

[Potier 1977] D. Potier, "Analysis of Demand Paging Policies with Swapped Working Sets," *Proceedings of the Sixth ACM Symposium on Operating Systems Principles* (November 1977), pages 125−131.

[Powell 1977] M. L. Powell, "The Demos File System," *Proceedings of the Sixth Symposium on Operating Systems Principles* (November 1977), pages 33−42.

[Presser 1975] L. Presser, "Multiprogramming Coordination," *Computing Surveys*, Volume 7, Number 1 (March 1975), pages 21−44.

[Prieve and Fabry 1976] B. G. Prieve and R. S. Fabry "VMIN — An Optimal Variable Space Page Replacement algorithm," *Communications of the ACM*, Volume 19, Number 5 (May 1976), pages 295−297.

[Quarterman 1990] J. S. Quarterman, *The Matrix Computer Networks and Conferencing Systems Worldwide*, Digital Press, Bedford, MA (1990).

[Quarterman and Hoskins 1986], J. S. Quarterman and H. C. Hoskins, "Notable Computer Networks," *Communications of the ACM*, Volume 29, Number 10 (October 1986), pages 932−971.

[Randell 1969] B. Randell, "A Note on Storage Fragmentation and Program Segmentation," *Communications of the ACM*, Volume 12, Number 7 (July 1969), pages 365−372.

[Randell and Kuehner 1968] B. Randell and C. J. Kuehner, "Dynamic Storage Allocation Systems," *Communications of the ACM*, Volume 11, Number 5 (May 1968), pages 197−304.

[Raynal 1986] M. Raynal, *Algorithms for Mutual Exclusion*, MIT Press, Cambridge, MA (1986).

[Rashid and Robertson 1981] R. Rashid and G. Robertson, "Accent: A Communication Oriented Network Operating System Kernel," *Proceedings of the Eighth Symposium on Operating System Principles* (December 1981), pages 64−75.

[Redell 1974] D. D. Redell, "Naming and Protection in Extendible Operating Systems," PhD. Thesis, University of California at Berkeley, CA (1974).

[Redell and Fabry 1974] D. D. Redell and R. S. Fabry, "Selective Revocation of Capabilities," *Proceedings of the IRIA International Workshop on Protection in Operating Systems* (1974), pages 197−210.

[Redell et al. 1980] D. D. Redell, Y. K. Dalal, T. R. Horseley, H. C. Lauer, W. C. Lynch, P. R. McJones, H. C. Murray, and S. C. Purcell, "Pilot: An Operating System for a Personal Computer," *Communications of the ACM*, Volume 23, Number 2 (February 1980), pages 81−92.

[Reed and Kanodia 1979] D. P. Reed and R. K. Kanodia, "Synchronization with Eventcounts and Sequences," *Communications of the ACM*, Volume 22, Number 2 (February 1979), pages 115−123.

[Reid 1987] B. Reid, "Reflections on Some Recent Widespread Computer Break-Ins," *Communications of the ACM*, Volume 30, Number 2 (February 1987), pages 103−105.

[Ricart and Agrawala 1981] G. Ricart and A. K. Agrawala, "An Optimal Algorithm for Mutual Exclusion in Computer Networks," *Communications of the ACM*, Volume 24, Number 1 (January 1981), pages 9−17.

[Richards 1969] M. Richards, "BCPL: A Tool for Compiler Writing and System Programming," *Proceedings of the AFIPS Spring Joint Computer Conference* (1969), pages 557−566.

[Ritchie 1979] D. Ritchie, "The Evolution of the UNIX Time-Sharing System," *Language Design and Programming Methodology, Lecture Notes on Computer Science*, Volume 79, Springer-Verlag (1979).

[Ritchie and Thompson 1974] D. M. Ritchie and K. Thompson, "The UNIX Time-Sharing System," *Communications of the ACM*, Volume 17, Number 7 (July 1974), pages 365−375; a later version appeared in *Bell System Technical Journal*, Volume 57, Number 6 (July-August 1978), pages 1905−1929.

[Rivest et al. 1978] R. L. Rivest, A. Shamir, and L. Adleman, "On Digital Signatures and Public Key Cryptosystems," *Communications of the ACM*, Volume 21, Number 2 (February 1978), pages 120−126.

[Rosen 1967] S. Rosen, Ed., *Programming Systems and Languages*, McGraw-Hill, New York, NY (1967).

[Rosen 1969] S. Rosen, "Electronic Computers: A Historical Survey," *Computing Surveys*, Volume 1, Number 1 (March 1969), pages 7−36.

[Rosenkrantz et al. 1978] D. J. Rosenkrantz, R. E. Stearns, and P. M. Lewis, II, "System Level Concurrency Control for Distributed Database Systems," *ACM Transactions on Database Systems*, Volume 3, Number 2 (June 1978), pages 178−198.

[Rosin 1969] R. F. Rosin, "Supervisory and Monitor Systems," *Computing Surveys*, Volume 1, Number 1 (March 1969), pages 37−54.

[Ruschitzka and Fabry 1977] M. Ruschizka and R. S. Fabry, "A Unifying Approach to Scheduling," *Communications of the ACM*, Volume 20, Number 7 (July 1977), pages 469−477.

[Rushby 1981] J. M. Rushby, "Design and Verification of Secure Systems," *Proceedings of the Eighth Symposium on Operating System Principles* (December 1981), pages 12−21.

[Rushby and Randell 1983] J. Rushby and B. Randell, "A Distributed Secure System," *Computer*, Volume 16, Number 7 (July 1983), pages 55−67.

[Saltzer 1974] J. H. Saltzer, "Protection and the Control of Information Sharing in Multics," *Communications of the ACM*, Volume 17, Number 7 (July 1974), pages 388−402.

[Saltzer and Schroeder 1975] J. H. Saltzer and M. D. Schroeder, "The Protection of Information in Computer Systems," *Proceedings of the IEEE*, Volume 63, Number 9 (September 1975), pages 1278−1308.

[Sammet 1971] J. E. Sammet, "Brief Survey of Languages Used in Systems Implementation," *ACM SIGPLAN Notices*, Volume 6, Number 9 (September 1971), pages 2−19.

[Sandberg 1987] R. Sandberg, *The Sun Network File System: Design, Implementation, and Experience*, Sun Microsystems, Inc., Mountain View, CA (1987).

[Sandberg et al 1985] R. Sandberg, D. Goldberg, S. Kleiman, D. Walsh, and B. Lyon, "Design and Implementation of the Sun Network Filesystem," *Proceedings of the 1985 USENIX Summer Conference* (June 1985), pages 119−130.

[Sanguinetti 1986] J. Sanguinetti, "Performance of a Message-Based Multiprocessor," *Computer*, Volume 19, Number 9 (September 1986), pages 47−56.

[Sarisky 1983] L. Sarisky, "Will Removable Hard Disks Replace the Floppy?" *Byte* (March 1983), pages 110−117.

[Satyanarayanan 1980a] M. Satyanarayanan, *Multiprocessors: A Comparative Study*, Prentice-Hall, Englewood Cliffs, NJ (1980).

[Satyanarayanan 1930b] M. Satyanarayanan, "Commercial Multiprocessing Systems," *Computer*, Volume 13, Number 5 (May 1980), pages 75−96.

[Satyanarayanan 1981] M. Satyanarayanan, "A Study of File Sizes and Functional Lifetimes," *Proceedings of the Eighth Symposium on Operating Systems Principles* (December 1981), pages 96−108.

[Satyanarayanan et al. 1985] M. Satyanarayanan, J. H. Howard, D. N. Nichols, R. N. Sidebotham, A. Z. Spector, and M. J. West, "The ITC Distributed File System: Principles and Design," *Proceedings of the Tenth ACM Symposium on Operating Systems Principles* (December 1985), pages 35−50.

[Sauer and Chandy 1981] C. H. Sauer and K. M. Chandy, *Computer Systems Performance Modeling*, Prentice-Hall, Englewood Cliffs, NJ (1981).

[Saxena and Bredt 1975] A. R. Saxena and T. H. Bredt, "A Structured Specification of a Hierarchical Operating System," *Proceedings of the ACM International Conference on Reliable Software* (June 1975), pages 310−318.

[Schell 1983] R. R. Schell, "A Security Kernel for a Multiprocessor Microcomputer," *Computer*, Volume 16, Number 7 (July 1983), pages 47−53.

[Schlichting and Schneider 1982] R. D. Schlichting and F. B. Schneider, "Understanding and Using Asynchronous Message Passing Primitives," *Proceedings of the Symposium on Principles of Distributed Computing* (August 1982), pages 141−147.

[Schmid 1976] H. A. Schmid, "On the Efficient Implementation of Conditional Critical Regions and the Construction of Monitors," *Acta Informatica*, Volume 6, Number 3 (1976), pages 227−279.

[Schneider 1982] F. B. Schneider, "Synchronization in Distributed Programs," *ACM Transactions on Programming Languages and Systems*, Volume 4, Number 2 (April 1982), pages 125−148.

[Schrage 1967] L. E. Schrage, "The Queue M/G/I with Feedback to Lower Priority Queues," *Management Science*, Volume 13 (1967), pages 466−474.

[Schroeder and Saltzer 1972] M. D. Schroeder and J. H. Saltzer, "A Hardware Architecture for Implementing Protection Rings," *Communications of the ACM*, Volume 15, Number 3 (March 1972), pages 157–170.

[Schultz 1988] B. Schultz, "VM: The Crossroads of Operating Systems," *Datamation*, Volume 34, Number 14 (July 1988), pages 79–84.

[Schwartz and Weissman 1967] J. I. Schwartz and C. Weissman, "The SDC Time-Sharing System Revisited," *Proceedings of the ACM National Meeting* (August 1967), pages 263–271.

[Schwartz et al. 1964] J. I. Schwartz, E. G. Coffman, and C. Weissman, "A General Purpose Time-Sharing System," *Proceedings of the AFIPS Spring Joint Computer Conference* (April 1964), pages 397–411.

[Schwemm 1972] R. E. Schwemm, "Experience Gained in the Development and Use of TSS," *Proceedings of the AFIPS Spring Joint Computer Conference*, (1972), pages 559–569.

[Seawright and MacKinnon 1979] L. H. Seawright and R. A. MacKinnon, "VM/370 — A Study of Multiplicity and Usefulness," *IBM Systems Journal*, Volume 18, Number 1 (1979), pages 4–17.

[Shneiderman 1984] B. Shneiderman, "Response Time and Display Rate in Human Performance with Computers," *ACM Computing Surveys*, Volume 16, Number 3 (September 1984), pages 265–285.

[Shore 1975] J. E. Shore, "On the External Storage Fragmentation Produced by First-Fit and Best-Fit Allocation Strategies," *Communications of the ACM*, Volume 18, Number 8 (August 1975), pages 433–440.

[Shoshani and Coffman 1970] A. Shoshani and E. G. Coffman, "Prevention, Detection, and Recovery from System Deadlocks," *Proceedings of the Fourth Annual Princeton Conference on Information Sciences and Systems* (March 1970).

[Silberschatz et al. 1977] A. Silberschatz, R. B. Kieburtz, and A. J. Bernstein, "Extending Concurrent Pascal to Allow Dynamic Resource Management," *IEEE Transactions on Software Engineering*, Volume SE-3, Number 3 (May 1977), pages 210–217.

[Silverman 1983] J. M. Silverman, "Reflections on the Verification of the Security of an Operating System Kernel," *Proceedings of the Ninth Symposium on Operating Systems Principles*, ACM, Volume 17, Number 5 (October 1983), pages 143–154.

[Simmons 1979] G. J. Simmons, "Symmetric and Asymmetric Encryption," *Computing Surveys*, Volume 11, Number 4 (December 1979), pages 304–330.

[Smith 1976] A. J. Smith, "A Modified Working Set Paging Algorithm," *IEEE Transactions on Computers*, Volume C-25, Number 9 (September 1976), pages 907–914.

[Smith 1978] A. J. Smith, "Bibliography on Paging and Related Topics," *Operating Systems Review*, Volume 12, Number 4 (October 1978), pages 39–56.

[Smith 1981] A. J. Smith, "Bibliography on File and I/O System Optimization and Related Topics," *Operating Systems Review*, Volume 15, Number 4 (October 1981), pages 39–54.

[Smith 1982] A. J. Smith, "Cache Memories," *ACM Computing Surveys*, Volume 14, Number 3 (September 1982), pages 473–530.

[Smith 1985] A. J. Smith, "Disk Cache-Miss Ratio Analysis and Design Considerations," *ACM Transactions on Computer Systems*, Volume 3, Number 3 (August 1985), pages 161–203.

[Stallings 1984] W. Stallings, "Local Networks," *Computing Surveys*, Volume 16, Number 1 (March 1984), pages 1–41.

[Stankovic 1982] J. S. Stankovic, "Software Communication Mechanisms: Procedure Calls Versus Messages," *Computer*, Volume 15, Number 4 (April 1982).

[Staustrup 1982] J. Staustrup, "Message Passing Communication versus Procedure Call Communication," *Software—Practice and Experience*, Volume 12, Number 3 (March 1982), pages 223–234.

[Stephenson 1983] C. J. Stephenson, "Fast Fits: A New Method for Dynamic Storage Allocation," *Proceedings of the Ninth Symposium on Operating Systems Principles* (December 1983), pages 30–32.

[Stone 1980] H. S. Stone, "The Coming Revolution in Operating Systems Courses," *Operating Systems Review*, Volume 14, Number 4 (October 1980), pages 72–77.

[Stone 1982] H. S. Stone, *Microcomputer Interfacing*, Addison-Wesley, Reading, MA (1982).

[Stone and Fuller 1973] H. S. Stone and S. H. Fuller, "On the Near Optimality of the Shortest-Latency-Time-First Drum Scheduling Discipline," *Communications of the ACM*, Volume 16, Number 6 (June 1973), pages 352–353.

[Strachey 1959] C. Strachey, "Time Sharing in Large Fast Computers," *Proceedings of the International Conference on Information Processing* (June 1959), pages 336–341.

[Stuart et al. 1984] D. Stuart, G. Buckley, and A. Silberschatz, "A Centralized Deadlock Detection Algorithm," Technical Report, University of Texas at Austin (1984).

[Sun Microsystems 1990] Sun Microsystems, *Network Programming Guide*, Sun Microsystems, Inc., Mountain View, CA (1990), pages 168–186.

[Svobodova 1976] L. Svobodova, *Computer Performance Measurement and Evaluation*, Elsevier North-Holland, New York, NY (1976).

[Svobodova 1984] L. Svobodova, "File Servers for Network-Based Distributed Systems," *ACM Computing Surveys*, Volume 16, Number 4 (December 1984), pages 353–398.

[Swinehart et al. 1979] D. Swinehart, G. McDaniel, and D. R. Boggs, "WFS: A Simple Shared File System for a Distributed Environment," *Proceedings of the Seventh Symposium on Operating System Principles* (December 1979), pages 9–17.

[Tanenbaum 1987] A. S. Tanenbaum, *Operating System Design and Implementation*, Prentice-Hall, Englewood Cliffs, NJ (1987).

[Tanenbaum 1988] A. S. Tanenbaum, *Computer Networks*, Second Edition, Prentice-Hall, Englewood Cliffs, NJ (1988).

[Tanenbaum and Van Renesse 1985] A. S. Tanenbaum and R. Van Renesse, "Distributed Operating Systems," *ACM Computing Surveys*, Volume 17, Number 4 (December 1985), pages 419–470.

[Teorey 1972] T. J. Teorey, "Properties of Disk Scheduling Policies in Multiprogrammed Computer Systems," *Proceedings of the AFIPS Fall Joint Computer Conference* (1972), pages 1–11.

[Teorey and Pinkerton 1972] T. J. Teorey and T. B. Pinkerton, "A Comparative Analysis of Disk Scheduling Policies," *Communications of the ACM*, Volume 15, Number 3 (March 1972), pages 177–184.

[Tevanian, et al. 1987a] A. Tevanian, Jr., R. F. Rashid, D. B. Golub, D. L. Black, E. Cooper, and M. W. Young, "Mach Threads and the Unix Kernel: The Battle for Control," *Proceedings of the Summer 1987 USENIX Conference*, (July 1987).

[Tevanian et al. 1987b] A. Tevanian, Jr., R. F. Rashid, M. W. Young, D. B. Golub, M. R. Thompson, W. Bolosky, and R. Sanzi; "A UNIX Interface for Shared Memory and Memory Mapped Files Under Mach," Technical Report, Carnegie Mellon University, Pittsburg, PA (July 1987).

[Thompson 1978] K. Thompson, "UNIX Implementation," *The Bell System Technical Journal*, Volume 57, Number 6, Part 2 (July-August 1978), pages 1931–1946.

[Thurber and Freeman 1980] K. J. Thurber and H. A. Freeman, "Updated Bibliography on Local Computer Networks," *Computer Architecture News*, Volume 8 (April 1980), pages 20–28.

[Toueg 1980] S. Toueg, "Deadlock- and Livelock-Free Packet Switching Networks," *Proceedings of the ACM Symposium on the Theory of Computing* (May 1980).

[Toueg and Ullman 1979] S. Toueg and J. D. Ullman, "Deadlock-Free Packet Switching Networks," *Proceedings of the ACM Symposium on the Theory of Computing* (May 1979).

[Treese 1988] G. W. Treese, "Berkeley Unix on 1000 Workstations: Athena Changes to 4.3BSD," *Proceedings of the Winter 1988 USENIX Conference* (February 1988), pages 175–182.

[Tsichritzis and Bernstein 1974] D. C. Tsichritzis and P. A. Bernstein, *Operating Systems*, Academic Press, New York, NY (1974).

[Unger 1972] C. Unger, Ed., *Command Languages*, North-Holland, Amsterdam (1972).

[Vantilborgh and Van Lamsweerde 1972] H. Vantilborgh and A. Van Lamsweerde, "On an Extension of Dijkstra's Semaphore Primitives," *Information Processing Letters*, Volume 1 (1972), pages 181–186.

[Vareha et al. 1969] A. L. Vareha, R. M. Rutledge, and M. M. Gold, "Strategies for Structuring Two-Level Memories in a Paging Environment," *Proceedings of the Second ACM Symposium on Operating System Principles* (October 1969), pages 54–59.

[Vuillemin 1978] A. Vuillemin, "A Data Structure for Manipulating Priority Queues," *Communications of the ACM*, Volume 21, Number 4 (April 1978), pages 309–315.

[Wah 1984] B. W. Wah, "File Placement on Distributed Computer Systems," *Computer*, Volume 17, Number 1 (January 1984), pages 23–32.

[Walker et al. 1983] B. Walker, G. J. Popek, R. English, C. Kline, and G. Theil, "The LOCUS Distributed Operating System," *Proceedings of the Ninth Symposium on Operating Systems Principles* (December 1983), pages 49–70.

[Walmer and Thompson 1989] L. R. Walmer and M. R. Thompson, "A Programmer's Guide to the Mach System Calls," Technical Report, Carnegie Mellon University, Pittsburg, PA (December 1989).

[Watson 1970] R. W. Watson, *Timesharing System Design Concepts*, McGraw-Hill, New York, NY (1970).

[Weingarten 1966] A. Weingarten, "The Eschenbach Drum Scheme," *Communications of the ACM*, Volume 9, Number 7 (July 1966), pages 509–512.

[Weizer 1981] N. Weizer, "A History of Operating Systems," *Datamation* (January 1981), pages 119–126.

[Welch 1979] T. A Welch, "Analysis of Memory Hierarchies for Sequential Data Access," *IEEE Computer*, Volume 12, Number 5 (May 1979), pages 16–26.

[Wilhelm 1976] N. C. Wilhelm, "An Anomaly in Disk Scheduling: A Comparison of FCFS and SSTF Seek Scheduling Using an Empirical Model for Disk Accesses," *Communications of the ACM*, Volume 19, Number 1 (January 1976), pages 13–17.

[Wilkes 1975] M. V. Wilkes, *Time-Sharing Computer Systems*, Third Edition, Macdonald, London (1975).

[Winograd et al. 1971] J. Winograd, S. J. Morganstein, and R. Herman, "Simulation Studies of a Virtual Memory, Time-Shared, Demand Paging Operating System," *Proceedings of the Third ACM Symposium on Operating Systems Principles* (October 1971), pages 149–155.

[Wirth 1968] N. Wirth, "PL360 — A Programming Language for the 360 Computers," *Journal of the ACM*, Volume 15, Number 1 (January 1968), pages 37–74.

[Wood and Kochan 1985] P. Wood and S. Kochan, *UNIX System Security*, Hayden, Hasbrouck Heights, NJ (1985).

[Wulf 1969] W. A. Wulf, "Performance Monitors for Multiprogramming Systems," *Proceedings of the Second ACM Symposium on Operating System Principles* (October 1969), pages 175–181.

[Wulf et al. 1971] W. A. Wulf, D. B. Russell, and A. N. Habermann, "BLISS: A Language for Systems Programming," *Communications of the ACM*, Volume 14, Number 12 (December 1971), pages 780–790.

[Wulf et al. 1974] W. A. Wulf, E. S. Cohen, W. M. Corwin, A. K. Jones, R. Levin, C. Pierson, and F. J. Pollack, "Hydra: The Kernel of a Multiprocessor Operating System," *Communications of the ACM*, Volume 17, Number 6 (June 1974), pages 337–345.

[Wulf et al. 1981] W. A. Wulf, R. Levin, and S. P. Harbison, *Hydra/C. mmp: An Experimental Computer System*, McGraw-Hill, New York, NY (1981).

[X3J11 1989] *X3.159 Standard for Programming Language C*, American National Standards Institute (1989).

[Zobel 1983] D. Zobel, "The Deadlock Problem: A Classifying Bibliography," *Operating Systems Review*, Volume 17, Number 4 (October 1983), pages 6−16.

INDEX

A

Abate, J., 361, 641
Abbot, C., 133, 641
Abort, 95
Abrams, M. D., 433, 641
Absolute code, 230
Absolute path, 381, 554
Abstract data types, 399
Abu-Sufah, W., 328, 641
Accent operating system, 194
Accetta, M., 85, 194, 629, 641
Access control problem, 175
Access groups, 388
Access lists, 388, 402
Access matrix, 400-405
Access-right expressions, 422
Access right, 399
Address binding, 230
Aditham, R., 656
Adleman, L., 671
Agrawal, D. P., 50, 641, 644
Agrawala, A. K., 489, 670
Ahituv, N., 433, 641
Aho, A. V., 327, 642

AIX, 72, 548
Akl, S. G., 433, 641
Alderson, A., 328
Alexander, M. T., 639
Allan, S. J., 360, 667
Allen, L., 434, 653
Allocation of frames, 301-304
Almes, G. T., 541, 642
Ammon, G. J., 360, 642
Amplification, 415
Andrew File System, 376, 461, 497, 503, 521-526
Andrews, G. R., 433, 665
Anyanwu, J. A., 395, 596, 642
Apollo computer, 47
Apollo's domain, 461
Apple, 50, 85, 360, 642
Apple Macintosh, 24, 46
Application program, 68
Arden, B., 328, 642
Arpanet, 591
Arpanet reference model, 591
Associative registers, 255
Asymmetric multiprocessing, 45, 122

Athena, 460

Atlas system, 26, 86, 327, 394, 631-633

Atomic operations, 150

Atwood, J. W., 132, 642

Audit log, 427

Authentication problem, 425

Automatic job sequencing, 9

Auxiliary rights, 415

B

Babaoglu, O., 547, 596, 642

Bach M. J, 595, 642

Background job, 561

Background processes, 118

Backing store, 282

Baer, J. L., 50, 328, 642, 658

Bakery algorithm, 144-147

Balkovich, E., 461, 642

Banker's algorithm, 207-210

Barak A., 461, 643

Baron, R., 641

Barron, D. W., 26, 643

Base register, 39-40, 240

Baskett, F., 132, 643

Batch processing systems, 8-11

Batson, A. P., 328, 643, 664

Bayer, R., 643

Bays, C., 274, 360, 643

BCPL, 86

Belady, L. A., 327, 328, 643

Belady's anomaly, 293

Bennett, B. T., 652

Bensoussan, A., 327, 643

Bernstein, A. J., 85, 432, 643, 652, 673

Bernstein, P. A., 676

Bershad, B. N., 433, 643

Best-fit placement strategy, 244, 337

Bhuyan, L. N., 50, 644

Bic, L., 27, 644

Binary semaphore, 188

Birman, K., 461, 644

Birrell, A. D., 194, 540, 644

Bit map, 334

Bit vector, 334

Black, A. P., 541, 629, 642, 644

Black, D. L., 629, 644, 675

Blair, G. S., 595, 644

Bliss, 86

Bobrow, D. G., 327, 394, 639, 644

Boettner, D., 328, 642

Boggs, D. R., 460, 666, 675

Boldt, I. V., 26, 645

Bolosky, W., 641, 675

Boot block, 580

Boorstyn, R. R., 460, 644

Bounded-buffer problem, 136, 155

Bounded waiting, 139

Bourne shell, 563

Bourne, S. R., 85, 563, 595, 644

Bozman, G., 274, 644

Branstad, D. K., 433, 645

Bratman, H., 26, 645

Brawn, B., 327, 328, 645

Brede. D. W., 656

Bredt, T. H., 85, 672

Brinch Hansen, P., 84, 85, 132, 173, 193-194, 634-636, 645

Bron, C., 327, 633, 645

Brown, G. D., 26, 645

Brown, H., 84, 645

Brownbridge, D. R., 541, 645

Brumfield, J. A., 27, 646

Brunt, R. F., 85, 646

Bryant, P., 328, 646

Budzinski, R. L., 328, 646

Buckley, G., 675

Buco, W., 644

Buffering, 14-15, 180-182

Bully Algorithm, 486

Bunt, R. B., 132, 646

Burchfiel, J. D., 644

Burkhard, W. A., 541, 650

Burns, J. E., 192, 193, 646

Burroughs systems, 274, 328, 430
Busy waiting, 30
Buzen, J. P., 132, 646
Byzantine Generals problem, 482

C

C-lists, 587
C-LOOK disk scheduling, 350
C-Threads Package, 605
C-SCAN disk scheduling, 350
C shell, 563
C threads package, 623
Cache-consistency, 499, 503-504
Cache management, 356
Caching, 499-505, 530
Cain, E., 596, 647
CAL system, 404, 411
Calabria, J. A., 642
Callback, 503, 524
Cambridge CAP system, 394, 416
Cambridge Digital Communication Ring, 448
Capabilities, 402-405, 415-417
Capability lists, 402-403
Carr, W. R., 327, 647
Carrier sense with multiple access (CSMA), 447
Carvalho, O. S. F., 489, 489, 647
Cascading mount, 520
Cascading termination, 95
Caswell, D., 629
CCI Tahoe system, 548
CDC 6600, 639
Cerf, V. G., 193, 596, 647
Chambers, J., 595, 647
Chandy, K. M., 132, 672
Chang, A., 647
Chang, E., 489, 647
Chansler, R. J., Jr., 659
Checksums, 184
Cherenson, A. R., 668
Cheriton, D. R., 85, 194, 460, 647
Chi, S., 361, 647

CHKDSK program, 395
Chorus, 549
Chow, J., 669
Chu, W. W., 327, 328, 540, 648, 668
Cigarette smoker's problem, 190
Cipher text, 428
Circuit switching, 446
Circular wait deadlock condition, 197, 203
Clark, D. D., 460, 648
Clark, W. A., 665
Clear text, 428
Client, 492
Client interface, 492
Client mobility, 522
Client-server model, 67, 590
Clingen, C. T., 643, 649
CMS system, 77
Codewords, 432
Coffman, E. G., 132, 133, 225, 327, 328, 360, 648, 665, 673
Cohen, E. S., 432, 648, 663, 677
Collision detection, 447
Comandos, 549
Comber, E. V., 433
Comeau, L. W., 327, 648
Comer, D., 27, 84, 596, 648, 649
Command interpreter, 56-57, 68
Communication links, 176
Communication processors, 451
Compaction, 247-249
Compatible Time-sharing System (CTSS), 26, 133, 546, 636
Computer networks, 460
Concurrent Pascal, 80, 84, 635, 636
Concurrent processes, 93-97
Condition variable, 169, 606
Conditional critical region, 163, 606
Conditional-wait construct, 174
Confinement, 424
Conner, M. H., 666

Context switch, 106
Contiguous allocation, 337-339
Control cards, 10
Control card interpreter, 10
Control program, 5
Conway, M., 193, 433, 649
Conway, R. W., 132, 648
Cooper, E. C., 629, 649, 675
Cooperating processes, 95-96, 135, 633
Cooprider, 655
Copeland, G., 360, 649
Copy on reference, 603
Corbato, F. J., 26, 133, 636, 637, 649
Coroutine, 193
Corwin, W. M., 663, 677
Courtois, P. J., 193, 649
Cox, G. W., 85, 649
CP/M, 639
CP/67, 85, 639
CPU burst, 103
CPU scheduling, 101, 103-106, 569-570, 607-609
CPU utilization, 107
CPU-bound process, 15, 103
CPU-I/O burst cycle, 103-104
CPU scheduler, 104
Creasy, R. J., 85, 649
Critical region, 162-168
Critical section problem, 139-147
Crowther, W. R., 460, 649
CSRG, 85, 549, 650
CTSS, 26, 133, 546, 636
Current directory, 381
Cylinder, 332

D

Dameon process, 67, 413
Dalal, Y. K., 670
Daley, R. C., 327, 394, 636, 643, 650
Daly, T. P., 644

DARPA, 588, 598
Data capability, 417
Data Encryption Standard, 428
Davcev, 541, 650
Davidson, E., 646
Davies, D. W., 433, 650
Deadlocks
    avoidance, 204-211
    Banker's algorithm, 207-210
    characterization, 197-201
    detection, 211-216, 473
    necessary condition, 197-198
    prevention, 201-204
    safe state, 205
Deadly embrace (see deadlock)
deBruijn, N. G., 192, 650
DEC-20 system, 639
DEC VAX, 598
DEC-VAXcluster, 456
Degree of multiprogramming, 102
Deitel, H. M., 27, 650
Dekker's algorithm, 187, 192
Demand paging, 277-286, 572
Demand segmentation, 277, 318-319
DeMeis, W. M., 328
Denning, D., 433, 651
Denning, P. J., 26, 27, 85, 132, 133, 327, 328, 432, 434, 642, 648, 651, 655
Dennis, J. B., 274, 327, 432, 636, 651
DEQ synchronization operation, 188
Deterministic modeling, 123
Device
    controller, 30
    directory, 334, 368
    driver, 7, 33
    independence, 13
    interrupt, 30-33
    management, 66
    queue, 99
Device status table, 35

Devillers, R., 225, 651
Diffie, W., 433, 651
Dijkstra, E. W., 85, 132, 192, 193, 224, 633, 651, 652
Dining philosophers problem, 158-160, 171-172
Dion, J., 540, 652, 666
Direct access, 372
Direct Memory Access (DMA), 29, 33
Directories, 576-577
Directory structure, 368, 376-386
Dirty bit, 289
Disabled interrupt, 32
Disk controller, 332
Disk drive, 332
Disk mirroring, 354
Disk scheduling, 345-352
Disk shadowing, 354
Disk stripping, 353
Disk structure, 330-334, 578-580
Dispatcher, 106
Distributed
    deadlock detection, 471-480
    deadlock prevention, 470-471
    file system, 491-541
    mutual exclusion, 466-470
    operating systems, 453
    system, 21-23, 437-540
Doll, D. R., 460, 652
Domain bit, 412
Domain name system, 451
Domain of protection, 399-400
Domain switching, 405-409, 412
Donnelley, J. E., 460, 652
Donovan, J. J., 84, 664
Doran, R. W., 192, 328, 651, 652
Douglis, F., 668
Draves, R. P., 629, 649
Dubner, H., 361, 641
Dual mode, 36-38
Durham, I., 659
Dynamic linking, 232
Dynamic loading, 232

Dynamic protection structures, 405-409
Dynamic routing, 445
Dynamic storage-allocation, 244, 337
Dynamically linked libraries, 232

E

Earhart, S. V., 642
Easton, M. C., 328, 652
Edison system, 84
Edwards, D. B. G., 660, 669
Effective access time, 284-286
Eisenberg, M. A., 192, 652
Ekanadham, K., 432, 652
Election algorithms, 485-488
Electronic mail, 23, 68, 439, 446, 449,
Ellis, C. S., 541, 652
Elphick, M. J., 648
EL X8 computer, 634
Enabled interrupt, 32
Encore, 45
Encore Multimax. 598
Encryption, 427-429
English, R., , 676
ENQ synchronization operation, 188
Enslow, P. H., 50, 460, 652
Ethernet, 589, 591
Event ordering, 463
Exception conditions, 182
Exception handling, 609-611
EXEC II system, 26
Execve system call, 94, 557
Exit system call, 95
Exponential average, 111
External fragmentation, 245, 338

F

Fabry, R. S., 132, 327, 432, 662, 665, 669, 670, 671

Fail-soft system, 44
Failure detection, 480
Fajman, R., 639
False deadlocks, 474
Farrow, R., 433, 652
FCFS (see First-Come, First-Served)
Feedback queue, 118-121
Feng, T., 460, 653
Fernandez, G., 434, 652
Ferranti computer, 632
Ferrari, D., 328, 652, 664
FIFO (see First-In, First-Out)
Fifty-percent rule, 245
File-allocation table (FAT), 341
File handle, 515
File management, 55
File manipulation, 65-66
File migration, 494
File operations, 370-372
File protection, 386-390
File replication, 493, 507-508
File session, 375
File system, 574-583
File-system organization, 365-370
File Transfer Protocol (FTP), 591
Filipski, A., 433, 653
Fine, G. H., 328, 653
Finkel, R. A., 27, 85, 490, 653, 664
First-Come, First-Served (FCFS)
  cpu scheduling, 108-109
  disk scheduling, 346
First-fit placement strategy, 244, 337
First-In, First-Out (FIFO)
  queue, 104
  page replacement, 292
Fischer, M. J., 434, 646
Fixed-head disk, 330
Fixed routing, 445
Fixed-size memory partitions, 242, 274
Flon, L., 655

Floppy disk, 332
Floyd, R. A., 541, 652
Fontao, R. O., 225, 653
Foreground processsses, 118, 561
Fork system call, 94, 557
Forsdick, H. C., 460, 653
Fortier, P. J., 460, 653
Fotheringham, J., 631, 653
Fragmentation
  external, 245, 338
  internal, 246, 368
Frailey, D. J., 224, 653
Frame-allocation algorithm, 290
Frames, 251
Frame table, 259
Frank, G. R., 85, 361, 653
Frank, H., 460, 644
Franklin, M. A., 328, 655
Franz LISP, 547
Free-space management, 334-336
Free-space list, 334
Freedman, D. H., 360, 653
Freeman, H. A., 460, 676
Freibergs, I. F., 328, 653
Fridrich, M., 540, 654
FTP, 591
Fujitani, L., 360, 654
Fuller, S. H., 361, 654, 674

G

Gait, J., 360, 654
Gantt chart, 108
Garbage collection, 386
Garcia-Molina, H., 490, 654
GE-635, 637
GE-645, 268, 274, 313, 327
Gecsei, J., 665
Gelernter, D., 490, 654
General graph directory, 385-386
Gerald, J., 328, 656
Gerla, M., 460, 654
Gibson, G. 668
Gien, M., 461, 540, 654

Gifford, D. K., 433, 654
Gligor, V. D., 489, 654
Global page replacement, 304
Global replacement, 310
Gold, E. M., 225, 654
Gold, M. M., 676
Goldberg, D., 672
Goldberg, R. P., 85, 654
Golden, D., 394, 654
Golub, D. B., 641, 644, 675
Gordon, R. C.,
Gotlieb, C. C., 361, 655
Graceful degradation, 44
Graham, G. S., 432, 655, 662
Graham, R. M., 643, 655
Gram, C., 84, 655
Grampp, F. T., 433, 596, 655
Grosshans, D., 394, 655
Gula, J. L., 50
Gupta, R. K., 328, 655
Gustavson, F. G., 327, 328, 645, 655

H

Habermann, A. N., 85, 193, 224, 655, 668, 677
Hall, D. E., 85, 655
Hamilton, J. A., 662
Hand shaking, 480
Hands-on system, 19
Hanko, J., 434, 653
Happened-before relation, 463, 464-465
Harbison, S. P., 677
Hard link, 554
Hardware protection, 38-42
Harker, J. M., 360, 656
Harrison, M. A., 432, 656
Hartmann, T. C., 85, 656
HASP, 26
Hatfield, D., 328, 656
Havender, J. W., 656
Havender's algorithm, 224

Hecht, M. S., 434, 656
Hellman, M. E., 433, 651
Henderson, P., 193, 656
Hendricks, E. C., 85, 656
Hennessy, J. L., 327, 647
Herman, R., 677
Hertweck, F. R., 84, 655
Heterogeneous system, 121
Hewlett-Packard Spectrum, 316
Heymans, F., 649
Hit ratio, 256
Hoagland, A. S., 361, 656
Hoare, C. A. R., 26, 173, 193, 274, 328, 656
Hofri, M., 361, 657
Holley, L. H., 85, 657
Holt, R. C., 224, 596, 657
Homogeneous system, 121
Horning, J. J., 132, 657
Horseley, T. R., 670
Hoskins, J., 460, 669
Houston Automatic Spooling Program (HASP), 26
Howard, J. H., 193, 225, 541. 631, 657, 666, 672
Howarth, D. J., 657, 660
Hsiao, D. K., 433, 657
Hydra, 415-416
Hyman, H., 187, 657

I

Iacobucci, E., 85, 328, 360, 657
I/O-bound process (job), 15, 103
I/O burst, 103
I/O interlock, 314-316
I/O system structure, 34-36, 54, 583-587
ICMP protocol, 591
IBM 360 series, 21, 84, 274, 637
IBM 370 series, 273, 313, 328
IBM 650, 632
IBM 1401, 12
IBM 7090, 636, 637

IBM 7094, 637, 638
IBM CP/67, 85, 638
IBM Fortran Monitor system, 26
IBM PC, 24
IBM RT, 316, 598
IBM Series/1, 45, 121
IBM system/38, 316
IBM VM, 75, 77, 85, 639
Iliffe, J. K., 432, 658
Immutable shared files, 376
Indefinite blocking, 114, 154
Independent processes, 95
Indexed allocation, 341-344
Indexed Sequential Access Method (ISAM), 375
Inode, 575
Intel systems, 38, 80-81, 261, 274, 318, 328, 360, 551, 658
Interactive system, 19
Interdata 8/32, 546
Intermachine interface, 492
Internal fragmentation, 246, 368
International Standards Organization (ISO), 448, 591
Internet domain, 588, 589
Internet Protocol (IP), 592
Interprocess communication (IPC), 175-186, 587, 611-617
Interrupt-based systems, 29-34
Interrupt vector, 38
Inverted page table, 316-317
IP protocol, 591, 592
ISAM, 375
Isloor, S. S., 225, 658
ISO, 448, 591, 658
ISO-OSI networking, 549
Israel, J., 540, 658

J

Jackson, C. W., 646, 653
Janakiram, V. K., 641
Jefferson, D., 432, 648
Jensen, E. D., 133, 658

Jessop, W. H., 541, 658
Jacobson, D. M., 658
Job control, 61-65, 564
Job Control Languages (JCL), 10, 638
Job queue, 99
Job scheduler, 101
Jodeit, J. G., 432, 658
Johri, A., 656
Jones, A. K., 50, 85, 432, 433, 460, 658, 659, 677
Jones, M. B., 652
Joseph, T., 461, 644
Joy, W. N., 547, 563, 596, 642, 662, 665
Ju, S., 643

K

Kahn, R., 460, 659
Kajla, A., 360, 662
Kameda, T., 225, 659
Kanodia, R. K., 489, 670
Karels, K. J., 662, 665
Katz, R. H., 668
Kay, J., 133, 659
Kazar, M. L., 657
KDF9 computer, 86
Kenley, G., 360, 668
Kenville, R. F., 360, 659
Kepecs, J. H., 460, 659
Kernel stack, 567
Kernighan, B. W., 86, 596, 659
Kerr, D. S., 657
Kessels, J. L. W., 191, 193, 659
Kieburtz, R. B., 433, 659, 673
Kilburn, T., 26, 274, 327, 631, 660
Kitts, D. L., 360, 668
Kleiman, S., 672
Kleinrock, L., 132, 133, 460, 648, 654, 660
Kline, C. S., 669, 676
Knuth, D. E., 192, 193, 274, 360, 660

Koch, D. L., 360, 660
Kochan, S. G., 433, 596, 677
Konigsford, W. L., 27, 663
Korn shell, 563
Korn, D., 563, 596, 660
Kornatzky Y., 461, 643
Kosaraju, S., 193, 660
Krakowiak, S., 27, 660
Kramer, S. M., 434, 660
Kuehner, C. J., 327, 328, 643, 670

L

Lamport, L., 192, 193, 432, 433,
    489, 490, 660, 661, 669
Lampson, B. W., 132, 133, 274,
    432, 633, 661
LAN, 448-449
Landwehr, C. E., 433, 661
Lang, C. A., 86, 661
Language-based protection, 417-
    422
Lanigan, M. J., 660
Lapid, Y., 641
Larson, P., 662
Latency time, 346
Lauder, P., 133, 659
Lauer, H. C., 628, 662, 670
Lauesen, S., 132, 224, 634, 662
Layered design, 72-75
Layland, J. W., 133, 663
Lazowska, E. D., 132, 642, 662
Lazy evaluation, 603
Lazy swapper, 278
Leach, P. J., 461, 561, 662
Least Frequently Used (LFU)
    page replacement, 298
Least Recently Used (LRU) page
    replacement, 294-297,
Leffler, S. J., 595, 596, 662, 665
Lehmann, F., 433, 662
Le Lann, G., 489, 490, 662
Lempel, A., 433, 662
Lett, A. L., 27, 663

Levin, R., 432, 663, 677
Levine, P. H., 662
Levy, H. M., 328, 541, 663
Levy, E, 663
Lewis, P. M. II, 671
LFU page replacement, 298
Library routines, 561
Lichtenberger, W. W., 26, 274,
    633, 663
Lightweight processes, 96, 526
Limit register, 39, 40
Linden, T. A., 434, 663
Link, 383
Linkage editor, 68, 230
Linked allocation, 339-341
Lipman, P. H., 328, 663
Lipner, S., 432, 663
Liptay, J. S., 328, 663
Lipton, R., 193, 663
Liskov, B. H., 85, 132, 433, 634,
    658, 663
Lister, A. M., 193, 663
Little, J. D. C., 133, 663
Little's formula, 125
Liu, C. L., 132, 663
Load balancing, 455
Load sharing, 22, 121, 438
Loader, 68
Lobel, J., 433, 664
Local Area Network (LAN), 448
Local name space, 521
Local page replacement, 305, 310
Locality of reference, 282
Location independence, 493
Location transparancy, 493
Locke, C. D., 658
Lock-key mechanism, 403
Locus system, 460, 497, 531-534
Logical address space, 242
Logical clock, 465
Logical devices, 579
Lomet, D., 225, 664
Long-term scheduler, 101
LOOK disk scheduling, 350

Loosely coupled multiprocessing, 21, 437
Loucks, L. K., 85, 664
LRU page replacement, 294-297
Lua, E. J., 328, 664
Lucas, H. C., 133, 664
Lynch, N. A., 193, 646
Lynch, W. C., 26, 133, 361, 664, 670
Lyon, B., 672

M

MacEwen, G. H., 361, 655
Mach operating system, 184-186, 549, 597-629
MacKinnon, R. A., 85, 664, 673
Madduri, H., 490, 664
Madison, A. W., 328, 664
Madnick, S. E., 84, 657, 664
Maekawa, M., 27, 664
Mailbox, 179-180
Malcolm, M. A., 647
Malone, J. R., 644
Maples, C., 50, 665
Mariani, J. A., 644
Marshall, L. F., 395, 596, 642
Masked interrupt, 32
Master Control Program (MCP), 80, 85, 639
Master File Directory (MFD), 378
Masuda, T., 328, 665
Mattson, R. L., 327, 328, 665
Maxwell, W. L., 649
Mayeda, W., 646
Maynard, K. J., 193, 663
McDaniel, G., 675
McGilton, H., 595, 665
McGraw, J. R., 433, 665
McGuire, M. R., 192, 652
McIsaac, P. V., 653
McJones, P. R., 670
McKeag, R. M., 274, 328, 633, 639, 656

McKellar, A., 327, 665
McKeon, B., 361, 665
McKinney, J. M., 133, 665
McKusick, M. K., 395, 596, 662, 665
MCP, 80, 85, 639
Mealy, G. H., 637, 665
Mechanisms and policies, 79-80, 398-399
Medium-term scheduling, 102
Medusa system, 460
Melen, L. S., 647
Memory management, 229-337, 571-574, 617-623
Memory object, 602-617
Memory protection, 38-40
Menasce, D., 489, 665
Menees, S. G., 657
Merlin, P. M., 490, 665, 666
Merwin-Daggett, M., 649
Message passing, 66-67
Message slots, 447
Message switching, 446
Message system, 176
Metcalfe, R. M., 460, 666
Metzner, J. R., 27, 666
Meyer, R. A., 85, 638, 666
MFT memory management , 242, 274
MFU page replacement, 299
Michigan Terminal System (MTS), 639
Microsoft, 50, 85, 328, 395, 666
Miller, L. W., 649
Minidisk, 76
Minix operating system, 549
Minoura, T., 225, 666
Mips system, 81, 551
Mitchell, J. G., 540, 658, 666
Mode-bit, 37
Modify bit, 289
Monitor call, 42
Monitor mode, 37
Monitor program type, 168-175

Morgan, H. L., 649, 665
Morgan, R., 596, 665
Morganstein, S. J., 677
Morris, D., 631, 666
Morris, J. H., 433, 541, 666
Morris, R. H., 433, 596, 655, 666
Morshedian, P. D., 433, 666
Most Frequently Used (MFU) page replacement, 299
Motorola systems, 81, 367, 274, 328, 360, 551, 667
Mount operation, 513
Mount protocol, 515
Moving-head disk, 330
MS-DOS, 24, 38, 46, 64, 70-71, 85, 341, 380, 395, 395, 639
MS-DOS FAT system, 360
Mullender, S. J., 394, 460, 540, 667
Multiaccess bus network, 443
MULTICS, 26, 47, 267, 269, 313, 327, 394, 413-415, 545, 636-637
Multilevel feedback queue scheduling, 119-121
Multilevel queues, 118-119
Multimax computer, 45
Multiple base registers, 249-250
Multiple-partition allocation, 242-249
Multipleprocessor scheduling, 121-122
Multiprocessor systems, 43-46, 437
Multiprogramming, 17-18, 38-42, 97-103, 242-249
Multitasking, 18-21
Muntz, R. R., 489, 665
Murphy, D. L., 644
Murray, H. C., 670
Mutual exclusion, 197, 202
Mutual-exclusion deadlock condition,
Mutual suspicion, 423

MVS, 79, 313, 638

N

National 32032, 551
Need-to-know principle, 399
Needham, R. M., 432, 460, 540, 628, 644, 662, 667
Nelson, B. J., 194, 644
Nelson, M., 541, 667, 668
Nelson, R. A., 643
Network File System (NFS), 395, 454, 495, 513-521
Network Operating Systems, 453
Network Topology, 439-443
Neumann, S., 641
Newcastle connection, 510-511
Newton, G., 27, 667
NeXt workstation, 598
NFS, 395, 454, 495, 513, 517
Nichols, D. A., 657
Nichols, D. N., 672
Noe, J. D., 642, 658
No preemption deadlock condition, 198, 203
No Remote Memory Access (NORMA), 599
Nonpreemptive scheduling, 105
Non-Uniform Memory Access (NUMA), 598, 599
Norton, P., 50, 360, 395, 667
Nutt, G. J., 50, 667

O

O'Leary, B. T., 360, 668
Obermarck, R., 490, 668
Object-oriented paradigm, 601
Off-line operation, 11-14
Oldehoeft, A. E., 664
Oldehoeft, R. R., 274, 360, 664, 668
Older, W., 540, 654
Olsen, R. P., 360, 667

On-line file system, 20
Opderbeck, H., 647
Open software foundation (OSF), 549, 598, 668
Operating system services, 57-59
Operdeck, H., 327, 328, 648, 668
Optimal page replacement, 293-294
Orange book, 433
Organick, E. I., 274, 327, 394, 432, 595, 636, 668
OS/2, 24, 46, 75, 85, 318, 328, 341, 360
OS/360, 26, 637-639
OS/MFT, 638
OS/MVS, 79, 313, 638
OS/MVT, 274, 638
OS/VS1, 638
OS/VS2, 638
Ousterhout, J. K., 460, 541, 667, 668
Overlays, 233-235
Overlay loaders, 68

P

P synchronization operation, 150
Packet switching, 446
Packs, 533
Padua, D. A., 328, 641
Page fault, 280
Page-Fault Frequency model (PFF), 309-310
Page fault handler, 28-281
Page fault rate, 290
Page replacement, 286-290
Page replacement algorithms, 290-300
Page size, 311-313
Page table, 251
Page-table base register (PTBR), 255
Page-table length register (PTLP), 258

Paged segmentation, 267-269
Pager, 278
Paging, 250-259
Paris, J. F., 541, 668
Parmelee, R. P., 639, 657, 668
Parnas, D. L., 193, 649, 668
Passwords, 388, 425
Path name, 379
Pathak, G. C., 641
Patil, S., 193, 668
Patterson, D. A., 360, 669
Pattison, R. E., 656
Payne, R. B., 657, 660
PCB, 91-92, 566
PDP-10, 86
PDP-11 system, 546
Pease, M., 490, 661, 669
Pechura, M., 360, 394, 654, 669
Perros, H. G., 361, 669
Perrott, R. H., 656
Personal computers, 24, 46-47
Peterson, G. L., 192, 646, 669
Peterson, T. I., 668
Physical address space, 242
Physical containers, 533
Pierson, C., 677
Pike, R., 596, 659
Pilot operating system, 394
Pinkerston, C. B., 433, 643
Pinkerton, T. B., 361, 675
Pipe, 558, 588
Pipeline, 564
Pirtle, M. W., 27, 274, 633, 663
PL/360, 86
Podell, H. J., 433, 641
Pogran, K. T., 648
Pollack, F. J., 663, 677
Polling, 34
Ports, 179, 498, 601-602, 612
Popek, G. J., 432, 434, 460, 541, 669, 676
POSIX standard, 549
Potier, D., 328, 669
Powell, M. L., 394, 669

Pradeep, S. S., 668
Preemptive scheduling, 105
Prefix table, 527
Prepaging, 310-311
Presser, L., 132, 669
Prieve, B. G., 327, 669
Primary copy, 533
Primos operating system, 80
Priority replacement algorithm, 305
Priority scheduling, 113
Privileged instruction, 38
Proberen, 150
Process concept, 89-92
Process control, 61-65
Process control blocks (PCB), 91-92, 566
Process creation, 93
Process management, 52, 604-611
Process migration, 455
Process sharing, 116
Process state, 90-91
Process termination, 94
Producer-consumer problem, 135
Programmer interface, 71
Programmer's Work Bench (PWB), 546
Proportional allocation, 303
Protection 38-42, 55, 397-433
Pu, C, 658
Public key encryption, 428, 433
Purcell, S. C., 670
Pure demand paging, 282
PV chunks, 193
PV general, 193
PV multiples, 193
Pyke, T., 460

Q

Quarterman, J., 460. 595, 596, 647, 662, 669
Queue
  feedback, 118-121
FIFO 104
  priority, 113-114
  ready, 99
Queueing
  models, 124
  network analysis, 125
  sector, 352-353

R

RAID disk organization, 353, 360
Randell, B., 132, 274, 328, 433, 541, 657, 670, 671
Random-Access Memory, (RAM), 331
Rashid, R., 194, 629, 641, 644, 670, 675
Raw device interfaces, 586-587
Raynal, M., 193, 670
RC 4000 system, 132, 194, 431, 634-635
RCA Spectra 70/46, 274
Reaching agreement, 482-485
Read-Only Memory (ROM), 23
Readers and writers problem, 155-158, 166-168
Ready queue, 99
Ready state, 91
Real-time systems, 23-24
Real user identifier, 559
Recovery from deadlock, 216-218
Redell, D. D., 394, 432, 670
Reed, D. P., 489, 648, 670
Reentrant code, 257
Reference bit, 297
Reference string, 290
Register
  associative, 255
  base, 39-40, 240, 242-249
Reid, B., 433, 670
Relative path name, 381, 554
Relocatable code, 232
Relocatable loaders, 68
Relocation register, 240

Remote File System (RFS), 546
Remote link, 528
Remote Job Entry (RJE), 45
Remote procedure call (RPC), 182, 454, 497, 498, 501
Remote services, 497-499
Rendezvous, 180
Resident monitor, 9
Resource-allocation graph, 198-201
Resource preemption, 217
Response time, 20, 107
Revocation, 410-411
Ricart, G., 489, 670
Richards, M., 86, 670
Rights amplification, 415
Ritchie, D. M., 86, 394, 545, 549, 551, 559, 595, 596, 659, 670, 671
Rivest, R. L., 433, 671
Robertson, G., 194, 629, 670
Roisin, 549
ROM, 23
Root file system, 580
Rosen, S., 26, 671
Rosenkrantz, D. J., 489, 671
Rosenthal, D. S. H., 666
Rosin, R. F., 671
Roucairol, G., 489, 647
Round-robin (RR) scheduling, 114-118
Routers, 451
Routing table, 445
RPC, 497, 498, 501, 526
RSX operating system, 639
Rudisin, G., 669
Running state, 91
Ruschitzka, M., 132, 671
Rushby, J. M., 433, 671
Russell, D. B., 677
Rutledge, R. M., 676
Ruzzo, W. L., 656
Ryan, T. A., 328, 647

S

Safe state, 205
Sager, G. R., 328, 642, 647
Salisbury, C. A., 657
Saltzer, J. H., 432, 433, 649, 671, 673
Sammet, J. E., 85, 671
Sandberg, R., 395, 541, 671, 672
Sanguinetti, J., 50, 672
Santana, G. R., 656
Sanzi, R., 675
Sarisky, L., 360, 672
Satellite processing, 12
Satyanarayanan, M., 50, 394, 461, 541, 657, 666, 672
Sauer, C. H., 85, 132, 664, 672
Saul, D. N., 657
Saxena, A. R., 85, 672
SCAN disk scheduling, 349-350
Scelza, D. A., 668
Schantz, R. E., 653
Scheduler,
  cpu, 101, 103-106
  disk, 345-346
  long-term, 101
  medium-term, 102
  priority, 113
  short-term, 101
Scheduling algorithms, 106-121
Scheduling concepts, 97-103
Scheduling queues, 99-101
Schell, R. R., 433, 672
Scherrer, D. K., 655
Schlichting, R. D., 194, 672
Schmid, H. A., 193, 672
Schneider, F. B., 194, 489, 672
Schneiderman, B., 132, 673
Schoeffler, J. D., 360, 669
Schrage, L. E., 133, 672
Schroeder, M. D., 395, 432, 433, 671, 673
Schultz, B., 85, 673

Schwans, K., 659
Schwartz, J. I., 26, 673
Schwartz, S. C., 328, 651, 659
Schwarz, P., 50
Schweitzer, P. J., 490, 665, 666
Schwemm, R. E., 673
Scrambled messages, 184
SCOPE operating system, 639
Scott, M. A.,
SDC Q-32 system, 26
Seal primitives, 417, 421, 433
Seawright, L. H., 85, 638, 666, 673
Second-chance page replacement, 298
Secondary storage management, 54
Sectors, 332
Sector queuing, 352-353
Security, 425-426
Seegmuller, G., 643
Seek time, 346
Segment descriptors, 318
Segment table, 262
Segment table base register (STBR), 264
Segment table length register (STLR), 264
Segmentation, 260-267
Semaphores, 149-155
Sequent system, 598
Sequential access, 372
Sequential process, 90
Session semantics, 376
Set-uid bit, 412
Sevcik, K. C., 662
Shamir, A., 671
Shared libraries, 233
Shared name space, 521
Shattuck, S. H., 489, 654
Shaw, A. C., 27, 644
Shedler, G. S., 643
Shell, 563

Shell script, 564
Shneiderman, B., 132, 673
Shore, J. E., 274, 360, 673
Shortest-Job-First scheduling (SJF), 109
Shortest-Remaining-Time-First scheduling , 112
Shortest-Seek-Time-First scheduling (SSTF), 347
Short-term scheduling, 101, 104
Shoshani, A., 225, 648, 673
Shostak, R., 661, 669
Sidebotham, R. N., 657, 672
Siegel, P., 85, 643
Signal operation, 150
Signals, 559
Signal synchronization operation, 150
Silberschatz, A., 433, 659, 663, 673, 675
Silverman, J. M., 433, 673
Simmons, G. J., 433, 673
Simple monitor, 8-11
Single-level directory, 377
Single-partition allocation, 238-242
Single-User systems, 24
SJF, 109
Sleepy barber problem, 189
Slutz, D. R., 328, 651, 665
Smith, A. J., 27, 274, 328, 361, 674
Smith, F. D., 666
Sockets, 588, 591
SODA system, 460
Soft link, 554
Software capability, 417, 421
Software generated interrupt, 34
Solo operating system, 80, 84, 636
Solomon, M. H., 460, 659
Source Code Control System (SCCS), 552

SPARC, 81
Spector, A. Z., 672
Spectra 70/46, 274
Spinlock, 152
Spooling, 15-17
Sprite, 526-531
SSTF scheduling, 347
Stack algorithm, 297
Staging a tape, 17
Stallings, W., 460, 674
Standard I/O, 564
Stanford, 639
Stankovic, J. S., 194, 674
StarOS system, 460
Starvation, 114, 154
Stateful file service, 505-506
Stateless file server, 505-506
Staustrup, J. A., 194, 674
Stearns, R. E., 671
Stephenson, C. J., 274, 674
Stone, H. S., 27, 50, 361, 646, 674
Storage Hierarchy, 354-356
Strachey, C., 26, 674
Stream I/O system, 546
Stuart, D., 489, 675
Stub, 233
Stump, B. L., 662
Sturgis, H. E., 432, 540, 658, 661
Sumner, F. H., 657, 660, 666
Sun, 47, 395, 541, 675
Sun sparc, 551
Superblock, 580
Supervisor mode, 37
Sventek, J. S., 655
Svobodova, L., 133, 541, 675
Swap instruction, 148
Swap space, 282
Swapper, 571
Swapping, 102, 235-238, 571
Swinehart, D., 540, 675
Symbolic link, 383, 554
Symmetric multiprocessing, 45
Synchronization hardware, 147-
    149

SYSGEN, 81
System calls, 35, 42, 59-67
System data segment, 567
System-development time, 78
System generation, 81-83
System mode, 37
System model, 195
System programs, 67-69

T

Taft, L. G., 656
Tanenbaum, A. S., 27, 394, 460,
    540, 596, 667, 675
Tasks, 89, 601
TCP/IP, 588, 589, 593
TCP protocol, 588, 591, 592
TENEX system, 327, 394, 547, 639
Teorey, T. J., 361, 675
Test-and-set instruction, 147
Tevanian, A., 629, 641, 644, 675
Tezlaff, W. H., 644
THE operating system, 73, 85,
    132, 327, 633
Theil, G., 669, 676
Thomas, D. T., 642
Thomas, L. K., 192, 652
Thomas, R. H., 653
Thompson, K., 394, 433, 545,
    550, 551, 595, 596, 666, 671,
    676
Thompson, M. R., 652, 675, 676
Thoth system, 194
Thrashing, 304-310
Threads, 96, 601, 604
Threat monitoring, 427
Throughput, 98, 107
Thurber, K. J., 460, 676
TI-990, 85
Tichy, W. F., 541, 668
Tightly coupled multiprocessing,
    21, 437
Tillman, C. C.,
Time quantum, 114

Timeout, 183, 483
Time Sharing Option (TSO), 21, 638
Time-sharing systems, 18-21
Time-slice, 41
Time-stamp, 465
Timer, 41
Token passing, 447
Token-ring, 591
Tokuda, H., 658
Tomlinson, R. S., 644
TOPS-10 system, 43, 394
TOPS-20 system, 366, 547, 639
Toueg, S., 490, 676
Trace tape, 126
Tracks, 330
Traiger, I. L., 665
Transient operating-system code, 240
Translation look-aside buffers (TLBs), 255
Transmission Control Protocol, (TCP), 592
Trap, 34
Trap door, 424
Tree-structured directories, 380-382
Treese, G. W., 460, 676
Trojan horse, 423
Tsichritzis, D. C., 676
TSO, 21, 638
TSS/360, 27, 638
Tuffs, D. E., 85, 646
Turnaround time, 19, 107

U

U structure, 567
UDP protocol, 589, 591
UDP/IP protocol, 513-521
Ullman, J. D., 490, 642, 656, 676
Ultrix, 548
Unbounded buffer problem, 136
Unger, C., 84, 676

UNIBUS, 571
Uniform Memory Access (UMA), 598-599
Universal Product Codes (UPC), 374
UNIX 4.3BSD, 545-596
UNIX domain, 588
UNIX united, 508
Unreliable communication, 483
Unseal primitive, 417, 421, 433
UPC, 374
Urban, M.,
USENIX Assocation, 548
User File Directory, (UFD), 378
User mobility, 515
User mode, 37
UUCP network, 451, 591

V

V kernel, 460
V synchronization operation, 150
Valid-invalid bit, 279
Van Horn, E. C., 432, 651
Van Lamsweerde, A., 193, 676
Van Renesse, R., 460, 675
Vantilborgh, H., 193, 676
Vareha, A. L., 328, 676
Varian, L. C., 327, 328, 648
VAX/VMS, 300, 328
Vaxstation computer, 47
Vegdahl, S. R., 659
Venus operating system, 73, 85, 132, 524, 634
Verhogen, 150
Vfork system call, 567
Vice, 521
Virtual address space, 276
Virtual File System (VFS), 517
Virtual machines, 75-79
Virtual memory, 275-328
Virtual routing, 445
Virtue protocol, 521
Virus, 47, 424

VM operating system, 75, 77, 85, 639

VMS operating system, 547, 639

Vnode, 517

Volatile storage, 329

Volume table, 368

Vuillemin, A., 133, 676

Vyssotsky, V. A., 26, 636, 649

W

Wah, B. W. 541, 676

Wait-Die deadlock scheme, 470

Wait-for graph, 214

Wait system call, 95, 558

Waiting time, 107

Waiting state, 91

Wait synchronization operation, 150

Walker, B., 460, 541, 669, 676

Walker, R. D. H., 432, 667

Walmer, L. R., 676

Walsh, D., 672

WAN, 450

Watson, R. W., 27, 394, 677

Wei, T. J., 656

Weingarten, A., 361, 677

Weissman, C., 26, 433, 673

Weizer, N., 26, 677

Welch, B., 361, 667, 668

Welch, T. A., 677

West, M. J., 672

Wheeler, D. J., 460

Whole file caching, 522

Wide Area Network (WAN), 449

Wilhelm, N. C., 361, 677

Wilkes, M. V., 394, 460, 677

Wilson, R., 633, 639

Wilton, R., 50, 360, 395, 667

Winograd, J., 327, 677

Wirth, N., 86, 677

Witt, B. I., 665

Wood, D., 643

Wood, P. H., 433, 596, 677

Working set model, 306-309

Workstation, 47

Worm, 47, 424

Worst-fit placement strategy, 244, 337

Wound-Wait deadlock scheme, 471

Wulf, W. A., 85, 86, 328, 432, 662, 677

Wylbur system, 639

Wyld, M. T., 666

X

X window system, 564, 565

X3J11, 677

XDR, 515

XDS 930, 633

XDS-940, 26, 274, 546, 633

XENIX, 548

Xerox Network System (XNS) protocol, 593

Xinu operating system, 549

Y

Yang, Q., 644

Young, M., 641, 644, 675

Z

Zahorjan, J., 662

Zalcstein, Y., 193, 656

Zobel, D., 27, 225, 678

Zombie process, 558

Zwaenepoel, W. Z., 460, 647